Baron Stow, Richard Fuller, Jeremiah Bell Jeter, S. F. Smith

The Psalmist with Music

A Manual for the Service of Sacred Song in Baptist Congregations and Choirs

Baron Stow, Richard Fuller, Jeremiah Bell Jeter, S. F. Smith

The Psalmist with Music
A Manual for the Service of Sacred Song in Baptist Congregations and Choirs

ISBN/EAN: 9783337296773

Printed in Europe, USA, Canada, Australia, Japan

Cover: Foto ©Lupo / pixelio.de

More available books at **www.hansebooks.com**

THE PSALMIST,

With Music:

A

MANUAL FOR THE SERVICE OF SACRED SONG

IN

BAPTIST CONGREGATIONS AND CHOIRS,

The Tunes

BEING ADAPTED TO THE COLLECTION OF HYMNS COMPILED BY

BARON STOW AND S. F. SMITH:

AND TO THE

SUPPLEMENT APPENDED BY RICHARD FULLER AND J. B. JETER.

Collated

By B. F. Edmands,

CONDUCTOR OF MUSIC AT BALDWIN PLACE CHURCH, BOSTON.

PHILADELPHIA:
AMERICAN BAPTIST PUBLICATION SOCIETY.
BOSTON: GOULD AND LINCOLN.
NEW YORK: SHELDON AND COMPANY.
CINCINNATI: GEO. S. BLANCHARD.
1860.

PREFATORY NOTE.

The Board of Directors of the American Baptist Publication and Sunday School Society, induced by the numerous and urgent calls which, for a long time, have been made from various sections of the country, for a new collection of Hymns, that should be adapted to the wants of the churches generally, resolved, in the year 1841, to take immediate measures for the accomplishment of this object. With this view, a committee, consisting of Rev. W. T. Brantly, D. D., of South Carolina, Rev. J. L. Dagg, of Alabama, Rev. R. B. C. Howell, of Tennessee, Rev. S. W. Lynd, D. D., of Ohio, Rev. J. B. Taylor, of Virginia, Rev. S. P. Hill, of Maryland, Rev. G. B. Ide and R. W. Griswold, of Pennsylvania, and Rev. W. R. Williams, D. D., of New York, was appointed to prepare and superintend the proposed selection. It was, however, subsequently ascertained that a similar work had been undertaken by Messrs. Gould, Kendall, and Lincoln, Publishers, of Boston; and that Rev. B. Stow and Rev. S. F. Smith, whose services they had engaged, had already commenced their labor. From the well-known ability of these gentlemen, there seemed good reason to expect a valuable collection, and one that would fully meet the end which the Board contemplated. In order, therefore, to avoid the unnecessary multiplication of Hymn Books, it was deemed expedient, by the Board, to unite, if possible, with the above-named Publishers. Accordingly, the manuscript of Messrs. Stow and Smith having been examined, and found quite satisfactory, arrangements were made to have the sheets, as they were issued from the press, submitted to the committee of the Board, with the understanding, that, if, after such alterations and improvements as might be suggested, it should meet their approval, the Board would adopt it as their own. This approval having been obtained, the Board voted, unanimously, to adopt and publish the work, and have negotiated with Gould, Kendall, and Lincoln, to that effect.

Signed by order and on behalf of the Board.

J. M. PECK,

Cor. Sec. Amer. Bap. Pub. Soc.

PHILADELPHIA, *May* 18, 1843.

CERTIFICATE.

The undersigned, having been requested, by the Board of Directors of the American Baptist Publication and Sunday School Society, to examine the proof-sheets of "The Psalmist," edited by the Rev. B. Stow and Rev. S. F. Smith, and to suggest such emendations as might seem expedient to render the work more acceptable to the churches throughout our country, hereby certify that they have performed the service assigned them, and unite in recommending the work as one well adapted to the purpose for which it was designed.

William R. Williams
George B. Ide
Rufus W. Griswold
Stephen P. Hill
James B Taylor
J. L. Dagg
W. T. Brantly
R. B. C. Howell
Samuel W. Lynd

EDITORIAL PREFACE.

A PREFACE, being the key by which to judge of the design of a work, may properly in this instance commence by adverting to the fact that a difference exists between, *first*, the preparation, *ab initio*, of a strictly normal Congregational Tune and Psalm Book, and, *second*, an adaptation of music to a Collection of Psalms and Hymns already published and in use.

In regard to such a 'normal collection,' it will be sufficient for our present purpose to intimate that, in our opinion, not only a much more limited range of *tunes*, but also of *psalms* and *hymns*, than collections usually contain, would be indispensable in order to insure entire success.

It is simply an adaptation of music to the Psalmist, — a work that, from long and general use in the Baptist churches, can now claim the title of a Denominational Hymn Book, — that is embodied in the following pages; the design being to meet the present demand for a manual of hymns and tunes for congregational use, and to furnish it in such form as to render it most speedily and conveniently available.

The attention which in late years has been given to the instruction of the young in the art of singing, and the silent but powerful influence of numerous well-instructed choirs upon our congregations, has prepared the way for the successful introduction and use of many melodies which are so complicated in rhythm that they would not, under a contrary state of things, be practicable for congregational singing, but which, being familiar, cannot now be omitted from a work of this kind without causing disappointment and dissatisfaction. This consideration has had the effect to enlarge the range, both rhythmic and melodic, from which selections have been made While, therefore, in the following pages some tunes will be noticed which rigid judgment would exclude from congregational use, the book should not be condemned on that account; because in the chorals, the choral-like tunes, and the more simple of the hymn tunes, — with the hymns annexed to them, — will be found music adapted to the wants of any congregation, whether of extended or of more limited musical ability. The enlarged number, moreover, will render the work more acceptable and useful for choir use: indeed, as a collection of standard tunes, it will be a valuable choir book even where congregational singing is not practised

An effort to respond to the expressed wishes of many kind friends in different parts of the country, who have manifested an interest in regard to the selection of music, has also had a conducent effect to enlarge the number of tunes; but comparison will show, nevertheless, that the aggregate in proportion to that of the hymns, is less than in most other similar works.

Care has been exercised to bring into as near juxtaposition as possible those hymns and tunes which have mutual associations, and to secure correspondence between the peculiarities in the poetical and the rhythmical structure of hymns and tunes, as well as to effect a general adaptation of the melodic and harmonic language and spirit of the music to that of the poetry. The necessity of conforming to the Psalmist, (as published without music,) in grouping the hymns under the same general topical headings, as well as in the indexical arrangements, so that both editions may be used simultaneously, may in some few instances have interfered with that greater nicety in peculiar adaptations which might have been made had an entirely new work been in hand: on this point, however, criticism is not anticipated, except from those accustomed to judge by their own standard of adaptation for choirs rather than of what is available for congregations.

Preference has been given to those melodies which have been in past years, and now are, familiar to the elder portion of our congregations; some of which have been laid aside, not on account of a want of excellence, but through the influence of authors and publishers of new collections, whose pecuniary interests mainly have been consulted in substituting *new* music. So long have some of these beautiful old sacred melodies been suffered to slumber that they will now be found new to many, if not to the majority, of younger singers of the present day, and will present to them the novelty and charm of absolutely fresh compositions. In the use of this class of tunes, the more aged — relying upon, or aided by, association and their recollections of the melodies sung in their youthful days, — and the young — in the exercise of their ability to read psalmody at sight, — will be enabled to unite their voices in the devotional service of the sanctuary, with comparatively little preparatory practice. The chorals which bear the most ancient dates will be found in some cases so old that even the fathers in the church may never have sung or heard them: but, having been composed with the special design to be sung by masses, they are effective mainly through the simplicity and dignity of their melodies, and are therefore easily learned. That they have been preserved so long, and handed down as models of church music, is a guarantee for their appropriateness, as well as for their intrinsic excellence. An effort has been made to give the melodies as originally written, as far as possible.

The old standard tunes will be found greatly to predominate in the old established metres; the new tunes appearing mostly in connection with the *peculiar and mixed metres*, which, being of comparatively modern origin, and having no corresponding old tunes, require new compositions, adaptations, and arrangements.

The absence of some tunes which have recently obtained place in manuals professedly of sacred music (such as "Bonnie Doon," "Auld Lang Syne," "Drink to me only," "Coming through the rye," "Paddy Carey," &c.) will be noticed; especially by those who (in ignorance of their origin and associations) have acquired a love for them on account of their pleasing melodies. There may be comparatively little objection to this use of some secular tunes; but the introduction of such music, commencing with the least objectionable, has opened the way for still greater departures from the true standard of dignity which church music should maintain, and has led to the adoption of tunes more and more objectionable, till at length the churches have now in very general use many graceless and unworthy melodies which have literally originated in the low comic songs of a degraded theatre, or the burlesque opera. Tolerance of such music and its use by religious assemblies seems strangely inconsistent with that jealous watchfulness which condemns the use of "arrangements" of the choicest strains of the more elevated opera, or the oratorio, by choirs. Surely a reform in this respect is needed, and a return to a correct standard of church music desirable.

Relying upon the ecclesiastical character of the chorals, &c., admitted, and upon an endeavor to keep within the confines of the field of *sacred music*, and free from compositions which have had objectionable antecedent associations, the editor confidently believes that every opening of the book will present music to which the hymns there appearing may be devotionally sung. Where a tune appears which is comparatively new or difficult, it is designed that one easier or better known shall in all cases be found upon the opposite page. The singing, therefore, need not always be confined to music upon the same page with a hymn; for not unfrequently the tune opposite will be found quite as appropriate, and sometimes the only one proper or available: the taste and judgment of the precentor must govern in this matter.

The general courtesy and kind favors of authors and publishers have opened as wide a field for selection of music as could be desired. In one instance only was permission to copy coupled with terms for compensation so exorbitant as to amount to a prohibition. But this happily was with reference only to a single class of tunes, so simple, and which by use are so impressed upon the memory of all accustomed to sing, that the brief quotations of signature with the few opening notes of their melodies, inserted occasionally at appropriate points through the book for the benefit of precentors, will render these tunes available wherever they are known, and insure that they will be taken up correctly whenever they may be sung from memory. With this qualification, it may be assumed that the insertion of every tune desired has been accomplished; which is a feature not always attainable.

Though it is believed that a selection of tunes *at random* for insertion in this Denominational Tune and Hymn Book could not affect unfavorably the rights or interests of the proprietors of music books compiled for general choir use or for other denominations, nevertheless infringements upon such rights have been studiously, and it is believed successfully, avoided. A desirable melody has not been omitted merely because some particular arrangement was not available; while, therefore, in some cases new arrangements have been made, it has sometimes been difficult to avoid the various readings under which a tune has appeared, and at the same time effect a satisfactory harmonization: for instance, the tune Howard (p. 100) is claimed, as it stands in Dr. Mason's works, as copyrighted property, while the tune differs in harmony or melody at several points in five, at least, of his books; — and this is not an isolated case. Some melodies which are extensively sung with Dr. Mason's harmonies appear in these pages as harmonized by other composers: in such cases, the arrangement best known would have been preferred if permitted; but those given are believed to be quite as correct and effective, and are such as would undoubtedly have been as popular under circumstances of as oft-repeated insertion in music books. These considerations are presented merely to account for whatever may be found in these pages which would without this explanation be considered an arbitrary alteration of old and familiar tunes.

Those tunes which are the copyrighted property of others have been inserted by the special permission of the composers or proprietors; whose names, as well as the titles of the collections from which the tunes have been taken, or in which they appear, are given in connection with the tunes, or are so particularly noticed in the index that an enumeration here would be superfluous: — our thanks are tendered to all those individuals thus noticed as having granted their generous favors. Their permission is indicated by the abbreviature ℘ which appears, with their names, prefixed to the tunes.

Acknowledgments are also tendered to those who have presented original compositions, and to SUMNER HILL, Esq., for special favor in granting free access to his valuable musical library.

It is unnecessary to offer, as is usual in prefaces, any remarks upon the classification or distinctive features of tunes, because the indexes are accompanied with notes and annotations which will furnish a key to all information necessary on such points; and they will exhibit at one view the character of the entire selection. Some remarks for the guidance of those who use the work will be found in the chapter of "DIRECTIONS," &c., at p. 16.

As by far the greater part of our congregations is composed of mere 'rote' singers, the general rule obtains that all should sing the melody; or at most, the women and children the melody, and the men the bass: — and even among the men many will be found who cannot learn any part but the melody. As, therefore, the soprano and bass parts only should be attempted by the congregation, the notation of those parts is given in the larger type, the legibility of which is increased by contrast with the smaller type in which the alto and tenor parts are printed. The parts thus given in small notes, generally sung by the younger portion of a congregation, should be attempted only by those whose knowledge of music enables them to read easily therefrom; and it would as a general rule be better to leave them entirely to the choir and instrument.

While the design has been to furnish available and not too difficult music, yet it will be found the melodies have not all been crippled by the fear that voices cannot reach extreme notes, nor the harmonies made monotonous by that rigid sameness of style which would inevitably result from an unbending determination to confine selections to that range of melody and harmony *which is most easily sung*, or to rearrange the harmonies *with that view alone.* It has been said above that the true congregational method is *for all to sing the melody:* — this is a general rule, the exceptions to which prevail when congregations become competent to sing correctly in parts. If, therefore, any notes are found too high in the scale for a congregation which practises according to the general rule, the precentor can easily remedy the difficulty by causing the tune to be taken in a lower key. The gathering together of tunes as written or arranged by so many composers must insure a more satisfactory and pleasing variety of harmonization than would an entire new arrangement of all the harmony by any one individual.

The same numbering of the hymns (though not the regular numerical sequence) has been preserved, so that a given hymn has the same number in this book, as in those without music in use in the churches. The pages, however, differ; but an announcement from the pulpit both of the number of the hymn and the page of this book, which will be necessary wherever this book is used, will obviate every inconvenience which may be anticipated from the use of this book in connection with the editions without music.

Differences of opinion and disappointments will undoubtedly arise, on first examinations, relative to the size of the book, the type, &c. It should be borne in mind that a large book is objectionable as a manual for frequent use, and that a large type is incompatible with a small book. A medium has therefore been adopted, which, it is believed, will happily meet the wishes of the greatest number, and be found to unite more features generally desirable than could be combined by any other form.

The general subject of congregational singing is too voluminous for profitable condensation within the reasonable limits of a preface, and will therefore not be attempted here; especially as the book is designed for use after the adoption of that mode of worship upon a conscientious examination and consideration of arguments and authorities, rather than as a work to gain proselytes to the cause. The editor, however, desires to be allowed to lift a warning voice against that form of the demand for change which seeks to build up this mode upon the ruins of choirs, merely to avoid effort and expense. He believes that singing by a congregation cannot be long maintained, even in its simplest form, without stated opportunities for combined practice, duly improved on the part of the people, and under the direction of a competent master of sacred song; and that it cannot go successfully a step beyond the strictly choral style without the aid of a distinct choir, or such instruction as shall constitute the congregation a choir in itself; and moreover, that upon the maintenance of a good choir system depends the preservation of church music from deterioration and decay. In this view he thinks he is sustained by the best writers on the subject. Dr. Mason, who has thought and said as much as any one upon the subject, thus writes, in the prefaces of his Sabbath Tune Book and National Psalmist — works especially designed to promote the cause: —

"It is to be regretted that some, in their zeal for congregational singing, have supposed it necessary to set their faces against choirs.

"Let it be remembered that while we would urge this as an essential form of church music, we would press with equal earnestness the importance of choirs and the choiral style. Choirs are not only necessary to sustain congregational singing, but the higher style or forms of musical expression can never be reached without them. We feel certain that delight and edification may unitedly result from a well-directed choiral performance in religious service. To reject a choir, then, is to reject the means of spiritual progress and happiness; it is to reject one of the most effective means of music's influence, to clip its wings, and limit its power over the heart. While, therefore, we are decidedly friendly to congregational singing, we are equally so to choir singing: they are both legitimate forms of musical truth derived from the nature of the art, and sanctioned by common experience, and by the word of God.

"The history of psalmody in New England certainly proves that if congregational singing be left to itself, it will not only decline, lose its interest and power, but become intolerable — a hinderance and not a help to devotion. The fact, too, that singing is almost universally so wretched in the parochial churches in England seems to prove that congregational singing cannot be sustained without the aid of a choir.

"Success in congregational singing cannot be expected without effort. There must be a willingness on the part of the people to make and persevere in this effort."

Such extracts might be much multiplied — tending to show that the two methods should exist together, and that if one only can be preserved, it should be the choir system, *because* that alone will preserve the standard, and at the same time is adapted to lead "the great congregation" in silent mental and spiritual participation in the 'service of sacred song' in like manner as the minister leads it in prayer.

With such effort and attention as the importance of the subject demands, both modes may be maintained, and made to move in mutual influence in religious worship, and together form a perfect system.

If this book shall contribute to the maintenance of this mode of worship, taken up in the church from convictions of duty, and well and properly sustained in the same spirit which induces or impels religious societies to contribute of their substance, energies, and talents towards the support of the worship of God in other departments of our established service, then can those engaged in its preparation feel that their labor and efforts have not been in vain.

B. F. Edmands.

Boston, December, 1859.

INDEX

FROM HYMNS TO PAGES.

THE hymns will here be found arranged in separate tablets of *fifty numbers each*, with the initial number of each tablet at its head in large type; the numbers of the hymns being placed in decimal columns. Thus, the *first* tablet contains the numbers of hymns, 1 to 49 inclusive; the *second*—Nos. 50 to 99 inclusive; the *third*—100 to 149 inclusive, &c., &c. This peculiarity of arrangement being designed to suggest to the mind, *primarily*, the particular locality of the number sought for, and to direct the eye most quickly to it among the mass of figures.

EXAMPLES.

To find Hymn 35. Look first for the tablet, containing the first fifty numbers, and having the initial number 1, at its head; then refer to the column commencing with **30**, and opposite to **35** in that column will be found 19, which is the page upon which stands the hymn sought for.

To find Hymn 825. Look first for the tablet, having 800 at its head; then refer to the column commencing with **820**, and opposite to the figure **5** in that column will be found 65, which is the page upon which stands the hymn sought for.

1.

Hymn.	Page.	Hymn.	Page.	Hymn.	Page.	Hymn.	Page.	Hymn.	Page.
1	18	**10**	270	**20**	17	**30**	235	**40**	236
2	17	**11**	235	**21**	94	**31**	18	**41**	23
3	92	**12**	299	**22**	95	**32**	235	**42**	378
4	93	**13**	270	**23**	340	**33**	96	**43**	99
5	19	**14**	93	**24**	94	**34**	99	**44**	277
6	18	**15**	94	**25**	306	**35**	19	**45**	236
7	92	**16**	95	**26**	18	**36**	96	**46**	99
8	93	**17**	92	**27**	95	**37**	378	**47**	327
9	93	**18**	96	**28**	306	**38**	276	**48**	236
10	270	**19**	324	**29**	95	**39**	99	**49**	20

50.

Hymn.	Page.	Hymn.	Page.	Hymn.	Page.	Hymn.	Page.	Hymn.	Page.
50	23	**60**	306	**70**	24	**80**	26	**90**	278
51	99	**61**	306	**71**	381	**81**	101	**91**	305
52	20	**62**	329	**72**	379	**82**	101	**92**	278
53	277	**63**	340	**73**	307	**83**	102	**93**	26
54	20	**64**	19	**74**	364	**84**	100	**94**	24
55	20	**65**	340	**75**	26	**85**	100	**95**	25
56	307	**66**	100	**76**	23	**86**	26	**96**	237
57	100	**67**	277	**77**	328	**87**	237	**97**	101
58	100	**68**	277	**78**	101	**88**	101	**98**	300
59	99	**69**	307	**79**	236	**89**	237	**99**	300

100.

Hymn.	Page.	Hymn.	Page.	Hymn.	Page.	Hymn.	Page.	Hymn.	Page.
100	103	110	103	120	364	130	29	140	28
1	24	11	102	21	278	1	100	1	28
2	102	12	103	2	238	2	31	2	29
3	27	13	25	3	27	3	106	3	28
4	24	14	27	4	104	4	107	4	380
5	102	15	307	5	104	5	109	5	290
6	25	16	104	6	109	6	32	6	28
7	103	17	27	7	105	7	105	7	106
8	25	18	279	8	106	8	280	8	107
9	328	19	104	9	30	9	105	149	105

150.

Hymn.	Page.	Hymn.	Page.	Hymn.	Page.	Hymn.	Page.	Hymn.	Page.
150	108	160	105	170	111	180	114	190	111
1	29	1	107	1	32	1	111	1	239
2	29	2	281	2	32	2	238	2	31
3	108	3	110	3	282	3	239	3	111
4	280	4	238	4	110	4	239	4	354
5	328	5	110	5	112	5	31	5	240
6	108	6	111	6	112	6	31	6	282
7	281	7	109	7	113	7	113	7	30
8	107	8	111	8	377	8	113	8	112
9	107	9	110	9	113	9	239	199	30

200.

Hymn.	Page.	Hymn.	Page.	Hymn.	Page.	Hymn.	Page.	Hymn.	Page.
200	386	210	118	220	374	230	34	240	116
1	328	11	114	1	119	1	242	1	294
2	382	12	32	2	294	2	33	2	116
3	284	13	115	3	240	3	308	3	285
4	340	14	114	4	119	4	308	4	34
5	131	15	240	5	341	5	308	5	369
6	283	16	118	6	33	6	283	6	115
7	308	17	115	7	331	7	241	7	34
8	241	18	118	8	339	8	34	8	116
9	329	19	33	9	118	9	115	249	285

250.

Hymn.	Page.	Hymn.	Page.	Hymn.	Page.	Hymn.	Page.	Hymn.	Page.
250	117	260	119	270	37	280	123	290	243
1	37	1	285	1	329	1	243	1	244
2	37	2	243	2	120	2	323	2	123
3	38	3	38	3	119	3	243	3	244
4	242	4	309	4	121	4	39	4	40
5	38	5	309	5	309	5	324	5	40
6	39	6	122	6	242	6	341	6	41
7	120	7	37	7	121	7	40	7	122
8	38	8	120	8	322	8	40	8	123
9	121	9	241	9	39	9	122	299	39

300.

350.

400.

450.

700.

750.

800.

850.

900.

950.

1000.

1050.

1100.

1150.

(See page 390, in the Supplement.)

NOTES.

The Index of First Lines of Hymns may be found at pp. 419 in the Chant edition, or 442 in the Supplement edition.

The Index of Tunes will be found at the end of the volume, at p. 425 in the Chant edition, or 449 to 456 in the Supplement edition. Embodied in it is much information relative to the music contained in the work.

The Particular Index of Subjects, and that of **Scriptures,** have not been reproduced in the "Psalmist with Music," for the reasons, that, being composed to so great an extent of figures, they would be much extended and rendered quite complex by the addition of the page-figures; and because it is presumed that all who would be likely to consult them would have at hand the editions without music, in which these Indexes may be found.

DIRECTIONS

TO THOSE WHO USE THIS BOOK.

MINISTERS — in giving out Hymns from the Psalmist (whether of this edition or any other) — should in all cases announce the NUMBER *of the Hymn*, and the PAGE on which it may be found in *this book*; thus, "THE 387TH HYMN, PAGE 47." Those who have this edition will then look *first* for the *page*, and upon it they will find the *hymn*, (and also a *tune*;) those who have editions *without* music, will simply look for the *hymn* in the regular order of arrangement.

PRECENTORS, or those having the selection and direction of the music, need not always be confined to the tune on the same page with a hymn: — frequently the tune on the opposite page will be found quite as appropriate and more available than that on the page where the hymn occurs. (*See notes on page 15 relative to Indexes.*)

INDEXES, ARRANGEMENT OF HYMNS, &c.

The number of a hymn being known, its location in this book can be ascertained by reference to the preceding "INDEX FROM HYMNS TO PAGES." (See. p. 9.)

The first line of a hymn being known, its *number* and *page* may be found in the "INDEX OF FIRST LINES," at the end of the volume. (See p. 419 Chant edition, or 442 Sup. edition.)

The Hymns of each Metre are grouped together: thus, *Long metre* hymns on pages 17 to 91; — *Common metre* hymns on pages 92 to 234; — *Short metre* hymns on pages 235 to 275, inclusive; and so on through the whole.

The General Topical Arrangement of the Original Psalmist — which was "*agreeable to the order of mental association and Christian experience*" — has been adhered to under each metre; (except a few slight deviations, unavoidable, especially in the mixed metres;) so that hymns on any general subject may be found in their proper relative positions in each metre successively. It will be seen that, by means of these *metrical* and *topical* arrangements combined, the General Subjects can be found quite as easily as through an *Index*.

Hymns on particular subjects, or on passages of Scripture, must be sought for through the proper *Indexes* in the edition *without music*.

MUSICAL SIGNS AND ABBREVIATIONS.

The "doubled" bar (See No. 1 above) indicates that a line of a stanza *ends* at the close of a full measure; or, that the succeeding line *begins* with the first note of a measure.

As it is musically improper to use either a single or double bar, except to divide full measures one from another, the sign No. 2 has been adopted to denote the point of closing or beginning a line of poetry in the midst of a measure; it has no musical value whatever, being simply a guide to the eye in applying the lines of a stanza to its appropriate section of a tune.

The close of a tune is indicated by the sign No. 3, or by the word "FINE."

A repeat, indicated by the dots between the staff-lines (See No. 4.), requires the intermediate or preceding music to be sung *twice* before passing to what follows.

Da Capo, at the otherwise apparent end of a tune, requires that it be taken up again at the beginning, and sung as far as "*the close.*" **D. C.** is an abbreviation of the words *Da Capo*.

The sign 𝄐 (See No. 5) is called a *Pause* or *Hold*; and indicates that the note, or chord, should be prolonged beyond the due value of the notes. The ear should be held sensitive to the slightest indication from the precentor, or organ, that the next note is to be sung.

The sign ℘ (an authorized abbreviature of the syllable "*per*") has been adopted to signify that the "permission" of the proprietors of copyright or composers of tunes has been granted. Tunes so marked are considered the property of others, inserted here by special permission; such insertion invalidating no rights.

Tunes will be found which are "*abbreviated*" by a repetition of the music of the first line in singing the third line of the stanza, and then passing to the music for the fourth line. A thorough understanding of the manner of applying the tune *Medway* (p. 29) to a stanza, will be sufficient to enable any one to understand all similar cases in the work.

The words "**1st time,**" over or under any measure which immediately precedes a repeat mark, imply that the measure is to be omitted when singing the strain the second time, — and the measure marked "**2d time**" is to be sung instead.

THE PSALMIST.

WORSHIP.

OLD HUNDRED. L. M. G. Franc. Dates previous to 1543.

2. L. M. Watts.

1 Before Jehovah's awful throne,
Ye nations, bow with sacred joy;
Know that the Lord is God alone;
He can create, and he destroy.

2 His sovereign power, without our aid,
Made us of clay, and formed us men;
And when, like wandering sheep, we strayed,
He brought us to his fold again.

3 We are his people; we his care;
Our souls, and all our mortal frame:
What lasting honors shall we rear,
Almighty Maker, to thy name?

4 We'll crowd thy gates, with thankful songs,
High as the heaven our voices raise;
And Earth, with her ten thousand tongues,
Shall fill thy courts with sounding praise.

5 Wide as the world is thy command;
Vast as eternity thy love;
Firm as a rock thy truth shall stand,
When rolling years shall cease to move.

20. L. M. Watts.

1 Great God, attend, while Zion sings
The joy that from thy presence springs:
To spend one day with thee on earth
Exceeds a thousand days of mirth.

2 Might I enjoy the meanest place
Within thy house, O God of grace,
Not tents of ease, nor thrones of power,
Should tempt my feet to leave thy door.

3 God is our sun — he makes our day,
God is our shield — he guards our way
From all th' assaults of hell and sin;
From foes without and foes within.

4 All needful grace will God bestow,
And crown that grace with glory too:
He gives us all things, and withholds
No real good from upright souls.

5 O God, our King, whose sovereign sway
The glorious host of heaven obey,
Display thy grace, exert thy power,
Till all on earth thy name adore.

OLD "TEN COMMANDMENTS" TUNE. ‡ J. BAPTIST BONOMETTI. 1560.

The "Audi Israel" of ancient and "Bava" of modern collections ‡ Sung by the Puritans from Ainsworth's Psalms.

1. L. M. TATE & BRADY.

1 WITH one consent, let all the earth
To God their cheerful voices raise;
Glad homage pay, with hallowed mirth,
And sing before him songs of praise;—

2 Assured that he is God alone,
From whom both we and all proceed,—
We, whom he chooses for his own,
The flock which he delights to feed.

3 O, enter, then, his temple gate;
Thence to his courts devoutly press;
And still your grateful hymns repeat,
And still his name with praises bless;

4 For he's the Lord, supremely good;
His mercy is forever sure;
His truth, which always firmly stood,
To endless ages shall endure.

6. L. M. WATTS.

1 YE nations round the earth, rejoice
Before the Lord, your sovereign King;
Serve him with cheerful heart and voice;
With all your tongues his glory sing.

2 The Lord is God; 'tis he alone
Doth life, and breath, and being, give;
We are his work, and not our own,
The sheep that on his pastures live.

3 Enter his gates with songs of joy;
With praises to his courts repair;
And make it your divine employ
To pay your thanks and honours there.

4 The Lord is good; the Lord is kind;
Great is his grace, his mercy sure;
And all the race of man shall find
His truth from age to age endure.

26. L. M. WATTS.

1 COME, gracious Lord, descend and dwell,
By faith and love, in every breast;
Then shall we know, and taste, and feel,
The joys that cannot be expressed.

2 Come, fill our hearts with inward strength,
Make our enlargéd souls possess,
And learn the height, and breadth, and length,
Of thine eternal love and grace.

3 Now to the God whose power can do
More than our thoughts and wishes know,
Be everlasting honors done,
By all the church, through Christ, his Son.

31. L. M. SIR J. E. SMITH.

1 PRAISE waits in Zion, Lord, for thee;
Thy saints adore thy holy name;
Thy creatures bend th' obedient knee,
And, humbly, thy protection claim.

2 Thy hand has raised us from the dust;
The breath of life thy Spirit gave;
Where, but in thee, can mortals trust?
Who, but our God, has power to save?

3 Eternal Source of truth and light,
To thee we look, on thee we call;
Lord, we are nothing in thy sight,
But thou to us art all in all.

4 Still may thy children in thy word
Their common trust and refuge see;
O, bind us to each other, Lord,
By one great tie,—the love of thee.

5 Here, at the portal of thy house,
We leave our mortal hopes and fears,
Accept our prayer, and bless our vows,
And dry our penitential tears.

WARE. L. M.

N. D. Gould.
National Church Harmony, 1833. ℗ ‡

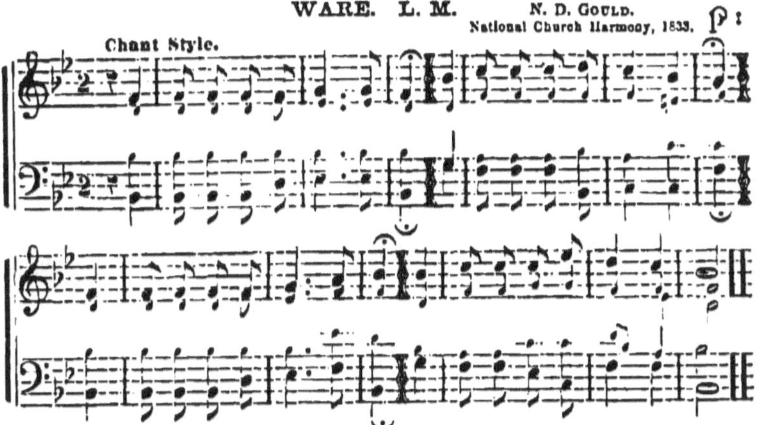

‡ The mark ℗ indicates "permission" from composers and proprietors of copyrights, throughout the book.

6 So shall our sun of hope arise,
  With brighter still and brighter ray,
Till thou shalt bless our longing eyes
  With beams of everlasting day.

5. L. M. Watts.

1 How pleasant, how divinely fair,
  O Lord of hosts, thy dwellings are!
With long desire my spirit faints
  To meet th' assemblies of thy saints.

2 My flesh would rest in thine abode;
  My panting heart cries out for God;
My God, my King, why should I be
  So far from all my joys and thee?

3 Blest are the saints, who dwell on high,
  Around thy throne, above the sky;
Thy brightest glories shine above,
  And all their work is praise and love.

4 Blest are the souls who find a place
  Within the temple of thy grace;
There they behold thy gentler rays,
  And seek thy face, and learn thy praise.

5 Blest are the men whose hearts are set
  To find the way to Zion's gate;
God is their strength; and, through the road,
  They lean upon their helper, God.

6 Cheerful they walk, with growing strength,
  Till all shall meet in heaven at length;
Till all before thy face appear,
  And join in nobler worship there.

35. L. M. J. Stennett.

1 Another six days' work is done,
  Another Sabbath is begun;
Return, my soul, enjoy thy rest,
  Improve the day that God hath blest.

2 O that our thoughts and thanks may rise,
  As grateful incense, to the skies,
And draw from heaven that sweet repose
  Which none but he that feels it knows!

3 A heavenly calm pervades the breast,
  The earnest of that glorious rest
Which for the church of God remains,
  The end of cares, the end of pains.

4 With joy, great God, thy works we view,
  In various scenes, both old and new:
With praise, we think on mercies past;
  With hope, we future pleasures taste.

5 In holy duties let the day,
  In holy pleasures, pass away;
How sweet, a Sabbath thus to spend,
  In hope of one that ne'er shall end!

64. L. M. Hart.

1 Dismiss us with thy blessing, Lord;
  Help us to feed upon thy word;
All that has been amiss, forgive,
  And let thy truth within us live.

2 Though we are guilty, thou art good;
  Wash all our works in Jesus' blood;
Give every burdened soul release,
  And bid us all depart in peace.

The following form has been adopted for suggesting to Precentors the proper key to tunes, so familiar that the objection of copyright proprietors to their insertion in this work will not operate to suppress their use in our churches.

WARD.

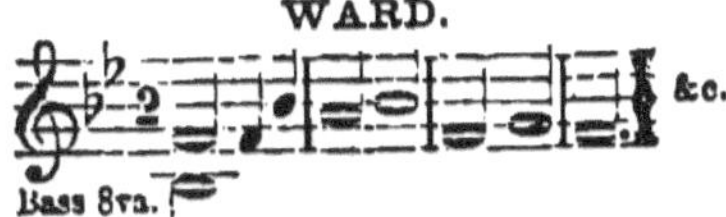

ANGELS' HYMN.‡ L. M. ORLANDO GIBBONS.
From Withers' Songs of the Church. 1623.

‡ Called also "Angels' Song." Has been arranged in many differing forms of rhythm and harmony.

49. L. M. BARBAULD.

1 WHEN, as returns this solemn day,
Man comes to meet his Maker, God,
What rites, what honors shall he pay?
How spread his sovereign name abroad?

2 From marble domes and gilded spires
Shall curling clouds of incense rise,
And gems, and gold, and garlands, deck
The costly pomp of sacrifice?

3 Vain, sinful man! creation's Lord
Thy golden offerings well may spare;
But give thy heart, and thou shalt find
Here dwells a God who heareth prayer.

4 O, grant us, in this solemn hour,
From earth and sin's allurements free,
To feel thy love, to own thy power,
And raise each raptured thought to thee!

52. L. M. BATHURST.

1 THIS day the Lord hath called his own;
O, let us, then, his praise declare,
Fix our desires on him alone,
And seek his face with fervent prayer.

2 Lord, in thy love we would rejoice,
Which bids the burdened soul be free,
And, with united heart and voice,
Devote these sacred hours to thee.

3 Now let the world's delusive things
No more our grovelling thoughts employ,
But Faith be taught to stretch her wings,
In search of heaven's unfailing joy.

4 O, let these earthly Sabbaths, Lord,
Be to our lasting welfare blest;
The purest comfort here afford,
And fit us for eternal rest.

54. L. M. RAFFLES.

1 BLEST hour, when mortal man retires
To hold communion with his God,
To send to heaven his warm desires,
And listen to the sacred word.

2 Blest hour, when earthly cares resign
Their empire o'er his anxious breast;
While, all around, the calm divine
Proclaims the holy day of rest.

3 Blest hour, when God himself draws nigh,
Well pleased his people's voice to hear,
To hush the penitential sigh,
And wipe away the mourner's tear.

4 Blest hour! for, where the Lord resorts,
Foretastes of future bliss are given,
And mortals find his earthly courts
The house of God, the gate of heaven.

55. L. M. DODDRIDGE.

1 THINE earthly Sabbaths, Lord, we love;
But there's a nobler rest above;
To that our longing souls aspire,
With cheerful hope and strong desire.

2 No more fatigue, no more distress,
Nor sin, nor death, shall reach the place;
No groans shall mingle with the songs
Which dwell upon immortal tongues;—

3 No rude alarms of angry foes;
No cares, to break the long repose;
No midnight shade, no clouded sun,
But sacred, high, eternal noon.

4 O, long-expected day, begin;
Dawn on these realms of pain and sin;
With joy we'll tread th' appointed road,
And sleep in death, to rest with God.

‡ Composed in $\frac{3}{2}$ time, by Crasselius, Lutheran Presbyter, of Dusseldorf; altered here only in rhythm.

1 From "A Hymn to the blessed Trinity," written in Gregorian notes in one part, as sung by "The Laudesi," the oldest musical society on record, founded A. D. 1310, by the Friars of All Saints, at Florence. The melody is unaltered in the first and third lines, but is slightly varied in the others. The rhythm is unchanged.

DEVOTION. L. M. Read.

41. L. M. Epis. Col.

1 My opening eyes with rapture see
The dawn of thy returning day ;
My thoughts, O God, ascend to thee,
While thus my early vows I pay.

2 I yield my heart to thee alone,
Nor would receive another guest :
Eternal King, erect thy throne,
And reign sole monarch in my breast.

3 O, bid this trifling world retire,
And drive each carnal thought away ;
Nor let me feel one vain desire,
One sinful thought, through all the day.

4 Then, to thy courts when I repair,
My soul shall rise on joyful wing,
The wonders of thy love declare,
And join the strains which angels sing.

5 Then shall I see, and hear, and know,
All I desired or wished below,
And every power find sweet employ
In that eternal world of joy.

50. L. M. Watts.

1 Sweet is the work, my God, my King,
To praise thy name, give thanks, and sing ;
To show thy love by morning light,
And talk of all thy truth at night.

2 Sweet is the day of sacred rest ;
No mortal care shall fill my breast ;
O, may my heart in tune be found,
Like David's harp, of solemn sound.

3 My heart shall triumph in the Lord,
And bless his works, and bless his word :
His works of grace, how bright they shine !
How deep his counsels, how divine !

4 And I shall share a glorious part,
When grace hath well refined my heart,
And fresh supplies of joy are shed,
Like holy oil, to cheer my head.

76. L. M. Watts.

1 The heavens declare thy glory, Lord ;
In every star thy wisdom shines ;
But when our eyes behold thy word,
We read thy name in fairer lines.

2 The rolling sun, the changing light,
And nights, and days, thy power confess ;
But that blest volume thou hast writ
Reveals thy justice and thy grace.

3 Sun, moon, and stars, convey thy praise
Around the earth, and never stand ;
So, when thy truth began its race,
It touched and glanced on every land.

4 Nor shall thy spreading gospel rest
Till through the world thy truth has run,
Till Christ has all the nations blest
That see the light or feel the sun.

5 Great Sun of Righteousness, arise ;
O, bless the world with heavenly light ;
Thy gospel makes the simple wise ;
Thy laws are pure, thy judgments right.

6 Thy noblest wonders here we view,
In souls renewed and sins forgiven ;
Lord, cleanse my sins, my soul renew,
And make thy word my guide to heaven.

UXBRIDGE.

OLD HUNDRED. L. M. G. Franc. Dates previous to 1542.

‡ The application of tunes not necessarily confined to hymns on the same page.

70. L. M. Tate & Brady.

1 Be thou, O God, exalted high;
And as thy glory fills the sky,
So let it be on earth displayed,
Till thou art here, as there, obeyed.

2 O God, my heart is fixed; 'tis bent
Its thankful tribute to present;
And, with my heart, my voice I'll raise
To thee, my God, in songs of praise.

3 Thy praises, Lord, I will resound
To all the listening nations round;
Thy mercy highest heaven transcends;
Thy truth beyond the clouds extends.

4 Be thou, O God, exalted high;
And as thy glory fills the sky,
So let it be on earth displayed,
Till thou art here, as there, obeyed.

94. L. M. Blacklock.

1 Come, O my soul, in sacred lays
Attempt thy great Creator's praise:
But, O, what tongue can speak his fame?
What verse can reach the lofty theme?

2 Enthroned amid the radiant spheres,
He glory like a garment wears;
To form a robe of light divine,
Ten thousand suns around him shine.

3 In all our Maker's grand designs,
Almighty power, with wisdom, shines;
His works, through all this wondrous frame,
Declare the glory of his name.

4 Raised on devotion's lofty wing,
Do thou, my soul, his glories sing;
And let his praise employ thy tongue
Till listening worlds shall join the song.

101. L. M. Watts.

1 Nature, with all her powers, shall sing
Her great Creator and her King;
Nor air, nor earth, nor skies, nor seas,
Deny the tribute of their praise.

2 Ye seraphs, who sit near his throne,
Begin to make his glories known;
Tune high your harps, and spread the sound
Throughout creation's utmost bound.

3 O, may our ardent zeal employ
Our loftiest thoughts and loudest songs;
Let there be sung, with warmest joy,
Hosanna from ten thousand tongues.

4 Yet, mighty God, our feeble frame
Attempts in vain to reach thy name;
The highest notes that angels raise
Fall far below thy glorious praise.

104. L. M. Watts.

1 Loud hallelujahs to the Lord,
From distant worlds, where creatures dwell;
Let heaven begin the solemn word,
And sound it dreadful down to hell.

2 Wide as his vast dominion lies,
Make the Creator's name be known;
Loud as his thunder shout his praise,
And sound it lofty as his throne.

3 Jehovah! — 'tis a glorious word;
O, may it dwell on every tongue;
But saints, who best have known the Lord,
Are bound to raise the noblest song.

4 Speak of the wonders of that love
Which Gabriel plays on every chord;
From all below, and all above,
Loud hallelujahs to the Lord.

DUKE STREET. L. M. J. HATTON. ‡

‡ Attributed also to REED.

95. L. M. WATTS.

1 PRAISE ye the Lord: my heart shall join
In work so pleasant, so divine;
My days of praise shall ne'er be past,
While life, and thought, and being, last.

2 Happy the man whose hopes rely
On Israel's God: he made the sky,
And earth, and seas, with all their train;
And none shall find his promise vain.

3 His truth forever stands secure;
He saves th' oppressed, he feeds the poor;
He helps the stranger in distress,
The widow and the fatherless.

4 He loves the saints; he knows them well,
But turns the wicked down to hell:
Thy God, O Zion, ever reigns;
Praise him in everlasting strains.

106. L. M. WATTS.

1 WITH all my powers of heart and tongue,
I'll praise my Maker in my song;
Angels shall hear the notes I raise,
Approve the song, and join the praise.

2 To God I cried, when troubles rose;
He heard me, and subdued my foes;
He did my rising fears control,
And strength diffused through all my soul.

3 Amid a thousand snares I stand,
Upheld and guarded by his hand;
His words my fainting soul revive,
And keep my dying faith alive.

4 I'll sing thy truth and mercy, Lord;
I'll sing the wonders of thy word;
Not all the works and names below,
So much thy power and glory show.

108. L. M. WATTS.

1 MY God, my King, thy various praise
Shall fill the remnant of my days;
Thy grace employ my humble tongue,
Till death and glory raise the song.

2 The wings of every hour shall bear
Some thankful tribute to thine ear;
And every setting sun shall see
New works of duty done for thee.

3 Thy works with boundless glory shine,
And speak thy majesty divine;
Let every realm with joy proclaim
The sound and honor of thy name.

4 Let distant times and nations raise
The long succession of thy praise,
And unborn ages make my song
The joy and triumph of their tongue.

113. L. M. WATTS.

1 BE thou exalted, O my God,
Above the heavens, where angels dwell;
Thy power on earth be known abroad,
And land to land thy wonders tell.

2 My heart is fixed; my song shall raise
Immortal honors to his name;
Awake, my tongue, to sound his praise,
His wondrous goodness to proclaim.

3 High o'er the earth his mercy reigns,
And reaches to the utmost sky;
His truth to endless years remains,
When lower worlds dissolve and die.

4 Be thou exalted, O my God,
Above the heavens, where angels dwell;
Thy power on earth be known abroad,
And land to land thy wonders tell.

GROTON. L. M.‡ Zinck. From Sacred Minstrel.

‡ For Hymn 75 repeat without pause.

75. L. M. Mrs. Opie.

1 There seems a voice in every gale,
A tongue in every opening flower,
Which tells, O Lord, the wondrous tale
Of thy indulgence, love, and power;
The birds, that rise on quivering wing,
Appear to hymn their Maker's praise,
And all the mingling sounds of spring
To thee a general anthem raise.

2 And shall my voice, great God, alone
Be mute 'midst Nature's loud acclaim,
Nor let my heart, with answering tone,
Breathe forth in praise thy holy name?
All Nature's debt is small to mine,
For Nature soon shall cease to be,
But — matchless proof of love divine —
Thou gav'st immortal life to me.

80. L. M. Watts.

1 Come, let our voices join to raise
A sacred song of solemn praise;
God is a sovereign King: rehearse
His honor in exalted verse.

2 Come, let our souls address the Lord,
Who framed our natures by his word;
He is our Shepherd: we, the sheep
His mercy chose, his pastures keep.

3 Come, let us hear his voice to-day,
The counsels of his love obey;
Nor let our hardened hearts renew
The sins and plagues that Israel knew.

4 Come, let us turn, with holy fear,
To him who now invites us near,
Accept the offered grace to-day,
Nor lose the blessing by delay.

5 Come, seize the promise while it waits,
And march to Zion's heavenly gates;
Believe, and take the promised rest;
Obey, and be forever blest.

86. L. M. Tate & Brady.

1 O praise the Lord in that blest place
From whence his goodness largely flows;
Praise him in heaven, where he his face
Unveiled in perfect glory shows.

2 Praise him for all the mighty acts
Which he in our behalf hath done;
His kindness this return exacts,
With which our praise should equal run.

3 Let all, who vital breath enjoy,
The breath he doth to them afford
In just returns of praise employ;
Let every creature praise the Lord.

93. L. M. Steele.

1 Awake, my soul; awake, my tongue;
My God demands the grateful song;
Let all my inmost powers record
The wondrous mercy of the Lord.

2 Divinely free his mercy flows,
Forgives my sins, allays my woes,
And bids approaching death remove,
And crowns me with indulgent love.

3 His mercy, with unchanging rays,
Forever shines, while time decays;
And children's children shall record
The truth and goodness of the Lord.

4 While all his works his praise proclaim,
And men and angels bless his name,
O, let my heart, my life, my tongue,
Attend, and join the blissful song.

HEBRO. L. M. Arranged by the Editor for this work.

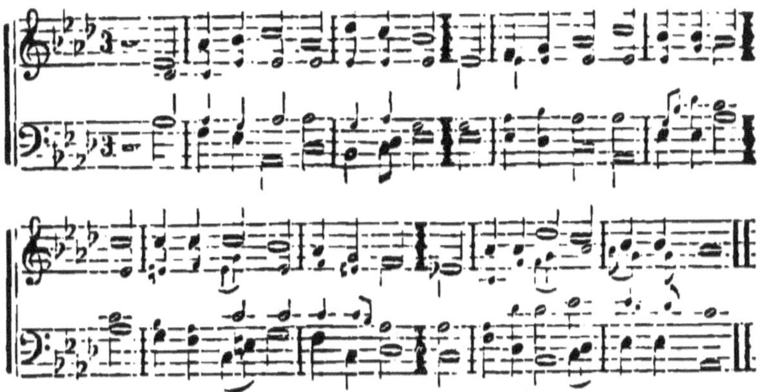

From a German choral; melody rhythmically changed.

103. L. M. Doddridge.

1 God of my life, through all my days
I'll tune the grateful notes of praise;
The song shall wake with opening light,
And warble to the silent night.

2 When anxious care would break my rest,
And grief would tear my throbbing breast,
The notes of praise, ascending high,
Shall check the murmur and the sigh.

3 When death o'er nature shall prevail,
And all the powers of language fail,
Joy through my swimming eyes shall break,
And mean the thanks I cannot speak.

4 But, O, when that last conflict's o'er,
And I am chained to earth no more,
With what glad accents shall I rise
To join the music of the skies!

5 Then shall I learn th' exalted strains
That echo through the heavenly plains,
And emulate, with joy unknown,
The glowing seraphs round thy throne.

114. L. M. Watts.

1 Almighty Ruler of the skies,
Through all the earth thy name is spread,
And thine eternal glories rise
Above the heavens thy hands have made.

2 To thee the voices of the young
Their sounding notes of honor raise,
And babes, with uninstructed tongue,
Declare the wonders of thy praise.

3 Amidst thy temple children throng
To see their great Redeemer's face;
The Son of David is their song,
And loud hosannas fill the place.

117. L. M. Watts.

1 Blest be the Father and his love,
To which celestial source we owe
Rivers of endless joy above,
And rills of comfort here below.

2 All praise to thee, great Son of God,
From whose dear, wounded body rolls
A precious stream of vital blood—
A fount of life for dying souls.

3 We give thee, sacred Spirit, praise,
Who, in our hearts of sin and woe,
Mak'st living springs of grace arise,
And into boundless glory flow.

4 Thus God the Father, God the Son,
And God the Spirit, we adore—
That sea of life and love unknown,
Without a bottom or a shore.

123. L. M. Bickersteth's Col.

1 Father of heaven, whose love profound
A ransom for our souls hath found,
Before thy throne we, sinners, bend;
To us thy pardoning love extend

2 Almighty Son, incarnate Word,
Our Prophet, Priest, Redeemer, Lord,
Before thy throne we, sinners, bend;
To us thy saving grace extend.

3 Eternal Spirit, by whose breath
The soul is raised from sin and death,
Before thy throne we, sinners, bend;
To us thy quickening power extend.

4 Jehovah! Father, Spirit, Son!
Eternal Godhead! Three in One!
Before thy throne we, sinners, bend;
Grace, pardon, life, to us extend.

JAH.: L. M. German.

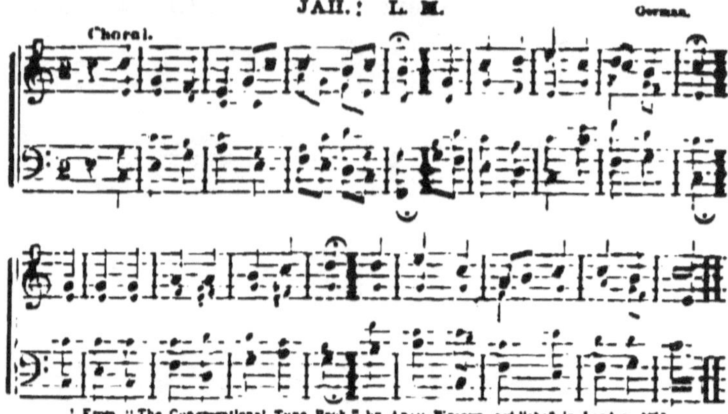

: From "The Congregational Tune Book," by ADAM WRIGHT, published in London, 1851.

140. L. M. NEEDHAM.

1 AWAKE, my tongue; thy tribute bring
To Him who gave thee power to sing;
Praise Him who has all praise above,
The source of wisdom and of love.

2 How vast his knowledge! how profound!
A depth where all our thoughts are drowned!
The stars he numbers, and their names
He gives to all those heavenly flames.

3 Through each bright world above, behold
Ten thousand thousand charms unfold,
Earth, air, and mighty seas, combine
To speak his wisdom all divine.

4 But in redemption, O, what grace!
Its wonders, O, what thought can trace!
Here wisdom shines forever bright;
Praise him, my soul, with sweet delight.

141. L. M. WATTS

1 JEHOVAH reigns; he dwells in light,
Arrayed with majesty and might;
The world, created by his hands,
Still on its firm foundation stands.

2 But ere this spacious world was made
Or had its first foundation laid,
His throne eternal ages stood;
Himself the ever-living God.

3 Like floods the angry nations rise,
And aim their rage against the skies;
Vain floods, that aim their rage so high;
At his rebuke, the billows die.

4 Forever shall his throne endure;
His promise stands forever sure;
And everlasting holiness
Becomes the dwellings of his grace.

143. L. M. WATTS.

1 JEHOVAH reigns; his throne is high;
His robes are light and majesty;
His glory shines with beams so bright,
No mortal can sustain the sight.

2 His terrors keep the world in awe;
His justice guards his holy law;
His love reveals a smiling face;
His truth and promise seal the grace.

3 Through all his works his wisdom shines,
And baffles Satan's deep designs;
His power is sovereign to fulfil
The noblest counsels of his will.

4 And will this glorious Lord descend
To be my Father and my Friend?
Then let my songs with angels' join;
Heaven is secure, if God be mine.

146. L. M. KIPPIS.

1 GREAT God, in vain man's narrow view
Attempts to look thy nature through;
Our laboring powers with reverence own
Thy glories never can be known.

2 Not the high seraph's mighty thought,
Who countless years his God has sought,
Such wondrous height or depth can find,
Or fully trace thy boundless mind.

3 Yet, Lord, thy kindness deigns to show
All that we mortals need to know;
While wisdom, goodness, power divine,
Through all thy works and conduct shine.

4 O, may our souls with rapture trace
Thy works of nature and of grace;
Adore thy sacred name, and still
Press on to know and do thy will.

MEDWAY. L. M. PERGOLESI.

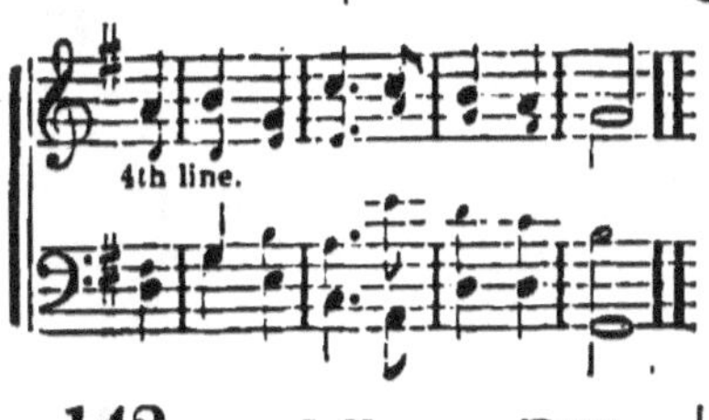

142. L. M. WATTS.

1 LORD, we adore thy vast designs,
Th' obscure abyss of providence,
Too deep to sound with mortal lines,
Too dark to view with feeble sense.

2 When thou dost clothe thine awful face
In angry frowns, without a smile,
We, through the cloud, believe thy grace,
Secure of thy compassion still.

3 Through seas and storms of deep distress
We sail by faith, and not by sight;
Faith guides us, in the wilderness,
Through all the terrors of the night.

4 Dear Father, if thy lifted rod
Resolves to scourge us here below,
Still let us lean upon our God;
Thine arm shall bear us safely through.

152. L. M. S. S. CUTTING.

1 GOD of the world! thy glories shine,
Through earth and heaven, with rays divine;
Thy smile gives beauty to the flower,
Thine anger to the tempest power.

2 God of our lives! the throbbing heart
Doth at thy beck its action start,—
Throbs on, obedient to thy will,
Or ceases, at thy fatal chill.

3 God of eternal life! thy love
Doth every stain of sin remove;
The cross, the cross — its hallowed light
Shall drive from earth her cheerless night.

4 God of all goodness! to the skies
Our hearts in grateful anthems rise;
And to thy service shall be given
The rest of life — the whole of heaven.

130. L. M. NOEL'S COL.

1 WHERE can we hide, or whither fly,
Lord, to escape thy piercing eye?
With thee it is not day and night,
But darkness shineth as the light.

2 Where'er we go, whate'er pursue,
Our ways are open to thy view,
Our motives read, our thoughts explored,
Our hearts revealed to thee, O Lord.

3 Is there, throughout all worlds, one spot,
One lonely wild, where thou art not?
The hosts of heaven enjoy thy care,
And those of hell know thou art there.

4 Awake, asleep, where none intrude,
Or 'midst the thronging multitude,
In every land, on every sea,
We are surrounded still with thee.

5 Search us, O God, and know each heart;
With every idol bid us part;
Make us to keep thy holy ways,
And live to utter forth thy praise.

151. L. M. WATTS.

1 HIGH in the heavens, eternal God,
Thy goodness in full glory shines;
Thy truth shall break through every cloud
That veils thy just and wise designs.

2 Forever firm thy justice stands,
As mountains their foundations keep;
Wise are the wonders of thy hands;
Thy judgments are a mighty deep.

3 O God, how excellent thy grace,
Whence all our hope and comfort spring!
The sons of Adam, in distress,
Fly to the shadow of thy wing.

4 In the provisions of thy house
We still shall find a sweet repast;
There mercy, like a river, flows,
And brings salvation to our taste.

5 Life, like a fountain, rich and free,
Springs from the presence of my Lord;
And in thy light our souls shall see
The glories promised in thy word.

ALFRETON. L. M. ‡ W. BEASTALL, 1708.

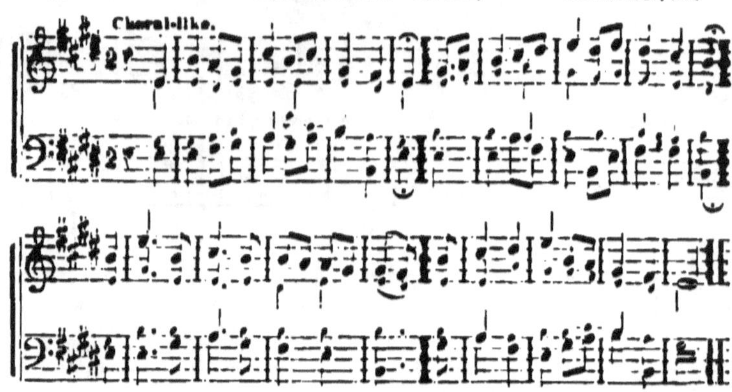

‡ Or, 6 lines by repeating the upper brace: for hymns below.

—IN HIMSELF.

129. L. M. 6 L. MOORE.

1 THOU art, O God, the life and light
  Of all this wondrous world we see;
Its glow by day, its smile by night,
  Are but reflections caught from thee;
Where'er we turn, thy glories shine,
And all things fair and bright are thine.

2 When day, with farewell beam, delays
  Among the opening clouds of even,
And we can almost think we gaze,
  Through opening vistas, into heaven,—
Those hues, that mark the sun's decline,
So soft, so radiant, Lord, are thine.

3 When night, with wings of starry gloom,
  O'ershadows all the earth and skies,
Like some dark, beauteous bird, whose plume
  Is sparkling with unnumbered eyes,—
That sacred gloom, those fires divine,
So grand, so countless, Lord, are thine.

4 When youthful Spring around us breathes,
  Thy spirit warms her fragrant sigh;
And every flower that Summer wreathes
  Is born beneath thy kindling eye:
Where'er we turn, thy glories shine,
And all things fair and bright are thine.

BELVILLE.

197. L. M. 6 L. ADDISON.

1 THE Lord my pasture shall prepare,
  And feed me with a shepherd's care;
  His presence shall my wants supply,
  And guard me with a watchful eye;
  My noonday walks he shall attend,
  And all my midnight hours defend.

2 When in the sultry glebe I faint,
  Or on the thirsty mountain pant,
  To fertile vales and dewy meads
  My weary, wandering steps he leads,
  Where peaceful rivers, soft and slow,
  Amid the verdant landscape flow.

3 Though in the paths of death I tread,
  With gloomy horrors overspread,
  My steadfast heart shall fear no ill,
  For thou, O Lord, art with me still:
  Thy friendly rod shall give me aid,
  And guide me through the dreadful shade.

4 Though in a bare and rugged way,
  Through devious, lonely wilds I stray,
  Thy presence shall my pains beguile;
  The barren wilderness shall smile,
  With sudden greens and herbage crowned,
  And streams shall murmur all around.

199. L. M. WATTS.

1 THOUGH I walk through the gloomy vale,
  Where death and all its terrors are,
  My heart and hope shall never fail,
  For God my Shepherd 's with me there.

2 Amid the darkness and the deeps,
  Thou art my comfort, thou my stay;
  Thy staff supports my feeble steps,
  Thy rod directs my doubtful way.

OLIVET. L. M.‡

‡ Or 6 lines by repeating the upper brace.

132. L. M. Spir. of Psalms.

1 Father of spirits, nature's God,
Our inmost thoughts are known to thee;
Thou, Lord, canst hear each idle word,
And every private action see.

2 Could we, on morning's swiftest wings,
Pursue our flight through trackless air,
Or dive beneath deep ocean's springs,
Thy presence still would meet us there.

3 In vain may guilt attempt to fly,
Concealed beneath the pall of night;
One glance from thy all-piercing eye
Can kindle darkness into light.

4 Search thou our hearts, and there destroy
Each evil thought, each secret sin,
And fit us for those realms of joy,
Where nought impure shall enter in.

185. L. M. Doddridge.

1 Ye sons of men, with joy record
The various wonders of the Lord;
And let his power and goodness sound
Through all your tribes, the earth around.

2 Let the high heavens your songs invite,—
Those spacious fields of brilliant light,
Where sun, and moon, and planets roll,
And stars that glow from pole to pole.

3 But, O, that brighter world above,
Where lives and reigns incarnate Love!
God's only Son, in flesh arrayed,
For man a bleeding victim made.

4 Thither, my soul, with rapture soar;
There, in the land of praise, adore;
The theme demands an angel's lay,
Demands an everlasting day.

186. L. M. Watts.

1 Bless, O my soul, the living God;
Call home thy thoughts, that rove abroad;
Let all the powers within me join
In work and worship so divine.

2 Bless, O my soul, the God of grace;
His favors claim thy highest praise;
Let not the wonders he hath wrought
Be lost in silence, and forgot.

3 'Tis he, my soul, that sent his Son
To die for crimes which thou hast done:
He owns the ransom, and forgives
The hourly follies of our lives.

4 Let every land his power confess;
Let all the earth adore his grace:
My heart and tongue, with rapture, join
In work and worship so divine.

192. L. M. Watts.

1 Great God, indulge my humble claim;
Thou art my hope, my joy, my rest;
The glories that compose thy name
Stand all engaged to make me blest.

2 Thou great and good, thou just and wise,
Thou art my Father and my God;
And I am thine, by sacred ties,
Thy son, thy servant, bought with blood.

3 With early feet I love t' appear
Among thy saints, and seek thy face;
Oft have I seen thy glory there,
And felt the power of sovereign grace.

4 I'll lift my hands, I'll raise my voice,
While I have breath to pray or praise;
This work shall make my heart rejoice,
And bless the remnant of my days.

NAZARETH. L. M. (Melcombe.) Attributed to S. Webbe. ‡

‡ Thought by some to be an arrangement from a Gregorian melody.

136. L. M. Watts.

1 Lord, thou hast searched and seen me through;
Thine eye commands, with piercing view,
My rising and my resting hours,
My heart and flesh, with all their powers.

2 My thoughts, before they are my own,
Are to my God distinctly known;
He knows the words I mean to speak,
Ere from my opening lips they break.

3 Within thy circling power I stand;
On every side I find thy hand;
Awake, asleep, at home, abroad,
I am surrounded still with God.

4 Amazing knowledge, vast and great!
What large extent! what lofty height!
My soul, with all the powers I boast,
Is in the boundless prospect lost.

5 O, may these thoughts possess my breast
Where'er I rove, where'er I rest!
Nor let my weaker passions dare
Consent to sin, for God is there.

171. L. M. Anon.

1 When thickly beat the storms of life,
And heavy is the chastening rod,
The soul, beyond the waves of strife,
Views the eternal rock — her God.

2 What hope dispels the spirit's gloom,
When sinking 'neath affliction's shock?
Faith, through the vista of the tomb,
Points to the everlasting Rock.

3 Is there a man who cannot see
That joy and grief are from above?
O, let him humbly bend the knee,
And own his Father's chastening love.

4 Hope, Grace, and Truth, with gentle hand,
Shall lead a bleeding Saviour's flock,
And show them, in the promised land,
The shelter of th' eternal Rock.

172. L. M. Watts.

1 God is the refuge of his saints,
When storms of sharp distress invade;
Ere we can offer our complaints,
Behold him present with his aid.

2 Loud may the troubled ocean roar;
In sacred peace our souls abide,
While every nation, every shore,
Trembles, and dreads the swelling tide.

3 There is a stream whose gentle flow
Supplies the city of our God;
Life, love, and joy, still gliding through,
And watering our divine abode.

4 That sacred stream, thine holy word,
Supports our faith, our fear controls;
Sweet peace thy promises afford,
And give new strength to fainting souls.

5 Zion enjoys her Monarch's love,
Secure against a threatening hour;
Nor can her firm foundation move,
Built on his truth, and armed with power.

212. L. M. Watts.

1 Not to condemn the sons of men,
Did Christ, the Son of God, appear;
No weapons in his hands are seen,
No flaming sword nor thunder there.

ALTON. L. M. From Sacred Minstrel.‡ 1833.

‡ This and all the tunes from the Sacred Minstrel are inserted by special permission.

2 Such was the pity of our God,
He loved the race of man so well,
He sent his Son to bear our load
Of sins, and save our souls from hell.

3 Sinners, believe the Saviour's word;
Trust in his mighty name, and live;
A thousand joys his lips afford,
His hands a thousand blessings give.

232. L. M. WATTS.

1 HE dies! — the Friend of sinners dies;
Lo! Salem's daughters weep around;
A solemn darkness veils the skies;
A sudden trembling shakes the ground.

2 Ye saints, approach! — the anguish view
Of him who groans beneath your load;
He gives his precious life for you;
For you he sheds his precious blood.

3 Here's love and grief beyond degree;
The Lord of glory dies for men;
But, lo! what sudden joys we see!
Jesus, the dead, revives again.

4 The rising God forsakes the tomb;
Up to his Father's court he flies;
Cherubic legions guard him home,
And shout him welcome to the skies.

5 Break off your tears, ye saints, and tell
How high our great Deliverer reigns;
Sing how he spoiled the hosts of hell,
And led the tyrant Death in chains.

6 Say, "Live forever, glorious King,
Born to redeem, and strong to save!"
Then ask, "O Death, where is thy sting?
And where thy victory, boasting Grave?"

219. L. M. W. B. TAPPAN.

1 'Tis midnight; and on Olive's brow
The star is dimmed that lately shone;
'Tis midnight; in the garden, now,
The suffering Saviour prays alone.

2 'Tis midnight; and, from all removed,
The Saviour wrestles lone, with fears;
E'en that disciple whom he loved
Heeds not his Master's grief and tears.

3 'Tis midnight; and for others' guilt
The man of sorrows weeps in blood;
Yet he that hath in anguish knelt
Is not forsaken by his God.

4 'Tis midnight; and from ether plains
Is borne the song that angels know;
Unheard by mortals are the strains
That sweetly soothe the Saviour's woe.

226. L. M. STEELE.

1 STRETCHED on the cross, the Saviour dies;
Hark! his expiring groans arise;
See, from his hands, his feet, his side,
Descends the sacred, crimson tide.

2 And didst thou bleed? — for sinners bleed?
And could the sun behold the deed?
No; he withdrew his cheering ray,
And darkness veiled the mourning day.

3 Can I survey this scene of woe,
Where mingling grief and mercy flow,
And yet my heart so hard remain,
Unmoved by either love or pain!

4 Come, dearest Lord, thy grace impart,
To warm this cold, this stupid heart,
Till all its powers and passions move
In melting grief and ardent love.

TIMSBURY. L. M.

I. Smith.

Hymn 230 admits widely different adaptations: occasion and circumstances should have influence.

230. L. M. S. Stennett.

1 "'Tis finished!" — so the Saviour cried,
And meekly bowed his head and died:
'Tis finished! — yes, the race is run,
The battle fought, the victory won.

2 'Tis finished! — this his dying groan
Shall sins of deepest hue atone,
And millions be redeemed from death
By Jesus' last, expiring breath.

3 'Tis finished! — Heaven is reconciled,
And all the powers of darkness spoiled;
Peace, love, and happiness, again
Return, and dwell with sinful men.

4 'Tis finished! — let the joyful sound
Be heard through all the nations round:
'Tis finished! — let the triumph rise,
And swell the chorus of the skies.

238. L. M. Butcher.

1 Hosanna! let us join to sing
The glories of our rising King;
Recount his deeds of might, and tell
How Jesus triumphed when he fell.

2 Soon as the morning's early ray
Brings on the third, th' appointed day,
Behold the angel cleave the skies,
Roll back the stone, and Jesus rise.

3 With strength immortal forth he comes,
And power and life from God resumes;
The days of pain and sorrow past,
His triumph shall forever last.

4 Hosanna! sons of men, record
The glories of your rising Lord;
The triumphs of the Saviour tell,
Who died, and conquered when he fell.

244. L. M. Watts.

1 Now for a tune of lofty praise
To great Jehovah's equal Son;
Awake, my voice, in heavenly lays,
And tell the wonders he hath done.

2 Sing how he left the worlds of light,
And those bright robes he wore above;
How swift and joyful was his flight,
On wings of everlasting love!

3 Deep in the shades of gloomy death,
Th' almighty Captive prisoner lay; —
Th' almighty Captive left the earth,
And rose to everlasting day.

4 Among a thousand harps and songs,
Jesus, the God, exalted reigns:
His sacred name fills all their tongues,
And echoes through the heavenly plains.

247. L. M. Watts.

1 Lord, when thou didst ascend on high,
Ten thousand angels filled the sky;
Those heavenly guards around thee wait,
Like chariots, that attend thy state.

2 Not Sinai's mountain could appear
More glorious, when the Lord was there;
While he pronounced his holy law,
And struck the chosen tribes with awe.

3 How bright the triumph none can tell,
When all the rebel powers of hell,
That thousand souls had captive made,
Were all in chains, like captives, led.

4 Raised by his Father to the throne,
He sent his promised Spirit down,
With gifts and grace for rebel men,
That God might dwell on earth again.

! See Note page 22.

STERLING. L. M.
Chant Style.
GOULD'S CHANT. L. M. (Hope.)
N. D. Gould.
OLD HUNDRED. L. M.
G. Franc.
Choral.

OLD "TEN COMMANDMENTS" TUNE. J. BAPTIST BONOMETTI. 1560.

251. L. M. WATTS.

1 NATURE with open volume stands,
 To spread her Maker's praise abroad;
And every labor of his hands
 Shows something worthy of a God.

2 But in the grace that rescued man
 His brightest form of glory shines;
Here, on the cross, 'tis fairest drawn,
 In precious blood and crimson lines.

3 Here I behold his inmost heart,
 Where truth and mercy strangely join
To pierce his Son with keenest smart,
 And make the purchased pleasures mine.

4 O the sweet wonders of that cross,
 Where God, the Saviour, loved and died!
Her noblest life my spirit draws
 From his dear wounds and bleeding side.

5 I would forever speak his name,
 In sounds to mortal ears unknown,
With angels join to praise the Lamb,
 And worship at his Father's throne.

252. L. M. WATTS.

1 Now to the power of God supreme
 Be everlasting honors given;
He saves from hell, — we bless his name, —
 He guides our wandering feet to heaven.

2 Not for our duties or deserts,
 But of his own abundant grace,
He works salvation in our hearts,
 And forms a people for his praise.

3 'Twas his own purpose that begun
 To rescue rebels doomed to die;
He gave us grace in Christ his Son,
 Before he spread the starry sky.

4 Jesus, the Lord, appears at last,
 And makes his Father's counsels known,
Declares the great transaction past,
 And brings immortal blessings down.

5 He died, and, in that dreadful night,
 Did all the powers of hell destroy;
He rose, and brought our heaven to light,
 And took possession of the joy.

267. L. M. WATTS.

1 SALVATION is forever nigh
 The souls who fear and trust the Lord;
And grace, descending from on high,
 Fresh hopes of glory shall afford.

2 Mercy and truth on earth are met,
 Since Christ the Lord came down from heaven.
By his atonement, so complete,
 Justice is pleased, and peace is given.

3 His righteousness is gone before,
 To give us free access to God;
Our wandering feet shall stray no more,
 But mark his steps, and keep the road.

270. L. M. ANON.

1 INSCRIBED upon the cross we see,
 In glowing letters, "God is love;"
He bears our sins upon the tree;
 He brings us mercy from above.

2 The cross! it takes our guilt away;
 It holds the fainting spirit up;
It cheers with hope the gloomy day,
 And sweetens every bitter cup; —

3 The balm of life, the cure of woe,
 The measure and the pledge of love,
The sinner's refuge here below,
 The angel's theme in heaven above.

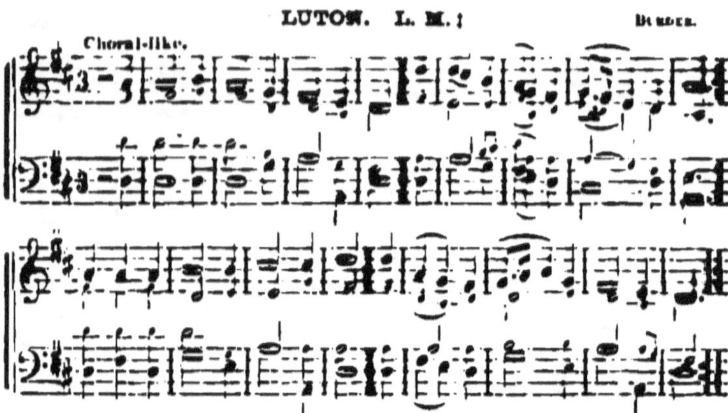

‡ May be sung to a 6 line hymn by repeating upper brace.

253. L. M. WATTS.

1 NO more, my God, I boast no more
 Of all the duties I have done;
I quit the hopes I held before,
 To trust the merits of thy Son.

2 Now, for the love I bear his name,
 What was my gain I count my loss;
My former pride I call my shame,
 And nail my glory to his cross.

3 Yes, and I must and will esteem
 All things but loss for Jesus' sake;
O, may my soul be found in him,
 And of his righteousness partake.

4 The best obedience of my hands
 Dares not appear before thy throne;
But Faith can answer thy demands,
 By pleading what my Lord has done.

255. L. M. WATTS.

1 DEEP in our hearts let us record
 The deeper sorrows of our Lord;
Behold, the rising billows roll,
 To overwhelm his holy soul.

2 Yet, gracious God, thy power and love
 Have made the curse a blessing prove;
Those dreadful sufferings of thy Son
 Atoned for sins that we had done.

3 The pangs of our expiring Lord
 The honors of thy law restored;
His sorrows made thy justice known,
 And paid for follies not his own.

4 O, for his sake our guilt forgive,
 And let the mourning sinner live:
The Lord will hear us in his name,
 Nor shall our hope be turned to shame.

258. L. M. S. STENNETT.

1 HOW shall the sons of men appear,
 Great God, before thine awful bar?
How may the guilty hope to find
 Acceptance with th' Eternal Mind?

2 Not vows, nor groans, nor broken cries,
 Not the most costly sacrifice,
Not infant blood profusely spilt,
 Will expiate a sinner's guilt.

3 Thy blood, dear Jesus, thine alone,
 Hath sovereign virtue to atone:
Here will we rest our only plea,
 When we approach, great God, to thee.

263. L. M. ANON.

1 COME, guilty sinners, come and see
 Your great atoning Sacrifice:
Behold, on yonder gory tree,
 The King of kings for rebels dies.

2 How gracious, how severe thou art,
 Just God, in thy redeeming plan!
The spear that pierced Immanuel's heart
 Revealed the fount of life for man.

3 Hail, hallowed cross, accursed no more;
 Rich tree of life to all our race;
Blest tree of Paradise, which bore
 The choicest fruit — the gift of grace.

4 Lord, shall our grief or joy prevail?
 Our heart is rent amidst their strife;
Shall we the Victim's death bewail,
 Or hail it as our way to life?

5 Thy dying, living, boundless love,
 While here below, shall tune our tongue,
And, when we join the choir above,
 Thy love be our triumphant song.

PROSPECT HILL. L. M. ‡ R. GILCHRIST.

‡ Or 6 lines by repeating upper brace.

256. L. M. FAWCETT.

1 BEHOLD the sin-atoning Lamb,
With wonder, gratitude, and love;
To take away our guilt and shame,
See him descending from above.

2 Our sins and griefs on him were laid;
He meekly bore the mighty load;
Our ransom-price he fully paid
In groans and tears, in sweat and blood.

3 To save a guilty world, he dies;
Sinners, behold the bleeding Lamb;
To him lift up your longing eyes,
And hope for mercy in his name.

4 Pardon and peace through him abound;
He can the richest blessings give;
Salvation in his name is found;
He bids the dying sinner live.

299. L. M. 6 L. URWICK'S COL.

1 JESUS, thou source of calm repose,
All fulness dwells in thee divine;
Our strength, to quell the proudest foes;
Our light, in deepest gloom to shine;
Thou art our fortress, strength, and tower,
Our trust, and portion, evermore.

2 Jesus, our Comforter thou art;
Our rest in toil, our ease in pain;
The balm to heal each broken heart;
In storms our peace, in loss our gain;
Our joy, beneath the worldling's frown;
In shame our glory and our crown;—

3 In want, our plentiful supply;
In weakness, our almighty power;
In bonds, our perfect liberty;
Our refuge in temptation's hour;
Our comfort, 'midst all grief and thrall;
Our life in death; our all in all.

284. L. M. 6 L. ENG. BAP. COL.

1 STILL nigh me, O my Saviour, stand,
And guard in fierce temptation's hour;
Support by thy almighty hand;
Show forth in me thy saving power;
Still be thine arm my sure defence;
Nor earth nor hell shall pluck me thence.

2 In suffering be thy love my peace;
In weakness be thy love my power;
And, when the storms of life shall cease,
O Saviour, in that trying hour,
In death, as life, be thou my Guide,
And save me, who for me hast died.

279. L. M. STEELE.

1 DEEP are the wounds which sin has made;
Where shall the sinner find a cure?
In vain, alas! is Nature's aid;
The work exceeds her utmost power.

2 But can no sovereign balm be found?
And is no kind physician nigh,
To ease the pain, and heal the wound,
Ere life and hope forever fly?

3 There is a great Physician near;
Look up, O fainting soul, and live;
See, in his heavenly smiles appear
Such help as nature cannot give.

4 See, in the Saviour's dying blood,
Life, health, and bliss, abundant flow:
'Tis only that dear, sacred flood
Can ease thy pain, and heal thy woe.

"THE SAVIOUR LIVES." L. M. Fr. Handel's Messiah. Ar. by B. F. Edmands.

‡ The arrangement of the whole hymn for choir and congregation, is published in sheet form.

287. L. M. Steele.

1 When sins and fears, prevailing, rise,
And fainting hope almost expires,
To thee, O Lord, I lift my eyes;
To thee I breathe my soul's desires.

2 Art thou not mine, my living Lord?
And can my hope, my comfort, die?
'Tis fixed on thine almighty word —
That word which built the earth and sky.

3 If my immortal Saviour lives,
Then my immortal life is sure;
His word a firm foundation gives;
Here I may build, and rest secure.

4 Here let my faith unshaken dwell;
Forever sure the promise stands;
Not all the powers of earth or hell
Can e'er dissolve the sacred bands.

5 Here, O my soul, thy trust repose;
If Jesus is forever mine,
Not death itself — that last of foes —
Shall break a union so divine.

288. L. M. Cowper.

1 Jesus, where'er thy people meet,
There they behold thy mercy-seat;
Where'er they seek thee, thou art found,
And every place is hallowed ground.

2 For thou, within no walls confined,
Dost dwell within the humble mind;
Such ever bring thee where they come,
And, going, take thee to their home.

3 Great Shepherd of thy chosen few,
Thy former mercies here renew;
Here, to our waiting hearts, proclaim
The sweetness of thy saving name.

294. L. M. Watts.

1 He lives! he lives! and sits above,
Forever interceding there:
Who shall divide us from his love,
Or what should tempt us to despair?

2 Shall persecution, or distress,
Shall famine, sword, or nakedness?
He who hath loved us bears us through,
And makes us more than conquerors too.

3 Faith hath an overcoming power;
It triumphs in the dying hour:
Christ is our life, our joy, our hope;
Nor can we sink with such a prop.

4 Not all that men on earth can do,
Nor powers on high, nor powers below,
Shall cause his mercy to remove,
Or wean our hearts from Christ, our love.

295. L. M. Pratt's Col.

1 The Saviour lives, no more to die;
He lives, the Lord enthroned on high;
He lives, triumphant o'er the grave;
He lives, eternally to save.

2 He lives, to still his servants' fears;
He lives, to wipe away their tears;
He lives, their mansions to prepare;
He lives, to bring them safely there.

3 Ye mourning souls, dry up your tears;
Dismiss your gloomy doubts and fears;
With cheerful hope your hearts revive,
For Christ, the Lord, is yet alive.

4 His saints he loves, and never leaves;
The contrite sinner he receives:
Abundant grace will he afford,
Till all are present with the Lord.

WINCHESTER. L. M. DR. CROFT.

This has been one of the most popular tunes extant.

296. L. M. STEELE.

1 He lives! the great Redeemer lives!
What joy the blest assurance gives!
And now, before his Father, God,
He pleads the merits of his blood.

2 Repeated crimes awake our fears,
And justice, armed with frowns, appears;
But in the Saviour's lovely face
Sweet mercy smiles, and all is peace.

3 Hence, then, ye dark, despairing thoughts;
Above our fears, above our faults,
His powerful intercessions rise;
And guilt recedes, and terror dies.

4 Great Advocate, almighty Friend,
On thee our humble hopes depend;
Our cause can never, never fail,
For thou dost plead, and must prevail.

321. L. M. WATTS.

1 Now to the Lord, who makes us know
The wonders of his dying love,
Be humble honors paid below,
And strains of nobler praise above.

2 'Twas he who cleansed us from our sins,
And washed us in his precious blood;
'Tis he who makes us priests and kings,
And brings us rebels near to God.

3 To Jesus, our atoning Priest,
To Jesus, our eternal King,
Be everlasting power confessed;
Let every tongue his glory sing.

4 Behold, on flying clouds he comes,
And every eye shall see him move;
Though with our sins we pierced him once,
Now he displays his pardoning love.

5 The unbelieving world shall wail,
While we rejoice to see the day:
Come, Lord, nor let thy promise fail,
Nor let thy chariot long delay.

333. L. M. WATTS.

1 Now be my heart inspired to sing
The glories of my Saviour King;
He comes with blessings from above,
And wins the nations to his love.

2 Thy throne, O God, forever stands;
Grace is the sceptre in thy hands:
Thy laws and works are just and right,
But truth and mercy thy delight.

3 Let endless honors crown thy head;
Let every age thy praises spread;
Let all the nations know thy word,
And every tongue confess thee Lord.

344. L. M. WATTS.

1 What equal honors shall we bring
To thee, O Lord our God, the Lamb,
When all the notes that angels sing
Are far inferior to thy name?

2 Worthy is he that once was slain,
The Prince of life, that groaned and died,
Worthy to rise, and live and reign
At his almighty Father's side.

3 Honor immortal must be paid,
Instead of scandal and of scorn;
While glory shines around his head,
He wears a crown without a thorn.

4 Blessings forever on the Lamb,
Who bore the curse for wretched men;
Let angels sound his sacred name,
And every creature say, "Amen."

TRURO. L. M. Dr. Charles Burney.

A tune almost universally found in standard collections.

319. L. M. Watts.

1 Now to the Lord a noble song;
Awake, my soul; awake, my tongue;
Hosanna to th' eternal name,
And all his boundless love proclaim.

2 See where it shines in Jesus' face,
The brightest image of his grace;
God in the person of his Son
Has all his mightiest works outdone.

3 The spacious earth and spreading flood
Proclaim the wise, the powerful God,
And thy rich glories from afar
Sparkle in every rolling star.

4 But in his looks a glory stands,
The noblest labor of thine hands:
The pleasing lustre of his eyes
Outshines the wonders of the skies.

5 Grace, 'tis a sweet, a charming theme;
My thoughts rejoice at Jesus' name;
Ye angels, dwell upon the sound;
Ye heavens, reflect it to the ground.

6 O, may I reach the happy place
Where he unveils his lovely face;
His beauties there may I behold,
And sing his name to harps of gold.

331. L. M. Campbell's Col.

1 What are those soul reviving strains,
Which echo thus from Salem's plains?
What anthems loud, and louder still,
So sweetly sound from Zion's hill?

2 Lo! 'tis an infant chorus sings
Hosanna to the King of kings:
The Saviour comes! — and babes proclaim
Salvation, sent in Jesus' name.

3 Nor these alone their voice shall raise,
For we will join this song of praise;
Still Israel's children forward press
To hail the Lord their Righteousness.

4 Messiah's name shall joy impart
Alike to Jew and Gentile heart:
He bled for us; he bled for you;
And we will sing hosanna too.

5 Proclaim hosannas loud and clear;
See David's Son and Lord appear!
All praise on earth to him be given,
And glory shout through highest heaven.

349. L. M. Percy Chapel Col.

1 The countless multitude on high,
Who tune their songs to Jesus' name,
All merit of their own deny,
And Jesus' worth alone proclaim.

2 Firm, on the ground of sovereign grace,
They stand before Jehovah's throne;
The only song in that blest place
Is, "Thou art worthy, thou alone."

3 With spotless robes of purest white,
And branches of triumphal palm,
They shout, with transports of delight,
The ceaseless, universal psalm, —

4 "Salvation's glory all be paid
To Him who sits upon the throne,
And to the Lamb, whose blood was shed;
Thou, thou art worthy, thou alone."

ROCKINGHAM.

&c.

CLARE. L. M.‡ EDWARD HAMILTON. From The Sanctus.

‡ This, and all the tunes from "The Sanctus," are inserted by special permission.

354. L. M. DODDRIDGE.

1 COME, sacred Spirit, from above,
And fill the coldest heart with love;
O, turn to flesh the flinty stone,
And let thy sovereign power be known.

2 O, let a holy flock await,
In crowds, around thy temple gate,
Each pressing on with zeal, to be
A living sacrifice to thee.

357. L. M. BEDDOME.

1 COME, thou eternal Spirit, come
From heaven, thy glorious dwelling-place;
O, make my sinful heart thy home,
And consecrate it by thy grace.

2 There fix, O Lord, thy blest abode,
And drive thy foes forever thence;
There shed a Saviour's love abroad,
And light, and life, and joy, dispense.

3 My wants supply; my fears suppress;
Direct my way, and hold me up;
Teach me, in times of deep distress,
To pray in faith, and wait in hope.

358. L. M. BURDER'S COL.

1 COME, Holy Spirit, calm my mind,
And fit me to approach my God;
Remove each vain, each worldly thought,
And lead me to thy blest abode.

2 Hast thou imparted to my soul
A living spark of holy fire?
O, kindle now the sacred flame,
And make me burn with pure desire.

3 A brighter faith and hope impart,
And let me now my Saviour see,
O, soothe and cheer my burdened heart,
And bid my spirit rest in thee.

364. L. M. ENG. BAP. COL.

1 As showers on meadows newly mown,
Our God shall send his Spirit down:
Eternal Source of grace divine,
What soul-refreshing drops are thine!

2 That heavenly influence let us find
In holy silence of the mind,
While every grace maintains its bloom,
Diffusing wide its rich perfume.

3 Nor let these blessings be confined
To us, but poured on all mankind,
Till earth's rude wastes in verdure rise,
And Eden's beauty greet our eyes.

383. L. M. T. SCOTT.

1 O LORD, and shall our fainting souls
Thy just displeasure ever mourn?
Thy Spirit grieved, and long withdrawn,
Will he no more to us return?

2 Great Source of light and peace, return,
Nor let us mourn and sigh in vain:
Come, repossess our longing hearts
With all the graces of thy train.

3 This temple, hallowed by thine hand,
Once more be with thy presence blest;
Here be thy grace anew displayed;
Be this thine everlasting rest.

UXBRIDGE.

HAYTI. L. M. LEONARD MARSHALL. From The Hosanna. ‡

‡ This, and the other tunes from "The Hosanna," are inserted by permission.

368. L. M. BROWNE.

1 COME, gracious Spirit, heavenly Dove,
With light and comfort from above;
Be thou our Guardian, thou our Guide;
O'er every thought and step preside.

2 To us the light of truth display,
And make us know and choose thy way;
Plant holy fear in every heart,
That we from God may ne'er depart.

3 Lead us to holiness — the road
Which we must take to dwell with God;
Lead us to Christ — the living way;
Nor let us from his pastures stray;—

4 Lead us to God, — our final rest, —
To be with him forever blest;
Lead us to heaven, its bliss to share —
Fulness of joy forever there.

369. L. M. BEDDOME.

1 COME, blessed Spirit, Source of light,
Whose power and grace are unconfined,
Dispel the gloomy shades of night,
The thicker darkness of the mind.

2 To mine illumined eyes display
The glorious truth thy words reveal;
Cause me to run the heavenly way;
Make me delight to do thy will.

3 Thine inward teachings make me know
The wonders of redeeming love,
The vanity of things below,
And excellence of things above.

4 While through this dubious maze I stray,
Spread, like the sun, thy beams abroad;
O, show the dangers of the way,
And guide my feeble steps to God.

376. L. M. WATTS.

1 ETERNAL Spirit, we confess
And sing the wonders of thy grace;
Thy power conveys our blessings down
From God the Father and the Son.

2 Enlightened by thine heavenly ray,
Our shades and darkness turn to day;
Thine inward teachings make us know
Our danger, and our refuge too.

3 Thy power and glory work within,
And break the chains of reigning sin;
Our wild, imperious lusts subdue,
And form our wretched hearts anew.

4 The troubled conscience knows thy voice,
Thy cheering words awake our joys;
Thy words allay the stormy wind,
And calm the surges of the mind.

380. L. M. C. WESLEY.

1 STAY, thou insulted Spirit, stay,
Though I have done thee such despite;
Cast not a sinner quite away,
Nor take thine everlasting flight.

2 Though I have most unfaithful been
Of all who e'er thy grace received, —
Ten thousand times thy goodness seen,
Ten thousand times thy goodness grieved, —

3 Yet, O, the chief of sinners spare,
In honor of my great High Priest;
Nor, in thy righteous anger, swear
I shall not see thy people's rest.

4 My weary soul, O God, release;
Uphold me with thy gracious hand;
O, guide me into perfect peace,
And bring me to the promised land.

HEBRO. L. M. Arranged by the Editor for this work.

EVENTIDE. L. M. Edward Hamilton. From The Sanctus.

HAMBOROUGH. L. M. Arranged; and harmonized by B. F. Edmands, 1833.

‡ See Note page 22.

STERLING. L. M.
Chant Style.
Ancient.
SHOEL. L. M.
Shoel.
OLD HUNDRED. L. M.
Choral.
G. Franc.
Dates previous to 1543.

WINCHELSEA. L. M. PRELLEUR.

‡ Observe the peculiarity in the rhythm of these measures.

387. L. M. HIGGINBOTHAM.

1 Now let my soul, eternal King,
To thee its grateful tribute bring;
My knee with humble homage bow;
My tongue perform its solemn vow.

2 All nature sings thy boundless love,
In worlds below, and worlds above;
But in thy blessed word I trace
Diviner wonders of thy grace.

3 There, what delightful truths I read!
There I behold the Saviour bleed;
His name salutes my listening ear,
Revives my heart, and checks my fear.

4 There, Jesus bids my sorrow cease,
And gives my laboring conscience peace;
There, lifts my grateful passions high,
And points to mansions in the sky.

5 For love like this, O, let my song,
Through endless years, thy praise prolong;
Let distant climes thy name adore,
Till time and nature are no more.

388. L. M. WATTS.

1 Let everlasting glories crown
Thy head, my Saviour and my Lord;
Thy hands have brought salvation down,
And stored the blessings in thy word.

2 In vain the trembling conscience seeks
Some solid ground to rest upon;
With long despair the spirit breaks,
Till we apply to Christ alone.

3 How well thy blessed truths agree!
How wise and holy thy commands!
Thy promises, how firm they be!
How firm our hope and comfort stands!

4 Should all the forms that men devise
Assault my faith with treacherous art,
I'd call them vanity and lies,
And bind the gospel to my heart!

400. L. M. WATTS.

1 'Twas by an order from the Lord,
The ancient prophets spoke his word;
His Spirit did their tongues inspire,
And warm their hearts with heavenly fire.

2 Great God, mine eyes with pleasure look
On all the pages of thy book;
There my Redeemer's face I see,
And read his name who died for me.

3 Let the false raptures of the mind
Be lost and vanish in the wind:
Here I can fix my hope secure;
This is thy word, and must endure.

404. L. M. BEDDOME.

1 God, in the gospel of his Son,
Makes his eternal counsels known:
Here love in all its glory shines,
And truth is drawn in fairest lines.

2 Here, sinners of an humble frame
May taste his grace, and learn his name;
May read, in characters of blood,
The wisdom, power, and grace of God.

3 Here, faith reveals to mortal eyes
A brighter world beyond the skies;
Here shines the light which guides our way
From earth to realms of endless day.

4 O grant us grace, almighty Lord,
To read and mark thy holy word,
Its truths with meekness to receive,
And by its holy precepts live.

406. L. M. BOWRING.

1 How sweetly flowed the gospel sound
From lips of gentleness and grace,
When listening thousands gathered round,
And joy and gladness filled the place!

2 From heaven he came, of heaven he spoke,
To heaven he led his followers' way;
Dark clouds of gloomy night he broke,
Unveiling an immortal day.

3 "Come, wanderers, to my Father's home;
Come, all ye weary ones, and rest:"
Yes, sacred Teacher, we will come,
Obey thee, love thee, and be blest.

4 Decay, then, tenements of dust;
Pillars of earthly pride, decay:
A nobler mansion waits the just,
And Jesus has prepared the way.

409. L. M. WATTS.

1 This is the word of truth and love,
Sent to the nations from above;
Jehovah here resolves to show
What his almighty grace can do.

2 This remedy did wisdom find,
To heal diseases of the mind —
This sovereign balm, whose virtues can
Restore the ruined creature, man.

3 The gospel bids the dead revive;
Sinners obey the voice, and live:
Dry bones are raised, and clothed afresh,
And hearts of stone are turned to flesh.

4 May but this grace my soul renew,
Let sinners gaze and hate me too;
The word that saves me does engage
A sure defence from all their rage.

414. L. M. BICKERSTETH'S COL.

1 Wanderer from God, return, return;
And seek an injured Father's face;
Those warm desires, that in thee burn,
Were kindled by reclaiming grace.

2 Wanderer from God, return, return;
Thy Father hears that deep-felt sigh;
He sees thy softened spirit mourn;
And mercy's voice invites thee nigh.

3 Wanderer from God, return, return;
Renounce thy fears; thy Saviour lives;
Go to his bleeding cross, and learn
How freely, fully, he forgives.

421. L. M. STEELE.

1 Come, weary souls, with sin distressed,
Come, and accept the promised rest;
The Saviour's gracious call obey,
And cast your gloomy fears away.

2 Oppressed with sin, a painful load,
O, come and spread your woes abroad:
Divine compassion, mighty love,
Will all the painful load remove.

3 Here mercy's boundless ocean flows,
To cleanse your guilt and heal your woes;
Pardon, and life, and endless peace;
How rich the gift! how free the grace!

4 Lord, we accept, with thankful heart,
The hope thy gracious words impart;
We come with trembling, yet rejoice,
And bless the kind, inviting voice.

5 Dear Saviour, let thy wondrous love
Confirm our faith, our fears remove;
O, sweetly influence every breast,
And guide us to eternal rest.

417. L. M. WATTS.

1 "COME hither, all ye weary souls,
Ye heavy-laden sinners, come;
I'll give you rest from all your toils,
And raise you to my heavenly home.

2 "They shall find rest who learn of me:
I'm of a meek and lowly mind;
But passion rages like the sea,
And pride is restless as the wind.

3 "Blest is the man whose shoulders take
My yoke, and bear it with delight:
My yoke is easy to the neck;
My grace shall make the burden light."

4 Jesus, we come at thy command;
With faith, and hope, and humble zeal,
Resign our spirits to thy hand,
To mould and guide us at thy will.

437. L. M. DODDRIDGE.

1 WHY will ye waste on trifling cares
That life which God's compassion spares;
While, in the various range of thought,
The one thing needful is forgot?

2 Shall God invite you from above?
Shall Jesus urge his dying love?
Shall troubled conscience give you pain,
And all these pleas unite in vain?

3 Not so your eyes will always view
Those objects which you now pursue;
Not so will heaven and hell appear,
When death's decisive hour is near.

4 Almighty God, thy grace impart;
Fix deep conviction on each heart;
Nor let us waste on trifling cares
That life which thy compassion spares.

5

450. L. M. WATTS.

1 O, SINNER, why so thoughtless grown?
Why in such dreadful haste to die?—
Daring to leap to worlds unknown!
Heedless against thy God to fly!

2 Wilt thou despise eternal fate,
Urged on by sin's delusive dreams,
Madly attempt th' infernal gate,
And force thy passage to the flames?

3 Stay, sinner, on the gospel plains,
And hear the Lord of life unfold
The glories of his dying pains,—
Forever telling, yet untold.

451. L. M. DWIGHT.

1 WHILE life prolongs its precious light,
Mercy is found, and peace is given;
But soon, ah, soon, approaching night
Shall blot out every hope of heaven.

2 While God invites, how blest the day!
How sweet the gospel's charming sound!
Come, sinners, haste, O haste away,
While yet a pardoning God is found.

3 Soon, borne on time's most rapid wing,
Shall death command you to the grave,
Before his bar your spirits bring,
And none be found to hear or save.

4 In that lone land of deep despair,
No Sabbath's heavenly light shall rise,
No God regard your bitter prayer,
No Saviour call you to the skies.

5 Now God invites; how blest the day!
How sweet the gospel's charming sound!
Come, sinners, haste, O haste away,
While yet a pardoning God is found.

‡ Minor tunes should be preferred for penitential hymns, like 467, 468, and 470.

467. L. M. Watts.

1 O THOU that hear'st when sinners cry,
Though all my crimes before thee lie,
Behold them not with angry look,
But blot their memory from thy book.

2 Create my nature pure within,
And form my soul averse to sin;
Let thy good Spirit ne'er depart,
Nor hide thy presence from my heart.

3 I cannot live without thy light,
Cast out and banished from thy sight;
Thy holy joys, my God, restore,
And guard me that I fall no more.

4 Though I have grieved thy Spirit, Lord,
His help and comfort still afford,
And let a wretch come near thy throne,
To plead the merits of thy Son.

468. L. M. Watts.

1 A BROKEN heart, my God, my King,
Is all the sacrifice I bring;
The God of grace will ne'er despise
A broken heart for sacrifice.

2 My soul is humbled in the dust,
And owns thy dreadful sentence just;
Look down, O Lord, with pitying eye,
And save the soul condemned to die.

3 Then will I teach the world thy ways;
Sinners shall learn thy sovereign grace;
I'll lead them to my Saviour's blood,
And they shall praise a pardoning God.

4 O, may thy love inspire my tongue;
Salvation shall be all my song;
And all my powers shall join to bless
The Lord, my strength and righteousness.

470. L. M. Watts.

1 O LORD, I fall before thy face;
My only refuge is thy grace:
No outward forms can make me clean;
The leprosy lies deep within.

2 No bleeding bird, nor bleeding beast,
Nor hyssop branch, nor sprinkling priest,
Nor running brook, nor flood, nor sea,
Can wash the dismal stain away.

3 Jesus, my God, thy blood alone
Hath power sufficient to atone;
Thy blood can make me white as snow;
No human power could cleanse me so.

4 While guilt disturbs and breaks my peace,
Nor flesh nor soul hath rest or ease;
Lord, let me hear thy pardoning voice,
And make my broken bones rejoice.

497. L. M. Watts.

1 WHAT shall the dying sinner do,
Who seeks relief for all his woe?
Where shall the guilty sufferer find
A balm to soothe his anguished mind?

2 In vain we search, in vain we try,
Till Jesus brings his gospel nigh;
'Tis there we find a sure relief,
A soothing balm for inward grief.

3 Be this the pillar of our hope;
This bears the fainting spirit up;
We read the grace, we trust the word,
And find salvation in the Lord.

4 Then let his name, who shed his blood
To bring the guilty nigh to God,
Be great in all the earth, and sung
In every land, by every tongue.

WELLS. L. M. Composed before 1740. ‡

‡ Ascribed to Broderip, and to Holdroyd.

484. L. M. WATTS.

1 SHOW pity, Lord; O Lord, forgive;
Let a repenting rebel live;
Are not thy mercies large and free?
May not a sinner trust in thee?

2 My crimes, though great, cannot surpass
The power and glory of thy grace;
Great God, thy nature hath no bound;
So let thy pardoning love be found.

3 O, wash my soul from every sin,
And make my guilty conscience clean;
Here, on my heart, the burden lies,
And past offences pain mine eyes.

4 My lips, with shame, my sins confess,
Against thy law, against thy grace;
Lord, should thy judgment grow severe,
I am condemned, but thou art clear.

5 Should sudden vengeance seize my breath,
I must pronounce thee just in death;
And if my soul were sent to hell,
Thy righteous law approves it well.

6 Yet save a trembling sinner, Lord,
Whose hope, still hovering round thy word,
Would light on some sweet promise there,
Some sure support against despair.

487. L. M. STEELE.

1 JESUS demands this heart of mine,
Demands my love, my joy, my care;
But, ah, how dead to things divine,
How cold, my best affections are!

2 'Tis sin, alas! with dreadful power,
Divides my Saviour from my sight;
O for one happy, shining hour
Of sacred freedom, sweet delight!

3 Come, gracious Lord; thy love can raise
My captive powers from sin and death,
And fill my heart and life with praise,
And tune my last, expiring breath.

496. L. M. WATTS.

1 WHILE I keep silence, and conceal
My heavy guilt within my heart,
What torments doth my conscience feel!
How keen the pangs of inward smart!

2 I spread my sins before the Lord,
And all my secret faults confess;
Thy gospel speaks a pardoning word,
Thy Holy Spirit seals the grace.

3 For this shall every humble soul
Make swift addresses at thy feet;
When floods of strong temptation roll,
There shall they find a blest retreat.

4 How safe beneath thy wings I lie,
When days grow dark and storms appear!
And, when I walk, thy watchful eye
Shall guide me safe from every snare.

515. L. M. WATTS.

1 'TIS by the faith of joys to come
We walk through deserts dark as night;
Till we arrive at heaven, our home,
Faith is our guide, and faith our light.

2 The want of sight she well supplies;
She makes the pearly gates appear;
Far into distant worlds she pries,
And brings eternal glories near.

3 With joy we tread the desert through,
While faith inspires a heavenly ray,
Though lions roar, and tempests blow,
And rocks and dangers fill the way.

BERTRAM. L. M. Rev. W. H. Havergall.

From London Congregational Tune Book.

489. L. M. Collyer.

1 Return, my wandering soul, return,
And seek an injured Father's face;
Those warm desires that in thee burn
Were kindled by redeeming grace.

2 Return, my wandering soul, return,
And seek a Father's melting heart;
His pitying eyes thy grief discern,
His heavenly balm shall heal thy smart.

3 Return, my wandering soul, return;
Thy dying Saviour bids thee live;
Go, view his bleeding side, and learn
How freely Jesus can forgive.

4 Return, my wandering soul, return,
And wipe away the falling tear;
'Tis God who says, "No longer mourn;"
'Tis mercy's voice invites thee near.

490. L. M. Doddridge.

1 Return, my roving heart, return,
And life's vain shadows chase no more;
Seek out some solitude to mourn,
And thy forsaken God implore.

2 O thou great God, whose piercing eye
Distinctly marks each deep retreat,
In these sequestered hours draw nigh,
And let me here thy presence meet.

3 Through all the windings of my heart,
My search let heavenly wisdom guide,
And still its radiant beams impart
Till all be known and purified.

4 Then let the visits of thy love
My inmost soul be made to share,
Till every grace combine to prove
That God has fixed his dwelling there.

475. L. M. Beddome.

1 Lord, with a grieved and aching heart,
To thee I look, to thee I cry;
Supply my wants, and ease my smart;
O, hear an humble prisoner's sigh.

2 Here on my soul the burden lies;
No human power can ease the load;
My numerous sins against me rise,
And far remove me from my God.

3 Break, break, O Lord, these tyrant chains,
And set the struggling captive free;
Redeem from everlasting pains,
And bring me safe to heaven and thee.

---

523. L. M. Watts.

1 From deep distress and troubled thoughts,
To thee, my God, I raise my cries;
If thou severely mark our faults,
No flesh can stand before thine eyes.

2 But thou hast built thy throne of grace,
Dispensing pardons freely there,
That sinners may approach thy face,
And hope and love, as well as fear.

3 As the benighted pilgrims wait,
And long and wish for breaking day,
So waits my soul before thy gate,
When will my God his face display?

4 My trust is fixed upon thy word,
Nor shall I trust thy word in vain;
Let mourning souls address the Lord,
And find relief from all their pain.

5 His love is great, and large his grace,
Through the redemption of his Son;
He turns our feet from sinful ways,
And pardons what our hands have done.

WINDHAM. L. M. Melody by M. LUTHER.‡ Arr. by READ, 1800.

‡ Originally in equal notes: may be so sung, as a choral.

548. L. M. STEELE.

1 THOU only Sovereign of my heart,
My refuge, my almighty Friend,
And can my soul from thee depart,
On whom alone my hopes depend?

2 Whither, ah, whither shall I go,
A wretched wanderer from my Lord?
Can this dark world of sin and woe
One glimpse of happiness afford?

3 Eternal life thy words impart;
On these my fainting spirit lives;
Here sweeter comforts cheer my heart
Than all the round of nature gives.

4 Let earth's alluring joys combine;
While thou art near, in vain they call;
One smile, one blissful smile of thine,
My gracious Lord, outweighs them all.

5 Low at thy feet my soul would lie;
Here safety dwells, and peace divine;
Still let me live beneath thine eye,
For life, eternal life, is thine.

755. L. M. WATTS.

1 LORD, what a thoughtless wretch was I,
To mourn, and murmur, and repine,
To see the wicked, placed on high,
In pride and robes of honor shine!

2 But, O, their end, their dreadful end!
Thy faithful word hath taught me so;
On slippery rocks I see them stand,
And fiery billows roll below.

3 Now I esteem their mirth and wine
Too dear to purchase with my blood;
Lord, 'tis enough that thou art mine,
My life, my portion, and my God.

684. L. M. KELLY.

1 O, WHERE is now that glowing love
That marked our union with the Lord?
Our hearts were fixed on things above,
Nor could the world a joy afford.

2 Where is the zeal that led us then
To make our Saviour's glory known?
That freed us from the fear of men,
And kept our eye on him alone?

3 Where are the happy seasons spent
In fellowship with Him we loved?
The sacred joy, the sweet content,
The blessedness that then we proved.

4 Behold, again we turn to thee;
O, cast us not away, though vile:
No peace we have, no joy we see,
O Lord our God, but in thy smile.

686. L. M. WATTS.

1 BROAD is the road that leads to death,
And thousands walk together there;
But wisdom shows a narrow path,
With here and there a traveller.

2 "Deny thyself and take thy cross,"
Is the Redeemer's great command:
Nature must count her gold but dross,
If she would gain this heavenly land.

3 The fearful soul that tires and faints,
And walks the ways of God no more,
Is but esteemed almost a saint,
And makes his own destruction sure.

4 Lord, let not all my hopes be vain;
Create my heart entirely new —
Which hypocrites could ne'er attain,
Which false apostates never knew.

This choral is elaborately arranged, by MENDELSSOHN, in the Oratorio "St. Paul."

563. L. M. WATTS.

1 How oft have sin and Satan strove
To rend my soul from thee, my God!
But everlasting is thy love,
And Jesus seals it with his blood.

2 The oath and promise of the Lord
Join to confirm the wondrous grace;
Eternal power performs the word,
And fills all heaven with endless praise.

3 Amidst temptations, sharp and long,
My soul to this dear refuge flies;
Hope is my anchor, firm and strong,
While tempests blow and billows rise.

4 The gospel bears my spirit up;
A faithful and unchanging God
Lays the foundation for my hope
In oaths, and promises, and blood.

569. L. M. SIR J. E. SMITH.

1 WHEN power divine, in mortal form,
Hushed with a word the raging storm,
In soothing accents Jesus said,
"Lo, it is I; be not afraid."

2 So, when in silence nature sleeps,
And his lone watch the mourner keeps,
One thought shall every pang remove —
Trust, feeble man, thy Maker's love.

3 God calms the tumult and the storm;
He rules the seraph and the worm;
No creature is by him forgot
Of those who know, or know him not.

4 And when the last, dread hour shall come,
While trembling Nature waits her doom,
This voice shall wake the pious dead —
"Lo, it is I; be not afraid."

630. L. M. WATTS.

1 MY God, permit me not to be
A stranger to myself and thee;
Amidst a thousand thoughts I rove,
Forgetful of my highest love.

2 Why should my passions mix with earth,
And thus debase my heavenly birth?
Why should I cleave to things below,
And let my God, my Saviour, go?

3 Call me away from flesh and sense;
One sovereign word can draw me thence;
I would obey the voice divine,
And all inferior joys resign.

4 Be earth, with all her scenes withdrawn;
Let noise and vanity begone:
In secret silence of the mind
My heaven, and there my God, I find.

672. L. M. J. F. OBERLIN.

1 O LORD, thy heavenly grace impart,
And fix my frail, inconstant heart;
Henceforth my chief desire shall be
To dedicate myself to thee.

2 Whate'er pursuits my time employ,
One thought shall fill my soul with joy;
That silent, secret thought shall be,
That all my hopes are fixed on thee.

3 Thy glorious eye pervadeth space;
Thy presence, Lord, fills every place;
And, wheresoe'er my lot may be,
Still shall my spirit cleave to thee.

4 Renouncing every worldly thing,
And safe beneath thy spreading wing,
My sweetest thought henceforth shall be,
That all I want I find in thee.

WARE. L. M. N. D. GOULD.
National Church Harmony, 1833.

605. L. M. NORTON.

1 MY God, I thank thee: may no thought
E'er deem a Father's hand severe;
But may this heart, by sorrow taught,
Calm each wild wish, each idle fear.

2 Thy mercy bids all nature bloom;
The sun shines bright, and man is gay;
Thine equal mercy spreads the gloom
That darkens o'er his little day.

3 Full many a throb of grief and pain
Thy frail and erring child must know;
But not one prayer is breathed in vain,
Nor does one tear unheeded flow.

4 Thy various messengers employ;
Thy purposes of love fulfil;
And, 'mid the wreck of human joy,
Let humble faith adore thy will.

609. L. M. WATTS.

1 HOW blest the man whose cautious feet
Avoid the way that sinners go,
Who hates the place where atheists meet,
And fears to talk as scoffers do!

2 He loves t' employ his morning light
Among the statutes of the Lord,
And spends the wakeful hours of night
With pleasure pondering o'er the word.

3 He, like a plant by gentle streams,
Shall flourish in immortal green;
And heaven will shine with kindest beams
On every work his hands begin.

4 But sinners find their counsels crossed;
As chaff before the tempest flies,
So shall their hopes be blown and lost,
When the last trumpet shakes the skies.

614. L. M. STEELE.

1 WHERE is my God? does he retire
Beyond the reach of humble sighs?
Are these weak breathings of desire
Too languid to ascend the skies?

2 He hears the breathings of desire;
The weak petition, if sincere,
Is not forbidden to aspire,
And hope to reach his gracious ear.

3 Look up, my soul, with cheerful eye;
See where the great Redeemer stands,
The glorious Advocate on high,
With precious incense in his hands.

4 He sweetens every humble groan;
He recommends each broken prayer;
Recline thy hope on him alone,
Whose power and love forbid despair.

636. L. M. STOWELL.

1 FROM every stormy wind that blows,
From every swelling tide of woes,
There is a calm, a sure retreat;
'Tis found before the mercy-seat.

2 There is a place where Jesus sheds
The oil of gladness on our heads—
A place of all on earth most sweet;
It is the blood-bought mercy-seat.

3 There is a scene where spirits blend,
Where friend holds fellowship with friend;
Though sundered far, by faith they meet
Around one common mercy-seat.

4 There, there, on eagle wings we soar,
And sin and sense molest no more;
And heaven comes down our souls to greet,
And glory crowns the mercy-seat.

The change of mode renders this peculiarly adapted for Hymn 517.

517. L. M. WATTS.

1 BURIED in shadows of the night
We lie, till Christ restores the light,
Till he descends to heal the blind,
And chase the darkness of the mind.

2 Our guilty souls are drowned in tears,
Till his atoning blood appears;
Then we awake from deep distress,
And sing the Lord our Righteousness.

3 Jesus beholds where Satan reigns
And binds his slaves in heavy chains;
He sets the prisoners free, and breaks
The iron bondage from our necks.

4 Poor, helpless worms in thee possess
Grace, wisdom, power, and righteousness;
Thou art our mighty All, and we
Give our whole selves, O Lord, to thee.

526. L. M. T. SCOTT.

1 WHY droops my soul, with grief oppressed?
Whence these wild tumults in my breast?
Is there no balm to heal my wound?
No kind physician to be found?

2 Raise to the cross thy tearful eyes;
Behold, the Prince of glory dies:
He dies, extended on the tree,
And sheds a sovereign balm for thee.

3 Blest Saviour, at thy feet I lie,
Here to receive a cure or die;
But grace forbids that painful fear—
Almighty grace, which triumphs here.

4 Thou wilt withdraw the poisoned dart,
Bind up and heal the wounded heart,
With blooming health my face adorn,
And change the gloomy night to morn.

531. L. M. WATTS.

1 HERE at thy cross, incarnate God,
I lay my soul beneath thy love,—
Beneath the droppings of thy blood,—
Nor shall it, Jesus, e'er remove.

2 Should worlds conspire to drive me thence,
Unmoved and firm this heart should lie;
Resolved,—for that's my last defence,—
If I must perish, there to die.

3 But speak, my Lord, and calm my fear;
Am I not safe beneath thy shade?
Thy justice will not strike me here,
Nor Satan dare my soul invade.

4 Yes, I'm secure beneath thy blood,
And all my foes shall lose their aim;
Hosanna to my Saviour God,
And my best honors to his name.

532. L. M. STEELE.

1 IN vain the world's alluring smile
Would my unwary heart beguile;
Deluding world! its brightest day—
Dream of a moment—flits away.

2 To nobler bliss my soul aspires;
Come, Lord, and fill these large desires
With power, and light, and love divine;
O, speak, and tell me thou art mine.

3 The blissful word, with joy replete,
Shall bid my gloomy fears retreat;
And heavenly hope, serenely bright,
Illume and cheer my darkest night.

4 So shall my joyful spirit rise,
On wings of faith, above the skies,
Then dwell forever near thy throne,
In joys to mortal thought unknown.

MEROE. L. M.

Comp. for Hymn 551. Wm. B. Bradbury, 1847. From Mendelssohn Col.

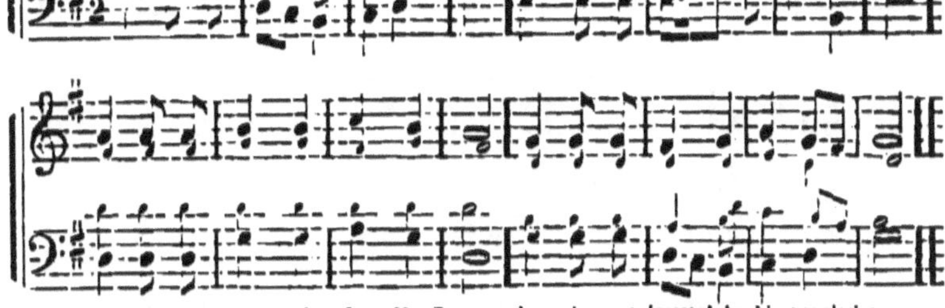

This, and all the tunes taken from Mr. Bradbury's works, are inserted by his permission.

549. L. M. C. Wesley.

1 Jesus, thy boundless love to me
 No thought can reach, no tongue declare:
Unite my thankful heart to thee,
 And reign without a rival there.

2 Thy love, how cheering is its ray!
 All pain before its presence flies;
Care, anguish, sorrow, melt away
 Where'er its healing beams arise.

3 O, let thy love my soul inflame,
 And to thy service sweetly bind;
Transfuse it through my inmost frame,
 And mould me wholly to thy mind.

4 Thy love, in sufferings, be my peace;
 Thy love, in weakness, make me strong;
And when the storms of life shall cease,
 Thy love shall be in heaven my song.

554. L. M. Grigg.

1 Jesus, and shall it ever be —
 A mortal man ashamed of thee!
Ashamed of thee, whom angels praise,
 Whose glories shine through endless days!

2 Ashamed of Jesus! — that dear Friend
 On whom my hopes of heaven depend!
No! — when I blush, be this my shame, —
 That I no more revere his name.

3 Ashamed of Jesus! — yes, I may,
 When I've no guilt to wash away,
No tear to wipe, no good to crave,
 No fears to quell, no soul to save.

4 Till then — nor is my boasting vain —
 Till then, I boast a Saviour slain;
And, O, may this my glory be, —
 That Christ is not ashamed of me.

546. L. M. Watts.

1 Let me but hear my Saviour say,
 "Strength shall be equal to thy day," —
Then I rejoice in deep distress,
 Upheld by all-sufficient grace.

2 I can do all things, or can bear
 All suffering, if my Lord be there;
Sweet pleasures mingle with the pains,
 While he my sinking head sustains.

3 I glory in infirmity,
 That Christ's own power may rest on me;
When I am weak, then I am strong;
 Grace is my shield, and Christ my song.

556. L. M. Doddridge.

1 My gracious Lord, I own thy right
 To every service I can pay,
And call it my supreme delight
 To hear thy dictates, and obey.

2 What is my being but for thee —
 Its sure support, its noblest end?
'Tis my delight thy face to see,
 And serve the cause of such a Friend.

3 I would not sigh for worldly joy,
 Or to increase my worldly good;
Nor future days nor powers employ
 To spread a sounding name abroad.

4 'Tis to my Saviour I would live —
 To him who for my ransom died;
Nor could all worldly honor give
 Such bliss as crowns me at his side.

5 His work my hoary age shall bless,
 When youthful vigor is no more,
And my last hour of life confess
 His saving love, his glorious power.

‡ John Huss suffered martyrdom at the stake A. D. 1415.

539. L. M. WATTS.

1 I SEND the joys of earth away;
Away, ye tempters of the mind,
False as the smooth, deceitful sea,
And empty as the whistling wind.

2 Your streams were floating me along
Down to the gulf of dark despair;
And while I listened to your song,
Your streams had e'en conveyed me there.

3 Lord, I adore thy matchless grace,
That warned me of that dark abyss,
That drew me from those treacherous seas,
And bade me seek superior bliss.

4 Now to the shining realms above
I stretch my hands and glance my eyes;
O for the pinions of a dove,
To bear me to the upper skies!

703. L. M. WATTS.

1 HAD I the tongues of Greeks and Jews,
And nobler speech than angels use,
If love be absent, I am found,
Like tinkling brass, an empty sound.

2 Were I inspired to preach and tell
All that is done in heaven and hell, —
Or could my faith the world remove, —
Still I am nothing without love.

3 Should I distribute all my store
To feed the hungry, clothe the poor, —
Or give my body to the flame,
To gain a martyr's glorious name, —

4 If love to God and love to men
Be absent, all my hopes are vain;
Nor tongues, nor gifts, nor fiery zeal,
The work of love can e'er fulfil.

704. L. M. WATTS.

1 MY dear Redeemer and my Lord,
I read my duty in thy word;
But in thy life the law appears,
Drawn out in living characters.

2 Such was thy truth, and such thy zeal,
Such deference to thy Father's will,
Such love, and meekness so divine,
I would transcribe, and make them mine.

3 Cold mountains and the midnight air
Witnessed the fervor of thy prayer;
The desert thy temptations knew,
Thy conflict and thy victory too.

4 Be thou my pattern; make me bear
More of thy gracious image here;
Then God, the Judge, shall own my name
Among the followers of the Lamb.

706. L. M. WATTS.

1 So let our lips and lives express
The holy gospel we profess;
So let our works and virtues shine
To prove the doctrine all divine.

2 Thus shall we best proclaim abroad
The honors of our Saviour God,
When his salvation reigns within,
And grace subdues the power of sin.

3 Our flesh and sense must be denied,
Ambition, envy, lust, and pride;
While justice, temperance, truth, and love,
Our inward piety approve.

4 Religion bears our spirits up,
While we expect that blessed hope,
The bright appearance of the Lord;
And faith stands leaning on his word.

DUKE STREET. L. M. J. HATTON. ‡

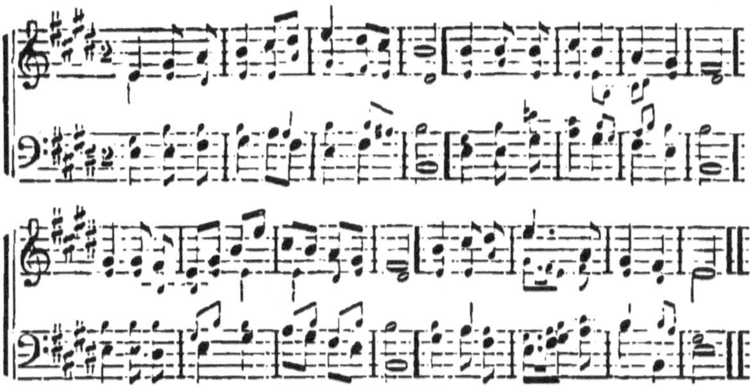

‡ Attributed also to REED.

575. L. M. STEELE.

1 IN vain my roving thoughts would find
A portion worthy of the mind;
On earth my soul can never rest,
For earth can never make me blest.

2 Can lasting happiness be found
Where seasons roll their hasty round,
And days and hours, with rapid flight,
Sweep cares and pleasures out of sight?

3 Arise, my thoughts; my heart, arise;
Leave this vain world, and seek the skies:
There purest joys forever last,
When seasons, days, and hours, are past.

4 Come, Lord, thy powerful grace impart;
Thy grace can raise my wandering heart
To pleasure, perfect and sublime,
Unmeasured by the wing of time.

720. L. M. WATTS.

1 STAND up, my soul, shake off thy fears,
And gird the gospel armor on;
March to the gates of endless joy,
Where Jesus, thy great Captain, 's gone.

2 Hell and thy sins resist thy course;
But hell and sin are vanquished foes;
Thy Saviour nailed them to the cross,
And sung the triumph when he rose.

3 Then let my soul march boldly on —
Press forward to the heavenly gate;
There peace and joy eternal reign,
And glittering robes for conquerors wait.

4 There shall I wear a starry crown,
And triumph in almighty grace,
While all the armies of the skies
Join in my glorious Leader's praise.

725. L. M. WATTS.

1 AWAKE, our souls; away, our fears;
Let every trembling thought be gone;
Awake, and run the heavenly race,
And put a cheerful courage on.

2 True, 'tis a strait and thorny road,
And mortal spirits tire and faint;
But they forget the mighty God,
Who feeds the strength of every saint; —

3 The mighty God, whose matchless power
Is ever new and ever young,
And firm endures, while endless years
Their everlasting circles run.

4 From thee, the overflowing spring,
Our souls shall drink a full supply;
While those who trust their native strength
Shall melt away, and droop, and die.

5 Swift as an eagle cuts the air,
We'll mount aloft to thine abode;
On wings of love our souls shall fly,
Nor tire amid the heavenly road.

779. L. M. WATTS.

1 WHO can describe the joys that rise,
Through all the courts of Paradise,
To see a penitent return, —
To see an heir of glory born?

2 With joy the Father does approve
The fruit of his eternal love;
The Son with joy looks down, and sees
The purchase of his agonies.

3 The Spirit takes delight to view
The holy soul he formed anew;
And saints and angels join to sing
The growing empire of their King.

MEDWAY. L. M. PERGOLESI.

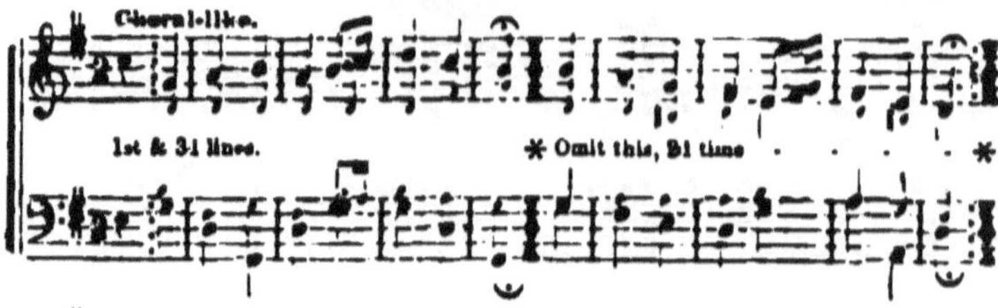

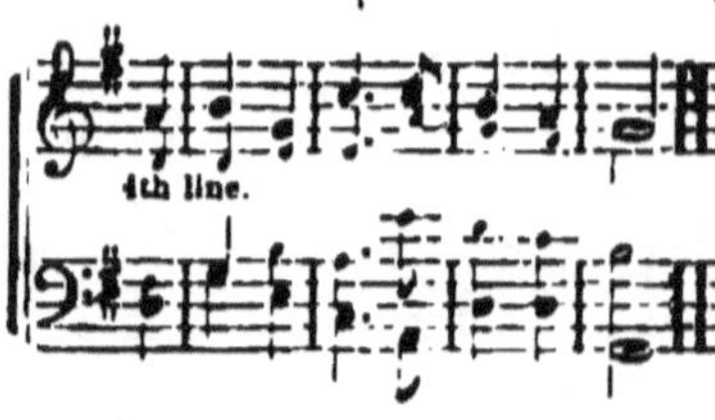

522. L. M. MERRICK.

1 O, TURN, great Ruler of the skies,
Turn from my sin thy searching eyes;
Nor let th' offences of my hand
Within thy book recorded stand.

2 Give me a will to thine subdued,
A conscience pure, a soul renewed;
Nor let me, wrapped in endless gloom,
An outcast from thy presence roam.

3 O, let thy Spirit to my heart
Once more his quickening aid impart,
My mind from every fear release,
And soothe my troubled thoughts to peace.

601. L. M. WATTS.

1 MY spirit looks to God alone;
My rock and refuge is his throne;
In all my fears, in all my straits,
My soul for his salvation waits.

2 Trust him, ye saints, in all your ways;
Pour out your hearts before his face;
When helpers fail and foes invade,
God is our all-sufficient aid.

618. L. M. WATTS.

1 UP to the fields where angels lie,
And living waters gently roll,
Fain would my thoughts ascend on high;
But sin hangs heavy on my soul.

2 O, might I once mount up and see
The glories of the eternal skies,
How vain a thing this world would be!
How empty all its fleeting joys!

3 Great All in All, eternal King,
Let me but view thy lovely face,
And all my powers shall bow and sing
Thine endless grandeur and thy grace.

756. L. M. WATTS.

1 MY spirit sinks within me, Lord;
But I will call thy grace to mind,
And times of past distress record,
When I have found my God was kind.

2 Yet will the Lord command his love,
When I address his throne by day,
Nor in the night his grace remove;
The night shall hear me sing and pray.

3 I'll chide my heart, that sinks so low;
Why should my soul indulge in grief?
Hope in the Lord, and praise him too;
He is my rest, my sure relief.

4 O God, thou art my hope, my joy;
Thy light and truth shall guide me still;
Thy word shall my best thoughts employ,
And lead me to thy heavenly hill.

776. L. M. WATTS.

1 CHILDREN, in years and knowledge young,
Your parents' hope, your parents' joy,
Attend the counsels of my tongue;
Let pious thoughts your minds employ.

2 If you desire a length of days,
And peace to crown your mortal state,
Restrain your feet from sinful ways,
Your lips from slander and deceit.

3 The eyes of God regard his saints;
His ears are open to their cries;
He sets his frowning face against
The sons of violence and lies.

4 To humble souls and broken hearts,
God, with his grace, is ever nigh;
Pardon and hope his love imparts,
When men in deep contrition lie.

5 He tells their tears; he counts their groans;
His Son redeems their souls from death;
His Spirit heals their broken bones;
They in his praise employ their breath.

WARD.

The tune should be repeated, without pause or interlude, for Hymn 525.

525. L. M. Collyer.

1 Soft be the gently-breathing notes
That sing the Saviour's dying love,
Soft as the evening zephyr floats,
And soft as tuneful lyres above;
Soft as the morning dews descend,
While warbling birds exulting soar,
So soft to our almighty Friend
Be every sigh our bosoms pour.

2 Pure as the sun's enlivening ray,
That scatters life and joy abroad;
Pure as the lucid orb of day,
That wide proclaims its Maker, God;
Pure as the breath of vernal skies;
So pure let our contrition be;
And purely let our sorrows rise
To Him who bled upon the tree.

698. L. M. Barbauld.

1 How blest the sacred tie that binds,
In sweet communion, kindred minds!
How swift the heavenly course they run,
Whose hearts, whose faith, whose hopes, are one!

2 To each the soul of each how dear!
What tender love, what holy fear!
How doth the generous flame within
Refine from earth, and cleanse from sin!

3 Nor shall the glowing flame expire,
When dimly burns frail nature's fire;
Then shall they meet in realms above,
A heaven of joy, a heaven of love.

FEDERAL STREET.

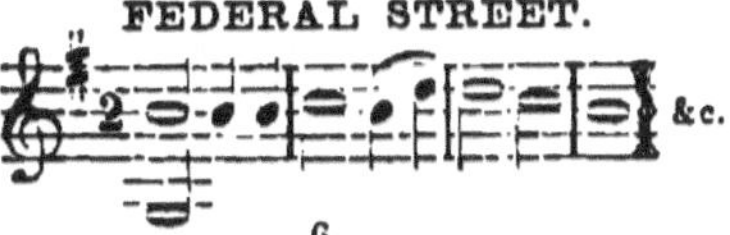

739. L. M. Ch. Psalmody.

1 Thou God of hope, to thee we bow;
Thou art our refuge in distress;
The husband of the widow thou,
The father of the fatherless.

2 The poor are thy peculiar care;
To them thy promises are sure;
Thy gifts the poor in spirit share;
O, may we always thus be poor.

3 May we thy law of love fulfil,
To bear each other's burdens here,
Endure and do thy righteous will,
And walk in all thy faith and fear.

4 Thou God of hope, to thee we bow;
Thou art our refuge in distress;
The husband of the widow thou,
The father of the fatherless.

750. L. M. Watts.

1 Blest are the men whose mercies move
To acts of kindness and of love:
From Christ, the Lord, shall they obtain
Like sympathy and love again.

2 Blest are the pure, whose hearts are clean,
Who never tread the ways of sin;
With endless pleasure they shall see
A God of spotless purity.

3 Blest are the men of peaceful life,
Who quench the coals of growing strife;
They shall be called the heirs of bliss,
The sons of God — the God of peace.

4 Blest are the faithful, who partake
Of pain and shame for Jesus' sake;
Their souls shall triumph in the Lord;
Eternal life is their reward.

524. L. M. 6 L. COLLYER.

1 FATHER of mercies, God of love,
O, hear an humble suppliant's cry;
Bend from thy lofty seat above,
Thy throne of glorious majesty;
O, deign to listen to my voice,
And bid my drooping heart rejoice.

2 I urge no merits of my own,
No worth, to claim thy gracious smile;
And when I bow before the throne,
Dare to converse with God a while,
Thy name, blest Saviour, is my plea —
Dearest and sweetest name to me.

3 Father of mercies, God of love,
Then hear thy humble suppliant's cry;
Bend from thy lofty seat above,
Thy throne of glorious majesty:
One pardoning word can make me whole,
And soothe the anguish of my soul.

585. L. M. 6 L. BOWRING.

1 O, LET my trembling soul be still,
While darkness veils this mortal eye,
And wait thy wise, thy holy will:
Wrapped yet in fears and mystery,
I cannot, Lord, thy purpose see;
Yet all is well, since ruled by thee.

2 When, mounted on thy clouded car,
Thou send'st thy darker spirits down,
I can discern thy light afar —
Thy light, sweet beaming through thy frown;
And, should I faint a moment, then
I think of thee, and smile again.

3 So, trusting in thy love, I tread
The narrow path of duty on:
What though some cherished joys are fled;
What though some fluttering dreams are gone;
Yet purer, brighter joys remain:
Why should my spirit, then, complain?

---

419. L. M. 6 L. EPIS. COL.

1 PEACE, troubled soul, whose plaintive moan
Hath taught the rocks the notes of woe;
Cease thy complaint, suppress thy groan,
And let thy tears forget to flow:
Behold, the precious balm is found,
To lull thy pain, to heal thy wound.

2 Come, freely come, by sin oppressed;
Unburden here thy weighty load;
Here find thy refuge and thy rest,
And trust the mercy of thy God;
Thy God's thy Saviour — glorious word!
Forever love and praise the Lord.

Hymn 419. "PEACE, TROUBLED SOUL." L. M. 6 L. MAZZINGHI.
Duett: or Trebles & Altos.
Inst.
Chorus.
ALDEN. L. M.
E. F. G.
From Nat. Church Harmony.
Chant Style.
Minor.
Major.

‡ From the Congregational Tune Book, London.

BURROUGHS. L. M. S. D. HADLEY.

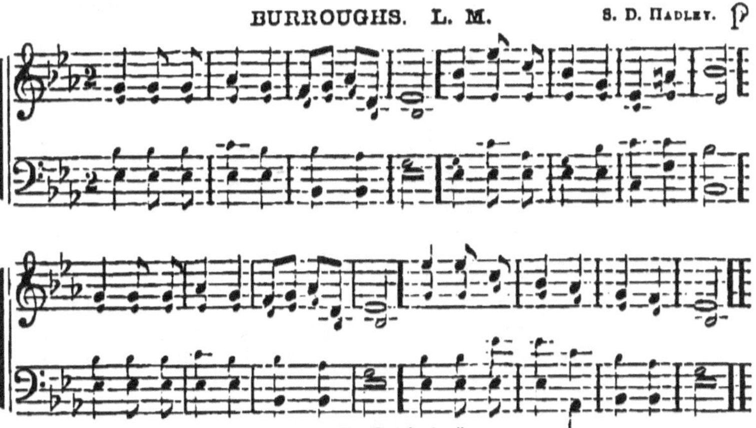

From "The Well Spring."

804. L. M. JUDSON.

1 OUR Saviour bowed beneath the wave,
And meekly sought a watery grave:
Come, see the sacred path he trod —
A path well pleasing to our God.

2 His voice we hear, his footsteps trace,
And hither come to seek his face,
To do his will, to feel his love,
And join our songs with songs above.

3 Hosanna to the Lamb divine!
Let endless glories round him shine;
High o'er the heavens forever reign,
O Lamb of God, for sinners slain.

805. L. M. WATTS.

1 Do we not know that solemn word,
That we are buried with the Lord?
Baptized into his death, and then
Put off the body of our sin?

2 Our souls receive diviner breath,
Raised from corruption, guilt, and death;
So from the grave did Christ arise,
And lives to God above the skies.

3 No more let sin or Satan reign
Within our mortal flesh again;
The various lusts we served before
Shall have dominion now no more.

807. L. M. JUDSON.

1 COME, Holy Spirit, Dove divine,
On these baptismal waters shine,
And teach our hearts, in highest strain,
To praise the Lamb, for sinners slain.

2 We love thy name, we love thy laws,
And joyfully embrace thy cause;
We love thy cross, the shame, the pain,
O Lamb of God, for sinners slain.

3 We sink beneath thy mystic flood;
O, bathe us in thy cleansing blood;
We die to sin, and seek a grave,
With thee, beneath the yielding wave.

4 And as we rise, with thee to live,
O, let the Holy Spirit give
The sealing unction from above,
The breath of life, the fire of love.

813. L. M. BEDDOME.

1 BLEST Saviour, we thy will obey:
Not of constraint, but with delight;
Thy servants hither come to-day
To honor thine appointed rite.

2 Descend, descend, celestial Dove,
On these dear followers of the Lord;
Exalted Head of all the church,
Thy promised aid to them afford.

3 Let faith, assisted now by signs,
The wonders of thy love explore,
And, washed in thy redeeming blood,
Let them depart, and sin no more.

825. L. M. DODDRIDGE.

1 'TIS done; the great transaction's done;
I am my Lord's, and he is mine:
He drew me, and I followed on,
Rejoiced to own the call divine.

2 Now rest, my long-divided heart;
Fixed on this blissful centre, rest;
Here have I found a nobler part;
Here heavenly pleasures fill my breast.

3 High Heaven, that hears the solemn vow,
That vow renewed shall daily hear,
Till in life's latest hour I bow,
And bless in death a bond so dear.

ALFRETON. L. M. W. BEASTALL, 1708.

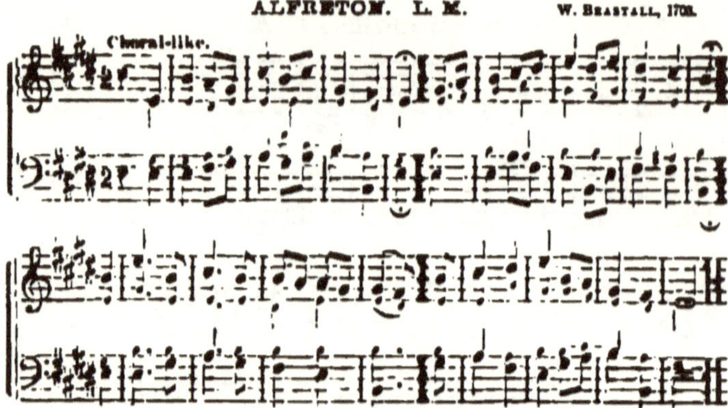

799. L. M. BALDWIN.

1 COME, happy souls, adore the Lamb,
Who loved our race ere time began,
Who veiled his Godhead in our clay,
And in an humble manger lay.

2 To Jordan's stream the Spirit led,
To mark the path his saints should tread;
With joy they trace the sacred way,
To see the place where Jesus lay.

3 Baptized by John in Jordan's wave,
The Saviour left his watery grave;
Heaven owned the deed, approved the way,
And blessed the place where Jesus lay.

4 Come, all who love his precious name,
Come, tread his steps, and learn of him:
Happy beyond expression they
Who find the place where Jesus lay.

816. L. M. BEDDOME.

1 ETERNAL Spirit, heavenly Dove,
On these baptismal waters move,
That we, through energy divine,
May have the substance with the sign.

2 All ye that love Immanuel's name,
And long to feel th' increasing flame,
'Tis you, ye children of the light,
The Spirit and the bride invite.

820. L. M. S. P. HILL.

1 COME, saints, adore your Saviour, God,
Who led your willing footsteps here;
Walk in the blessed paths he trod,
Nor duty dread, nor danger fear.

2 Come, sacred Dove, in peace descend,
As once thou didst on Jordan's wave;
Now with this scene thine influence blend,
And hover o'er this solemn grave.

826. L. M. KELLY.

1 COME in, thou blessed of the Lord;
O, come in Jesus' precious name:
We welcome thee with one accord,
And trust the Saviour does the same.

2 Thy name, 'tis hoped, already stands
Within the book of life above;
And now to thine we join our hands,
In token of fraternal love.

3 Those joys which earth cannot afford
We'll seek in fellowship to prove,
Joined in one spirit to our Lord,
Together bound by mutual love.

4 And while we pass this vale of tears,
We'll make our joys and sorrows known;
We'll share each other's hopes and fears,
And count a brother's case our own.

5 Once more our welcome we repeat;
Receive assurance of our love;
O, may we all together meet
Around the throne of God above.

828. L. M. NEWTON.

1 KINDRED in Christ, for his dear sake,
A hearty welcome here receive;
May we together now partake
The joys which only he can give.

2 May He by whose kind care we meet
Send his good Spirit from above,
Make our communications sweet,
And cause our hearts to burn with love

3 Forgotten be each worldly theme,
When Christians see each other thus;
We only wish to speak of Him
Who lived, and died, and reigns for us.

LUTON. L. M. BURDER.

Choral-like.

4 We'll talk of all he did, and said,
And suffered, for us here below,
The path he marked for us to tread,
And what he's doing for us now.

5 Thus, as the moments pass away,
We'll love, and wonder, and adore,
And long to see the glorious day
When we shall meet to part no more.

829. L. M. BEDDOME.

1 BELIEVING souls, of Christ beloved,
Who have yourselves to him resigned,
Your faith and practice, both approved,
A hearty welcome here shall find.

2 Now saved from sin and Satan's wiles,
Though by a scorning world abhorred,
Now share with us the Saviour's smiles;
Come in, ye ransomed of the Lord.

3 In fellowship we join our hands,
And you an invitation give;
Unite with us in sacred bands;
The pledges of our love receive.

4 Do Thou, who art the church's Head,
This union with thy blessing crown;
And still, O Lord, revive the dead,
Till thousands more thy name shall own.

836. L. M. WATTS

1 NOW let our mournful songs record
The dying sorrows of our Lord,
When he complained in tears and blood,
Like one forsaken of his God.

2 But God, his Father, heard his cry;
Raised from the dead, he reigns on high;
The nations learn his righteousness,
And humble sinners taste his grace.

831. L. M. WATTS.

1 'TWAS on that dark, that doleful night,
When powers of earth and hell arose
Against the Son of God's delight,
And friends betrayed him to his foes,—

2 Before the mournful scene began,
He took the bread, and blessed, and brake;
What love through all his actions ran!
What wondrous words of grace he spake!

3 "This is my body, broke for sin;
Receive and eat the living food;"
Then took the cup, and blessed the wine;
"'Tis the new covenant in my blood."

4 "Do this," he cried, "till time shall end,
In memory of your dying Friend;
Meet at my table, and record
The love of your departed Lord."

5 Jesus, thy feast we celebrate;
We show thy death, we sing thy name,
Till thou return, and we shall eat
The marriage supper of the Lamb.

833. L. M. WATTS.

1 OUR spirits join to praise the Lamb;
O that our feeble lips could move
In strains immortal as his name,
And melting as his dying love!

2 Was ever equal pity found?
The Prince of heaven resigns his breath,
And pours his life out on the ground
To ransom guilty worms from death.

3 In vain our mortal voices strive
To speak compassion so divine;
Had we a thousand lives to give,
A thousand lives should all be thine.

STONEFIELD. L. M. S. STANLEY.

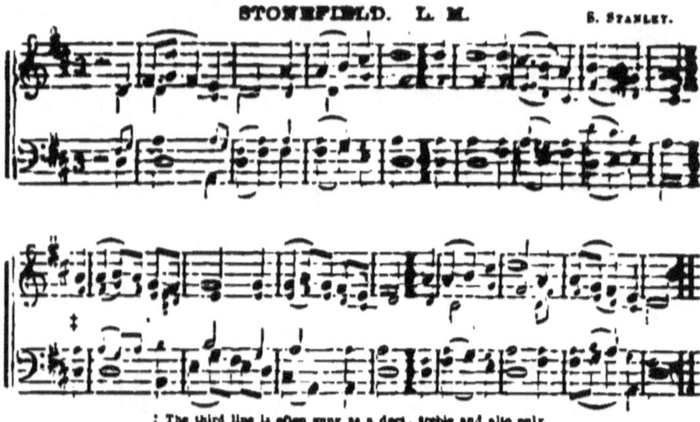

‡ The third line is often sung as a duet, treble and alto only.

834. L. M. WATTS.

1 WHEN I survey the wondrous cross,
On which the Prince of glory died,
My richest gain I count but loss,
And pour contempt on all my pride.

2 Forbid it, Lord, that I should boast,
Save in the death of Christ, my God;
All the vain things that charm me most,
I sacrifice them to his blood.

3 See, from his head, his hands, his feet,
Sorrow and love flow mingled down:
Did e'er such love and sorrow meet,
Or thorns compose so rich a crown?

4 Were all the realm of nature mine,
That were a present far too small;
Love so amazing, so divine,
Demands my soul, my life, my all.

844. L. M. KRISHNA PAL.

1 O THOU, my soul, forget no more
The Friend who all thy sorrows bore;
Let every idol be forgot;
But, O my soul, forget him not.

2 Renounce thy works and ways, with grief,
And fly to this divine relief;
Nor Him forget, who left his throne,
And for thy life gave up his own.

3 Eternal truth and mercy shine
In him, and he himself is thine;
And canst thou, then, with sin beset,
Such charms, such matchless charms, forget?

4 O, no; till life itself depart,
His name shall cheer and warm my heart;
And, lisping this, from earth I'll rise,
And join the chorus of the skies.

845. L. M. WATTS.

1 JESUS is gone above the skies,
Where our weak senses reach him not;
And carnal objects court our eyes,
To thrust our Saviour from our thought.

2 He knows what wandering hearts we have,
Apt to forget his lovely face;
And, to refresh our minds, he gave
These kind memorials of his grace.

3 Let sinful joys be all forgot,
And earth grow less in our esteem,
Christ and his love fill every thought,
And faith and hope be fixed on him.

4 While he is absent from our sight,
'Tis to prepare our souls a place,
That we may dwell in heavenly light,
And live forever near his face.

849. L. M. WATTS.

1 FAR from my thoughts, vain world, be gone;
Let my religious hours alone;
Fain would my eyes my Saviour see;
I wait a visit, Lord, from thee.

2 O, warm my heart with holy fire,
And kindle there a pure desire;
Come, sacred Spirit, from above,
And fill my soul with heavenly love.

3 Blest Saviour, what delicious fare!
How sweet thy entertainments are!
Ne'er did the angels taste above
Redeeming grace and dying love.

4 Hail, great Immanuel, all divine!
In thee thy Father's glories shine;
Thy glorious name shall be adored,
And every tongue confess thee, Lord.

BRIDGEWATER. L. M. EDSON.

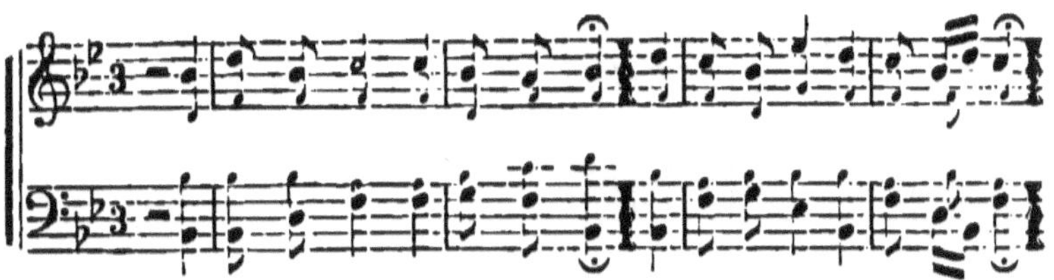

852. L. M. WATTS.

1 "Go, preach my gospel," saith the Lord;
"Bid the whole earth my grace receive:
He shall be saved that trusts my word,
And he condemned who'll not believe.

2 "I'll make your great commission known;
And ye shall prove my gospel true,
By all the works that I have done,
By all the wonders ye shall do.

3 "Teach all the nations my commands;
I'm with you till the world shall end;
All power is trusted in my hands;
I can destroy, and I defend."

4 He spake; and light shone round his head;
On a bright cloud to heaven he rode:
They to the farthest nations spread
The grace of their ascended God.

MISS'Y CHANT.

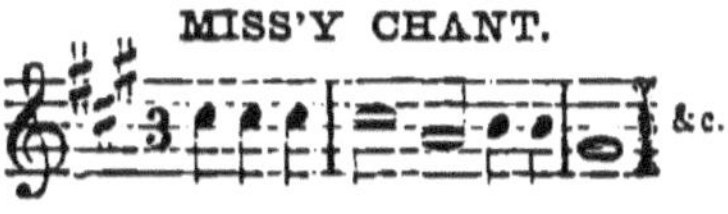

854. L. M. WATTS.

1 JESUS shall reign where'er the sun
Does his successive journeys run;
His kingdom stretch from shore to shore
Till moons shall wax and wane no more.

2 For him shall endless prayer be made,
And endless praises crown his head;
His name, like sweet perfume, shall rise
With every morning sacrifice.

3 People and realms of every tongue
Dwell on his love with sweetest song;
And infant voices shall proclaim
Their early blessings on his name.

4 Blessings abound where'er he reigns;
The joyful prisoner bursts his chains;
The weary find eternal rest;
And all the sons of want are blest.

5 Let every creature rise, and bring
Peculiar honors to our King;
Angels descend with songs again,
And earth repeat the loud Amen.

OLD HUNDRED. L. M. G. Franc. Dates previous to 1543.

853. L. M. Watts.

1 Great God, whose universal sway
The known and unknown worlds obey,
Now give the kingdom to thy Son;
Extend his power, exalt his throne.

2 As rain on meadows newly mown,
So shall he send his influence down;
His grace on fainting souls distils,
Like heavenly dew on thirsty hills.

3 The heathen lands that lie beneath
The shades of overspreading death,
Revive at his first dawning light,
And deserts blossom at the sight.

4 The saints shall flourish in his days,
Dressed in the robes of joy and praise;
Peace, like a river, from his throne,
Shall flow to nations yet unknown.

855. L. M. Voke.

1 Behold, the heathen waits to know
The joy the gospel will bestow;
The exiled captive to receive
The freedom Jesus has to give.

2 Come, let us, with a grateful heart,
In this blest labor share a part;
Our prayers and offerings gladly bring
To aid the triumphs of our King.

3 Our hearts exult in songs of praise,
That we have seen these latter days,
When our Redeemer shall be known
Where Satan long hath held his throne.

4 Where'er his hand hath spread the skies,
Sweet incense to his name shall rise,
And slave and freeman, Greek and Jew,
By sovereign grace be formed anew.

860. L. M. Slinn

1 Arise in all thy splendor, Lord;
Let power attend thy gracious word;
Unveil the beauties of thy face,
And show the glories of thy grace.

2 Diffuse thy light and truth abroad,
And be thou known th' almighty God;
Make bare thine arm, thy power display,
While truth and grace thy sceptre sway.

3 Send forth thy messengers of peace;
Make Satan's reign and empire cease;
Let thy salvation, Lord, be known,
That all the world thy power may own.

909. L. M. Pratt's Col.

1 Arise, arise; with joy survey
The glory of the latter day:
Already is the dawn begun
Which marks at hand a rising sun.

2 "Behold the way," ye heralds, cry;
Spare not, but lift your voices high;
Convey the sound from pole to pole,
"Glad tidings" to the captive soul.

3 "Behold the way to Zion's hill,
Where Israel's God delights to dwell:
He fixes there his lofty throne,
And calls the sacred place his own."

4 The north gives up; the south no more
Keeps back her consecrated store;
From east to west the message runs,
And either India yields her sons.

5 Auspicious dawn, thy rising ray
With joy we view, and hail the day.
Great Sun of Righteousness, arise,
And fill the world with glad surprise.

857. L. M. Anon.

1 Awake, all-conquering Arm, awake,
And Satan's mighty empire shake;
Assert the honors of thy throne,
And make this ruined world thy own.

2 Thine all-successful power display,
Convert a nation in a day;
Until the universe shall be
But one great temple, Lord, for thee.

861. L. M. Burder's Col.

1 Arm of the Lord, awake, awake;
Put on thy strength, the nations shake;
Now let the world, adoring, see
Triumphs of mercy wrought by thee.

2 Say to the heathen, from thy throne,
"I am Jehovah, God alone:"
Thy voice their idols shall confound,
And cast their altars to the ground.

3 Let Zion's time of favor come;
O, bring the tribes of Israel home;
Soon may our wondering eyes behold
Gentiles and Jews in Jesus' fold.

4 Almighty God, thy grace proclaim
Through every clime, of every name;
Let adverse powers before thee fall,
And crown the Saviour Lord of all.

865. L. M. Pratt's Col.

1 Sovereign of worlds, display thy power;
Be this thy Zion's favored hour:
O, bid the morning star arise;
O, point the heathen to the skies.

2 Set up thy throne where Satan reigns,
In western wilds and eastern plains;
Far let the gospel's sound be known;
Make thou the universe thine own.

3 Speak, and the world shall hear thy voice;
Speak, and the desert shall rejoice;
Dispel the gloom of heathen night;
Bid every nation hail the light.

869. L. M. Bacon.

1 Though now the nations sit beneath
The darkness of o'erspreading death,
God will arise with light divine,
On Zion's holy towers to shine.

2 That light shall beam o'er distant lands,
And heathen tribes, in joyful bands,
Come with exulting haste to prove
The power and greatness of his love.

3 Lord, spread the triumphs of thy grace;
Let truth, and righteousness, and peace,
In mild and lovely forms display
The glories of the latter day.

896. L. M. Pratt's Col.

1 Zion, awake; thy strength renew;
Put on thy robes of beauteous hue;
Church of our God, arise and shine,
Bright with the beams of truth divine.

2 Soon shall thy radiance stream afar,
Wide as the heathen nations are;
Gentiles and kings thy light shall view;
All shall admire and love thee too.

903. L. M. Ch. Psalmody.

1 Soon may the last, glad song arise
Through all the myriads of the skies —
That song of triumph, which records
That all the earth is now the Lord's.

2 Let thrones, and powers, and kingdoms be
Obedient, mighty God, to thee;
And over land, and stream, and main,
Now wave the sceptre of thy reign.

3 O, let that glorious anthem swell;
Let host to host the triumph tell,
That not one rebel heart remains,
But over all the Saviour reigns.

911. L. M. Watts.

1 Now let the angel sound on high;
Let shouts be heard through all the sky;
Kings of the earth, with glad accord,
Give up your kingdoms to the Lord.

2 Almighty God, thy power assume,
Who wast, and art, and art to come;
Jesus, the Lamb, that once was slain,
Forever live, forever reign.

920. L. M. Anon.

1 O Thou, who once on Israel's ground
A homeless wanderer was found,—
Redeemer, on thy heavenly throne,
Still call those ancient tribes thine own.

2 Bid their departed light return;
Thy holy splendor round them burn;
From prostrate Judah's ruins raise
A living temple to thy praise.

926. L. M. Watts.

1 From all who dwell below the skies
Let the Creator's praise arise;
Let the Redeemer's name be sung,
Through every land, by every tongue.

2 Eternal are thy mercies, Lord;
Eternal truth attends thy word;
Thy praise shall sound from shore to shore,
Till suns shall rise and set no more.

CLARE. L. M. EDWARD HAMILTON.

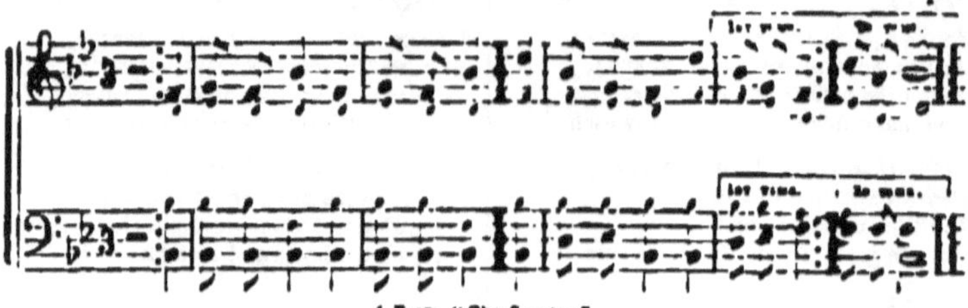

‡ From "The Sanctus."

878. L. M. A. BALFOUR.

1 Go, messenger of peace and love,
To people plunged in shades of night;
Like angels sent from fields above,
Be thine to shed celestial light.

2 On barren rock and desert isle,
Go, bid the rose of Sharon bloom;
Till arid wastes around thee smile,
And bear to heaven a sweet perfume.

3 Go to the hungry — food impart;
To paths of peace the wanderer guide;
And lead the thirsty, panting heart
Where streams of living water glide.

4 Go, bid the bright and morning star
From Bethlehem's plains resplendent shine,
And, piercing through the gloom afar,
Shed heavenly light and love divine.

5 O, faint not in the day of toil,
When harvest waits the reaper's hand;
Go, gather in the glorious spoil,
And joyous in his presence stand.

6 Thy love a rich reward shall find
From Him who sits enthroned on high;
For they who turn the erring mind
Shall shine like stars above the sky.

882. L. M. WINCHELL'S SEL.

1 YE Christian heralds, — go, proclaim
Salvation in Immanuel's name;
To distant climes the tidings bear,
And plant the rose of Sharon there.

2 He'll shield you with a wall of fire,
With holy zeal your hearts inspire;
Bid raging winds their fury cease,
And calm the savage breast to peace.

3 And when our labors all are o'er,
Then shall we meet to part no more —
Meet, with the blood-bought throng to fall,
And crown the Saviour Lord of all.

914. L. M. COLLYER.

1 ASSEMBLED at thy great command,
Before thy face, dread King, we stand:
The voice that marshalled every star
Has called thy people from afar.

2 We meet, through distant lands to spread
The truth for which the martyrs bled;
Along the line — to either pole —
The anthem of thy praise to roll.

3 Our prayers assist; accept our praise;
Our hopes revive; our courage raise;
Our counsels aid; to each impart
The single eye, the faithful heart.

4 Forth with thy chosen heralds come
Recall the wandering spirits home:
From Zion's mount send forth the sound,
To spread the spacious earth around.

922. L. M. PRATT'S COL.

1 WHY, on the bending willows hung,
O Israel, sleeps thy tuneful string? —
Still mute remains thy sullen tongue,
And Zion's song declines to sing?

2 Awake! thy sweetest raptures raise:
Let harp and voice unite their strains:
Thy promised King his sceptre sways;
And Jesus, thy Messiah, reigns.

3 No taunting foes the song require;
No strangers mock thy captive chain;
But friends invite the silent lyre,
And brethren ask the holy strain.

4 Nor fear thy Salem's hills to wrong,
If other lands thy triumph share;
A heavenly city claims thy song;
A brighter Salem rises there.

5 By foreign streams no longer roam:
Nor, weeping, think of Jordan's flood:
In every clime behold a home;
In every temple see thy God.

931. L. M. WATTS.

1 HAPPY the church, thou sacred place,
The seat of thy Creator's grace;
Thine holy courts are his abode,
Thou earthly palace of our God.

2 Thy walls are strength; and at thy gates
A guard of heavenly warriors waits;
Nor shall thy deep foundation move,
Fixed on his counsels and his love.

3 Thy foes in vain designs engage;
Against thy throne in vain they rage,
Like rising waves with angry roar,
That dash and die upon the shore.

4 God is our shield, and God our sun;
Swift as the fleeting moments run,
On us he sheds new beams of grace;
And we reflect his brightest praise.

MISSIONARY CHANT.

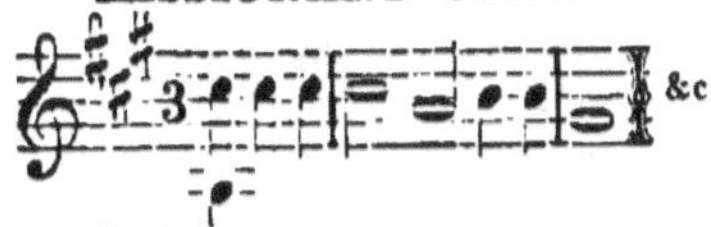

934. L. M. MONTGOMERY.

1 HERE, in thy name, eternal God,
We build this earthly house for thee;
O, choose it for thy fixed abode,
And guard it long from error free.

2 Here, when thy people seek thy face,
And dying sinners pray to live,
Hear thou, in heaven, thy dwelling place,
And when thou hearest, Lord, forgive.

3 Here, when thy messengers proclaim
The blessed gospel of thy Son,
Still by the power of his great name
Be mighty signs and wonders done.

4 When children's voices raise the song,
Hosanna! to their heavenly King,
Let heaven with earth the strain prolong;
Hosanna! let the angels sing.

5 But will, indeed, Jehovah deign
Here to abide, no transient guest?
Here will our great Redeemer reign,
And here the Holy Spirit rest?

6 Thy glory never hence depart;
Yet choose not, Lord, this house alone;
Thy kingdom come to every heart;
In every bosom fix thy throne.

935. L. M. WATTS.

1 WHERE shall we go to seek and find
A habitation for our God?
A dwelling for th' Eternal Mind
Among the sons of flesh and blood?

2 The God of Jacob chose the hill
Of Zion for his ancient rest;
And Zion is his dwelling still;
His church is with his presence blest.

3 Here will he meet the hungry poor,
And fill their souls with living bread;
Here sinners, waiting at the door,
With sweet provision shall be fed.

4 "Here will I fix my gracious throne,
And reign forever," saith the Lord;
"Here shall my power and love be known,
And blessings shall attend my word."

938. L. M. WILLIS.

1 THE perfect world, by Adam trod,
Was the first temple built by God;
His fiat laid the corner stone;
He spake, and lo! the work was done.

2 He hung its starry roof on high,
The broad expanse of azure sky;
He spread its pavement, green and bright,
And curtained it with morning light.

3 The mountains in their places stood,
The sea, the sky; and all was good;
And when its first pure praises rung,
The morning stars together sung.

4 Lord, 'tis not ours to make the sea,
And earth, and sky, a house for thee;
But in thy sight our offering stands,
An humble temple built with hands.

941. L. M. DODDRIDGE.

1 AND will the great, eternal God
On earth establish his abode?
And will he, from his heavenly throne,
Avow our temples for his own?

2 We bring the tribute of our praise,
And sing that condescending grace
Which to our notes will lend an ear,
And call us, sinful mortals, near.

3 These walls we to thy honor raise;
Long may they echo with thy praise,
And thou, descending, fill the place
With choicest tokens of thy grace.

4 Here let the great Redeemer reign,
With all the graces of his train;
While power divine his words attends,
To conquer foes and cheer his friends.

5 And in the great, decisive day,
When God the nations shall survey,
May it before the world appear
That crowds were born to glory here.

ALL SAINTS. L. M.

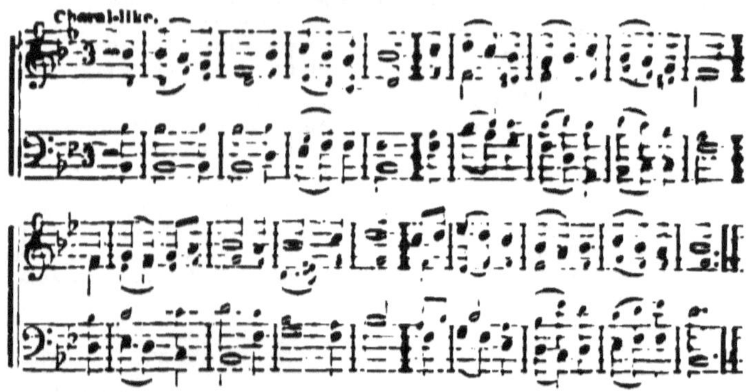

942. L. M. H. S. WASHBURN.

1 ALMIGHTY God, thy constant care
Hath been our sure support and stay,
And hither gladly we repair,
Our early sacrifice to pay.

2 Accept our vows: in humble trust
This house we consecrate to thee;
O, may thy promise to the just
Forever, Lord, our portion be.

3 And may that stream which maketh glad
The city of our God below,
Revive the drooping, cheer the sad,
As still its healing waters flow.

4 So let thy people here enjoy
The blessings which thy grace hath given,
That they may hail, with purer joy,
The unseen, perfect bliss of heaven.

945. L. M. DODDRIDGE.

1 FATHER of mercies, in thy house
We pay our homage and our vows,
While with a grateful heart we share
These pledges of our Saviour's care.

2 The Saviour, when to heaven he rose
In splendid triumph o'er his foes,
Conferred his gifts on men below;
And wide his royal bounties flow.

3 Hence sprung th' apostle's honored name,
Sacred beyond all earthly fame;
In lowlier forms, to bless our eyes,
Our pastors hence and teachers rise.

4 So shall the bright succession run
Through latest courses of the sun;
While numerous churches, by their care,
Shall rise and flourish, large and fair.

946. L. M. BEDDOME.

1 FATHER of mercies, bow thine ear,
Attentive to our earnest prayer:
We plead for those who plead for thee;
Successful pleaders may they be.

2 How great their work! how vast their charge!
Do thou their anxious souls enlarge:
Their best endowments are our gain;
We share the blessings they obtain.

3 O, clothe with energy divine
Their words; and let those words be thine;
To them thy sacred truth reveal;
Suppress their fear; inflame their zeal.

4 Teach them to sow the precious seed;
Teach them thy chosen flock to feed;
Teach them immortal souls to gain;
And thus reward their toil and pain.

5 Let thronging multitudes around
Hear from their lips the joyful sound,
In humble strains thy grace implore,
And feel thy Spirit's living power.

950. L. M. MONTGOMERY.

1 WE bid thee welcome in the name
Of Jesus, our exalted Head:
Come as a servant: so he came;
And we receive thee in his stead.

2 Come as a shepherd: guard and keep
This fold from Satan and from sin,
Nourish the lambs and feed the sheep;
The wounded heal, the lost bring in.

3 Come as a watchman: take thy stand
Upon thy tower on Zion's height;
And when the sword comes on the land,
Warn us to fly, or teach to fight.

GREGORY. L. M.

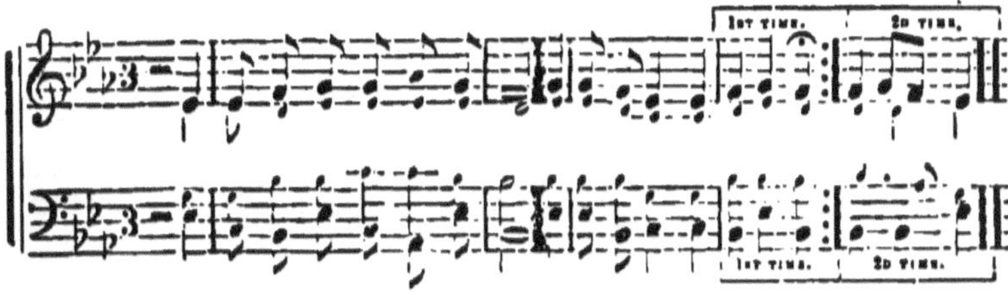

4 Come as an angel, hence to guide
A band of pilgrims on their way;
That, safely walking at thy side,
We never fail, nor faint, nor stray.

5 Come as a teacher sent from God,
Charged his whole counsel to declare;
Lift o'er our ranks the prophet's rod,
While we uphold thy hands with prayer.

6 Come as a messenger of peace,
Filled with the Spirit, fired with love;
Live to behold our large increase,
And die to meet us all above.

951. L. M. S. F. Smith.

1 'Tis done — th' important act is done —
Heaven, earth, its solemn purport know;
Its fruits, when time its race has run,
Shall through eternal ages flow.

2 The covenants of this sacred hour,
Great Shepherd of thy people, seal;
Spirit of grace, diffuse thy power,
Our vows accept, thy might reveal.

3 Behold our guide, and deign to crown
His toils, O Lamb of God, with love;
His lips inspire; each effort own;
Breathe, dwell within him, heavenly Dove.

4 Behold his charge; what wealth shall dare
With its most priceless worth to vie?
Suns, systems, worlds, how mean they are,
Compared with souls, that cannot die!

5 The sun may set in endless gloom,
The planets from their stations flee,
Creation fill oblivion's tomb,
But souls can never cease to be.

6 O, when, before the judgment-seat,
The wicked quake in dread despair,
May we, all reverent at thy feet,
Pastor and flock, find mercy there.

ROCKINGHAM.

&c.

953. L. M. S. F. Smith.

1 Spirit of peace and holiness,
This new-created union bless;
Bind each to each in ties of love,
And ratify our work above.

2 Saviour, who carest for thy sheep,
The shepherd of thy people keep;
Guide him in every doubtful way,
Nor let his feet from duty stray.

3 Gird thou his heart with strength divine;
Let Christ through all his conduct shine;
Faithful in all things may he be —
Dead to the world, alive to thee.

4 O thou, whose love doth never fail,
Breathe on this dry and thirsty vale;
And may it, from this hour, appear
That thy reviving power is there.

5 Lord of the Sabbath, unto thee
Our spirits rise in harmony;
Accept our praise, our sins remove,
And fit us for thy courts above.

954. L. M. S. F. Smith.

1 And now the solemn deed is done;
The vow is pledged, the toil begun;
Seal thou, O God, the oath above,
And ratify the pledge of love.

2 The shepherd of thy people bless;
Gird him with thy own holiness;
In duty may his pleasure be,
His glory in his zeal for thee.

3 Here let the ardent prayer arise,
Faith fix its grasp beyond the skies,
The tear of penitence be shed,
And myriads to the Saviour led.

4 Come, Spirit, here consent to dwell,
The mists of earth and sin dispel;
Blest Saviour, thy own rights maintain;
Supreme in every bosom reign.

5 O, let our humble worship be
A grateful tribute, Lord, to thee;
And may these hallowed scenes of love
Fit us for purer joys above.

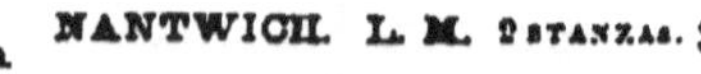

NANTWICH. L. M. 2 STANZAS. ‡

Adapted to Hymn 959. Dr. Madan.

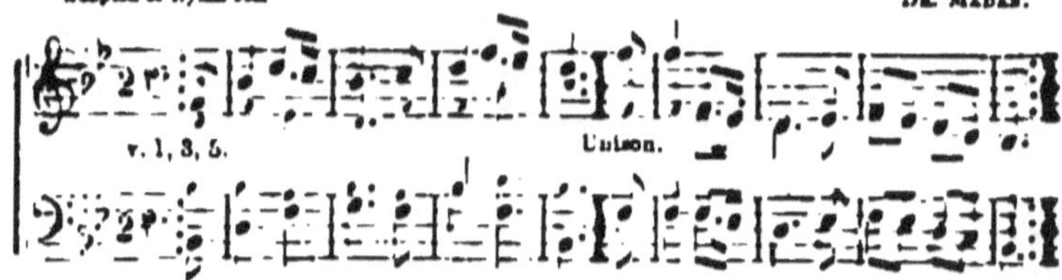

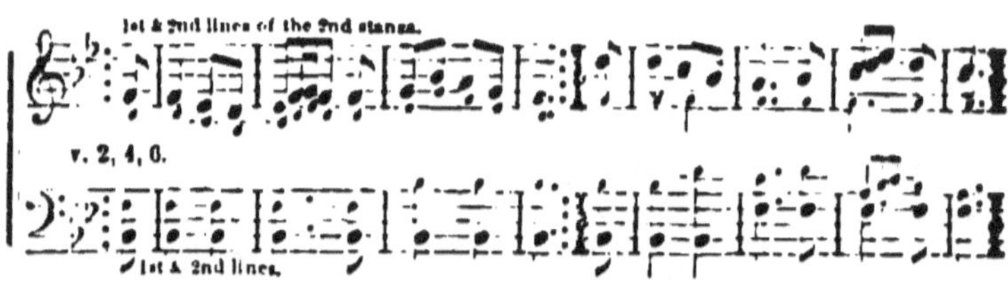

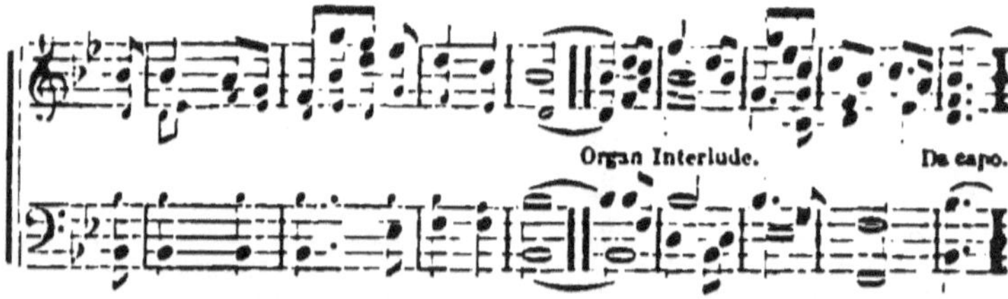

959. L. M. H. K. White.

1 When, marshalled on the nightly plain,
The glittering host bestud the sky,
One star alone, of all the train,
Can fix the sinner's wandering eye.

2 Hark! hark! to God the chorus breaks,
From every host, from every gem;
But one alone the Saviour speaks, —
It is the Star of Bethlehem!

3 Once on the raging seas I rode;
The storm was loud, the night was dark;
The ocean yawned, and rudely blowed
The wind that tossed my foundering bark.

4 Deep horror then my vitals froze;
Death struck, I ceased the tide to stem;
When suddenly a star arose, —
It was the Star of Bethlehem!

5 It was my guide, my light, my all;
It bade my dark forebodings cease;
And, through the storm and danger's thrall,
It led me to the port of peace.

6 Now, safely moored, my perils o'er,
I'll sing, first in night's diadem,
Forever, and forevermore, —
The Star — the Star of Bethlehem!

963. L. M. Watts.

1 Would you behold the works of God,
His wonders in the world abroad?
With hardy mariners survey
The unknown regions of the sea.

2 They leave their native shores behind,
And seize the favor of the wind;
Till God command, and tempests rise
That heave the ocean to the skies.

3 When land is far, and death is nigh,
Bereaved of hope, to God they cry:
His mercy hears their loud address,
And sends salvation in distress.

4 He bids the winds their wrath assuage,
And stormy tempests cease to rage;
The grateful band their fears give o'er,
And hail with joy their native shore.

5 O, may the sons of men record
The wondrous goodness of the Lord;
Let them their purest offerings bring,
And in the church his glory sing.

---

‡ The tune above may be sung as a four line tune — a single verse at a time — by omitting all the repeats. In the last line are choosing notes for those treble voices which cannot reach the high notes.

GERMANIA. L. M. (Lotha.) ‡ J. H. SCHEIN. Died 1631.

Choral.

Called also Leipsic. One of the best of chorals.

957. L. M. COWPER.

1 THE billows swell; the winds are high;
Clouds overcast my wintry sky:
Out of the depths to thee I call;
My fears are great; my strength is small.

2 O Lord, the pilot's part perform,
And guide and guard me through the storm;
Defend me from each threatening ill;
Control the waves; say, "Peace! be still."

3 Amidst the roaring of the sea,
My soul still hangs her hope on thee;
Thy constant love, thy faithful care,
Is all that saves me from despair.

4 Dangers of every shape and name
Attend the followers of the Lamb,
Who leave the world's deceitful shore,
And leave it to return no more.

5 Though tempest-tossed, and half a wreck,
My Saviour through the floods I seek;
Let neither winds nor stormy rain
Force back my shattered bark again.

962. L. M. L. H. SIGOURNEY.

1 PRAYER may be sweet in cottage homes,
Where sire and child devoutly kneel,
While through the open casement nigh
The vernal blossoms fragrant steal.

2 Prayer may be sweet in stately halls,
Where heart with kindred heart is blent,
And upward to th' eternal throne
The hymn of praise melodious sent.

3 But he who fain would know how warm
The soul's appeal to God may be,
From friends and native land should turn,
A wanderer on the faithless sea;—

4 Should hear its deep, imploring tone
Rise heavenward o'er the foaming surge,
When billows toss the fragile bark,
And fearful blasts the conflict urge.

5 Nought, nought appears but sea and sky;
No refuge where the foot may flee;
How will he cast, O Rock divine,
The anchor of his soul on thee!

967. L. M. UNION COL.

1 ASSEMBLED in our school once more,
O Lord, thy blessing we implore;
We meet to read, and sing, and pray;
Be with us, then, through this thy day.

2 Our fervent prayer to thee ascends
For parents, teachers, foes, and friends;
And when we in thy house appear,
Help us to worship in thy fear.

3 When we on earth shall meet no more,
May we above to glory soar,
And praise thee in more lofty strains
Where one eternal Sabbath reigns.

992. L. M. PRESB. COL.

1 JOIN, every tongue, to praise the Lord;
All nature rests upon his word;
Mercy and truth his courts maintain,
And own his universal reign.

2 Seasons and times obey his voice;
The evening and the morn rejoice
To see the earth made soft with showers,
Enriched with fruit, and dressed in flowers.

3 Thy works pronounce thy power divine;
In all the earth thy glories shine;
Through every month thy gifts appear;
Great God, thy goodness crowns the year.

985. L. M. Dyer.

1 Great Maker of unnumbered worlds,
And whom unnumbered worlds adore,
Whose goodness all thy creatures share,
While nature trembles at thy power, —

2 Thine is the hand that moves the spheres
That wakes the wind, and lifts the sea;
And man, who moves the lord of earth,
Acts but the part assigned by thee.

3 While suppliant crowds implore thine aid,
To thee we raise the humble cry;
Thine altar is the contrite heart,
Thine incense the repentant sigh.

4 O, may our land, in this her hour,
Confess thy hand, and bless the rod,
By penitence make thee her Friend,
And find in thee a guardian God.

998. L. M. Higginbotham.

1 Great God, let all my tuneful powers
Awake and sing thy mighty name:
Thy hand revolves my circling hours —
Thy hand, from whence my being came.

2 Seasons and moons, still rolling round
In beauteous order, speak thy praise;
And years, with smiling mercy crowned,
To thee successive honors raise.

3 My life, my health, my friends, I owe
All to thy vast, unbounded love;
Ten thousand precious gifts below,
And hope of nobler joys above.

4 Thus will I sing till nature cease,
Till sense and language are no more,
And after death thy boundless grace,
Through everlasting years, adore.

994. L. M. Doddridge.

1 Eternal Source of every joy,
Thy praise may well our lips employ,
While in thy temple we appear,
Whose goodness crowns the circling year.

2 Wide as the wheels of nature roll,
Thy hand supports the steady pole;
The sun is taught by thee to rise,
And darkness when to veil the skies.

3 The flowery spring, at thy command,
Embalms the air and paints the land;
The summer rays with vigor shine
To raise the corn and cheer the vine.

4 Thy hand in autumn richly pours
Through all our coasts abundant stores;
And winters, softened by thy care,
No more a dreary aspect wear.

5 Still be the cheerful homage paid
With morning light and evening shade;
Seasons, and months, and weeks, and days
Demand successive songs of praise.

995. L. M. Campbell's Col.

1 Great God, as seasons disappear,
And changes mark the rolling year,
Thy favor still doth crown our days,
And we would celebrate thy praise.

2 The harvest song we would repeat:
"Thou givest us the finest wheat,"
"The joy of harvest" we have known:
The praise, O Lord, is all thine own.

3 Our tables spread, our garners stored —
O, give us hearts to bless thee, Lord;
Forbid it, Source of light and love,
That hearts and lives should barren prove

ARNHEIM.‡ L. M. S. HOLYOKE. 1785.

‡ The first tune published by HOLYOKE, and the last he sang five days previous to his death in 1816. The melody is given here as in the original, except in descending to the lower octave in treble part, last line; the upper small notes are the originals, and *may* be sung with the others at pleasure; the lower should be preferred in congregational singing.

4 Another harvest comes apace;
Mature our spirits by thy grace,
That we may calmly meet the blow
The sickle gives to lay us low;—

5 That so, when angel reapers come
To gather sheaves to thy blest home,
Our spirits may be borne on high
To thy safe garner in the sky.

1001. L. M. PRES. COL.

1 GREAT God of nations, now to thee
Our hymn of gratitude we raise;
With humble heart and bending knee,
We offer thee our song of praise.

2 Thy name we bless, almighty God,
For all the kindness thou hast shown
To this fair land the pilgrims trod,—
This land we fondly call our own.

3 Here Freedom spreads her banner wide,
And casts her soft and hallowed ray;
Here thou our fathers' steps didst guide
In safety through their dangerous way.

4 We praise thee that the gospel's light
Through all our land its radiance sheds,
Dispels the shades of error's night,
And heavenly blessings round us spreads.

5 Great God, preserve us in thy fear;
In dangers still our Guardian be;
O, spread thy truth's bright precepts here;
Let all the people worship thee.

1006. L. M. PRATT'S COL.

1 LORD, let thy goodness lead our land,
Still saved by thine almighty hand,
The tribute of its love to bring
To thee, our Saviour and our King.

2 Let every public temple raise
Triumphant songs of holy praise;
Let every peaceful, private home
A temple, Lord, to thee become.

3 Still be it our supreme delight
To walk as in thy glorious sight;
Still in thy precepts and thy fear,
Till life's last hour, to persevere.

1010. L. M. WATTS.

1 GOD of the morning, at thy voice
The cheerful sun makes haste to rise,
And like a giant doth rejoice
To run his journey through the skies.

2 O, like the sun may I fulfil
Th' appointed duties of the day;
With ready mind and active will
March on, and keep my heavenly way.

3 Lord, thy commands are clean and pure,
Enlightening our beclouded eyes;
Thy threatenings just, thy promise sure;
Thy gospel makes the simple wise.

4 Give me thy counsels for my guide,
And then receive me to thy bliss;
All my desires and hopes beside
Are faint and cold compared with this.

ST. AUSTIN. L. M.

From the Psalter.

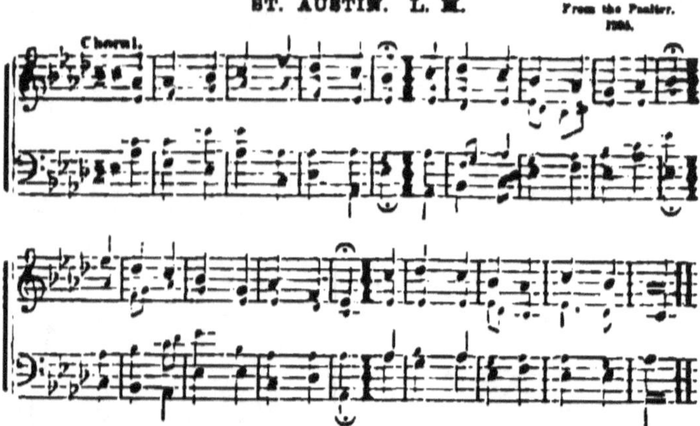

1011. L. M. WATTS.

1 My God, how endless is thy love!
Thy gifts are every evening new;
And morning mercies from above
Gently distil like early dew.

2 Thou spread'st the curtains of the night,
Great Guardian of my sleeping hours;
Thy sovereign word restores the light,
And quickens all my drowsy powers.

3 I yield my powers to thy command;
To thee I consecrate my days;
Perpetual blessings from thy hand
Demand perpetual songs of praise.

1017. L. M. KENN.

1 Awake, my soul, and with the sun
Thy daily stage of duty run;
Shake off dull sloth, and joyful rise
To pay thy morning sacrifice.

2 Wake, and lift up thyself, my heart,
And with the angels bear thy part,
Who all night long unwearied sing
High praises to th' eternal King.

3 Glory to thee, who safe hast kept,
And hast refreshed me while I slept:
Grant, Lord, when I from death shall wake
I may of endless life partake.

4 Lord, I to thee my vows renew;
Dispel my sins as morning dew;
Guard my first springs of thought and will,
And with thyself my spirit fill.

5 Direct, control, suggest, this day,
All I design, or do, or say,
That all my powers, with true delight,
In thy sole glory may unite.

1022. L. M. ANON.

1 Still evening comes, with gentle shade,
Sweet harbinger of balmy rest
From toilsome hours, and anxious thoughts
Revolving in the pensive breast.

2 Refulgent day in darkness sets;
The noisy crowds are hushed in sleep;
Harsh sounds to gentle murmurs turn,
As o'er the fields the zephyrs sweep.

3 The hour is sweet when tumults cease;
The scene obscured inspires my eye,
And darkness marks the loved retreat
Where pleasures live, and sorrows die.

4 Retirement solemn, yet serene,
And undisturbed by human voice,
Invites repose on Jesus' arm,
And bids my soul in God rejoice.

1023. L. M. WATTS.

1 Thus far the Lord has led me on;
Thus far his power prolongs my days;
And every evening shall make known
Some fresh memorial of his grace.

2 Much of my time has run to waste,
And I, perhaps, am near my home;
But he forgives my follies past,
He gives me strength for days to come.

3 I lay my body down to sleep;
Peace is the pillow for my head;
While well appointed angels keep
Their watchful stations round my bed.

4 Thus, when the night of death shall come,
My flesh shall rest beneath the ground,
And wait thy voice to break my tomb,
With sweet salvation in the sound.

CLARE. L. M.

EDWARD HAMILTON.
From The Sanctus.

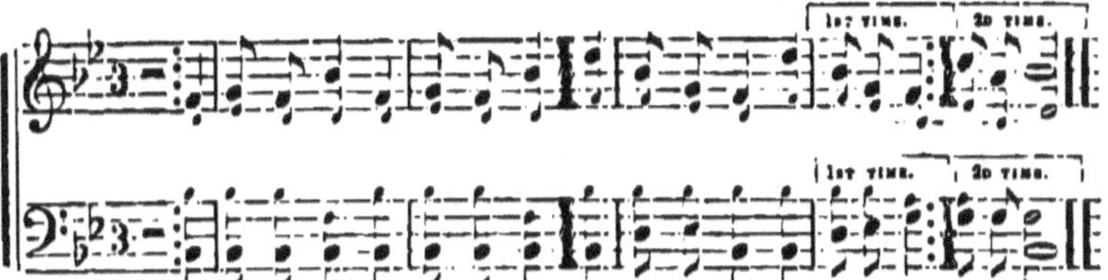

1025. L. M. STEELE.

1 GREAT God, to thee my evening song,
With humble gratitude, I raise;
O, let thy mercy tune my tongue,
And fill my heart with lively praise.

2 My days, unclouded as they pass,
And every gently-rolling hour,
Are monuments of wondrous grace,
And witness to thy love and power.

3 And yet this thoughtless, wretched heart,
Too oft regardless of thy love,
Ungrateful, can from thee depart,
And, fond of trifles, vainly rove.

4 Seal my forgiveness in the blood
Of Jesus: his dear name alone
I plead for pardon, gracious God,
And kind acceptance, at thy throne.

5 Let this blest hope mine eyelids close;
With sleep refresh my feeble frame;
Safe in thy care may I repose,
And wake with praises to thy name.

1031. L. M. KENN.

1 GLORY to thee, my God, this night,
For all the blessings of the light:
Keep me, O keep me, King of kings,
Beneath the shadow of thy wings.

2 Forgive me, Lord, for thy dear Son,
The ills which I this day have done;
That with the world, myself, and thee,
I, ere I sleep, at peace may be.

3 Teach me to live that I may dread
The grave as little as my bed;
Teach me to die that so I may
With joy behold the judgment day.

4 Be thou my Guardian while I sleep;
Thy watchful station near me keep;
My heart with love celestial fill,
And guard me from th' approach of ill.

5 Lord, let my heart forever share
The bliss of thy paternal care:
'Tis heaven on earth, 'tis heaven above,
To see thy face and sing thy love.

1044. L. M. DODDRIDGE.

1 GOD of eternity, from thee
Did infant Time his being draw;
Moments, and days, and months, and years,
Revolve by thine unvaried law.

2 Silent and slow they glide away;
Steady and strong the current flows,
Lost in eternity's wide sea—
The boundless gulf from whence it rose.

3 With it the thoughtless sons of men
Upon the rapid streams are borne
Swift on to their eternal home,
Whence not one soul can e'er return.

4 Yet, while the shore, on either side,
Presents a gaudy, flattering show,
We gaze, in fond amazement lost,
Nor think to what a world we go.

5 Great Source of wisdom, teach my heart
To know the price of every hour,
That time may bear me on to joys
Beyond its measure and its power.

1046. L. M. DODDRIDGE.

1 OUR Helper, God, we bless his name,
Whose love forever is the same;
The tokens of whose gracious care
Begin, and crown, and close the year.

2 Amid ten thousand snares, we stand
Supported by his guardian hand;
And see, when we review our ways,
Ten thousand monuments of praise.

3 Thus far his arm hath led us on;
Thus far we make his mercy known;
And while we tread this desert land,
New mercies shall new songs demand.

4 Our grateful souls on Jordan's shore
Shall raise one sacred pillar more,
Then bear, in his bright courts above,
Inscriptions of immortal love.

FEDERAL STREET.

&c.

GERMANIA. L. M. (Lotha.) J. H. Schein. Died 1631.

Called also Leipsic. One of the best of chorals.

1051. L. M. Doddridge.

1 Great God, we sing that mighty hand,
By which supported still we stand:
The opening year thy mercy shows;
Let mercy crown it till it close.

2 By day, by night, at home, abroad,
Still we are guarded by our God;
By his incessant bounty fed,
By his unerring counsel led.

3 With grateful hearts the past we own;
The future — all to us unknown —
We to thy guardian care commit,
And peaceful leave before thy feet.

4 In scenes exalted or depressed,
Be thou our joy, and thou our rest;
Thy goodness all our hopes shall raise,
Adored through all our changing days.

5 When death shall close our earthly songs,
And seal in silence mortal tongues,
Our Helper, God, in whom we trust,
In brighter worlds our souls shall boast.

HAMBURG.

1056. L. M. Spir. of the Psalms.

1 Ere mountains reared their forms sublime,
Or heaven and earth in order stood,
Before the birth of ancient time,
From everlasting thou art God.

2 A thousand ages, in their flight,
With thee are as a fleeting day;
Past, present, future, to thy sight
At once their various scenes display.

3 But our brief life's a shadowy dream,
A passing thought, that soon is o'er,
That fades with morning's earliest beam,
And fills the musing mind no more.

4 To us, O Lord, the wisdom give,
Each passing moment so to spend,
That we at length with thee may live
Where life and bliss shall never end.

HAMBORO'. Harmony, p. 22.

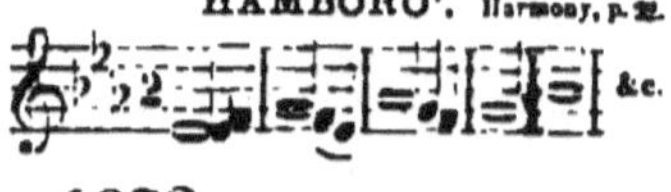

1073. L. M. Watts.

1 Through every age, eternal God,
Thou art our rest our safe abode:
High was thy throne ere heaven was made,
Or earth, thy humble footstool, laid.

2 Long hadst thou reigned ere time began,
Or dust was fashioned into man:
And long thy kingdom shall endure,
When earth and time shall be no more.

3 But man, weak man, is born to die,
Made up of guilt and vanity:
Thy dreadful sentence, Lord, is just —
"Return, ye sinners, to your dust."

4 Death, like an ever flowing stream,
Sweeps us away: our life's a dream —
An empty tale — a morning flower,
Cut down and withered in an hour.

5 Teach us, O Lord, how frail is man,
And kindly lengthen out our span,
Till, cleansed by grace, we all may be
Prepared to die, and dwell with thee.

From the "Dead March," in the oratorio, Saul.

1071. L. M. WATTS.

1 IT is the Lord our Saviour's hand
Impairs our strength amid the race;
Disease and death, at his command
Arrest us, and cut short our days.

2 Spare, gracious Lord, O, spare, we pray,
Nor let our sun go down at noon:
Thy years are one eternal day;
And must thy children die so soon?

3 Yet, in the midst of death and grief,
This thought our sorrows shall assuage—
"Our Father and our Saviour lives;
Thou art the same through every age."

4 Before thy face thy church shall live,
And on thy throne thy children reign;
This fading world shall they survive,
And rise to glorious life again.

1072. L. M. WATTS.

1 WHY should we start, and fear to die?
What timorous worms we mortals are!
Death is the gate of endless joy,
And yet we dread to enter there.

2 The pains, the groans, and dying strife,
Fright our approaching souls away;
Still we shrink back again to life,
Fond of our prison and our clay.

3 O, if my Lord would come and meet,
My soul should stretch her wings in haste,
Fly, fearless, through death's iron gate,
Nor feel the terrors as she passed.

4 Jesus can make a dying bed
Feel soft as downy pillows are,
While on his breast I lean my head,
And breathe my life out sweetly there.

1078. L. M. WATTS.

1 UNVEIL thy bosom, faithful tomb;
Take this new treasure to thy trust,
And give these sacred relics room
To slumber in the silent dust.

2 Nor pain, nor grief, nor anxious fear,
Invades thy bounds; no mortal woes
Can reach the peaceful sleeper here,
While angels watch the soft repose.

3 So Jesus slept; God's dying Son
Passed through the grave, and blest the bed:
Rest here, blest saint, till from his throne
The morning break, and pierce the shade.

4 Break from his throne, illustrious morn;
Attend, O earth, his sovereign word;
Restore thy trust; a glorious form
Shall then arise to meet the Lord.

1095. L. M. EPIS. COL.

1 As vernal flowers that scent the morn,—
But wither in the rising day,—
Thus lovely was this infant's dawn,
Thus swiftly fled his life away.

2 He died before his infant soul
Had ever burnt with wrong desires,
Had ever spurned at heaven's control,
Or ever quenched its sacred fires.

3 He died to sin; he died to care;
But for a moment felt the rod;
Then, rising on the viewless air,
'Spread his light wings, and soared to God.

4 This blessèd theme now cheers my voice;
The grave is not the loved one's prison;
The "stone" that covered half my joys
Is "rolled away," and, lo! "he's risen."

ROSEDALE. L. M.

George F. Root.
Composed 18[illegible].

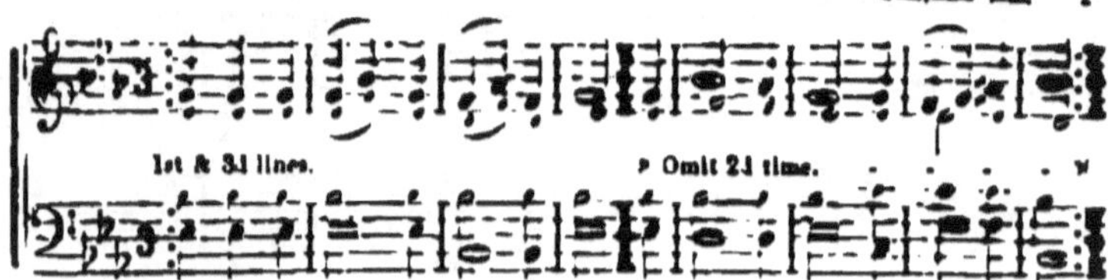

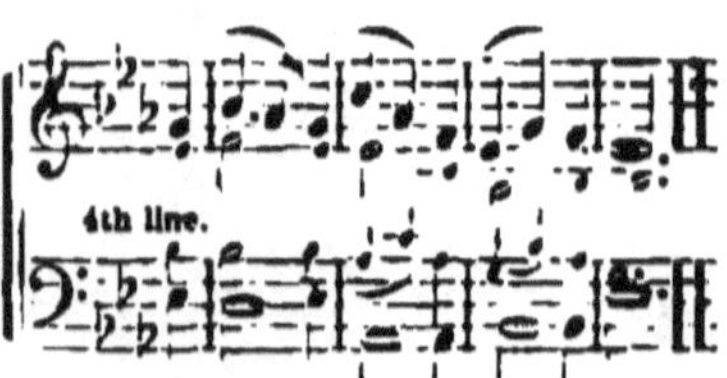

This and the other selections from "The Sabbath Bell" inserted by Mr. Root's permission.

1085. 8s & 4. Montgomery.

1 There is a calm for those who weep,
A rest for weary pilgrims found:
They softly lie, and sweetly sleep,
Low in the ground. *Low in the ground.*

2 The storm that sweeps the wintry sky
No more disturbs their deep repose,
Than summer evening's latest sigh,
That shuts the rose. *That, &c.*

3 Then, traveller in the vale of tears,
To realms of everlasting light,
Through time's dark wilderness of years,
Pursue thy flight. *Pursue, &c.*

4 Thy soul, renewed by grace divine,
In God's own image, freed from clay,
In heaven's eternal sphere shall shine,
A star of day. *A star, &c.*

1088. L. M. Steele.

1 So fades the lovely, blooming flower,
Frail, smiling solace of an hour;
So soon our transient comforts fly,
And pleasure only blooms to die.

2 Is there no kind, no healing art,
To soothe the anguish of the heart?
Spirit of grace, be ever nigh.
Thy comforts are not made to die.

3 Let gentle patience smile on pain,
Till dying hope revives again;
Hope wipes the tear from sorrow's eye,
And faith points upward to the sky.

1103. L. M. Barbauld.

1 How blest the righteous when he dies
When sinks the weary soul to rest!
How mildly beam the closing eyes!
How gently heaves the expiring breast!

2 So fades a summer cloud away;
So sinks the gale when storms are o'er;
So gently shuts the eye of day;
So dies a wave along the shore.

3 A holy quiet reigns around,
A calm which life nor death destroys;
And nought disturbs that peace profound
Which his unfettered soul enjoys.

4 Farewell, conflicting hopes and fears,
Where lights and shades alternate dwell;
How bright th' unchanging morn appears!
Farewell, inconstant world, farewell!

5 Life's labor done, as sinks the clay,
Light from its load the spirit flies,
While heaven and earth combine to say,
"How blest the righteous when he dies!"

1111. L. M. Bathurst.

1 How sweet the hour of closing day,
When all is peaceful and serene,
And when the sun, with cloudless ray,
Sheds mellow lustre o'er the scene!

2 Such is the Christian's parting hour;
So, peacefully he sinks to rest,
When faith, endued from heaven with power,
Sustains and cheers his languid breast.

3 Mark but that radiance of his eye,
That smile upon his wasted cheek:
They tell us of his glory nigh,
In language that no tongue can speak.

4 A beam from heaven is sent to cheer
The pilgrim on his gloomy road;
And angels are attending near,
To bear him to their bright abode.

5 Who would not wish to die like those
Whom God's own Spirit deigns to bless,
To sink into that soft repose;
Then wake to perfect happiness?

‡ Called also "Brighton."

1100. L. M. J. N. Brown.

1 Go, spirit of the sainted dead,
Go to thy longed-for, happy home:
The tears of man are o'er thee shed;
The voice of angels bids thee come.

2 If life be not in length of days,
In silvered locks, and furrowed brow,
But living to the Saviour's praise,
How few have lived so long as thou!

3 Though earth may boast one gem the less,
May not e'en heaven the richer be?
And myriads on thy footsteps press,
To share thy blest eternity.

1108. L. M. Norton.

1 O, stay thy tears; for they are blest,
Whose days are past, whose toil is done:
Here, midnight care disturbs our rest;
Here, sorrow dims the noonday sun.

2 How blest are they whose transient years
Pass like an evening meteor's flight!
Not dark with guilt, nor dim with tears;
Whose course is short, unclouded, bright.

3 O, cheerless were our lengthened way;
But Heaven's own light dispels the gloom,
Streams downward from eternal day,
And casts a glory round the tomb.

4 O, stay thy tears; the blest above
Have hailed a spirit's heavenly birth,
And sung a song of joy and love;
Then why should anguish reign on earth?

1105. L. M. 6 L. Winchell's Sel.

1 Sweet is the thought, the promise sweet,
That friends, long-severed friends, shall meet —
That kindred souls, on earth disjoined,
Shall meet, from earthly dross refined,
Their mortal cares and sorrows o'er,
And mingle hearts to part no more.

2 But for this hope, this blessèd stay,
When earthly comforts all decay,
O, who could view th' expiring eye,
Nor wish, with those they love, to die?
Who could receive their parting breath,
Nor long to follow them in death?

3 But we have brighter hopes; we know
Short is this pilgrimage of woe;
We know that our Redeemer lives;
We trust the promises he gives;
And part in hope to meet above,
Where all is joy, and all is love.

In "The Jubilee," and several other of Mr. B.'s collections.

1109. L. M. Mackay.

1 Asleep in Jesus! blessèd sleep,
From which none ever wakes to weep—
A calm and undisturbed repose,
Unbroken by the last of foes.

2 Asleep in Jesus! O, how sweet
To be for such a slumber meet!
With holy confidence to sing
That Death has lost his venomed sting!

3 Asleep in Jesus! peaceful rest,
Whose waking is supremely blest:
No fear, no woe, shall dim that hour
That manifests the Saviour's power.

4 Asleep in Jesus! O, for me
May such a blissful refuge be:
Securely shall my ashes lie,
And wait the summons from on high.

5 Asleep in Jesus! far from thee
Thy kindred and their graves may be;
But thine is still a blessèd sleep,
From which none ever wakes to weep.

1128. L. M. Watts.

1 When God is nigh, my faith is strong;
His arm is my almighty prop;
Be glad, my heart; rejoice, my tongue;
My dying flesh shall rest in hope.

2 Though in the dust I lay my head,
Yet, gracious God, thou wilt not leave
My soul forever with the dead,
Nor lose thy children in the grave.

3 My flesh shall thy first call obey,
Shake off the dust, and rise on high;
Then shalt thou lead the wondrous way
To yonder throne above the sky.

4 There streams of endless pleasure flow,
And full discoveries of thy grace,
Which we but tasted here below,
Spread heavenly joys through all the place.

MISSIONARY CHANT.

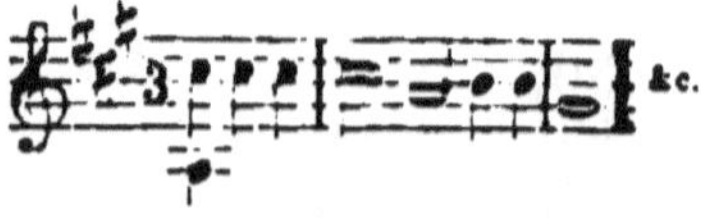

1134. L. M. Watts.

1 He reigns! the Lord the Saviour reigns!
Sing to his name in lofty strains;
Let all the earth in songs rejoice,
And in his praise exalt their voice.

2 Deep are his counsels, and unknown;
But grace and truth support his throne:
Though gloomy clouds his way surround,
Justice is their eternal ground.

3 In robes of judgment, lo! he comes,
Shakes the wide earth and cleaves the tombs;
Before him burns devouring fire;
The mountains melt, the seas retire.

4 His enemies, with sore dismay,
Fly from the sight, and shun the day;
Then lift your heads, ye saints, on high,
And sing, for your redemption's nigh.

MONMOUTH. L. M. or, 8s & 7s, — peculiar. M. LUTHER. 1546.

1132. 8s & 7s, peculiar. LUTHER.

1 GREAT God, what do I see and hear?
The end of things created:
The Judge of man I see appear,
On clouds of glory seated:
The trumpet sounds; the graves restore
The dead which they contained before:
Prepare, my soul, to meet him.

2 The dead in Christ shall first arise,
At the last trumpet's sounding,
Caught up to meet him in the skies,
With joy their Lord surrounding:
No gloomy fears their souls dismay;
His presence sheds eternal day
On those prepared to meet him.

3 But sinners, filled with guilty fears,
Behold his wrath prevailing;
For they shall rise, and find their tears
And sighs are unavailing:
The day of grace is past and gone;
Trembling, they stand before the throne,
All unprepared to meet him.

4 Great God, what do I see and hear!
The end of things created:
The Judge of man I see appear,
On clouds of glory seated:
Before his cross I view the day
When heaven and earth shall pass away,
And thus prepare to meet him.

1130. L. M. W. SCOTT.

1 THE day of wrath, that dreadful day,
When heaven and earth shall pass away!—
What power shall be the sinner's stay?
How shall he meet that dreadful day?—

2 When, shrivelling like a parchéd scroll,
The flaming heavens together roll,
And louder yet, and yet more dread,
Resounds the trump that wakes the dead?

3 O, on that day, that wrathful day,
When man to judgment wakes from clay,
Be thou, O Christ, the sinners stay,
Though heaven and earth shall pass away.

1135. L. M. HEBER.

1 THE Lord will come; the earth shall quake;
The hills their ancient seats forsake;
And, withering, from the vault of night
The stars withdraw their feeble light.

2 The Lord will come; but not the same
As once in lowly form he came,—
A quiet Lamb to slaughter led,—
The bruised, the suffering, and the dead.

3 The Lord will come; a dreadful form,
With wreath of flame, and robe of storm,
On cherub wings, and wings of wind,
Anointed Judge of human kind.

4 Can this be he who wont to stray
A pilgrim on the world's highway,
By power oppressed, and mocked by pride?
O God, is this the Crucified?

5 Go, tyrants, to the rocks complain;
Go seek the mountain's cleft in vain;
But faith, victorious o'er the tomb,
Shall sing for joy, "The Lord is come."

NAZARETH. L. M. (Melcombe.) {Attributed to S. Webbe.

1149. L. M. Pratt's Col.

1 How vain is all beneath the skies!
How transient every earthly bliss!
How slender all the fondest ties
That bind us to a world like this!

2 The evening cloud, the morning dew,
The withering grass, the fading flower,
Of earthly hopes are emblems true —
The glory of a passing hour.

3 But though earth's fairest blossoms die,
And all beneath the skies is vain,
There is a brighter world on high,
Beyond the reach of care and pain.

4 Then let the hope of joys to come
Dispel our cares, and chase our fears:
If God be ours, we're travelling home,
Though passing through a vale of tears.

1172. L. M. Anon.

1 There is a land mine eye hath seen,
In visions of enraptured thought,
So bright that all which spreads between
Is with its radiant glory fraught; —

2 A land upon whose blissful shore
There rests no shadow, falls no stain;
There those who meet shall part no more,
And those long parted meet again.

3 Its skies are not like earthly skies,
With varying hues of shade and light;
It hath no need of suns to rise,
To dissipate the gloom of night.

4 There sweeps no desolating wind
Across that calm, serene abode;
The wanderer there a home may find,
Within the Paradise of God.

1179. L. M. Sac. Lyrics.

1 Lo! round the throne, at God's right hand,
The saints, in countless myriads, stand,
Of every tongue, redeemed to God,
Arrayed in garments washed in blood.

2 Through tribulation great they came;
They bore the cross; despised the shame:
From all their labors now they rest,
In God's eternal glory blest.

3 Hunger and thirst they feel no more;
Nor sin, nor pain, nor death deplore:
The tears are wiped from every eye,
And sorrow yields to endless joy.

4 They see their Saviour face to face,
And sing the triumphs of his grace;
Him day and night they ceaseless praise;
To him their loud hosannas raise.

5 Worthy the Lamb, for sinners slain,
Through endless years to live and reign,
Thou hast redeemed us by thy blood,
And made us kings and priests to God.

1180. L. M. Beddome.

1 O happy saints, who dwell in light,
And walk with Jesus, clothed in white;
Safe landed on that peaceful shore
Where pilgrims meet to part no more.

2 Released from sorrow, toil, and strife,
And welcomed to an endless life,
Their souls have now begun to prove
The height and depth of Jesus' love.

3 There, gazing on his beauteous face,
They tell the wonders of his grace,
And, while they sing with rapture sweet,
They bow, adoring, at his feet.

LEWIS. L. M.
H. H. Hawley.
OLIVET. L. M.
ST. AUSTIN. L. M.
From the Psalter. 1595.
Choral.

‡ The authorship not subject to doubts which attach to some other chorals ascribed to him.

1154. L. M. WATTS.

1 O FOR a sight, a pleasing sight
Of our almighty Father's throne!
There sits our Saviour, crowned with light,
Clothed with a body like our own.

2 Adoring saints around him stand,
And thrones and powers before him fall;
The God shines gracious through the man,
And sheds bright glories on them all.

3 O, what amazing joys they feel,
While to their golden harps they sing,
And echo, from each heavenly hill,
The glorious triumphs of their King!

4 When shall the day, O Lord, appear,
That I shall mount to dwell above,
And stand and bow among them there,
And view thy face, and sing thy love?

1165. L. M. WATTS.

1 WHAT sinners value I resign;
Lord, 'tis enough that thou art mine;
I shall behold thy blissful face,
And stand complete in righteousness.

2 This life's a dream — an empty show;
But that bright world to which I go
Hath joys substantial and sincere:
When shall I wake, and find me there?

3 O glorious hour! O blest abode!
I shall be near and like my God;
And flesh and sin no more control
The sacred pleasures of my soul.

4 My flesh shall slumber in the ground
Till the last trumpet's joyful sound,
Then burst the chains, with glad surprise,
And in my Saviour's image rise.

1174. L. M. TUCK.

1 There is a region lovelier far
Than sages tell or poets sing,
Brighter than noonday glories are,
And softer than the tints of spring.

2 It is not fanned by summer's gale;
'Tis not refreshed by vernal showers;
It never needs the moonbeam pale, —
For there are known no evening hours.

3 No; for that world is ever bright
With purest radiance all its own:
The streams of uncreated light
Flow round it from th' eternal throne.

4 It is all holy and serene,
The land of glory and repose;
No cloud obscures the radiant scene;
There not a tear of sorrow flows.

5 In vain the curious, searching eye
May seek to view the fair abode,
Or find it in the starry sky:
It is the dwelling place of God.

OLD HUNDRED. L. M.

G. FRANC.
Dates previous to 1543.

Choral.

DOXOLOGIES.

1. L. M.

PRAISE God, from whom all blessings flow;
Praise him, all creatures here below;
Praise him above, ye heavenly host;
Praise Father, Son, and Holy Ghost.

2. L. M.

To God the Father, God the Son,
And God the Spirit, three in one,
Be honor, praise, and glory given,
By all on earth and all in heaven.

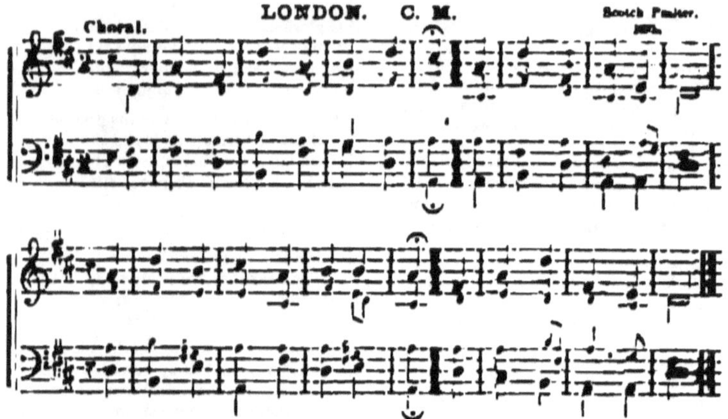

3. C. M. WATTS.

1 How did my heart rejoice to hear
My friends devoutly say,
"In Zion let us all appear,
And keep the solemn day"!

2 I love her gates; I love the road;
The church, adorned with grace,
Stands like a palace built for God,
To show his milder face.

3 Up to her courts, with joy unknown,
The holy tribes repair;
The Son of David holds his throne,
And sits in judgment there.

4 He hears our praises and complaints;
And, while his awful voice
Divides the sinners from the saints,
We tremble and rejoice.

5 Peace be within this sacred place,
And joy a constant guest;
With holy gifts and heavenly grace
Be her attendants blest.

6 My soul shall pray for Zion still,
While life or breath remains;
Here my best friends, my kindred, dwell;
Here God, my Saviour, reigns.

7. C. M. WATTS.

1 I LOVE to see the Lord below;
His church displays his grace;
But upper worlds his glory know,
And view him face to face.

2 I love to worship at his feet,
Though sin annoy me there,
But saints, exalted near his seat,
Have no assaults to fear.

3 I love to meet him in his court,
And taste his heavenly love;
But still his visits seem too short,
Or I too soon remove.

4 He shines, and I am all delight;
He hides, and all is pain:
When will he fix me in his sight,
And ne'er depart again?

5 O Lord, I love thy service now;
Thy church displays thy power;
But soon in heaven I hope to bow
And praise thee evermore.

17. C. M. H. M. WILLIAMS.

1 WHILE thee I seek, protecting Power,
Be my vain wishes stilled;
And may this consecrated hour
With better hopes be filled.

2 Thy love the power of thought bestowed;
To thee my thoughts would soar;
Thy mercy o'er my life has flowed;
That mercy I adore.

3 In each event of life, how clear
Thy ruling hand I see!
Each blessing to my soul more dear,
Because conferred by thee.

4 In every joy that crowns my days,
In every pain I bear,
My heart shall find delight in praise,
Or seek relief in prayer.

5 When gladness wings my favored hour,
Thy love my thoughts shall fill;
Resigned, when storms of sorrow lower,
My soul shall meet thy will.

6 My lifted eye, without a tear,
The gathering storm shall see;
My steadfast heart shall know no fear;
That heart shall rest on thee.

PETERBORO'. C. M. ENGLISH.

4. C. M. WATTS.

1 YE that obey th' immortal King,
Attend his holy place;
Bow to the glories of his name,
And sing his wondrous grace.

2 Lift up your hands by morning light,
And raise your thanks on high;
Send your admiring thoughts, by night,
Above the starry sky.

3 The God of Zion cheers your hearts
With rays of quickening grace:
'Tis he that spreads the heavens abroad,
Whose presence fills the place.

8. C. M. WATTS.

1 LORD, in the morning thou shalt hear
My voice ascending high;
To thee will I direct my prayer,
To thee lift up mine eye;—

2 Up to the hills where Christ is gone
To plead for all his saints,
Presenting at his Father's throne
Our songs and our complaints.

3 Thou art a God before whose sight
The wicked shall not stand;
Sinners shall ne'er be thy delight,
Nor dwell at thy right hand.

4 But to thy house will I resort,
To taste thy mercies there;
I will frequent thine holy court,
And worship in thy fear.

5 O, may thy Spirit guide my feet
In ways of righteousness,
Make every path of duty straight
And plain before my face.

9. C. M. JERVIS.

1 WITH sacred joy we lift our eyes
To those bright realms above,
That glorious temple in the skies,
Where dwells eternal Love.

2 Before the gracious throne we bow
Of heaven's almighty King;
Here we present the solemn vow,
And hymns of praise we sing.

3 O Lord, while in thy house we kneel,
With trust and holy fear,
Thy mercy and thy truth reveal,
And lend a gracious ear.

4 With fervor teach our hearts to pray,
And tune our lips to sing;
Nor from thy presence cast away
The sacrifice we bring.

14. C. M. WATTS.

1 MY soul, how lovely is the place
To which thy God resorts!
'Tis heaven to see his smiling face,
Though in his earthly courts.

2 There the great monarch of the skies
His saving power displays;
And light breaks in upon our eyes
With kind and quickening rays.

3 With his rich gifts the heavenly Dove
Descends and fills the place,
While Christ reveals his wondrous love,
And sheds abroad his grace.

4 There, mighty God, thy words declare
The secrets of thy will;
And still we seek thy mercy there,
And sing thy praises still.

CLARENDON. C. M. Isaac Tucker.

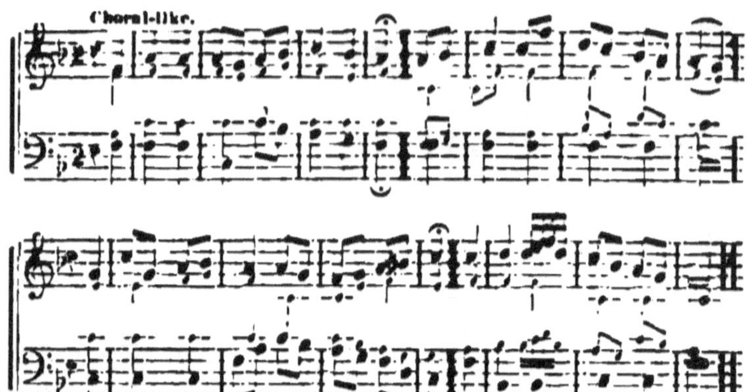

15. C. M. Watts.

1 What shall I render to my God,
For all his kindness shown?
My feet shall visit thine abode,
My songs address thy throne.

2 Among the saints who fill thy house,
My offering shall be paid;
There shall my zeal perform the vows
My soul, in anguish, made.

3 How much is mercy thy delight,
Thou ever-blessed God!
How dear thy servants in thy sight!
How precious is their blood!

4 How happy all thy servants are!
How great thy grace to me!
My life, which thou hast made thy care,
Lord, I devote to thee.

5 Now, I am thine, — forever thine, —
Nor shall my purpose move;
Thy hand hath loosed my bonds of pain,
And bound me with thy love.

6 Here, in thy courts, I leave my vow,
And thy rich grace record;
Witness, ye saints, who hear me now,
If I forsake the Lord.

24. C. M. Montgomery.

1 Lord, teach thy servants how to pray
With reverence and with fear:
Though dust and ashes, yet we may,
We must, to thee draw near.

2 We come, then, God of grace, to thee;
Give broken, contrite hearts;
Give — what thine eye delights to see —
Truth in the inward parts.

3 Give deep humility; the sense
Of godly sorrow give;
A strong, desiring confidence
To see thy face and live.

4 Give faith in that one sacrifice
Which can for sin atone;
To cast our hopes, to fix our eyes,
On Christ, and Christ alone.

5 Give patience, still to wait and weep,
Though mercy long delay;
Courage, our fainting souls to keep,
And trust thee, though thou slay.

6 Give these, and then thy will be done:
Thus strengthened with all might,
We through thy Spirit and thy Son,
Shall pray, and pray aright.

21. C. M. Sacred Poetry.

1 Lord, when we bow before thy throne,
And our confessions pour,
O, may we feel the sins we own,
And hate what we deplore.

2 Our contrite spirits, pitying, see;
True penitence impart;
And let a healing ray from thee
Beam hope on every heart.

3 When we disclose our wants in prayer,
O, let our wills resign,
And not a thought our bosom share
Which is not wholly thine.

4 Let faith each meek petition fill,
And waft it to the skies,
And teach our hearts 'tis goodness, still,
That grants it, or denies.

ROCHESTER. C. M. Composer unknown.

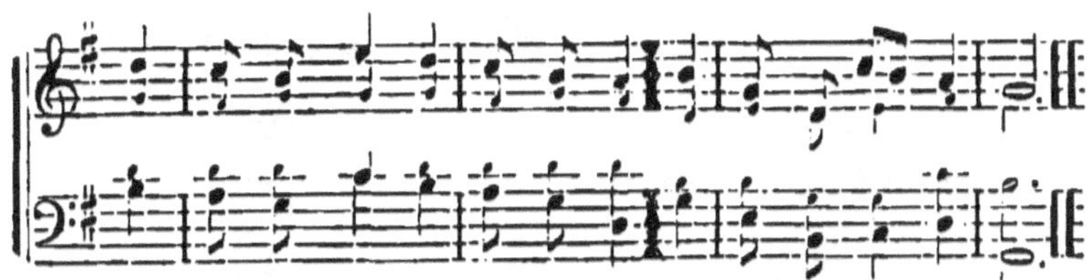

Generally ascribed to WILLIAMS. It is in DIBDIN's "Standard Tune Book" in notes of equal length.

16. C. M. NEWTON.

1 GREAT Shepherd of thy people, hear;
Thy presence now display;
We kneel within thy house of prayer;
O, give us hearts to pray.

2 The clouds which veil thee from our sight,
In pity, Lord, remove;
Dispose our minds to hear aright
The message of thy love.

3 Help us, with holy fear and joy,
To kneel before thy face;
O, make us, creatures of thy power,
The children of thy grace.

27. C. M. PRATT'S COL.

1 AGAIN our earthly cares we leave,
And to thy courts repair;
Again, with joyful feet, we come
To meet our Saviour here.

2 Within these walls let holy peace,
And love, and concord, dwell;
Here give the troubled conscience ease,
The wounded spirit heal.

3 The feeling heart, the melting eye,
The humble mind, bestow;
And shine upon us from on high,
To make our graces grow.

4 May we in faith receive thy word,
In faith present our prayers,
And in the presence of our Lord
Unbosom all our cares.

5 Show us some token of thy love,
Our fainting hope to raise,
And pour thy blessing from above,
That we may render praise.

22. C. M. STEELE.

1 COME, O thou King of all thy saints,
Our humble tribute own,
While, with our praises and complaints,
We bow before thy throne.

2 How should our songs, like those above,
With warm devotion rise!
How should our souls, on wings of love,
Mount upward to the skies!

3 But, ah, the song, how faint it flows!
How languid our desire!
How dim the sacred passion glows
Till thou the heart inspire!

4 Dear Saviour, let thy glory shine,
And fill thy dwellings here,
Till life, and love, and joy divine,
A heaven on earth appear.

29. C. M. PRESB. COL.

1 WITHIN thy house, O Lord, our God,
In glory now appear;
Make this a place of thine abode,
And shed thy blessings here.

2 When we thy mercy-seat surround,
Thy Spirit, Lord, impart;
And let thy gospel's joyful sound
With power reach every heart.

3 Here let the blind their sight obtain;
Here give the mourners rest;
Let Jesus here triumphant reign,
Enthroned in every breast.

4 Here let the voice of sacred joy
And humble prayer arise,
Till higher strains our tongues employ
In realms beyond the skies.

TALLIS CHANT. C. M. Thomas Tallis. 1560.

18. C. M. Watts.

1 Early, my God, without delay,
I haste to seek thy face;
My thirsty spirit faints away
Without thy cheering grace.

2 So pilgrims, on the scorching sand,
Beneath a burning sky,
Long for a cooling stream at hand;
And they must drink, or die.

3 I've seen thy glory, and thy power,
Through all thy temple shine;
My God, repeat that heavenly hour,
That vision so divine.

4 Not all the blessings of a feast
Can please my soul so well,
As when thy richer grace I taste,
And in thy presence dwell.

5 Not life itself, with all its joys,
Can my best passions move,
Or raise so high my cheerful voice,
As thy forgiving love.

6 Thus, till my last, expiring day,
I'll bless my God and King;
Thus will I lift my hands to pray,
And tune my lips to sing.

36. C. M. Kelly.

1 And now another week begins;
This day we call the Lord's;
This day he rose who bore our sins,
For so his word records.

2 Hark, how the angels sweetly sing!
Their voices fill the sky;
They hail their great, victorious King,
And welcome him on high.

3 We'll catch the note of lofty praise;
Their joys, O, may we feel;
Our thankful song with them we'll raise,
And emulate their zeal.

4 Come then, ye saints, and grateful sing
Of Christ, our risen Lord;
Of Christ, the everlasting King;
Of Christ, th' incarnate Word.

5 Hail, mighty Saviour! thee we hail,
High on thy throne above;
Till heart and flesh together fail,
We'll sing thy matchless love.

33. C. M. Edmeston.

1 When the worn spirit wants repose,
And sighs her God to seek,
How sweet to hail the evening's close,
That ends the weary week!

2 How sweet to hail the early dawn,
That opens on the sight,
When first that soul reviving morn
Sheds forth new rays of light!

3 Sweet day! thine hours too soon will cease,
Yet, while they gently roll,
Breathe, heavenly Spirit, source of peace,
A Sabbath o'er my soul.

4 When will my pilgrimage be done,
The world's long week be o'er,
That Sabbath dawn, which needs no sun,
That day, which fades no more?

AZMON.

LANESBORO'. C. M.
AUGUSTUS. C. M.
W. W. JOHNSON.
From Sacred Minstrel.
Slow.
Lento.
ST. SEBASTIAN. C. M. (Melbourne.)
ENGLISH TUNE.
Col Soprani, ad lib.

‡ "French" is the original name. The original "Dundee" is the tune we call "Windsor," p. 142.

34. C. M. WATTS.

1 THIS is the day the Lord hath made;
He calls the hours his own;
Let heaven rejoice, let earth be glad,
And praise surround the throne.

2 To-day he rose, and left the dead;
And Satan's empire fell;
To-day the saints his triumph spread,
And all his wonders tell.

3 Hosanna to th' anointed King,
To David's holy Son;
Help us, O Lord; descend, and bring
Salvation from thy throne.

4 Blest be the Lord, who comes to men
With messages of grace;
Who comes, in God the Father's name,
To save our sinful race.

5 Hosanna in the highest strains
The church on earth can raise!
The highest heavens, in which he reigns,
Shall give him nobler praise.

39. C. M. DE COURCY'S COL.

1 COME, let us join, with sweet accord,
In hymns around the throne;
This is the day our rising Lord
Hath made and called his own.

2 This is the day which God hath blest,
The brightest of the seven —
A type of that eternal rest
Which saints enjoy in heaven.

43. C. M. SPIR. OF PSALMS.

1 WITH joy we hail the sacred day
Which God has called his own;
With joy the summons we obey,
To worship at his throne.

2 Thy chosen temple, Lord, how fair!
Where willing votaries throng
To breathe the humble, fervent prayer,
And pour the choral song.

3 Spirit of grace, O, deign to dwell
Within thy church below;
Make her in holiness excel,
With pure devotion glow.

4 Let peace within her walls be found;
Let all her sons unite
To spread, with grateful zeal, around,
Her clear and shining light.

5 Great God, we hail the sacred day
Which thou hast called thine own;
With joy the summons we obey,
To worship at thy throne.

46. C. M. MRS. FOLLEN.

1 HOW sweet, upon this sacred day,
The best of all the seven,
To cast our earthly thoughts away,
And think of God and heaven!

2 How sweet to be allowed to pray
Our sins may be forgiven!
With filial confidence to say,
"Father, who art in heaven"!

3 How sweet the words of peace to hear
From Him to whom 'tis given
To wake the penitential tear,
And lead the way to heaven!

4 And if, to make our sins depart,
In vain the will has striven,
He who regards the inmost heart
Will send his grace from heaven.

5 Then hail, thou sacred, blessèd day,
The best of all the seven,
When hearts unite their vows to pay
Of gratitude to Heaven!

51. C. M. BARBAULD.

1 O FATHER, though the anxious fear
May cloud to-morrow's way,
Nor fear nor doubt shall enter here;
All shall be thine to-day.

2 We will not bring divided hearts
To worship at thy shrine;
But each unholy thought departs,
And leaves the temple thine.

3 Sleep, sleep to-day, tormenting cares,
Of earth and folly born;
Ye shall not dim the light that streams
From this celestial morn.

4 To-morrow will be time enough
To feel your harsh control;
Ye shall not desecrate, this day,
The Sabbath of the soul.

59. C. M. PRATT'S COL.

1 ALMIGHTY God, eternal Lord,
Thy gracious power make known;
Apply the virtue of thy word,
And melt the heart of stone.

2 Speak, with the voice that wakes the dead,
And bid the sleeper rise;
O, let his guilty conscience dread
The death that never dies.

3 Let us receive the word we hear,
Each in an honest heart;
Lay up the precious treasure there,
And never with it part.

HOWARD'S. C. M.† — Dr. Howard.‡

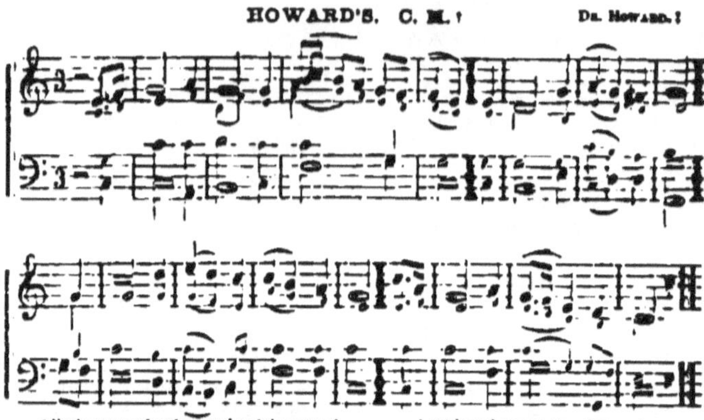

† Newly arranged and original melody restored.

‡ Attributed also to Mrs. Cummer.

57. C. M. Pratt's Col.

1 Eternal Sun of Righteousness,
Display thy beams divine,
And cause the glory of thy face
On all our hearts to shine.

2 Light in thy light, O, may we see;
Thy grace and mercy prove;
Revived, and cheered, and blessed by thee,
The God of pardoning love.

58. C. M. Wesley's Col.

1 Father of all, in whom, alone,
We live, and move, and breathe,
One bright, celestial ray send down,
And cheer thy sons beneath.

2 While in thy word we search for thee,
O, fill our souls with awe;
Thy light impart, that we may see
The wonders of thy law.

3 Now let our darkness comprehend
The light that shines so clear;
Now thy revealing Spirit send,
And give us ears to hear.

4 Before us make thy goodness pass,
Which here, by faith, we know
Let us in Jesus see thy face,
And die to all below

---

66. C. M. Hemans.

1 Praise ye the Lord; on every height
Songs to his glory raise;
Ye angel hosts, ye stars of night
Join in immortal praise.

2 O fire and vapor, hail and snow,
Ye servants of his will;
O stormy winds, that only blow
His mandates to fulfil; —

3 Mountains and rocks, to heaven that rise;
Fair cedars of the wood;
Creatures of life that wing the skies,
Or track the plains for food; —

4 Judges of nations; kings, whose hand
Waves the proud sceptre high;
O youths and virgins of the land;
O age and infancy; —

5 Praise ye his name, to whom alone
All homage should be given,
Whose glory, from th' eternal throne,
Spreads wide o'er earth and heaven.

84. C. M. Watts.

1 O, all ye nations, praise the Lord,
Each with a different tongue;
In every language learn his word,
And let his name be sung.

2 His mercy reigns through every land;
Proclaim his grace abroad;
Forever firm his truth shall stand;
Praise ye the faithful God.

85. C. M. Wrangham.

1 O, all ye nations, praise the Lord,
His glorious acts proclaim;
The fulness of his grace record,
And magnify his name.

2 His love is great, his mercy sure,
And faithful is his word;
His truth forever shall endure;
Forever praise the Lord.

78. C. M. BARLOW.

1 AWAKE, my soul, to sound his praise;
Awake, my harp, to sing;
Join, all my powers, the song to raise,
And morning incense bring.

2 Among the people of his care,
And through the nations round,
Glad songs of praise will I prepare,
And there his name resound.

3 Be thou exalted, O my God,
Above the starry frame;
Diffuse thy heavenly grace abroad,
And teach the world thy name.

4 So shall thy chosen sons rejoice,
And throng thy courts above,
While sinners hear thy pardoning voice,
And taste redeeming love.

81. C. M. WATTS.

1 SING to the Lord Jehovah's name,
And in his strength rejoice;
When his salvation is our theme,
Exalted be our voice.

2 With thanks approach his awful sight,
And psalms of honor sing;
The Lord's a God of boundless might,
The whole creation's King.

3 Come, and with humble souls adore;
Come, kneel before his face:
O, may the creatures of his power
Be children of his grace.

4 Now is the time — he bends his ear,
And waits for your request;
Come, lest he rouse his wrath, and swear,
"Ye shall not see my rest."

97. C. M. ROWE.

1 BEGIN the high, celestial strain,
My raptured soul, and sing
A sacred hymn of grateful praise
To heaven's almighty King.

2 Ye curling fountains, as ye roll
Your silver waves along,
Repeat to all your verdant shores
The subject of the song.

3 Bear it, ye breezes, on your wings,
To distant climes away,
And round the wide-extended world
The lofty theme convey.

4 Take up the burden of his name,
Ye clouds, as ye arise,
To deck with gold the opening morn,
Or shade the evening skies.

5 Long let it warble round the spheres,
And echo through the sky;
Let angels, with immortal skill,
Improve the harmony;—

6 While we, with sacred rapture fired,
The blest Creator sing,
And chant our consecrated lays
To heaven's eternal King.

82. C. M. PRATT'S COL.

1 SING to the Lord in joyful strains;
Let earth his praise resound;
Let all the cheerful nations join
To spread his glory round.

2 Thou city of the Lord, begin
The universal song;
And let the scattered villages
The cheerful notes prolong;—

3 Till, 'midst the strains of distant lands,
The islands sound his praise;
And all, combined, with one accord,
Jehovah's glories raise.

88. C. M. WARDLAW.

1 LIFT up to God the voice of praise,
Whose breath our souls inspired;
Loud, and more loud, the anthems raise
With grateful ardor fired.

2 Lift up to God the voice of praise,
Whose goodness, passing thought,
Loads every moment, as it flies,
With benefits unsought.

3 Lift up to God the voice of praise,
From whom salvation flows,
Who sent his Son our souls to save
From everlasting woes.

4 Lift up to God the voice of praise,
For hope's transporting ray,
Which lights, thro' darkest shades of death,
To realms of endless day.

898. C. M. WATTS.

1 SHINE, mighty God, on Zion shine,
With beams of heavenly grace;
Reveal thy power through every land,
And show thy smiling face.

2 When shall thy name, from shore to shore,
Sound through the earth abroad,
And distant nations know and love
Their Saviour and their God?

3 Sing to the Lord, ye distant lands;
Sing loud, with joyful voice;
Let every tongue exalt his praise,
And every heart rejoice.

83. C. M. Watts.

1 All ye who love the Lord, rejoice,
And let your songs be new ;
Amid the church, with cheerful voice,
His later wonders show.

2 The Jews, the people of his grace,
Shall their Redeemer sing ;
And Gentile nations join the praise,
While Zion owns her King.

3 The Lord takes pleasure in the just,
Whom sinners treat with scorn ;
The meek, who lie despised in dust,
Salvation shall adorn.

105. C. M. Watts.

1 Praise waits in Zion, Lord, for thee ;
There shall our vows be paid ;
Thou hast an ear when sinners pray ;
All flesh shall seek thine aid.

2 O Lord, our guilt and fears prevail ;
But pardoning grace is thine,
And thou wilt grant us power and skill
To conquer every sin.

3 Blest are the men whom thou wilt choose
To bring them near thy face ;
Give them a dwelling in thy house,
To feast upon thy grace.

4 In answering what thy church requests
Thy truth and terror shine ;
And works of dreadful righteousness
Fulfil thy kind design.

5 Thus shall the wondering nations see
The Lord is good and just ;
And distant islands fly to thee,
And make thy name their trust.

102. C. M. Watts.

1 Come, let us lift our joyful eyes
Up to the courts above,
And smile to see our Father there,
Upon a throne of love.

2 Come, let us bow before his feet,
And venture near the Lord ;
No fiery cherub guards his seat,
Nor double-flaming sword.

3 The peaceful gates of heavenly bliss
Are opened by the Son ,
High let us raise our notes of praise,
And reach th' almighty throne.

4 To thee ten thousand thanks we bring
Great Advocate on high,
And glory to th' eternal King,
Who lays his anger by.

111. C. M. Watts.

1 Arise, my soul, my joyful powers,
And triumph in my God ;
Awake, my voice, and loud proclaim
His glorious grace abroad.

2 The arms of everlasting love
Beneath my soul be placed,
And on the Rock of Ages set
My slippery footsteps fast.

3 The city of my blest abode
Is walled around with grace ;
Salvation for a bulwark stands
To shield the sacred place.

4 Arise, my soul , awake, my voice,
And tunes of pleasure sing ;
Loud hallelujahs shall address
My Saviour and my King.

100. C. M. WATTS.

1 BEGIN, my tongue, some heavenly theme,
And speak some boundless thing;
The mighty works, or mightier name,
Of our eternal King.

2 Tell of his wondrous faithfulness,
And sound his power abroad;
Sing of the glory and the grace
Of our Redeemer, God.

3 Proclaim "salvation from the Lord,
For wretched, dying men;"
His hand inscribed the sacred word
With an immortal pen.

4 Recorded by eternal love,
Each promise clearly shines;
Nor can the powers of hell remove
Those everlasting lines.

5 His word of grace is sure and strong
As that which built the skies;
The voice that rolls the stars along
Speaks all the promises.

6 O, might I hear his heavenly tongue
But whisper, "Thou art mine,"
The gentle words should raise my song
To notes almost divine.

107. C. M. LUTH. COL.

1 HAIL, great Creator, wise and good;
To thee our songs we raise;
Nature, through all her various scenes,
Invites us to thy praise.

2 At morning, noon, and evening mild,
Fresh wonders strike our view;
And, while we gaze, our hearts exult,
With transports ever new.

3 Thy glory beams in every star
Which gilds the gloom of night,
And decks the smiling face of morn
With rays of cheerful light.

4 The lofty hill, the humble lawn,
With countless beauties shine;
The silent grove, the solemn shade,
Proclaim thy power divine.

5 Great nature's God, still may these scenes
Our serious hours engage;
Still may our grateful hearts consult
Thy works' instructive page.

6 And while, in all thy wondrous ways,
Thy varied love we see,
O, may our hearts, great God, be led,
Through all thy works, to thee.

110. C. M. HEGINBOTHAM.

1 MY soul shall praise thee, O my God,
Through all my mortal days,
And in eternity prolong
Thy vast, thy boundless praise.

2 In every smiling, happy hour,
Be this my sweet employ;
Thy praise refines my earthly bliss,
And heightens all my joy.

3 When anxious grief and gloomy care
Afflict my throbbing breast,
My tongue shall learn to speak thy praise,
And lull each pain to rest.

4 Nor shall my tongue alone proclaim
The honors of my God;
My life, with all its active powers,
Shall spread thy praise abroad.

5 And when these lips shall cease to move,
When death shall close these eyes,
My soul shall then to nobler heights
Of joy and transport rise.

6 My powers shall then, in lofty strains,
Their grateful tribute pay;
The theme demands an angel's tongue,
An everlasting day.

112. C. M. WRANGHAM.

1 To thee, my righteous King and Lord,
My grateful soul I'll raise;
From day to day thy works record,
And ever sing thy praise.

2 Thy greatness human thought exceeds;
Thy glory knows no end;
The lasting record of thy deeds
Through ages shall descend.

3 Thy wondrous acts, thy power, and might,
My constant theme shall be;
That song shall be my soul's delight,
Which breathes in praise to thee.

4 The Lord is bountiful and kind;
His anger slow to move;
His tender mercies all shall find,
And all his goodness prove.

5 From all thy works, O Lord, shall spring
The sound of joy and praise;
Thy saints shall of thy glory sing,
And show the world thy ways.

6 Throughout all ages shall endure
Thine everlasting reign;
And thy dominion, firm and sure,
Forever shall remain.

STAMFORD. C. M. TANSUR.

116. C. M. WATTS.

1 LET children hear the mighty deeds
Which God performed of old,
Which in our younger years we saw,
And which our fathers told.

2 He bids us make his glories known,
His works of power and grace;
And we'll convey his wonders down
Through every rising race.

3 Our lips shall tell them to our sons,
And they again to theirs,
That generations yet unborn
May teach them to their heirs.

4 Thus shall they learn, in God alone
Their hope securely stands,
That they may ne'er forget his works,
But practise his commands.

119. C. M. WATTS.

1 FATHER of glory, to thy name
Immortal praise we give,
Who dost an act of grace proclaim,
And bid us, rebels, live

2 Immortal honor to the Son,
Who makes thine anger cease;
Our lives he ransomed with his own,
And died to make our peace.

3 To thy almighty Spirit be
Immortal glory given,
Whose influence brings us near to thee,
And trains us up for heaven.

4 Let men, with their united voice,
Adore th' eternal God,
And spread his honors, and their joys,
Through nations far abroad.

124. C. M. WATTS.

1 LET them neglect thy glory, Lord,
Who never knew thy grace;
But our loud songs shall still record
The wonders of thy praise.

2 We raise our shouts, O God, to thee,
And send them to thy throne;
All glory to th' united Three,
The undivided One.

3 'Twas he — and we'll adore his name —
That formed us by a word;
'Tis he restores our ruined frame;
Salvation to the Lord.

4 Hosanna! let the earth and skies
Repeat the joyful sound;
Rocks, hills, and vales reflect the voice
In one eternal round.

125. C. M. WATTS.

1 GLORY to God the Father's name,
Who, from our sinful race,
Hath chosen myriads to proclaim
The honors of his grace.

2 Glory to God the Son be paid,
Who dwelt in humble clay,
And, to redeem us from the dead,
Gave his own life away.

3 Glory to God the Spirit give,
From whose almighty power
Our souls their heavenly birth derive,
And bless the happy hour.

4 Glory to God, that reigns above,
The holy Three in One,
Who, by the wonders of his love,
Has made his nature known.

5 Let faith, and love, and duty join
One general song to raise;
Let saints, in earth and heaven, combine
In harmony and praise.

---

127. C. M. Watts.

1 Eternal Wisdom, thee we praise;
Thee, all thy creatures sing;
While with thy name, rocks, hills, and seas,
And heaven's high palace, ring.

2 Thy hand, how wide it spread the sky!
How glorious to behold!
Tinged with a blue of heavenly dye,
And decked with sparkling gold.

3 Thy glories blaze all nature round,
And strike the gazing sight,
Through skies, and seas, and solid ground,
With terror and delight.

4 Almighty power, and equal skill,
Shine through the worlds abroad,
Our souls with vast amazement fill,
And speak the builder, God.

5 But still, the wonders of thy grace
Our warmer passions move;
Here we behold our Saviour's face,
And here adore his love.

149. C. M. Eng. Bap. Col.

1 Thy kingdom, Lord, forever stands,
While earthly thrones decay;
And time submits to thy commands,
While ages roll away.

2 Thy sovereign bounty freely gives
Its unexhausted store;
And universal nature lives
On thy sustaining power.

3 Holy and just in all its ways
Is providence divine;
In all its works immortal rays
Of power and mercy shine.

4 The praise of God — delightful theme! —
Shall fill my heart and tongue;
Let all creation bless his name
In one eternal song.

137. C. M. Martineau's Col.

1 'Twas God who fixed the rolling spheres,
And stretched the boundless skies,
Who formed the plan of endless years,
And bade the ages rise.

2 From everlasting is his might,
Immense and unconfined;
He pierces through the realms of light,
And rides upon the wind.

3 He darts along the burning sky;
Loud thunders round him roar;
Through worlds above his terrors fly,
While worlds below adore.

4 He speaks—great nature's wheels stand still,
And leave their wonted round;
The mountains melt; each trembling hill
Forsakes its ancient bound.

5 Ye worlds, and every living thing,
Fulfil his high command;
Pay grateful homage to your King,
And own his ruling hand.

139. C. M. H. K. White.

1 The Lord our God is clothed with might;
The winds obey his will;
He speaks, and in the heavenly height
The rolling sun stands still.

2 Rebel, ye waves, and o'er the land
With threatening aspect roar;
The Lord uplifts his awful hand,
And chains you to the shore.

3 Ye winds of night, your force combine;
Without his high behest,
Ye shall not, in the mountain pine,
Disturb the sparrow's nest.

4 His voice sublime is heard afar;
In distant peals it dies;
He binds the whirlwinds to his car,
And sweeps the howling skies.

5 Ye nations, bend; in reverence bend;
Ye monarchs, wait his nod,
And bid the choral song ascend
To celebrate our God.

160. C. M. Beddome.

1 The truth of God shall still endure,
And firm his promise stand;
Believing souls may rest secure
In his almighty hand.

2 Should earth and hell their forces join,
He would contemn their rage,
And render fruitless their design
Against his heritage.

3 The rainbow round about his throne
Proclaims his faithfulness;
He will his purposes perform,
His promises of grace.

4 The hills and mountains melt away;
But he is still the same:
Let saints to him their homage pay,
And magnify his name.

‡ In England next to "Old Hundred" in popularity.

128. C. M. Watts.

1 Great God, how infinite art thou!
What worthless worms are we;
Let all the race of creatures bow,
And pay their praise to thee.

2 Thy throne eternal ages stood
Ere seas or stars were made;
Thou art the ever-living God,
Were all the nations dead.

3 Eternity, with all its years,
Stands present in thy view;
To thee there's nothing old appears;
Great God, there's nothing new.

4 Our lives through various scenes are drawn,
And vexed with trifling cares;
While thine eternal thought, moves on
Thine undisturbed affairs.

5 Great God, how infinite art thou!
What worthless worms are we;
Let all the race of creatures bow,
And pay their praise to thee.

147. C. M. Watts.

1 Keep silence, all created things,
And wait your Maker's nod;
My soul stands trembling while she sings
The honors of her God.

2 Life, death, and hell, and worlds unknown,
Hang on his firm decree;
He sits on no precarious throne,
Nor borrows leave to be.

3 Before his throne a volume lies,
With all the fates of men;
With every angel's form and size,
Drawn by th' eternal pen.

4 His providence unfolds the book,
And makes his counsels shine;
Each opening leaf, and every stroke,
Fulfils some deep design.

5 Here, he exalts neglected worms
To sceptres and a crown;
And there, the following page he turns,
And casts the monarch down.

6 My God, I would not long to see
My fate, with curious eyes—
What gloomy lines are writ for me,
Or what bright scenes may rise.

7 In thy fair book of life and grace,
O, may I find my name
Recorded in some humble place,
Beneath my Lord, the Lamb.

133. C. M. Watts.

1 God is a spirit, just and wise;
He sees our inmost mind;
In vain to heaven we raise our cries
And leave our hearts behind.

2 Nothing but truth before his throne
With honor can appear;
The painted hypocrites are known,
Whate'er the guise they wear.

3 Their lifted eyes salute the skies,
Their bending knees the ground;
But God abhors the sacrifice
Where not the heart is found.

4 Lord, search my thoughts, and try my ways,
And make my soul sincere;
Then shall I stand before thy face,
And find acceptance there.

134. C. M. WATTS.

1 In all my vast concerns with thee,
In vain my soul would try
To shun thy presence, Lord, or flee
The notice of thine eye.

2 Thine all-surrounding sight surveys
My rising, and my rest,
My public walks, my private ways,
And secrets of my breast.

3 My thoughts lie open to the Lord
Before they're formed within;
And ere my lips pronounce the word,
He knows the sense I mean.

4 O, wondrous knowledge, deep and high!
Where can a creature hide?
Within thy circling arms I lie,
Enclosed on every side.

5 So let thy grace surround me still,
And like a bulwark prove,
To guard my soul from every ill,
Secured by sovereign love.

148. C. M. COWPER.

1 God moves in a mysterious way,
His wonders to perform;
He plants his footsteps in the sea,
And rides upon the storm.

2 Ye fearful saints, fresh courage take;
The clouds ye so much dread
Are big with mercy, and shall break
With blessings on your head.

3 Judge not the Lord by feeble sense,
But trust him for his grace,
Behind a frowning providence
He hides a smiling face.

4 His purposes will ripen fast,
Unfolding every hour;
The bud may have a bitter taste,
But sweet will be the flower.

5 Blind unbelief is sure to err,
And scan his work in vain;
God is his own interpreter,
And he will make it plain.

158. C. M. STEELE.

1 Eternal Power, Almighty God,
Who can approach thy throne?
Accessless light is thine abode,
To angel eyes unknown.

2 Before the radiance of thine eye
The heavens no longer shine;
And all the glories of the sky
Are but the shade of thine.

3 Great God, and wilt thou condescend
To cast a look below?
To this dark world thy notice bend —
These seats of sin and woe?

4 How strange, how wondrous, is thy love!
With trembling we adore:
Not all th' exalted minds above
Its wonders can explore.

5 While golden harps and angel tongues
Resound immortal lays,
Great God, permit our humble songs
To rise and speak thy praise.

159. C. M. NEEDHAM.

1 Holy and reverend is the name
Of our eternal King;
"Thrice holy Lord," the angels cry;
"Thrice holy," let us sing.

2 The deepest reverence of the mind,
Pay, O my soul, to God;
Lift, with thy hands, a holy heart
To his sublime abode.

3 With sacred awe pronounce his name,
Whom words nor thoughts can reach;
A contrite heart shall please him more
Than noblest forms of speech.

4 Thou holy God, preserve my soul
From all pollution free;
The pure in heart are thy delight,
And they thy face shall see.

161. C. M. WATTS.

1 My never-ceasing song shall show
The mercies of the Lord,
And make succeeding ages know
How faithful is his word.

2 The sacred truths his lips pronounce
Shall firm as heaven endure;
And if he speak a promise once,
Th' eternal grace is sure.

3 How long the race of David held
The promised Jewish throne!
But there's a nobler promise sealed
To David's greater Son.

4 His seed forever shall possess
A throne above the skies;
The meanest subject of his grace
Shall to that glory rise.

5 Lord God of hosts, thy wondrous ways
Are sung by saints above;
And saints on earth their honors raise
To thine unchanging love.

TALLIS. C. M. (Attalia.) Thomas Tallis. 1565.

150. C. M. Gibbons.

1 Thy goodness, Lord, our souls confess;
Thy goodness we adore; —
A spring whose blessings never fail;
A sea without a shore.

2 Sun, moon, and stars thy love declare
In every golden ray;
Love draws the curtains of the night,
And love brings back the day.

3 Thy bounty every season crowns
With all the bliss it yields,
With joyful clusters loads the vines,
With strengthening grain the fields.

4 But chiefly thy compassion, Lord,
Is in the gospel seen:
There, like a sun, thy mercy shines,
Without a cloud between.

5 There pardon, peace, and holy joy,
Through Jesus' name are given;
He on the cross was lifted high,
That we might reign in heaven.

153. C. M. Steele.

1 Ye humble souls, approach your God
With songs of sacred praise;
For he is good, supremely good,
And kind are all his ways.

2 All nature owns his guardian care;
In him we live and move;
But nobler benefits declare
The wonders of his love.

3 He gave his well belovéd Son
To save our souls from sin;
'Tis here he makes his goodness known,
And proves it all divine.

4 To this sure refuge, Lord, we come,
And here our hope relies;
A safe defence, a peaceful home,
When storms of trouble rise.

5 Thine eye beholds, with kind regard,
The souls who trust in thee;
Their humble hope thou wilt reward
With bliss divinely free.

6 Great God, to thy almighty love
What honors shall we raise?
Not all the raptured songs above
Can render equal praise.

156. C. M. G. Burder.

1 Come, ye that know and fear the Lord,
And lift your souls above;
Let every heart and voice accord,
To sing, that God is love.

2 This precious truth his word declares,
And all his mercies prove;
While Christ, th' atoning Lamb, appears,
To show, that God is love.

3 Behold his loving kindness waits
For those who from him rove,
And calls of mercy reach their hearts,
To teach them, God is love.

4 And O that you, whose hardened hearts
No fears of hell can move,
May hear the gospel's milder voice,
That tells you, God is love!

5 O, may we all, while here below,
This best of blessings prove;
Till warmer hearts, in brighter worlds,
Shall shout, that God is love.

SYME. C. M.

EDWARD HAMILTON. From The Sanctus.

126. C. M. WALLACE.

1 THERE'S not a star whose twinkling light
Illumes the distant earth,
And cheers the solemn gloom of night,
But goodness gave it birth.

2 There's not a cloud whose dews distil
Upon the parching clod,
And clothe with verdure vale and hill,
That is not sent by God.

3 There's not a place in earth's vast round,
In ocean deep, or air,
Where skill and wisdom are not found;
For God is every where.

4 Around, beneath, below, above,
Wherever space extends,
There Heaven displays its boundless love,
And power with goodness blends.

131. C. M. TATE & BRADY.

1 THROUGH endless years thou art the same,
O thou eternal God;
Each future age shall know thy name,
And tell thy works abroad.

2 The strong foundations of the earth
Of old by thee were laid;
By thee the beauteous arch of heaven
With matchless skill was made.

3 Soon shall this goodly frame of things,
Created by thy hand,
Be, like a vesture, laid aside,
And changed at thy command.

4 But thy perfections, all divine,
Eternal as thy days,
Through everlasting ages shine,
With undiminished rays.

10

135. C. M. H. K. WHITE.

1 THE Lord our God is Lord of all;
His station who can find?
I hear him in the waterfall,
I hear him in the wind.

2 If in the gloom of night I shroud,
His face I cannot fly;
I see him in the evening cloud,
And in the morning sky.

3 He lives, he reigns in every land,
From winter's polar snows,
To where, across the burning sand,
The blasting meteor glows.

4 He smiles, we live; he frowns, we die;
We hang upon his word;
He rears his mighty arm on high,
We fall before his sword.

5 He bids his gales the fields deform;
Then, when his thunders cease,
He paints his rainbow on the storm,
And lulls the winds to peace.

167. C. M. DRENNAN.

1 THE heaven of heavens cannot contain
The universal Lord;
Yet he in humble hearts will deign
To dwell and be adored.

2 Where'er ascends the sacrifice
Of fervent praise and prayer,
Or on the earth, or in the skies,
The God of heaven is there.

3 His presence is diffused abroad
Through realms and worlds unknown;
Who seek the mercies of our God
Are ever near his throne.

163. C. M. WATTS.

1 O LORD, our God, how wondrous great
 Is thine exalted name!
The glories of thy heavenly state
 Let every tongue proclaim.

2 Lord, what is man, or all his race,
 Who dwells so far below,
That thou shouldst visit him with grace,
 And love his nature so?—

3 That thine eternal Son should bear
 To take a mortal form,—
Made lower than his angels are,
 To save a dying worm?

4 Let him be crowned with majesty
 Who bowed his head to death,
And be his honors sounded high
 By all things that have breath.

5 Jesus, our Lord, how wondrous great
 Is thine exalted name!
The glories of thy heavenly state
 Let all the earth proclaim.

169. C. M. PITT.

1 ON God we build our sure defence;
 In God our hopes repose;
His hand protects our varying life,
 And guards us from our foes.

2 Our minds shall be serene and calm,
 Like Siloa's peaceful flood,
Whose soft and silver streams refresh
 The city of our God.

3 We to the mighty Lord of hosts
 Securely will resort;
For refuge fly to Jacob's God,
 Our succor and support.

165. C. M. TATE & BRADY.

1 O THOU, to whom all creatures bow
 Within this earthly frame,
Through all the world, how great art thou!
 How glorious is thy name!

2 When heaven, thy glorious work on high,
 Employs my wondering sight,—
The moon, that nightly rules the sky,
 With stars of feebler light,—

3 Lord, what is man, that thou shouldst choose
 To keep him in thy mind?
Or what his race, that thou shouldst prove
 To them so wondrous kind?

4 O Thou, to whom all creatures bow
 Within this earthly frame,
Through all the world, how great art thou!
 How glorious is thy name!

174. C. M. DODDRIDGE.

1 HOW firm the saint's foundation stands!
 His hopes can ne'er remove,
Sustained by God's almighty hand,
 And sheltered in his love.

2 God is the treasure of his soul,
 A source of sacred joy,
Which no afflictions can control,
 Nor death itself destroy.

3 Lord, may we feel thy cheering beams,
 And taste thy saints' repose;
We will not mourn the perished streams,
 While such a fountain flows.

LITCHFIELD.

166. C. M. MONTGOMERY.

1 FAITHFUL, O Lord, thy mercies are,
A rock that cannot move;
A thousand promises declare
Thy constancy of love.

2 Thou waitest to be gracious still;
Thou dost with sinners bear,
That, saved, we may thy goodness feel,
And all thy grace declare.

3 Its streams the whole creation reach,
So plenteous is the store;
Enough for all, enough for each,
Enough forevermore.

4 Throughout the universe it reigns;
It stands forever sure;
And while thy truth, O God, remains,
Thy goodness shall endure.

168. C. M. WATTS.

1 To heaven I lift my waiting eyes;
There all my hopes are laid;
The Lord, who built the earth and skies,
Is my perpetual aid.

2 Their steadfast feet shall never fall
Whom he designs to keep;
His ear attends their humble call,
His eyes can never sleep.

3 Israel, rejoice, and rest secure;
Thy keeper is the Lord;
His wakeful eyes employ his power
For thine eternal guard.

4 He guards thy soul, he keeps thy breath,
Where thickest dangers come;
Go and return, secure from death,
Till God shall call thee home.

170. C. M. TATE & BRADY.

1 No change of time shall ever shock
My trust, O Lord, in thee;
For thou hast always been my rock,
A sure defence to me.

2 Thou our deliverer art, O God;
Our trust is in thy power;
Thou art our shield from foes abroad,
Our safeguard, and our tower.

3 To thee will we address our prayer,
To whom all praise we owe;
O, may me, by thy watchful care,
Be saved from every foe.

4 Then let Jehovah be adored,
On whom our hopes depend;
For who, except the mighty Lord,
His people can defend?

181. C. M. * DOANE.

1 LORD, should we leave thy hallowed feet,
To whom should we repair?
Where else such holy comforts meet
As spring eternal there?

2 Earth has no fount of true delight,
No pure, perennial stream;
And sorrow's storm, and death's long night,
Obscure life's brightest beam.

3 Unmingled joys 'tis thine to give,
And undecaying peace;
For thou canst teach us so to live
That life shall never cease.

4 Thou only canst the cheering words
Of endless life supply,
Anointed of the Lord of lords,
The Son of God most high.

190. C. M. HERVEY.

1 SINCE all the varying scenes of time
God's watchful eye surveys,
O, who so wise to choose our lot,
Or to appoint our ways!

2 Good when he gives, — supremely good, —
Nor less when he denies;
E'en crosses, from his sovereign hand,
Are blessings in disguise.

3 Why should we doubt a Father's love,
So constant and so kind?
To his unerring, gracious will
Be every wish resigned.

4 In thy fair book of life divine,
My God, inscribe my name;
There let it fill some humble place,
Beneath my Lord, the Lamb.

193. C. M. TATE & BRADY.

1 THROUGH all the changing scenes of life,
In trouble and in joy,
The praises of my God shall still
My heart and tongue employ.

2 The hosts of God encamp around
The dwellings of the just;
Deliverance he affords to all
Who make his name their trust.

3 O, make but trial of his love,
Experience will decide
How blest are they, and only they,
Who in his truth confide.

4 Fear him, ye saints, and you will then
Have nothing else to fear;
Make you his service your delight,
He'll make your wants his care.

CANTERBURY. C. M.

In Este's Psalter. 1592.

175. C. M. WATTS.

1 GOD, my supporter and my hope,
My help forever near,
Thine arm of mercy held me up,
When sinking in despair.

2 Thy counsels, Lord, shall guide my feet
Through this dark wilderness;
Thine hand conduct me near thy seat,
To dwell before thy face.

3 Were I in heaven without my God,
'Twould be no joy to me;
And whilst this earth is my abode,
I long for none but thee.

4 What if the springs of life were broke,
And flesh and heart should faint;
God is my soul's eternal rock,
The strength of every saint.

5 Behold the sinners, that remove
Far from thy presence, die;
Not all the idol gods they love
Can save them when they cry.

6 But to draw near to thee, my God,
Shall be my sweet employ;
My tongue shall sound thy works abroad,
And tell the world my joy.

176. C. M. BEDDOME.

1 'Tis faith supports my feeble soul
In times of deep distress,
When storms arise and billows roll,
Great God, I trust thy grace.

2 Thy powerful arm still bears me up,
Whatever griefs befall;
Thou art my life, my joy, my hope,
And thou my all in all.

3 Bereft of friends, beset with foes,
With dangers all around,
To thee I all my fears disclose;
In thee my help is found.

4 In every want, in every strait,
To thee alone I fly;
When other comforters depart,
Thou art forever nigh.

198. C. M. WATTS.

1 MY Shepherd will supply my need;
Jehovah is his name;
In pastures fresh he makes me feed,
Beside the living stream.

2 He brings my wandering spirit back
When I forsake his ways,
And leads me, for his mercy's sake,
In paths of truth and grace.

3 When I walk through the shades of death,
Thy presence is my stay;
A word of thy supporting breath
Drives all my fears away.

4 Thy hand, in sight of all my foes,
Doth still my table spread;
My cup with blessings overflows;
Thine oil anoints my head.

5 The sure provision of my God,
Attend me all my days;
O, may thine house be mine abode,
And all my works be praise.

6 There would I find a settled rest,
While others go and come—
No more a stranger or a guest,
But like a child at home.

ABRIDGE. C. M. ISAAC SMITH. 1770.

177. C. M. STEELE.

1 My God, my Father,—blissful name,—
O, may I call thee mine?
May I with sweet assurance claim
A portion so divine?

2 This only can my fears control,
And bid my sorrows fly;
What harm can ever reach my soul
Beneath my Father's eye?

3 Whate'er thy holy will denies,
I calmly would resign;
For thou art good, and just, and wise;
O, bend my will to thine.

4 Whate'er thy sacred will ordains,
O, give me strength to bear;
And let me know my Father reigns,
And trust his tender care.

179. C. M. DODDRIDGE.

1 Great Ruler of all nature's frame,
We own thy power divine;
We hear thy breath in every storm,
For all the winds are thine.

2 Wide as they sweep their sounding way,
They work thy sovereign will;
And awed by thy majestic voice,
Confusion shall be still.

3 Thy mercy tempers every blast
To them that seek thy face,
And mingles with the tempest's roar
The whispers of thy grace.

4 Those gentle whispers let me hear,
Till all the tumult cease;
And gales of Paradise shall lull
My weary soul to peace.

187. C. M. WATTS.

1 Sweet is the memory of thy grace,
My God, my heavenly King;
Let age to age thy righteousness
In songs of glory sing.

2 God reigns on high, but ne'er confines
His goodness to the skies;
Through all the earth his bounty shines,
And every want supplies.

3 How kind are thy compassions, Lord!
How slow thine anger moves!
But soon he sends his pardoning word,
To cheer the souls he loves.

4 Sweet is the memory of thy grace,
My God, my heavenly King;
Let age to age thy righteousness
In songs of glory sing.

188. C. M. WATTS.

1 My God, my portion, and my love,
My everlasting all,
I've none but thee in heaven above,
Or on this earthly ball.

2 How vain a toy is glittering wealth,
If once compared to thee?
Or what's my safety, or my health,
Or all my friends, to me?

3 Were I possessor of the earth,
And called the stars my own,
Without thy graces, and thyself,
I were a wretch undone.

4 Let others stretch their arms like seas,
And grasp in all the shore;
Grant me the visits of thy grace,
And I desire no more.

‡ Ascribed by some to Dr. Croft.

180. C. M. Anon.

1 Jehovah lives, and be his name
By every heart adored;
From age to age he is the same,
The only God and Lord.

2 He is our rock when troubles rise,
And storms and tempests lower;
He rides triumphant in the skies,
And saves us by his power.

3 Salvation to the Lord belongs;
We give Jehovah praise;
Lift up our hearts, and holy songs
To our deliverer raise.

4 He saves from danger, death, and hell,
From fear, distress, and harm;
Makes every soul in safety dwell,
For mighty is his arm.

211. C. M. Doddridge.

1 Hark! the glad sound! the Saviour comes,
The Saviour promised long!
Let every heart prepare a throne,
And every voice a song.

2 He comes, the prisoner to release,
In Satan's bondage held;
The gates of brass before him burst,
The iron fetters yield.

3 He comes, from thickest films of vice
To clear the mental ray,
And on the eyes oppressed with night
To pour celestial day.

4 He comes, the broken heart to bind,
The bleeding soul to cure,
And, with the treasures of his grace,
Enrich the humble poor.

5 Our glad hosannas, Prince of Peace,
Thy welcome shall proclaim;
And heaven's eternal arches ring
With thy belovéd name.

214. C. M. Watts.

1 Sing to the Lord, ye distant lands,
Ye tribes of every tongue;
His new-discovered grace demands
A new and nobler song.

2 Say to the nations, Jesus reigns!
God's own Almighty Son;
His power the sinking world sustains,
And grace surrounds his throne.

3 Let heaven proclaim the joyful day;
Joy through the earth be seen;
Let cities shine in bright array,
And fields in cheerful green.

4 Let new seraphic joy surprise
The islands of the sea,
Ye mountains, sink; ye valleys, rise;
Prepare the Lord his way.

5 Behold, he comes! he comes to bless
The nations, as their God,
To show the world his righteousness,
And send his truth abroad.

6 But when his voice shall raise the dead,
And bid the world draw near,
How will the guilty nations dread
To see their Judge appear!

AZMON.

BRAY. C. M. N. Herman. 1550.

213. C. M. Watts.

1 Joy to the world! the Lord is come!
Let earth receive her King;
Let every heart prepare him room,
And heaven and nature sing.

2 Joy to the earth! the Saviour reigns!
Let men their songs employ;
While fields, and floods, rocks, hills, and plains,
Repeat the sounding joy.

3 No more let sins and sorrows grow,
Nor thorns infest the ground;
He comes to make his blessings flow
Far as the curse is found.

4 He rules the world with truth and grace,
And makes the nations prove
The glories of his righteousness,
And wonders of his love.

217. C. M. C. Wesley.

1 The race that long in darkness pined
Have seen a glorious light;
The people dwell in day, who dwelt
In death's surrounding night.

2 To hail thy rise, thou better Sun,
The gathering nations come
With joy, as when the reapers bear
The harvest treasures home.

3 To us a Child of hope is born,
To us a Son is given;
And him shall all the earth obey,
And all the hosts of heaven.

4 His name shall be the Prince of Peace,
Forevermore adored,
The Wonderful, the Counsellor,
The great and mighty Lord.

5 His power increasing still shall spread;
His reign no end shall know;
His throne shall justice guard above,
And peace abound below.

239. C. M. Percy Chapel Col.

1 The Sun of Righteousness appears,
To set in blood no more;
Exult; he banishes your fears;
Your rising God adore.

2 The saints, when he resigned his breath,
Unclosed their sleeping eyes;
He breaks again the bands of death;
Again the dead arise.

3 Alone the dreadful race he ran,
Alone the wine-press trod;
He died and suffered as a man;
He rises as a God.

4 In vain the stone, the watch, and seal
Forbid an early rise
To Him who shuts the gates of hell,
And opens Paradise.

246. C. M. Tate & Brady.

1 Lift up your heads, eternal gates,
Unfold, to entertain
The King of glory; — see, he comes
With his celestial train.

2 "Who is this King of glory? — who?"
The Lord, for strength renowned;
In battle mighty — o'er his foes
Eternal Victor crowned.

3 Lift up your heads, eternal gates,
Unfold, to entertain
The King of glory; — see, he comes
With all his shining train.

4 "Who is this King of glory? — who?"
The Lord of hosts renowned;
Of glory he alone is King,
Who is with glory crowned.

RINETON. C. M. (Marlow.) WILLIAMS.

240. C. M. WATTS.

1 BLEST morning, whose young dawning rays
Beheld our rising God;
That saw him triumph o'er the dust,
And leave his dark abode.

2 A silent prisoner in the tomb
The great Redeemer lay,
Till the revolving skies had brought
The third, th' appointed day.

3 Hell and the grave unite their force
To hold our God in vain:
The sleeping Conqueror arose,
And burst their feeble chain.

4 To thy great name, Almighty Lord,
These sacred hours we pay;
And loud hosannas shall proclaim
The triumph of the day.

5 Salvation and immortal praise
To our victorious King;
Let heaven and earth, and rocks and seas,
With glad hosannas ring.

242. C. M. WATTS.

1 HOSANNA to the Prince of Light,
Who clothed himself in clay,
Entered the iron gates of death,
And tore the bars away.

2 Death is no more the king of dread,
Since our Immanuel rose;
He took the tyrant's sting away,
And spoiled our hellish foes.

3 See how the Conqueror mounts aloft,
And to his Father flies,
With scars of honor in his flesh,
And triumph in his eyes.

4 There our exalted Saviour reigns,
And scatters blessings down;
Our Jesus fills the middle seat
Of the celestial throne.

5 Raise your devotion, mortal tongues
To reach his blest abode;
Sweet be the accents of your songs
To our incarnate God.

6 Bright angels, strike your loudest strings,
Your sweetest voices raise;
Let heaven, and all created things,
Sound our Immanuel's praise.

248. C. M. WATTS.

1 O FOR a shout of sacred joy
To God, the sovereign King!
Let every land their tongues employ,
And hymns of triumph sing.

2 Jesus, our God, ascends on high;
His heavenly guards around
Attend him, rising through the sky,
With trumpet's joyful sound.

3 While angels shout, and praise their King
Let mortals learn their strains;
Let all the earth his honors sing;
O'er all the earth he reigns.

4 Speak forth his praise with awe profound;
Let knowledge guide the song;
Nor mock him with a solemn sound
Upon a thoughtless tongue.

AZMON.

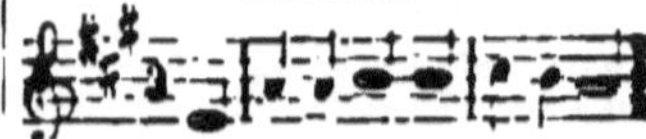

‡ Each stanza may be sung separately.

250. C. M. FANCH & TURNER.

1 BEYOND the glittering, starry sky,
Which God's right hand sustains,
There, in the boundless worlds of light,
Our great Redeemer reigns.

2 The host of angels, strong and fair,
In countless armies shine;
At his right hand, with golden harps,
They offer songs divine.

3 And when he stooped on earth to dwell,
And suffer rude disdain,
They cast their honors at his feet,
And waited in his train.

4 In all his toils and conflicts here
Their Sovereign they attend,
And pause, and wonder how, at last,
This scene of love will end.

5 When all the powers of hell combined
To fill his cup of woe,
Their wondering eyes beheld his tears
In blood and anguish flow.

6 As on the torturing cross he hung,
And darkness veiled the sky,
Amazed, they saw that awful sight,
The Lord of glory die.

7 They saw him break the bars of death,
Which none e'er broke before,
And rise in conquering majesty,
To stoop to death no more.

8 They brought his chariot from the skies,
To bear him to his throne;
Clapped their triumphant wings, and cried,
"The glorious work is done!"

3d, 4th, 5th, and 6th stanzas may be sung to the first half of the tune, separately.

TALLIS. C. M. (Attalia) T. Tallis. 1565.

210. C. M. Steele.

1 And did the holy and the just,
The Sovereign of the skies,
Stoop down to wretchedness and dust,
That guilty man might rise?

2 Yes, the Redeemer left his throne,
His radiant throne on high, —
Surprising mercy! love unknown! —
To suffer, bleed, and die.

3 He took the dying traitor's place,
And suffered in his stead;
For sinful man, — O, wondrous grace! —
For sinful man he bled.

4 O Lord, what heavenly wonders dwell
In thine atoning blood!
By this are sinners saved from hell,
And rebels brought to God.

218. C. M. Curtis's Col.

1 And didst thou, Jesus, condescend,
When veiled in human clay,
To heal the sick, the lame, the blind,
And drive disease away?

2 Didst thou regard the beggar's cry,
And cause the blind to see?
Thou Son of David, hear — O, hear —
Have mercy, too, on me.

3 And didst thou pity mortal woe,
And sight and health restore?
O, pity, Lord, and save my soul,
Which needs thy mercy more.

4 Didst thou thy trembling servant raise,
When sinking in the wave?
I perish, Lord; O, save my soul;
For thou alone canst save.

216. C. M. Watts.

1 The true Messiah now appears;
The types are all withdrawn:
So fly the shadows and the stars
Before the rising dawn.

2 The smoking sweet and bleeding lamb,
The kid and bullock slain,
And costly spice of every name,
Would all be burnt in vain.

3 Aaron must lay his robes away,
His mitre and his vest,
When Christ, the Lord, comes down to be
The offering and the priest.

4 He took our mortal flesh, to show
The wonders of his love;
For us he paid his life below,
And prays for us above.

5 "Forgive," he cries, "forgive their sins,
For I myself have died;"
And then he shows his open veins,
And pleads his wounded side.

229. C. M. Epis. Col.

1 From whence these direful omens round,
Which heaven and earth amaze?
And why do earthquakes cleave the ground?
Why hides the sun his rays?

2 Well may the earth astonished shake,
And nature sympathize,
The sun, as darkest night, be black;
Their Maker, Jesus, dies!

3 Behold, fast streaming from the tree,
His all-atoning blood:
Is this the Infinite? 'Tis he,
My Saviour and my God.

4 For me these pangs his soul assail;
For me this death is borne;
My sins gave sharpness to the nail,
And pointed every thorn.

5 Let sin no more my soul enslave;
Break, Lord, its tyrant chain;
O, save me, whom thou cam'st to save,
Nor bleed nor die in vain.

CUPAR. C. M.

From Scotch Psalter. 1635.

Choral.

221. C. M. HAWEIS.

1 DARK was the night, and cold the ground
On which the Lord was laid;
His sweat, like drops of blood ran down;
In agony he prayed,—

2 "Father, remove this bitter cup,
If such thy sacred will;
If not, content to drink it up,
Thy pleasure I fulfil."

3 Go to the garden, sinner; see
Those precious drops that flow;
The heavy load he bore for thee;
For thee he lies so low.

4 Then learn of him the cross to bear;
Thy Father's will obey;
And, when temptations press thee near,
Awake to watch and pray.

224. C. M. PERCY CHAPEL COL.

1 BEHOLD the Saviour of mankind
Upon the shameful tree:
How great the love that him inclined
To bleed and die for me!

2 "My God," he cries; all nature shakes,
And earth's strong pillars bend;
The gate of death in sunder breaks;
The solid marbles rend.

3 "'Tis finished; now the ransom's paid
Receive my soul," he cries;
Behold, he bows his sacred head;
He bows his head, and dies!

4 But soon he'll break death's tyrant chain,
And in full glory shine:
O Lamb of God, was ever pain,
Was ever love, like thine?

260. C. M. WATTS.

1 BEHOLD what pity touched the heart
Of God's eternal Son;
Descending from the heavenly court,
He left his Father's throne.

2 His living power, and dying love,
Redeemed unhappy men,
And raised the ruins of our race
To life and God again.

3 To thee, O Lord, our noblest powers
We joyfully resign;
Blest Jesus, take us for thy own,
For we are doubly thine.

273. C. M. HOSKINS.

1 BEHOLD, behold the Lamb of God,
Who takes away our guilt;
Behold th' atoning, precious blood
That for our sins he spilt.

2 O sinners, now to Christ draw near,
Invited by his word;
The chief of sinners need not fear;
Behold the Lamb of God.

3 Backsliders, too, the Saviour calls,
And washes in his blood:
Arise, return from grievous falls;
Behold the Lamb of God.

4 In every state, and time, and place,
Nought plead but Jesus' blood;
However wretched be your case,
Behold the Lamb of God.

5 Spirit of grace, to us apply
Immanuel's precious blood,
That we may, with thy saints on high,
Behold the Lamb of God.

This and other of Dr. Hastings' tunes inserted by his special permission.

257. C. M. S. Stennett.

1 Majestic sweetness sits enthroned
Upon the Saviour's brow ;
His head with radiant glories crowned ;
His lips with grace o'erflow.

2 No mortal can with him compare,
Among the sons of men ;
Fairer is he than all the fair
Who fill the heavenly train.

3 He saw me plunged in deep distress,
And flew to my relief;
For me he bore the shameful cross,
And carried all my grief.

4 To him I owe my life and breath,
And all the joys I have ;
He makes me triumph over death,
And saves me from the grave.

5 To heaven, the place of his abode,
He brings my weary feet,
Shows me the glories of my God,
And makes my joys complete.

6 Since from his bounty I receive
Such proofs of love divine,
Had I a thousand hearts to give,
Lord, they should all be thine.

268. C. M. Watts.

1 Come, happy souls, approach your God
With new, melodious songs ;
Come, render to almighty grace
The tribute of your tongues.

2 So strange, so boundless was the love
That pitied dying men,
The Father sent his equal Son
To give them life again.

3 Thy hands, dear Jesus, were not armed
With a revenging rod ;
No hard commission to perform
The vengeance of a God :

4 But all was mercy, all was mild,
And wrath forsook the throne,
When Christ on mercy's errand came,
And brought salvation down.

5 Here, sinners, you may heal your wounds,
And wipe your sorrows dry :
Trust in the mighty Saviour's name,
And you shall never die.

6 See, dearest Lord, our willing souls
Accept thine offered grace ;
We bless the great Redeemer's love,
And give the Father praise.

272. C. M. Campbell's Col.

1 In vain we seek for peace with God
By methods of our own :
Blest Saviour, nothing but thy blood
Can bring us near the throne.

2 The threatenings of thy broken law
Impress the soul with dread :
If God his sword of justice draw,
It strikes the spirit dead.

3 But thy atoning sacrifice
Hath answered all demands ;
And peace and pardon from the skies
Are blessings from thy hands.

4 'Tis by thy death we live, O Lord ;
'Tis on thy cross we rest :
Forever be thy love adored,
Thy name forever blest.

FOUNTAIN. C. M.

† By permission of Dr. T. Hastings. ‡ May end here.

259. C. M. GIBBONS.

1 Jesus, th' eternal Son of God,
Whom seraphim obey,
The bosom of the Father leaves,
And enters human clay.

2 From heaven to sinful earth he comes,
The messenger of grace,
And on the bloody tree expires,
A victim in our place.

3 Transgressors of the deepest stain
In him salvation find:
His blood removes the foulest guilt,
His Spirit heals the mind.

4 He saves our souls from sin and hell;
His words are true and sure,
And on this rock our faith may rest
Immovable, secure.

274. C. M. COWPER.

1 There is a fountain filled with blood,
Drawn from Immanuel's veins;
And sinners, plunged beneath that flood,
Lose all their guilty stains.

2 The dying thief rejoiced to see
That fountain, in his day;
O, may I there, though vile as he,
Wash all my sins away.

3 Thou dying Lamb, thy precious blood
Shall never lose its power,
Till all the ransomed church of God
Are saved, to sin no more.

4 E'er since, by faith, I saw the stream
Thy flowing wounds supply,
Redeeming love has been my theme,
And shall be, till I die.

5 And when this feeble, faltering tongue
Lies silent in the grave,
Then, in a nobler, sweeter song,
I'll sing thy power to save.

277. C. M. WATTS.

1 Salvation! O, the joyful sound!
'Tis pleasure to our ears,
A sovereign balm for every wound,
A cordial for our fears.

2 Buried in sorrow, and in sin,
At hell's dark door we lay;
But we arise, by grace divine,
To see a heavenly day.

3 Salvation! let the echo fly
The spacious earth around,
While all the armies of the sky
Conspire to raise the sound.

BELCHER. C. M.

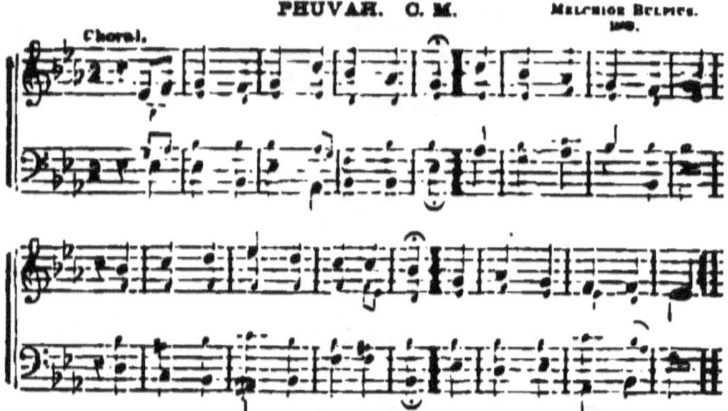

266. C. M. Watts.

1 Lord, we confess our numerous faults,
How great our guilt has been;
Foolish and vain were all our thoughts,
And all our lives were sin.

2 But, O my soul, forever praise,
Forever love his name,
Who turns thy feet from dangerous ways
Of folly, sin, and shame.

3 'Tis not by works of righteousness
Which our own hands have done;
But we are saved by sovereign grace,
Abounding through his Son.

4 'Tis from the mercy of our God
That all our hopes begin;
'Tis by the water and the blood
Our souls are washed from sin.

5 'Tis through the purchase of his death
Who hung upon the tree,
The Spirit is sent down to breathe
On such dry bones as we.

6 Raised from the dead, we live anew;
And, justified by grace,
We shall appear in glory too,
And see our Father's face.

289. C. M. Swain.

1 A Friend there is — your voices join,
Ye saints, to praise his name —
Whose truth and kindness are divine,
Whose love's a constant flame.

2 When most we need his helping hand,
This Friend is always near:
With heaven and earth at his command,
He waits to answer prayer.

3 When frowns appear to veil his face,
And clouds surround his throne,
He hides the purpose of his grace,
To make it better known.

4 And, if our dearest comforts fall
Before his sovereign will,
He never takes away our all;
Himself he gives us still.

5 Our sorrows in the scale he weighs,
And measures out our pains;
The wildest storm his word obeys;
His word its rage restrains.

297. C. M. Doddridge.

1 Now let our cheerful eyes survey
Our great High Priest above,
And celebrate his constant care
And sympathizing love.

2 Though raised to heaven's exalted throne,
Where angels bow around,
And high o'er all the hosts of light,
With matchless honors crowned,—

3 The names of all his saints he bears,
Deep graven on his heart;
Nor shall the meanest Christian say
That he hath lost his part.

4 Those characters shall fair abide,
Our everlasting trust,
When gems, and monuments, and crowns,
Are mouldered down to dust.

5 So, gracious Saviour, on our breasts
May thy dear name be worn,—
A sacred ornament and guard,
To endless ages borne.

DEDHAM. C. M. Wm. Gardiner.

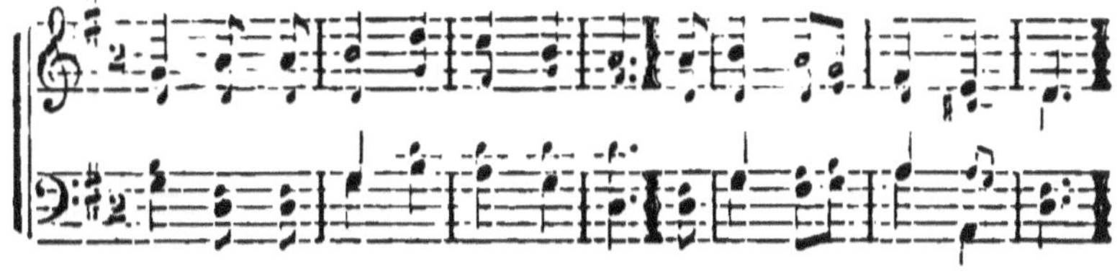

280. C. M. Doane.

1 Thou art the way; to thee alone
From sin and death we flee;
And he who would the Father seek,
Must seek him, Lord, through thee.

2 Thou art the truth; thy word alone
True wisdom can impart;
Thou, only, canst instruct the mind,
And purify the heart.

3 Thou art the life; the rending tomb
Proclaims thy conquering arm;
And those who put their trust in thee,
Nor death nor hell shall harm.

4 Thou art the way, the truth, the life;
Grant us to know that way,
That truth to keep, that life to win
Which lead to endless day.

292. C. M. Higginbotham.

1 To thee, my Shepherd and my Lord,
A grateful song I raise;
O, let the feeblest of thy flock
Attempt to speak thy praise.

2 But how shall mortal tongues express
A subject so divine?
Do justice to so vast a theme,
Or praise a love like thine?

3 My life, my joy, my hope, I owe
To this amazing love;
Ten thousand thousand comforts here,
And nobler bliss above.

4 To thee my trembling spirit flies,
With sin and grief oppressed;
Thy gentle voice dispels my fears,
And lulls my cares to rest.

298. C. M. Watts.

1 With joy we meditate the grace
Of our High Priest above:
His heart is full of tenderness;
His bosom glows with love.

2 Touched with a sympathy within,
He knows our feeble frame;
He knows what sore temptations mean,
For he has felt the same.

3 He, in the days of feeble flesh,
Poured out his cries and tears,
And in his measure feels afresh
What every member bears.

4 Then let our humble faith address
His mercy and his power;
We shall obtain delivering grace
In each distressing hour.

302. C. M. Steele.

1 Jesus, in thy transporting name
What glories meet our eyes!
Thou art the seraph's lofty theme,
The wonder of the skies.

2 Well might the heavens with wonder view
A love so strange as thine;
No thought of angels ever knew
Compassion so divine.

3 And didst thou, Saviour, leave the sky,
To sink beneath our woes?
Didst thou descend to bleed and die
For thy rebellious foes?

4 O, may our willing hearts confess
Thy sweet, thy gentle sway;
Glad captives of thy matchless grace
Thy righteous rule obey.

ARLINGTON. C. M. ‡ Dr. Arne.

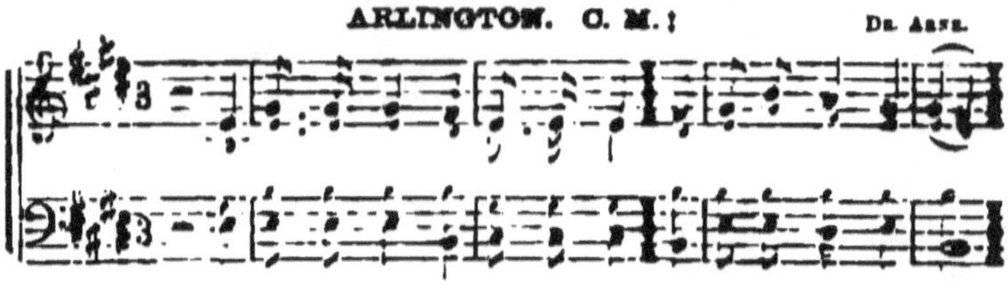

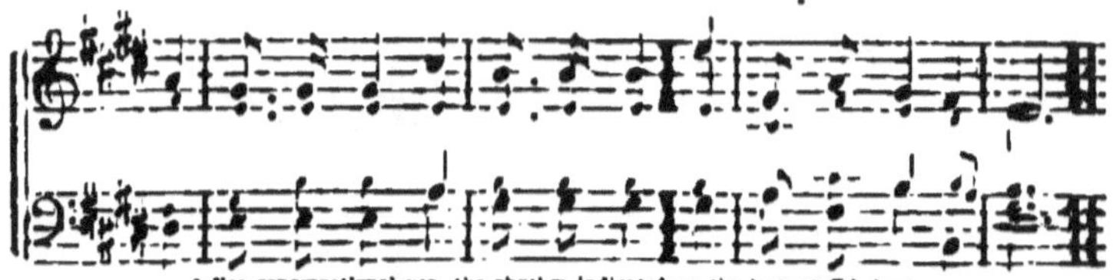

‡ For congregational use, the rhythm indicated on the bass staff is best.

305. C. M. Beddome.

1 Jesus! delightful, charming name!
It spreads a fragrance round;
Justice and mercy, truth and peace,
In union here are found.

2 He is our life, our joy, our strength;
In him all glories meet;
He is a shade above our heads,
A light to guide our feet.

3 The thickest clouds are soon dispersed,
If Jesus shows his face;
To weary, heavy-laden souls
He is the resting-place.

4 When storms arise and tempests blow,
He speaks the stilling word;
The threatening billows cease to flow,
The winds obey their Lord.

5 Through every age he's still the same;
But we ungrateful prove;
Forget the savor of his name,
The sweetness of his love.

306. C. M. Doddridge.

1 Jesus, I love thy charming name;
'Tis music to my ear;
Fain would I sound it out so loud
That earth and heaven might hear.

2 Yes, thou art precious to my soul,
My transport and my trust:
Jewels to thee are gaudy toys,
And gold is sordid dust.

3 All my capacious powers can wish
In thee doth richly meet;
Nor to my eyes is light so dear,
Nor friendship half so sweet.

4 Thy grace shall dwell upon my heart,
And shed its fragrance there, —
The noblest balm of all its wounds,
The cordial of its care.

5 I'll speak the honors of thy name
With my last, laboring breath,
And, dying, clasp thee in my arms,
The antidote of death.

307. C. M. Watts.

1 Dearest of all the names above,
My Saviour and my God,
Who can resist thy heavenly love,
Or trifle with thy blood?

2 'Tis by the merits of thy death
The Father smiles again;
'Tis by thine interceding breath
The Spirit dwells with men.

3 Till God in human flesh I see,
My thoughts no comfort find;
The holy, just, and sacred Three
Are terrors to my mind.

4 But if Immanuel's face appear,
My hope, my joy, begin;
His name forbids my slavish fear;
His grace removes my sin.

5 While Jews on their own law rely,
And Greeks of wisdom boast,
I love th' incarnate mystery,
And there I fix my trust.

DOWNS.

&c.

DUNFERMLINE. C. M. RAVENSCROFT'S Book of Psalms.
Specimen of the melody and harmony of 1621.

309. C. M. STEELE.

1 THE Saviour, O! what endless charms
Dwell in that blissful sound!
Its influence every fear disarms,
And spreads delight around.

2 Here pardon, life, and joy divine,
In rich profusion flow,
For guilty rebels, lost in sin,
And doomed to endless woe.

3 The mighty Former of the skies
Descends to our abode,
While angels view with wondering eyes,
And hail th' incarnate God.

4 How rich the depths of love divine!
Of bliss, a boundless store!
Dear Saviour, let me call thee mine;
I cannot wish for more.

5 On thee alone my hope relies;
Beneath thy cross I fall,
My Lord, my life, my sacrifice,
My Saviour, and my all.

342. C. M. BEDDOME.

1 JESUS, my Saviour and my God,
Thy wondrous love reveal;
Let angels spread thy name abroad,
And men thy glories tell

2 Let all, with sweet and cheerful voice,
Harmonious anthems raise;
Be thou the spring of all their joys,
The life of all their praise.

3 Be thou exalted in the heavens,
And o'er this earthly ball;
Let creatures into nothing sink,
And Christ be all in all.

RINETON. C. M. (Marlow.) WILLIAMS.

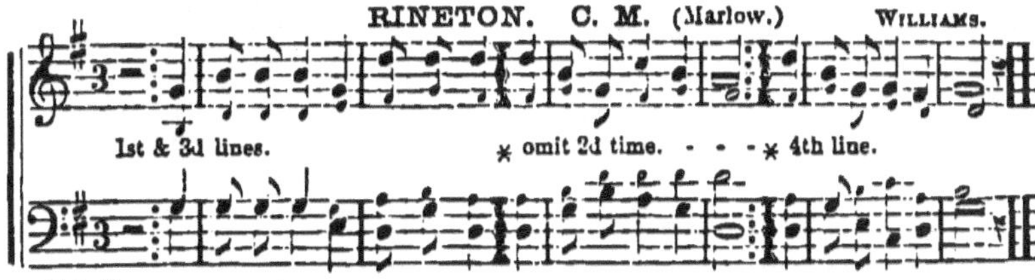

315. C. M. WATTS.

1 FATHER, I sing thy wondrous grace;
I bless my Saviour's name;
He bought salvation for the poor,
And bore the sinner's shame.

2 His deep distress has raised us high;
His duty and his zeal
Fulfilled the law which mortals broke,
And finished all thy will.

3 Zion is thine, most holy God;
Thy Son shall bless her gates;
And glory, purchased by his blood,
For thine own Israel waits.

4 Let heaven, and all that dwell on high,
To God their voices raise;
While lands and seas assist the sky,
And join t' advance his praise.

HOWARD'S. C. M.† Dr. Howard.‡

† Newly arranged and original melody restored. ‡ Attributed also to Mrs. Covansay.

310. C. M. Steele.

1 To our Redeemer's glorious name
Awake the sacred song!
O, may his love — immortal flame —
Tune every heart and tongue.

2 His love what mortal thought can reach!
What mortal tongue display!
Imagination's utmost stretch
In wonder dies away!

3 Dear Lord, while we, adoring, pay
Our humble thanks to thee,
May every heart with rapture say,
"The Saviour died for me."

4 O, may the sweet, the blissful theme
Fill every heart and tongue,
Till strangers love thy charming name,
And join the sacred song.

311. C. M. Beddome.

1 How great the wisdom, power, and grace
Which in redemption shine!
The heavenly host with joy confess
The work is all divine.

2 Before his feet they cast their crowns, —
Those crowns which Jesus gave, —
And, with ten thousand thousand tongues,
Proclaim his power to save.

3 They tell the triumphs of his cross,
The sufferings which he bore,
How low he stooped, how high he rose,
And rose to stoop no more.

4 O, let them still their voices raise,
And still their songs renew;
Salvation well deserves the praise
Of men, and angels too.

ADAGIO. C. M. Gregorian.

* Omit these chords in last line, and sing the last two chords instead.

316. C. M. Percy Chapel Col.

1 O, sing to Him who loved and bled;
Ye heaven-born sinners, sing;
'Twas Jesus suffered in your stead;
Own him your God and King.

2 He washed us, in his precious blood,
From every guilty stain;
He made us kings and priests to God,
And we shall with him reign.

3 Sing of his everlasting love,
From whence salvation flows;
Sing to him here, then sing above,
Of all that he bestows.

4 To him that loved us when depraved,
When guilty, blind, and poor;
To him that loved, and died, and saved,
Be glory evermore.

N. DOUGALL.

324. C. M. WATTS.

1 MY Saviour, my almighty Friend,
When I begin thy praise,
Where will the growing numbers end,
The numbers of thy grace?

2 Thou art my everlasting trust;
Thy goodness I adore;
And since I knew thy graces first,
I speak thy glories more.

3 When I am filled with sore distress
For some surprising sin,
I'll plead thy perfect righteousness,
And mention none but thine.

4 How will my lips rejoice to tell
The victories of my King!
My soul, redeemed from sin and hell,
Shall thy salvation sing.

329. C. M. STEELE.

1 AWAKE, awake the sacred song
To our incarnate Lord;
Let every heart and every tongue
Adore th' eternal Word.

2 When Jesus left his throne above,
To dwell with sinful worms,
Then shone almighty power and love,
In all their glorious forms.

3 To dwell with sorrow here below,
The Saviour left the skies,
And stooped to wretchedness and woe,
That worthless man might rise.

4 Adoring angels tuned their songs,
To hail the joyful day;
With rapture, then, let mortal tongues
Their grateful worship pay.

330. C. M. STEELE.

1 COME, ye that love the Saviour's name,
And joy to make it known,
The Sovereign of your hearts proclaim,
And bow before his throne.

2 When in his earthly courts we view
The glories of our King,
We long to love as angels do,
And wish like them to sing.

3 And shall we long and wish in vain?
Lord, teach our songs to rise:
Thy love can raise our humble strain,
And bid it reach the skies.

4 O, happy period! glorious day!
When heaven and earth shall raise,
With all their powers, their raptured lay,
To celebrate thy praise.

335. C. M. WATTS.

1 JESUS, our Lord, ascend thy throne,
And near thy Father sit:
In Zion shall thy power be known,
And make thy foes submit.

2 What wonders shall thy gospel do!
Thy converts shall surpass
The numerous drops of morning dew,
And own thy sovereign grace.

3 Jesus, our Priest, forever lives,
To plead for us above;
Jesus, our King, forever gives
The blessings of his love.

4 God shall exalt his glorious head,
And his high throne maintain;
Shall strike the powers and princes dead,
Who dare oppose his reign.

CORONATION. C. M. O. HOLDEN.

338. C. M. DUNCAN.

1 ALL hail the power of Jesus' name!
Let angels prostrate fall;
Bring forth the royal diadem,
And crown him Lord of all!

2 Ye chosen seed of Israel's race, —
A remnant weak and small, —
Hail him, who saves you by his grace,
And crown him Lord of all!

3 Ye Gentile sinners, ne'er forget
The wormwood and the gall;
Go, spread your trophies at his feet,
And crown him Lord of all!

4 Let every kindred, every tribe,
On this terrestrial ball,
To him all majesty ascribe,
And crown him Lord of all!

5 O that, with yonder sacred throng,
We at his feet may fall;
We'll join the everlasting song,
And crown him Lord of all!

350. C. M. WATTS.

1 HOSANNA to our conquering King!
All hail, incarnate Love!
Ten thousand songs and glories wait
To crown thy head above.

2 Thy victories and thy deathless fame
Through all the world shall run,
And everlasting ages sing
The triumphs thou hast won.

MILES' LANE. C. M. Peculiar. SHRUBSOLE.

DEVIZES. C. M. Tucker. Old arrangement.

332. C. M. WATTS.

1 LET earth, with every isle and sea,
Rejoice; the Saviour reigns:
His word, like fire, prepares his way,
And mountains melt to plains.

2 His presence sinks the proudest hills,
And makes the valleys rise;
The humble soul enjoys his smiles,
The haughty sinner dies.

3 Adoring angels, at his birth,
Made our Redeemer known;
Thus shall he come to judge the earth,
And angels guard his throne.

4 His foes shall tremble at his sight,
And hills and seas retire;
His children take their upward flight,
And leave the world on fire.

5 The seeds of joy and glory sown
For saints in darkness here,
Shall rise and spring in worlds unknown,
And a rich harvest bear.

343. C. M. WATTS.

1 BEHOLD the glories of the Lamb
Amid his Father's throne;
Prepare new honors for his name,
And songs before unknown.

2 Let elders worship at his feet,
The church adore around,
With vials full of odors sweet,
And harps of sweeter sound.

3 Those are the prayers of all the saints,
And these the hymns they raise:
Jesus is kind to our complaints;
He loves to hear our praise.

4 Now to the Lamb, that once was slain,
Be endless blessings paid;
Salvation, glory, joy remain
Forever on thy head.

5 Thou hast redeemed our souls with blood;
Hast set the prisoner free;
Hast made us kings and priests to God,
And we shall reign with thee.

348. C. M. C. WESLEY.

1 O FOR a thousand tongues to sing
My dear Redeemer's praise —
The glories of my God and King,
The triumphs of his grace!

2 My gracious Master and my God,
Assist me to proclaim,
To spread through all the earth abroad,
The honors of thy name.

3 Jesus! the name that calms our fears,
That bids our sorrows cease;
'Tis music in the sinner's ears;
'Tis life, and health, and peace.

4 He breaks the power of reigning sin;
He sets the prisoner free;
His blood can make the foulest clean;
His blood availed for me.

351. C. M. C. WESLEY.

1 O FOR a thousand seraph tongues
To bless th' incarnate Word!
O for a thousand thankful songs
In honor of my Lord!

2 Come, tune afresh your golden lyres,
Ye angels round the throne;
Ye saints, in all your sacred choirs,
Adore th' eternal Son.

LAUENBURG. C. M. German.

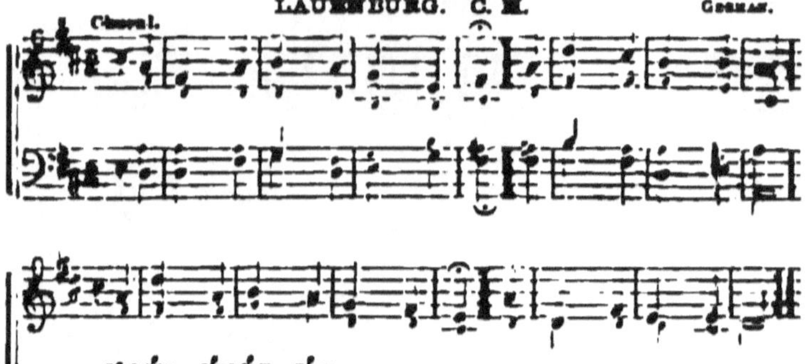

318. C. M. Watts.

1 Father, how wide thy glory shines!
How high thy wonders rise!
Known through the earth by thousand signs,
By thousand through the skies.

2 Those mighty orbs proclaim thy power;
Their motions speak thy skill;
And on the wings of every hour
We read thy patience still.

3 But when we view thy strange design
To save rebellious worms,
Where justice and compassion join
In their divinest forms,—

4 Here the whole Deity is known;
Nor dares a creature guess
Which of the glories brightest shone,
The justice or the grace.

5 Now the full glories of the Lamb
Adorn the heavenly plains;
Bright seraphs chant Immanuel's name,
And try their choicest strains.

6 O, may I bear some humble part
In that immortal song;
Wonder and joy shall tune my heart,
And love command my tongue.

337. C. M. Wallin.

1 Hail, mighty Jesus! how divine
Is thy victorious sword!
The stoutest rebel must resign
At thy commanding word.

2 How deep the wounds thine arrows give!
They pierce the hardest heart;
Thy smiles of grace the slain revive,
And joy succeeds to smart.

3 Still gird thy sword upon thy thigh;
Ride with majestic sway;
Go forth, great Prince, triumphantly,
And make thy foes obey.

4 And, when thy victories are complete,—
When all the chosen race
Shall round the throne of glory meet
To sing thy conquering grace,—

5 O, may my humble soul be found
Among that glorious throng;
And I with them thy praise will sound
In heaven's immortal song.

346. C. M. Watts.

1 Come, let us join our cheerful songs
With angels round the throne;
Ten thousand thousand are their tongues,
But all their joys are one.

2 "Worthy the Lamb that died," they cry,
"To be exalted thus:"
"Worthy the Lamb," our lips reply,
"For he was slain for us."

3 Jesus is worthy to receive
Honor and power divine;
And blessings, more than we can give,
Be, Lord, forever thine.

4 Let all that dwell above the sky,
And air, and earth, and seas,
Conspire to lift thy glories high,
And speak thy endless praise.

5 The whole creation join in one
To bless the sacred name
Of Him who sits upon the throne,
And to adore the Lamb.

ADAGIO. C. M.

Gregorian.

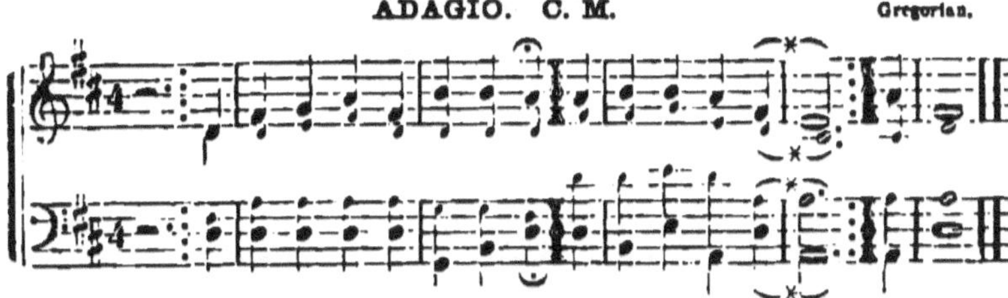

* Omit these chords in last line, and sing the last two chords instead.

308. C. M. WATTS.

1 PLUNGED in a gulf of dark despair,
We wretched sinners lay,
Without one cheerful beam of hope,
Or spark of glimmering day.

2 With pitying eyes the Prince of grace
Beheld our helpless grief;
He saw, and — O, amazing love! —
He flew to our relief.

3 Down from the shining seats above,
With joyful haste he fled,
Entered the grave in mortal flesh,
And dwelt among the dead.

4 O, for this love, let rocks and hills
Their lasting silence break,
And all harmonious human tongues
The Saviour's praises speak.

5 Angels, assist our mighty joys;
Strike all your harps of gold;
But when you raise your highest notes,
His love can ne'er be told.

WOODSTOCK. C. M.

DUTTON.

See note p. 124.

4 O'er the blue depths of Galilee
There comes a holier calm,
And Sharon waves, in solemn praise,
Her silent groves of palm.

5 "Glory to God!" the sounding skies
Aloud with anthems ring;
"Peace to the earth, good-will to men,
From heaven's eternal King!"

205. C. M. E. H. SEARS.

1 CALM on the listening ear of night
Come heaven's melodious strains,
Where wild Judea stretches far
Her silver-mantled plains:

2 Celestial choirs, from courts above,
Shed sacred glories there,
And angels, with their sparkling lyres,
Make music on the air.

3 The joyous hills of Palestine
Send back the glad reply,
And greet, from all their holy heights,
The dayspring from on high.

355. C. M. BICKERSTETH'S COL.

1 COME, Holy Spirit, from above,
With thy celestial fire;
Come, and with flames of zeal and love
Our hearts and tongues inspire.

2 The Spirit, by his heavenly breath,
New life creates within;
He quickens sinners from the death
Of trespasses and sin.

3 The things of Christ the Spirit takes,
And to our hearts reveals;
Our bodies he his temple makes,
And our redemption seals.

ST. MAGNUS. (Nottingham.) C. M. Jer. Clark. Died 1707.

367. C. M. Haweis.

1 Great Spirit, by whose mighty power
All creatures live and move,
On us thy benediction shower;
Inspire our souls with love.

2 Hail, Source of light! arise and shine;
All gloom and doubt dispel;
Give peace and joy, for we are thine;
In us forever dwell.

3 From death to life our spirits raise;
Complete redemption bring;
New tongues impart to speak the praise
Of Christ, our God and King.

4 Thine inward witness bear, unknown
To all the world beside;
Exulting, then, we feel and own
Our Saviour glorified.

382. C. M. Watts.

1 Why should the children of a King
Go mourning all their days?
Great Comforter, descend, and bring
Some tokens of thy grace.

2 Dost thou not dwell in all thy saints,
And seal them heirs of heaven?
When wilt thou banish my complaints,
And show my sins forgiven?

3 Assure my conscience of her part
In my Redeemer's blood,
And bear thy witness, with my heart,
That I am born of God.

4 Thou art the earnest of his love,
The pledge of joys to come;
And thy soft wings, celestial Dove,
Will safely bear me home.

373. C. M. Doddridge.

1 Great Father of our feeble race,
Behold, thy servants wait;
With longing eyes and lifted hands,
We flock around thy gate.

2 O, shed abroad that royal gift,
Thy Spirit, from above,
To bless our eyes with sacred light,
And fire our hearts with love.

3 With speedy flight may he descend,
And solid comfort bring,
And o'er our languid souls extend
His all reviving wing.

4 Blest earnest of eternal joy,
Declare our sins forgiven,
And bear, with energy divine,
Our raptured thoughts to heaven.

5 Diffuse, O God, refreshing showers,
That earth its fruit may yield,
And change this barren wilderness
To Carmel's flowery field.

353. C. M. Watts.

1 Come, Holy Spirit, heavenly Dove,
With all thy quickening powers,
Come, shed abroad a Saviour's love
In these cold hearts of ours.

2 Look! how we grovel here below,
Fond of these trifling toys!
Our souls can neither fly nor go,
To reach eternal joys.

3 In vain we tune our formal songs;
In vain we strive to rise;
Hosannas languish on our tongues,
And our devotion dies.

BALDWIN PLACE. C. M. B. F. EDMANDS.‡ 1850.

‡ The first three measures (rhythm excepted) from a German choral.

4 Dear Lord, and shall we ever live
At this poor, dying rate—
Our love so faint, so cold to thee,
And thine to us so great?

5 Come, Holy Spirit, heavenly Dove,
With all thy quickening powers,
Come, shed abroad a Saviour's love,
And that shall kindle ours.

360. C. M. PRATT'S COL.

1 ETERNAL Spirit, God of truth,
Our contrite hearts inspire;
Revive the flame of heavenly love,
And feed the pure desire.

2 'Tis thine to soothe the sorrowing mind,
With guilt and fear oppressed;
'Tis thine to bid the dying live,
And give the weary rest.

3 Subdue the power of every sin,
Whate'er that sin may be,
That we, with humble, holy heart,
May worship only thee.

4 Then with our spirits witness bear
That we are sons of God,
Redeemed from sin, from death, and hell,
Through Christ's atoning blood.

384. C. M. S. F. SMITH.

1 SPIRIT of holiness, descend;
Thy people wait for thee;
Thine ear, in kind compassion, lend;
Let us thy mercy see.

2 Behold, thy weary churches wait
With wishful, longing eyes;
Let us no more lie desolate;
O, bid thy light arise.

3 Thy light, that on our souls hath shone,
Leads us in hope to thee;
Let us not feel its rays alone—
Alone thy people be.

4 O, bring our dearest friends to God;
Remember those we love;
Fit them, on earth, for thine abode;
Fit them for joys above.

5 Spirit of holiness, 'tis thine
To hear our feeble prayer;
Come,—for we wait thy power divine,—
Let us thy mercy share.

385. C. M. BATHURST.

1 SPIRIT of holiness, look down,
Our fainting hearts to cheer;
And, when we tremble at thy frown,
O, bring thy comforts near.

2 The fear which thy convictions wrought,
O, let thy grace remove;
And may the souls which thou hast taught
To weep, now learn to love.

3 Now let thy saving mercy heal
The wounds it made before;
Now on our hearts impress thy seal,
That we may doubt no more.

4 Complete the work thou hast begun,
And make our darkness light,
That we a glorious race may run,
Till faith be lost in sight.

5 Then, as our wondering eyes discern
The Lord's unclouded face,
In fitter language we shall learn
To sing triumphant grace.

TALLIS. C. M. (Attalia) T. TALLIS. 1565.

375. C. M. CAMPBELL'S COL.

1 THY Spirit pour, O gracious Lord,
On all assembled here;
Let us receive th' ingrafted word
With meekness and with fear.

2 By faith in thee, the soul receives
New life, though dead before;
And he who in thy name believes
Shall live, to die no more.

3 Preserve the power of faith alive
In those who love thy name;
For sin and Satan daily strive
To quench the sacred flame.

4 Thy grace and mercy first prevailed
From death to set us free;
And, often since, our life had failed,
Unless renewed by thee.

5 To thee we look; to thee we bow;
To thee for help we call;
Our life, our resurrection, thou,
Our hope, our joy, our all.

377. C. M. WATTS.

1 NOT all the outward forms on earth,
Nor rites that God has given,
Nor will of man, nor blood, nor birth,
Can raise a soul to heaven.

2 The sovereign will of God alone
Creates us heirs of grace,
Born in the image of his Son,
A new, peculiar race.

3 The Spirit, like some heavenly wind,
Breathes on the sons of flesh,
Creates anew the carnal mind,
And forms the man afresh.

4 Our quickened souls awake, and rise
From their long sleep of death;
On heavenly things we fix our eyes,
And praise employs our breath.

379. C. M. BEDDOME.

1 THE blessèd Spirit, like the wind,
Blows when and where he please:
How happy are the men who feel
The soul-enlivening breeze!

2 He moulds the carnal mind afresh,
Subdues the power of sin,
Transforms the heart of stone to flesh,
And plants his grace within.

3 He sheds abroad the Father's love,
Applies redeeming blood,
Bids both our guilt and fear remove,
And brings us home to God.

4 Lord, fill each dead, benighted soul
With light, and life, and joy:
None can thy mighty power control
Or shall thy work destroy.

381. C. M. CAMPBELL'S COL.

1 THE God of grace will never leave
Or cast away his own;
And yet, when we his Spirit grieve,
His comforts are withdrawn.

2 If noisy war, or strife, abound,
We grieve the peaceful Dove;
His gracious aid is ever found
In paths of truth and love.

3 Should we indulge one secret sin,
Or disregard his laws,
His succor and support, within,
The Spirit, vexed, withdraws.

4 Forbid it, gracious Lord, that we,
Who, from thy hand, receive
The Spirit's power to make us free,
Should e'er that Spirit grieve.

HANLEY.

HOLDEN'S GLASGOW. C. M. HOLDEN.

386. C. M. WATTS.

1 LET all the heathen writers join
To form one perfect book,
Great God, if once compared with thine,
How mean their writings look!

2 Not the most perfect rules they gave
Could show one sin forgiven,
Nor lead a step beyond the grave;
But thine conduct to heaven.

3 I've seen an end of what we call
Perfection here below —
How short the powers of nature fall,
And can no farther go.

4 Yet men would fain be just with God,
By works their hands have wrought;
But thy commands, exceeding broad,
Extend to every thought.

5 In vain we boast perfection here,
While sin defiles our frame,
And sinks our virtues down so far,
They scarce deserve the name.

6 Our faith, and love, and every grace,
Fall far below thy word;
But perfect truth and righteousness
Dwell only with the Lord.

397. C. M. STEELE.

1 FATHER of mercies, in thy word
What endless glory shines!
Forever be thy name adored,
For these celestial lines.

2 'Tis here the tree of knowledge grows,
And yields a free repast;
Here purer sweets than nature knows
Invite the longing taste.

3 'Tis here the Saviour's welcome voice
Spreads heavenly peace around,
And life, and everlasting joys,
Attend the blissful sound.

4 O, may these heavenly pages be
My ever-dear delight;
And still new beauties may I see,
And still increasing light.

5 Divine Instructor, gracious Lord,
Be thou forever near;
Teach me to love thy sacred word,
And view my Saviour here.

401. C. M. STENNETT.

1 LET worldly men, from shore to shore,
Their chosen good pursue;
Thy word, O Lord, we value more
Than treasures of Peru.

2 Here mines of knowledge, love, and joy,
Are opened to our sight;
The purest gold without alloy,
And gems divinely bright.

3 The counsels of redeeming grace
These sacred leaves unfold;
And here the Saviour's lovely face
Our raptured eyes behold.

4 Here light, descending from above,
Directs our doubtful feet;
Here promises of heavenly love
Our ardent wishes meet.

5 Our numerous griefs are here redressed,
And all our wants supplied:
Nought we can ask to make us blest
Is in this book denied.

389. C. M. WATTS.

1 O, HOW I love thy holy law!
'Tis daily my delight;
And thence my meditations draw
Divine advice by night.

2 My waking eyes prevent the day,
To meditate thy word;
My soul with longing melts away,
To hear thy gospel, Lord.

3 Thy heavenly words my heart engage,
And well employ my tongue,
And, through my weary pilgrimage,
Yield me a heavenly song.

4 When nature sinks, and spirits droop,
Thy promises of grace
Are pillars to support my hope,
And there I write thy praise.

395. C. M. COWPER.

1 WHAT glory gilds the sacred page!
Majestic, like the sun,
It gives a light to every age;
It gives, but borrows none.

2 The power that gave it still supplies
The gracious light and heat:
Its truths upon the nations rise;
They rise, but never set.

3 Let everlasting thanks be thine
For such a bright display
As makes a world of darkness shine
With beams of heavenly day.

4 My soul rejoices to pursue
The steps of Him I love,
Till glory breaks upon my view
In brighter worlds above.

396. C. M. CAMPBELL'S COL.

1 A GLORY in the word we find,
When grace restores our sight;
But sin has darkened all the mind,
And veiled the heavenly light.

2 When God the Spirit clears our view,
How bright the doctrines shine!
Their holy fruits and sweetness show
The Author is divine.

3 How blest are we with open face
To view thy glory, Lord,
And all thy image here to trace
Reflected in thy word!

4 O, teach us, as we look, to grow
In holiness and love,
That we may long to see and know
Thy glorious face above.

402. C. M. WATTS.

1 LORD, I have made thy word my choice,
My lasting heritage;
There shall my noblest powers rejoice,
My warmest thoughts engage.

2 I'll read the histories of thy love,
And keep thy laws in sight,
While through the promises I rove,
With ever-fresh delight.

3 'Tis a broad land, of wealth unknown,
Where springs of life arise,
Seeds of immortal bliss are sown,
And hidden glory lies.

4 The best relief that mourners have,
It makes our sorrows blest;
Our fairest hope beyond the grave,
And our eternal rest.

DURHAM. C. M. Scotch Psalter. [1] 1635.

[1] Rhythm changed; — may be sung in equal notes.

392. C. M. FAWCETT.

1 How precious is the book divine,
By inspiration given!
Bright as a lamp its doctrines shine,
To guide our souls to heaven.

2 It sweetly cheers our drooping hearts
In this dark vale of tears;
Life, light, and joy, it still imparts,
And quells our rising fears.

3 This lamp, through all the tedious night
Of life shall guide our way,
Till we behold the clearer light
Of an eternal day.

393. C. M. EPIS. COL.

1 GREAT God, with wonder and with praise
On all thy works I look;
But still thy wisdom, power, and grace,
Shine brightest in thy book.

2 Here are my choicest treasures hid;
Here my best comfort lies,
Here my desires are satisfied;
And here my hopes arise.

3 Lord, make me understand thy law;
Show what my faults have been;
And from thy gospel let me draw
The pardon of my sin.

398. C. M. WATTS.

1 LADEN with guilt, and full of fears,
I fly to thee, my Lord;
And not a gleam of hope appears,
But in thy written word.

2 The volume of my Father's grace
Does all my grief assuage;
Here I behold my Saviour's face
In almost every page.

3 This is the field where hidden lies
The pearl of price unknown;
That merchant is divinely wise
Who makes this pearl his own.

4 Here consecrated water flows,
To quench my thirst of sin;
'Tis here the tree of knowledge grows;
No danger dwells therein.

399. C. M. EVAN. MAG.

1 HAIL, sacred truth! whose piercing rays
Dispel the shades of night,
Diffusing o'er the mental world
The healing beams of light.

2 Thy word, O Lord, with friendly aid,
Restores our wandering feet,
Converts the sorrows of the mind
To joys divinely sweet.

3 O, send thy light and truth abroad
In all their radiant blaze,
And bid th' admiring world adore
The glories of thy grace.

408. C. M. WATTS.

1 BLEST are the souls that hear and know
The gospel's joyful sound;
Peace shall attend the paths they go,
And light their steps surround.

2 Their joy shall bear their spirits up,
Through their Redeemer's name;
His righteousness exalts their hope,
Nor Satan dares condemn.

3 The Lord, our glory and defence,
Strength and salvation gives;
Israel, thy King forever reigns,
Thy God forever lives.

ST. STEPHEN'S. C. M. Rev. Wm. Jones.

410. C. M. Medley.

1 O, what amazing words of grace
Are in the gospel found!
Suited to every sinner's case
Who hears the joyful sound.

2 Come, then, with all your wants and wounds,
Your every burden bring;
Here love, unchanging love, abounds,
A deep, celestial spring.

3 This spring with living water flows,
And heavenly joy imparts:
Come, thirsty souls, your wants disclose,
And drink with thankful hearts.

4 A host of sinners, vile as you,
Have here found life and peace;
Come, then, and prove its virtues too,
And drink, adore, and bless.

411. C. M. Watts.

1 Christ and his cross are all our theme;
The mysteries that we speak
Are scandal in the Jews' esteem,
And folly to the Greek.

2 But souls enlightened from above
With joy receive the word;
They see what wisdom, power, and love
Shine in their dying Lord.

3 The vital savor of his name
Restores their fainting breath;
But unbelief perverts the same
To guilt, despair, and death.

4 Till God diffuse his graces down,
Like showers of heavenly rain,
In vain Apollos sows the ground,
And Paul may plant in vain.

423. C. M. Steele.

1 The Saviour calls; let every ear
Attend the heavenly sound;
Ye doubting souls, dismiss your fear;
Hope smiles reviving round.

2 For every thirsty, longing heart,
Here streams of bounty flow;
And life, and health, and bliss impart,
To banish mortal woe.

3 Ye sinners, come; 'tis mercy's voice;
That gracious voice obey;
'Tis Jesus calls to heavenly joys;
And can you yet delay?

4 Dear Saviour, draw reluctant hearts;
To thee let sinners fly,
And take the bliss thy love imparts,
And drink, and never die.

425. C. M. Doddridge.

1 Come, let us join our souls to God
In everlasting bands,
And seize the blessings he bestows
With eager hearts and hands.

2 Come, let us to his temple haste,
And seek his favor there,
Before his footstool humbly bow,
And offer fervent prayer.

3 Come, let us share, without delay,
The blessings of his grace;
Nor shall the years of distant life
Their memory e'er efface.

4 O, may our children ever haste
To seek their fathers' God,
Nor e'er forsake the happy path
Their fathers' feet have trod.

418. C. M. HUNTINGDON'S COL.

1 COME, sinner, to the gospel feast;
O, come without delay;
For there is room in Jesus' breast
For all who will obey.

2 There's room in God's eternal love
To save thy precious soul;
Room in the Spirit's grace above
To heal and make thee whole.

3 There's room within the church, redeemed
With blood of Christ divine;
Room in the white-robed throng, convened,
For that dear soul of thine.

4 There's room in heaven among the choir,
And harps and crowns of gold,
And glorious palms of victory there,
And joys that ne'er were told.

5 There's room around thy Father's board
For thee and thousands more;
O, come and welcome to the Lord;
Yea, come this very hour.

420. C. M. STEELE.

1 YE wretched, hungry, starving poor,
Behold a royal feast,
Where Mercy spreads her bounteous store
For every humble guest.

2 There Jesus stands with open arms;
He calls — he bids you come:
Though guilt restrains, and fear alarms,
Behold, there yet is room.

3 O, come, and with his children taste
The blessings of his love;
While hope expects the sweet repast
Of nobler joys above.

4 There, with united heart and voice,
Before th' eternal throne,
Ten thousand thousand souls rejoice,
In songs on earth unknown.

5 And yet ten thousand thousand more
Are welcome still to come:
Ye longing souls, the grace adore,
And enter while there's room.

433. C. M. E. JONES.

1 COME, weary sinner, in whose breast
A thousand thoughts revolve;
Come, with your guilt and fear oppressed,
And make this last resolve: —

2 "I'll go to Jesus, though my sin
Hath like a mountain rose;
I know his courts; I'll enter in,
Whatever may oppose.

3 "I'll prostrate lie before his throne,
And there my guilt confess;
I'll tell him I'm a wretch undone,
Without his sovereign grace.

4 "I'll to the gracious King approach,
Whose sceptre pardon gives;
Perhaps he may command my touch,
And then the suppliant lives.

5 "Perhaps he will admit my plea,
Perhaps will hear my prayer;
But, if I perish, I will pray,
And perish only there.

6 "I can but perish if I go;
I am resolved to try;
For if I stay away, I know
I must forever die."

‡ Ascribed by some to Dr. Croft.

422. C. M. WATTS.

1 LET every mortal ear attend,
And every heart rejoice;
The trumpet of the gospel sounds
With an inviting voice.

2 Ho! all ye hungry, starving souls,
That feed upon the wind,
And vainly strive with earthly toys
To fill an empty mind,—

3 Eternal Wisdom has prepared
A soul-reviving feast,
And bids your longing appetites
The rich provision taste.

4 Ho! ye that pant for living streams,
And pine away, and die,
Here you may quench your raging thirst
With springs that never dry.

5 The happy gates of gospel grace
Stand open night and day;
Lord, we are come to seek supplies,
And drive our wants away.

424. C. M. DODDRIDGE.

1 THE King of heaven his table spreads,
And dainties crown the board:
Not Paradise, with all its joys,
Could such delight afford.

2 Ye hungry poor, that long have strayed
In sin's dark mazes, come;
Come from your most obscure retreats,
And grace shall find you room.

3 Millions of souls, in glory now,
Were fed and feasted here;
And millions more, still on the way,
Around the board appear.

4 Yet are his house and heart so large,
That millions more may come;
Nor could the whole assembled world
O'erfill the spacious room.

5 All things are ready; come away,
Nor weak excuses frame:
Come, taste the dainties of the feast,
And bless the Master's name.

428. C. M. WATTS.

1 JESUS, thy blessings are not few,
Nor is thy gospel weak;
Thy grace can melt the stubborn Jew,
And bow th' aspiring Greek.

2 Wide as the reach of Satan's rage
Doth thy salvation flow;
'Tis not confined to sex or age,
The lofty or the low.

3 While grace is offered to the prince,
The poor may take their share;
No mortal has a just pretence
To perish in despair.

4 Come, all ye vilest sinners, come;
He'll form your souls anew:
His gospel and his heart have room
For rebels such as you.

5 His doctrine is almighty love;
There's virtue in his name
To turn the raven to a dove,
The lion to a lamb.

ALBANY.

RINETON. C. M. (Marlow.) WILLIAMS.

434. C. M. HYMNS OF ZION.

1 AMAZING sight! the Saviour stands
And knocks at every door!
Ten thousand blessings in his hands,
To satisfy the poor.

2 "Behold," he saith, "I bleed and die
To bring you to my rest:
Hear, sinners, while I'm passing by,
And be forever blest.

3 "Will you despise my bleeding love,
And choose the way to hell?
Or in the glorious realms above,
With me, forever dwell?

4 "Say, will you hear my gracious voice,
And have your sins forgiven?
Or will you make that wretched choice,
And bar yourselves from heaven?"

447. C. M. FAWCETT.

1 SINNER, the voice of God regard;
His mercy speaks to-day;
He calls you, by his sovereign word,
From sin's destructive way.

2 Like the rough sea, that cannot rest,
You live devoid of peace;
A thousand stings within your breast
Deprive your soul of ease.

3 Why will you in the crooked ways
Of sin and folly go?
In pain you travel all your days,
To reap immortal woe.

4 But he who turns to God shall live,
Through his abounding grace;
His mercy will the guilt forgive
Of those who seek his face.

5 Bow to the sceptre of his word,
Renouncing every sin;
Submit to him, your sovereign Lord,
And learn his will divine.

6 His love exceeds your highest thoughts;
He pardons like a God;
He will forgive your numerous faults
Through our Redeemer's blood.

456. C. M. EPIS. COL.

1 SEE, in the vineyard of the Lord
A barren fig-tree stands;
It yields no fruit, no blossom bears,
Though planted by his hands.

2 From year to year he seeks for fruit,
And still no fruit is found;
It stands, amid the living trees,
A cumberer of the ground.

3 But, see, an Intercessor pleads,
The barren tree to spare;
"Let Justice still withhold his hand,
And grant another year.

4 "Perhaps some means of grace untried
May reach the stony heart;
The softening dews of heavenly grace
May life anew impart.

5 "But if these means should prove in vain,
And still no fruit is found,
Then Mercy shall no longer plead,
But Justice cut it down."

LITCHFIELD.

452. C. M. Doddridge.

1 "Repent!" the voice celestial cries;
No longer dare delay:
The soul that scorns the mandate, dies,
And meets a fiery day.

2 No more the sovereign eye of God
O'erlooks the crimes of men;
His heralds now are sent abroad
To warn the world of sin.

3 O sinners, in his presence bow,
And all your guilt confess;
Accept the offered Saviour now,
Nor trifle with his grace.

4 Soon will the awful trumpet sound,
And call you to his bar;
His mercy knows th' appointed bound,
And yields to justice there.

5 Amazing love, that yet will call,
And yet prolong our days!
Our hearts, subdued by goodness, fall,
And weep, and love, and praise.

458. C. M. Harbottle.

1 See how the fruitless fig-tree stands
Beneath the owner's frown;
The axe is lifted in his hands,
To cut the cumberer down.

2 "Year after year, I come," he cries,
"And still no fruit is shown;
I see but empty leaves arise;
Then cut the cumberer down.

3 "The axe of death, at one sharp stroke,
Shall make my justice known;
Each bough shall tremble at the shock
Which cuts the cumberer down."

4 Sinner, beware! — the axe of death
Is raised, and aimed at thee:
A while thy Maker spares thy breath;
Beware, O barren tree!

459. C. M. Addison.

1 When, rising from the bed of death,
O'erwhelmed with guilt and fear,
I see my Maker face to face, —
O, how shall I appear!

2 If yet, while pardon may be found,
And mercy may be sought,
My heart with inward terror shrinks,
And trembles at the thought, —

3 When thou, O Lord, shalt stand disclosed
In majesty severe,
And sit in judgment on my soul, —
O, how shall I appear!

4 But there's forgiveness, Lord, with thee;
Thy nature is benign;
Thy pardoning mercy I implore,
For mercy, Lord, is thine.

508. C. M. Percy Chapel Col.

1 Father, I stretch my hands to thee;
No other help I know;
If thou withdraw thyself from me,
Ah, whither shall I go?

2 What did thine only Son endure
Before I drew my breath!
What pain, what labor, to secure
My soul from endless death!

3 Author of faith, to thee I lift
My weary, longing eyes;
O, may I now receive that gift;
My soul, without it, dies.

‡ The first three measures (rhythm excepted) from a German choral.

460. C. M. MIDDLETON.

1 As o'er the past my memory strays,
Why heaves the secret sigh?
'Tis that I mourn departed days,
Still unprepared to die.

2 The world and wordly things beloved
My anxious thoughts employed;
And time, unhallowed, unimproved,
Presents a fearful void.

3 Yet, holy Father, wild despair
Chase from my laboring breast:
Thy grace it is which prompts the prayer;
That grace can do the rest.

4 My life's brief remnant all be thine;
And when thy sure decree
Bids me this fleeting breath resign,
O, speed my soul to thee.

461. C. M. STEELE.

1 DEAR Saviour, when my thoughts recall
The wonders of thy grace,
Low at thy feet, ashamed I fall,
And hide this wretched face.

2 Shall love like thine be thus repaid?
Ah, vile, ungrateful heart!
By earth's low cares detained, betrayed,
From Jesus to depart;—

3 From Jesus, who alone can give
True pleasure, peace, and rest;—
When absent from my Lord, I live
Unsatisfied, unblest.

4 But he, for his own mercy's sake,
My wandering soul restores;
He bids the mourning heart partake
The pardon it implores.

5 O, while I breathe to thee, my Lord,
The penitential sigh,
Confirm the kind, forgiving word,
With pity in thine eye.

6 Then shall the mourner, at thy feet,
Rejoice to seek thy face;
And, grateful, own how kind, how sweet,
Is thy forgiving grace.

473. C. M. S. STENNETT.

1 WITH tears of anguish I lament,
Here at thy cross, my God,
My passion, pride, and discontent,
And vile ingratitude.

2 O, was there e'er a heart so base,
So false, as mine has been —
So faithless to its promises,
So prone to every sin?

3 Yet, I remember, thy commands
Are holy, just, and true;
I feel that what my God demands
Is his most rightful due.

4 Thy word I hear, thy counsels weigh,
And all thy works approve:
Still, nature finds it hard t' obey,
And harder yet to love.

5 How long, dear Saviour, shall I feel
This warfare in my breast?
In mercy bow this stubborn will,
And give my spirit rest.

CORINTH.

YORK. C. M. Psalter, 1615

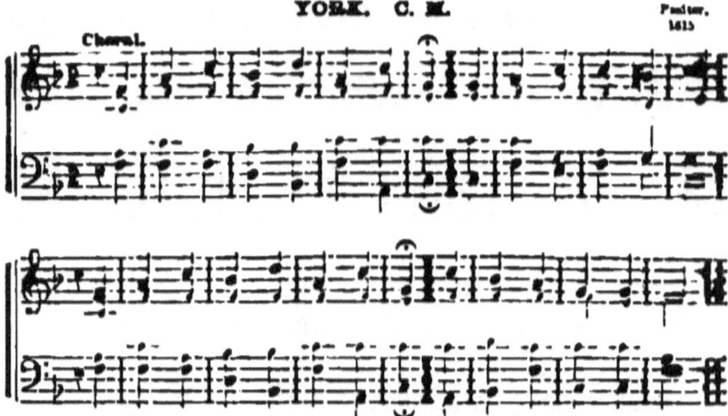

466. C. M. Anon.

1 With guilt oppressed, bowed down with sin,
Beneath its load I groan;
Give me, O Lord, a heart of flesh;
Remove this heart of stone.

2 A burdened sinner, lo! I come,
In dread of death and hell;
O, seal my pardon with thy blood,
And all my fears dispel.

3 Nor peace, nor rest, my soul can find,
Till thy dear cross I see;
Till there in humble faith I cry,
"The Saviour died for me."

4 O, give this true and living faith,
This soul supporting view;
Till old things be forever past,
And all within be new.

469. C. M. Newton.

1 In evil long I took delight,
Unawed by shame or fear,
Till a new object struck my sight,
And stopped my wild career.

2 I saw one hanging on a tree,
In agonies and blood;
He fixed his languid eyes on me,
As near his cross I stood.

3 O, never, till my latest breath,
Shall I forget that look;
It seemed to charge me with his death,
Though not a word he spoke.

4 My conscience felt and owned the guilt;
It plunged me in despair;
I saw my sins his blood had spilt,
And helped to nail him there.

5 A second look he gave, which said,
"I freely all forgive;
This blood is for thy ransom paid;
I die that thou mayst live."

6 Thus, while his death my sin displays
In all its darkest hue,
Such is the mystery of grace,
It seals my pardon too.

478. C. M. Watts.

1 Lord, how secure my conscience was,
And felt no inward dread!
I was alive without the law,
And thought my sins were dead.

2 My hopes of heaven were firm and bright;
But since the precept came
With such convincing power and light,
I find how vile I am.

3 My guilt appeared but small before,
Till I with terror saw
How perfect, holy, just, and pure
Is thine eternal law.

4 Then felt my soul the heavy load;
My sins revived again;
I had provoked a dreadful God,
And all my hopes were slain.

5 My God, I cry with every breath,
Exert thy power to save;
O, break the yoke of sin and death,
And thus redeem the slave.

485. C. M. Watts.

1 O God of mercy, hear my call;
My load of guilt remove;
Break down this separating wall
That bars me from thy love.

WINDSOR. C. M. English Psalter, 1592.

2 Give me the presence of thy grace;
Then my rejoicing tongue
Shall speak aloud thy righteousness,
And make thy praise my song.

3 No blood of goats, nor heifer slain,
For sin could e'er atone;
The death of Christ shall still remain
Sufficient and alone.

4 A soul, oppressed with sin's desert,
My God will ne'er despise;
A broken and a contrite heart
Is our best sacrifice.

486. C. M. Watts.

1 And are we, wretches, yet alive?
And do we yet rebel?
'Tis boundless, 'tis amazing love,
That bears us up from hell.

2 The burden of our weighty guilt
Would sink us down to flames;
And threatening terror rolls above,
To crush our feeble frames.

3 Almighty Goodness cries, "Forbear,"
And straight the thunder stays;
And dare we now provoke his wrath,
And weary out his grace?

4 Lord, we have long abused thy love,
Too long indulged our sin;
Our aching hearts now bleed to see
What rebels we have been.

5 No more, ye lusts, shall ye command;
No more will we obey;
Stretch out, O God, thy conquering hand,
And drive thy foes away.

492. C. M. Watts.

1 Great King of glory and of grace,
We own, with humble shame,
How vile is our degenerate race,
And our first father's name.

2 We live estranged, afar from God,
And love the distance well;
With haste we run the dangerous road
That leads to death and hell.

3 And can such rebels be restored?
Such natures made divine?
Let sinners see thy glory, Lord,
And feel this power of thine.

4 We raise our Father's name on high,
Who his own Spirit sends
To bring rebellious strangers nigh,
And turn his foes to friends.

494. C. M. Watts.

1 Vain are the hopes the sons of men
On their own works have built;
Their hearts by nature all unclean,
And all their actions guilt.

2 Let Jew and Gentile silent bow,
Without a murmuring word;
Let all the race of man confess
Their guilt before the Lord.

3 In vain we ask God's righteous law
To justify us now;
Since to convince and to condemn
Is all the law can do.

4 Jesus, how glorious is thy grace!
When in thy name we trust,
Our faith receives a righteousness
That makes the sinner just.

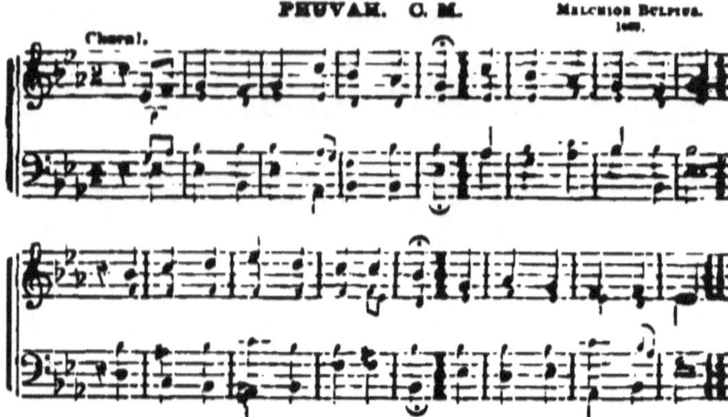

488. C. M. C. WESLEY.

1 O FOR that tenderness of heart
Which bows before the Lord,
That owns how just and good thou art,
And trembles at thy word!

2 O for those humble, contrite tears,
Which from repentance flow,
That sense of guilt, which, trembling, fears
The long-suspended blow!

3 O Lord, to me in pity give
For sin the deep distress,
The pledge thou wilt at last receive,
And bid me die in peace.

4 O, fill my soul with faith and love,
And strength to do thy will;
Raise my desires and hopes above;
Thyself to me reveal.

499. C. M. STEELE.

1 AND will the Lord thus condescend
To visit sinful worms?
Thus at the door shall Mercy stand,
In all her winning forms?

2 Surprising grace!—and shall my heart
Unmoved and cold remain?
Has it no soft, no tender part?
Must Mercy plead in vain?

3 Shall Jesus for admission sue,
His charming voice unheard?
And shall my heart, his rightful due,
Remain forever barred?

4 O Lord, exert thy conquering grace;
Thy mighty power display;
One beam of glory from thy face
Can melt my sin away.

504. C. M. PRES. COL.

1 O LORD, when billows o'er me rise,
When deep cries out to deep,
When angry clouds obscure the skies,
My soul in safety keep.

2 Thy promise has in troubles past
My staff of succor been;
Support me now, while trials last,
Nor leave me in my sin.

3 No sacrifice my soul can plead,
But that rich offering paid,
When Christ on Calvary deigned to bleed,
And full atonement made.

4 Forever here I rest my cause;
In faith I make this plea:
Christ hath obeyed thy righteous laws;
Christ hath expired for me.

514. C. M. WATTS.

1 MISTAKEN souls that dream of heaven,
And make their empty boast
Of inward joys, and sins forgiven,
While they are slaves to lust!

2 How vain are fancy's airy flights,
If faith be cold and dead;
None but a living power unites
To Christ, the living Head.

3 'Tis faith that purifies the heart;
'Tis faith that works by love;
That bids all sinful joys depart,
And lifts the thoughts above.

4 This faith shall every fear control
By its celestial power,
With holy triumph fill the soul
In death's approaching hour.

HAMMOND. C. M. No. 1. N. D. Gould. From N. C. Har.

463. C. M. Heginbotham.

1 And can mine eyes, without a tear,
A weeping Saviour see?
Shall I not weep his groans to hear,
Who groaned and died for me?

2 Blest Jesus, let those tears of thine
Subdue each stubborn foe;
Come, fill my heart with love divine,
And bid my sorrows flow.

481. C. M. Village Hymns.

1 The long-lost son, with streaming eyes,
From folly just awake,
Reviews his wanderings with surprise;
His heart begins to break.

2 "I starve," he cries, "nor can I bear
The famine in this land,
While servants of my Father share
The bounty of his hand.

3 "With deep repentance I'll return
And seek my Father's face;
Unworthy to be called a son,
I'll ask a servant's place."

4 Far off the Father saw him move,
In pensive silence mourn,
And quickly ran, with arms of love,
To welcome his return.

5 Through all the courts the tidings flew,
And spread the joy around;
The angels tuned their harps anew;
The long-lost son is found!

HAMMOND. C. M. No. 2. N. D. Gould. From N. C. Har.

MARTYRS. C. M. ‡ Ravenscroft's Psalter. 1621.

‡ "Plaintive Martyrs, worthy of the name." — *Burns.*

472. C. M. Watts.

1 Alas! and did my Saviour bleed?
And did my Sovereign die?
Would he devote that sacred head
For such a worm as I?

2 Was it for crimes that I had done
He groaned upon the tree?
Amazing pity! grace unknown!
And love beyond degree!

3 Well might the sun in darkness hide,
And shut his glories in,
When Christ, the mighty Maker, died
For man the creature's sin.

4 Thus might I hide my blushing face
While his dear cross appears,
Dissolve my heart in thankfulness,
And melt mine eyes to tears.

5 But drops of grief can ne'er repay
The debt of love I owe:
Here, Lord, I give myself away;
'Tis all that I can do.

503. C. M. Needham.

1 Kind are the words that Jesus speaks
To cheer the drooping saint:
"My grace sufficient is for you,
Though nature's powers may faint.

2 "My grace its glories shall display,
And make your griefs remove;
Your weakness shall the triumphs tell
Of boundless power and love."

3 What though my griefs are not removed?
Yet why should I despair?
For, if my Saviour's arm support,
I can the burden bear.

4 O thou, my Saviour and my Lord,
'Tis good to trust thy name:
Thy power, thy faithfulness, and love,
Will ever be the same.

5 Weak as I am, yet through thy grace
I all things can perform,
And, smiling, triumph in thy name
Amid the raging storm.

521. C. M. Cotterill's Col.

1 Out of the deeps, O Lord, we call,
While guilty fears oppress;
Do thou, with ear attentive, hear
The voice of our distress.

2 If thou our sins severely mark,
And strict account demand,
O, who, of all the sons of men,
Before thy face shall stand:

3 But, Lord, 'tis thine to spare and save —
With mercy souls to win;
For mercy binds the grateful heart,
And makes it fear to sin.

4 We trust in thee; in thee, O Lord,
Is full redemption found;
Thy mercy pardons every sin,
And closes every wound.

560. C. M. Pratt's Col.

1 Still on the Lord thy burden roll,
Nor let a care remain,
His mighty arm shall bear thy soul,
And all thy griefs sustain.

2 Ne'er will the Lord his aid deny
To those who trust his love:
The men, who on his grace rely,
Nor earth nor hell shall move.

BARBY. C. M. TANSUR.

500. C. M. WATTS.

1 How sad our state by nature is!
Our sin, how deep it stains!
And Satan binds our captive minds
Fast in his slavish chains.

2 But, hark! a voice of sovereign love!
'Tis Christ's inviting word—
"Ho! ye despairing sinners, come,
And trust upon the Lord."

3 My soul obeys th' almighty call,
And runs to this relief;
I would believe thy promise, Lord;
O, help my unbelief.

4 To the dear fountain of thy blood,
Incarnate God, I fly;
Here let me wash my spotted soul
From stains of deepest dye.

5 A guilty, weak, and helpless worm,
On thy kind arms I fall;
Be thou my strength and righteousness,
My Saviour and my all.

501. C. M. WATTS.

1 I WAITED patient for the Lord;
He bowed to hear my cry;
He saw me resting on his word,
And brought salvation nigh.

2 He raised me from a gloomy pit,
Where, mourning, long I lay,
And from my bonds released my feet—
Deep bonds of miry clay.

3 Firm on a rock he made me stand,
And taught my cheerful tongue
To praise the wonders of his hand,
In new and thankful song.

4 I'll spread his works of grace abroad;
The saints with joy shall hear,
And sinners learn to make my God
Their only hope and fear.

5 How many are thy thoughts of love!
Thy mercies, Lord, how great!
We have not words nor hours enough
Their numbers to repeat.

509. C. M. STEELE.

1 THOU lovely Source of true delight,
Unseen whom I adore,
Unveil thy beauties to my sight,
That I may love thee more.

2 Thy glory o'er creation shines;
But in thy sacred word
I read, in fairer, brighter lines,
My bleeding, dying Lord.

3 'Tis here, whene'er my comforts droop,
And sins and sorrows rise,
Thy love, with cheerful beams of hope,
My fainting heart supplies.

4 But, ah, too soon the pleasing scene
Is clouded o'er with pain;
My gloomy fears arise between,
And I again complain.

5 Jesus, my Lord, my life, my light,
O, come with blissful ray;
Break, radiant through the shades of night,
And chase my fears away.

6 Then shall my soul with rapture trace
The wonders of thy love;
Then shall I see thy glorious face
In endless joy above.

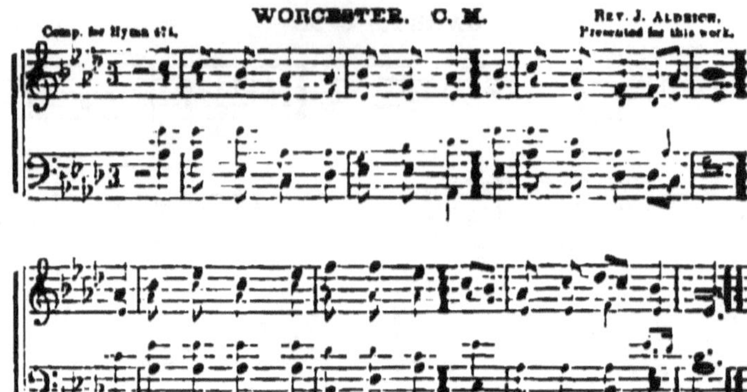

474. C. M. S. Stennett.

1 Dear Saviour, prostrate at thy feet
A guilty rebel lies,
And upward to thy mercy-seat
Presumes to lift his eyes.

2 If tears of sorrow would suffice
To pay the debt I owe,
Tears should from both my weeping eyes
In ceaseless torrents flow.

3 But no such sacrifice I plead
To expiate my guilt;
No tears, but those which thou hast shed —
No blood, but thou hast spilt.

4 I plead thy sorrows, gracious Lord;
Do thou my sins forgive:
Thy justice will approve the word
That bids the sinner live.

482. C. M. Steele.

1 O Lord, thy tender mercy hears
Contrition's humble sigh;
Thy hand, indulgent, wipes the tears
From sorrow's weeping eye.

2 See, low before thy throne of grace,
A sinful wanderer mourn;
Hast thou not bid me seek thy face?
Hast thou not said, "Return"?

3 O, shine on this benighted heart,
With beams of mercy shine;
And let thy healing voice impart
A taste of joys divine.

4 Thy presence only can bestow
Delights which never cloy;
Be this my solace here below,
And my eternal joy.

493. C. M. Jervis.

1 Sweet is the friendly voice which speaks
The words of life and peace;
That bids the penitent rejoice,
And sin and sorrow cease.

2 No healing balm on earth, like this,
Can cheer the contrite heart;
No flattering dreams of earthly bliss
Such pure delight impart.

3 Thou still art merciful and kind;
Thy mercy, Lord, reveal:
The broken heart thy grace can bind,
The wounded spirit heal.

4 Let thy bright presence, Lord, restore
True peace within my breast;
Conduct me in the path that leads
To everlasting rest.

510. C. M. Beddome.

1 'Tis faith that lays the sinner low,
And covers him with shame;
Renouncing all self righteousness,
It trusts in Jesus' name.

2 Faith works with power, but will not plead
The best of works when done;
It knows no other ground of trust
But in the Lord alone.

3 It gives no title, but receives;
No blessing it procures;
Yet, where it truly lives and reigns,
All blessings it insures.

4 Its sole dependence and its stay
Is Jesus' righteousness;
'Tis thus salvation is by faith,
And all of sovereign grace.

COMMUNION NEW. C. M. SUMNER HILL. From The Sanctus.

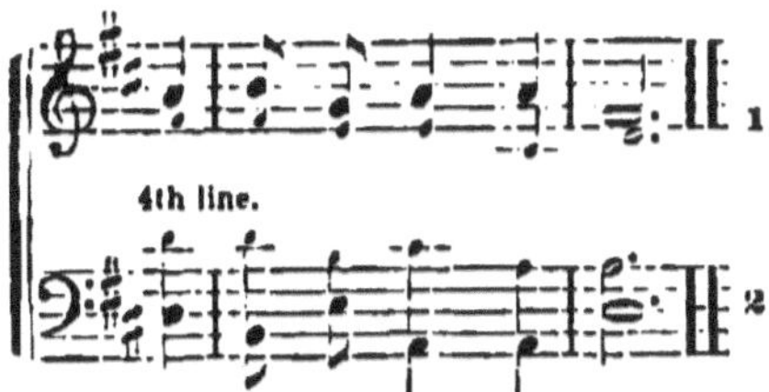

5 The more this principle prevails,
The more is grace adored;
No glory it assumes; but gives
All glory to the Lord.

511. C. M. BATH COL.

1 O FOR a faith that will not shrink,
Though pressed by every foe,
That will not tremble on the brink
Of any earthly woe! —

2 That will not murmur nor complain
Beneath the chastening rod,
But, in the hour of grief or pain,
Will lean upon its God; —

3 A faith that shines more bright and clear
When tempests rage without;
That when in danger knows no fear,
In darkness feels no doubt; —

4 That bears, unmoved, the world's dread frown,
Nor heeds its scornful smile; —
That seas of troubles cannot drown,
Nor Satan's arts beguile; —

5 A faith that keeps the narrow way
Till life's last hour is fled,
And with a pure and heavenly ray
Lights up a dying bed; —

6 Lord, give us such a faith as this:
And then, whate'er may come,
We'll taste, e'en here, the hallowed bliss
Of an eternal home.

ALBANY.

&c.

506. C. M. WATTS.

1 FAITH is the brightest evidence
Of things beyond our sight;
It pierces through the veil of sense,
And dwells in heavenly light.

2 It sets time past in present view,
Brings distant prospects home,
Of things a thousand years ago,
Or thousand years to come.

3 By faith we know the world was made
By God's almighty word;
We know the heavens and earth shall fade,
And be again restored.

4 Abrah'm obeyed the Lord's command,
From his own country driven;
By faith he sought a promised land,
But found his rest in heaven.

5 Thus through life's pilgrimage we stray,
The promise in our eye;
By faith we walk the narrow way,
That leads to joy on high.

507. C. M. TURNER.

1 FAITH adds new charms to earthly bliss,
And saves us from its snares;
It yields support in all our toils,
And softens all our cares.

2 The wounded conscience knows its power
The healing balm to give;
That balm the saddest heart can cheer,
And make the dying live.

3 Unveiling wide the heavenly world,
Where endless pleasures reign,
It bids us seek our portion there,
Nor bids us seek in vain.

4 Faith shows the promise fully sealed
With our Redeemer's blood;
It helps our feeble hope to rest
Upon a faithful God.

5 There, still unshaken, would we rest,
Till this frail body dies,
And then, on faith's triumphant wing,
To endless glory rise.

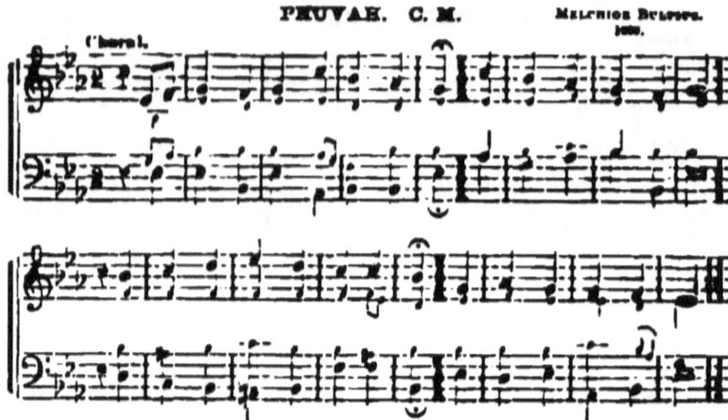

518. C. M. Steele.

1 How helpless guilty nature lies,
Unconscious of its load!
The heart, unchanged, can never rise
To happiness and God.

2 Can aught beneath a power divine
The stubborn will subdue?
'Tis thine, eternal Spirit, thine
To form the heart anew.

3 'Tis thine the passions to recall,
And upward bid them rise,
And make the scales of error fall
From reason's darkened eyes.

4 To chase the shades of death away,
And bid the sinner live,
A beam of heaven, a vital ray,
'Tis thine alone to give.

5 O, change these wretched hearts of ours,
And give them life divine;
Then shall our passions and our powers,
Almighty Lord, be thine.

519. C. M. Newton.

1 Lord, I approach the mercy-seat,
Where thou dost answer prayer;
There humbly fall before thy feet,
For none can perish there.

2 Thy promise is my only plea;
With this I venture nigh;
Thou callest burdened souls to thee,
And such, O Lord, am I.

3 Bowed down beneath a load of sin,
By Satan sorely pressed,
By wars without, and fears within,
I come to thee for rest.

4 Be thou my shield and hiding-place,
That, sheltered near thy side,
I may my fierce accuser face,
And tell him thou hast died.

5 O, wondrous love! — to bleed and die,
To bear the cross and shame,
That guilty sinners, such as I
Might plead thy gracious name.

536. C. M. Doddridge.

1 Blest Jesus, while in mortal flesh
I hold my frail abode,
Still would my spirit rest on thee,
My Saviour and my God.

2 On thy dear cross I fix my eyes,
Then raise them to thy seat;
Till love dissolves my inmost soul,
At my Redeemer's feet.

3 Be dead, my heart, to worldly charms;
Be dead to every sin;
And tell the boldest foe without
That Jesus reigns within.

541. C. M. Steele.

1 Source of eternal joys divine,
To thee my soul aspires;
O, could I say, "The Lord is mine,"
'Tis all my soul desires.

2 My hope, my trust, my life, my Lord,
Assure me of thy love;
O, speak the kind, transporting word,
And bid my fears remove:

3 Then shall my thankful powers rejoice,
And triumph in my God,
Till heavenly rapture tune my voice
To spread thy praise abroad.

533. C. M. STEELE.

1 Ye earthly vanities, depart;
Forever hence remove;
For Christ alone deserves my heart,
And every thought of love.

2 His heart, where love and pity dwelt
In all their softest forms,
Sustained the heavy load of guilt
For lost, rebellious worms.

3 Can I my bleeding Saviour view,
And yet ungrateful prove,
And pierce his wounded heart anew,
And grieve his injured love?

4 Great God, forbid: O, bind this heart,
This roving heart, of mine,
So firm, — that it may ne'er depart, —
In chains of love divine.

534. C. M. STEELE.

1 Ye glittering toys of earth, adieu;
A nobler choice be mine;
A heavenly prize attracts my view,
A treasure all divine.

2 Jesus, to multitudes unknown, —
O name divinely sweet! —
Jesus, in thee, in thee alone,
True wealth and honor meet.

3 Should earth's vain treasures all depart,
Of this dear gift possessed,
I'd clasp it to my joyful heart,
And be forever blest.

4 Dear portion of my soul's desires,
Thy love is bliss divine;
Accept the wish that love inspires,
And let me call thee mine.

535. C. M. BEDDOME.

1 This world would be a wilderness,
If banished, Lord, from thee;
And heaven, without thy smiling face,
Would be no heaven to me.

2 My Friend art thou where'er I go,
The object of my love,
My kind Protector here below,
And my reward above.

3 When foes intrude, or tyrants frown,
Thou art my sure relief;
To thee I make my sorrows known,
And tell thee all my grief.

4 'Mid rising winds and beating storms,
Reclining on thy breast,
I find in thee a hiding-place,
And there securely rest.

538. C. M. J. RYLAND.

1 O Lord, I would delight in thee,
And on thy care depend;
To thee in every trouble flee,
My best, my only Friend.

2 When all created streams are dried,
Thy fulness is the same;
May I with this be satisfied,
And glory in thy name.

3 No good in creatures can be found,
But may be found in thee;
I must have all things, and abound,
While God is God to me.

4 O Lord, I cast my care on thee;
I triumph and adore;
My great concern shall ever be
To love and please thee more.

543. C. M. WATTS.

1 My soul forsakes her vain delight,
And bids the world farewell;
On things of sense why fix my sight?
Why on its pleasures dwell?

2 There's nothing round this spacious earth
That suits my soul's desire;
To boundless joy and solid mirth
My nobler thoughts aspire.

3 No longer will I ask its love,
Nor seek its friendship more;
The happiness that I approve
Is not within its power.

4 O for the pinions of a dove,
T' ascend the heavenly road:
There shall I share my Saviour's love;
There shall I dwell with God.

558. C. M. BEDDOME.

1 And must I part with all I have,
My dearest Lord, for thee?
It is but right, since thou hast done
Much more than this for me.

2 Yes, let it go! one look from thee
Will more than make amends
For all the losses I sustain
Of honor, riches, friends.

3 Ten thousand worlds, ten thousand lives,
How worthless they appear,
Compared with thee, — supremely good,
Divinely bright and fair!

4 Saviour of souls, could I from thee
A single smile obtain,
The loss of all things I could bear,
And glory in my gain.

DUNDEE. C. M.

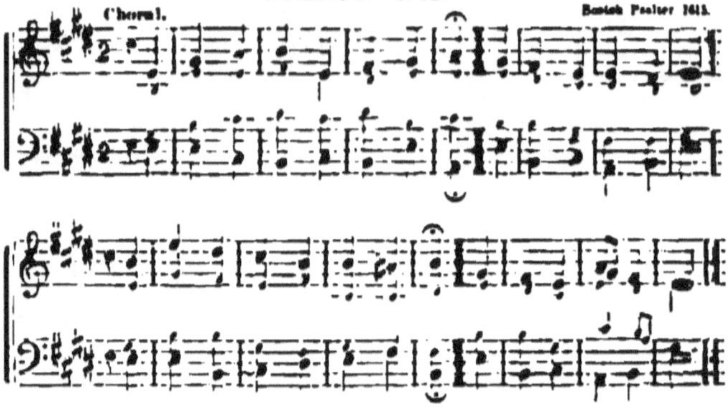

Choral. Scotch Psalter 1615.

550. C. M. WATTS.

1 In vain we lavish out our lives
To gather empty wind;
The choicest blessings earth can yield
Will starve a hungry mind.

2 But God can every want supply,
And fill our hearts with peace;
He gives by promise, and by oath,
The riches of his grace.

3 Come, and he'll cleanse our spotted souls,
And wash away our stains
In that rich fountain, which his Son
Poured from his dying veins.

4 There shall his sacred Spirit dwell,
And deep engrave his law,
And every motion of our souls
To swift obedience draw.

5 Thus will he pour salvation down,
And we shall render praise;
We, the dear people of his love,
And he, our God of grace.

557. C. M. BOURNE'S COL.

1 O SAVIOUR, welcome to my heart;
Possess thy humble throne;
Bid every rival hence depart,
And claim me for thy own.

2 The world and Satan I forsake;
To thee I all resign;
My longing heart, O Saviour, take,
And fill with love divine.

3 O, may I never turn aside,
Nor from thy bosom flee;
Let nothing here my heart divide;
I give it all to thee.

566. C. M. BEDDOME.

1 O LORD, if in the book of life
My worthless name should stand,
In fairest characters, inscribed
By thine unerring hand, —

2 My soul thou wilt by grace prepare
For crowns above the skies,
And on my way, from heavenly stores,
Wilt grant me fresh supplies:

3 Then I to thee, in sweetest strains,
Will grateful anthems raise:
But life's too short, my powers too weak,
To utter half thy praise.

4 Had I ten thousand thousand tongues,
Not one should silent be;
Had I ten thousand thousand hearts,
I'd give them all to thee.

570. C. M. REL. SOUVENIR.

1 O FATHER, good or evil send,
As seemeth best to thee,
And teach my stubborn soul to bend
In love to thy decree.

2 Whatever come, if thou wilt bless
The brightness and the gloom,
And temper joy, and soothe distress,
I fear no earthly doom.

3 Life cannot give a cureless sting;
Death can but crown my bliss,
And waft me far, on angel's wing,
To perfect happiness.

CORINTH.

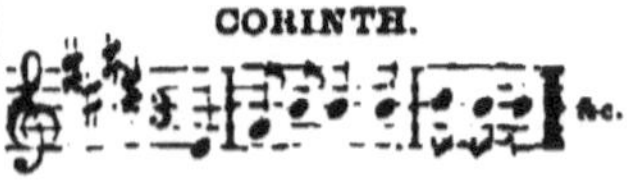

&c.

YORK. C. M.

Scotch Psalter, 1615.

581. C. M. Haweis.

1 Submissive to thy will, my God,
I all to thee resign,
And bow before thy chastening rod;
I mourn, but not repine.

2 Why should my foolish heart complain,
When wisdom, truth, and love
Direct the stroke, inflict the pain,
And point to joys above?

3 How short are all my sufferings here!
How needful every cross!
Away, my unbelieving fear,
Nor call my gain my loss.

4 Then give, O Lord, or take away,
I'll bless thy sacred name:
Jesus, to-day, and yesterday,
And ever, is the same.

582. C. M. Montgomery.

1 I cannot call affliction sweet;
And yet 'twas good to bear:
Affliction brought me to thy feet,
And I found comfort there.

2 My wearied soul was all resigned
To thy most gracious will:
O, had I kept that better mind,
Or been afflicted still!

3 Where are the vows which then I vowed?
The joys which then I knew?
Those, vanished like the morning cloud;
These, like the early dew.

4 Lord, grant me grace for every day,
Whate'er my state may be;
Through life, in death, with truth to say,
"My God is all to me."

584. C. M. Drummond.

1 Bereft of all, when hopeless care
Would sink us to the tomb,
O, what can save us from despair?
What dissipate the gloom?

2 No balm that earthly plants distil
Can soothe the mourner's smart;
No mortal hand, with lenient skill,
Bind up the broken heart.

3 But one alone, who reigns above,
Our woe to joy can turn,
And light the lamp of joy and love
That long has ceased to burn.

4 Then, O my soul, to Jesus flee;
To him thy woes reveal;
His eye alone thy wounds can see,
His hand alone can heal.

587. C. M. T. Green.

1 It is the Lord, enthroned in light,
Whose claims are all divine,
Who has an undisputed right
To govern me and mine.

2 It is the Lord, who gives me all
My wealth, my friends, my ease;
And of his bounties may recall
Whatever part he please.

3 It is the Lord, my faithful God,—
Thrice blessèd be his name,—
Whose gracious promise, sealed with blood,
Must ever be the same.

4 And can my soul, with hopes like these,
Be faithless or repine?
No, gracious God; take what thou please;
To thee I all resign.

588. C. M. Merrick's Col.

1 Author of good, to thee we turn;
Thine ever-wakeful eye
Alone can all our wants discern,
Thy hand alone supply.

2 O, let thy love within us dwell,
Thy fear our footsteps guide;
That love shall vainer loves expel,
That fear all fears beside.

3 And, O, by error's force subdued,
Since oft, with stubborn will,
We blindly shun the latent good,
And grasp the specious ill,—

4 Not what we wish, but what we want,
Let mercy still supply:
The good we ask not, Father, grant;
The ill we ask, deny.

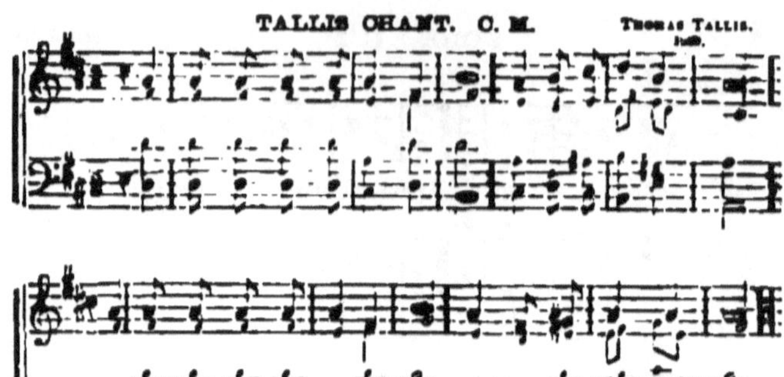

551. C. M. WINCHELL'S SEL.

1 BRIGHT was the guiding star, that led,
With mild, benignant ray,
The Gentiles to the lowly bed
Where our Redeemer lay.

2 But, lo! a brighter, clearer light
Now points to his abode;
It shines through sin and sorrow's night,
To guide us to our Lord.

3 O, haste to follow where it leads;
The gracious call obey,
Be rugged wilds, or flowery meads,
The Christian's destined way.

4 O, gladly tread the narrow path,
While light and grace are given;
Who meekly follow Christ on earth
Shall reign with him in heaven.

552. C. M. WATTS.

1 I'M not ashamed to own my Lord,
Or to defend his cause,
Maintain the honor of his word,
The glory of his cross.

2 Jesus, my God, I know his name;
His name is all my trust;
Nor will he put my soul to shame,
Nor let my hope be lost.

3 Firm as his throne his promise stands,
And he can well secure
What I've committed to his hands
Till the decisive hour.

4 Then will he own my worthless name
Before his Father's face,
And in the New Jerusalem
Appoint my soul a place.

565. C. M. NOEL'S COL.

1 THE God of grace and glory calls,
And leads the wondrous way
To his own palace, where he reigns
In uncreated day.

2 Jesus, the Herald of his love,
Displays the glorious prize,
And shows the purchase of his blood
To our admiring eyes.

3 He perfects what his hand begins,
And stone on stone he lays,
Till firm and fair the building rise,
A temple to his praise.

4 The songs of everlasting years
That mercy shall attend
Which leads, through sufferings of an hour,
To joys that never end.

594. C. M. WATTS.

1 SOON as I heard my Father say,
"Ye children, seek my grace,"
My heart replied, without delay,
"I'll seek my Father's face."

2 Let not thy face be hid from me,
Nor frown my soul away;
God of my life, I fly to thee
In each distressing day.

3 Should friends and kindred, near and dear,
Leave me to want, or die,
My God will make my life his care,
And all my need supply.

4 Wait on the Lord, ye trembling saints,
And keep your courage up:
He'll raise your spirit when it faints,
And far exceed your hope.

RINETON. C. M. (Marlow.)
WILLIAMS.
ANDOVER. C. M.
From Nat. Ch. Harmony
DUNDEE. C. M.
Choral.
Scotch Psalter, 1615.

BLANDFORD. C. M.
Choral-like.
HOWARD'S. C. M.
Dr. Howard.
ST. SEBASTIAN. C. M. (Melbourne)
English Tune.

561. C. M. WATTS.

1 FIRM as the earth thy gospel stands,
My Lord, my hope, my trust;
If I am found in Jesus' hands,
My soul can ne'er be lost.

2 His honor is engaged to save
The meanest of his sheep;
All, whom his heavenly Father gave,
His hands securely keep.

3 Nor death nor hell shall e'er remove
His favorites from his breast;
Within the bosom of his love
They must forever rest.

562. C. M. WATTS.

1 OUR God, how firm his promise stands
E'en when he hides his face!
He trusts in our Redeemer's hands
The kingdom of his grace.

2 Then why, my soul, these sad complaints?
Christ and his flock are one:
Thy God is faithful to his saints,
Is faithful to his Son.

3 Beneath his smile my heart has lived,
And heavenly joy possessed:
I'll render thanks for grace received,
And trust him for the rest.

654. C. M. RAFFLES.

1 THOU boundless Source of every good,
Our best desires fulfil;
We would adore thy wondrous grace,
And mark thy sovereign will.

2 In all thy mercies may our souls
Thy bounteous goodness see;
Nor let the gifts thy hand imparts
Estrange our hearts from thee.

3 Teach us, in time of deep distress
To own thy hand, O God,
And in submissive silence, learn
The lessons of thy rod.

4 In every changing scene of life,
Whate'er that scene may be,
Give us a meek and humble mind,—
A mind at peace with thee.

5 Do thou direct our steps aright;
Help us thy name to fear;
And give us grace to watch and pray,
And strength to persevere.

6 Then may we close our eyes in death,
Without a fear or care;
For death is life, and labor rest,
If thou art with us there.

604. C. M. WATTS.

1 THE Lord of glory is my light,
And my salvation too;
God is my strength, nor will I fear
What all my foes can do.

2 One blessing, Lord, my heart desired;
O, grant me mine abode
Among the churches of thy saints,
The temples of my God.

3 There shall I offer my requests,
And see thy glory still;
Shall hear thy messages of love,
And learn thy holy will.

4 When troubles rise, and storms appear,
There may his children hide;
God has a strong pavilion, where
He makes my soul abide.

5 Now shall my head be lifted high
Above my foes around,
And songs of joy and victory
Within thy temple sound.

631. C. M. ANON.

1 THOU Power supreme, whose mighty scheme
These woes of mine fulfil,
Here, firm, I rest; they must be best,
Because they are thy will.

2 Then all I want,—O, do thou grant
This one request of mine,—
Since to enjoy thou dost deny,
Assist me to resign.

681. C. M. WATTS.

1 MY God, the spring of all my joys,
The life of my delights,
The glory of my brightest days,
And comfort of my nights!

2 In darkest shades, if he appear,
My dawning is begun;
He is my soul's bright morning star,
And he my rising sun.

3 The opening heavens around me shine
With beams of sacred bliss,
While Jesus shows his love is mine,
And whispers, I am his.

4 My soul would leave this heavy clay,
At that transporting word,
And run with joy the shining way,
To meet my gracious Lord.

5 Fearless of hell and ghastly death,
I break through every foe:
The wings of love and arms of faith
Shall bear me conqueror through.

CRUCIFIX. C. M. R. F. EDWARDS

Minor.

555. C. M. ANON.

1 BEHOLD the Lamb of God, who bore
  Thy guilt upon the tree,
And paid in blood the dreadful score,
  The ransom due for thee.

2 Behold him till the sight endears
  The Saviour to thy heart;
His piercéd feet bedew with tears,
  Nor from his cross depart.

3 Behold him till his dying love
  Thy every thought control;
Its vast, constraining influence prove
  O'er body, spirit, soul.

4 Behold him as the race you run,
  Your never failing Friend;
He will complete the work begun:
  And grace in glory end.

617. C. M. STEELE.

1 DEAR Refuge of my weary soul,
  On thee, when sorrows rise,
On thee, when waves of trouble roll,
  My fainting hope relies.

2 To thee I tell each rising grief,
  For thou alone canst heal;
Thy word can bring a sweet relief
  For every pain I feel.

3 But, O, when gloomy doubts prevail,
  I fear to call thee mine;
The springs of comfort seem to fail,
  And all my hopes decline.

4 Yet, gracious God, where shall I flee?
  Thou art my only trust;
And still my soul would cleave to thee,
  Though prostrate in the dust.

590. C. M. WATTS.

1 CONSIDER all my sorrows, Lord,
  And thy deliverance send;
My soul for thy salvation faints;
  When will my troubles end?

2 Yet I have found 'tis good for me
  To bear my Father's rod;
Affliction made me learn thy law,
  And live upon my God.

3 Had not thy word been my delight
  When earthly joys were fled,
My soul, oppressed with sorrow's weight,
  Had sunk among the dead.

4 Before I knew thy chastening rod,
  My feet were apt to stray;
But now I learn to keep thy word,
  Nor wander from thy way.

657. C. M. EXETER COL.

1 LORD, through the dubious paths of life
  Thy feeble servant guide;
Supported by thy powerful arm,
  My footsteps shall not slide.

2 To thee, O my unerring Guide,
  I would myself resign:
In all my ways acknowledge thee,
  And form my will by thine.

3 Thus shall each blessing of thy hand
  Be doubly sweet to me:
And in new griefs I still shall have
  A refuge, Lord, in thee.

4 Lord, by thy counsel, while I live,
  O, guide my wandering feet;
And when my course on earth is run,
  Conduct me to thy seat.

MARTYRDOM. C. M. (Avon.) ‡ H. WILSON. Scotch Tune.

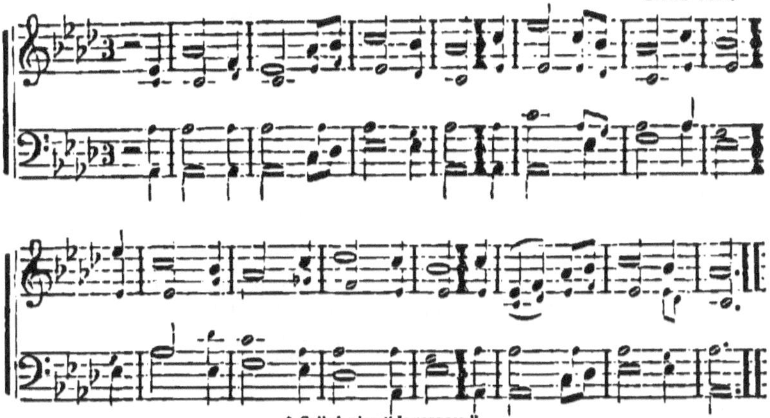

‡ Called also "Inverness."

559. C. M. DODDRIDGE.

1 THOU Lord of all the worlds on high,
Allow my humble claim;
Nor, while a child would raise its cry,
Disdain a Father's name.

2 My Father, God, how sweet the sound!
How tender and how dear!
Not all the melody of heaven
Could so delight the ear.

3 Come, sacred Spirit, seal the name
On my believing heart,
And show that in Jehovah's grace
I share a filial part.

4 By such a heavenly signal cheered,
Unwavering I believe,
And Abba, Father, humbly cry;
Nor can the sign deceive.

5 On wings of everlasting love
The Comforter is come;
All terrors at his voice disperse,
And endless pleasures bloom.

572. C. M. WATTS.

1 NAKED, as from the earth we came
And rose to life at first,
We to the earth return again,
And mingle with the dust.

2 The dear delights we here enjoy,
And fondly call our own,
Are only favors borrowed now,
To be repaid anon.

3 'Tis God who lifts our comforts high,
Or sinks them in the grave;
He gives, and blessèd be his name,
He takes but what he gave.

4 Peace, all our angry passions, then;
Let each rebellious sigh
Be silent at his sovereign will,
And every murmur die.

5 If smiling mercy crown our lives,
Its praises shall be spread;
And we'll adore the justice, too,
That strikes our comforts dead.

593. C. M. STEELE.

1 IN vain I trace creation o'er
In search of solid rest;
The whole creation is too poor
To make me truly blest.

2 Let earth and all her charms depart,
Unworthy of the mind;
In God alone this restless heart
Enduring bliss can find.

3 Thy favor, Lord, is all I want;
Here would my spirit rest:
O, seal the rich, the boundless grant,
And make me fully blest

595. C. M. EDMESTON.

1 O THOU whose mercy guides my way,
Though now it seem severe,
Forbid my unbelief to say
There is no mercy here.

2 O, grant me to desire the pain
That comes in kindness down,
More than the world's alluring gain
Succeeded by a frown.

3 Then, though thou bow my spirit low,
Love only shall I see;
The very hand that strikes the blow
Was wounded once for me.

576. C. M. Beddome.

1 Be thou, O Lord, my treasure here,
And fix my thoughts above ;
Unveil thy glories to my view,
And bid me taste thy love.

2 The world how mean, with all its store,
Compared with thee, my lord !
Its vain and fleeting joys how few !
How little they afford !

3 The goods of earth are empty things,
And pleasures soon decay ;
Its honors are but noisy breath,
And sceptres pass away.

4 Ye vain and glittering toys, begone ;
Ye false delights, adieu ;
My glorious Lord fills all the space,
And leaves no room for you.

578. C. M. Hudson.

1 How happy is the Christian's state !
His sins are all forgiven ;
A cheering ray confirms the grace,
And lifts his hopes to heaven.

2 Though, in the rugged path of life,
He heaves the pensive sigh,
Yet, trusting in the Lord, he finds
Supporting grace is nigh.

3 If, to prevent his wandering steps,
He feels the chastening rod,
The gentle stroke shall bring him back
To his forgiving God.

4 And when the welcome message comes,
To call his soul away,
His soul in raptures will ascend
To everlasting day.

586. C. M. Watts.

1 With earnest longings of the mind,
My God, to thee I look ;
So pants the hunted hart to find
And taste the cooling brook.

2 When shall I see thy courts of grace,
And meet my God again ?
So long an absence from thy face
My heart endures with pain.

3 'Tis with a mournful pleasure now
I think on ancient days ;
Then to thy house did numbers go,
And all our work was praise.

4 But why, my soul, sunk down so far,
Beneath this heavy load ?
Why do my thoughts indulge despair,
And sin against my God ?

5 Hope in the Lord, whose mighty hand
Can all thy woes remove ;
For I shall yet before him stand,
And sing restoring love.

597. C. M. Anon.

1 O God, to thee my sinking soul
In deep distress doth fly ;
Thy love can all my griefs control,
And all my wants supply.

2 How oft, when dark misfortune's hand
Around their victim stood,
The seeming ill, at thy command,
Hath changed to real good !

3 The tempest that obscured the sky
Hath set my bosom free
From earthly care and sensual joy,
And turned my thoughts to thee.

4 Affliction's blast hath made me learn
To feel for others' woe,
And humbly seek, with deep concern,
My own defects to know.

5 Then rage, ye storms ; ye billows, roar ;
My heart defies your shock ;
Ye make me cling to God the more —
To God, my sheltering rock.

591. C. M. STEELE.

1 WHEN fainting in the sultry waste,
And parched with thirst extreme,
The weary pilgrim longs to taste
The cool, refreshing stream.

2 So longs the weary, fainting mind,
Oppressed with sins and woes,
Some soul-reviving spring to find,
Whence heavenly comfort flows.

3 O, may I thirst for thee, my God,
With ardent, strong desire;
And still, through all this desert road,
To taste thy grace aspire.

4 Then shall my prayer to thee ascend,
A grateful sacrifice;
My mourning voice thou wilt attend,
And grant me full supplies.

592. C. M. LOGAN.

1 WHAT though no flowers the fig-tree clothe,
Though vines their fruit deny,
The labor of the olive fail,
And fields no meat supply;—

2 Though from the fold, with sad surprise,
My flock cut off I see;
Though famine reign in empty stalls,
Where herds were wont to be;—

3 Yet in the Lord will I be glad,
And glory in his love;
In him I'll joy, who will the God
Of my salvation prove.

4 God is the treasure of my soul,
The source of lasting joy—
A joy which want shall not impair,
Nor death itself destroy.

603. C. M. DODDRIDGE.

1 ETERNAL God, our wondering souls
Admire thy matchless grace—
That thou wilt walk, that thou wilt dwell,
With such a sinful race.

2 Cheered with thy presence, I can trace
The desert with delight:
Through all the gloom, one smile of thine
Can dissipate the night.

3 Nor shall I through eternal days
A restless pilgrim roam;
Thy hand, that now directs my course,
Will soon convey me home.

4 With joy my spirit will consent
To drop its mortal load,
And hail the messenger of death,
That bids it rise to God.

596. C. M. BEDDOME.

1 MY times of sorrow and of joy,
Great God, are in thy hand;
My choicest comforts come from thee,
And go at thy command?

2 If thou shouldst take them all away,
Yet would I not repine;
Before they were possessed by me,
They were entirely thine.

3 Nor would I drop a murmuring word,
Though all the world were gone,
But seek enduring happiness
In thee, and thee alone.

611. C. M. BEDDOME.

1 YE trembling souls, dismiss your fears,
Be mercy all your theme;
For mercy like a river flows,
In one perpetual stream.

2 "Fear not" the powers of earth and hell;
God will those powers restrain;
His arm will all their rage repel,
And make their efforts vain.

3 "Fear not" the want of outward good;
For his he will provide,
Grant them supplies of daily food,
And give them heaven beside.

4 "Fear not" that he will e'er forsake,
Or leave his work undone;
He's faithful to his promises,
And faithful to his Son.

5 "Fear not" the terrors of the grave,
Nor death's relentless sting;
He will from endless wrath preserve,
To endless glory bring.

612. C. M. WATTS.

1 BEHOLD thy waiting servant, Lord,
Devoted to thy fear;
Remember and confirm thy word,
For all my hopes are there.

2 Hast thou not sent salvation down,
And promised quickening grace?
Doth not my heart address thy throne?
And yet thy love delays.

3 Mine eyes for thy salvation fail;
O, bear thy servant up;
Nor let the scoffing lips prevail,
That dare reproach my hope.

4 Is not my faith thy gift, O Lord?
Then let thy truth appear:
Saints shall rejoice in my reward,
And trust as well as fear.

ST. MAGNUS. (Nottingham.) C. M. JER. CLARK. Died 1707.

Choral.

589. C. M. WATTS.

1 WITH my whole heart I've sought thy face;
O, let me never stray
From thy commands, O God of grace,
Nor tread the sinner's way.

2 Thy word I've hid within my heart,
To keep my conscience clean,
And be an everlasting guard
From every rising sin.

3 I'm a companion of the saints,
Who fear and love the Lord;
My sorrows rise, my nature faints,
When men transgress thy word.

4 My heart with sacred reverence hears
The threatenings of thy word;
My flesh with holy trembling fears
The judgments of the Lord.

5 My God, I long, I hope, I wait,
For thy salvation still;
Thy holy law is my delight,
And I obey thy will.

615. C. M. WATTS.

1 THOU art my portion, O my God;
Soon as I know thy way,
My heart makes haste t' obey thy word,
And suffers no delay.

2 I choose the path of heavenly truth,
And glory in my choice;
Not all the riches of the earth
Could make me so rejoice.

3 Thy precepts and thy heavenly grace
I set before my eyes;
Thence I derive my daily strength,
And there my comfort lies.

4 If once I wander from thy path,
I think upon my ways,
Then turn my feet to thy commands,
And trust thy pardoning grace.

5 Now I am thine, forever thine;
O, save thy servant, Lord;
Thou art my shield, my hiding place;
My hope is in thy word.

616. C. M. WATTS.

1 FOREVER blessèd be the Lord,
My Saviour and my shield;
He sends his Spirit with his word,
To arm me for the field.

2 When sin and hell their force unite,
He makes my soul his care,
Instructs me to the heavenly fight,
And guards me through the war.

3 A Friend and Helper so divine
Doth my weak courage raise;
He makes the glorious victory mine,
And his shall be the praise.

621. C. M. WATTS.

1 UNSHAKEN as the sacred hill,
And firm as mountains be, —
Firm as a rock, the soul shall rest,
That leans, O Lord, on thee.

2 Not walls nor hills could guard so well
Old Salem's happy ground,
As those eternal arms of love,
That every saint surround.

3 Deal gently, Lord, with souls sincere,
And lead them safely on,
Within the gates of Paradise,
Where Christ, their Lord, is gone.

602. C. M. NEWTON.

1 How happy they who know the Lord, —
With whom he deigns to dwell!
He cheers and guides them by his word;
His arm supports them well.

2 His presence sweetens all their cares,
And makes their burdens light;
A word from him dispels their fears,
And gilds the gloom of night.

608. C. M. CAMPBELL'S COL.

1 SUPREME, in wisdom as in power,
The Rock of Ages stands,
Though him thou canst not see, nor trace
The workings of his hands.

2 He gives the conquest to the weak,
Supports the sinking heart;
And courage, in the evil hour,
His heavenly aids impart.

3 Mere human power shall fast decay,
And youthful vigor cease;
But they who wait upon the Lord
In strength shall still increase.

4 They with unwearied feet shall tread
The path of life divine,
With growing ardor onward move,
With growing brightness shine.

5 On eagles' wings they mount, they soar;
Their wings are faith and love;
Till, past the cloudy regions here,
They rise to heaven above.

629. C. M. WATTS.

1 MY thoughts surmount these lower skies,
And look within the veil:
There springs of endless pleasure rise;
The waters never fail.

2 There I behold, with sweet delight,
The blessèd Three in One;
And strong affections fix my sight
On God's incarnate Son.

3 His promise stands forever firm;
His grace shall ne'er depart:
He binds my name upon his arm,
And seals it on his heart.

4 Light are the pains that nature brings;
How short our sorrows are,
When with eternal future things
The present we compare!

5 I would not be a stranger still
To that celestial place,
Where I forever hope to dwell
Near my Redeemer's face.

623. C. M. WATTS.

1 WHENCE do our mournful thoughts arise?
And where's our courage fled?
Has restless sin or raging hell
Struck all our comforts dead?

2 Have we forgot th' almighty name
That formed the earth and sea?
And can an all-creating arm
Grow weary or decay?

3 Almighty strength and boundless grace
In our Jehovah dwell!
He gives the conquest to the weak,
And dooms their foes to hell.

4 Mere mortal power shall fade and die,
And youthful vigor cease;
But we, that wait upon the Lord,
Shall feel our strength increase.

658. C. M. JUDSON.

1 OUR Father, God, who art in heaven,
All hallowed be thy name;
Thy kingdom come; thy will be done
In heaven and earth the same.

2 Give us this day our daily bread;
And as we those forgive
Who sin against us, so may we
Forgiving grace receive.

3 Into temptation lead us not;
From evil set us free;
And thine the kingdom, thine the power,
And glory, ever be.

692. C. M. WATTS.

1 MY soul lies cleaving to the dust;
Lord, give me life divine;
From vain desires, and every lust,
Turn off these eyes of mine.

2 I need the influence of thy grace
To speed me in thy way,
Lest I should loiter in my race,
Or turn my feet astray.

3 Are not thy mercies sovereign still,
And thou a faithful God?
Wilt thou not grant me warmer zeal
To run the heavenly road?

4 Does not my heart thy precepts love,
And long to see thy face?
And yet how slow my spirits move
Without enlivening grace!

5 Then shall I love thy gospel more,
And ne'er forget thy word,
When I have felt its quickening power
To draw me near the Lord.

PHILLIPS. C. M. F. Hubbard.

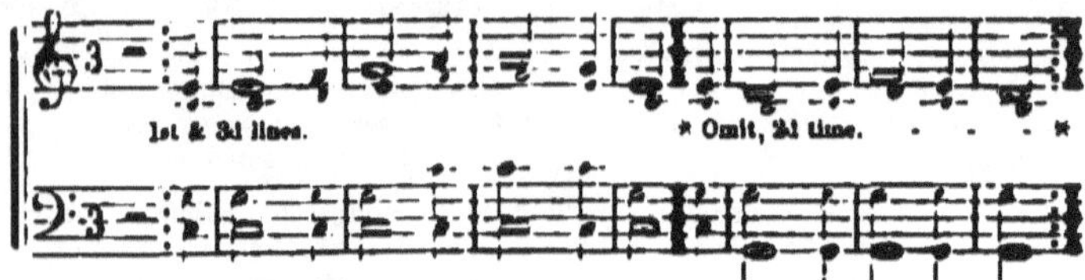

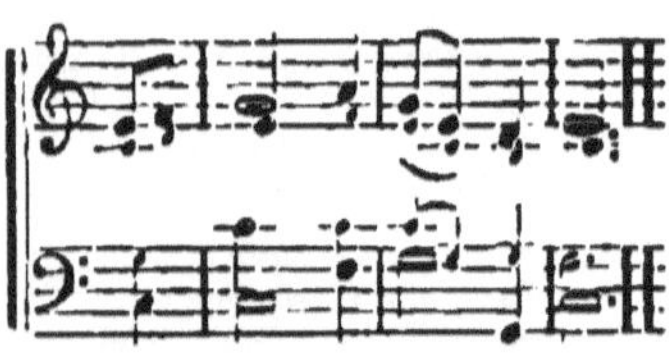

624. C. M. Higginbotham.

1 When sickness shakes the languid frame,
Each phantom pleasure flies;
Vain hopes of bliss no more obscure
Our long-deluded eyes.

2 The tottering frame of mortal life
Shall crumble into dust;
Nature shall faint; but learn, my soul,
On nature's God to trust.

3 The man whose pious heart is fixed
Securely on his God,
In every frown may comfort find,
And kiss the chastening rod.

4 Nor him shall death itself alarm;
On heaven his soul relies;
With joy he views his Maker's love,
And with composure dies.

661. C. M. Ch. Psalmody.

1 O, could I find, from day to day,
A nearness to my God,
Then would my hours glide sweet away,
While leaning on his word.

2 Lord, I desire with thee to live
Anew from day to day,
In joys the world can never give,
Nor ever take away.

3 Blest Jesus, come, and rule my heart,
And make me wholly thine,
That I may never more depart,
Nor grieve thy love divine.

4 Thus, till my last, expiring breath,
Thy goodness I'll adore;
And when my frame dissolves in death,
My soul shall love thee more.

637. C. M. Mrs. Brown.

1 I love to steal a while away
From every cumbering care,
And spend the hours of setting day
In humble, grateful prayer.

2 I love in solitude to shed
The penitential tear,
And all his promises to plead
Where none but God can hear.

3 I love to think on mercies past,
And future good implore,
And all my cares and sorrows cast
On him whom I adore.

4 I love by faith to take a view
Of brighter scenes in heaven;
The prospect doth my strength renew,
While here by tempests driven.

5 Thus, when life's toilsome day is o'er,
May its departing ray
Be calm as this impressive hour,
And lead to endless day.

646. C. M. Watts.

1 O that I knew the secret place
Where I might find my God!
I'd spread my wants before his face,
And pour my woes abroad.

2 I'd tell him how my sins arise;
What sorrows I sustain;
How grace decays, and comfort dies,
And leaves my heart in pain.

3 He knows what arguments I'd take
To wrestle with my God;
I'd plead for his own mercy's sake,
And for my Saviour's blood.

4 My God will pity my complaints,
And heal my broken bones;
He takes the meaning of his saints,
The language of their groans.

5 Arise, my soul, from deep distress,
And banish every fear;
He calls thee to his throne of grace,
To spread thy sorrows there.

619. C. M. STEELE.

1 DEAR Father, to thy mercy-seat
My soul for shelter flies:
'Tis here I find a safe retreat
When storms and tempests rise.

2 My cheerful hope can never die,
If thou, my God, art near;
Thy grace can raise my comforts high,
And banish every fear.

3 My great Protector and my Lord,
Thy constant aid impart;
O, let thy kind, thy gracious word
Sustain my trembling heart.

4 O, never let my soul remove
From this divine retreat;
Still let me trust thy power and love,
And dwell beneath thy feet.

626. C. M. B. W. NOEL.

1 WHEN musing sorrow weeps the past,
And mourns the present pain,
'Tis sweet to think of peace at last,
And feel that death is gain.

2 'Tis not that murmuring thoughts arise,
And dread a Father's will;
'Tis not that meek submission flies,
And would not suffer still.

3 It is that heaven-born Faith surveys
The path that leads to light,
And longs her eagle plumes to raise,
And lose herself in sight.

4 It is that troubled conscience feels
The pangs of struggling sin,
And sees, though far, the hand that heals,
And ends the strife within.

5 O, let me wing my hallowed flight
From earth-born woe and care,
And soar above these clouds of night,
My Saviour's bliss to share.

628. C. M. COTTON.

1 WHY, O my soul, O, why depressed,
And whence thine anxious fears?
Let former favors fix thy trust,
And check thy rising tears.

2 Affliction is a stormy deep,
Where wave succeeds to wave;
Though o'er my head the billows roll,
I know the Lord can save.

3 On him I trust and build my hope,
Nor murmur at his rod;
In vain the waves of trouble roll,
While he is still my God.

627. C. M. TOPLADY.

1 WHEN languor and disease invade
This trembling house of clay,
'Tis sweet to look beyond my pain,
And long to fly away;—

2 Sweet to look inward, and attend
The whispers of his love;
Sweet to look upward, to the place
Where Jesus pleads above;—

3 Sweet to look back, and see my name
In life's fair book set down;
Sweet to look forward, and behold
Eternal joys my own;—

4 Sweet on his faithfulness to rest,
Whose love can never end;
Sweet on the promise of his grace
For all things to depend;—

5 Sweet, in the confidence of faith,
To trust his firm decrees;
Sweet to lie passive in his hands,
And know no will but his.

6 If such the sweetness of the stream,
What must the fountain be,
Where saints and angels draw their bliss
Directly, Lord, from thee!

656. C. M. MILMAN.

1 O, HELP us, Lord; each hour of need
Thy heavenly succor give;
Help us in thought, and word, and deed,
Each hour on earth we live.

2 O, help us, when our spirits bleed,
With contrite anguish sore;
And when our hearts are cold and dead,
O, help us, Lord, the more.

3 O, help us, through the prayer of faith,
More firmly to believe;
For still the more the servant hath,
The more shall he receive.

4 O, help us, Father, from on high;
We know no help but thee:
O, help us so to live and die,
As thine in heaven to be.

754. C. M. WATTS.

1 I LOVE the Lord: he heard my cries,
And pitied every groan:
Long as I live, when troubles rise,
I'll hasten to his throne.

2 I love the Lord: he bowed his ear,
And chased my grief away:
O, let my heart no more despair,
While I have breath to pray.

3 The Lord beheld me sore distressed;
He bade my pains remove;
Return, my soul, to God, thy rest,
For thou hast known his love.

620. C. M. WATTS.

1 How can I sink with such a prop
As my eternal God,
Who bears the earth's huge pillars up,
And spreads the heavens abroad?

2 How can I die while Jesus lives,
Who rose and left the dead?
Pardon and grace my soul receives
From my exalted Head.

3 All that I am, and all I have,
Shall be forever thine;
Whate'er my duty bids me give,
My cheerful hands resign.

4 Yet if I might make some reserve,
And duty did not call,
I love my God with zeal so great,
That I should give him all.

641. C. M. RIPPON'S COL.

1 FATHER divine, thy piercing eye
Sees through the darkest night,
In deep retirement thou art nigh,
With heart-discerning sight.

2 May that observing eye survey
My faithful homage paid,
With every morning's dawning ray,
And every evening's shade.

3 O, let thy own celestial fire
The incense still inflame,
While fervent vows to thee aspire,
Through my Redeemer's name.

4 So shall the visits of thy love
My soul in secret bless;
So wilt thou deign, in worlds above,
Thy suppliant to confess.

643. C. M. COBBIN.

1 A THRONE of grace! then let us go
And offer up our prayer,
A gracious God will mercy show
To all that worship there.

2 A throne of grace! O, at that throne
Our knees have often bent,
And God has showered his blessings down
As often as we went.

3 A throne of grace! rejoice, ye saints,
That throne is open still;
To God unbosom your complaints,
And then inquire his will.

4 A throne of grace we yet shall need
Long as we draw our breath,
A Saviour, too, to intercede,
Till we are changed by death.

5 The throne of glory then shall glow
With beams from Jesus' face,
And we no longer want shall know,
Nor need a throne of grace.

649. C. M. CAPPE'S COL.

1 ETERNAL Source of life and light,
Supremely good and wise,
To thee we bring our grateful vows,
To thee lift up our eyes.

2 Our dark and erring minds illume
With truth's celestial rays,
Inspire our hearts with sacred love,
And tune our lips to praise.

3 Conduct us safely, by thy grace,
Through life's perplexing road,
And place us, when that journey's o'er,
At thy right hand, O God.

BOWDOIN STREET. C. M. B. F. EDMANDS. 1859.

632. C. M. MONTGOMERY.

1 PRAYER is the soul's sincere desire,
Unuttered or expressed,
The motion of a hidden fire,
That trembles in the breast.

2 Prayer is the burden of a sigh,
The falling of a tear,
The upward glancing of an eye,
When none but God is near.

3 Prayer is the simplest form of speech
That infant lips can try;
Prayer, the sublimest strains that reach
The majesty on high.

4 Prayer is the Christian's vital breath,
The Christian's native air,
His watchword at the gates of death;
He enters heaven with prayer.

633. C. M. MONTGOMERY.

1 PRAYER is the contrite sinner's voice,
Returning from his ways,
While angels in their songs rejoice,
And cry, "Behold, he prays."

2 The saints in prayer appear as one
In word, and deed, and mind,
While with the Father and the Son
Sweet fellowship they find.

3 Nor prayer is made on earth alone;
The Holy Spirit pleads,
And Jesus, on th' eternal throne,
For sinners intercedes.

4 O Thou, by whom we come to God,—
The life, the truth, the way,—
The path of prayer thyself hast trod;
Lord, teach us how to pray.

634. C. M. BEDDOME.

1 PRAYER is the breath of God in man,
Returning whence it came;
Love is the sacred fire within,
And prayer the rising flame.

2 It gives the burdened spirit ease,
And soothes the troubled breast;
Yields comfort to the mourners here,
And to the weary, rest.

3 When God inclines the heart to pray,
He hath an ear to hear;
To him there's music in a groan,
And beauty in a tear.

4 The humble suppliant cannot fail
To have his wants supplied,
Since He for sinners intercedes
Who once for sinners died.

640. C. M. ANON.

1 SWEET is the prayer whose holy stream
In earnest pleading flows;
Devotion dwells upon the theme,
And warm and warmer glows.

2 Faith grasps the blessing she desires;
Hope points the upward gaze;
And Love, celestial Love, inspires
The eloquence of praise.

3 But sweeter far the still small voice,
Unheard by human ear,
When God has made the heart rejoice,
And dried the bitter tear.

4 No accents flow, no words ascend;
All utterance faileth there;
But sainted spirits comprehend,
And God accepts the prayer.

NEW HAVEN. C. M. Double. GIARDINI.

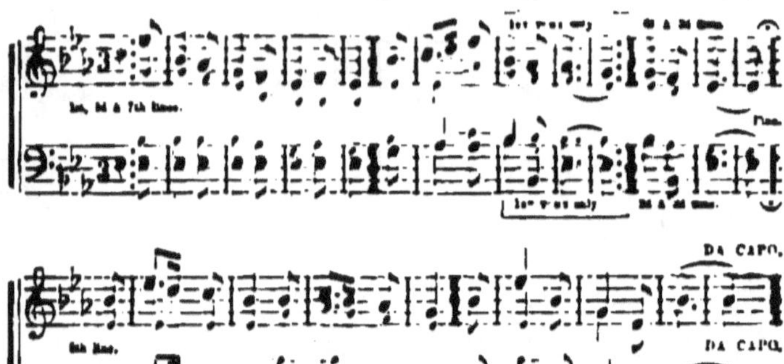

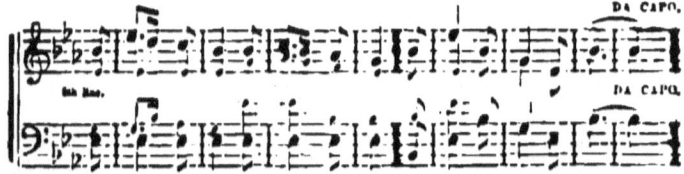

529. C. M. SPIR. OF PSALMS.

1 GREAT God, wert thou severe to mark
The deeds we do amiss,
Before thy presence who could stand?
Who claim thy promised bliss?
But, O, thou merciful and just,
Thy love surpasseth thought;
A gracious Saviour has appeared,
And peace and pardon brought.

2 Thy servants in the temple watched
The dawning of the day,
Impatient with its earliest beams
Their holy vows to pay;
And chosen saints far off beheld
That great and glorious morn,
When the glad dayspring from on high
Auspiciously should dawn.

3 On us the Sun of Righteousness
Its brightest beams hath poured;
With grateful hearts and holy zeal,
Lord, be thy love adored;
And let us look with joyful hope
To that more glorious day,
Before whose brightness sin, and death,
And grief, shall flee away.

571. C. M. AVELINO.

1 WHENE'ER the clouds of sorrow roll,
And trials whelm the mind, —
When, faint with grief, thy wearied soul
No joys on earth can find, —
Then lift thy voice to God on high,
Dry up the trembling tear,
And hush the low, complaining sigh:
"Fear not;" thy God is near.

2 When dark temptations spread their snares,
And earth with charms allures,
And when thy soul, oppressed with fears,
The world's assault endures,
Then let thy Father's friendly voice
Thy fainting spirit cheer,
And bid thy trembling heart rejoice:
"Fear not;" thy God is near.

3 And when the final hour shall come,
That calls thee to thy rest,
To dwell within thy heavenly home,
A welcome, joyful guest,
Be calm; though Jordan's waves may roll,
No ills shall meet thee there;
Angels shall whisper to thy soul,
"Fear not;" thy God is near.

660. C. M. PERCY CHAPEL COL.

1 FATHER, I know thy ways are just,
Although to me unknown;
O, grant me grace thy love to trust,
And cry, "Thy will be done."

2 If thou shouldst hedge with thorns my path,
Should wealth and friends be gone,
Still, with a firm and lively faith,
I'll cry, "Thy will be done."

3 Although thy steps I cannot trace,
Thy sovereign right I'll own;
And, as instructed by thy grace,
I'll cry, "Thy will be done."

4 'Tis sweet thus passively to lie
Before thy gracious throne,
Concerning every thing to cry,
"My Father's will be done."

COMFORT C. M. or, 8s & 6s.‡
Mrs. P. Gibson.
CODA.
For Hymn 571. Fear not; fear not; Fear not; thy God is near.
Hymns 659, 660. Thy will; thy will; Thy will, my God, be done.
For Hymn 736. A hope — a hope — a hope — a bless - ed hope.
A star — a star — a star — a love - ly star.
A voice — a voice — a voice — a cheer - ing voice.
That hope — that hope — that hope, the hope of heaven.

‡ This tune may be sung with or without the coda. If sung to Hymn 571, repeat the tune before singing the coda.

659. 8s & 6. Anon.

1 My God, my Father, while I stray
Far from my home, on life's rough way,
O, teach me from my heart to say,
"Thy will, my God, be done."

2 Though dark my path, and sad my lot,
Let me be still, and murmur not,
And breathe the prayer divinely taught,
"Thy will, my God, be done."

3 What though in lonely grief I sigh
For friends beloved no longer nigh;
Submissive still would I reply,
"Thy will, my God, be done."

4 If thou shouldst call me to resign
What most I prize, — it ne'er was mine, —
I only yield thee what is thine;
"Thy will, my God, be done."

5 Should pining sickness waste away
My life in premature decay,
In life or death teach me to say,
"Thy will, my God, be done."

6 Renew my will from day to day,
Blend it with thine, and take away
Whate'er now makes it hard to say,
"Thy will, my God, be done."

736. C. M. H. H. Hawley.

1 There is a hope, a blessèd hope,
More precious and more bright
Than all the joyless mockery
The world esteems delight.

2 There is a star, a lovely star,
That lights the darkest gloom,
And sheds a peaceful radiance o'er
The prospects of the tomb.

3 There is a voice, a cheering voice,
That lifts the soul above,
Dispels the painful, anxious doubt,
And whispers, "God is love."

4 That voice, aloud from Calvary's height,
Proclaims the soul forgiven;
That star is revelation's light;
That hope the hope of heaven.

ST. STEPHEN'S. C. M. Rev. Wm. Jones.

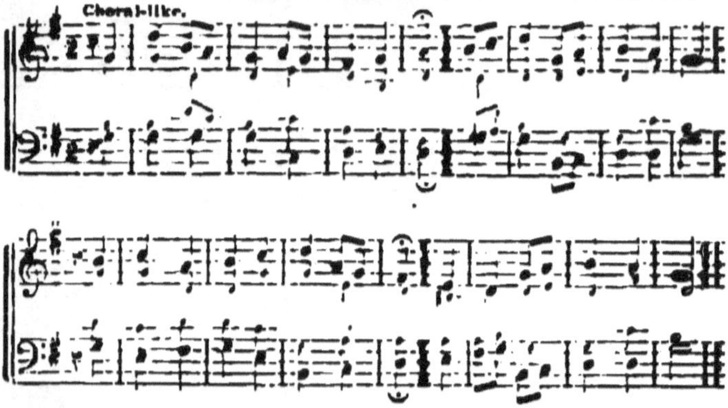

Choral-like.

647. C. M. Urwick's Col.

1 Father of all our mercies, thou
In whom we move and live,
Hear us in heaven, thy dwelling, now,
And answer, and forgive.

2 When, harassed by ten thousand foes,
Our helplessness we feel,
O, give the weary soul repose,
The wounded spirit heal.

3 When dire temptations gather round,
And threaten or allure,
By storm or calm, in thee be found
A refuge strong and sure.

4 When age advances, may we grow
In faith, in hope, and love,
And walk in holiness below
To holiness above.

663. C. M. C. Wesley.

1 O for a heart to praise my God!
A heart from sin set free!
A heart that's sprinkled with the blood
So freely shed for me!

2 O for a heart submissive, meek,
My great Redeemer's throne,
Where only Christ is heard to speak,
Where Jesus reigns alone!

3 O for an humble, contrite heart,
Believing, true, and clean,
Which neither life nor death can part
From him that dwells within!

4 Thy temper, gracious Lord, impart;
Come quickly from above;
O, write thy name upon my heart;
Thy name, O God, is love.

669. C. M. Watts.

1 O that thy statutes every hour
Might dwell upon my mind!
Thence I derive a quickening power,
And daily peace I find.

2 To meditate thy precepts, Lord,
Shall be my sweet employ;
My soul shall ne'er forget thy word;
Thy word is all my joy.

3 How would I run in thy commands,
If thou my heart discharge
From sin and Satan's hateful chains,
And set my feet at large!

4 My lips with courage shall declare
Thy statutes and thy name,
I'll speak thy word though kings should hear,
Nor yield to sinful shame.

673. C. M. Steele.

1 And can my heart aspire so high
To say, "My Father," God?
Lord, at thy feet I fain would lie,
And learn to kiss the rod.

2 I would submit to all thy will;
For thou art good and wise;
Let each rebellious thought be still,
Nor one faint murmur rise.

3 Thy love can cheer the darkest gloom,
And bid me wait serene,
Till hopes and joys immortal bloom,
And brighten all the scene.

4 "My Father, God," permit my heart
To plead her humble claim,
And ask the bliss those words impart,
In my Redeemer's name.

CHARITY. C. M. N. D. GOULD.

Peculiar Hymn Tune. From the Sacred Minstrel.

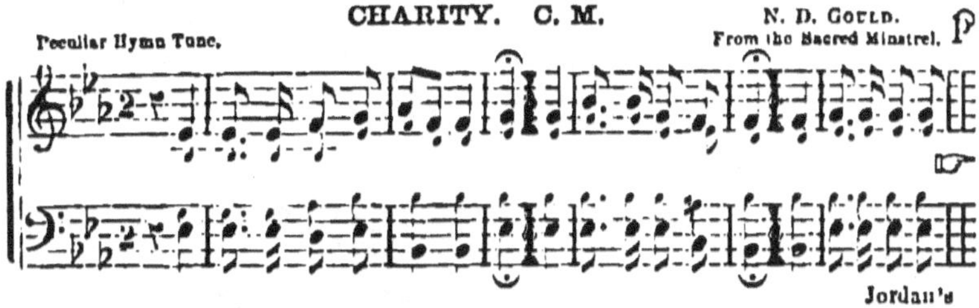
Jordan's

may be omitted.
—swelling tide, O Lord, O Lord, O Lord, remember me, O Lord, remember me.

For Hymn 667, sing the whole tune.

☞ In the 1st, 2d, and 3d stanzas of Hymn 666 omit all the notes between the double bars and the signs ☞ . . . . ☜.

667. C. M. HAWEIS.

1 O THOU from whom all goodness flows,
I lift my soul to thee;
In all my sorrows, conflicts, woes,
O Lord, remember me.

2 When, with an aching, burdened heart,
I seek relief of thee,
Thy pardon grant, new peace impart;
O Lord, remember me.

3 When trials sore obstruct my way,
And ills I cannot flee,
O, let my strength be as my day;
O Lord, remember me.

4 If, for thy sake, upon my name
Reproach and shame shall be,
I'll hail reproach, and welcome shame:
O Lord, remember me.

5 When worn, with pain, disease, and grief,
This feeble body see;
Grant patience, rest, and kind relief;
O Lord, remember me.

6 When, in the solemn hour of death,
I wait thy just decree,
By this the prayer of my last breath,—
O Lord, remember me.

7 And when before thy throne I stand,
And lift my soul to thee,
Then, with the saints at thy right hand,
O Lord, remember me.

666. C. M. ANON.

1 "REMEMBER me," my Saviour God,
Whilst here on earth I stay;
Give strength to bear affliction's rod,
And faith to watch and pray.

2 "Remember me," when fortune smiles,
And scenes are bright and fair,
Lest I should fall, through Satan's wiles,
Beneath his baneful snare.

3 "Remember me;" thy voice I'll greet
In all thy dealings here;
O, let thy Spirit guide my feet,
And I shall never fear.

4 "Remember me;" stand near my side,
Where'er my lot may be;
And when by Jordan's swelling tide,
O Lord, "remember me."

Hymn 563 on opposite page may be sung to the above tune in same manner as 666, the 4th verse having a peculiar last line.

EVAN.

&c.

675. C. M. Meth. Col.

1 Shepherd divine, our wants relieve,
In this our evil day;
To all thy tempted followers give
The heart to trust and pray.

2 Long as our fiery trials last,
Long as the cross we bear,
O, let our souls on thee be cast,
In never-ceasing prayer.

3 Thy Holy Spirit's praying grace
Give us in faith to claim,
To wrestle till we see thy face,
And know thy hidden name.

4 Till thou the Father's love impart,
Till thou thyself bestow,
Be this the cry of every heart —
"I will not let thee go."

677. C. M. Epis. Col.

1 Thou Fount of blessing, God of love,
To thee our hearts we raise;
Thine all-sustaining power we prove,
And gladly sing thy praise.

2 Thine, wholly thine, we long to be;
Our sacrifice receive;
Made, and preserved, and saved, by thee,
To thee ourselves we give

3 To thee our every wish aspires,
For all thy mercy's store,
The sole return thy love requires
Is, that we ask for more.

4 For more we ask; we open, Lord,
Our hearts t' embrace thy will:
Renew us by thy quickening word,
And from thy fulness fill.

679. C. M. Watts.

1 'Twas in the watches of the night
I thought upon thy power;
I kept thy lovely face in sight,
Amid the darkest hour.

2 While I lay resting on my bed,
My soul arose on high;
My God, my life, my hope, I said,
Bring thy salvation nigh.

3 I strive to mount thy holy hill;
I walk the heavenly road;
Thy glories all my spirit fill,
While I commune with God.

4 Thy mercy stretches o'er my head
The shadow of thy wing;
My heart rejoices in thine aid,
And I thy praises sing.

705. C. M. Kirkham.

1 Didst thou, dear Saviour, suffer shame,
And bear the cross for me?
And shall I fear to own thy name,
Or thy disciple be?

2 Inspire my soul with life divine,
And make me truly bold;
Let knowledge, faith, and meekness shine,
Nor love nor zeal grow cold.

3 Let mockers scoff, the world defame,
And treat me with disdain;
Still may I glory in thy name,
And count reproach my gain.

4 To thee I cheerfully submit,
And all my powers resign;
Let wisdom point out what is fit,
And I'll no more repine.

ARLINGTON. C. M. ‡ DR. ARNE.

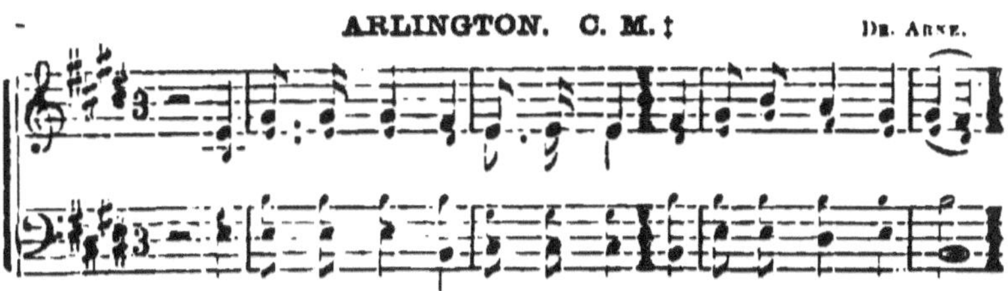

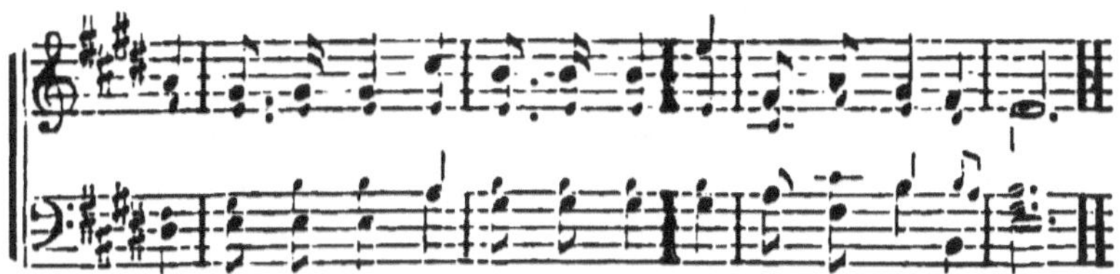

‡ For congregational use the rhythm indicated in the bass staff is best.

688. C. M. WATTS.

1 STRAIT is the way, the door is strait
That leads to joys on high:
'Tis but a few that find the gate,
While crowds mistake and die.

2 Belovéd self must be denied,
The mind and will renewed,
Passion suppressed, and patience tried,
And vain desires subdued.

3 Lord, can a feeble, helpless worm
Fulfil a task so hard?
Thy grace must all the work perform,
And give the free reward.

709. C. M. WATTS.

1 O THAT the Lord would guide my ways,
To keep his statutes still;
O that my God would grant me grace
To know and do his will!

2 O, send thy Spirit down, to write
Thy law upon my heart;
Nor let my tongue indulge deceit,
Nor act the liar's part.

3 From folly turn away my eyes;
Let no corrupt design,
Nor covetous desire, arise
Within this soul of mine.

4 Direct my footsteps by thy word,
And make my heart sincere;
Let sin have no dominion, Lord,
But keep my conscience clear.

5 Make me to walk in thy commands, —
'Tis a delightful road, —
Nor let my head, nor heart, nor hands,
Offend against my God.

690. C. M. STEELE.

1 HOW oft, alas! this wretched heart
Has wandered from the Lord!
How oft my roving thoughts depart,
Forgetful of his word!

2 Yet sovereign mercy calls, "Return;"
Dear Lord, and may I come?
My vile ingratitude I mourn;
O, take the wanderer home.

3 And canst thou, wilt thou, yet forgive,
And bid my crimes remove?
And shall a pardoned rebel live
To speak thy wondrous love?

4 Thy pardoning love, so free, so sweet,
Blest Saviour, I adore;
O, keep me at thy sacred feet,
And let me rove no more.

716. C. M. CAMPBELL'S COL.

1 THE Saviour bids us watch and pray,
Through life's brief, fleeting hour,
And gives the Spirit's quickening ray
To those who seek his power.

2 The Saviour bids us watch and pray,
Maintain a warrior's strife;
Help, Lord, to hear thy voice to-day;
Obedience is our life.

3 The Saviour bids us watch and pray;
For soon the hour will come
That calls us from the earth away,
To our eternal home.

4 O Saviour, we would watch and pray,
And hear thy sacred voice,
And walk, as thou hast marked the way,
To heaven's eternal joys.

HAEFFNER. C. M.

691. C. M. Cowper.

1 O for a closer walk with God!
A calm and heavenly frame!
A light to shine upon the road
That leads me to the Lamb!

2 Where is the blessedness I knew
When first I saw the Lord?
Where is the soul-refreshing view
Of Jesus and his word?

3 What peaceful hours I then enjoyed!
How sweet their memory still!
But now I find an aching void
The world can never fill.

4 Return, O holy Dove, return,
Sweet messenger of rest;
I hate the sins that made thee mourn,
And drove thee from my breast.

5 The dearest idol I have known,
Whate'er that idol be,
Help me to tear it from thy throne,
And worship only thee.

6 So shall my walk be close with God,
Calm and serene my frame;
So purer light shall mark the road
That leads me to the Lamb.

697. C. M. Swain.

1 How sweet, how heavenly, is the sight
When those that love the Lord
In one another's peace delight,
And thus fulfil his word! —

2 When each can feel his brother's sigh,
And with him bear a part;
When sorrow flows from eye to eye,
And joy from heart to heart! —

3 When, free from envy, scorn, and pride,
Our wishes all above,
Each can his brother's failings hide,
And show a brother's love!

4 Love is the golden chain that binds
The happy souls above;
And he's an heir of heaven that finds
His bosom glow with love.

699. C. M. Watts.

1 Lo! what an entertaining sight
Those friendly brethren prove,
Whose cheerful hearts in bands unite
Of harmony and love! —

2 Where streams of bliss from Christ, the spring,
Descend to every soul,
And heavenly peace, with balmy wing,
Shades and bedews the whole!

3 'Tis pleasant as the morning dews
That fall on Zion's hill,
Where God his mildest glory shows,
And makes his grace distil.

701. C. M. Spir. of Psalms.

1 Spirit of peace, celestial Dove,
How excellent thy praise!
No richer gift than Christian love
Thy gracious power displays.

2 Sweet as the dew on herb and flower,
That silently distils,
At evening's soft and balmy hour,
On Zion's fruitful hills, —

3 So, with mild influence from above,
Shall promised grace descend,
Till universal peace and love
O'er all the earth extend.

ST. MARTIN'S. C. M. TANSUR. 1735.

702. C. M. BEDDOME.

1 In duties and in sufferings too,
Thy path, my Lord, I'd trace;
As thou hast done, so would I do,
Depending on thy grace.

2 Inflamed with zeal, 'twas thy delight
To do thy Father's will;
O, may that zeal my soul excite
Thy precepts to fulfil.

3 Unsullied meekness, truth, and love,
Through all thy conduct shine;
O, may my whole deportment prove
A copy, Lord, of thine.

712. C. M. BOWRING.

1 The Saviour now is gone before
To yon blest realms of light:
O, thither may our spirits soar,
And wing their upward flight.

2 Lord, make us to those joys aspire,
That spring from love to thee,
That pass the carnal heart's desire,
And faith alone can see.

3 To guide us to thy glories, Lord,
To lift us to the sky,
O, may thy Spirit still be poured
Upon us from on high.

713. C. M. DODDRIDGE.

1 My soul, triumphant in the Lord,
Proclaim thy joys abroad,
And march with holy vigor on,
Supported by thy God.

2 Through every winding maze of life
His hand has been my guide;
And in his long-experienced care
My heart shall still confide.

3 His grace through all the desert flows,
An unexhausted stream;
That grace, on Zion's sacred mount,
Shall be my endless theme.

4 Beyond the choicest joys of time,
Thy courts on earth I love;
But, O, I burn with strong desire
To dwell with thee above.

5 There, joined with all the shining band,
My soul would thee adore,
A pillar in thy temple fixed,
To be removed no more.

714. C. M. DODDRIDGE.

1 Awake, my drowsy soul, awake,
And view the threatening scene;
See how thy foes encamp around,
And treason lurks within.

2 'Tis not this mortal life alone
These hostile powers assail:
How canst thou hope for future bliss,
If their attempts prevail?

3 Then to the work of God awake;
Behold thy Master near;
The various, arduous task pursue
With vigor and with fear.

4 The awful register goes on;
Th' account will surely come;
And opening day, or closing night,
May bear me to my doom.

5 Tremendous thought! how deep it strikes!
Yet like a dream it flies,
Till God's own voice the slumbers chase
From these deluded eyes.

SOLOMON. C. M. From Handel.

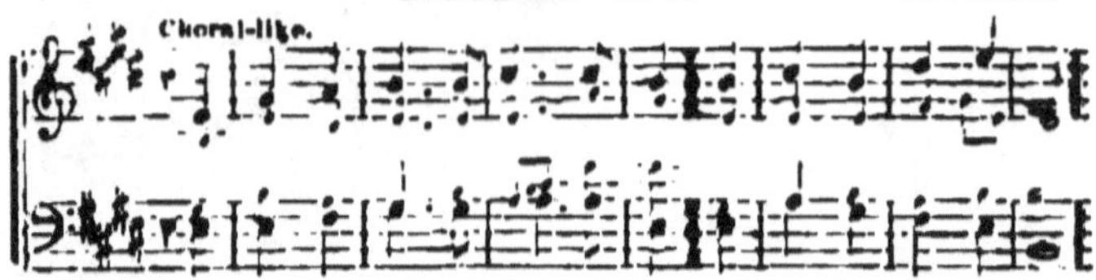

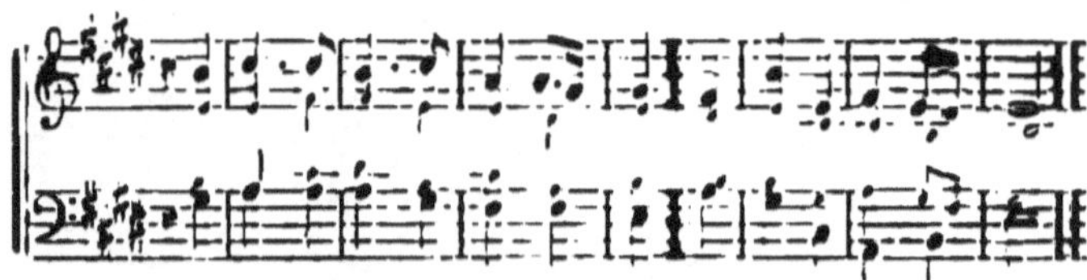

664. C. M. Steele.

1 Father, whate'er of earthly bliss
  Thy sovereign will denies,
Accepted at thy throne of grace,
  Let this petition rise: —

2 Give me a calm, a thankful heart,
  From every murmur free;
The blessings of thy grace impart,
  And make me live to thee.

3 Let the sweet hope that thou art mine
  My life and death attend;
Thy presence through my journey shine,
  And crown my journey's end.

693. C. M. Addison.

1 When all thy mercies, O my God,
  My rising soul surveys,
Transported with the view, I'm lost
  In wonder, love, and praise.

2 Unnumbered comforts on my soul
  Thy tender care bestowed,
Before my infant heart conceived
  From whom those comforts flowed.

3 When in the slippery paths of youth
  With heedless steps I ran,
Thine arm, unseen, conveyed me safe,
  And led me up to man.

4 Ten thousand thousand precious gifts
  My daily thanks employ;
Nor is the least a cheerful heart,
  That tastes those gifts with joy.

5 Through every period of my life,
  Thy goodness I'll pursue;
And after death, in distant worlds,
  The glorious theme renew.

6 Through all eternity, to thee
  A grateful song I'll raise:
But, O, eternity's too short
  To utter all thy praise.

710. C. M. Watts.

1 To thee, before the dawning light,
  My gracious God, I pray;
I meditate thy name by night,
  And keep thy law by day.

2 My spirit faints to see thy grace:
  Thy promise bears me up;
And, while salvation long delays,
  Thy word supports my hope.

3 When midnight darkness veils the skies,
  I call thy works to mind;
My thoughts in warm devotion rise,
  And sweet acceptance find.

731. C. M. Watts.

1 God of my childhood and my youth,
  The Guide of all my days,
I have declared thy heavenly truth,
  And told thy wondrous ways.

2 Wilt thou forsake my hoary hairs,
  And leave my fainting heart?
Who shall sustain my sinking years,
  If God, my strength, depart?

3 Let me thy power and truth proclaim
  Before the rising age,
And leave a savor of thy name
  When I shall quit the stage.

4 The land of silence and of death
  Attends my next remove;
O, may these poor remains of breath
  Teach all the world thy love.

MARTYRDOM. C. M. (Avon.)
H. WILSON.
Scotch Tune.
AUGUSTUS. C. M.
W. W. JOHNSON.
From Sacred Minstrel.
Lento
REFUGE. C. M.
N. DOUGALL.

ST. MARTIN'S. C. M.
DUNFERMLINE. C. M.
Choral.
PETERBORO'. C. M.
ENGLISH.

729. C. M. Barbauld.

1 Our country is Immanuel's ground;
We seek that promised soil:
The songs of Zion cheer our hearts,
While strangers here we toil.

2 We tread the path our Master trod;
We bear the cross he bore;
And every thorn that wounds our feet
His temples pierced before.

3 Our powers are oft dissolved away
In ecstasies of love;
And while our bodies wander here,
Our souls are fixed above.

4 We purge our mortal dross away,
Refining as we run;
But while we die to earth and sense,
Our heaven is here begun.

732. C. M. Watts.

1 My God, my everlasting hope,
I live upon thy truth;
Thy hands have held my childhood up,
And strengthened all my youth.

2 Still has my life new wonders seen,
Repeated every year;
Behold, my days that yet remain,
I trust them to thy care.

3 Cast me not off when strength declines,
When hoary hairs arise;
And round me let thy glory shine,
Whene'er thy servant dies.

4 Then, in the history of my age,
When men review my days,
They'll read thy love in every page,
In every line thy praise.

733. C. M. Sad. Recreations.

1 In trouble and in grief, O God,
Thy smile hath cheered my way;
And joy hath budded from each thorn
That round my footsteps lay.

2 The hours of pain have yielded good
Which prosperous days refused;
As herbs, though scentless when entire,
Spread fragrance when they're bruised.

3 The oak strikes deeper, as its boughs
By furious blasts are driven;
So life's tempestuous storms the more
Have fixed my heart in heaven.

4 All-gracious Lord, whate'er my lot
In other times may be,
I'll welcome still the heaviest grief
That brings me near to thee.

734. C. M. Watts.

1 Lord, what a wretched land is this,
That yields us no supply —
No cheering fruits, no wholesome trees,
No streams of living joy!

2 Our journey is a thorny maze;
But we march upward still,
Forget those troubles of the ways,
And press to Zion's hill.

3 There, on a green and flowery mount,
Our weary souls shall sit,
And with transporting joy recount
The labors of our feet.

4 Eternal glory to the King
Whose hand conducts us through;
Our tongues shall never cease to sing,
And endless praise renew.

735. C. M. Watts.

1 Death may dissolve my body now,
And bear my spirit home:
Why do my days so sluggish move,
Nor my salvation come?

2 God has laid up in heaven for me
A crown which cannot fade;
The righteous Judge, at that great day,
Shall place it on my head.

3 Jesus, the Lord, will guard me safe
From every ill design,
And to his heavenly kingdom take
This feeble soul of mine.

4 God is my everlasting aid,
My portion and my friend;
To him be highest glory paid,
Through ages without end.

738. C. M. Watts.

1 How blest is he who fears the Lord,
And follows his commands,
Who lends the poor without reward,
Or gives with liberal hands!

2 As pity dwells within his breast
To all the sons of need,
So God shall answer his request
With blessings on his seed.

3 In times of danger and distress,
Some beams of light shall shine,
To show the world his righteousness,
And give him peace divine.

4 His works of piety and love
Remain before the Lord;
Sweet peace on earth, and joys above,
Shall be his sure reward.

CHRISTMAS. C. M. HANDEL.

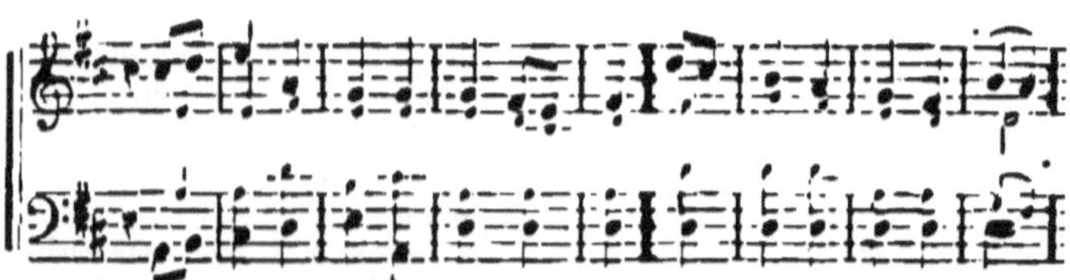

721. C. M. WATTS.

1 AM I a soldier of the cross,
A follower of the Lamb?
And shall I fear to own his cause,
Or blush to speak his name?

2 Must I be carried to the skies
On flowery beds of ease,
While others fought to win the prize,
And sailed through bloody seas?

3 Are there no foes for me to face?
Must I not stem the flood?
Is this vile world a friend to grace,
To help me on to God?

4 Sure I must fight, if I would reign;
Increase my courage, Lord:
I'll bear the toil, endure the pain,
Supported by thy word.

5 Thy saints in all this glorious war
Shall conquer, though they die;
They see the triumph from afar,
And seize it with their eye.

6 When that illustrious day shall rise,
And all thy armies shine
In robes of victory through the skies,
The glory shall be thine.

726. C. M. DODDRIDGE.

1 AWAKE, my soul; stretch every nerve,
And press with vigor on;
A heavenly race demands thy zeal,
And an immortal crown.

2 A cloud of witnesses around
Hold thee in full survey;
Forget the steps already trod,
And onward urge thy way.

3 'Tis God's all-animating voice
That calls thee from on high;
'Tis his own hand presents the prize
To thine uplifted eye;—

4 That prize, with peerless glories bright,
Which shall new lustre boast,
When victors' wreaths and monarchs' gems
Shall blend in common dust.

728. C. M. NEEDHAM.

1 RISE, O my soul, pursue the path
By ancient worthies trod;
Aspiring, view those holy men
Who lived and walked with God.

2 Though dead, they speak in reason's ear,
And in example live;
Their faith, and hope, and mighty deeds,
Still fresh instruction give.

3 'Twas thro' the Lamb's most precious blood
They conquered every foe;
To his almighty power and grace
Their crowns of life they owe.

4 Lord, may I ever keep in view
The patterns thou hast given,
And ne'er forsake the blessed road
That led them safe to heaven.

722. C. M. ANON.

1 O, SPEED thee, Christian, on thy way,
And to thy armor cling;
With girded loins the call obey
That grace and mercy bring.

2 There is a battle to be fought,
An upward race to run,
A crown of glory to be sought,
A victory to be won.

3 The shield of faith repels the dart
That Satan's hand may throw;
His arrow cannot reach thy heart,
If Christ control the bow.

4 The glowing lamp of prayer will light
Thee on thy anxious road;
'Twill keep the goal of heaven in sight,
And guide thee to thy God.

5 O, faint not, Christian, for thy sighs
Are heard before his throne;
The race must come before the prize,
The cross before the crown.

727. C. M. WATTS.

1 GIVE me the wings of faith, to rise
Within the veil, and see
The saints above, how great their joys,
How bright their glories be.

2 Once they were mourning here below,
And bathed their couch with tears;
They wrestled hard, as we do now,
With sins, and doubts, and fears.

3 I ask them whence their victory came;
They, with united breath,
Ascribe their conquest to the Lamb,
Their triumph to his death.

4 They marked the footsteps that he trod;
His zeal inspired their breast;
And, following their incarnate God,
Possessed the promised rest.

5 Our glorious Leader claims our praise,
For his own pattern given;
While the long cloud of witnesses
Shows the same path to heaven.

746. C. M. DODDRIDGE.

1 JESUS, our Lord, how rich thy grace!
Thy bounties, how complete!
How shall we count the matchless sum?
How pay the mighty debt?

2 High on a throne of radiant light
Dost thou exalted shine;
What can our poverty bestow,
When all the worlds are thine?

3 But thou hast brethren here below,
The partners of thy grace,
And wilt confess their humble names
Before thy Father's face.

4 In them thou mayst be clothed, and fed,
And visited, and cheered;
And in their accents of distress
Our Saviour's voice is heard.

5 Thy face, with reverence and with love,
We in thy poor would see;
O, rather let us beg our bread,
Than hold it back from thee.

764. C. M. WATTS.

1 FROM thee, O God, our joys shall rise,
And run eternal rounds,
Beyond the limits of the skies,
And all created bounds.

2 The holy triumphs of our souls
Shall death itself outbrave,
Leave dull mortality behind,
And fly beyond the grave.

3 There, where our blessèd Saviour reigns,
In heaven's unmeasured space,
We'll spend a long eternity
In pleasure and in praise.

4 Blest Saviour, every smile of thine
Shall fresh endearments bring,
And thousand tastes of new delight
From all thy graces spring.

5 Haste, our belovèd, bear our souls
Up to thy blest abode;
Haste, for our spirits long to see
Our Saviour and our God.

780. C. M. NEEDHAM.

1 O, HOW divine, how sweet the joy,
When but one sinner turns,
And, with an humble, broken heart,
His sins and errors mourns!

2 Pleased with the news, the saints below
In songs their tongues employ;
Beyond the skies the tidings go,
And heaven is filled with joy.

3 Well pleased the Father sees and hears
The conscious sinner's moan;
Jesus receives him in his arms,
And claims him for his own.

4 Nor angels can their joys contain,
But kindle with new fire;
"The sinner lost is found," they sing,
And strike the sounding lyre.

TALLIS. C. M. (Attalia.) T. TALLIS. 1565.

Choral.

1st & 3d lines. * omit, 2d time - - - - - - - - *

744. C. M. W. CROSWELL.

1 LORD, lead the way the Saviour went,
By lane and cell obscure,
And let our treasures still be spent,
Like his, upon the poor.

2 Like him, through scenes of deep distress,
Who bore the world's sad weight,
We, in their gloomy loneliness
Would seek the desolate.

3 For thou hast placed us side by side
In this wide world of ill;
And that thy followers may be tried,
The poor are with us still.

4 Small are the offerings we can make;
Yet thou hast taught us, Lord,
If given for the Saviour's sake,
We lose not our reward.

748. C. M. SPIR. OF PSALMS.

1 HOW blest the children of the Lord,
Who, walking in his sight,
Make all the precepts of his word
Their study and delight!

2 That precious wealth shall be their dower,
Which cannot know decay,
Which moth or rust shall ne'er devour,
Nor spoiler take away.

3 For them that heavenly light shall spread,
Whose cheering rays illume
The darkest hours of life, and shed
A halo round the tomb.

4 Their works of piety and love,
Performed through Christ, their Lord,
Forever registered above,
Shall meet a sure reward.

741. C. M. BARBAULD.

1 BLEST is the man whose softening heart
Feels all another's pain;
To whom the supplicating eye
Is never raised in vain;—

2 Whose breast expands with generous warmth
A brother's woes to feel,
And bleeds in pity o'er the wound
He wants the power to heal.

3 He spreads his kind, supporting arms
To every child of grief;
His secret bounty largely flows,
And brings unasked relief.

4 To gentle offices of love
His feet are never slow;
He views, through mercy's melting eye,
A brother in a foe.

5 Himself, through Christ, hath mercy found—
Free mercy from above;
That mercy moves him to fulfil
The perfect law of love.

760. C. M. WATTS.

1 O GOD, our help in ages past,
Our hope for years to come,
Our shelter from the stormy blast,
And our eternal home,—

2 Beneath the shadow of thy throne
Thy saints have dwelt secure;
Sufficient is thine arm alone,
And our defence is sure.

3 Before the hills in order stood,
Or earth received her frame,
From everlasting thou art God,
To endless years the same.

4 Thy word commands our flesh to dust,—
"Return, ye sons of men;"
All nations rose from earth at first,
And turn to earth again.

5 O God, our help in ages past,
Our hope for years to come,
Be thou our guard while troubles last,
And our eternal home.

724. C. M. STEELE.

1 ALAS! what hourly dangers rise!
What snares beset my way!
To heaven, O, let me lift mine eyes,
And hourly watch and pray.

2 How oft my mournful thoughts complain,
And melt in flowing tears!
My weak resistance, ah, how vain!
How strong my foes and fears!

3 O gracious God, in whom I live,
My feeble efforts aid;
Help me to watch, and pray, and strive,
Though trembling and afraid.

4 Increase my faith, increase my hope,
When foes and fears prevail;
O, bear my fainting spirit up,
Or soon my strength will fail.

5 Whene'er temptations lure my heart,
Or draw my feet aside,
My God, thy powerful aid impart,
My Guardian and my Guide.

6 O, keep me in thy heavenly way,
And bid the tempter flee;
And let me never, never stray
From happiness and thee.

743. C. M. BODEN.

1 BRIGHT Source of everlasting love,
To thee our souls we raise,
And to thy sovereign bounty rear
A monument of praise.

2 Thy mercy gilds the path of life
With every cheering ray,
And kindly checks the rising tear,
Or wipes that tear away.

3 What shall we render, bounteous Lord,
For all the grace we see?
The goodness feeble man can yield
Extendeth not to thee.

4 To scenes of woe, to beds of pain,
We'll cheerfully repair,
And, with the gifts thy hand bestows,
Relieve the sufferers there.

5 The widow's heart shall sing for joy;
The orphan shall be glad;
And hungering souls we'll gladly point
To Christ, the living bread.

6 Thus, what our heavenly Father gave
Shall we as freely give;
Thus copy him who lived to save,
And died that we might live.

742. C. M. DODDRIDGE.

1 FATHER of mercies, send thy grace,
All powerful, from above,
To form in our obedient souls
The image of thy love.

2 O, may our sympathizing breasts
That generous pleasure know,
Kindly to share in others' joy,
And weep for others' woe.

3 When poor and helpless sons of grief
In deep distress are laid,
Soft be our hearts their pains to feel,
And swift our hands to aid.

4 So Jesus looked on dying man,
When throned above the skies,
And, in the Father's bosom blest,
He felt compassion rise.

5 On wings of love the Saviour flew
To raise us from the ground;
For us he shed his precious blood —
A balm for every wound.

749. C. M. WATTS.

1 HAPPY the heart where graces reign,
Where love inspires the breast:
Love is the brightest of the train,
And strengthens all the rest.

2 Knowledge, alas! 'tis all in vain,
And all in vain our fear:
Our stubborn sins will fight and reign,
If love be absent there.

3 'Tis love that makes our cheerful feet
In swift obedience move;
The devils know, and tremble too;
But they can never love.

4 This is the grace that lives and sings
When faith and hope shall cease;
'Tis this shall strike our joyful strings
In brightest realms of bliss.

763. C. M. BODEN'S COL.

1 "FATHER, forgive," the Saviour cried,
With his expiring breath,
And drew eternal blessings down
On those who wrought his death.

2 Jesus, this wondrous love we sing,
And whilst we sing, admire;
Breathe on our souls, and kindle there
The same celestial fire.

3 By thine example ever swayed,
We for our foes will pray;
With love their hatred, and their curse
With blessings, will repay.

BALERMA. C. M. R. SIMPSON.

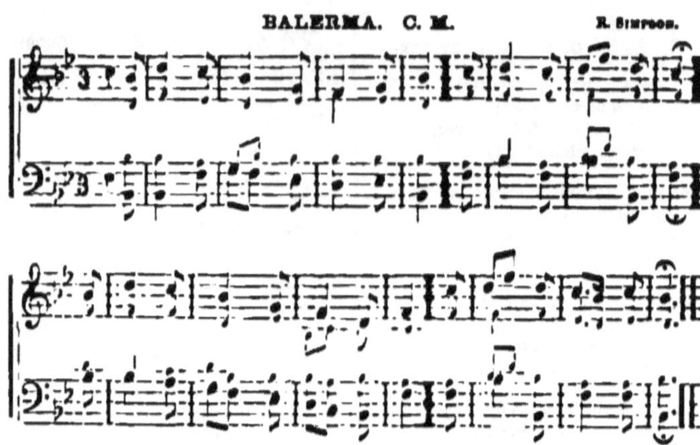

Attributed also to H. Wilson.

757. C. M. DODDRIDGE.

1 THESE mortal joys, how soon they fade !
How swift they pass away !
The dying flower reclines its head,
The beauty of a day.

2 Soon are those earthly treasures lost
We fondly call our own ;
We scarcely can possession boast,
Before we find them gone.

3 But there are joys which cannot die,
With God laid up in store,
Treasures beyond the changing sky,
More bright than golden ore.

4 The seeds which piety and love
Have scattered here below,
In fair and fertile fields above
To ample harvests grow.

766. C. M. DODDRIDGE.

1 O HAPPY Christian, who can boast,
"The Son of God is mine"!
Happy, though humbled in the dust—
Rich in this gift divine.

2 He lives the life of heaven below,
And shall forever live ;
Eternal streams from Christ shall flow,
And endless vigor give.

3 That life we ask with bended knee ;
Nor will the Lord deny,
Nor will celestial mercy see
Its humble suppliants die.

4 That life obtained, for praise alone
We wish continued breath ;
And, taught by blest experience, own
That praise can live in death.

765. C. M. FAWCETT.

1 RELIGION is the chief concern
Of mortals here below ;
May we its great importance learn,
Its sovereign virtue know.

2 Religion should our thoughts engage
Amid our youthful bloom ;
'Twill fit us for declining age,
And for the solemn tomb.

3 O, may our hearts, by grace renewed,
Be our Redeemer's throne ;
And be our stubborn wills subdued,
His government to own.

4 Let deep repentance, faith, and love
Be joined with godly fear,
And all our conversation prove
Our hearts to be sincere.

5 Let lively hope our souls inspire ;
Let warm affections rise ;
And may we wait with strong desire
To mount above the skies.

769. C. M. PRATT'S COL.

1 WHILE in the tender years of youth,
In nature's smiling bloom,
Ere age arrive, and trembling waits
Its summons to the tomb,—

2 Remember thy Creator, God ;
For him thy powers employ ;
Make him thy fear, thy love, thy hope,
Thy portion, and thy joy.

3 He will in safety guide thy course
O'er life's uncertain sea,
And bring thee to that peaceful shore
Where happy spirits be.

770. C. M. WATTS.

1 How shall the young secure their hearts,
And guard their lives from sin?
Thy word the choicest rules imparts
To keep the conscience clean.

2 'Tis like the sun, a heavenly light,
That guides us all the day,
And, through the dangers of the night,
A lamp to lead our way.

3 Thy precepts make us truly wise;
We hate the sinner's road;
We hate our own vain thoughts that rise;
But love thy law, O God.

4 Thy word is everlasting truth:
How pure is every page!
That holy book shall guide our youth,
And well support our age.

772. C. M. EPIS. COL.

1 O IN the morn of life, when youth
With vital ardor glows,
And shines in all the fairest charms
That beauty can disclose,—

2 Deep in thy soul, before its powers
Are yet by vice enslaved,
Be thy Creator's glorious name
And character engraved;—

3 Ere yet the shades of sorrow cloud
The sunshine of thy days,
And cares and toils, in endless round,
Encompass all thy ways;—

4 Ere yet thy heart the woes of age,
With vain regret, deplore,
And sadly muse on former joys,
That now return no more.

5 True wisdom, early sought and gained,
In age will give thee rest;
O, then, improve the morn of life,
To make its evening blest.

773. C. M. HEBER.

1 BY cool Siloam's shady rill
How fair the lily grows!
How sweet the breath, beneath the hill,
Of Sharon's dewy rose.

2 Lo! such the child whose early feet
The paths of peace have trod,
Whose secret heart, with influence sweet,
Is upward drawn to God.

3 By cool Siloam's shady rill
The lily must decay;
The rose, that blooms beneath the hill,
Must shortly fade away.

4 And soon, too soon, the wintry hour
Of man's maturer age
Will shake the soul with sorrow's power
And stormy passion's rage.

5 O Thou who givest life and breath,
We seek thy grace alone,
In childhood, manhood, age, and death,
To keep us still thine own.

774. C. M. COWPER.

1 BESTOW, O Lord, upon our youth
The gift of saving grace,
And let the seed of sacred truth
Fall in a fruitful place.

2 Grace is a plant, where'er it grows,
Of pure and heavenly root,
But fairest in the youngest shows,
And yields the sweetest fruit.

3 Ye careless ones, O, hear betimes
The voice of sovereign love;
Your youth is stained with many crimes,
But mercy reigns above.

4 For you the public prayer is made;
O, join the public prayer:
For you the secret tear is shed;
O, shed yourselves a tear.

5 We pray that you may early prove
The Spirit's power to teach;
You cannot be too young to love
That Jesus whom we preach.

775. C. M. LOGAN.

1 How happy is the child who hears
Instruction's warning voice,
And who celestial Wisdom makes
His early, only choice!

2 For she has treasures greater far
Than east or west unfold,
And her rewards more precious are
Than all their stores of gold.

3 She guides the young with innocence
In pleasure's path to tread;
A crown of glory she bestows
Upon the hoary head.

4 According as her labors rise,
So her rewards increase;
Her ways are ways of pleasantness
And all her paths are peace.

YORK. C. M.

Psalter. 1615.

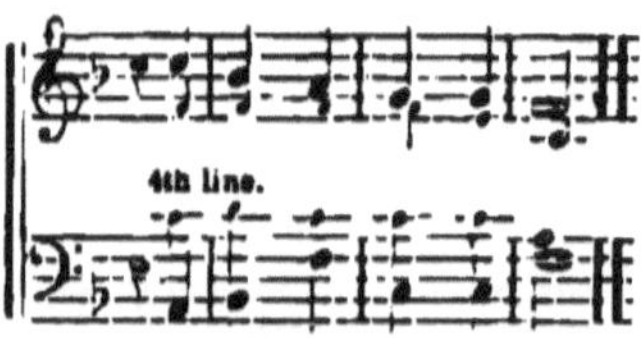

758. C. M. WATTS.

1 LONG have we heard the joyful sound
Of thy salvation, Lord;
And still how weak our faith is found,
And knowledge of thy word!

2 How cold and feeble is our love!
How negligent our fear!
How low our hope of joys above!
How few affections there!

3 Great God, thy sovereign power impart,
To give thy word success;
Write thy salvation in each heart,
And make us learn thy grace.

4 Show our forgetful feet the way
That leads to joys on high,
Where knowledge grows without decay,
And love shall never die.

785. C. M. ANON.

1 ETERNAL Saviour, God of Love,
Abused, insulted Friend,
O, from thy lofty throne above,
Thy saving mercy send.

2 Here lies my naked, guilty heart,
Before thy piercing eye;
To me thy healing touch impart;
O, reach me, for I die.

3 All that my future life shall know
Of love, and joy, and light,
Shall burn for thee, and shine and glow
By thine effectual might.

4 Thus to thy claim my trembling soul
Her sweet submission brings,
And thee, while changing ages roll,
Shall rest beneath thy wings.

751. C. M. WATTS.

1 HOW vain are all things here below!
How false, and yet how fair!
Each pleasure hath its poison too,
And every sweet a snare.

2 The brightest things below the sky
Shine with deceiving light;
We should suspect some danger nigh,
Where we possess delight.

3 Our dearest joys, our nearest friends, —
The partners of our blood, —
How they divide our wavering minds,
And leave but half for God!

4 The fondness of a creature's love,
How strong it strikes the sense!
'Tis there the warm affections move,
Nor can we call them thence.

5 Dear Saviour, let thy beauties be
My soul's eternal food,
And grace command my heart away
From all created good.

759. C. M. NEWTON.

1 SWEET was the time when first I felt
The Saviour's pardoning blood
Applied to cleanse my soul from guilt,
And bring me home to God.

2 Soon as the morn the light revealed,
His praises tuned my tongue,
And when the evening shades prevailed,
His love was all my song.

3 In prayer my soul drew near the Lord,
And saw his glory shine;
And when I read his holy word,
I called each promise mine.

4 But now, when evening shade prevails,
My soul in darkness mourns;
And when the morn the light reveals,
No light to me returns.

5 Rise, Lord, and help me to prevail;
O, make my soul thy care;
I know thy mercy cannot fail;
Let me that mercy share.

GIDEONI. C. M.

J. OSGOOD, 1853.
From Melodia Sacra

This, and other of Mr. OSGOOD's tunes, copied by his permission.

747. C. M. BEDDOME.

1 HAPPY, forever happy he
Whose heart is cleansed from sin;
His life is from reproaches free,
His conscience is serene.

2 Remote from anger, noise, and strife,
Submissive and resigned,
He leads a holy, peaceful life,
Is loved of all mankind.

3 With tender pity for the poor,
He hears their plaintive cries,
And, out of his increasing store,
Their urgent want supplies.

4 In sickness God will soothe his grief,
And be his constant Friend;
At death will yield him kind relief,
And crown his journey's end.

5 Whene'er the tempting foe alarms,
Or spreads the fatal snare,
I'll fly to my Redeemer's arms;
For safety must be there.

6 My Guardian, my almighty Friend,
On thee my soul would rest;
On thee alone my hopes depend;
In thee I'm ever blest.

671. C. M. STEELE.

1 PERMIT me, Lord, to seek thy face,
Obedient to thy call —
To seek the presence of thy grace,
My strength, my life, my all.

2 All I can wish is thine to give:
My God, I ask thy love —
That greatest boon I can receive,
That bliss of heaven above.

3 To heaven my restless heart aspires;
O for some quickening ray,
To animate my faint desires,
And cheer the tiresome way!

4 While sin and Satan join their art
To keep me from my Lord,
O Saviour, guard my trembling heart,
And guide me by thy word.

762. C. M. DODDRIDGE.

1 MY God, thy service well demands
The remnant of my days;
Why was this fleeting breath renewed,
But to renew thy praise?

2 Thine arms of everlasting love
Did this weak frame sustain,
When life was hovering o'er the grave,
And nature sunk with pain.

3 I calmly bowed my fainting head
On thy dear, faithful breast,
And waited for my Father's call
To his eternal rest.

4 Into thy hands, my Saviour God,
Did I my soul resign,
In firm dependence on that truth
Which made salvation mine.

5 Back from the borders of the grave,
At thy command, I come;
Nor will I ask a speedier flight
To my celestial home.

6 Where thou appointest mine abode,
There would I choose to be;
For in thy presence death is life,
And earth is heaven with thee.

‡ Each stanza may be sung separately.

782. C. M. Watts.

1 When God revealed his gracious name,
And changed my mournful state,
My rapture seemed a pleasing dream,
The grace appeared so great.

2 The world beheld the glorious change,
And did thy hand confess;
My tongue broke out in unknown strains,
And sung surprising grace.

3 "Great is the work," my neighbors cried,
And owned thy power divine:
"Great is the work," my heart replied,
"And be the glory thine."

4 The Lord can clear the darkest skies,
Can give us day for night,
Make drops of sacred sorrow rise
To rivers of delight.

5 Let those who sow in sadness wait
Till the fair harvest come;
They shall confess their sheaves are great,
And shout the blessings home.

781. C. M. C. Wesley.

1 Eternal Father, God of love,
To thee our hearts we raise;
Thy all-sustaining power we prove,
And gladly sing thy praise.

2 Thine, wholly thine, O, let us be;
Our sacrifice receive;
Made, and preserved, and saved by thee,
To thee ourselves we give.

3 Come, Holy Ghost, the Saviour's love
Shed in our hearts abroad;
So shall we ever live, and move,
And be, with Christ in God.

DEDHAM. C. M. Wm. Gardiner.

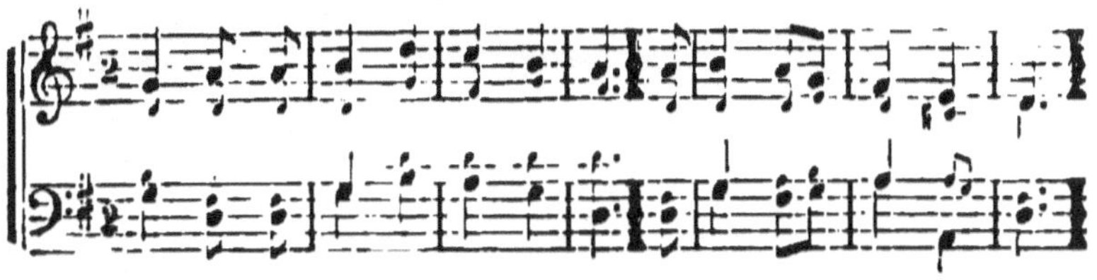

789. C. M. Watts.

1 Not to the terrors of the Lord,
The tempest, fire, and smoke;
Not to the thunder of that word
Which God on Sinai spoke;—

2 But we are come to Zion's hill,
The city of our God,
Where milder words declare his will,
And spread his love abroad.

3 Behold the great, the glorious host
Of angels clothed in light;
Behold the spirits of the just,
Whose faith is turned to sight.

4 Behold the blest assembly there,
Whose names are writ in heaven,
And God, the Judge, who doth declare
Their vilest sins forgiven.

5 The saints on earth, and all the dead,
But one communion make;
All join in Christ, their living Head,
And of his grace partake.

6 In such society as this
Our weary souls would rest;
The man who dwells where Jesus is
Must be forever blest.

791. C. M. C. Wesley.

1 Come, let us join our friends above,
Who have obtained the prize,
And on the eagle wings of love
To joy celestial rise.

2 Let saints below in concert sing
With those to glory gone;
For all the servants of our King
In heaven and earth are one.

3 One family, we dwell in him;
One church above, beneath;
Though now divided by the stream—
The narrow stream—of death.

4 One army of the living God,
To his command we bow;
Part of the host have crossed the flood,
And part are crossing now.

5 E'en now to their eternal home
Some happy spirits fly;
And we are to the margin come,
And soon expect to die.

6 O Saviour, be our constant Guide;
Then, when the word is given,
Bid Jordan's narrow stream divide,
And land us safe in heaven.

793. C. M. C. Wesley.

1 Happy the souls to Jesus joined,
And saved by grace alone:
Walking in all his ways, they find
Their heaven on earth begun.

2 The church triumphant in thy love,
Their mighty joys we know:
They sing the Lamb in hymns above,
And we in hymns below.

3 Thee in thy glorious realm they praise,
And bow before thy throne;
We in the kingdom of thy grace:
The kingdoms are but one.

4 The holy to the holiest leads:
From thence our spirits rise;
And he that in thy statutes treads
Shall meet thee in the skies.

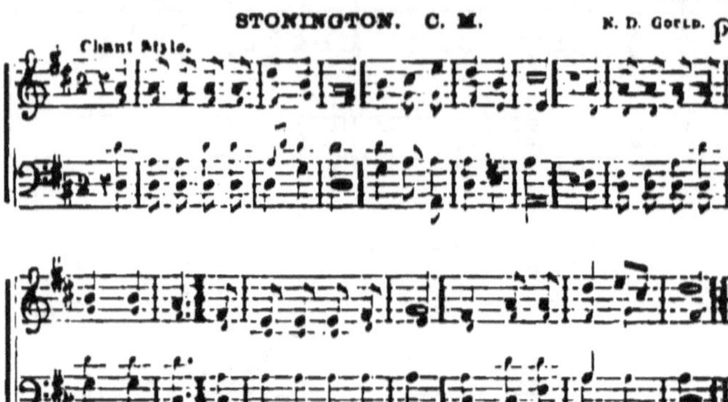

787. C. M. WATTS.

1 BEHOLD the sure foundation stone,
Which God in Zion lays,
To build our heavenly hopes upon,
And his eternal praise.

2 Chosen of God, to sinners dear,
Let saints adore the name;
They trust their whole salvation here,
Nor shall they suffer shame.

3 The foolish builders, scribe and priest,
Reject it with disdain;
Yet on this rock the church shall rest,
And envy rage in vain.

4 What though the gates of hell withstood;
Yet must this building rise:
'Tis thine own work, almighty God,
And wondrous in our eyes.

796. C. M. BEDDOME.

1 A HOST of spirits round the throne
In humble posture stand,
On every head a starry crown,
A palm in every hand.

2 From different regions of the globe
These happy spirits came;
In Jesus' blood they washed their robes,
And triumphed in his name.

3 One glorious body now they make—
More glorious far their Head;
Their souls to rapturous joys awake;
Their sorrows all are fled.

4 Without a jarring note, they join
In ceaseless songs of praise,
And to the sacred Three in One
Loud hallelujahs raise.

790. C. M. MONTGOMERY.

1 IN one fraternal bond of love,
One fellowship of mind,
The saints below and saints above
Their bliss and glory find.

2 Here, in their house of pilgrimage,
Thy statutes are their song;
There, through one bright, eternal age,
Thy praises they prolong.

3 Lord, may our union form a part
Of that thrice happy whole,
Derive its pulse from thee, the heart,
Its life from thee, the soul.

DOWNS.

823. C. M. ENG. BAP. COL.

1 O LORD, we in thy footsteps tread,
With joy thy cause maintain;
Like Jesus numbered with the dead,
Like him we rise and reign.

2 Down to the hallowed grave we go,
Obedient to thy word;
'Tis thus the world around shall know,
We're buried with the Lord.

3 'Tis thus we bid its pomps adieu,
And boldly venture in:
O, may we rise to live anew,
And only die to sin.

BOWDOIN STREET. C. M. B. F. EDMANDS.

800. C. M. FELLOWS.

1 O LORD, and will thy pardoning love
Embrace a wretch so vile?
Wilt thou my load of guilt remove,
And bless me with thy smile?

2 Hast thou the cross for me endured,
And all its shame despised?
And shall I be ashamed, O Lord,
With thee to be baptized?

3 Didst thou the great example lead,
In Jordan's swelling flood?
And shall my pride disdain the deed,
That's worthy of my God?

4 O Lord, the ardor of thy love
Reproves my cold delays;
And now my willing footsteps move
In thy delightful ways.

801. C. M. ANON.

1 LORD, I am thine, and in thy aid
I place my firmest trust;
How large the price thy love has paid
For vile, polluted dust!

2 In thine assembly now I stand;
My vows to thee I bring,
Obedient to thy great command,
My Saviour and my King.

3 I stand before the sacred flood;
Thy gracious words invite:
How poor an offering, O my God,
I make thee in this rite!

4 Thine ordinance, great Saviour, bless;
Support me all my days;
May I each gospel truth confess,
And walk in all thy ways.

17

803. C. M. S. F. SMITH.

1 WHILE in this sacred rite of thine,
We yield our spirits now,
Shine o'er the waters, Dove divine,
And seal the cheerful vow.

2 All glory be to Him whose life
For ours was freely given,
Who aids us in the spirit's strife,
And makes us meet for heaven.

3 To thee we gladly now resign
Our life and all our powers;
Accept us in this rite divine,
And bless these hallowed hours.

4 O, may we die to earth and sin,
Beneath the mystic flood;
And when we rise, may we begin
To live anew for God.

822. C. M. DODDRIDGE.

1 BAPTIZED into our Saviour's death,
Our souls to sin must die;
With Christ our Lord we live anew,
With Christ ascend on high.

2 There, by his Father's side he sits,
Enthroned divinely fair,
Yet owns himself our Brother still,
And our Forerunner there.

3 Rise from these earthly trifles, rise
On wings of faith and love;
Above, our choicest treasure lies,—
And be our hearts above.

4 But earth and sin will draw us down,
When we attempt to fly;
Lord, send thy strong, attractive power
To fix our souls on high.

SOLOMON. C. M.

From Handel.

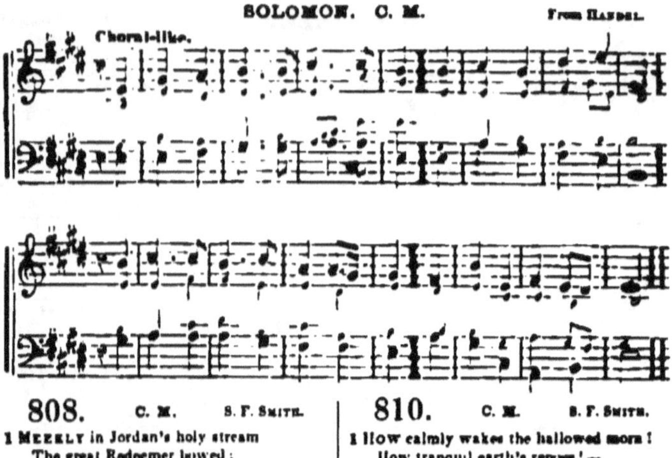

808. C. M. S. F. Smith.

1 Meekly in Jordan's holy stream
The great Redeemer bowed;
Bright was the glory's sacred beam
That hushed the wondering crowd.

2 Thus God descended to approve
The deed that Christ had done;
Thus came the emblematic Dove,
And hovered o'er the Son.

3 So, blessèd Spirit, come to-day
To our baptismal scene:
Let thoughts of earth be far away,
And every mind serene.

4 This day we give to holy joy;
This day to heaven belongs:
Raised to new life, we will employ
In melody our tongues.

810. C. M. S. F. Smith.

1 How calmly wakes the hallowed morn!
How tranquil earth's repose! —
Meet emblem of the Sabbath morn,
When, early, Jesus rose.

2 How fair, along the rippling wave,
The radiant light is cast! —
A symbol of the mystic grave
Through which the Saviour passed.

3 Around this scene of sacred love
The peace of heaven is shed:
So came the Spirit, like a dove,
To rest on Jesus' head.

4 Lord, meet us in this path of thine;
We come thy right to seal;
Move o'er the waters, Dove divine,
And all thy grace reveal.

DUNDEE. C. M.

Scotch Psalter, 1615.

A. A. GOULD.
From Nat. Ch. Harmony.

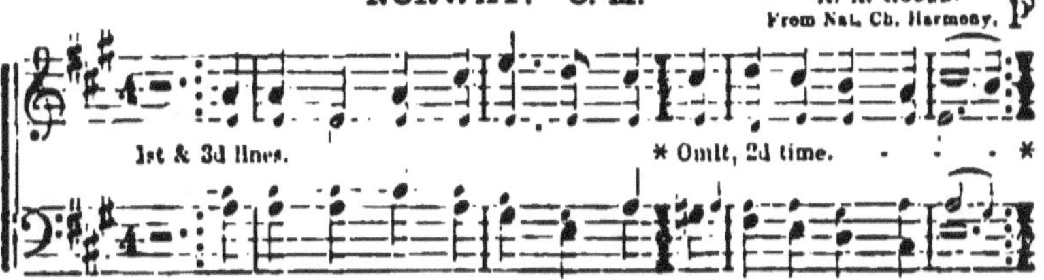

802. C. M. BEDDOME.

1 BURIED beneath the yielding wave
The great Redeemer lies;
Faith views him in the watery grave,
And thence beholds him rise.

2 Thus do his willing saints, to-day,
Their ardent zeal express,
And, in the Lord's appointed way,
Fulfil all righteousness.

3 With joy we in his footsteps tread,
And would his cause maintain,—
Like him be numbered with the dead,
And with him rise and reign.

4 His presence oft revives our hearts,
And drives our fears away;
When he commands, and strength imparts,
We cheerfully obey.

5 Now we, blest Saviour, would to thee
Our grateful voices raise;
Washed in the fountain of thy blood,
Our lives shall all be praise.

824. C. M. JAS. NEWTON.

1 LET plenteous grace descend on those,
Who, hoping in thy word,
This day have solemnly declared
That Jesus is their Lord.

2 With cheerful feet may they advance,
And run the Christian race,
And, through the troubles of the way,
Find all-sufficient grace.

3 Lord, plant us all into thy death,
That we thy life may prove—
Partakers of thy cross beneath,
And of thy crown above.

811. C. M. ENG. BAP. COL.

1 'TIS God the Father we adore
In this baptismal sign;
'Tis he whose voice on Jordan's shore
Proclaimed the Son divine.

2 The Father owned him; let our breath,
In answering praise, ascend,
As in the image of his death
We own our heavenly Friend.

3 We seek the consecrated grave
Along the path he trod:
Receive us in the hallowed wave,
Thou holy Son of God.

4 Let earth and heaven our zeal record,
And future witness bear,
That we to Zion's mighty Lord
Our full allegiance swear.

5 O that our conscious souls may own,
With joy's serene survey,
Inscribed upon his judgment throne,
The transcript of this day.

812. C. M. J. RYLAND.

1 IN all my Lord's appointed ways
My journey I'll pursue;
"Hinder me not," ye much-loved saints,
For I must go with you.

2 Through floods and flames, if Jesus lead,
I'll follow where he goes;
"Hinder me not," shall be my cry,
Though earth and hell oppose.

3 Through duties, and through trials too,
I'll go at his command;
"Hinder me not;" for I am bound
To my Immanuel's land.

4 And, when my Saviour calls me home,
Still this my cry shall be,—
"Hinder me not;" come, welcome, death;
I'll gladly go with thee.

AZMON.

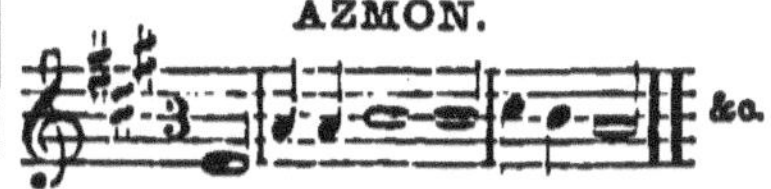

ABRIDGE. C. M. — Isaac Smith.

827. C. M. MONTGOMERY.

1 COME in, thou blessèd of the Lord:
 Stranger nor foe art thou:
We welcome thee with warm accord,
 Our friend, our brother now.

2 The hand of fellowship, the heart
 Of love, we offer thee:
Leaving the world, thou dost but part
 From lies and vanity.

3 The cup of blessing which we bless,
 The heavenly bread we break,—
Our Saviour's blood and righteousness,—
 Freely with us partake.

4 In weal or woe, in joy or care,
 Thy portion shall be ours;
Christians their mutual burdens bear;
 They lend their mutual powers.

5 Come with us; we will do thee good,
 As God to us hath done;
Stand but in him, as those have stood
 Whose faith the victory won.

6 And when, by turns, we pass away,
 As star by star grows dim,
May each, translated into day,
 Be lost, and found in him.

830. C. M. BADDOME.

1 YE men and angels, witness now,—
 Before the Lord we speak;
To him we make our solemn vow,—
 A vow we dare not break,—

2 That, long as life itself shall last,
 Ourselves to Christ we yield;
Nor from his cause will we depart,
 Or ever quit the field.

3 We trust not in our native strength,
 But on his grace rely;
May he, with our returning wants,
 All needful aid supply.

4 O, guide our doubtful feet aright,
 And keep us in thy ways;
And, while we turn our vows to prayers,
 Turn thou our prayers to praise.

850. C. M. ANON.

1 LET vain pursuits and vain desires
 Be banished from the heart,
The Saviour's love fill every breast,
 And light and life impart.

2 He knows how frail our nature is,
 Our souls how apt to stray;
How much we need his gracious help
 To keep us in the way!

3 These faithful pledges of his love
 His mercy did ordain,
To bring refreshment to our souls,
 And faith and hope sustain.

4 Since such his condescending grace,
 Let us, with hearts sincere,
Obedient to his holy will,
 His table now draw near.

5 And while we join to celebrate
 The sufferings of our Lord,
May we receive new grace and power,
 T' obey his holy word.

HERMON.

DUNFERMLINE. C. M. Ravenscroft's Book of Psalms.
Specimen of the melody and harmony of 1621.

835. C. M. Watts.

1 How sweet and awful is the place,
With Christ within the doors,
While everlasting Love displays
The choicest of her stores!

2 While all our hearts, and every song,
Join to admire the feast,
Each of us cries, with thankful tongue,
"Lord, why was I a guest?

3 "Why was I made to hear thy voice,
And enter while there's room,
When thousands make a wretched choice,
And rather starve than come?"

4 'Twas the same love that spread the feast
That sweetly forced us in;
Else we had still refused to taste,
And perished in our sin.

5 Pity the nations, O our God;
Constrain the earth to come;
Send thy victorious word abroad,
And bring the strangers home.

6 We long to see thy churches full,
That all the chosen race
May, with one voice, and heart, and soul,
Sing thy redeeming grace.

841. C. M. Pratt's Col.

1 Prepare us, Lord, to view thy cross,
Who all our griefs hast borne;
To look on thee, whom we have pierced—
To look on thee, and mourn.

2 While thus we mourn, we would rejoice;
And, as thy cross we see,
Let each exclaim, in faith and hope,
"The Saviour died for me!"

837. C. M. J. Stennett.

1 Lord, at thy table we behold
The wonders of thy grace,
But most of all admire that we
Should find a welcome place;—

2 We, who are all defiled with sin,
And rebels to our God;
We, who have crucified thy Son,
And trampled on his blood.

3 What strange, surprising grace is this,
That we, so lost, have room!
Jesus our weary souls invites,
And freely bids us come.

4 Ye saints below, and hosts of heaven,
Join all your sacred powers:
No theme is like redeeming love;
No Saviour is like ours.

838. C. M. Watts.

1 "The promise of my Father's love
Shall stand forever good,"
He said; and gave his soul to death,
And sealed the grace with blood.

2 To this dear covenant of thy word
I set my worthless name;
I seal the promise to my Lord,
And make my humble claim.

3 I call that legacy my own
Which Jesus did bequeath;
'Twas purchased with a dying groan,
And ratified in death.

4 The light and strength, the pardoning grace,
And glory, shall be mine:
My life and soul, my heart and flesh,
And all my powers, are thine.

WOODLAND. C. M. N. D. GOULD. From the Sacred Minstrel.

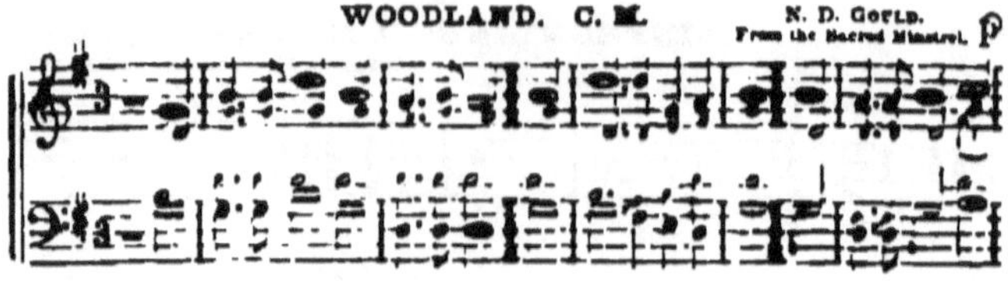

839. C. M. S. STENNETT.

1 HERE at thy table, Lord, we meet,
 To feed on food divine:
Thy body is the bread we eat,
 Thy precious blood the wine.

2 Here peace and pardon sweetly flow:
 O, what delightful food!
We eat the bread, and drink the wine,
 But think on nobler good.

3 Deep was the suffering he endured
 Upon th' accursèd tree;
"For me," each welcome guest may say,
 "'Twas all endured for me."

4 Sure there was never love so free —
 Dear Saviour — so divine:
Well thou mayst claim that heart of me,
 Which owes so much to thine.

842. C. M. B. W. NOEL.

1 IF human kindness meets return,
 And owns the grateful tie;
If tender thoughts within us burn
 To feel a friend is nigh; —

2 O, shall not warmer accents tell
 The gratitude we owe
To Him who died our fears to quell,
 And save from endless woe?

3 While yet his anguished soul surveyed
 Those pangs he would not flee,
What love his latest words displayed! —
 "Meet and remember me."

4 Remember thee! thy death, thy shame,
 The griefs which thou didst bear!
O memory, leave no other name
 But his recorded there.

840. C. M. WATTS.

1 HOW condescending and how kind
 Was God's eternal Son!
Our misery reached his heavenly mind,
 And pity brought him down.

2 This was compassion like a God,
 That, when the Saviour knew
The price of pardon was his blood,
 His pity ne'er withdrew.

3 Here let our hearts begin to melt,
 While we his death record,
And, with our joy for pardoned guilt,
 Mourn that we pierced the Lord.

846. C. M. WARDLAW.

1 REMEMBER thee, redeeming Lord!
 While memory holds her place,
Can we forget the Prince of life,
 Who saves us by his grace?

2 The Lord of life, with glory crowned,
 On heaven's exalted throne,
Remembers those for whom, on earth,
 He heaved his dying groan.

3 His glory now no tongue of man
 Or seraph bright can tell;
Yet 'tis the chief of all his joys
 That souls are saved from hell.

4 For this he came and dwelt on earth;
 For this his life was given,
For this he fought and vanquished death;
 For this he pleads in heaven.

5 Join, all ye saints beneath the sky,
 Your grateful praise to give;
Sing loud hosannas to the Lord,
 Who died that you might live.

LIND. C. M. German.

848. C. M. E. Taylor.

1 O, here, if ever, God of love,
Let strife and hatred cease,
And every heart harmonious move,
And every thought be peace.

2 Not here, where, met to think on Him
Whose latest thoughts were ours,
Shall mortal passions come to dim
The prayer devotion pours.

3 No, gracious Master, not in vain
Thy life of love hath been;
The peace thou gav'st may yet remain,
Though thou no more art seen.

4 "Thy kingdom come:" we watch, we wait
To hear thy cheering call,
When heaven shall ope its glorious gate,
And God be all in all.

851. C. M. Scotch Col.

1 To Him who loved the souls of men,
And washed us in his blood,
To royal honors raised our head,
And made us priests to God, —

2 To him let every tongue be praise,
And every heart be love,
All grateful honors paid on earth,
And nobler songs above.

---

862. C. M. W. Ward.

1 Great God, the nations of the earth
Are by creation thine;
And in thy works, by all beheld,
Thy radiant glories shine.

2 But, Lord, thy greater love has sent
Thy gospel to mankind,
Unveiling what rich stores of grace
Are treasured in thy mind.

3 O, when shall these glad tidings spread
The spacious earth around,
Till every tribe and every soul
Shall hear the joyful sound?

4 Smile, Lord, on each divine attempt
To spread the gospel's rays,
And build on sin's demolished throne
The temples of thy praise.

875. C. M. Montgomery.

1 Spirit of power and might, behold
A world by sin destroyed:
Creator Spirit, as of old,
Move on the formless void.

2 Give thou the Word: that healing sound
Shall quell the deadly strife,
And earth again, like Eden crowned,
Bring forth the tree of life.

3 If sang the morning stars for joy
When nature rose to view,
What strains will angel harps employ
When thou shalt all renew!

4 And if the sons of God rejoice
To hear a Saviour's name,
How will the ransomed raise their voice,
To whom that Saviour came!

5 Lo! every kindred, tongue, and tribe,
Assembling round the throne,
The new creation shall ascribe
To sovereign love alone.

LUTZEN. C. M. NICOL. HERRMAN. 1561.

864. C. M. GIBBONS.

1 LORD, send thy word, and let it fly,
Armed with thy Spirit's power:
Ten thousands shall confess its sway,
And bless the saving hour.

2 Beneath the influence of thy grace
The barren wastes shall rise,
With sudden greens and fruits arrayed,
A blooming paradise.

3 True holiness shall strike its root
In each regenerate heart;
Shall in a growth divine arise,
And heavenly fruits impart.

4 Peace, with her olives crowned, shall stretch
Her wings from shore to shore;
No trump shall rouse the rage of war,
No murderous cannon roar.

5 Lord, for those days we wait; those days
Are in thy word foretold;
Fly swifter, sun and stars, and bring
This promised age of gold.

6 "Amen," with joy divine, let earth's
Unnumbered myriads cry;
"Amen," with joy divine, let heaven's
Unnumbered choirs reply.

866. C. M. S. F. SMITH.

1 MOST gracious to fulfil thy word,
Almighty to defend,—
To reap thy ripened harvest, Lord,
Thy chosen servants send.

2 Send to the east the valiant band:
Send to each distant pole;
Send to the west; o'er every land
Salvation's current roll.

3 Heralds of peace, we come! we come!
On love's swift wings we fly;
Ye dead in sin, O, live; ye dumb,
In hallelujahs cry.

4 O Zion, spread more wide thy tent;
Stretch forth thy straining cords;
The promise dawns; the clouds are rent;
Earth, thou shalt be the Lord's.

5 Haste, haste, ye years of toil and woe;
Heaven, earth, break forth and sing,
"The kingdoms of the world are now
Thy conquest, peerless King."

6 Amen, amen; let echoing praise
Swell like the sounding sea;
To God, to God, those rapturous lays,
That tide of praise, shall be.

888. C. M. MORELL.

1 GO, and the Saviour's grace proclaim,
Ye favored men of God;
Go, publish, through Immanuel's name,
Salvation bought with blood.

2 Go, with determined courage go,
And armed with power divine;
Your God will needful strength bestow,
And on your labors shine.

3 He who has called you to the war
Will soon reward your pains;
Before Messiah's conquering car
Shall mountains sink to plains.

4 Shrink not, though earth and hell oppose,
But plead your Master's cause,
Assured that e'en your mightiest foes
Shall bow before his cross.

NORWAY. C. M. A. A. GOULD. From Nat. Ch. Harmony.

858. C. M. LYTE.

1 Be merciful to us, O God;
Upon thy people shine;
And spread thy saving truth abroad,
Till all that live be thine.

2 Give light and comfort to thine own;
And let that light extend
Till thy prevailing name be known
To earth's remotest end.

3 Let all the people praise thee, Lord;
Let all their homage bring;
From sea to sea be thou adored,
Redeemer, Judge, and King.

870. C. M. BURDER'S COL.

1 JESUS, immortal King, arise;
Assert thy rightful sway;
Till earth, subdued, its tribute brings,
And distant lands obey.

2 Ride forth, victorious Conqueror, ride,
Till all thy foes submit,
And all the powers of hell resign
Their trophies at thy feet.

3 Send forth thy word, and let it fly
This spacious earth around,
Till every soul beneath the sun
Shall hear the joyful sound.

4 O, may the great Redeemer's name
Through every clime be known,
And heathen gods, forsaken, fall,
And Jesus reign alone.

5 From sea to sea, from shore to shore,
May Jesus be adored,
And earth, with all her millions, shout
Hosannas to the Lord.

894. C. M. MONTGOMERY.

1 DAUGHTER of Zion, from the dust
Exalt thy fallen head;
Again in thy Redeemer trust;
He calls thee from the dead.

2 Awake, awake; put on thy strength,
Thy beautiful array;
The day of freedom dawns at length,
The Lord's appointed day.

3 Rebuild thy walls, thy bounds enlarge,
And send thy heralds forth;
Say to the south, "Give up thy charge,"
And, "Keep not back, O north."

4 They come! they come! thine exiled bands,
Where'er they rest or roam,
Have heard thy voice in distant lands,
And hasten to their home.

5 Thus, though the universe shall burn,
And God his works destroy,
With songs thy ransomed shall return,
And everlasting joy.

899. C. M. LOGAN.

1 BEHOLD, the mountain of the Lord,
In latter days, shall rise
Above the mountains and the hills,
And draw the wondering eyes.

2 To this the joyful nations round,
All tribes and tongues, shall flow:
"Up to the hill of God," they say,
"And to his house, we'll go."

3 The beam that shines on Zion's hill
Shall lighten every land:
The King who reigns in Zion's towers
Shall all the world command.

4 No strife shall vex Messiah's reign,
Or mar the peaceful years;
To ploughshares men shall beat their swords,
To pruning-hooks their spears.

5 Come, then, O, come from every land,
To worship at his shrine;
And, walking in the light of God,
With holy beauty shine.

‡ A model of a choral in triple time.

885. C. M. Morell.

1 Father of mercies, condescend
  To hear our fervent prayer,
While these our brethren we commend
  To thy paternal care.

2 Before them set an open door;
  Their various efforts bless;
On them thy Holy Spirit pour,
  And crown them with success.

3 Endow them with a heavenly mind;
  Supply their every need;
Make them in spirit meek, resigned,
  But bold in word and deed.

4 In every tempting, trying hour,
  Uphold them by thy grace,
And guard them by thy mighty power
  Till they shall end their race.

5 Then, followed by a numerous train,
  Gathered from heathen lands,
A crown of life may they obtain
  From their Redeemer's hands.

886. C. M. Anon.

1 Kindred, and friends, and native land,
  How shall we say, "Farewell"?
How, — when our swelling sails expand, —
  How will our bosoms swell!

2 Yes, nature, all thy soft delights
  And tender ties we know;
But love, more strong than death, unites
  To Him that bids us go.

3 Thus, when, our every passion moved,
  The gushing tear-drop starts,
The cause of Jesus, more beloved,
  Shall glow within our hearts.

4 The sighs we breathe for precious souls,
  Where he is yet unknown,
Might waft us to the distant poles,
  Or to the burning zone.

5 With warm desire our bosoms swell,
  Our glowing powers expand;
"Farewell," then we can say, "farewell,
  Our friends, our native land."

895. C. M. Watts.

1 Let Zion and her sons rejoice;
  Behold the promised hour;
Her God hath heard her mourning voice,
  And comes t' exalt his power.

2 Her dust and ruins, that remain,
  Are precious in his eyes;
These ruins shall be built again,
  And all that dust shall rise.

3 The Lord will raise Jerusalem,
  And stand in glory there;
All nations bow before his name,
  And kings attend with fear.

4 He sits, a Sovereign, on his throne,
  With pity in his eyes;
He hears the dying prisoners' groan,
  And sees their sighs arise.

5 He frees the soul condemned to death;
  Nor, when his saints complain,
Shall it be said that praying breath
  Was ever spent in vain.

6 This shall be known when we are dead,
  And left on long record,
That ages yet unborn may read,
  And praise and trust the Lord.

NORTHFIELD. C. M. INGALLS.

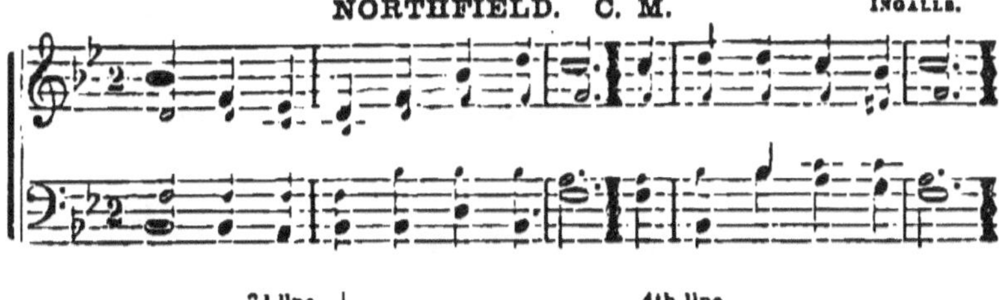

898. C. M. WATTS.

1 SHINE, mighty God, on Zion shine
With beams of heavenly grace;
Reveal thy power through every land,
And show thy smiling face.

2 When shall thy name, from shore to shore
Sound through the earth abroad,
And distant nations know and love
Their Saviour and their God?

3 Sing to the Lord, ye distant lands;
Sing loud, with joyful voice;
Let every tongue exalt his praise,
And every heart rejoice.

905. C. M. WATTS.

1 LO! what a glorious sight appears
To our believing eyes!
The earth and seas are passed away,
And fled the rolling skies.

2 From highest heaven, where God resides,
That holy, happy place,
The new Jerusalem comes down,
Adorned with shining grace.

3 Attending angels shout for joy,
And heavenly armies sing —
"Ye saints, behold the sacred seat
Of your descending King.

4 "The God of glory down to men
Removes his blest abode;
His saints the objects of his grace,
And he their faithful God.

5 "His own soft hand shall wipe the tears
From every weeping eye,
And pains, and groans, and griefs, and fears,
And death itself, shall die."

6 How long, dear Saviour, O, how long
Shall this bright hour delay?
Fly swifter round, ye wheels of time,
And bring the welcome day.

923. C. M. W. B. TAPPAN.

1 HARK! 'tis the Prophet of the skies
Proclaims redemption near:
The night of death and bondage flies;
The dawning tints appear.

2 Zion, from deepest shades of gloom,
Awakes to glorious day;
Her desert wastes with verdure bloom,
Her shadows flee away.

3 To heal her wounds, her night dispel,
The heralds cross the main;
On Calvary's mournful brow they tell
That Jesus lives again.

4 From Salem's towers the Islam sign
With holy zeal is hurled;
'Tis there Immanuel's symbols shine;
His banner is unfurled.

5 The gladdening news, conveyed afar,
Remotest nations hear;
To welcome Judah's rising star,
The ransomed tribes appear.

6 Again in Bethl'em swells the song;
The choral breaks again;
While Jordan's shores the strains prolong,
"Good-will and peace to men."

MEAR. C. M. Author unknown.

May be sung in notes of equal length throughout, i. e., in 2-2 time.

924. C. M. Moore.

1 But who shall see the glorious day,
When, throned on Zion's brow,
The Lord shall rend that veil away
Which binds the nations now?

2 When earth no more beneath the fear
Of his rebuke shall lie,—
When pain shall cease, and every tear
Be wiped from every eye,—

3 Then, Judah, thou no more shalt mourn
Beneath the heathen's chain;
Thy days of splendor shall return,
And all be new again.

4 The fount of life shall then be quaffed
In peace by all who come,
And every wind that blows shall waft
Some long-lost exile home.

927. C. M. Watts.

1 Arise, O King of grace, arise,
And enter to thy rest;
Behold, thy church, with longing eyes
Waits to be owned and blest.

2 Enter, with all thy glorious train,
Thy Spirit and thy Word;
All that the ark did once contain
Could no such grace afford.

3 Here, mighty God, accept our vows;
Here let thy praise be spread;
Bless the provisions of thy house,
And fill thy poor with bread.

4 Here let the Son of David reign,
Let God's Anointed shine;
Justice and truth his court maintain,
With love and power divine.

5 Here let him hold a lasting throne;
And, as his kingdom grows,
Fresh honors shall adorn his crown,
And shame confound his foes.

DOWNS.

929. C. M. S. F. Smith.

1 Planted in Christ, the living vine,
This day, with one accord,
Ourselves, with humble faith and joy,
We yield to thee, O Lord.

2 Joined in one body may we be;
One inward life partake;
One be our heart; one heavenly hope
In every bosom wake.

3 In prayer, in effort, tears, and toils,
One wisdom be our guide;
Taught by one Spirit from above,
In thee may we abide.

4 Complete in us, whom grace hath called,
Thy glorious work begun,
O Thou, in whom the church on earth
And church in heaven are one.

5 Around this feeble, trusting band
Thy sheltering pinions spread,
Nor let the storms of trial beat
Too fiercely on our head.

6 Then, when, among the saints in light,
Our joyful spirits shine,
Shall anthems of immortal praise,
O Lamb of God, be thine.

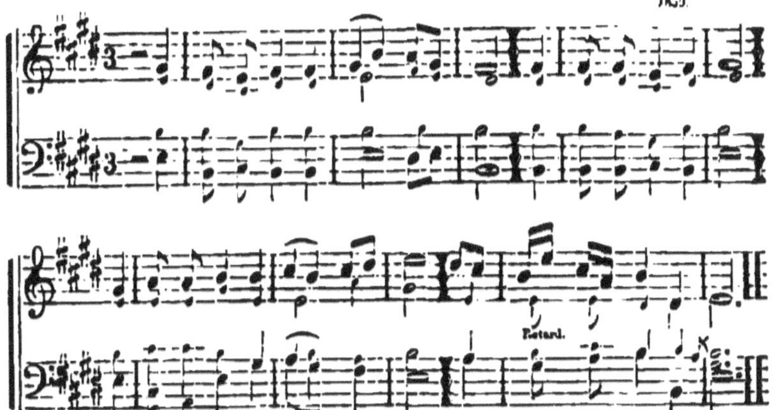

936. C. M. Dobell's Col.

1 Great Sovereign of the earth and sky,
And Lord of all below,
Before thy glorious majesty
Ten thousand seraphs bow.

2 Yet thou art not confined above;
Thy presence knows no bound;
Where'er thy praying people meet,
There thou art always found.

3 Behold a temple raised for thee;
O, meet thy people here;
Here, O thou King of saints, reside,
And in thy church appear.

4 Within these walls let holy peace,
And love, and concord, dwell;
Here give the troubled conscience ease,
The wounded spirit heal.

5 Here may salvation be proclaimed
By thy most precious blood;
Let sinners know the joyful sound,
And own their Saviour, God.

937. C. M. Reed.

1 Spirit divine, attend our prayer,
And make this house thy home;
Descend with all thy gracious power;
O, come, great Spirit, come.

2 Come as the light: to us reveal
Our sinfulness and woe,
And lead us in the paths of life,
Where all the righteous go.

3 Come as the fire, and purge our hearts,
Like sacrificial flame;
Let every soul an offering be
To our Redeemer's name.

4 Come as a dove, and spread thy wings,—
The wings of peaceful love,—
And let the church on earth become
Blest as the church above.

5 Spirit divine, attend our prayer,
And make this house thy home;
Descend with all thy gracious power;
O, come, great Spirit, come.

939. C. M. J. D. Knowles.

1 O God, though countless worlds of light
Thy power and glory show;
Though round thy throne, above all height,
Immortal seraphs glow,—

2 Yet oft to men of ancient time
Thy glorious presence came,
And in Moriah's fane sublime
Thou didst record thy name.

3 And now, where'er thy saints apart
Are met for praise and prayer,
Wherever sighs a contrite heart,
Thou, gracious God, art there.

4 With grateful joy, thy children rear
This temple, Lord, to thee;
Long may they sing thy praises here,
And here thy beauty see.

5 Here, Saviour, deign thy saints to meet;
With peace their hearts to fill;
And here, like Sharon's odors sweet,
May grace divine distil.

6 Here may thy truth fresh triumphs win;
Eternal Spirit, here,
In many a heart now dead in sin
A living temple rear.

WOODLAND. C. M. N. D. Gould.
From the Sacred Minstrel.

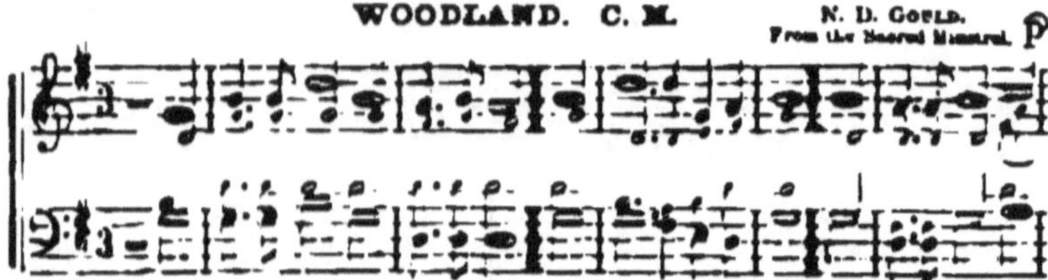

943. C. M. Shepherd's Col.

1 Will God in very deed descend,
And dwell with men below?
An ear to mortal worship lend?
To us his glory show?

2 While heaven's exalted spheres resound
With hymns which angels sing,
Will God in mercy so abound,
T' accept the praise we bring?

3 Allowed within thy courts to meet,
Thy presence we implore;
Smile on us from thy mercy-seat,
And we desire no more.

4 Here let thy gospel be declared;
Here make thy power be known;
May every heart, by grace prepared,
Be the Redeemer's throne.

5 Here make thyself a glorious name,
And form us for thy praise;
Thy promised presence, Lord, we claim,
And supplicate thy grace.

LITCHFIELD.

944. C. M. J. R. Scott.

1 To thee this temple we devote,
Our Father and our God;
Accept it thine, and seal it now
Thy Spirit's blest abode.

2 Here may the prayer of faith ascend,
The voice of praise arise;
O, may each lowly service prove
Accepted sacrifice.

3 Here may the sinner learn his guilt,
And weep before his Lord;
Here, pardoned, sing a Saviour's love,
And here his vows record.

4 Here may affliction dry the tear,
And learn to trust in God,
Convinced it is a Father smites,
And love that guides the rod.

5 Peace be within these sacred walls;
Prosperity be here;
Long smile upon thy people, Lord,
And evermore be near.

---

947. 8s & 6s. S. F. Smith.

1 Blest is the hour when cares depart,
And earthly scenes are far,—
When tears of woe forget to start,
And gently dawns upon the heart
Devotion's holy star.

2 Blest is the place where angels bend
To hear our worship rise,
Where kindred thoughts their musings blend,
And all the soul's affections tend
Beyond the veiling skies.

3 Blest are the hallowed vows that bind
Man to his work of love—
Bind him to cheer the humble mind,
Console the weeping, lead the blind,
And guide to joys above.

4 Sweet shall the song of glory swell,
Spirit divine, to thee,
When they whose work is finished well,
In thy own courts of rest shall dwell,
Blest through eternity.

948. C. M. M. A. Collier.

1 The sun, that lights yon broad, blue sky,
May see his radiance dim; —
The stars, that circle bright and high,
May hush their joyous hymn; —

2 The spring may breathe her balmy airs,
Yet earth no verdure show; —
The purest love a mother bears
May lose its wonted glow; —

3 But still within the Saviour's breast
There dwells a quenchless flame:
The earth may sink, the hills depart,
It lives, it burns the same.

4 O ransomed church, the Son of God
Still loves thy children well;
For thee the paths of death he trod;
'Tis thine his grace to tell.

5 Saviour, thy messenger we greet
Within this hallowed spot;
O, may we here thy presence meet:
Our God, forsake us not.

955. C. M. Doddridge.

1 Let Zion's watchmen all awake,
And take th' alarm they give;
Now let them from the mouth of God
Their awful charge receive.

2 'Tis not a cause of small import
The pastor's care demands,
But what might fill an angel's heart,
And filled a Saviour's hands.

3 They watch for souls, for which the Lord
Did heavenly bliss forego, —
For souls, which must forever live,
In rapture or in woe.

4 May they that Jesus, whom they preach,
Their own Redeemer, see;
And watch thou daily o'er their souls,
That they may watch for thee.

---

968. C. M. Jane Taylor.

1 There is a glorious world of light
Above the starry sky,
Where saints departed, clothed in white,
Adore the Lord most high.

2 And hark! amid the sacred songs
Those heavenly voices raise,
Ten thousand thousand infant tongues
Unite in perfect praise.

3 Those are the hymns that we shall know,
If Jesus we obey;
That is the place where we shall go,
If found in wisdom's way.

969. C. M. Strachan.

1 Be ours the bliss in wisdom's way
To guide untutored youth,
And lead the mind that went astray
To virtue and to truth.

2 Delightful work, young souls to win,
And turn the rising race
From the deceitful paths of sin
To seek redeeming grace!

3 Almighty God, thine influence shed
To aid this good design;
The honors of thy name be spread,
And all the glory thine.

972. C. M. Union Col.

1 Great God, in whom we live and move,
Accept our feeble praise,
For all the mercy, grace, and love,
Which crowns our youthful days.

2 For countless mercies, love unknown,
Lord, what can we impart?
Thou dost require one gift alone —
The offering of the heart.

3 Incline us, Lord, to give it thee;
Preserve us by thy grace,
Till death shall bring us all to see
Thy glory face to face.

973. C. M. Union Col.

1 How should our souls delight to bless
The God of truth and grace,
Who crowns our labors with success,
Among the rising race.

2 Their joyful tongues unite to praise
His all-redeeming love,
To him their sweet hosannas raise,
While they his mercies prove.

---

975. C. M. Sel. Hymns.

1 Great God, we would to thee make known
Each fond, maternal care;
For this we gather round thy throne,
And bring our children there.

2 We ask not wealth, long life, or fame,
Or aught the world can give,
May they but glorify thy name,
And to thy honor live.

3 This is the burden of our prayer —
When from our bosoms riven,
May they be objects of thy care,
And heirs, at last, of heaven.

WOODSTOCK. C. M. DUTTON, JR.

See note to "Arlington," p. 131.

977. C. M. DODDRIDGE.

1 SEE Israel's gentle Shepherd stand,
With all-engaging charms;
Hark! how he calls the tender lambs,
And folds them in his arms!

2 "Permit them to approach," he cries,
"Nor scorn their humble name;
For 'twas to bless such souls as these
The Lord of angels came."

3 We bring them, Lord, by fervent prayer,
And yield them up to thee;
With humble trust that we are thine,
Thine let our offspring be.

4 If orphans they are left behind,
Thy guardian care we trust;
That care shall heal our bleeding hearts,
If weeping o'er their dust.

978. C. M. MOTHERS' HYMNS.

1 O LORD, behold us at thy feet,
A needy, sinful band;
As suppliants round thy mercy-seat,
We come at thy command.

2 'Tis for our children we would plead,
The offspring thou hast given;
Where shall we go in time of need,
But to the God of heaven?

3 We ask not for them wealth or fame,
Amid the worldly strife;
But, in the all prevailing Name,
We ask eternal life.

4 We seek the Spirit's quickening grace,
To make them pure in heart,
That they may stand before thy face,
And see thee as thou art.

979. C. M. CH. PSALMIST.

1 HOW can we see the children, Lord,
In love whom thou hast given,
Remain regardless of thy word,
Without a hope of heaven?

2 How can we see them tread the path
That leads to endless death;
Thus adding to thy fearful wrath,
With every moment's breath?

3 Lord, hear the parents' earnest cry,
And save our children dear:
Now send thy Spirit from on high,
And fill them with thy fear.

4 O, make them love thy holy law,
And joyful walk therein;
Their hearts to new obedience draw;
Save them from every sin.

982. C. M. ANON.

1 ON, through Judea's palmy plain,
By Jordan's silv'ry shore,
The Saviour leads the thronging train,
Who follow to adore.

2 'Midst youth, and sire, and blooming maid,
He marked the listening child;
His hand upon its head he laid,
And blest in accents mild.

3 Lord, though no more thy hallowed form
Can greet our children's sight,
Grant that, whilst life their breasts shall warm,
Thy word may guide them right.

4 They may not feel thine earthly touch,
But be thy Spirit given,
To make them holy; "for of such
The kingdom is of heaven."

CANTERBURY. C. M. — In Este's Psalter. 1592.

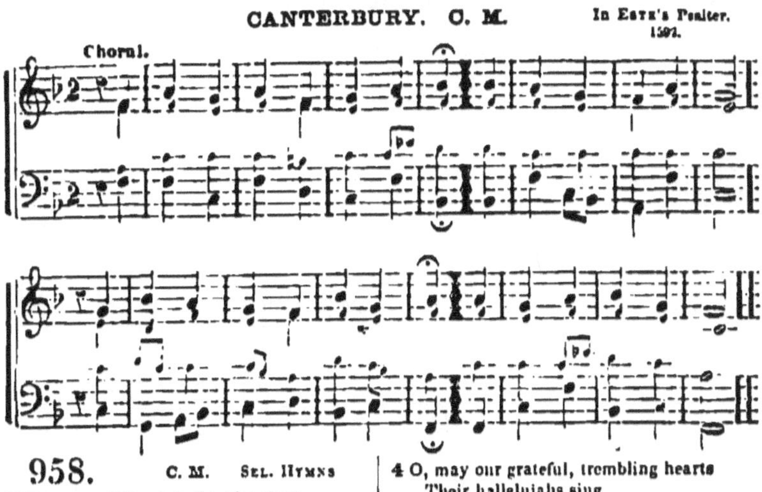

958. C. M. — Sel. Hymns

1 We come, O Lord, before thy throne,
And, with united pleas,
We meet and pray for those who roam
Far off upon the seas.

2 O, may the Holy Spirit bow
The sailor's heart to thee,
Till tears of deep repentance flow
Like rain-drops in the sea.

3 Then may a Saviour's dying love
Pour peace into his breast,
And waft him to the port above
Of everlasting rest.

961. C. M. — Madan's Col.

1 Our little bark, on boisterous seas,
By cruel tempests tost,
Without one cheerful beam of hope,
Expecting to be lost, —

2 We to the Lord, in humble prayer,
Breathed out our sad distress;
Though feeble, yet with contrite hearts,
We begged return of peace.

3 Then ceased the stormy winds to blow;
The surges ceased to roll;
And soon again a placid sea
Spoke comfort to the soul.

4 O, may our grateful, trembling hearts
Their hallelujahs sing
To Him who hath our lives preserved, —
Our Saviour and our King.

964. C. M. — Addison.

1 How are thy servants blest, O Lord!
How sure is their defence!
Eternal Wisdom is their guide,
Their help, Omnipotence.

2 In foreign realms, and lands remote,
Supported by thy care,
Through burning climes they pass unhurt,
And breathe in tainted air.

3 When by the dreadful tempest borne
High on the broken wave,
They know thou art not slow to hear,
Nor impotent to save.

4 The storm is laid; the winds retire,
Obedient to thy will;
The sea, that roars at thy command,
At thy command is still.

5 In midst of dangers, fears, and deaths,
Thy goodness we'll adore;
We'll praise thee for thy mercies past,
And humbly hope for more.

ADAGIO. C. M. — Gregorian.

* Omit these chords in last line, and sing the last two chords instead.

W. Tansur's Col. 1736.

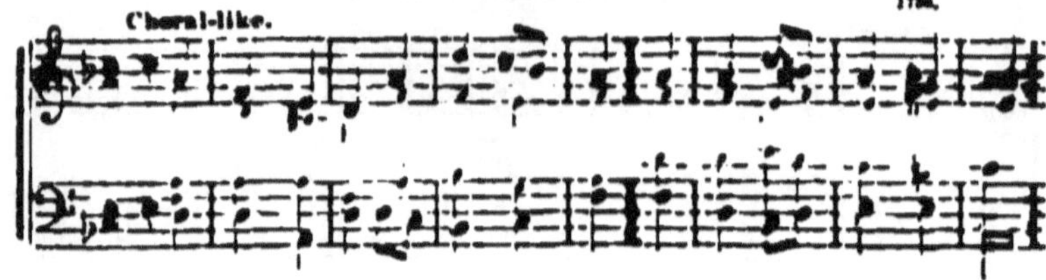

983. C. M. Hart.

1 Lord, look on all assembled here,
Who in thy presence stand
To offer up united prayer
For this our sinful land.

2 O, may we all, with one consent,
Fall low before thy throne,
With tears the nation's sins lament,
The church's, and our own.

3 And should the dread decree be past,
And we must feel the rod,—
Let faith and patience hold us fast
To our correcting God.

984. C. M. Rippon's Col.

1 When Abrah'm, full of sacred awe,
Before Jehovah stood,
And, with an humble, fervent prayer,
For guilty Sodom sued,—

2 With what success, what wondrous grace,
Was his petition crowned!
The Lord would spare, if in this place
Ten righteous men were found.

3 And could a single pious soul
So rich a boon obtain?
Great God, and shall a nation cry,
And plead with thee in vain?

4 Are not the righteous dear to thee
Now, as in ancient times?
Or does this sinful land exceed
Gomorrah in her crimes?

5 Still we are thine; we bear thy name;
Here yet is thine abode;
Long has thy presence blessed our land:
Forsake us not, O God.

987. C. M. Watts.

1 Lord, thou hast scourged our guilty land;
Behold, thy people mourn;
Shall vengeance ever guide thy hand,
And mercy ne'er return?

2 Our Zion trembles at thy stroke,
And dreads thy lifted hand;
O, heal the people thou hast broke,
And spare our guilty land.

3 Then shall our loud and grateful voice
Proclaim our guardian God;
The nations round the earth rejoice,
And sound thy praise abroad.

988. C. M. Rippon's Col.

1 Almighty Lord, before thy throne
Thy mourning people bend;
'Tis on thy pardoning grace alone
Our dying hopes depend.

2 Dark judgments, from thy heavy hand,
Thy dreadful power display;
Yet mercy spares our guilty land,
And still we live to pray.

3 How changed, alas! are truths divine,
For error, guilt, and shame!
What impious numbers, bold in sin,
Disgrace the Christian name!

4 O, turn us, turn us, mighty Lord;
Convert us by thy grace;
Then shall our hearts obey thy word,
And see again thy face.

5 Then, should oppressing foes invade,
We will not yield to fear,
Secure of all-sufficient aid,
When thou, O God, art near.

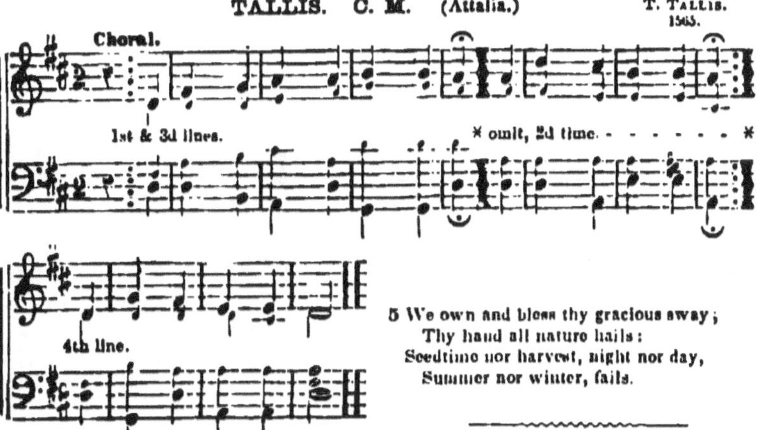

5 We own and bless thy gracious sway;
Thy hand all nature hails:
Seedtime nor harvest, night nor day,
Summer nor winter, fails.

986. C. M. BREVIARY.

1 O SINNER, bring not tears alone,
Or outward form of prayer;
But let it in thy heart be known
That penitence is there.

2 To smite the breast, the clothes to rend,
God asketh not of thee:
Thy secret soul he bids thee bend
In true humility.

3 O, let us, then, with heartfelt grief,
Draw near unto our God,
And pray to him to grant relief,
And stay the lifted rod.

4 O righteous Judge, if thou wilt deign
To grant us what we need,
We pray for time to turn again,
And grace to turn indeed.

997. C. M. ANON.

1 FOUNTAIN of mercy, God of love,
How rich thy bounties are!
The rolling seasons, as they move,
Proclaim thy constant care.

2 When in the bosom of the earth
The sower hid the grain,
Thy goodness marked its secret birth,
And sent the early rain.

3 The spring's sweet influence, Lord, was thine;
The plants in beauty grew;
Thou gav'st refulgent suns to shine,
And gav'st refreshing dew.

4 These various mercies from above
Matured the swelling grain;
A kindly harvest crowns thy love,
And plenty fills the plain.

1002. C. M. ANON.

1 To Him from whom our blessings flow,
Who all our wants supplies,
This day the choral song and vow
From grateful hearts shall rise

2 'Twas he who led the pilgrim band
Across the stormy sea;
'Twas he who stayed the tyrant's hand,
And set our country free.

3 When shivering on a strand unknown,
In sickness and distress,
Our fathers looked to God alone,
To save, protect, and bless.

4 Be thou our nation's strength and shield,
In manhood as in youth;
Thine arm for our protection wield,
And guide us by thy truth.

1003. C. M. WEXFORD.

1 LORD, while for all mankind we pray,
Of every clime and coast,
O, hear us for our native land,—
The land we love the most.

2 O, guard our shores from every foe,
With peace our borders bless,
With prosperous times our cities crown,
Our fields with plenteousness.

3 Unite us in the sacred love
Of knowledge, truth, and thee;
And let our hills and valleys shout
The songs of liberty.

4 Lord of the nations, thus to thee
Our country we commend;
Be thou her refuge and her trust,
Her everlasting friend.

REFUGE. C. M. N. DOUGALL.

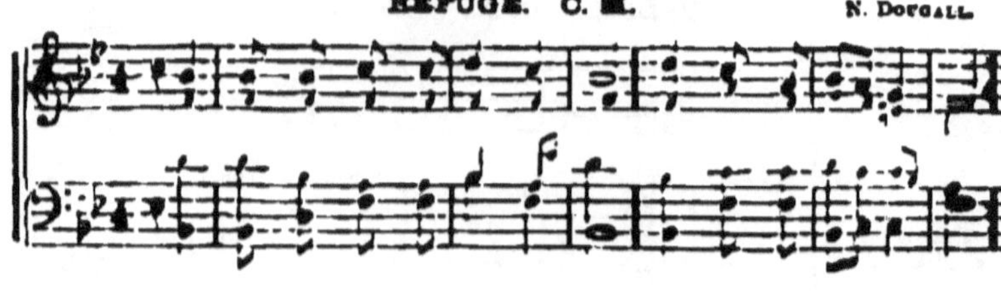

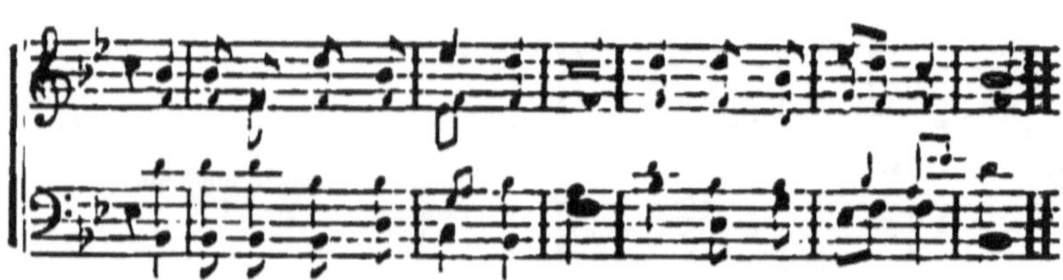

1008. C. M. ANON.

1 When morning's first and hallowed ray
Breaks with its trembling light,
To chase the pearly dews away, —
Bright tear-drops of the night, —

2 My heart, O Lord, forgets to rove,
But rises, gladly free,
On wings of everlasting love,
And finds its home in thee.

3 When evening's silent shades descend,
And nature sinks to rest,
Still to my Father and my Friend
My wishes are addressed.

4 And e'en when midnight's solemn gloom
Above, around, is spread,
Sweet dreams of everlasting bloom
Are hovering o'er my head.

5 I dream of that fair land, O Lord,
Where all thy saints shall be;
I wake to lean upon thy word,
And still delight in thee.

1012. C. M. SAC. OFFERING.

1 Again, from calm and sweet repose,
I rise to hail the dawn;
Again my waking eyes unclose,
To view the smiling morn.

2 Great God of love, thy praise I'll sing;
For thou hast safely kept
My soul beneath thy guardian wing,
And watched me while I slept.

3 Glory to thee, eternal Lord;
O, teach my heart to pray,
And thy blest Spirit's help afford,
To guide me through the day.

4 Let every thought and word accord
With thy most holy will;
Each deed the precepts of thy word
With pious aim fulfil.

5 From danger, sin, and every ill,
My constant Guardian prove;
O, sanctify my heart, and fill
With thoughts of holy love.

1015. C. M. STEELE.

1 God of my life, my morning song
To thee I cheerful raise;
Thine acts of love 'tis good to sing,
And pleasant 'tis to praise.

2 Preserved by thy almighty arm,
I passed the shades of night,
Serene, and safe from every harm,
To see the morning light.

3 While numbers spent the night in sighs,
And restless pains and woes,
In gentle sleep I closed my eyes,
And woke from sweet repose.

4 O, let the same almighty care
Through all this day attend;
From every danger, every snare,
My heedless steps defend.

5 Smile on my minutes as they roll,
And guide my future days,
And let thy goodness fill my soul
With gratitude and praise.

HERMON.

PETERBORO'. C. M. ENGLISH.

1009. C. M. WATTS.

1 ONCE more, my soul, the rising day
Salutes thy waking eyes;
Once more, my voice, thy tribute pay
To Him who rules the skies.

2 Night unto night his name repeats;
The day renews the sound,
Wide as the heavens on which he sits,
To turn the seasons round.

3 'Tis he supports my mortal frame;
My tongue shall speak his praise;
My sins would rouse his wrath to flame,
And yet his wrath delays.

4 How many wretched souls have fled
Since the last setting sun!
And yet thou lengthenest out my thread,
And yet my moments run.

5 Great God, let all my hours be thine,
While I enjoy the light;
Then shall my sun in smiles decline,
And bring a peaceful night.

1018. C. M. KIPPIS.

1 ON thee, each morning, O my God,
My waking thoughts attend,
In whom are founded all my hopes,
In whom my wishes end.

2 My soul, in pleasing wonder lost,
Thy boundless love surveys,
And, fired with grateful zeal, prepares
The sacrifice of praise.

3 When evening slumbers press my eyes,
With thy protection blest,
In peace and safety I commit
My weary limbs to rest.

4 My spirit, in thy hands secure,
Fears no approaching ill;
For, whether waking or asleep,
Thou, Lord, art with me still.

5 Then will I daily to the world
Thy wondrous acts proclaim,
Whilst all with me shall praise and sing,
And bless thy sacred name.

6 At morn, at noon, at night, I'll still
The pleasing work pursue,
And thee alone will praise, to whom
All praise is ever due.

1019. C. M. WATTS.

1 HOSANNA, with a cheerful sound,
To God's upholding hand!
Ten thousand snares attend us round,
And yet secure we stand.

2 That was a most amazing power
That raised us with a word;
And every day, and every hour,
We lean upon the Lord.

3 The rising morn cannot assure
That we shall end the day;
For death stands ready at the door
To hurry us away.

4 Our life is forfeited by sin
To God's most righteous law;
We own thy grace, immortal King,
In every breath we draw.

5 God is our sun, whose daily light
Our joy and safety brings;
Our feeble frame lies safe at night
Beneath his guardian wings.

1024. C. M. WATTS.

1 DREAD Sovereign, let my evening song
Like holy incense rise;
Assist the offering of my tongue
To reach the lofty skies.

2 Through all the dangers of the day
Thy hand was still my guard;
And still to drive my wants away
Thy mercy stood prepared.

3 Perpetual blessings from above
Encompass me around;
But, O, how few returns of love
Hath my Redeemer found!

4 What have I done for him who died
To save my guilty soul?
Alas! my sins are multiplied,
Fast as my minutes roll.

5 Yet, with this guilty heart of mine,
Lord, to thy cross I flee,
And to thy grace my soul resign,
To be renewed by thee.

1029. C. M. SAC. OFFERING.

1 ETERNAL God of love and power,
I will thy praise resound,
And tell how every passing hour
Is with thy goodness crowned.

2 Throughout the day, thy tender care
Has all my wants supplied,
And deigned from every baneful snare
My erring steps to guide.

3 But, O, my tongue in vain essays
Thy bounty to declare;
It ne'er can tell, in mortal lays,
How great thy mercies are.

4 But yet thine all-discerning eye
My grateful heart can see;
And all its warm emotions lie,
O Lord, exposed to thee.

5 Now, while mine eyes are closed in sleep,
Wilt thou my Guardian be,
And deign my wearied frame to keep
From every danger free.

1034. C. M. WATTS.

1 LORD, thou wilt hear me when I pray;
I am forever thine:
I fear before thee all the day,
Nor would I dare to sin.

2 And while I rest my weary head,
From cares and business free,
'Tis sweet conversing on my bed
With my own heart and thee.

3 I pay this evening sacrifice,
And when my work is done,
Great God, my faith, my hope relies
Upon thy grace alone.

4 Thus with my thoughts composed to peace,
I'll give mine eyes to sleep,
Thy hand in safety keeps my days,
And will my slumbers keep

1035. C. M. WATTS.

1 WITH songs and honors sounding loud,
Address the Lord on high;
O'er all the heavens he spreads his cloud,
And waters veil the sky.

2 He sends his showers of blessings down,
To cheer the plains below;
He makes the grass the mountains crown,
And corn in valleys grow.

3 His steady counsels change the face
Of each declining year;
He bids the sun cut short his race,
And wintry days appear.

4 On us his providence has shone,
With gentle, smiling rays;
O, may our lips and lives make known
His goodness and his praise.

1036. C. M. STEELE.

1 When verdure clothes the fertile vale,
And blossoms deck the spray,
And fragrance breathes in every gale,
How sweet the vernal day!

2 Hark! how the feathered warblers sing!
'Tis nature's cheerful voice;
Soft music hails the lovely spring,
And woods and fields rejoice.

3 O God of nature and of grace,
Thy heavenly gifts impart;
Then shall my meditation trace
Spring, blooming in my heart.

4 Inspired to praise, I then shall join
Glad nature's cheerful song,
And love and gratitude divine
Attune my joyful tongue.

1038. C. M. W. B. PEABODY.

1 When brighter suns and milder skies
Proclaim the opening year,
What various sounds of joy arise!
What prospects bright appear!

2 Earth and her thousand voices give
Their thousand notes of praise;
And all, that by his mercy live,
To God their offering raise.

3 The streams, all beautiful and bright,
Reflect the morning sky;
And there, with music in his flight,
The wild bird soars on high.

4 Thus, like the morning, calm and clear,
That saw the Saviour rise,
The spring of heaven's eternal year
Shall dawn on earth and skies.

5 No winter there, no shades of night,
Obscure those mansions blest,
Where, in the happy fields of light,
The weary are at rest.

1042. C. M. STEELE.

1 Stern Winter throws his icy chains,
Encircling nature round;
How bleak, how comfortless the plains,
Late with gay verdure crowned!

2 The sun withholds his vital beams,
And light and warmth depart;
And drooping, lifeless nature seems
An emblem of my heart.

3 Return, O blissful sun, and bring
Thy soul-reviving ray:
This mental winter shall be spring,
This darkness cheerful day.

4 O happy state! divine abode,
Where spring eternal reigns,
And perfect day, the smile of God,
Fills all the heavenly plains.

5 Great Source of light, thy beams display,
My drooping joys restore,
And guide me to the seats of day,
Where winter frowns no more.

BLANDFORD. C. M. T. JACKSON.

1039. C. M. NEWTON.

1 At length the wished-for spring has come:
How altered is the scene!
The trees and shrubs are dressed in bloom,
The earth arrayed in green

2 O, let my inmost soul confess,
With grateful joy and love,
The bounteous hand that deigns to bless
The garden, field, and grove.

3 Inspired to praise, my heart would join
Glad nature's cheerful song;
While love and gratitude combine
To tune my joyful tongue.

4 My faith exults, that yet the spring
Of righteousness and praise
Our gracious God will surely bring,
And in all nations raise.

1043. C. M. WATTS.

1 The hoary frost, the fleecy snow,
Descend, and clothe the ground,
The liquid streams forbear to flow,
In icy fetters bound

2 When, from his dreadful stores on high,
God pours the sounding hail,
The man that does his power defy
Shall find his courage fail.

3 God sends his word, and melts the snow;
The fields no longer mourn;
He calls the warmer gales to blow,
And bids the spring return.

4 The changing wind, the flying cloud,
Obey his mighty word;
With songs and honors sounding loud,
Praise ye the sovereign Lord.

1047. C. M. DODDRIDGE.

1 Awake, ye saints, and raise your eyes,
And lift your voices high;
Awake, and praise that sovereign love
That shows salvation nigh.

2 On all the wings of time it flies;
Each moment brings it near:
Then welcome each declining day;
Welcome each closing year.

3 Not many years their rounds shall run,
Nor many mornings rise,
Ere all its glories stand revealed
To our admiring eyes.

4 Ye wheels of nature, speed your course;
Ye mortal powers, decay;
Fast as ye bring the night of death,
Ye bring eternal day.

1053. C. M. NEWTON.

1 Now, gracious Lord, thine arm reveal,
And make thy glory known;
Now let us all thy presence feel,
And soften hearts of stone.

2 From all the guilt of former sin
May mercy set us free;
And let the year, we now begin,
Begin and end with thee.

3 Send down thy Spirit from above,
That saints may love thee more,
And sinners now may learn to love,
Who never loved before.

4 And when before thee we appear,
In our eternal home,
May growing numbers worship here,
And praise thee in our room.

H. H. Hawley.

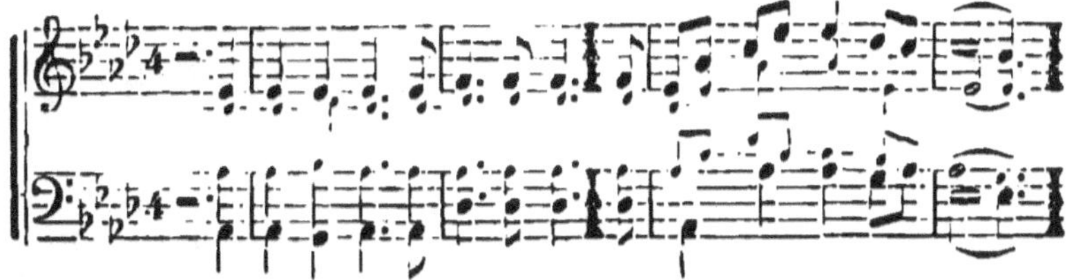

1045. C. M. Anon.

1 And now, my soul, another year
Of thy short life is past;
I cannot long continue here,
And this may be my last.

2 Much of my hasty life is gone,
Nor will return again;
And swift my passing moments run,—
The few that yet remain.

3 Awake, my soul; with utmost care
Thy true condition learn:
What are thy hopes? how sure? how fair?
What is thy great concern?

4 Behold, another year begins;
Set out afresh for heaven;
Seek pardon for thy former sins,
In Christ so freely given.

5 Devoutly yield thyself to God,
And on his grace depend;
With zeal pursue the heavenly road,
Nor doubt a happy end.

1048. C. M. Doddridge.

1 Remark, my soul, the narrow bound
Of each revolving year;
How swift the weeks complete their round!
How short the months appear!

2 So fast eternity comes on,
And that important day
When all that mortal life hath done
God's judgment shall survey.

3 Yet like an idle tale we pass
The swift-revolving year,
And study artful ways t' increase
The speed of its career.

4 Awake, O God, my careless heart
Its great concerns to see,
That I may act the Christian part,
And give the year to thee.

5 So shall their course more grateful roll,
If future years arise;
Or this shall bear my waiting soul
To joy beyond the skies.

1052. C. M. Higginbotham.

1 God of our lives, thy various praise
Our voices shall resound:
Thy hand directs our fleeting days,
And brings the seasons round.

2 To thee shall grateful songs arise,
Our Father and our Friend,
Whose constant mercies from the skies
In genial streams descend.

3 In every scene of life, thy care,
In every age, we see;
And constant as thy favors are,
So let our praises be.

4 Still may thy love, in every scene,
In every age, appear;
And let the same compassion deign
To bless the opening year.

5 If mercy smile, let mercy bring
Our wandering souls to God:
In our affliction we shall sing,
If thou wilt bless the rod.

MELODY.

BANGOR. C. M. W. Tansur's Col. 1.M.

Choral-like.

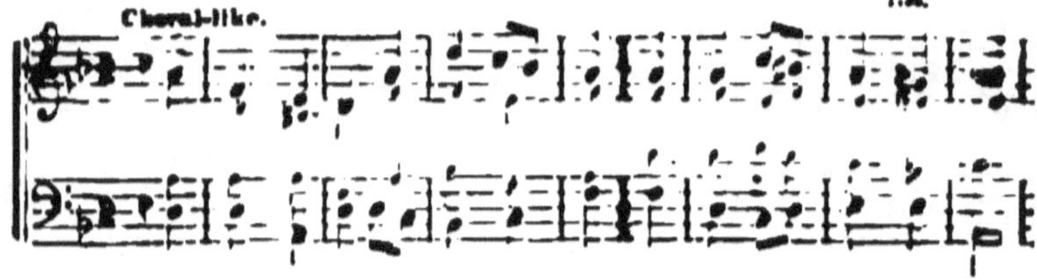

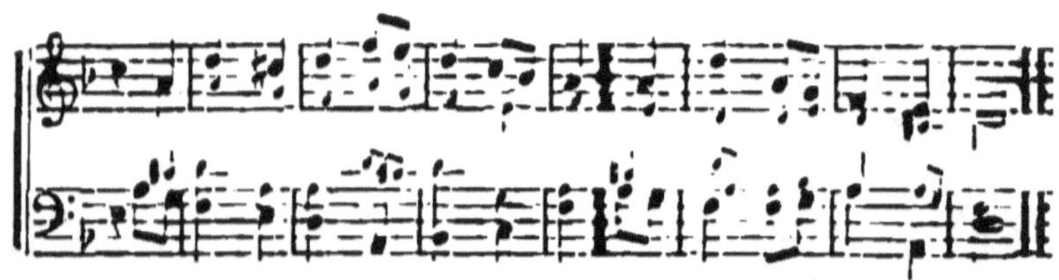

1054. C. M. Watts.

1 How short and hasty is our life!
How vast our soul's affairs!
Yet foolish mortals vainly strive
To lavish out their years

2 Our days run thoughtlessly along,
Without a moment's stay;
Just like a story, or a song,
We pass our lives away.

3 God from on high invites us home;
But we march heedless on,
And, ever hastening to the tomb,
Stoop downward as we run.

4 Draw us, O God, with sovereign grace,
And lift our thoughts on high,
That we may end this mortal race,
And see salvation nigh.

1055. C. M. Watts.

1 Teach me the measure of my days,
Thou Maker of my frame;
I would survey life's narrow space,
And learn how frail I am.

2 A span is all that we can boast;
How short the fleeting time!
Man is but vanity and dust,
In all his flower and prime.

3 What can I wish, or wait for, then,
From creatures — earth and dust?
They make our expectations vain,
And disappoint our trust.

4 Now I forbid my carnal hope,
My fond desire recall;
I give my mortal interest up,
And make my God my all.

1057. C. M. J. Q. Adams.

1 How swift, alas! the moments fly!
How rush the years along!
Scarce here, yet gone already by,
The burden of a song.

2 See childhood, youth, and manhood pass,
And age, with furrowed brow;
Time was — time shall be — but, alas!
Where, where in time is now?

3 Time is the measure but of change;
No present hour is found;
The past, the future, fill the range
Of time's unceasing round.

4 Where, then, is now? In realms above,
With God's atoning Lamb,
In regions of eternal love,
Where sits enthroned I AM.

5 Then, pilgrim, let thy joys and fears
On time no longer lean;
But henceforth all thy hopes and fears
From earth's affections wean.

6 To God let grateful accents rise;
With truth, with virtue, live;
So, all the bliss that time denies
Eternity shall give.

1061. C. M. Watts.

1 Thee we adore, Eternal Name,
And humbly own to thee
How feeble is our mortal frame,
What dying worms are we.

2 The year rolls round, and steals away
The breath that first it gave;
Whate'er we do, where'er we be,
We're travelling to the grave.

COMMUNION NEW. C. M.

3 Great God, on what a slender thread
Hang everlasting things! —
The final state of all the dead
Upon life's feeble strings!

4 Eternal joy, or endless woe,
Attends on every breath;
And yet how unconcerned we go
Upon the brink of death!

5 Awake, O Lord, our drowsy sense,
To walk this dangerous road;
And if our souls are hurried hence,
May they be found with God.

1067. C. M. Anon.

1 When floating on life's troubled sea,
By storms and tempests driven,
Hope, with her radiant finger, points
To brighter scenes in heaven.

2 She bids the storms of life to cease,
The troubled breast be calm,
And in the wounded heart she pours
Religion's healing balm.

3 Her hallowed influence cheers life's hours
Of sadness and of gloom;
She guides us, through this vale of tears
To joys beyond the tomb.

4 And when our fleeting days are o'er,
And life's last hour draws near,
With still unwearied wing she hastes
To wipe the falling tear.

5 She bids the anguished heart rejoice:
Though earthly ties are riven,
We still may hope to meet again
In yonder peaceful heaven.

1069. C. M. Reed.

1 Come, let us strike our harps afresh
To great Jehovah's name;
Sweet be the accents of our tongues
When we his love proclaim.

2 'Twas by his bidding we were called
In pain a while to part;
'Tis by his care we meet again,
And gladness fills our heart.

3 Blest be the hand that has preserved
Our feet from every snare,
And blest the goodness of the Lord,
Which to this hour we share.

4 O, may the Spirit's quickening power
Now sanctify our joy,
And warm our zeal in works of love
Our talents to employ.

5 Fast, fast our minutes fly away;
Soon shall our wanderings cease;
Then with our Father we shall dwell,
A family of peace.

1097. C. M. Dale.

1 Dear as thou wert, and justly dear,
We will not weep for thee:
One thought shall check the starting tear;
It is, that thou art free.

2 And thus shall faith's consoling power
The tears of love restrain:
O, who that saw thy parting hour
Could wish thee here again?

3 Triumphant in thy closing eye
The hope of glory shone;
Joy breathed in thy expiring sigh,
To think the race was run.

4 Thy passing spirit gently fled,
Sustained by grace divine;
O, may such grace on us be shed,
And make our end like thine.

FUNERAL THOUGHT. C. M.

J. Smith.
Arnold's Psalms, 1791.

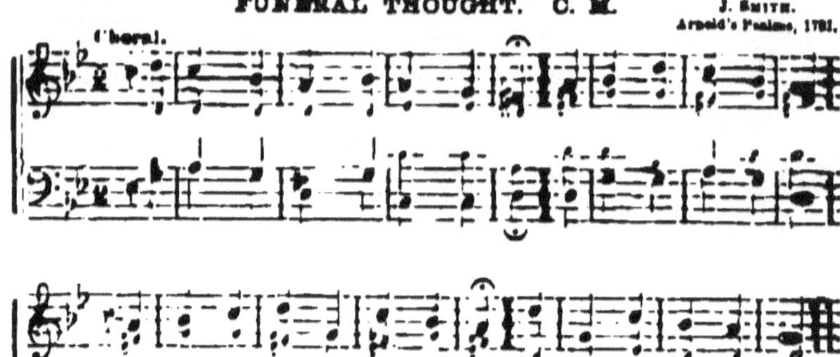

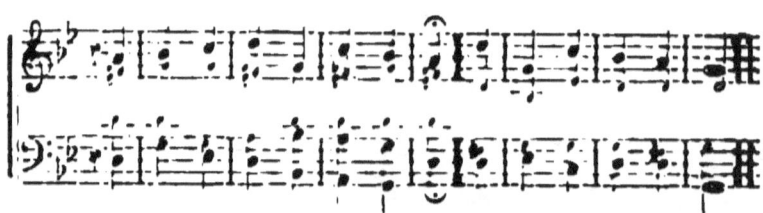

1079. C. M. Watts.

1 Hark! from the tombs a warning sound;
My ears, attend the cry —
"Ye living men, come view the ground
Where you must shortly lie.

2 "Princes, this clay must be your bed,
In spite of all your towers;
The tall, the wise, the reverend head,
Must lie as low as ours."

3 Great God, is this our certain doom?
And are we still secure? —
Still walking downward to the tomb,
And yet prepare no more?

4 Grant us the power of quickening grace,
To fit our souls to fly;
Then, when we drop this dying flesh,
We'll rise above the sky.

1081. C. M. Heber.

1 Beneath our feet and o'er our head
Is equal warning given:
Beneath us lie the countless dead;
And far above is heaven.

2 Death rides on every passing breeze,
And lurks in every flower;
Each season has its own disease,
Its peril every hour.

3 Turn, sinner, turn: thy danger know:
Where'er thy foot can tread,
The earth rings hollow from below,
And warns thee of her dead.

4 Turn, Christian, turn: thy soul apply
To truths which hourly tell
That they who underneath thee lie
Shall live in heaven — or hell.

1074. C. M. Collyer.

1 When, bending o'er the brink of life,
My trembling soul shall stand,
And wait to pass death's awful flood,
Great God, at thy command, —

2 Thou Source of life and joy supreme,
Whose arm alone can save,
Dispel the darkness that surrounds
The entrance to the grave.

3 Lay thy supporting, gentle hand
Beneath my sinking head,
And let a beam of life divine
Illume my dying bed.

1082. C. M. Doddridge.

1 Heaven has confirmed the dread decree,
That Adam's race must die:
One general ruin sweeps them down,
And low in dust they lie.

2 Ye living men, the tomb survey,
Where you must shortly dwell;
Hark! how the awful summons sounds
In every funeral knell!

3 Once you must die, and once for all;
The solemn purport weigh;
For know that heaven or hell depends
On that important day.

4 Those eyes, so long in darkness veiled,
Must wake, the Judge to see;
And every word, and every thought,
Must pass his scrutiny.

5 O, may I in the Judge behold
My Saviour and my Friend,
And, far beyond the reach of death,
With all his saints ascend.

ORTONVILLE. C. M. Dr. Thos. Hastings. From The Psalmista.

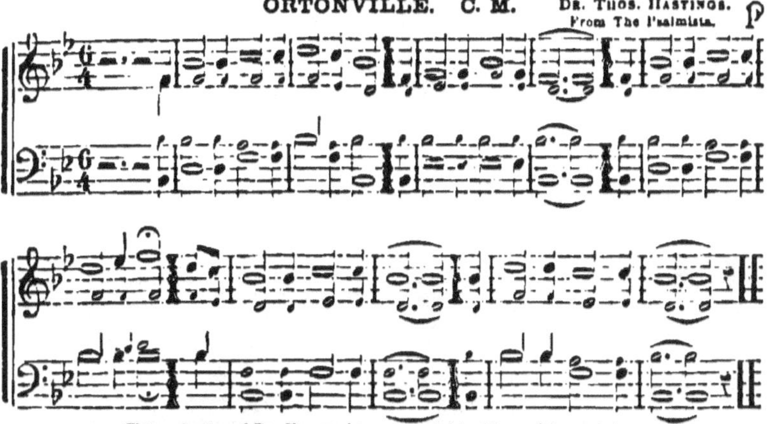

This and other of Dr. Hastings' tunes inserted by his special permission.

1075. C. M. Watts.

1 Death cannot make our souls afraid,
If God be with us there ;
We may walk through its darkest shade,
And never yield to fear.

2 I could renounce my all below,
If my Redeemer bid ;
And run, if I were called to go,
And die, as Moses did.

3 Might I but climb to Pisgah's top,
And view the promised land,
My flesh itself would long to drop,
And welcome the command.

4 Clasped in my heavenly Father's arms,
I would forget my breath,
And lose my life among the charms
Of so divine a death.

1077. C. M. Beddome.

1 If I must die, O, let me die
With hope in Jesus' blood —
The blood that saves from sin and guilt,
And reconciles to God.

2 If I must die, O, let me die
In peace with all mankind,
And change these fleeting joys below
For pleasures more refined.

3 If I must die, — and die I must, —
Let some kind seraph come,
And bear me on his friendly wing
To my celestial home.

4 Of Canaan's land, from Pisgah's top,
May I but have a view,
Though Jordan should o'erflow its banks,
I'll boldly venture through.

19 •

1104. C. M. Watts.

1 Hear what the voice from heaven proclaims
For all the pious dead :
"Sweet is the savor of their names,
And soft their sleeping bed.

2 "They die in Jesus, and are blest ;
How kind their slumbers are !
From suffering and from sin released,
They're freed from every snare.

3 "Far from this world of toil and strife,
They're present with the Lord ;
The labors of their mortal life
End in a large reward."

1113. C. M. Doddridge.

1 Ye golden lamps of heaven, farewell,
With all your feeble light ;
Farewell, thou ever-changing moon,
Pale empress of the night.

2 And thou, refulgent orb of day,
In brighter flames arrayed,
My soul, that springs beyond thy sphere,
No more demands thy aid.

3 Ye stars are but the shining dust
Of my divine abode,
The pavement of those heavenly courts
Where I shall see my God.

4 The Father of eternal light
Will there his beams display ;
Nor shall one moment's darkness blend
With that unvaried day.

EVAN.

DUNFERMLINE. C. M. Ravenscroft's Book of Psalms.
Specimen of the melody and harmony of 1621.

1091. C. M. Steele.

1 When blooming youth is snatched away
 By death's resistless hand,
Our hearts the mournful tribute pay,
 Which pity must demand.

2 While pity prompts the rising sigh,
 O, may this truth, impressed
With awful power, "I too must die,"
 Sink deep in every breast.

3 Let this vain world engage no more:
 Behold the opening tomb:
It bids us seize the present hour:
 To-morrow death may come.

4 O, let us fly — to Jesus fly,
 Whose powerful arm can save;
Then shall our hopes ascend on high,
 And triumph o'er the grave.

5 Great God, thy sovereign grace impart
 With cleansing, healing power;
This only can prepare the heart
 For death's surprising hour.

1092. C. M. Watts.

1 Why do we mourn departing friends,
 Or shake at death's alarms?
'Tis but the voice that Jesus sends
 To call them to his arms.

2 Are we not tending upward, too,
 As fast as time can move?
Nor would we wish the hours more slow,
 To keep us from our Love.

3 Why should we tremble to convey
 Their bodies to the tomb?
'Twas there the flesh of Jesus lay,
 And left a long perfume.

4 The graves of all the saints he blest,
 And softened every bed;
Where should the dying members rest,
 But with their dying Head?

5 Thence he arose, ascending high,
 And showed our feet the way;
Up to the Lord our souls shall fly,
 At the great rising day.

6 Then let the last loud trumpet sound,
 And bid our kindred rise:
Awake, ye nations under ground;
 Ye saints, ascend the skies.

Omit 1st note of the tune in singing hymn 1093.

1093. 7, 6s & 8. Noel's Col.

1 Brother, thou art gone to rest;
 We will not weep for thee;
For thou art now where oft on earth
 Thy spirit longed to be.

2 Brother, thou art gone to rest;
 Thine is an early tomb;
But Jesus summoned thee away;
 Thy Saviour called thee home.

3 Brother, thou art gone to rest;
 Thy toils and cares are o'er;
And sorrow, pain, and suffering, now
 Shall ne'er distress thee more.

4 Brother, thou art gone to rest;
 Thy sins are all forgiven;
And saints in light have welcomed thee
 To share the joys of heaven.

5 Brother, thou art gone to rest;
 And this shall be our prayer —
That, when we reach our journey's end,
 Thy glory we may share.

1087. C. M. WATTS.

1 GREAT God, I own thy sentence just,
And nature must decay;
I yield my body to the dust,
To dwell with fellow-clay.

2 Yet faith may triumph o'er the grave,
And trample on the tombs;
My great Redeemer ever lives,
My God, my Saviour, comes.

3 The mighty Conqueror shall appear,
High on a royal seat;
And Death, the last of all his foes,
Lie vanquished at his feet.

4 Then shall I see thy lovely face
With strong, immortal eyes,
And feast upon thy wondrous grace,
With pleasure and surprise.

1094. C. M. L. H. SIGOURNEY.

1 As, bowed by sudden storms, the rose
Sinks on the garden's breast,
Down to the grave our brother goes,
In silence there to rest.

2 No more with us his tuneful voice
The hymn of praise shall swell;
No more his cheerful heart rejoice
When peals the Sabbath bell.

3 Yet, if, in yonder cloudless sphere,
Amid a sinless throng,
He utters in his Saviour's ear
The everlasting song,—

4 No more we'll mourn the absent friend,
But lift our earnest prayer,
And daily every effort bend
To rise and join him there.

1102. C. M. PEABODY.

1 BEHOLD the western evening light!
It melts in deepening gloom;
So calmly Christians sink away,
Descending to the tomb.

2 The winds breathe low; the yellow leaf
Scarce whispers from the tree;
So gently flows the parting breath,
When good men cease to be.

3 How beautiful, on all the hills,
The crimson light is shed!
'Tis like the peace the Christian gives
To mourners round his bed.

4 How mildly on the wandering cloud
The sunset beam is cast!
So sweet the memory left behind,
When loved ones breathe their last.

5 And, lo! above the dews of night
The vesper star appears:
So faith lights up the mourner's heart,
Whose eyes are dim with tears.

6 Night falls, but soon the morning light
Its glories shall restore;
And thus the eyes that sleep in death
Shall wake, to close no more.

1110. C. M. ANON.

1 I LOOKED upon the righteous man,
And saw his parting breath,
Without a struggle or a sigh,
Serenely yield to death:
There was no anguish on his brow,
Nor terror in his eye:
The spoiler aimed a fatal dart,
But lost the victory.

2 I looked upon the righteous man,
And heard the holy prayer
Which rose above that breathless form,
To soothe the mourner's care,
And felt how precious was the gift
He to his loved ones gave—
The stainless memory of the just,
The wealth beyond the grave.

3 I looked upon the righteous man;
And all our earthly trust
Of pleasure, vanity, or pride,
Seemed lighter than the dust,
Compared with his celestial gain—
A home above the sky:
O, grant us, Lord, his life to live,
That we like him may die.

1115. C. M. DODDRIDGE.

1 WHAT though the arm of conquering death
Does God's own house invade;
What though our teacher and our friend
Is numbered with the dead;—

2 Though earthly shepherds dwell in dust,
The agéd and the young;
The watchful eye in darkness closed,
And dumb th' instructive tongue;—

3 Th' eternal Shepherd still survives,
His teaching to impart:
Lord, be our Leader and our Guide,
And rule and keep our heart.

4 Yes, while the dear Redeemer lives,
We have a boundless store,
And shall be fed with what He gives,
Who lives forevermore.

NAOMI.

&c.

RESIGNATION. C. M. T. CLARK. From Nat. Ch. Harmony.

1076. C. M. WATTS.

1 O FOR an overcoming faith,
To cheer my dying hours,
To triumph o'er the monster Death,
And all his frightful powers!

2 Joyful, with all the strength I have,
My quivering lips should sing —
"Where is thy boasted victory, Grave?
And where, O Death, thy sting?"

3 If sin be pardoned, I'm secure;
Death has no sting beside:
The law gives sin its damning power;
But Christ, my ransom died.

4 Now to the God of victory
Immortal thanks be paid,
Who makes us conquerors, while we die,
Through Christ, our living Head.

1126. C. M. WATTS.

1 BLEST be the everlasting God,
The Father of our Lord;
Be his abounding mercy praised,
His majesty adored.

2 When from the dead he raised his Son,
And called him to the sky,
He gave our souls a lively hope
That they should never die.

3 What though our inbred sins require
Our flesh to see the dust;
Yet as the Lord our Saviour rose,
So all his followers must.

4 There's an inheritance divine
Reserved against that day;
'Tis uncorrupted, undefiled,
And cannot fade away.

5 Saints by the power of God are kept
Till the salvation come;
We walk by faith as strangers here,
Till Christ shall call us home.

1129. C. M. H. K. WHITE.

1 THROUGH sorrow's night, and danger's path,
Amid the deepening gloom,
We, soldiers of a heavenly King,
Are marching to the tomb.

2 There, when the turmoil is no more,
And all our powers decay,
Our cold remains in solitude
Shall sleep the years away.

3 Our labors done, securely laid
In this our last retreat,
Unheeded o'er our silent dust
The storms of life shall beat.

4 Yet not thus lifeless, in the grave,
The vital spark shall lie;
For o'er life's wreck that spark shall rise,
To seek its kindred sky.

5 These ashes, too, — this little dust, —
Our Father's care shall keep,
Until the final trump shall break
The long and dreary sleep.

6 Then love's soft dew o'er every eye
Shall shed its mildest rays,
And our long-silent dust shall rise,
With shouts of endless praise!

HERMON.

TALLIS. C. M. (Attalia) T. TALLIS. 1565.

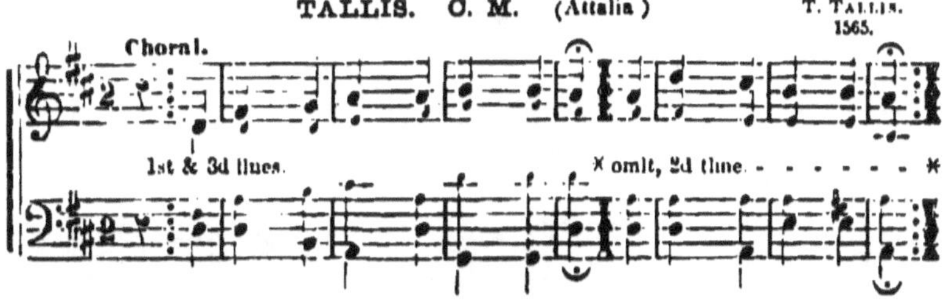

1121. C. M. SCOTCH COL.

1 WHEN the last trumpet's awful voice
This rending earth shall shake, —
When opening graves shall yield their charge,
And dust to life awake, —

2 Those bodies that corrupted fell
Shall incorrupted rise,
And mortal forms shall spring to life
Immortal in the skies.

3 Behold, what heavenly prophets sung
Is now at last fulfilled —
That Death should yield his ancient reign,
And, vanquished, quit the field

4 Let Faith exalt her joyful voice,
And thus begin to sing:
"O Grave, where is thy triumph now?
And where, O Death, thy sting?"

1123. C. M. STEELE.

1 LIFE is a span — a fleeting hour:
How soon the vapor flies!
Man is a tender, transient flower,
That e'en in blooming dies.

2 The once-loved form, now cold and dead,
Each mournful thought employs;
And Nature weeps her comforts fled,
And withered all her joys.

3 Hope looks beyond the bounds of time,
When what we now deplore
Shall rise in full, immortal prime,
And bloom to fade no more.

4 Cease, then, fond Nature, cease thy tears;
Thy Saviour dwells on high;
There everlasting spring appears;
There joys shall never die.

1124. C. M. WATTS.

1 How long shall Death, the tyrant, reign,
And triumph o'er the just?
How long the blood of martyrs slain
Lie mingled with the dust?

2 Lo! I behold the scattered shades;
The dawn of heaven appears;
The bright, immortal morning spreads
Its blushes round the spheres.

3 I see the Lord of glory come,
And flaming guards around;
The skies divide to make him room;
The trumpet shakes the ground.

4 I hear the voice, "Ye dead, arise!"
And, lo! the graves obey;
And waking saints, with joyful eyes,
Salute th' expected day.

5 O, may our humble spirits stand
Among them, clothed in white:
The meanest place at his right hand
Is infinite delight.

6 How will our joy and wonder rise,
When our returning King
Shall bear us homeward through the skies,
On love's triumphant wing!

1127. C. M. WATTS.

1 I SET the Lord before my face;
He bears my courage up;
My heart, my tongue, their joy express;
My flesh shall rest in hope.

2 My spirit, Lord, thou wilt not leave
Where souls departed are,
Nor quit my body in the grave,
To see destruction there.

3 Thou wilt reveal the path of life,
And raise me to thy throne;
Thy courts immortal pleasure give;
Thy presence, joys unknown.

EVAN.

CRUCIFIX. C. M. B. F. EDMANDS.

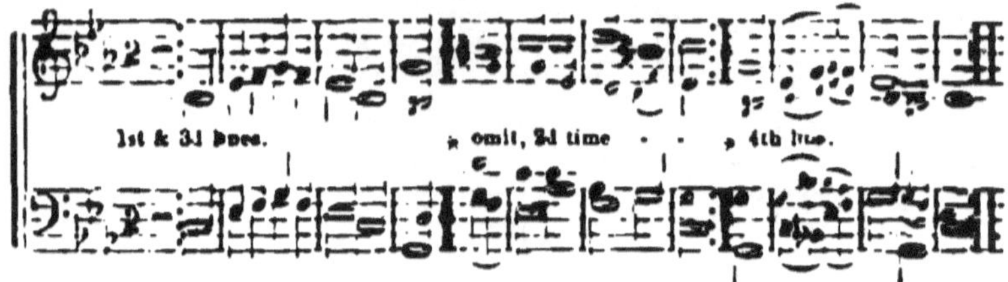

1137. C. M. DODDRIDGE.

1 THE day approaches, O my soul, —
The great, decisive day, —
Which from the verge of mortal life
Shall bear thee far away.

2 Another day more awful dawns,
And, lo! the Judge appears:
Ye heavens, retire before his face;
And sink, ye darkened stars.

3 Yet does one short, preparing hour —
One precious hour — remain:
Rouse, then, my soul, with all thy power,
Nor let it pass in vain.

1142. C. M. WATTS.

1 THAT awful day will surely come, —
The appointed hour makes haste, —
When I must stand before my Judge,
And pass the solemn test.

2 Thou lovely Chief of all my joys,
Thou Sovereign of my heart,
How could I bear to hear thy voice
Pronounce the sound, "Depart!"

3 O, wretched state of deep despair,
To see my God remove,
And fix my dreadful station where
I must not taste his love!

4 Jesus, I throw my arms around,
And hang upon thy breast;
Without one gracious smile from thee,
My spirit cannot rest.

5 O, tell me that my worthless name
Is graven on thy hands;
Show me some promise in thy book,
Where my salvation stands.

1147. C. M. WATTS.

1 THERE is a house not made with hands,
Eternal, and on high;
And here my spirit waiting stands
Till God shall bid it fly.

2 Shortly this prison of my clay
Must be dissolved and fall;
Then, O my soul, with joy obey
Thy heavenly Father's call.

3 'Tis he, by his almighty grace,
That forms thee fit for heaven,
And, as an earnest of the place,
Has his own Spirit given.

4 We walk by faith of joys to come;
Faith lives upon his word;
But while the body is our home,
We're absent from the Lord.

5 'Tis pleasant to believe thy grace,
But we had rather see;
We would be absent from the flesh,
And present, Lord, with thee.

1170. C. M. STEELE.

1 FAR from these narrow scenes of night,
Unbounded glories rise,
And realms of joy and pure delight,
Unknown to mortal eyes.

2 Fair, distant land! — could mortal eyes
But half its charms explore,
How would our spirits long to rise,
And dwell on earth no more!

3 No cloud those blissful regions know —
Realms ever bright and fair;
For sin, the source of mortal woe,
Can never enter there.

4 O, may the heavenly prospect fire
Our hearts with ardent love,
Till wings of faith, and strong desire,
Bear every thought above.

5 Prepare us, Lord, by grace divine,
For thy bright courts on high;
Then bid our spirits rise and join
The chorus of the sky.

MELODY.

&c.

WINDSOR. C. M.
English Psalter. 1592.
Choral.
Minor.
BALERMA. C. M.
R. SIMPSON.
ST. SEBASTIAN. C. M. (Melbourne)
ENGLISH TUNE.
Col Soprani, ad lib.

WOODRUFF. C. M.
H. H. Hawley.
WOODSTOCK. C. M.
Dutton, Jr.
WOODLAND. C. M.
N. D. Gould.
From the Sacred Minstrel.
3d line of stanza twice.

HILLSIDE. C. M.

Sumner Hill. From the Sanctus. P

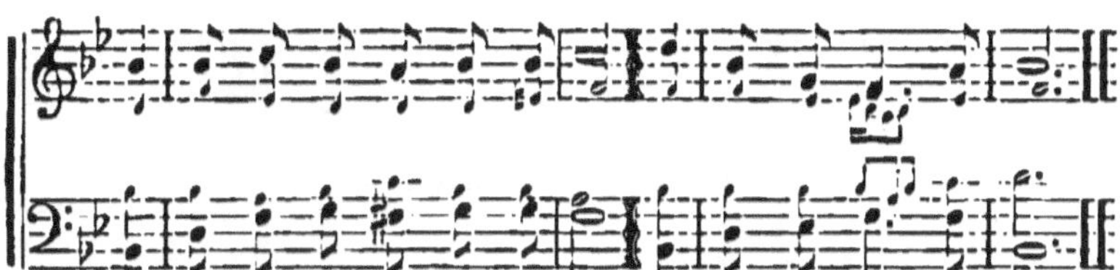

1156. C. M. Watts.

1 When I can read my title clear
To mansions in the skies,
I bid farewell to every fear,
And wipe my weeping eyes.

2 Should earth against my soul engage,
And fiery darts be hurled,
Then I can smile at Satan's rage,
And face a frowning world.

3 Let cares, like a wild deluge, come,
And storms of sorrow fall!
May I but safely reach my home,
My God, my heaven, my all.

4 There shall I bathe my weary soul
In seas of heavenly rest,
And not a wave of trouble roll
Across my peaceful breast.

1158. C. M. Steele.

1 Come, Lord, and warm each languid heart;
Inspire each lifeless tongue;
And let the joys of heaven impart
Their influence to our song.

2 Then to the shining realms of bliss
The wings of faith shall soar,
And all the charms of Paradise
Our raptured thoughts explore.

3 There shall the followers of the Lamb
Join in immortal songs,
And endless honors to his name
Employ their tuneful tongues.

4 Lord, tune our hearts to praise and love;
Our feeble notes inspire,
Till, in thy blissful courts above,
We join the heavenly choir.

20

1162. C. M. Moore.

1 The dove let loose in eastern skies,
Returning fondly home,
Ne'er stoops to earth her wing, nor flies,
Where idler warblers roam;—

2 But high she shoots through air and light,
Above all low delay,
Where nothing earthly bounds her flight,
Nor shadow dims her way.

3 So grant me, Lord, from every snare
Of sinful passion free,
Aloft, through faith's serener air,
To urge my course to thee;—

4 No sin to cloud, no lure to stay,
My soul, as home she springs,
Thy sunshine on her joyful way,
Thy freedom on her wings.

1167. C. M. W. B. Tappan.

1 There is an hour of hallowed peace
For those with cares oppressed,
When sighs and sorrowing tears shall cease,
And all be hushed to rest.

2 'Tis then the soul is freed from fears
And doubts which here annoy;
Then they that oft had sown in tears
Shall reap again in joy.

3 There is a home of sweet repose,
Where storms assail no more;
The stream of endless pleasure flows
On that celestial shore.

4 There purity with love appears,
And bliss without alloy;
There they that oft had sown in tears
Shall reap again in joy.

JORDAN. C. M. Double. BILLINGS.

1146. C. M. WATTS.

1 THERE is a land of pure delight,
  Where saints, immortal, reign;
Eternal day excludes the night,
  And pleasures banish pain.

2 There everlasting spring abides,
  And never fading flowers:
Death, like a narrow sea, divides
  That heavenly land from ours.

3 Sweet fields, beyond the swelling flood,
  Stand dressed in living green:
So to the Jews fair Canaan stood,
  While Jordan rolled between.

4 But timorous mortals start and shrink
  To cross this narrow sea,
And linger, trembling, on the brink,
  And fear to launch away.

5 O, could we make our doubts remove, —
  Those gloomy doubts that rise, —
And see the Canaan that we love
  With unbeclouded eyes, —

6 Could we but climb where Moses stood,
  And view the landscape o'er, —
Not Jordan's stream, nor death's cold flood,
  Should fright us from the shore.

1178. C. M. TOPLADY.

1 HOW happy are the souls above,
  From sin and sorrow free!
With Jesus they are now at rest,
  And all his glory see.

2 "Worthy the Lamb," aloud they cry,
  "That brought us near to God:"
In ceaseless hymns of praise they shout
  The virtue of his blood.

3 Sweet gratitude inspires their songs,
  Ambitious to proclaim,
Before the Father's awful throne,
  The honors of the Lamb.

4 With wondering joy their lips recount
  Their fears and dangers past,
And bless the wisdom, power, and love,
  Which brought them home at last.

5 Lord, let the merit of thy death
  To me, like them, be given;
And I, like them, will shout thy praise
  Through all the courts of heaven.

HANLEY.

WOODLAND. C. M.

N. D. Gould.
From the Sacred Minstrel.

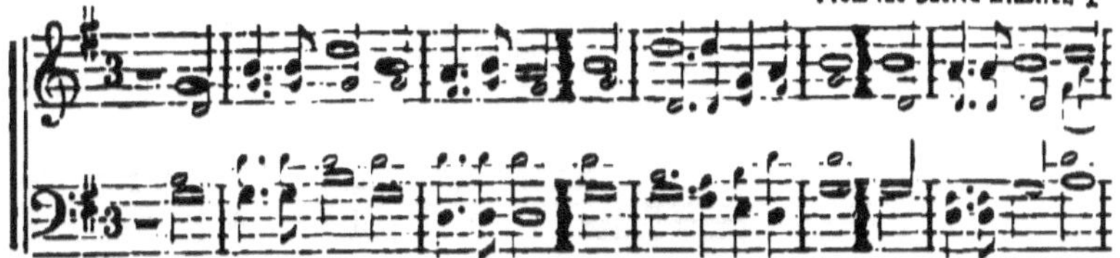

1153. C. M. Watts.

1 Nor eye hath seen, nor ear hath heard,
 Nor sense nor reason known,
What joys the Father has prepared
 For those that love his Son.

2 But the good Spirit of the Lord
 Reveals a heaven to come;
The beams of glory in his word
 Allure and guide us home.

3 Pure are the joys above the sky,
 And all the region peace:
No wanton lips, nor envious eye,
 Can see or taste the bliss.

4 Those holy gates forever bar
 Pollution, sin, and shame;
And none shall gain admittance there
 But followers of the Lamb.

1173. C. M. Stennett.

1 On Jordan's stormy banks I stand,
 And cast a wishful eye
To Canaan's fair and happy land,
 Where my possessions lie.

2 O the transporting, rapturous scene,
 That rises to my sight! —
Sweet fields, arrayed in living green,
 And rivers of delight.

3 O'er all those wide-extended plains
 Shines one eternal day;
There God the Son forever reigns,
 And scatters night away.

4 No chilling winds, nor poisonous breath,
 Can reach that healthful shore;
Sickness and sorrow, pain and death,
 Are felt and feared no more.

5 When shall I reach that happy place,
 And be forever blest?
When shall I see my Father's face,
 And in his bosom rest?

6 Filled with delight, my raptured soul
 Would here no longer stay;
Though Jordan's waves should round me roll,
 I'd fearless launch away.

Note. The direction — "third line of stanza repeated" — which appears with the above tune, applies only to hymns in common metre. In hymn 1168 no line of words is sung twice.

1168. 8s & 6s. W. B. Tappan.

1 There is an hour of peaceful rest
 To mourning wanderers given;
There is a joy for souls distressed,
A balm for every wounded breast;
 'Tis found alone in heaven.

2 There is a home for weary souls,
 By sins and sorrows driven,
When tossed on life's tempestuous shoals,
Where storms arise, and ocean rolls,
 And all is drear — 'tis heaven.

3 There faith lifts up the tearless eye,
 The heart no longer riven,
And views the tempest passing by,
Sees evening shadows quickly fly,
 And all serene in heaven.

4 There fragrant flowers immortal bloom,
 And joys supreme are given;
There rays divine disperse the gloom;
Beyond the dark and narrow tomb
 Appears the dawn of heaven.

HAMMOND. C. M. No. 1. N. D. Gould. From N. C. Har.

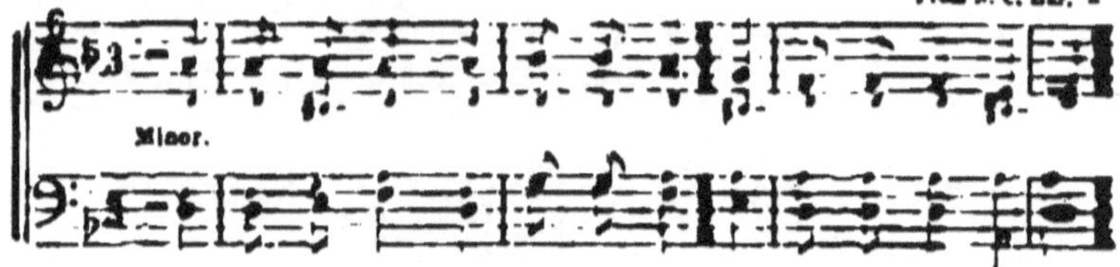

Composed for first two stanzas of Hymn 1155. See No. 2 opposite.

1171.‡ C. M. R. Turnbull.

1 There is a place of sacred rest,
  Far, far beyond the skies,
Where beauty smiles eternally,
  And pleasure never dies; —
My Father's house, my heavenly home,
  Where "many mansions" stand,
Prepared, by hands divine, for all
  Who seek the better land.

2 When tossed upon the waves of life,
  With fear on every side, —
When fiercely howls the gathering storm,
  And foams the angry tide, —
Beyond the storm, beyond the gloom,
  Breaks forth the light of morn,
Bright beaming from my Father's house,
  To cheer the soul forlorn.

3 Yes, even at that fearful hour,
  When death shall seize its prey,
And from the place that knows us now,
  Shall hurry us away, —
The vision of that heavenly home
  Shall cheer the parting soul,
And o'er it, mounting to the skies,
  A tide of rapture roll.

4 In that pure home of tearless joy
  Earth's parted friends shall meet,
With smiles of love that never fade,
  And blessedness complete:
There, there adieus are sounds unknown;
  Death frowns not on that scene,
But life, and glorious beauty, shine,
  Untroubled and serene.

‡ This hymn may be sung to either tune, by singing it twice to each stanza. The best adaptation for the 2d and 3d stanzas is to sing both tunes; which may be done with the lead of an organ, if previously rehearsed.

1155. C. M. Watts.

1 Our sins, alas! how strong they are!
  And, like a raging flood,
They break our duty, Lord, to thee,
  And force us from our God.

2 The waves of trouble, how they rise!
  How loud the tempests roar!
But death shall land our weary souls
  Safe on the heavenly shore.

3 Fulfilling there his high commands,
  Our cheerful feet shall move;
No sin shall clog our active zeal,
  Or cool our burning love.

4 We there shall ever sing and tell
  The wonders of his grace,
While heavenly raptures fire our hearts,
  And smile in every face.

5 Forever his dear, sacred name
  Shall dwell upon our tongue,
And Jesus and salvation be
  The close of every song.

1175. C. M. Watts.

1 "These glorious minds, how bright they shine!
  Whence all their white array?
How came they to the happy seats
  Of everlasting day?"

2 Lo! these are they from sufferings great
  Who came to realms of light,
And in the blood of Christ have washed
  Those robes, which shine so bright.

3 Now with triumphal palms they stand
  Before the throne on high,
And serve the God they love, amid
  The glories of the sky.

HAMMOND. C. M. No. 2. N. D. Gould. From N. C. Har.

Composed for 3d, 4th, & 5th stanzas of Hymn 1155. See No. 1, opposite.

4 His presence fills each heart with joy,
Tunes every lip to sing;
By day, by night, the sacred courts
With glad hosannas ring.

5 Their thirst and hunger ever flee;
Their joys forever last;
The fruit of life's immortal tree
Shall be their sweet repast.

6 The Lamb shall lead his heavenly flock
Where living fountains rise;
And love divine shall wipe away
The sorrows of their eyes.

1150. C. M. Village Hymns.

1 Bright glories rush upon my sight,
And charm my wondering eyes —
The regions of immortal light,
The beauties of the skies.

2 All hail, ye fair, celestial shores,
Ye lands of endless day;
A rich delight your prospect pours,
And drives my griefs away.

3 There's a delightful clearness now;
My clouds of doubt are gone;
Fled is my former darkness, too;
My fears are all withdrawn.

4 Short is the passage, short the space,
Between my home and me;
There, there behold the radiant place!
How near the mansions be!

5 Immortal wonders! boundless things
In those dear worlds appear:
Prepare me, Lord, to stretch my wings
And in those glories share.

1166. C. M. Montgomery's Col.

1 Jerusalem! my glorious home!
Name ever dear to me!
When shall my labors have an end,
In joy, and peace, and thee?

2 When shall these eyes thy heaven-built walls
And pearly gates behold?
Thy bulwarks with salvation strong,
And streets of shining gold?

3 O, when, thou city of my God,
Shall I thy courts ascend,
Where congregations ne'er break up,
And Sabbaths have no end?

4 There happier bowers than Eden's bloom,
Nor sin nor sorrow know:
Blest seats! through rude and stormy scenes
I onward press to you.

5 Why should I shrink at pain and woe?
Or feel at death dismay?
I've Canaan's goodly land in view,
And realms of endless day.

6 Apostles, martyrs, prophets, there,
Around my Saviour stand;
And soon my friends in Christ below
Will join the glorious band.

7 Jerusalem! my glorious home!
My soul still pants for thee;
Then shall my labors have an end,
When I thy joys shall see.

MELODY.

&c.

WATTS. C. M. N. D. Gould. From the Sacred Minstrel.

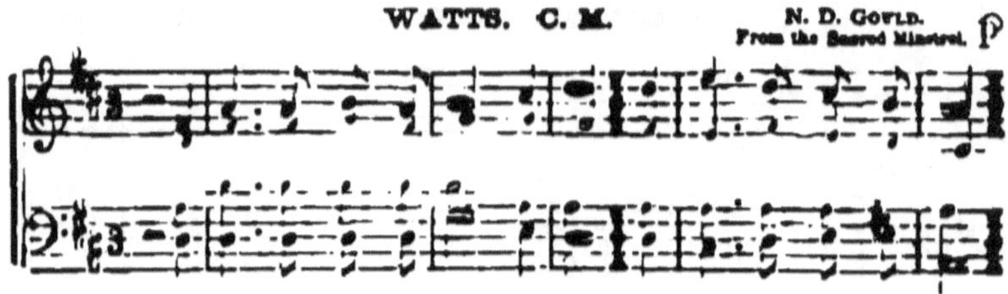

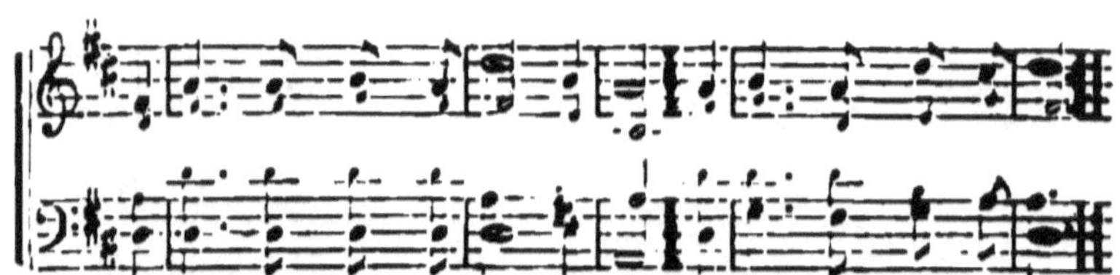

1157. C. M. Beddome.

1 There is a world of perfect bliss
Above the starry skies;
Oppressed with sorrows and with sins,
I thither lift my eyes.

2 'Tis there the weary are at rest,
And all is peace within;
The mind, with guilt no more oppressed,
Is tranquil and serene.

3 Discord and strife are banished thence,
Distrust and slavish fear;
No more we hear the pensive sigh,
Or see the falling tear.

4 Farewell to earth and earthly things:
In vain they tempt my stay:
Come, angels, spread your joyful wings,
And bear my soul away.

5 I long to see my Father's face,
And sing his praises too:
Adieu, companions, dearest friends;
Vain world, once more adieu.

1160. C. M. Ch. Psalmody.

1 Yes, there are joys that cannot die,
With God laid up in store —
Treasures, beyond the changing sky,
More bright than golden ore.

2 To that bright world my soul aspires,
With rapturous delight:
O for the Spirit's quickening powers,
To speed me in my flight!

HERMON.

&c.

1169. C. M. Steele.

1 O, let our thoughts and wishes fly
Above these gloomy shades,
To those bright worlds beyond the sky,
Which sorrow ne'er invades!

2 There, joys unseen by mortal eyes,
Or reason's feeble ray,
In ever-blooming prospect rise,
Exposed to no decay.

3 Lord, send a beam of light divine
To guide our upward aim;
With one reviving look of thine
Our languid hearts inflame.

4 O, then, on faith's sublimest wing,
Our ardent souls shall rise
To those bright scenes where pleasures spring
Immortal in the skies.

MEDFIELD.

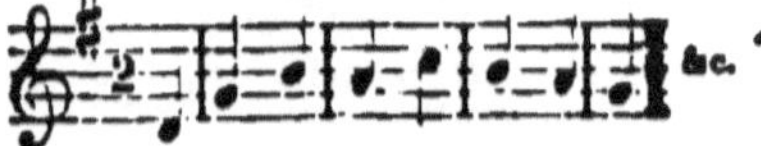

&c.

DOXOLOGIES.

3. C. M.

Let God the Father, and the Son,
And Spirit, be adored,
Where there are works to make him known,
Or saints to love the Lord.

4. C. M.

To Father, Son, and Holy Ghost,
One God, whom we adore,
Be glory as it was, is now,
And shall be evermore.

OLMUTZ. S. M. Gregorian. "Magnificat."

11. S. M. E. Taylor.

1 Come to the house of prayer,
O thou afflicted, come;
The God of peace shall meet thee there;
He makes that house his home.

2 Come to the house of praise,
Ye who are happy now;
In sweet accord your voices raise,
In kindred homage bow.

3 Ye aged, hither come,
For ye have felt his love;
Soon shall your trembling tongues be dumb,
Your lips forget to move.

4 Ye young, before his throne
Come, bow; your voices raise;
Let not your hearts his praise disown
Who gives the power to praise.

5 Thou, whose benignant eye
In mercy looks on all,—
Who seest the tear of misery,
And hear'st the mourner's call,—

6 Up to thy dwelling-place
Bear our frail spirits on,
Till they outstrip time's tardy pace,
And heaven on earth be won.

30. S. M. C. Wesley.

1 Jesus, we look to thee,
Thy promised presence claim;
Thou in the midst of us wilt be,
Assembled in thy name.

2 Thy name salvation is,
Which here we come to prove;
Thy name is life, and health, and peace,
And everlasting love.

3 We meet, the grace to take
Which thou hast freely given;
We meet on earth for thy dear sake,
That we may meet in heaven.

4 O, may thy quickening voice
The death of sin remove,
And bid our inmost souls rejoice
In hope of perfect love.

32. S. M. Urwick's Col.

1 How sweet to bless the Lord,
And in his praises join!
With saints his goodness to record,
And sing his power divine!

2 These seasons of delight
The dawn of glory seem,
Like rays of pure, celestial light,
Which on our spirits beam.

3 O, blest assurance this;
Bright morn of heavenly day;
Sweet foretaste of eternal bliss,
That cheers the pilgrim's way.

4 Thus may our joys increase,
Our love more ardent grow,
While rich supplies of Jesus' grace
Refresh our souls below.

5 But O, the bliss sublime,
When joy shall be complete,
In that unclouded, glorious clime
Where all thy servants meet!

6 Then shall the ransomed throng
The Saviour's love record,
And shout, in everlasting song,
"Salvation to the Lord!"

LISBON. S. M. READ.

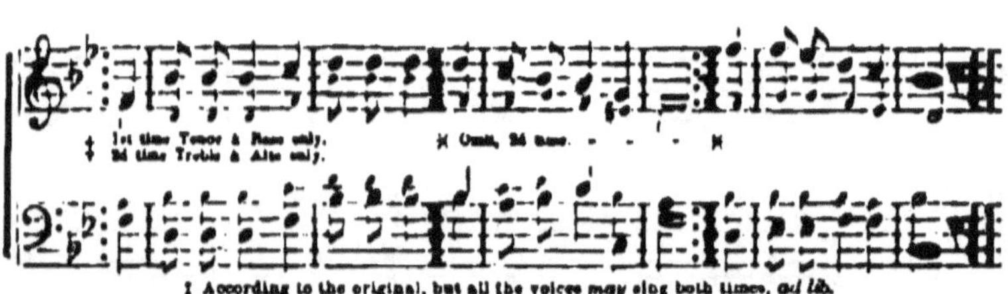

‡ According to the original, but all the voices may sing both times, *ad lib.*

40. S. M. WATTS.

1 WELCOME, sweet day of rest,
That saw the Lord arise;
Welcome to this reviving breast,
And these rejoicing eyes.

2 The King himself comes near,
And feasts his saints to-day;
Here we may sit, and see him here,
And love, and praise, and pray.

3 One day, amid the place
Where Christ, my Lord, has been,
Is sweeter than ten thousand days
Of pleasure, and of sin.

4 My willing soul would stay
In such a frame as this,
Till called to rise and soar away
To everlasting bliss.

45. S. M. SPIR. OF PSALMS.

1 SWEET is the work, O Lord,
Thy glorious name to sing,
To praise and pray, to hear thy word,
And grateful offerings bring;—

2 Sweet at the dawning light,
Thy boundless love to tell,
And, when approach the shades of night,
Still on the theme to dwell;—

3 Sweet, on this day of rest,
To join, in heart and voice,
With those who love and serve thee best,
And in thy name rejoice.

4 To songs of praise and joy
Be every Sabbath given,
That such may be our blest employ
Eternally in heaven.

48. S. M. BULFINCH.

1 HAIL to the Sabbath day!
The day divinely given,
When men to God their homage pay,
And earth draws near to heaven.

2 Lord, in this sacred hour,
Within thy courts we bend,
And bless thy love, and own thy power,
Our Father and our Friend.

3 But thou art not alone
In courts by mortals trod;
Nor only is the day thine own
When man draws near to God:

4 Thy temple is the arch
Of yon unmeasured sky;
Thy Sabbath, the stupendous march
Of grand eternity.

5 Lord, may that holier day
Dawn on thy servants' sight;
And purer worship may we pay
In heaven's unclouded light.

79. S. M. WATTS.

1 COME, sound his praise abroad,
And hymns of glory sing;
Jehovah is the sovereign God,
The universal King.

2 Come, worship at his throne;
Come, bow before the Lord;
We are his work, and not our own;
He formed us by his word.

3 To-day attend his voice,
Nor dare provoke his rod;
Come, like the people of his choice,
And own your gracious God.

SILVER STREET. S. M. J. SMITH.

87. S. M. MONTGOMERY.

1 ARISE, and bless the Lord,
Ye people of his choice;
Arise, and bless the Lord your God,
With heart, and soul, and voice.

2 Though high above all praise,
Above all blessing high,
Who would not fear his holy name,
And laud, and magnify?

3 O for the living flame
From his own altar brought,
To touch our lips, our souls inspire,
And wing to heaven our thought!

4 God is our strength and song,
And his salvation ours;
Then be his love in Christ proclaimed
With all our ransomed powers.

5 Arise, and bless the Lord;
The Lord your God adore;
Arise, and bless his glorious name,
Henceforth, forevermore.

96. S. M. MONTGOMERY.

1 O, BLESS the Lord, my soul;
His grace to thee, proclaim;
And all that is within me, join
To bless his holy name.

2 O, bless the Lord, my soul;
His mercies bear in mind;
Forget not all his benefits;
The Lord to thee is kind.

3 He will not always chide;
He will with patience wait;
His wrath is ever slow to rise,
And ready to abate.

4 The Lord forgives thy sins,
Prolongs thy feeble breath;
He healeth thine infirmities,
And ransoms thee from death.

5 He clothes thee with his love,
Upholds thee with his truth,
And, like the eagle, he renews
The vigor of thy youth.

6 Then bless his holy name
Whose grace hath made thee whole,
Whose loving kindness crowns thy days;
O, bless the Lord, my soul.

89. S. M. WATTS.

1 EXALT the Lord our God,
And worship at his feet;
His nature is all holiness,
And mercy is his seat.

2 When Israel was his church,
When Aaron was his priest,
When Moses cried, when Samuel prayed,
He gave his people rest.

3 Oft he forgave their sins,
Nor would destroy their race;
And oft he made his vengeance known,
When they abused his grace.

4 Exalt the Lord our God,
Whose grace is still the same:
Still he's a God of holiness,
And jealous for his name.

LABAN.

&c.

122. S. M. WESLEY'S COL.

1 FATHER, in whom we live,
In whom we are and move,
All glory, power, and praise, receive,
For thy creating love.

2 O thou incarnate Word,
Let all thy ransomed race
Unite in thanks, with one accord,
For thy redeeming grace.

3 Spirit of holiness,
Let all thy saints adore
Thy sacred gifts, and join to bless
Thy heart renewing power.

4 The grace on man bestowed,
Ye heavenly choirs, proclaim,
And cry, "Salvation to our God!
Salvation to the Lamb!"

164. S. M. WATTS.

1 O LORD, our heavenly King,
Thy name is all divine;
Thy glories round the earth are spread,
And o'er the heavens they shine.

2 When to thy works on high
I raise my wondering eyes,
And see the moon, complete in light,
Adorn the evening skies,—

3 When I survey the stars,
And all their shining forms,—
Lord, what is man, that worthless thing,
Akin to dust and worms?

4 Lord, what is worthless man,
That thou shouldst love him so?
Next to thine angels is he placed,
And Lord of all below.

5 How rich thy bounties are,
How wondrous are thy ways,
That, from the dust, thy power should frame
A monument of praise!

182. S. M. WATTS.

1 O, BLESS the Lord, my soul;
Let all within me join,
And aid my tongue to bless his name,
Whose favors are divine.

2 O, bless the Lord, my soul;
Nor let his mercies lie
Forgotten in unthankfulness,
And without praises die.

3 'Tis he forgives thy sins;
'Tis he relieves thy pain;
'Tis he that heals thy sicknesses,
And gives thee strength again.

4 He crowns thy life with love,
When ransomed from the grave;
He who redeemed my soul from hell,
Hath sovereign power to save.

5 He fills the poor with good;
He gives the sufferers rest:
The Lord hath judgments for the proud,
And justice for th' oppressed.

6 His wondrous works and ways
He made by Moses known,
But sent the world his truth and grace
By his belovéd Son.

LATHROP.

KINNICUT. S. M. H. H. HAWLEY.

Comp. for Hymn 183.

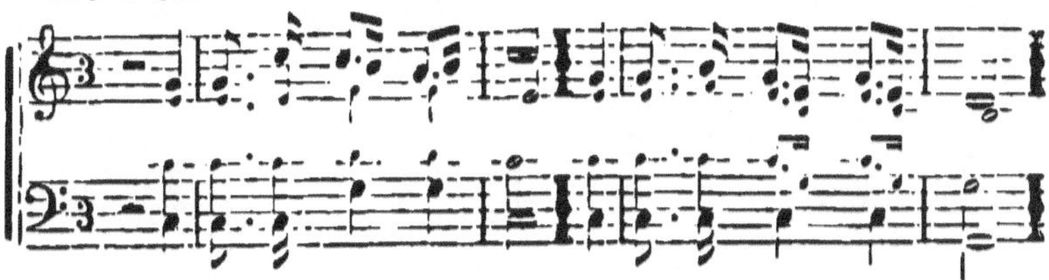

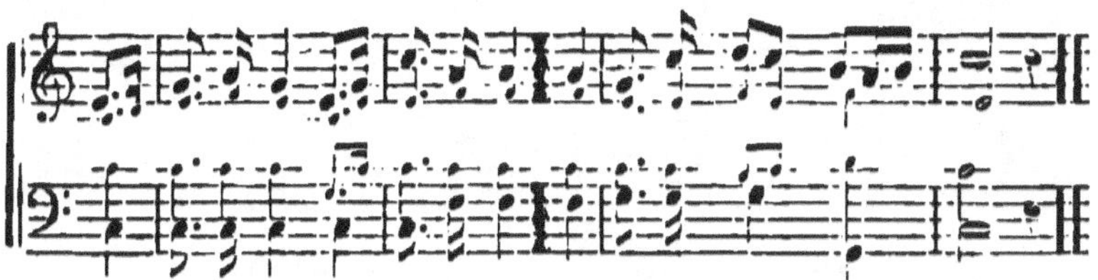

183. S. M. WATTS.

1 My soul, repeat his praise
  Whose mercies are so great,
Whose anger is so slow to rise,
  So ready to abate.

2 His power subdues our sins,
  And his forgiving love,
Far as the east is from the west,
  Doth all our guilt remove.

3 High as the heavens are raised
  Above the ground we tread,
So far the riches of his grace
  Our highest thoughts exceed.

184. S. M. WATTS.

1 THE pity of the Lord,
  To those that fear his name,
Is such as tender parents feel;
  He knows our feeble frame.

2 He knows we are but dust,
  Scattered with every breath;
His anger, like a rising wind,
  Can send us swift to death.

3 Our days are as the grass,
  Or like the morning flower;
When blasting winds sweep o'er the field,
  It withers in an hour.

4 But thy compassions, Lord,
  To endless years endure;
And children's children ever find
  Thy words of promise sure.

BOYLSTON.

189. S. M. BEDDOME.

1 GOD is the fountain whence
  Ten thousand blessings flow;
To him my life, my health, and friends,
  And every good, I owe.

2 The comforts he affords
  Are neither few nor small;
He is the source of fresh delights,
  My portion and my all.

3 He fills my heart with joy,
  My lips attunes for praise;
And to his glory I'll devote
  The remnant of my days.

191. S. M. WATTS.

1 BEHOLD, what wondrous grace
  The Father has bestowed
On sinners of a mortal race,
  To call them sons of God!

2 Nor doth it yet appear
  How great we must be made;
But when we see our Saviour here,
  We shall be like our Head.

3 A hope so much divine
  May trials well endure;
May purify our souls from sin,
  As Christ, the Lord, is pure.

4 If in my Father's love
  I share a filial part,
Send down thy Spirit like a dove,
  To rest upon my heart.

5 We would no longer lie
  Like slaves beneath the throne;
Our faith shall Abba, Father, cry,
  And thou the kindred own.

SWABIA. S. M. ANCIENT GERMAN. Dibdin's Standard Tune Book.

195. S. M. WATTS.

1 THE Lord my Shepherd is;
I shall be well supplied:
Since he is mine, and I am his,
What can I want beside?

2 He leads me to the place
Where heavenly pasture grows,
Where living waters gently pass,
And full salvation flows.

3 If e'er I go astray,
He doth my soul reclaim,
And guides me, in his own right way,
For his most holy name.

4 While he affords his aid,
I cannot yield to fear;
Tho' I should walk thro' death's dark shade,
My Shepherd's with me there.

5 In sight of all my foes,
Thou dost my table spread;
My cup with blessings overflows,
And joy exalts my head.

6 The bounties of thy love
Shall crown my future days;
Nor from thy house will I remove,
Nor cease to speak thy praise.

215. S. M. NEEDHAM.

1 BEHOLD, the Prince of Peace,
The chosen of the Lord,
God's well-belovéd Son, fulfils
The sure, prophetic word

2 No royal pomp adorns
This King of righteousness;
And meekness, patience, truth, and love,
Compose his princely dress.

3 The Spirit of the Lord,
In rich abundance shed,
On this great Prophet gently lights,
And rests upon his head.

4 He is the Light of men;
His doctrine life imparts;
O, may we feel its quickening power
To warm and cheer our hearts.

223. S. M. DODDRIDGE.

1 BEHOLD th' amazing sight,
The Saviour lifted high;
Behold the Son of God's delight
Expire in agony.

2 For whom, for whom, my heart,
Were all these sorrows borne?
Why did he feel that painful smart,
And meet that various scorn?

3 For us he hung and bled,
For us in torture died;
'Twas love that bowed his fainting head,
And oped his gushing side.

4 I see, and I adore
In sympathy of love;
I feel the strong, attractive power
To lift my soul above.

5 Drawn by such cords as these,
Let all the earth combine,
With cheerful ardor, to confess
The energy divine.

SHAWMUT.

COMMAND. S. M. EDWARD HAMILTON. From the Sanctus.

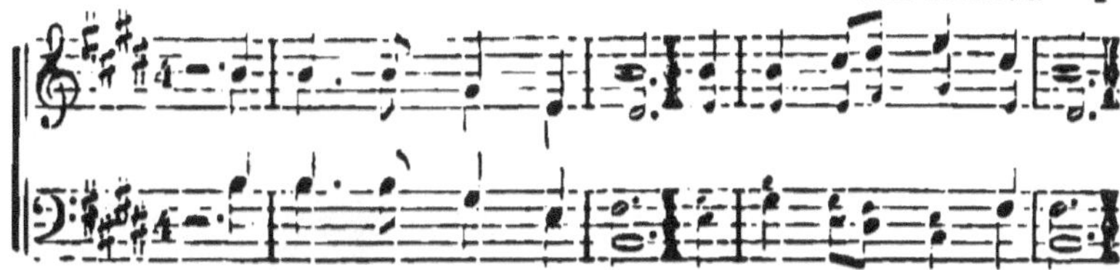

6 In thee our hearts unite,
Nor share thy griefs alone,
But from the cross pursue their flight
To thy triumphant throne.

208. S. M. WATTS.

1 BEHOLD, the grace appears,
The blessing promised long;
Angels announce the Saviour near,
In this triumphant song: —

2 "Glory to God on high,
And heavenly peace on earth;
Good-will to men, to angels joy,
At the Redeemer's birth."

3 In worship so divine
Let men employ their tongues;
With the celestial host we join,
And loud repeat their songs: —

4 "Glory to God on high,
And heavenly peace on earth;
Good-will to men, to angels joy,
At our Redeemer's birth."

237. S. M. KELLY.

1 "THE Lord is risen indeed;"
He lives to die no more;
He lives the sinner's cause to plead,
Whose curse and shame he bore.

2 "The Lord is risen indeed;"
Then hell has lost his prey;
With him is risen the ransomed seed,
To reign in endless day.

3 "The Lord is risen indeed;"
Attending angels, hear;
Up to the courts of heaven, with speed,
The joyful tidings bear.

4 Then wake your golden lyres,
And strike each cheerful chord;
Join, all ye bright, celestial choirs,
To sing our risen Lord.

269. S. M. WATTS.

1 RAISE your triumphant songs
To an immortal tune;
Let all the earth resound the deeds
Celestial grace has done.

2 Sing how eternal love
Its chief belovéd chose,
And bade him raise our ruined race
From their abyss of woes.

3 His hand no thunder bears;
No terror clothes his brow;
No bolts to drive our guilty souls
To fiercer flames below.

4 'Twas mercy filled the throne,
And wrath stood silent by,
When Christ was sent with pardons down
To rebels doomed to die.

5 Now, sinners, dry your tears;
Let hopeless sorrow cease;
Bow to the sceptre of his love
And take the offered peace.

6 Lord, we obey thy call;
We lay an humble claim
To the salvation thou hast brought;
And love and praise thy name.

LABAN.

AYLESBURY. S. M. Dr. Maurice Greene. Died 1755.

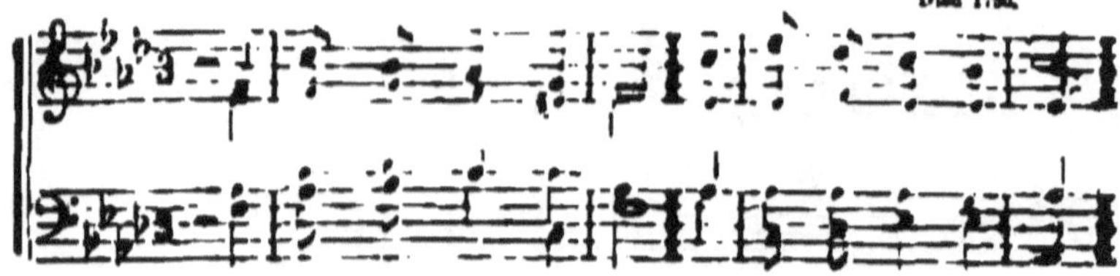

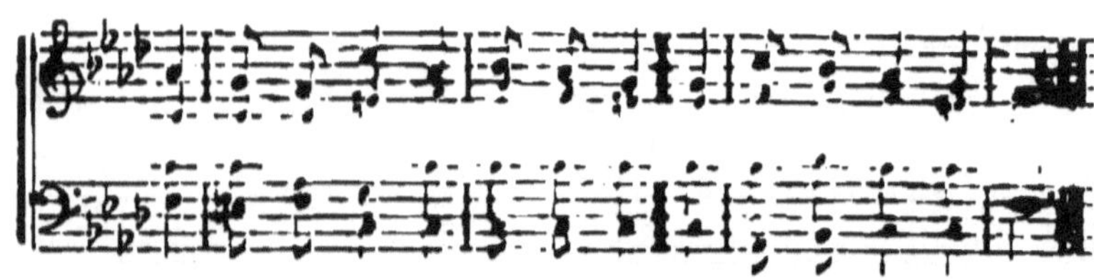

231. S. M. Watts.

1 Like sheep we went astray,
And broke the fold of God,
Each wandering in a different way,
But all the downward road.

2 How dreadful was the hour
When God our wanderings laid,
And did at once his vengeance pour,
Upon the Shepherd's head!

3 How glorious was the grace,
When Christ sustained the stroke!
His life and blood the Shepherd pays,
A ransom for the flock.

4 But God shall raise his head
O'er all the sons of men,
And let him see a numerous seed,
To recompense his pain.

5 "I'll give him," saith the Lord,
"A portion with the strong:
He shall possess a large reward,
And hold his honors long."

254. S. M. Watts.

1 Not all the blood of beasts,
On Jewish altars slain,
Could give the guilty conscience peace,
Or wash away the stain.

2 But Christ, the heavenly Lamb,
Takes all our sins away;
A sacrifice of nobler name,
And richer blood, than they.

3 My faith would lay her hand
On that dear head of thine,
While like a penitent I stand,
And there confess my sin.

4 My soul looks back, to see
The burdens thou didst bear
When hanging on the cursed tree,
And hopes her guilt was there.

5 Believing, we rejoice
To see the curse remove;
We bless the Lamb with cheerful voice,
And sing his bleeding love.

276. S. M. Anon.

1 O Christ, what gracious words
Are ever, ever thine!
Thy voice is music to the soul,
And life, and peace divine.

2 Grace, everlasting grace,
Glad tidings, full of joy,
Flow from thy lips, the lips of truth,
And flow without alloy.

3 The broken heart, the poor,
The bruised, the deaf, the blind,
The dumb, the dead, the captive wretch,
In thee compassion find.

4 Lord Jesus, speed the day,
The promised day of grace,
To all the poor, the dumb, the deaf,
The dead, of Adam's race.

5 One blissful anthem then
Around the earth shall roll,
And human nature shout thy name,
The life of every soul.

SHAWMUT.

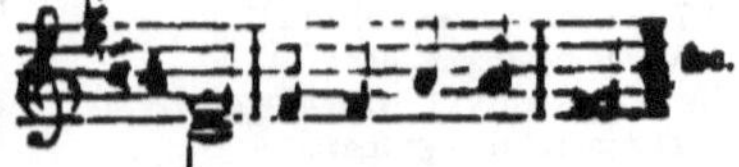

HUDSON. S. M. (Cambridge Old.) REV. R. HARRISON.

262. S. M. BEDDOME.

1 GOD'S holy law, transgressed,
Speaks nothing but despair;
Convinced of guilt, with grief oppressed,
We find no comfort there.

2 Not all our groans and tears,
Nor works which we have done,
Nor vows, nor promises, nor prayers,
Can e'er for sin atone.

3 Relief alone is found
In Jesus' precious blood:
'Tis this that heals the mortal wound,
And reconciles to God.

4 High lifted on the cross,
The spotless Victim dies:
This is salvation's only source;
Hence all our hopes arise.

283. S. M. HOSKINS.

1 BEHOLD the gift of God:
Sinners, adore his name,
Who shed for us his precious blood,
Who bore our curse and shame.

2 Behold the living bread
Which Jesus came to give,
By dying in the sinner's stead,
That he might ever live.

3 The Lord delights to give;
He knows you've nought to buy:
To Jesus haste; this bread receive,
And you shall never die.

BADEA.

281. S. M. LYRICA

1 JESUS, my truth, my way,
My sure, unerring light,
On thee my feeble soul I stay,
Which thou wilt lead aright.

2 My wisdom and my guide,
My counsellor thou art;
O, never let me leave thy side,
Or from thy paths depart.

290. S. M. DODDRIDGE.

1 MY soul, with joy attend
While Jesus silence breaks;
No angel's harp such music yields,
As what my Shepherd speaks.

2 "I know my sheep," he cries;
"My soul approves them well:
Vain is the world's delusive guise,
And vain the rage of hell.

3 "I freely feed them now
With tokens of my love;
But richer pastures I prepare,
And sweeter streams, above.

4 "Unnumbered years of bliss
I to my people give;
And while my throne unshaken stands
Shall all my chosen live.

5 "This tried, almighty hand
Is raised for their defence;
Where is the power shall reach them there,
Or what shall force them thence?"

6 "Enough, my gracious Lord,"
Let faith triumphant cry;
"My heart can on this promise live,—
Can with this promise die."

MOUNT EPHRAIM. S. M. B. Milgrove. About 1769.

293. S. M. Urwick's Col.

1 We sing the Saviour's love,
Who pitied wretched men,
Delighting in the thought of peace,
Ere time and worlds began.

2 We see its smiling beams,
Forth shining at his birth,
And trace its lustre day by day,
While he sojourned on earth.

3 But, in his closing hour,
How infinite his grace,
When, bowed beneath the curse, he died
To save the chosen race!

4 Ten thousand thousand songs,
With high, seraphic flame,
Fall far below the boundless praise
Of our Immanuel's name.

300. S. M. Campbell's Col.

1 Jesus, the Conqueror, reigns,
In glorious strength arrayed;
His kingdom over all maintains,
And bids the earth be glad.

2 Ye sons of men, rejoice
In Jesus' mighty love:
Lift up your heart, lift up your voice,
To him who rules above.

3 Extol his kingly power;
Adore th' exalted Son,
Who died, but lives, to die no more,
High on his Father's throne.

4 Our Advocate with God,
He undertakes our cause,
And spreads through all the earth abroad
The triumph of his cross.

291. S. M. Steele.

1 While my Redeemer's near,
My Shepherd and my Guide,
I bid farewell to every fear;
My wants are all supplied.

2 To ever-fragrant meads,
Where rich abundance grows,
His gracious hand indulgent leads,
And guards my sweet repose.

3 Dear Shepherd, if I stray,
My wandering feet restore;
And guard me with thy watchful eye,
And let me rove no more.

303. S. M. Doddridge.

1 Dear Saviour, we are thine
By everlasting bands;
Our hearts, our souls, we would resign
Entirely to thy hands.

2 To thee we still would cleave
With ever-growing zeal;
If millions tempt us Christ to leave,
O, let them ne'er prevail.

3 Thy Spirit shall unite
Our souls to thee, our Head;
Shall form us to thy image bright,
And teach thy paths to tread.

4 Death may our souls divide
From these abodes of clay;
But love shall keep us near thy side,
Through all the gloomy way.

5 Since Christ and we are one,
Why should we doubt or fear?
If he in heaven hath fixed his throne,
He'll fix his members there.

BATTISHILL. S. M.

BATTISHILL.
From a Chant.

313. S. M. HAMMOND.

1 AWAKE, and sing the song
Of Moses and the Lamb;
Wake every heart, and every tongue,
To praise the Saviour's name.

2 Sing of his dying love;
Sing of his rising power;
Sing how he intercedes, above,
For us, whose sins he bore.

3 Sing, till we feel our heart
Ascending with our tongue;
Sing, till the love of sin depart,
And grace inspire our song.

4 Sing on your heavenly way,
Ye ransomed sinners, sing;
Sing on, rejoicing every day
In Christ, th' eternal King.

5 Soon shall we hear him say,
"Ye blesséd children, come!"
Soon will he call us hence, away
To our eternal home.

6 There shall our raptured tongue
His endless praise proclaim,
And sweeter voices tune the song
Of Moses and the Lamb.

312. S. M. BEDDOME.

1 YE angels, bless the Lord,
And praise his sacred name;
Diffuse his glories all abroad,
His gracious acts proclaim.

2 Praise him, ye heavenly powers,
And make his goodness known;
Christ is your Head, as well as ours,
And ye surround his throne.

3 Praise him, ye hosts of light,
In accents sweet and high;
To him you owe your power and might;
At his command you fly.

4 Ye wingéd seraphim,
Your grateful voices raise;
Created and preserved by him,
Let him have all your praise.

5 The lofty song begin,
And tune your harps anew;
While we in sacred concert join,
And strive to vie with you.

CASWELL. S. M.

B. F. E.

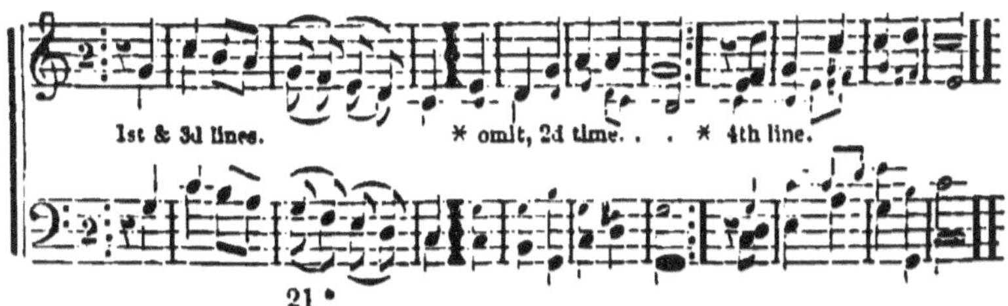

356. S. M. PRATT'S COL.

1 BLEST Comforter divine,
Let rays of heavenly love
Amid our gloom and darkness shine,
And guide our souls above.

2 Turn us, with gentle voice,
From every sinful way,
And bid the mourning saint rejoice,
Though earthly joys decay.

3 By thine inspiring breath
Make every cloud of care,
And e'en the gloomy vale of death,
A smile of glory wear.

4 O, fill thou every heart
With love to all our race;
Great Comforter, to us impart
These blessings of thy grace.

361. S. M. HART.

1 COME, Holy Spirit, come;
Let thy bright beams arise;
Dispel the sorrow from our minds,
The darkness from our eyes.

2 Convince us all of sin;
Then lead to Jesus' blood,
And to our wondering view reveal
The mercies of our God.

3 Revive our drooping faith,
Our doubts and fears remove,
And kindle in our breasts the flame
Of never-dying love.

4 'Tis thine to cleanse the heart,
To sanctify the soul,
To pour fresh life in every part,
And new-create the whole.

5 Dwell, Spirit, in our hearts;
Our minds from bondage free;
Then shall we know, and praise, and love
The Father, Son, and Thee.

362. S. M. BEDDOME.

1 COME, Holy Spirit, come,
With energy divine,
And on this poor, benighted soul
With beams of mercy shine.

2 Melt, melt this frozen heart;
This stubborn will subdue;
Each evil passion overcome,
And form me all anew.

3 Mine will the profit be,
But thine shall be the praise;
And unto thee will I devote
The remnant of my days.

363. S. M. ANON.

1 THOU, Holy Spirit, art
Of truth the promised seal;
Convincing power thou dost impart,
And Jesus' grace reveal.

2 O, breathe thy quickening breath,
And light and life afford;
Instruct us how to live by faith,
And glorify the Lord.

378. S. M. MONTGOMERY

1 'Tis God the Spirit leads
In paths before unknown:
The work to be performed is ours;
The strength is all his own.

2 Supported by his grace,
We still pursue our way,
And hope at last to reach the prize,
Secure in endless day.

ST. THOMAS. S. M. A. WILLIAMS.

3 'Tis he that works to will;
'Tis he that works to do;
The power by which we act is his,
And his the glory too.

390. S. M. BEDDOME.

1 O LORD, thy perfect word
Directs our steps aright;
Nor can all other books afford
Such profit or delight.

2 Celestial light it sheds,
To cheer this vale below;
To distant lands its glory spreads,
And streams of mercy flow.

3 True wisdom it imparts;
Commands our hope and fear;
O, may we hide it in our hearts,
And feel its influence there.

391. S. M. WATTS.

1 BEHOLD, the lofty sky
Declares its Maker, God,
And all his starry works on high
Proclaim his power abroad.

2 The darkness and the light
Still keep their course the same;
While night to day, and day to night,
Divinely teach his name.

3 In every different land
Their general voice is known;
They show the wonders of his hand,
And orders of his throne.

4 Ye Christian lands, rejoice;
Here he reveals his word;
We are not left to nature's voice
To bid us know the Lord.

403. S. M. WATTS.

1 BEHOLD, the morning sun
Begins his glorious way;
His beams through all the nations run,
And life and light convey.

2 But where the gospel comes,
It spreads diviner light;
It calls dead sinners from their tombs,
And gives the blind their sight.

3 How perfect is thy word!
And all thy judgments just!
Forever sure thy promise, Lord,
And we securely trust.

4 My gracious God, how plain
Are thy directions given!
O, may I never read in vain,
But find the path to heaven.

430. S. M. PRATT'S COL.

1 YE trembling captives, hear;
The gospel trumpet sounds:
No music more can charm the ear,
Or heal your heartfelt wounds.

2 'Tis not the trump of war,
Nor Sinai's awful roar:
Salvation's news it spreads afar,
And vengeance is no more.

3 Forgiveness, love, and peace,
Glad heaven aloud proclaims;
And earth the jubilee release,
With eager rapture, claims.

4 Far, far, to distant lands
The saving news shall spread,
And Jesus all his willing bands
In glorious triumph lead.

CHESTER. S. M. S. Stanley.

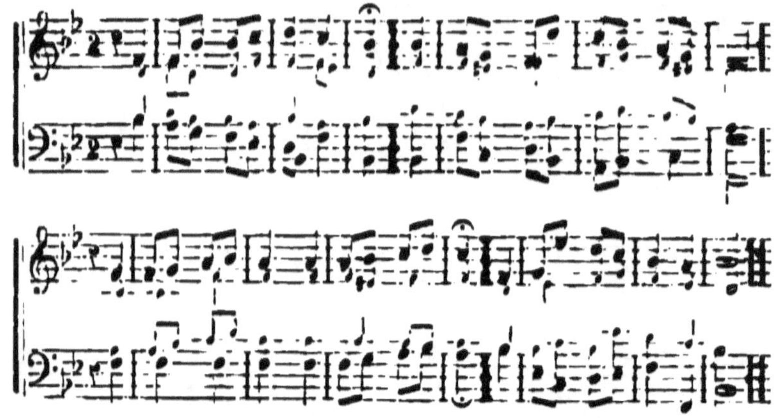

405. S. M. Watts.

1 The Lord on high proclaims
His Godhead from his throne ;
Mercy and justice are the names
By which he will be known.

2 Ye dying souls that sit
In darkness and distress,
Look from the borders of the pit
To his recovering grace.

3 Sinners shall hear the sound ;
Their thankful tongues shall own
Their righteousness and strength are found
In thee, O Lord, alone.

4 In thee shall Israel trust,
And see their guilt forgiven ;
Thou wilt pronounce the sinners just,
And take the saints to heaven.

412. S. M. Doddridge.

1 The Lord Jehovah calls ;
Be every ear inclined ;
May such a voice awake each heart,
And captivate the mind.

2 If he in thunder speak,
Earth trembles at his nod ;
But milder accents here proclaim
The condescending God.

3 O, harden not your hearts,
But hear his voice to-day ;
Lest, ere to-morrow's earliest dawn,
He call your souls away.

4 Almighty God, pronounce
The word of conquering grace ;
So shall the flint dissolve to tears,
And scorners seek thy face.

AYLESBURY. S. M. Dr. Maurice Greene. Died 1755.

431. S. M. Epis. Col.

1 The Spirit, in our hearts,
Is whispering, "Sinner, come;"
The bride, the church of Christ, proclaims
To all his children, "Come!"

2 Let him that heareth say
To all about him, "Come;"
Let him that thirsts for righteousness
To Christ, the fountain, come.

3 Yes, whosoever will,
O, let him freely come,
And freely drink the stream of life;
'Tis Jesus bids him come.

4 Lo! Jesus, who invites,
Declares, "I quickly come:"
Lord, even so; we wait thy hour;
O blest Redeemer, come.

432. S. M. Pratt's Col.

1 Ye sons of earth, arise,
Ye creatures of a day;
Redeem the time — be bold — be wise,
And cast your bonds away.

2 The year of gospel grace
With us rejoice to see,
And thankfully in Christ embrace
Your proffered liberty.

3 Blest Saviour, Lord of all,
Thee help us to receive;
Obedient to thy gracious call,
O, bid us turn and live.

4 Our former years misspent
Now let us deeply mourn,
And, softened by thy grace, repent,
And to thine arms return.

BLADEN. S. M. German.

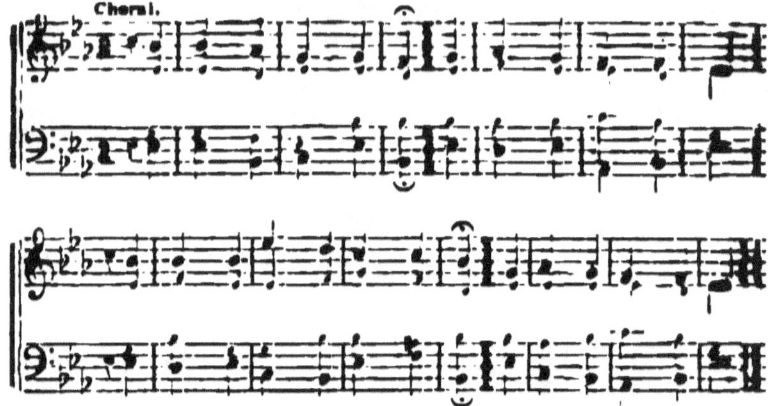

435. S. M. Dobell.

1 Now is th' accepted time;
Now is the day of grace;
Now, sinners, come, without delay,
And seek the Saviour's face.

2 Now is th' accepted time;
The Saviour calls to-day;
To-morrow it may be too late;
Then why should you delay?

3 Now is th' accepted time;
The gospel bids you come,
And every promise in his word
Declares there yet is room.

4 Lord, draw reluctant souls,
And feast them with thy love;
Then will the angels swiftly fly
To bear the news above.

442. S. M. Hyde.

1 And canst thou, sinner, slight
The call of love divine?
Shall God with tenderness invite,
And gain no thought of thine?

2 Wilt thou not cease to grieve
The Spirit from thy breast,
Till he thy wretched soul shall leave
With all thy sins oppressed?

3 To-day a pardoning God
Will hear the suppliant pray;
To-day, a Saviour's cleansing blood
Will wash thy guilt away.

4 But grace so dearly bought
If yet thou wilt despise,
Thy fearful doom, with sorrow fraught,
Will fill thee with surprise.

436. S. M. Select Hymns.

1 Now is the day of grace;
Now to the Saviour come;
The Lord is calling, "Seek my face,
And I will guide you home."

2 A Father bids you speed;
O, wherefore then delay?
He calls in love; he sees your need;
He bids you come to-day.

3 To-day the prize is won;
The promise is to save;
Then, O, be wise; to-morrow's sun
May shine upon your grave.

440. S. M. Dwight.

1 Ye sinners, fear the Lord,
While yet 'tis called to-day;
Soon will the awful voice of death
Command your souls away.

2 Soon will the harvest close,
The summer soon be o'er;
O sinners, then your injured God
Will heed your cries no more.

3 Then, while 'tis called to-day,
O, hear the gospel's sound;
Come, sinners, haste, O, haste away,
While pardon may be found.

443. S. M. Pratt's Col.

1 All yesterday is gone;
To-morrow's not our own;
O, sinner, come, without delay,
To bow before the throne.

2 O, hear his voice to-day,
And harden not your heart;
To-morrow, with a frown, he may
Pronounce the word, — "Depart."

ST. BRIDE. S. M. DR. HOWARD. 1760.

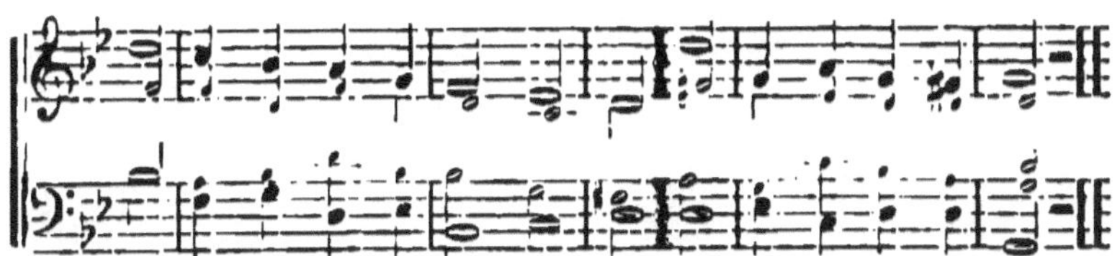

445. S. M. DODDRIDGE.

1 THE swift-declining day,
How fast its moments fly,
While evening's broad and gloomy shade
Gains on the western sky!

2 Ye mortals, mark its pace,
And use the hours of light;
For know, its Maker can command
An instant, endless night.

3 Give glory to the Lord,
Who rules the rolling sphere:
Submissive, at his footstool bow,
And seek salvation there.

4 Then shall new lustre break
Through all the heavy gloom,
And lead you to unchanging light,
In your celestial home.

446. S. M. VILLAGE HYMNS.

1 MY son, know thou the Lord;
Thy fathers' God obey;
Seek his protecting care by night,
His guardian hand by day.

2 Call while he may be found;
O, seek him while he's near;
Serve him with all thy heart and mind,
And worship him with fear.

3 If thou wilt seek his face,
His ear will hear thy cry;
Then shalt thou find his mercy sure,
His grace forever nigh.

4 But if thou leave thy God,
Nor choose the path to heaven,
Then shalt thou perish in thy sins,
And never be forgiven.

480. S. M. ANON.

1 ONCE more we meet to pray,
Once more our guilt confess;
Turn not, O Lord, thine ear away
From creatures in distress.

2 Our sins to heaven ascend,
And there for vengeance cry;
O God, behold the sinner's Friend,
Who intercedes on high.

3 Though we are vile indeed,
And well deserve thy curse,
The merits of thy Son we plead,
Who lived and died for us.

4 Now let thy bosom yearn,
As it hath done before;
Return to us, O God, return,
And ne'er forsake us more.

471. S. M. BEDDOME.

1 DID Christ o'er sinners weep,
And shall our cheeks be dry?
Let floods of penitential grief
Burst forth from every eye.

2 The Son of God in tears
The wondering angels see;
Be thou astonished, O my soul;
He shed those tears for thee.

3 He wept that we might weep;
Each sin demands a tear:
In heaven alone no sin is found,
And there's no weeping there.

DENNIS.

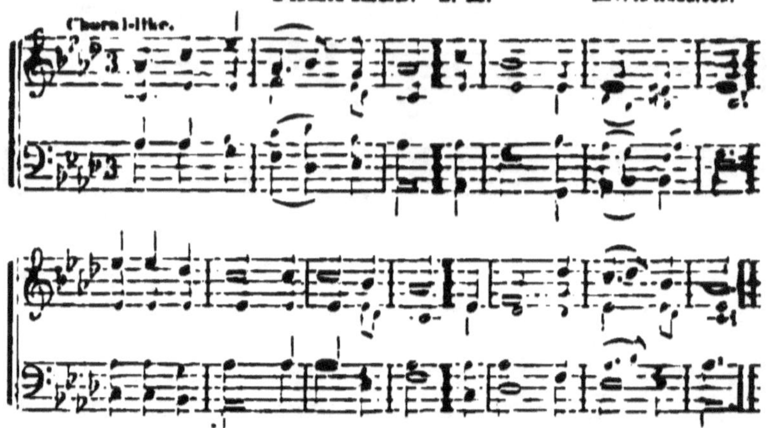

465. S. M. Rippon's Col.

1 Like Israel, Lord, am I;
My soul is at a stand;
A sea before, a host behind,
And rocks on either hand.

2 O Lord, I cry to thee,
And would thy word obey;
Bid me advance; and, through the sea,
Create a new-made way.

3 The time of greatest straits
Thy chosen time has been
To manifest thy power is great,
And make thy glory seen.

4 O, send deliverance down;
Display the arm divine;
So shall the praise be all thy own,
And I be doubly thine.

495. S. M. Watts.

1 O, blessed souls are they
Whose sins are covered o'er;
Divinely blest, to whom the Lord
Imputes their guilt no more.

2 They mourn their follies past,
And keep their hearts with care;
Their lips and lives without deceit,
Shall prove their faith sincere.

3 While I concealed my guilt,
I felt the festering wound,
Till I confessed my sins to thee,
And ready pardon found.

4 Let sinners learn to pray;
Let saints keep near the throne;
Our help in times of deep distress
Is found in God alone.

505. S. M. Beddome.

1 Faith is a precious grace,
Where'er it is bestowed;
It boasts a high, celestial birth,
And is the gift of God.

2 Jesus it owns as King,
And all-atoning Priest;
It claims no merit of its own,
But looks for all in Christ.

3 To him it leads the soul,
When filled with deep distress;
Flies to the fountain of his blood,
And trusts his righteousness.

4 Since 'tis thy work alone,
And that divinely free,
Lord, send the Spirit of thy Son,
To work this faith in me.

540. S. M. Campbell's Col.

1 Lord, I would come to thee,
A sinner all defiled;
O, take the stain of guilt away,
And own me as thy child.

2 I cannot live in sin,
And feel a Saviour's love:
Thy blood can make my spirit clean,
And write my name above.

3 Among thy little flock
I need the Shepherd's care;
Pour waters from the smitten Rock,
And pastures green prepare.

4 Blest Shepherd, I am thine;
Still keep me in thy fear;
Now fill my heart with grace divine;
Bring thy salvation near.

CRUCIFIX. S. M. D. F. EDMANDS.

* These slurs not to be observed in singing the third line.

464. S. M. EPIS. COL.

1 AH, how shall fallen man
Be just before his God!
If he contend in righteousness,
We fall beneath his rod.

2 If he our ways should mark
With strict, inquiring eyes,
Could we for one of thousand faults
A just excuse devise?

3 All-seeing, powerful God,
Who can with thee contend?
Or who that tries th' unequal strife
Shall prosper in the end?

4 The mountains, in thy wrath,
Their ancient seats forsake;
The trembling earth deserts her place;
Her rooted pillars shake.

5 Ah, how shall guilty man
Contend with such a God?
None, none can meet him, and escape,
But through the Saviour's blood.

479. S. M. TATE & BRADY.

1 HAVE mercy, Lord, on me,
As thou wert ever kind;
Let me, oppressed with loads of guilt,
Thy wonted pardon find.

2 Against thee, Lord, alone,
And only in thy sight,
Have I transgressed; and, though condemned,
Must own thy judgments right.

3 Blot out my crying sins,
Nor me in anger view;
Create in me a heart that's clean,
An upright mind renew.

4 Withdraw not thou thy help,
Nor cast me from thy sight,
Nor let thy Holy Spirit take
His everlasting flight.

5 The joy thy favor gives
Let me again obtain,
And thy free Spirit's firm support
My fainting soul sustain.

483. S. M. BEDDOME.

1 THOU Lord of all above,
And all below the sky,
Before thy feet I prostrate fall,
And for thy mercy cry.

2 Forgive my follies past,
The crimes which I have done;
O, bid a contrite sinner live,
Through thy incarnate Son.

3 Guilt, like a heavy load,
Upon my conscience lies;
To thee I make my sorrows known,
And lift my weeping eyes.

4 The burden which I feel,
Thou only canst remove;
Display, O Lord, thy pardoning grace,
And thy unbounded love.

5 One gracious look of thine
Will ease my troubled breast;
O, let me know my sins forgiven,
And I shall then be blest.

491. S. M. COWPER.

1 MY former hopes are fled;
My terror now begins;
I feel, alas! that I am dead
In trespasses and sins.

2 Ah, whither shall I fly?
I hear the thunder roar;
The law proclaims destruction nigh,
And vengeance at the door.

3 When I review my ways,
I dread impending doom;
But hark! a friendly whisper says,
"Flee from the wrath to come."

4 I see, or think I see,
A glimmering from afar,
A beam of day that shines for me,
To save me from despair.

5 Forerunner of the sun,
It marks the pilgrim's way;
I'll gaze upon it while I run,
And watch the rising day.

513. S. M. Noel's Col.

1 If on a quiet sea
Toward heaven we calmly sail,
With grateful hearts, O God, to thee,
We'll own the favoring gale.

2 But should the surges rise,
And rest delay to come,
Blest be the sorrow, kind the storm,
Which drives us nearer home.

3 Soon shall our doubts and fears
All yield at thy control;
Thy tender mercies shall illume
The midnight of the soul.

4 Teach us, in every state,
To make thy will our own,
And, when the joys of sense depart,
To live by faith alone.

545. S. M. Beddome.

1 When sorrows round us roll,
And comforts we have none,
Dear Saviour, say that thou art ours,
And all our griefs are gone.

2 Is there no friend to cheer
In times of deep distress, —
A smile from thee will help to bear,
Or make the burden less.

3 Though in the gloomy vale
Of death, we fear no harm,
Supported by thy powerful grace,
Reclining on thine arm.

4 This is our utmost wish,
O Lord, — that thou wouldst be,
Forever, ever near to us,
And keep us near to thee.

527. S. M. Rippon's Col.

1 Unto thine altar, Lord,
A broken heart I bring;
And wilt thou graciously accept
Of such a worthless thing?

2 To Christ, the bleeding Lamb,
My faith directs its eyes;
Thou may'st reject that worthless thing,
But not his sacrifice.

3 When he gave up his life,
The law was satisfied;
And now, to its severer claims
I answer, "Jesus died."

542. S. M. Anon.

1 I languish for a sight
Of Him who reigns on high, —
Jesus, my soul's supreme delight;
For Him alone I sigh.

2 O that I knew the place
Where I might find my God,
And make the arms of his embrace
My soul's secure abode!

3 Near to his mercy-seat,
Where grace triumphant reigns,
I'd come and worship at his feet,
And tell him all my pains.

4 The arguments I'd use
My troubles shall suggest;
Nor can my blessed Lord refuse
The cause of the distressed.

5 O Saviour, bring me near;
New life, new strength impart;
Cast out at once my slavish fear,
And dwell within my heart.

600. S. M. Sac. Songs.

1 How tender is thy hand,
O thou most gracious Lord!
Afflictions come at thy command,
And leave us at thy word.

2 How gentle was the rod
That chastened us for sin!
How soon we found a smiling God
Where deep distress had been.

3 A Father's hand we felt,
A Father's heart we knew;
'Mid tears of penitence we knelt,
And found his word was true.

4 Now we will bless the Lord,
And in his strength confide;
Forever be his name adored,
For there is none beside.

625. S. M. Watts.

1 When, overwhelmed with grief,
My heart within me dies,
Helpless, and far from all relief,
To heaven I lift mine eyes.

2 O, lead me to the Rock
That's high above my head,
And make the covert of thy wings
My shelter and my shade.

3 Within thy presence, Lord,
Forever I'll abide;
Thou art the tower of my defence,
The refuge where I hide.

4 Thou givest me the lot
Of those that fear thy name;
If endless life be their reward,
I shall possess the same.

639. S. M. Sac. Lyrics.

1 How sweet the melting lay,
Which breaks upon the ear,
When, at the hour of rising day,
Christians unite in prayer!

2 The breezes waft their cries
Up to Jehovah's throne;
He listens to their humble sighs,
And sends his blessings down.

3 So Jesus rose to pray
Before the morning light—
Once on the chilling mount did stay,
And wrestle all the night.

4 Glory to God on high,
Who sends his blessings down
To rescue souls condemned to die,
And make his people one.

642. S. M. Newton.

1 Behold the throne of grace!
The promise calls me near;
There Jesus shows a smiling face,
And waits to answer prayer.

2 Thine image, Lord, bestow,
Thy presence and thy love;
I ask to serve thee here below,
And reign with thee above.

3 Teach me to live by faith;
Conform my will to thine,
Let me victorious be in death,
And then in glory shine.

4 If thou these blessings give,
And wilt my portion be,
All worldly joys I'll cheerful leave,
And find my heaven in thee.

648. S. M. Pratt's Col.

1 My God, my prayer attend;
O, bow thine ear to me,
Without a hope, without a friend,
Without a help, but thee

2 O, guard my soul around,
Which loves and trusts thy grace;
Nor let the powers of hell confound
The hopes on thee I place.

3 Thy mercy I entreat;
Let mercy hear my cries,
While, humbly waiting at thy seat,
My daily prayers arise.

4 O, bid my heart rejoice,
And every fear control,
Since at thy throne, with suppliant voice,
To thee I lift my soul.

683. S. M. Watts.

1 Is this the kind return?
Are these the thanks we owe—
Thus to abuse eternal love,
Whence all our blessings flow?

2 To what a stubborn frame
Has sin reduced our mind!
What strange, rebellious wretches we!
And God as strangely kind!

3 Turn, turn us, mighty God,
And mould our souls afresh;
Break, sovereign grace, these hearts of stone,
And give us hearts of flesh.

4 Let past ingratitude
Provoke our weeping eyes,
And hourly, as new mercies fall,
Let hourly thanks arise.

HARTLAND. S. M. (Kentucky.) ‡ INGALS, 1805. Arr. by J. OSGOOD.

‡ Called also "Iowa," arranged in $\frac{3}{2}$ time.

547. S. M. WATTS.

1 NOT with our mortal eyes
Have we beheld the Lord;
Yet we rejoice to hear his name,
And love him in his word.

2 On earth we want the sight
Of our Redeemer's face;
Yet, Lord, our inmost thoughts delight
To dwell upon thy grace.

3 And, when we feel thy love,
Diviner joys arise;
On wings of faith we soar above,
To mansions in the skies.

655. S. M. WATTS.

1 MY God, permit my tongue
This joy — to call thee mine;
And let my early cries prevail
To taste thy love divine.

2 For life, without thy love,
No relish can afford;
No joy can be compared with this, —
To serve and please the Lord.

3 In wakeful hours of night,
I call my God to mind;
I think how wise thy counsels are,
And all thy dealings kind.

4 Since thou hast been my help,
To thee my spirit flies:
And on thy watchful providence
My cheerful hope relies.

5 The shadow of thy wings
My soul in safety keeps;
I follow where my Father leads,
And he supports my steps.

650. S. M. MONTGOMERY.

1 OUR heavenly Father, hear
The prayer we offer now;
Thy name be hallowed far and near,
To thee all nations bow.

2 Thy kingdom come; thy will
On earth be done in love,
As saints and seraphim fulfil
Thy perfect law above.

3 Our daily bread supply
While by thy word we live;
The guilt of our iniquity
Forgive, as we forgive.

4 From dark temptation's power,
From Satan's wiles, defend;
Deliver in the evil hour,
And guide us to the end.

5 Thine shall forever be
Glory and power divine;
The sceptre, throne, and majesty
Of heaven and earth are thine.

6 Thus humbly taught to pray
By thy belovéd Son,
Through him we come to thee, and say,
"All for his sake be done."

740. S. M. MONTGOMERY.

1 SOW in the morn thy seed;
At eve hold not thy hand;
To doubt and fear give thou no heed;
Broadcast it o'er the land, —

2 And duly shall appear,
In verdure, beauty, strength,
The tender blade, the stalk, the ear,
And the full corn at length.

PADDINGTON. S. M.

3 Thou canst not toil in vain;
Cold, heat, and moist, and dry,
Shall foster and mature the grain
For garners in the sky.

4 Thence, when the glorious end, —
The day of God, — shall come,
The angel-reapers shall descend,
And heaven cry, "Harvest home!"

723. S. M. C. Wesley.

1 Soldiers of Christ, arise,
And gird your armor on,
Strong in the strength which God supplies
Through his eternal Son.

2 Strong in the Lord of hosts,
And in his mighty power,
The man who in the Saviour trusts
Is more than conqueror.

3 Stand, then, in his great might,
With all his strength endued,
And take, to arm you for the fight,
The panoply of God: —

4 That, having all things done,
And all your conflicts past,
You may o'ercome through Christ alone,
And stand complete at last.

5 From strength to strength go on;
Wrestle, and fight, and pray;
Tread all the powers of darkness down,
And win the well-fought day.

6 Still let the Spirit cry,
In all his soldiers, "Come,"
Till Christ the Lord descends from high,
And takes the conquerors home.

737. S. M. L. H. Sigourney.

1 Laborers of Christ, arise,
And gird you for the toil;
The dew of promise from the skies
Already cheers the soil.

2 Go where the sick recline,
Where mourning hearts deplore;
And where the sons of sorrow pine,
Dispense your hallowed lore.

3 Urge, with a tender zeal,
The erring child along
Where peaceful congregations kneel,
And pious teachers throng.

4 Be faith, which looks above,
With prayer, your constant guest,
And wrap the Saviour's changeless love
A mantle round your breast.

5 So shall you share the wealth
That earth may ne'er despoil,
And the blest gospel's saving health
Repay your arduous toil.

781. S. M. Swain.

1 Who can forbear to sing,
Who can refuse to praise,
When Zion's high, celestial King
His saving power displays? —

2 When sinners at his feet,
By mercy conquered, fall?
When grace, and truth, and justice meet,
And peace unites them all?

3 Who can forbear to praise
Our high, celestial King,
When sovereign, rich, redeeming grace
Invites our tongues to sing?

CONCORD. S. M. O. HOLDEN.

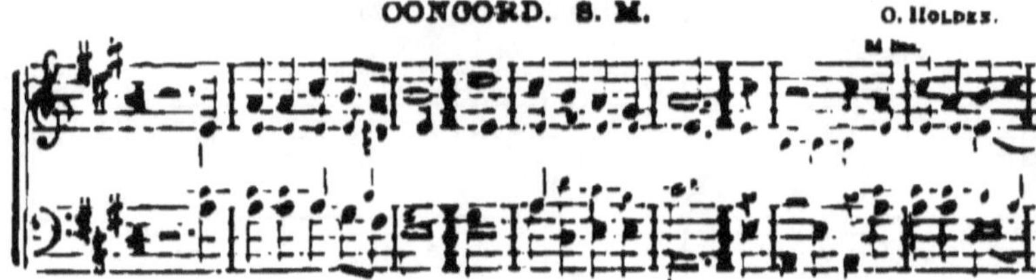

520. S. M. DODDRIDGE.

1 GRACE! 'tis a charming sound —
Harmonious to the ear;
Heaven with the echo shall resound,
And all the earth shall hear.

2 Grace first contrived the way
To save rebellious man;
And all the steps that grace display
Which drew the wondrous plan.

3 Grace led my roving feet
To tread the heavenly road;
And new supplies, each hour, I meet,
While pressing on to God.

4 Grace all the work shall crown,
Through everlasting days;
It lays in heaven the topmost stone,
And well deserves the praise.

715. S. M. DODDRIDGE.

1 YE servants of the Lord,
Each in his office wait:
With joy obey his heavenly word,
And watch before his gate.

2 Let all your lamps be bright,
And trim the golden flame;
Gird up your loins, as in his sight,
For awful is his name.

3 Watch! — 'tis your Lord's command;
And while we speak, he's near:
Mark every signal of his hand,
And ready all appear.

4 O, happy servant he,
In such a posture found!
He shall his Lord with rapture see,
And be with honor crowned.

717. S. M. HEATH.

1 MY soul, be on thy guard;
Ten thousand foes arise;
The hosts of sin are pressing hard
To draw thee from the skies.

2 O, watch, and fight, and pray;
The battle ne'er give o'er;
Renew it boldly every day,
And help divine implore.

3 Ne'er think the victory won,
Nor lay thine armor down;
Thy arduous work will not be done
Till thou obtain thy crown.

4 Fight on, my soul, till death
Shall bring thee to thy God;
He'll take thee, at thy parting breath,
To his divine abode.

730. S. M. MONTGOMERY.

1 OUR Captain leads us on;
He beckons from the skies;
He reaches out a starry crown,
And bids us take the prize.

2 "Be faithful unto death,
Partake my victory,
And thou shalt wear this glorious wreath,
And thou shalt reign with me:" —

3 'Tis thus the righteous Lord
To every soldier saith;
Eternal life is the reward
Of all victorious faith.

4 Who conquer in his might
The victor's meed receive;
They claim a kingdom in his right,
Which God will freely give.

NOLEN. S. M. (Common chord tune.) JOSEPH OSGOOD.
From Bay State Collection.

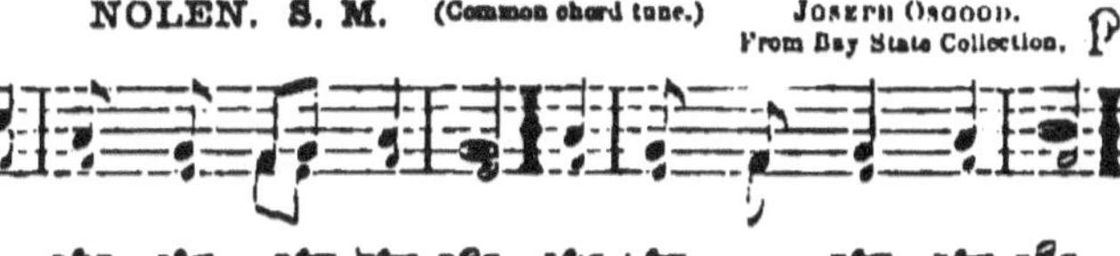

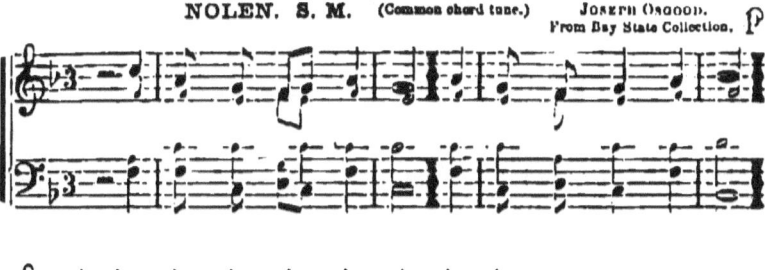

516. S. M. WATTS.

1 How heavy is the night
  That hangs upon our eyes,
Till Christ, with his reviving light,
  O'er our dark souls arise!

2 Our guilty spirits dread
  To meet the wrath of Heaven;
But, in his righteousness arrayed,
  We see our sin forgiven.

3 Unholy and impure
  Are all our thoughts and ways;
His hands infected nature cure
  With sanctifying grace.

4 The powers of hell agree
  To hold our souls in vain;
He sets the sons of bondage free,
  And breaks the cruel chain.

5 Lord, we adore thy ways
  To bring us near to God,
Thy sovereign power, thy healing grace,
  And thine atoning blood.

689. S. M. STEELE.

1 MY Maker and my King,
  To thee my all I owe;
Thy sovereign bounty is the spring
  Whence all my blessings flow.

2 The creature of thy hand,
  On thee alone I live;
My God, thy benefits demand
  More praise than I can give.

3 Lord, what can I impart,
  When all is thine before?
Thy love demands a thankful heart,—
  The gift, alas! how poor!

4 Shall I withhold thy due?
  And shall my passions rove?
Lord, form this wretched heart anew,
  And fill it with thy love.

5 O, let thy grace inspire
  My soul with strength divine;
Let all my powers to thee aspire,
  And all my days be thine.

694. S. M. WATTS.

1 BLEST are the sons of peace,
  Whose hearts and hopes are one,
Whose kind designs to serve and please
  Through all their actions run.

2 Blest is the pious house
  Where zeal and friendship meet;
Their songs of praise, their mingled vows,
  Make their communion sweet.

3 From those celestial springs
  Such streams of pleasure flow,
As no increase of riches brings,
  Nor honors can bestow.

4 Thus, when on Aaron's head
  They poured the rich perfume,
The oil through all his raiment spread,
  And fragrance filled the room.

5 Thus, on the heavenly hills,
  The saints are blessed above,
Where joy, like morning dew, distils,
  And all the air is love.

SHAWMUT.

LOUDON. S. M. T. OLMSTED.

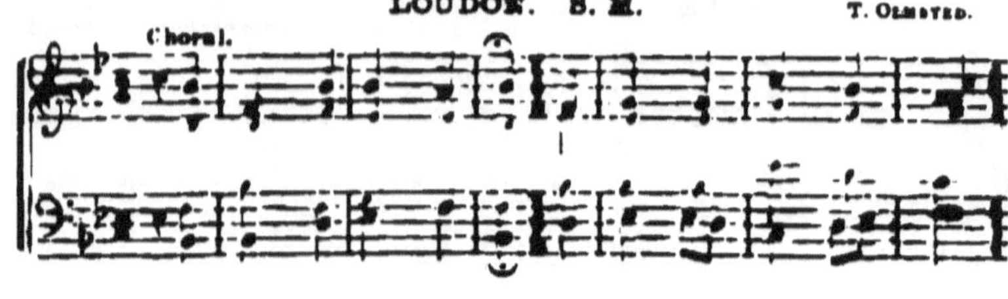

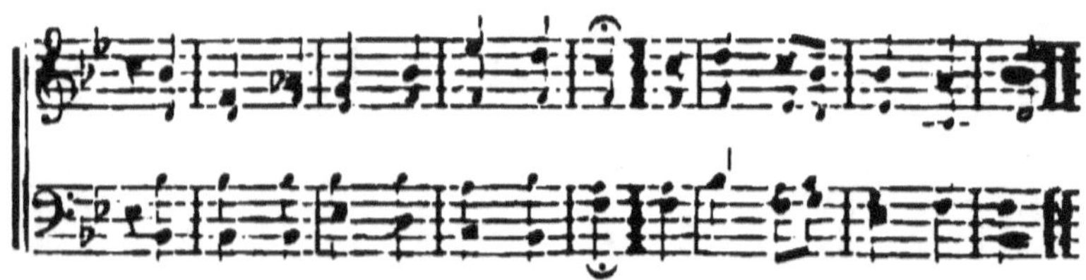

537. S. M. BEDDOME.

1 O LORD, thou art my Lord,
My portion and delight;
All other lords I now reject,
And cast them from my sight.

2 Thy sovereign right I own;
Thy glorious power confess;
Thy law shall ever rule my heart,
While I adore thy grace.

3 Too long my feet have strayed
In sin's forbidden way;
But since thou hast my soul reclaimed,
To thee my vows I'll pay.

4 My soul, to Jesus joined
By faith, and hope, and love,
Now seeks to dwell among thy saints,
And rest with them above.

5 Accept, O Lord, my heart;
To thee myself I give;
Nor suffer me from hence to stray,
Or cause thy saints to grieve.

665. S. M. MASON.

1 BLEST are the pure in heart,
For they shall see our God;
The secret of the Lord is theirs;
Their soul is his abode.

2 Still to the lowly soul
He doth himself impart,
And for his temple and his throne
Selects the pure in heart.

BOYLSTON.

668. S. M. ANON.

1 LORD, help me to resign
My doubting heart to thee,
And, whether cheerful or distressed,
Thine, thine alone to be.

2 My only aim be this,—
Thy purpose to fulfil,
In thee rejoice with all my strength,
And do thy holy will.

3 Lord, thy all-seeing eye
Keeps watch with sleepless care;
Thy great compassion never fails;
Thou hear'st my humble prayer.

4 So will I firmly trust
That thou wilt guide me still,
And guard me safe throughout the way
That leads to Zion's hill.

676. S. M. C. WESLEY.

1 O GOD, my strength, my hope,
On thee I cast my care,
With humble confidence look up,
And know thou hearest prayer.

2 O for a godly fear
A quick-discerning eye,
That looks to thee when sin is near,
And sees the tempter fly!—

3 A spirit still prepared,
And armed with jealous care,
Forever standing on its guard,
And watching unto prayer!

4 Lord, let me still abide,
Nor from my hope remove,
Till thou my patient spirit guide
To better worlds above.

564. S. M. WATTS.

1 To God, the only wise,
Our Saviour and our King,
Let all the saints below the skies
Their humble praises bring.

2 'Tis his almighty love,
His counsel, and his care,
Preserves us safe from sin and death,
And every hurtful snare.

3 He will present our souls,
Unblemished and complete,
Before the glory of his face,
With joys divinely great.

4 Then all the chosen seed
Shall meet around the throne,
Shall bless the conduct of his grace,
And make his wonders known.

718. S. M. WATTS.

1 I LIFT my soul to God;
My trust is in his name:
Let not my foes, that seek my blood,
Still triumph in my shame.

2 From early dawning light
Till evening shades arise,
For thy salvation, Lord, I wait,
With ever-longing eyes.

3 Remember all thy grace,
And lead me in thy truth;
Forgive the sins of riper days,
And follies of my youth.

4 The Lord is just and kind;
The meek shall learn his ways,
And every humble sinner find
The blessings of his grace.

613. S. M. EPIS. COL.

1 O, CEASE, my wandering soul,
On restless wing to roam;
All this wide world, to either pole,
Has not for thee a home.

2 Behold the ark of God;
Behold the open door;
O, haste to gain that dear abode,
And rove, my soul, no more.

3 There safe thou shalt abide,
There sweet shall be thy rest,
And every longing satisfied,
With full salvation blest.

682. S. M. WATTS.

1 MINE eyes and my desire
Are ever to the Lord;
I love to plead his promised grace,
And rest upon his word.

2 Turn, turn thee to my soul;
Bring thy salvation near;
When will thy hand release my feet
From every deadly snare?

3 When shall the sovereign grace
Of my forgiving God
Restore me from those dangerous ways
My wandering feet have trod?

4 O, keep my soul from death,
Nor put my hope to shame;
For I have placed my only trust
In my Redeemer's name.

5 With humble faith I wait
To see thy face again;
Of Israel it shall ne'er be said,
"He sought the Lord in vain."

HARTLAND. S. M. (Kentucky.) ‡ Ingals, 1805. Arr. by J. Osgood.

‡ Called also "Iowa," arranged in $\frac{3}{2}$ time.

761. S. M. Watts.

1 Let sinners take their course,
And choose the road to death;
But in the worship of my God
I'll spend my daily breath.

2 My thoughts address his throne,
When morning brings the light;
I seek his blessing every noon,
And pay my vows at night.

3 Thou wilt regard my cries,
O my eternal God,
While sinners perish in surprise,
Beneath thy holy rod.

4 Because they dwell at ease,
And no sad changes feel,
They neither fear nor trust thy name,
Nor learn to do thy will.

5 But I, with all my cares,
Will lean upon the Lord;
I'll cast my burdens on his arm,
And rest upon his word.

6 His arm shall well sustain
The children of his love;
The ground on which their safety stands
No earthly power can move.

768. S. M. Luth. Col.

1 When gloomy thoughts and fears
The trembling heart invade,
And all the face of nature wears
A universal shade,—

2 Religion can assuage
The tempest of the soul;
And every fear shall lose its rage
At her divine control.

3 Through life's bewildered way,
Her hand unerring leads;
And o'er the path her heavenly ray
A cheering lustre sheds.

4 When reason, tired and blind,
Sinks helpless and afraid,
Thou blest supporter of the mind,
How powerful is thine aid!

5 O, let us feel thy power,
And find thy sweet relief,
To cheer our every gloomy hour,
And calm our every grief.

771. S. M. Fawcett.

1 With humble heart and tongue,
My God, to thee I pray:
O, bring me now, while I am young,
To thee, the living way.

2 Make an unguarded youth
The object of thy care;
Help me to choose the way of truth,
And fly from every snare.

3 My heart, to folly prone,
Renew by power divine;
Unite it to thyself alone,
And make me wholly thine.

4 O, let thy word of grace
My warmest thoughts employ;
Be this, through all my following days,
My treasure and my joy.

5 To what thy laws impart
Be my whole soul inclined:
O, let them dwell within my heart,
And sanctify my mind.

PENTONVILLE. S. M.

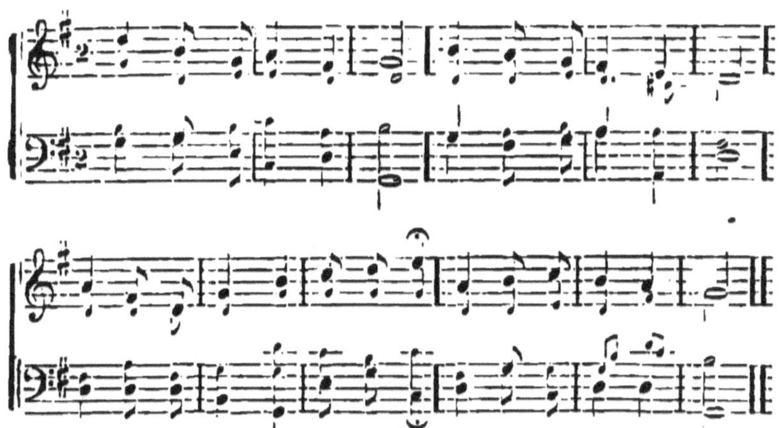

607. S. M. WATTS.

1 THE man is ever blest
Who shuns the sinners' ways,
Among their councils never stands,
Nor takes the scorner's place, —

2 But makes the law of God
His study and delight,
Amidst the labors of the day,
And watches of the night.

3 He, like a tree, shall thrive,
With waters near the root;
Fresh as the leaf his name shall live;
His works are heavenly fruit.

4 Not so th' ungodly race;
They no such blessings find:
Their hopes shall flee like empty chaff
Before the driving wind.

662. S. M. PERCY CHAP. COL.

1 MY Saviour, fill my soul
With holiness and peace;
Arise with healing in thy wings;
Bid sin and doubting cease.

2 May things beneath the sky
Engross my heart no more;
Be thou my first, my chief delight,
My soul's unbounded store.

3 In thee all treasures lie;
From thee all blessings flow;
Thou art the bliss of saints above,
The joy of saints below.

4 O, come and make me thine,
A sinner saved by grace:
Then shall I sing, with loudest strains,
In heaven, thy dwelling-place.

767. S. M. WATTS.

1 COME, we that love the Lord,
And let our joys be known;
Join in a song with sweet accord,
And thus surround the throne.

2 The sorrows of the mind
Be banished from the place;
Religion never was designed
To make our pleasures less.

3 Let those refuse to sing
Who never knew our God;
But children of the heavenly King
May speak their joys abroad.

4 The hill of Zion yields
A thousand sacred sweets,
Before we reach the heavenly fields,
Or walk the golden streets.

5 Then let our songs abound,
And every tear be dry;
We're marching through Immanuel's ground,
To fairer worlds on high.

708. S. M. TOPLADY.

1 YOUR harps, ye trembling saints,
Down from the willows take;
Loud, to the praise of love divine,
Bid every string awake.

2 Though in a foreign land,
We are not far from home;
And nearer to our house above
We every moment come.

3 His grace will to the end
Stronger and brighter shine;
Nor present things, nor things to come,
Shall quench the spark divine.

PADDINGTON. S. M.

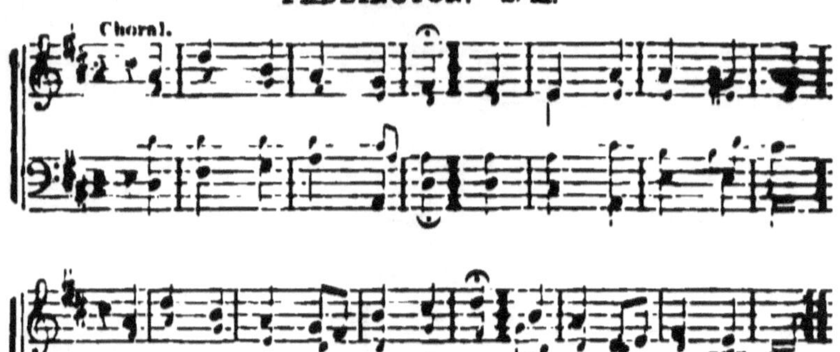

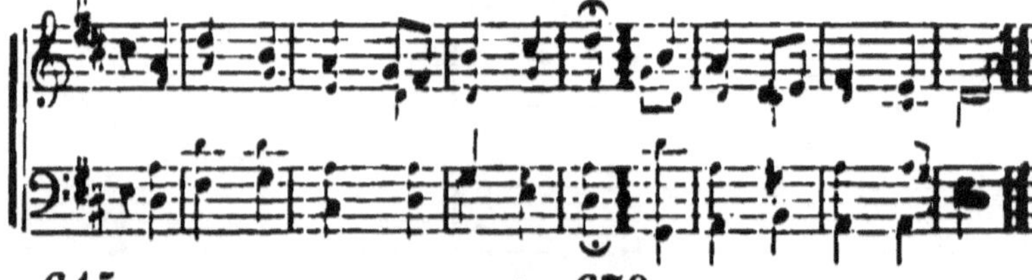

645. S. M. MEDLEY.

1 COME, praying souls, rejoice,
And bless your Father's name;
With joy to him lift up your voice,
And all his love proclaim.

2 Your mournful cry he hears;
He marks your feeblest groan,
Supplies your wants, dispels your fears,
And makes his mercy known.

3 To all his praying saints
He ever will attend,
And to their sorrows and complaints
His ear in mercy bend.

4 Then blessèd be the Lord,
Who has not turned away
His mercy, nor his precious word,
From those who love to pray.

5 No; still he bows his ear
In gentle pity down;
For praying breath he loves to hear,
And praying souls he'll crown.

6 Then let us still go on
In his appointed ways,
Rejoicing in his name alone,
In prayer and humble praise.

670. S. M. WATTS.

1 SHALL we go on to sin,
Because thy grace abounds?
Or crucify the Lord again,
And open all his wounds?

2 Forbid it, mighty God;
Nor let it e'er be said
That we, whose sins are crucified,
Should raise them from the dead.

3 We will be slaves no more,
Since Christ has made us free,
Has nailed our tyrants to his cross,
And bought our liberty.

696. S. M. BEDDOME.

1 LET party names no more
The Christian world o'erspread:
Gentile and Jew, and bond and free,
Are one in Christ, their Head.

2 Among the saints on earth
Let mutual love be found —
Heirs of the same inheritance,
With mutual blessings crowned.

3 Thus will the church below
Resemble that above,
Where streams of endless pleasure flow,
And every heart is love.

SELAH. S. M.

ST. THOMAS. S. M. A. WILLIAMS.

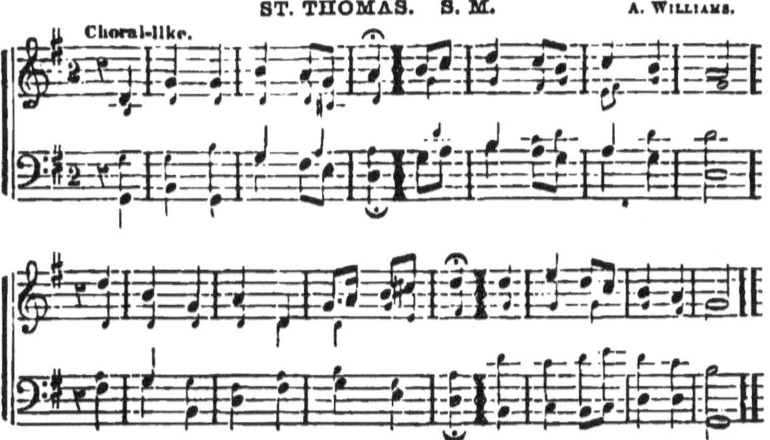

786. S. M. WATTS.

1 FAR as thy name is known
The world declares thy praise;
Thy saints, O Lord, before thy throne,
Their songs of honor raise.

2 With joy thy people stand
On Zion's chosen hill,
Proclaim the wonders of thy hand,
And counsels of thy will.

3 Let strangers walk around
The city where we dwell,
Survey with care thine holy ground,
And mark the building well,—

4 The order of thy house,
The worship of thy court,
The cheerful songs, the solemn vows,—
And make a fair report.

5 How decent, and how wise!
How glorious to behold!
Beyond the pomp that charms the eyes,
And rites adorned with gold.

6 The God we worship now
Will guide us till we die—
Will be our God while here below,
And ours above the sky.

794. S. M. WATTS.

1 How honored is the place
Where we adoring stand!
Zion, the glory of the earth,
And beauty of the land.

2 Bulwarks of grace defend
The city where we dwell,
While walls, of strong salvation made,
Defy th' assaults of hell.

3 Lift up th' eternal gates;
The doors wide open fling;
Enter, ye nations that obey
The statutes of your King.

4 Here taste unmingled joys,
And live in perfect peace,
You that have known Jehovah's name,
And ventured on his grace.

5 Trust in the Lord, ye saints,
And banish all your fears;
Strength in the Lord Jehovah dwells,
Eternal as his years.

797. S. M. WATTS.

1 GREAT is the Lord our God,
And let his praise be great;
He makes his churches his abode,
His most delightful seat.

2 In Zion God is known,
A refuge in distress:
How bright has his salvation shone,
Through all her palaces!

3 When kings against her joined,
And saw the Lord was there,
In wild confusion of the mind,
They fled with hasty fear.

4 Oft have our fathers told,
Our eyes have often seen,
How well our God secures the fold
Where his own sheep have been.

5 In every new distress
We'll to his house repair;
We'll call to mind his wondrous grace,
And seek deliverance there.

NOTE. — Dibdin's "Standard Psalm Tune Book" has this melody in $\frac{4}{2}$ time. The tune is there called Hampton, and the authorship stated to be uncertain.

788. S. M. DWIGHT.

1 I LOVE thy kingdom, Lord,
The house of thine abode,
The church our blest Redeemer saved
With his own precious blood.

2 I love thy church, O God;
Her walls before thee stand,
Dear as the apple of thine eye,
And graven on thy hand.

3 For her my tears shall fall;
For her my prayers ascend;
To her my cares and toils be given,
Till toil and cares shall end.

4 Beyond my highest joy
I prize her heavenly ways,
Her sweet communion, solemn vows,
Her hymns of love and praise.

5 Jesus, thou Friend divine,
Our Saviour and our King,
Thy hand, from every snare and foe,
Shall great deliverance bring.

6 Sure as thy truth shall last,
To Zion shall be given
The brightest glories earth can yield,
And brighter bliss of heaven.

798. S. M. S. F. SMITH.

1 WITH willing hearts we tread
The path the Saviour trod;
We love th' example of our Head,
The glorious Lamb of God.

2 On thee, on thee alone,
Our hope and faith rely,
O thou who didst for sin atone,
Who didst for sinners die.

3 We trust thy sacrifice;
To thy dear cross we flee;
O, may we die to sin, and rise
To life and bliss in thee.

SELAH. S. M.

ADMONITION. S. M. — REV. J. ALDRICH. From Sacred Lyre.

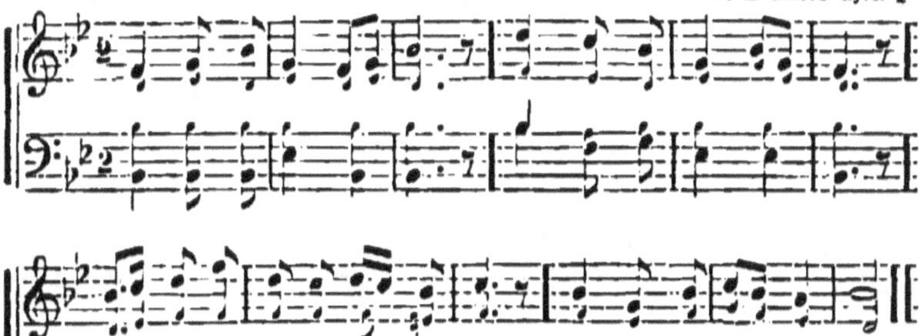

809. S. M. ENG. BAP. COL.

1 HERE, Saviour, we would come,
In thine appointed way;
Obedient to thy high commands,
Our solemn vows we pay.

2 O, bless this sacred rite,
To bring us near to thee;
And may we find that as our day
Our strength shall also be.

818. S. M. S. F. SMITH.

1 DOWN to the sacred wave
The Lord of life was led:
And he who came our souls to save
In Jordan bowed his head.

2 He taught the solemn way;
He fixed the holy rite;
He bade his ransomed ones obey,
And keep the path of light.

3 Blest Saviour, we will tread
In thy appointed way;
Let glory o'er these scenes be shed,
And smile on us to-day.

821. S. M. L. H. SIGOURNEY.

1 SAVIOUR, thy law we love,
Thy pure example bless,
And, with a firm, unwavering zeal,
Would in thy footsteps press.

2 Not to the fiery pains
By which the martyrs bled;
Not to the scourge, the thorn, the cross,
Our favored feet are led;—

3 But, at this peaceful tide,
Assembled in thy fear,
The homage of obedient hearts
We humbly offer here.

832. S. M. WATTS.

1 JESUS invites his saints
To meet around his board;
Here pardoned rebels sit, and hold
Communion with their Lord.

2 This holy bread and wine
Maintain our fainting breath,
By union with our living Lord,
And interest in his death.

3 Let all our powers be joined
His glorious name to raise;
Let holy love fill every mind,
And every voice be praise.

859. S. M. VILLAGE HYMNS.

1 O GOD of sovereign grace,
We bow before thy throne,
And plead, for all the human race,
The merits of thy Son.

2 Spread through the earth, O Lord,
The knowledge of thy ways,
And let all lands with joy record
The great Redeemer's praise.

925. S. M. WATTS.

1 THY name, almighty Lord,
Shall sound through distant lands:
Great is thy grace, and sure thy word;
Thy truth forever stands.

2 Far be thine honor spread,
And long thy praise endure—
Till morning light and evening shade
Shall be exchanged no more.

LABAN.

CROYDON. S. M.

From LATROBE'S SEL.

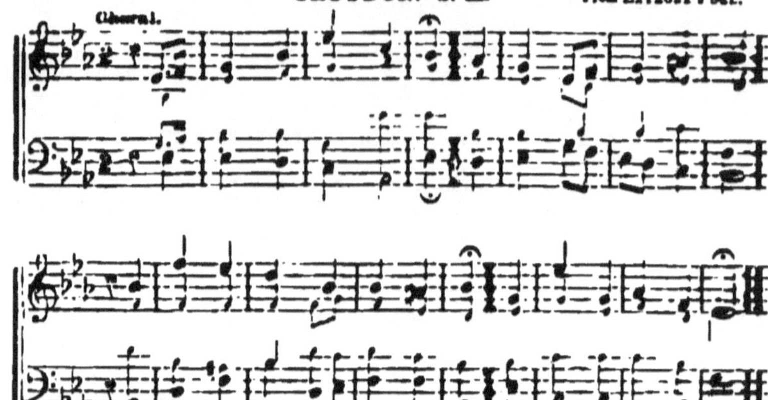

879. S. M. WARDLAW'S COL.

1 O LORD our God, arise,
  The cause of Truth maintain,
And wide o'er all the peopled world
  Extend her blessèd reign.

2 Thou Prince of life, arise,
  Nor let thy glory cease;
Far spread the conquests of thy grace,
  And bless the earth with peace.

3 O Holy Spirit, rise,
  Expand thy heavenly wing,
And o'er a dark and ruined world
  Let light and order spring.

4 O, all ye nations, rise;
  To God the Saviour sing;
From shore to shore, from earth to heaven,
  Let echoing anthems ring.

887. S. M. VOKE.

1 YE messengers of Christ,
  His sovereign voice obey;
Arise and follow where he leads,
  And peace attend your way.

2 The Master whom you serve
  Will needful strength bestow,
Depending on his promised aid,
  With sacred courage go.

3 Go, spread the Saviour's name;
  Go, tell his matchless grace;
Proclaim salvation, full and free,
  To Adam's guilty race.

4 We wish you, in his name,
  The most divine success;
Assured that he who sends you forth
  Will your endeavors bless.

918. S. M. TATE & BRADY.

1 To bless thy chosen race,
  In mercy, Lord, incline,
And cause the brightness of thy face
  On all thy saints to shine, —

2 That so thy wondrous way
  May through the world be known,
While distant lands their homage pay,
  And thy salvation own.

3 O, let them shout and sing
  Glad songs of pious mirth;
For thou, the righteous Judge and King,
  Shalt govern all the earth.

4 Let differing nations join
  To celebrate thy fame;
Let all the world, O Lord, combine
  To praise thy glorious name.

921. S. M. C. WESLEY.

1 LORD, send thy servants forth
  To call the Hebrews home;
From east and west, from south and north,
  Let all the wanderers come

2 Where'er, in lands unknown,
  The fugitives remain,
Bid every creature help them on,
  Thy holy mount to gain.

3 An offering to the Lord,
  There let them all be seen,
And washed with water and with blood,
  In soul and body clean.

4 With Israel's myriads sealed,
  Let all the nations meet,
And show the promises fulfilled, —
  Thy family complete.

WESTMINSTER. S. M. DR. BOYCE.

856. S. M. Eng. Epis. Col.

1 O God, to earth incline,
With mercies from above,
And let thy presence round us shine
With beams of heavenly love.

2 Through all the earth below
Thy ways of grace proclaim,
Till distant nations hear and know
The Saviour's blessèd name.

3 Now let the world agree
One general voice to raise,
Till all mankind present to thee
Their songs of grateful praise.

4 O, let the nations round
Their cheerful powers employ,
And earth's far-distant coasts resound
With shouts of sacred joy.

5 Then earth, thy grace confessed,
Shall pour its fruits abroad;
By thee thy numerous church be blest,
O Lord, our gracious God.

6 Thy blessing shall extend;
Thy saving grace appear;
And all, to earth's remotest end,
The Lord our Saviour fear.

949. S. M. Watts.

1 How beauteous are their feet
Who stand on Zion's hill:
Who bring salvation on their tongues,
And words of peace reveal!

2 How charming is their voice!
How sweet their tidings are! —
"Zion, behold thy Saviour King;
He reigns and triumphs here."

3 How happy are our ears,
That hear this joyful sound!
Which kings and prophets waited for,
And sought, but never found.

4 How blessèd are our eyes,
That see this heavenly light!
Prophets and kings desired it long,
But died without the sight.

5 The watchmen join their voice,
And tuneful notes employ;
Jerusalem breaks forth in songs,
And deserts learn the joy.

6 The Lord makes bare his arm
Through all the earth abroad;
Let every nation now behold
Their Saviour and their God.

989. S. M. E. Scott.

1 Thy bounties, gracious Lord,
With gratitude we own;
We praise thy providential care,
That showers its blessings down.

2 With joy thy people bring
Their offerings round thy throne;
With thankful souls, behold, we pay
A tribute of thine own.

3 O, may this sacrifice,
While at thy feet we bend,
An odor of a sweet perfume,
To thee, the Lord, ascend.

4 Well pleased our God will view
The products of his grace;
With endless life will he fulfil
His kindest promises.

CLAYTONVILLE. S. M. WM. B. BRADBURY. From the Psalmista.

974. S. M. CAMPBELL'S COL.

1 THOU God of sovereign grace,
In mercy now appear;
We long to see thy smiling face,
And feel that thou art near.

2 Receive these lambs to-day,
O Shepherd of the flock,
And wash the stains of guilt away
Beside the smitten Rock.

3 Thy saving health impart,
O Comforter divine;
Now make these children pure in heart;
Make them entirely thine.

4 To-day in love descend;
O, come this precious hour;
In mercy now their spirits bend
By thy resistless power.

5 Our laboring bosoms bleed
Till thou our griefs dispel;
Sure is the promise which we plead,
In all things ordered well.

6 Low bending at thy feet,
Our offspring we resign;
Thine arm is strong, thy love is great,
And high thy glories shine.

980. S. M. FELLOWS.

1 GREAT God, now condescend
To bless our rising race;
Soon may their willing spirits bend,
The subjects of thy grace.

2 O, what a pure delight
Their happiness to see!
Our warmest wishes all unite
To lead their souls to thee.

3 O grant thy Spirit, Lord,
Their hearts to sanctify;
Remember now thy gracious word:
Our hopes on thee rely.

4 Draw forth the melting tear,
The penitential sigh;
Inspire their hearts with faith sincere
And fix their hopes on high.

5 These children now are thine;
We give them back to thee;
O, lead them, by thy grace divine,
Along the heavenly way.

981. S. M. DODDRIDGE.

1 THE Saviour kindly calls
Our children to his breast;
He folds them in his gracious arms;
Himself declares them blest.

2 "Let them approach," he cries,
"Nor scorn their humble claim;
The heirs of heaven are such as these;
For such as these I came."

3 With joy we bring them, Lord,
Devoting them to thee,
Imploring that, as we are thine,
Thine may our offspring be.

1016. S. M. DWIGHT.

1 SERENE I laid me down,
Beneath his guardian care:
I slept — and I awoke and found
My kind Preserver near.

2 Thus does thine arm support
This weak, defenceless frame;
But whence these favors, Lord, to me,
All worthless as I am?

SELAH. S. M.

3 O, how shall I repay
The bounties of my God?
This feeble spirit pants beneath
The pleasing, painful load.

4 My life I would anew
Devote, O Lord, to thee,
And in thy service I would spend
A long eternity.

1028. S. M. Curtis's Col.

1 Another day is passed,
The hours forever fled,
And time is bearing us away
To mingle with the dead.

2 Our minds in perfect peace
Our Father's care shall keep;
We yield to gentle slumber now,
For thou canst never sleep.

3 How blessėd, Lord, are they
On thee securely stayed!
Nor shall they be in life alarmed,
Nor be in death dismayed.

1058. S. M. Watts.

1 Lord, what a feeble piece
Is this our mortal frame!
Our life, how poor a trifle 'tis,
That scarce deserves the name!

2 Alas! 'twas brittle clay
That formed our body first;
And every month and every day,
'Tis mouldering back to dust.

3 Our moments fly apace;
Nor will our minutes stay;
Just like a flood our hasty days
Are sweeping us away.

4 Well, if our days must fly,
We'll keep their end in sight;
We'll spend them all in wisdom's way,
And let them speed their flight.

5 They'll waft us sooner o'er
This life's tempestuous sea:
We soon shall reach the peaceful shore
Of blest eternity.

1062. S. M. Doddridge.

1 Our fathers! where are they,
With all they called their own?
Their joys and griefs, their hopes and cares,
Their wealth and honor gone!

2 But joy or grief succeeds
Beyond our mortal thought,
While still the remnant of their dust
Lies in the grave forgot.

3 God of our fathers, hear,
Thou everlasting Friend,
While we, as on life's utmost verge,
Our souls to thee commend.

4 Of all the pious dead
May we the footsteps trace,
Till with them, in the land of light,
We dwell before thy face.

1063. S. M. Doddridge.

1 To-morrow, Lord, is thine,
Lodged in thy sovereign hand;
And if its sun arise and shine,
It shines by thy command.

2 The present moment flies,
And bears our life away;
O, make thy servants truly wise,
That they may live to-day.

3 Since on this fleeting hour
Eternity is hung,
Awake, by thine almighty power,
The agėd and the young.

4 One thing demands our care;
O, be that still pursued,
Lest, slighted once, the season fair
Should never be renewed.

5 To Jesus may we fly,
Swift as the morning light,
Lest life's young, golden beams should die
In sudden, endless night.

1068. S. M. FAWCETT.

1 Blest be the tie that binds
Our hearts in Christian love;
The fellowship of kindred minds
Is like to that above.

2 Before our Father's throne
We pour our ardent prayers;
Our fears, our hopes, our aims are one,
Our comforts, and our cares.

3 We share our mutual woes,
Our mutual burdens bear;
And often for each other flows
The sympathizing tear.

4 When we asunder part,
It gives us inward pain;
But we shall still be joined in heart,
And hope to meet again.

5 This glorious hope revives
Our courage by the way;
While each in expectation lives,
And longs to see the day.

6 From sorrow, toil, and pain,
And sin, we shall be free,
And perfect love and friendship reign
Through all eternity.

1114. S. M. CH. PSALMODY.

1 O for the death of those
Who slumber in the Lord!
O, be like theirs my last repose,
Like theirs my last reward!

2 Their bodies in the ground,
In silent hope, may lie,
Till the last trumpet's joyful sound
Shall call them to the sky.

3 Their ransomed spirits soar,
On wings of faith and love,
To meet the Saviour they adore,
And reign with him above.

4 With us their names shall live
Through long-succeeding years,
Embalmed with all our hearts can give —
Our praises and our tears.

5 O for the death of those
Who slumber in the Lord!
O, be like theirs my last repose,
Like theirs my last reward!

1118. S. M. MONTGOMERY.

1 "Servant of God, well done;
Rest from thy loved employ:
The battle fought, the victory won,
Enter thy Master's joy."

2 The voice at midnight came;
He started up to hear;
A mortal arrow pierced his frame;
He fell, but felt no fear.

3 Tranquil amid alarms,
It found him on the field,
A veteran slumbering on his arms,
Beneath his red-cross shield.

4 The pains of death are past;
Labor and sorrow cease:
And, life's long warfare closed at last,
His soul is found in peace.

5 Soldier of Christ, well done;
Praise be thy new employ;
And, while eternal ages run,
Rest in thy Saviour's joy.

SWABIA. S. M.

Ancient German.
Dibdin's Standard Tune Book.

1122. S. M. Watts.

1 And must this body die?
This mortal frame decay?
And must these active limbs of mine
Lie mouldering in the clay?

2 God, my Redeemer, lives,
And often, from the skies,
Looks down, and watches all my dust,
Till he shall bid it rise.

3 Arrayed in glorious grace
Shall these vile bodies shine,
And every shape, and every face,
Look heavenly and divine.

4 These lively hopes we owe
To Jesus' dying love;
We would adore his grace below,
And sing his power above.

5 O Lord, accept the praise
Of these our humble songs,
Till strains of nobler sound we raise
With our immortal tongues.

CRUCIFIX. S. M.

D. F. Edmands.

* These slurs not to be observed in singing the third line.

1125. S. M. Luth. Col.

1 And am I born to die?
To lay this body down?
And must my trembling spirit fly
Into a world unknown?

2 Waked by the trumpet's sound,
I from the grave must rise,
And see the Judge with glory crowned,
And see the flaming skies.

3 How shall I leave my tomb,
With triumph, or regret?—
A fearful or a joyful doom,
A curse or blessing, meet?

4 I must from God be driven,
Or with my Saviour dwell;
Must come, at his command, to heaven,
Or else depart — to hell.

5 O Thou, that wouldst not have
One wretched sinner die,—
Who died thyself, my soul to save
From endless misery,—

6 Show me the way to shun
Thy dreadful wrath severe,
That, when thou comest on thy throne,
I may with joy appear.

FRANCONIA. S. M. — German Melody, 1738. From Havergal's Psalmody.

1141. S. M. Beddome.

1 Behold, the day is come;
The righteous Judge is near;
And sinners, trembling at their doom,
Shall soon their sentence hear.

2 Angels, in bright attire,
Conduct him through the skies;
Darkness and tempest, smoke and fire,
Attend him as he flies.

3 How awful is the sight!
How loud the thunders roar!
The sun forbears to give his light,
The stars are seen no more.

4 The whole creation groans;
But saints arise and sing:
They are the ransomed of the Lord,
And he their God and King.

1142. S. M. Doddridge.

1 And will the Judge descend?
And must the dead arise?
And not a single soul escape
His all-discerning eyes?

2 How will my heart endure
The terrors of that day,
When earth and heaven, before his face,
Astonished, shrink away?

3 But, ere the trumpet shakes
The mansions of the dead,
Hark! from the gospel's cheering sound
What joyful tidings spread!

4 Come, sinners, seek his grace,
Whose wrath ye cannot bear;
Fly to the shelter of his cross,
And find salvation there.

DOOMSDAY. S. M. — Wood.

CRUCIFIX. S. M.

B. F. EDMANDS.

* These slurs not to be observed in singing the third line.

1152. S. M. MONTGOMERY.

1 O, WHERE shall rest be found —
Rest for the weary soul?
'Twere vain the ocean depths to sound,
Or pierce to either pole.

2 The world can never give
The bliss for which we sigh:
'Tis not the whole of life to live,
Nor all of death to die.

3 Beyond this vale of tears,
There is a life above, —
Unmeasured by the flight of years —
And all that life is love.

4 There is a death, whose pang
Outlasts the fleeting breath:
O, what eternal terrors hang
Around the second death!

5 Lord God of truth and grace,
Teach us that death to shun,
Lest we be banished from thy face,
And evermore undone.

MY FATHER'S HOUSE. S. M.

Composed for Hymn 1159.

H. H. HAWLEY.
Presented for this work.

1159. S. M. MONTGOMERY.

1 MY Father's house on high!
Home of my soul! how near,
At times, to faith's foreseeing eye,
Thy golden gates appear!

2 I hear at morn and even,
At noon and midnight hour,
The choral harmonies of heaven
Seraphic music pour.

3 O, then my spirit faints
To reach the land I love —
The bright inheritance of saints,
My glorious home above.

5. DOXOLOGY. S. M.

YE angels round the throne,
And saints that dwell below,
Adore the Father, love the Son,
And bless the Spirit too.

BETHESDA. H. M. DR. GREEN.

10. H. M. WATTS.

1 LORD of the worlds above,
How pleasant and how fair
The dwellings of thy love,
Thine earthly temples are!
To thine abode | With warm desires
My heart aspires, | To see my God.

2 O, happy souls, who pray
Where God appoints to hear!
O, happy men, who pay
Their constant service there!
They praise thee still; | Who love the way
And happy they | To Zion's hill.

3 They go from strength to strength,
Through this dark vale of tears,
Till each arrives at length,
Till each in heaven appears:
O glorious seat, | Shall thither bring
When God, our King, | Our willing feet.

13. H. M. WATTS.

1 To spend one sacred day
Where God and saints abide,
Affords diviner joy
Than thousand days beside:
Where God resorts, | To keep the door
I love it more | Than shine in courts.

2 God is our sun and shield,
Our light and our defence;
With gifts his hands are filled;
We draw our blessings thence:
He will bestow | Peculiar grace,
On Jacob's race | And glory too.

3 The Lord his people loves;
His hand no good withholds
From those his heart approves,—
From pure and upright souls.
Thrice happy he, | Whose spirit trusts
O God of hosts, | Alone in thee.

---

38. H. M. COTTERILL.

1 AWAKE, ye saints, awake,
And hail the sacred day;
In loftiest songs of praise
Your joyful homage pay;
Come, bless the day | The type of heaven's
That God hath blest, | Eternal rest.

2 On this auspicious morn
The Lord of life arose,
And burst the bars of death,
And vanquished all our foes;
And now he pleads | And reaps the fruit
Our cause above, | Of all his love.

HADDAM. H. M. ENGLISH.

3 All hail, triumphant Lord!
Heaven with hosannas rings;
And earth, in humbler strains,
Thy praise responsive sings:
Worthy the Lamb, | Through endless years
That once was slain, | To live and reign.

44. H. M. HAYWARD.

1 WELCOME, delightful morn;
Sweet day of sacred rest,
I hail thy kind return;
Lord, make these moments blest:
From low desires | I soar to reach
And fleeting toys, | Immortal joys.

2 Now may the King descend,
And fill his throne of grace;
The sceptre, Lord, extend,
While saints address thy face:
Let sinners feel | And learn to know
Thy quickening word, | And fear the Lord.

3 Descend, celestial Dove,
With all thy quickening powers;
Disclose a Saviour's love,
And bless the sacred hours:
Then shall my soul | Nor Sabbaths be
New life obtain, | Enjoyed in vain.

53. H. M. BREVIARY.

1 HERE, gracious God, do thou
In mercy now draw nigh;
Accept each faithful prayer,
And mark each suppliant sigh;
In copious shower, | This holy day
On all who pray | Thy blessings pour.

2 Here may we find from heaven
The grace which we implore;
And may that grace, once given,
Be with us evermore —
Until that day | To endless rest
When all the blest | Are called away.

67. H. M. WATTS.

1 YE tribes of Adam, join
With heaven, and earth, and seas,
And offer notes divine
To your Creator's praise:
Ye holy throng | In worlds of light
Of angels bright, | Begin the song.

2 The shining worlds above
In glorious order stand,
Or in swift courses move,
By his supreme command:
He spake the word, | From nothing came
And all their frame | To praise the Lord.

3 Let all the nations fear
The God that rules above;
He brings his people near,
And makes them taste his love;
While earth and sky | His saints shall raise
Attempt his praise, | His honors high.

68. H. M. DWIGHT.

1 SING to the Lord most high;
Let every land adore;
With grateful voice make known
His goodness and his power;
With cheerful songs | And let his praise
Declare his ways, | Inspire your tongues.

2 Enter his courts with joy;
With fear address the Lord;
He formed us with his hand,
And quickened by his word;
With wide command, | O'er every sea
He spreads his sway | And every land.

3 His hands provide our food,
And every blessing give;
We feed upon his care,
And in his pastures live:
With cheerful songs | And let his praise
Declare his ways, | Inspire your tongues.

AMHERST. H. M. BILLINGS.

90. H. M. TATE & BRADY.

1 YE boundless realms of joy,
Exalt your Maker's name;
His praise your songs employ
Above the starry frame:
Your voices raise, | And seraphim,
Ye cherubim | To sing his praise.

2 Let all adore the Lord,
And praise his holy name,
By whose almighty word
They all from nothing came;
And all shall last, | His firm decree
From changes free; | Stands ever fast.

92. H. M. STEELE.

1 LET every creature join
To bless Jehovah's name,
And every power unite
To swell th' exalted theme;
Let nature raise, | A general song
From every tongue, | Of grateful praise.

2 But, O, from human tongues
Should nobler praises flow,
And every thankful heart
With warm devotion glow;
Your voices raise, | Above the rest,
Ye highly blest; | Declare his praise.

3 Assist me, gracious God;
My heart, my voice inspire;
Then shall I humbly join
The universal choir;
Thy grace can raise | And tune my song
My heart and tongue, | To lively praise.

121. H. M. WATTS.

1 To Him who chose us first,
Before the world began;
To Him who bore the curse
To save rebellious man;
To Him who formed | Are endless praise,
Our hearts anew, | And glory due.

2 The Father's love shall run
Through our immortal songs;
We bring to God the Son
The tribute of our tongues:
Our lips address | With equal praise,
The Spirit's name, | And zeal the same.

3 Let every saint above,
And angel round the throne,
Forever bless and love
The sacred Three in One.
Thus heaven shall raise | When earth and time
His honors high, | Grow old and die.

LENOX. H. M. EDSON.

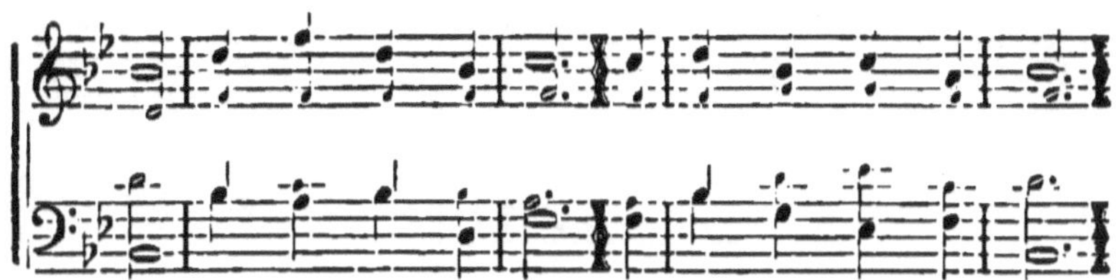

118. H. M. WATTS.

1 WE give immortal praise
For God the Father's love—
For all our comforts here,
And better hopes above:
He sent his own | To die for sins
Eternal Son | That we had done.

2 To God the Son belongs
Immortal glory too,
Who bought us with his blood
From everlasting woe:
And now he lives, | And sees the fruit
And now he reigns, | Of all his pains.

3 To God the Spirit's name
Immortal worship give,
Whose new-creating power
Makes the dead sinner live:
His work completes | And fills the soul
The great design, | With joy divine.

4 Almighty God, to thee
Be endless honors done,
The undivided Three,
The great and glorious One:
Where Reason fails, | There Faith prevails,
With all her powers, | And Love adores.

LUBEC. H. M.

ANCIENT MELODY
From a Geneva Collection.

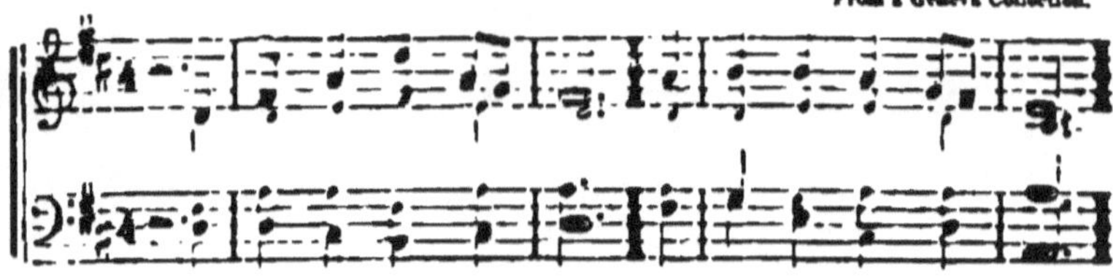

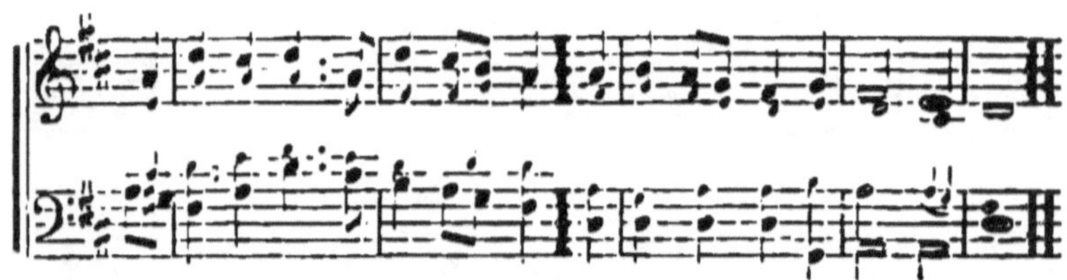

138. H. M. WATTS.

1 THE Lord Jehovah reigns;
His throne is built on high;
The garments he assumes
Are light and majesty;
His glories shine | No mortal eye
With beams so bright, | Can bear the sight.

2 The thunders of his hand
Keep all the world in awe;
His wrath and justice stand
To guard his holy law;
And where his love | His truth confirms
Resolves to bless, | And seals the grace.

3 Through all his ancient works
Surprising wisdom shines,
Confounds the powers of hell,
And breaks their fell designs:
Strong is his arm, | His great decrees,
And shall fulfil | His sovereign will.

4 And can this mighty King
Of glory condescend?
And will he write his name
My Father and my Friend?
I love his name; | Join, all my powers,
I love his word; | And praise the Lord.

154. H. M. WATTS.

1 GIVE thanks to God most high,
The universal Lord,
The sovereign King of kings,
And be his name adored:
Thy mercy, Lord, | And ever sure
Shall still endure; | Abides thy word.

2 How mighty is his hand!
What wonders hath he done!
He formed the earth and seas,
And spread the heavens alone:
His power and grace | And let his name
Are still the same; | Have endless praise.

3 He sent his only Son
To save us from our woe,
From Satan, sin, and death,
And every hurtful foe:
His power and grace | And let his name
Are still the same; | Have endless praise.

4 Give thanks aloud to God—
To God, the heavenly King;
And let the spacious earth
His works and glories sing:
Thy mercy, Lord, | And ever sure
Shall still endure; | Abides thy word.

WARSAW. H. M. T. CLARK.

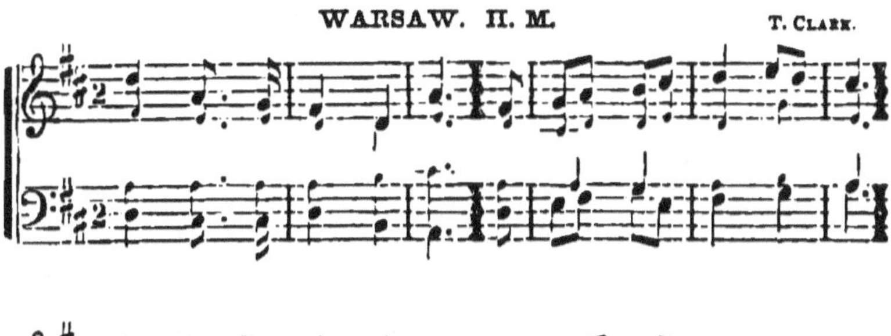

157. H. M. J. YOUNG.

1 O FOR a shout of joy,
Loud as the theme we sing!
To this divine employ
Your hearts and voices bring;
Sound, sound, through all the earth abroad,
The love, th' eternal love, of God.

2 Unnumbered myriads stand,
Of seraphs bright and fair,
Or bow at his right hand,
And pay their homage there;
But strive in vain, with loudest chord,
To sound the wondrous love of God.

3 Yet sinners saved by grace,
In songs of lower key,
In every age and place,
Have sung the mystery;
Have told, in strains of sweet accord,
The love, the sovereign love, of God.

4 Though earth and hell assail,
And doubts and fears arise,
The weakest shall prevail,
And grasp the heavenly prize;
And through an endless age record
The love, th' unchanging love, of God.

5 O for a shout of joy,
Loud as the theme we sing!
To this divine employ
Your hearts and voices bring;
Sound, sound, through all the earth abroad,
The love, th' eternal love, of God.

162. H. M. DODDRIDGE.

1 THE promises I sing,
Which sovereign love hath spoke;
Nor will th' eternal King
His words of grace revoke:
They stand secure | Not Zion's hill
And steadfast still; | Abides so sure.

2 The mountains melt away
When once the Judge appears,
And sun and moon decay,
That measure mortal years;
But still the same, | The promise shines
In radiant lines | Through all the flame.

3 Their harmony shall sound
Through my attentive ears,
When thunders cleave the ground,
And dissipate the spheres:
'Midst all the shock | I stand serene,
Of that dread scene, | Thy word my rock.

ROWE STREET. H. M.

Gregorian.
Arr. by R. F. [illegible]

173. H. M. Watts.

1 To heaven I lift mine eyes ;
From God is all my aid, —
The God who built the skies,
And earth and nature made :
God is the tower | His grace is nigh
To which I fly ; | In every hour.

2 My feet shall never slide,
And fall in fatal snares,
Since God, my guard and guide,
Defends me from my fears.
Those wakeful eyes, | Shall Israel keep
Which never sleep, | When dangers rise.

3 No burning heats by day,
Nor blasts of evening air,
Shall take my health away,
If God be with me there :
Thou art my sun, | To guard my head
And thou my shade, | By night or noon.

4 Hast thou not pledged thy word
To save my soul from death ?
And I can trust my Lord
To keep my mortal breath :
I'll go and come, | Till from on high
Nor fear to die, | Thou call me home.

196. H. M. Condee.

1 The Lord my Shepherd is,
And he my soul will keep,
He knoweth who are his,
And watcheth o'er his sheep ;
Away with every anxious fear ;
I cannot want while he is near.

2 His wisdom doth provide
The pasture where I feed ;
Where silent waters glide
Along the quiet mead,
He leads my feet, and, when I roam,
O'ertakes, and brings the wanderer home.

3 He leads, himself, the way
His faithful flock should take :
Them who his voice obey,
His love will ne'er forsake ;
And surely truth and mercy will
Attend me on my journey still.

4 Let me but feel him near —
Death's gloomy pass in view —
I'll walk without a fear
The shaded valley through ;
With rod and staff, my Shepherd's care
Will guide my steps and guard me there.

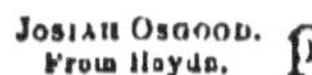

206. H. M. SALISBURY COL.

1 HARK! what celestial sounds!
What music fills the air!
Soft warbling to the morn,
It strikes the ravished ear:
Now all is still, | In tuneful notes,
Now wild it floats | Loud, sweet, and shrill.

2 Th' angelic hosts descend,
With harmony divine:
See how from heaven they bend,
And in full chorus join:
"Fear not," say they; | Jesus, your King,
"Great joy we bring: | Is born to-day."

3 He comes, your souls to save
From death's eternal gloom;
To realms of bliss and light
He lifts you from the tomb:
Your voices raise, | Your songs unite
With sons of light; | Of endless praise.

4 Glory to God on high!
Ye mortals, spread the sound,
And let your raptures fly
To earth's remotest bound;
For peace on earth, | To man is given,
From God in heaven, | At Jesus' birth.

236. H. M. DODDRIDGE.

1 YES, the Redeemer rose;
The Saviour left the dead,
And o'er our hellish foes
High raised his conquering head:
In wild dismay, | Fall to the ground,
The guards around | And sink away.

2 Behold, th' angelic bands
In full assembly meet,
To wait his high commands,
And worship at his feet:
With joy they come, | From realms of day
And wing their way | To Jesus' tomb.

3 Then back to heaven they fly,
The joyful news to bear:
Hark! as they soar on high,
What music fills the air!
Their anthems say, | Hath left the dead;
"The Lord, who bled, | He rose to-day."

4 Ye mortals, catch the sound,
Redeemed by him from hell,
And send the echo round
The globe on which you dwell:
Transported, cry, | Hath left the dead,
"The Lord, who bled, | No more to die."

203. H. M. Reed's Col.

1 Hark! hark! the notes of joy
 Roll o'er the heavenly plains,
And seraphs find employ
 For their sublimest strains:
Some new delight in heaven is known;
Loud sound the harps around the throne.

2 Hark! hark! the sounds draw nigh;
 The joyful hosts descend;
The Lord forsakes the sky;
 To earth, his footsteps bend:
He comes to bless our fallen race;
He comes with messages of grace.

3 Bear, bear the tidings round;
 Let every mortal know
What love in God is found,
 What pity he can show:
Ye winds that blow, ye waves that roll,
Convey the news from pole to pole.

4 Strike, strike the harps again,
 To great Immanuel's name:
Arise, ye sons of men,
 And all his grace proclaim:
Angels and men, wake every string;
'Tis God the Saviour's praise we sing.

241. H. M. T. Scott.

1 Awake, our drowsy souls,
 And burst the slothful band;
The wonders of this day
 Our noblest songs demand:
Auspicious morn, thy blissful rays
Bright seraphs hail, in songs of praise.

2 At thy approaching dawn,
 Reluctant death resigned
The glorious Prince of life
 In dark domains confined;
Th' angelic host around him bends,
And he amid their shouts ascends.

3 All hail, triumphant Lord!
 Heaven with hosannas rings;
While earth, in humbler strains,
 Thy praise responsive sings:
"Worthy art thou, who once wast slain,
Through endless years to live and reign."

4 Gird on, great Prince, thy sword;
 Ascend thy conquering car;
While justice, truth, and love,
 Maintain the glorious war:
Victorious, thou thy foes shalt tread,
And sin and hell in triumph lead.

243. H. M. BICKERSTETH'S COL.

1 THE happy morn is come:
  Triumphant o'er the grave,
 The Saviour leaves the tomb,
  Omnipotent to save:
Captivity is captive led;
For Jesus liveth, that was dead.

2 Who now accuseth them,
  For whom their Ransom died?
 Who now shall those condemn
  Whom God hath justified?
Captivity is captive led;
For Jesus liveth, that was dead.

3 Christ hath the ransom paid;
  The glorious work is done;
 On him our help is laid,
  By him our victory won:
Captivity is captive led;
For Jesus liveth, that was dead.

261. H. M. C. WESLEY.

1 ARISE, my soul, arise;
  Shake off thy guilty fears;
 The bleeding Sacrifice
  In my behalf appears:
Before the throne my Surety stands;
My name is written on his hands.

2 The bleeding wounds he bears,
  Received on Calvary,
 Now pour effectual prayers,
  And strongly speak for me:
"Forgive him, O, forgive," they cry,
"Nor let that ransomed sinner die."

3 The Father hears him pray,
  The dear Anointed One;
 He cannot turn away
  The pleading of his Son:
His Spirit answers to the blood,
And tells me I am born of God.

4 To God I'm reconciled;
  His pardoning voice I hear;
 He owns me for his child;
  I can no longer fear:
With filial trust I now draw nigh,
And "Father, Abba Father," cry.

249. H. M. DODDRIDGE.

1 O YE immortal throng
  Of angels round the throne,
 Join with our feeble song
  To make the Saviour known.
On earth ye knew | His beauteous face
His wondrous grace; | In heaven ye view.

2 Ye saw the holy Child
  In human flesh arrayed,
 Supremely meek and mild,
  While in the manger laid;
And praise to God, | For such a birth,
And peace on earth, | Proclaimed aloud.

3 Ye in the wilderness
  Beheld the tempter spoiled,
 Well known in every dress,
  In every combat foiled,
And joyed to crown | When Satan fled
The Victor's head, | Before his frown.

4 Around the bloody tree
  Ye pressed with strong desire,
 That wondrous sight to see,
  The Lord of life expire;
And could your eyes | Had dropped it there
Have known a tear, | In sad surprise.

5 Around his sacred tomb
  A willing watch ye keep,
 Till the blest moment come
  To rouse him from his sleep;
Then rolled the stone, | Your rising Lord
And all adored | With joy unknown.

6 When all arrayed in light
  The shining Conqueror rode,
 Ye hailed his rapturous flight
  Up to the throne of God,
And waved around | And struck your strings
Your golden wings, | Of sweetest sound.

301. H. M. WATTS.

1 JOIN all the glorious names
  Of wisdom, love, and power,
 That ever mortals knew,
  Or angels ever bore:
All are too mean | Too mean to set
To speak his worth, | The Saviour forth.

2 Great Prophet of our God,
  Our tongues shall bless thy name;
 By thee the joyful news
  Of our salvation came,—
The joyful news | Of hell subdued,
Of sins forgiven, | And peace with heaven.

3 Jesus, our great High Priest,
  Has shed his blood and died;
 Our guilty conscience needs
  No sacrifice beside:
His precious blood | And now it pleads
Did once atone, | Before the throne.

4 O thou almighty Lord,
  Our Conqueror and our King,
 Thy sceptre and thy sword,
  Thy reigning grace, we sing.
Thine is the power; | In willing bonds
O make us sit | Beneath thy feet.

DARWELL'S. H. M. Rev. W. Darwell.

322. H. M. Campbell's Col.

1 Come, ye who love the Lord,
And feel his quickening power,
Unite, with one accord,
His goodness to adore:
To heaven and earth aloud proclaim
Your great Redeemer's glorious name.

2 He left his throne above,
His glory laid aside,
Came down on wings of love,
And wept, and bled, and died:
The pangs he bore what tongue can tell,
To save our souls from death and hell?

3 He burst the grave; he rose
Victorious from the dead;
And thence his vanquished foes
In glorious triumph led:
Up through the heavens the Conqueror rode,
Triumphant, to the throne of God.

4 Soon he again will come —
His chariot will not stay —
To take his children home
To realms of endless day:
There shall we see him face to face,
And sing the triumphs of his grace.

325. H. M. C. Wesley.

1 Rejoice! the Lord is King;
Your God and King adore;
Mortals, give thanks, and sing,
And triumph evermore:
Lift up the heart; | Rejoice aloud;
Lift up the voice; | Ye saints, rejoice.

2 His kingdom cannot fail;
He rules o'er earth and heaven;
The keys of death and hell
Are to the Saviour given;
Lift up the heart; | Rejoice aloud;
Lift up the voice; | Ye saints, rejoice.

3 He every foe shall quell,
Shall all our sins destroy;
And every bosom swell
With pure seraphic joy:
Lift up the heart; | Rejoice aloud;
Lift up the voice; | Ye saints, rejoice.

4 Rejoice in glorious hope;
Jesus, the Judge, shall come,
And take his servants up
To their eternal home:
We soon shall hear | The trump of God
Th' archangel's voice; | Shall sound; rejoice.

FLANDERS. H. M. Old Flemish Air.‡ Arranged by Dr. T. Hastings.

‡ From "The Selah."

359. H. M. Campbell's Col.

1 O Thou that hearest prayer,
 Attend our humble cry,
And let thy servants share
 Thy blessing from on high:
We plead the promise of thy word;
Grant us thy Holy Spirit, Lord.

2 If earthly parents hear
 Their children when they cry,—
If they, with love sincere,
 Their varied wants supply,—
Much more wilt thou thy love display,
And answer when thy children pray.

3 Our heavenly Father, thou;
 We, children of thy grace:
O, let thy Spirit now
 Descend and fill the place:
So shall we feel the heavenly flame,
And all unite to praise thy name.

4 O, may that sacred fire,
 Descending from above,
Our languid hearts inspire
 With fervent zeal and love:
Enlighten our beclouded eyes,
And teach our grovelling souls to rise.

5 And send thy Spirit down
 On all the nations, Lord,
With great success to crown
 The preaching of thy word,
Till heathen lands shall own thy sway,
And cast their idol gods away.

407. H. M. Toplady.

1 Blow ye the trumpet, blow,
 The gladly-solemn sound;
Let all the nations know,
 To earth's remotest bound,
The year of jubilee is come;
Return, ye ransomed sinners, home.

2 Exalt the Lamb of God,
 The sin-atoning Lamb;
Redemption by his blood,
 Through all the lands, proclaim:
The year of jubilee is come;
Return, ye ransomed sinners, home.

3 Ye slaves of sin and hell,
 Your liberty receive,
And safe in Jesus dwell,
 And blest in Jesus live:
The year of jubilee is come;
Return, ye ransomed sinners, home.

4 The gospel trumpet hear,
 The news of pardoning grace:
Ye happy souls, draw near;
 Behold your Saviour's face:
The year of jubilee is come;
Return, ye ransomed sinners, home.

5 Jesus, our great High Priest,
 Has full atonement made;
Ye weary spirits, rest;
 Ye mourning souls, be glad:
The year of jubilee is come;
Return, ye ransomed sinners, home.

ALTAR. H. M.

Arr. by Dr. T. Hastings.

From "The Selah."

502. H. M. Beddome.

1 From thy dear, piercéd side,
Unspotted Lamb of God,
Came forth a mingled stream
Of water and of blood:
My sinful soul | Till every stain
There I would lay, | Is washed away.

2 'Tis from this sacred spring
A sovereign virtue flows,
To heal my painful wounds,
And cure my deadly woes:
Here, then, I'll bathe, | Till not a wound
And bathe again, | Or woe remain.

3 A fountain 'tis, unsealed,
Divinely rich and free;
Open for all who come,
And open, too, for me:
To this pure fount | Come, sinners, come;
Will I repair; | There's mercy there.

579. H. M. Bengel.

1 I'll think upon the woes,—
Most spotless Lamb of God,—
To which thou didst expose,
Upon th' accurséd wood,
Thyself for mine iniquity;
And bless thee still in chastening me.

2 Why should my will complain,
When all he means is kind?
Though great my grief and pain,
To him I'll be resigned;
Yes, wait and hope, as me behoves
The Father chastens whom he loves.

3 I cannot take amiss
These sufferings as too great;
Thou'rt good, though they increase;
Still patiently I'll wait:
Ill it becomes me to repine;
Make me in life and spirit thine.

4 My heart shall envy none
Who seem to prosper more:
Only may I be one
Of thine who so endure,
That here in piety they thrive,
Till heavenly perfectness arrive.

5 Thou fount of all delight,
And secret of my joy,
Though many a tearful night
May still my heart employ,
Yet will I hope one day to see
A blest eternity with thee.

544. H. M. Campbell's Col.

1 Hail, everlasting Spring!
Celestial Fountain, hail!
Thy streams salvation bring;
The waters never fail;
Still they endure, | For all our woe
And still they flow, | A sovereign cure.

2 Blest be his wounded side,
And blest his bleeding heart,
Who all in anguish died,
Such favors to impart;
His sacred blood | From every sin
Shall make us clean | And fit for God.

FLANDERS. H. M. OLD FLEMISH AIR.‡ Arranged by DR. T. HASTINGS.

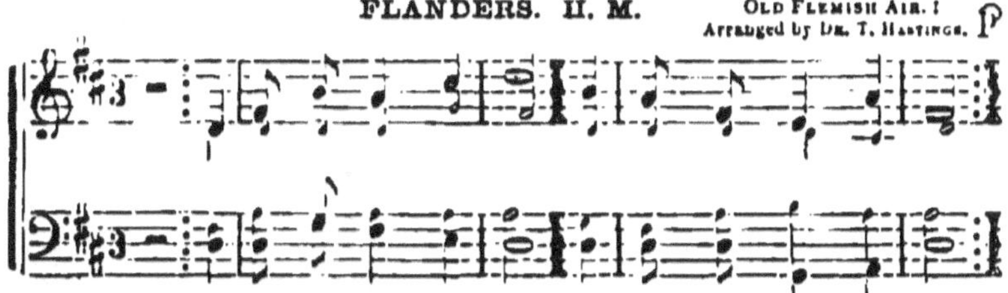

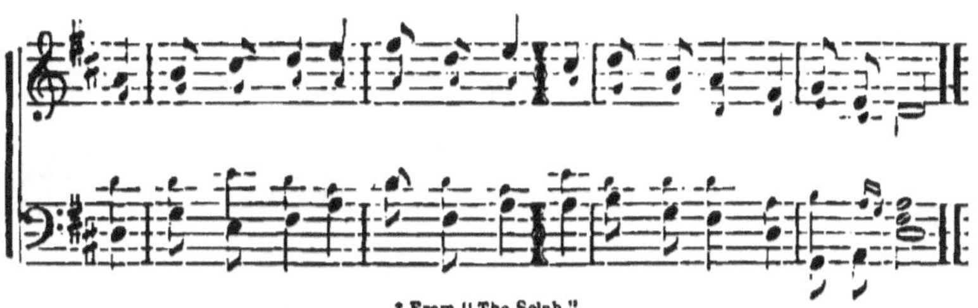

‡ From "The Selah."

3 To that dear source of love,
Our souls this day would come;
And thither, from above,
Lord, call the nations home;
That Jew and Greek, | On all their tongues,
With rapturous songs | Thy praise may speak.

685. H. M. WINCHELL'S SEL.

1 WHERE is my Saviour now,
Whose smiles I once possessed?
Till he return, I bow,
By heavy grief oppressed:
My days of happiness are gone,
And I am left to weep alone.

2 Where can the mourner go,
And tell his tale of grief?
Ah, who can soothe his woe,
And give him sweet relief?
Earth cannot heal the wounded breast,
Or give the troubled sinner rest.

3 Jesus, thy smiles impart;
My gracious Lord, return,
And ease my wounded heart,
And bid me cease to mourn:
Then shall this night of sorrow flee,
And peace and heaven be found in thee.

700. H. M. MONTGOMERY.

1 How beautiful the sight
Of brethren who agree
In friendship to unite
And bonds of charity!
'Tis like the precious ointment, shed
O'er all his robes, from Aaron's head.

2 'Tis like the dews that fill
The cups of Hermon's flowers;
Or Zion's fruitful hill,
Bright with the drops of showers,
When mingling odors breathe around,
And glory rests on all the ground.

3 For there the Lord commands
Blessings, a countless store,
From his unsparing hands;
Yea, life forevermore:
Thrice happy they who meet above
To spend eternity in love.

814. H. M. FELLOWS.

1 DESCEND, celestial Dove,
And make thy presence known;
Reveal our Saviour's love,
And seal us for thine own:
Unblest by thee, | Nor can we e'er
Our works are vain; | Acceptance gain.

2 When our incarnate God,
The sovereign Prince of light,
In Jordan's swelling flood
Received the holy rite,
In open view | And, dove-like, flew
Thy form came down, | The King to crown.

3 Continue still to shine,
And fill us with thy fire:
This ordinance is thine;
Do thou our souls inspire:
Thou wilt attend | "Till time shall end,"
On all thy sons: | Thy promise runs.

WARSAW. H. M. T. CLARK

867. H. M. BURDER.

1 RISE, Sun of glory, rise!
And chase the shades of night,
Which now obscure the skies,
And hide thy sacred light:
O, chase those dismal shades away,
And bring the bright, millennial day.

2 Now send thy Spirit down
On all the nations, Lord,
With great success to crown
The preaching of thy word;
That heathen lands may own thy sway,
And cast their idol gods away.

3 Then shall thy kingdom come
Among our fallen race,
And all the earth become
The temple of thy grace,
Whence pure devotion shall ascend,
And songs of praise, till time shall end.

ZEBULON.

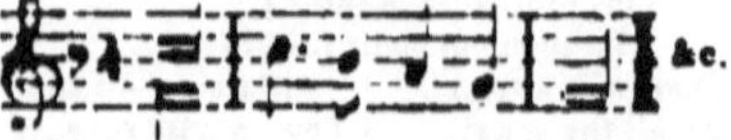

897. H. M. DODDRIDGE.

1 O ZION, tune thy voice,
And raise thy hands on high;
Tell all the earth thy joys,
And boast salvation nigh;
Cheerful in God, | While rays divine
Arise and shine, | Stream far abroad.

2 He gilds thy mourning face
With beams that cannot fade;
His all-resplendent grace
He pours around thy head;
The nations round | With lustre new,
Thy form shall view, | Divinely crowned.

3 In honor to his name,
Reflect that sacred light,
And loud that grace proclaim
Which makes thy darkness bright;
Pursue his praise, | In worlds above
Till sovereign love | The glory raise.

4 There, on his holy hill,
A brighter Sun shall rise,
And with his radiance fill
Those fairer, purer skies;
While, round his throne, | In nobler spheres
Ten thousand stars | His influence own.

DARWELL'S. H. M. REV. W. DARWELL.

863. H. M. VILLAGE HYMNS.

1 SOVEREIGN of worlds above,
And Lord of all below,
Thy faithfulness and love,
Thy power and mercy, show:
Fulfil thy word; | Let heathen live,
Thy Spirit give; | And praise the Lord.

2 Few be the years that roll
Ere all shall worship thee;
The travail of his soul
Soon let the Saviour see:
O God of grace, | Fill earth with joy,
Thy power employ, | And heaven with praise.

908. H. M. ANON.

1 ISLES of the south, awake!
The song of triumph sing;
Let mount, and hill, and vale
With hallelujahs ring:
Shout, for the idol's overthrown,
And Israel's God is God alone.

2 Wild wastes of Afric, shout!
Your shackled sons are free,
No mother wails her child
'Neath the banana-tree:
No slave-ship dashes on thy shore;
The clank of chains is heard no more.

3 Shout, vales of India, shout!
No funeral fires blaze high;
No idol song rings loud,
As rolls the death-car by:
The banner of the cross now waves
Where Christian heralds made their graves.

4 Shout, rocky hills of Greece!
The crescent head lies low;
No Moslem flings his chain
Around the Christian now;
But Greek and Moslem join in one
To praise the Saviour, God the Son.

5 Shout, hills of Palestine!
Have you forgot the groan,
The spear, the thorn, the cross,
The wine-press trod alone,
The dying prayer that rose from thee,
Thou garden of Gethsemane?

6 Hail, glad, millennial day!
O, shout, ye heavens above!
To-day the nations sing
The song, redeeming love:
Redeeming love the song shall be:
Hail, blessèd year of jubilee!

872. H. M. T. Scott.

1 All hail, incarnate God!
  The wondrous things foretold
Of thee, in sacred writ,
  With joy our eyes behold:
Still doth thine arm
New trophies wear,
And monuments
Of glory rear.

2 O, haste, victorious Prince,
  That glorious, happy day,
When souls, like drops of dew,
  Shall own thy gentle sway;
O, may it bless
Our longing eyes,
And bear our shouts
Beyond the skies.

3 All hail, triumphant Lord!
  Eternal be thy reign:
Behold, the nations wait
  To wear thy gentle chain:
When earth and time
Are known no more,
Thy throne shall stand
Forever sure.

---

933. H. M. Francis.

1 Great King of glory, come,
  And with thy favor crown
This temple as thy home,
  This people as thine own:
Beneath this roof, O, deign to show
How God can dwell with men below.

2 Here may thine ears attend
  Our interceding cries,
And grateful praise ascend,
  Like incense, to the skies:
Here may thy word melodious sound,
And spread celestial joys around.

3 Here may our unborn sons
  And daughters sound thy praise,
And shine, like polished stones,
  Through long succeeding days:
Here, Lord, display thy saving power,
While temples stand and men adore.

4 Here may the listening throng
  Imbibe thy truth and love;
Here Christians join the song
  Of seraphim above;
Till all who humbly seek thy face,
Rejoice in thy abounding grace.

928. H. M. Pratt's Col.

1 Fixed on the sacred hills,
  Its firm foundations rest;
The Lord his temple fills
  With all his glory blest:
He waits where'er
His saints adore;
But loves the gates
Of Zion more.

2 O Zion, sacred place!
  Thy name shall spread around
The city of his grace;
  His wonders there abound:
Thy glories will
Thy God declare;
And earth thy fame
Resound afar.

940. H. M. Doddridge.

1 Great Father of mankind,
  We bless that wondrous grace
Which could for Gentiles find
  Within thy courts a place:
How kind the care
Our God displays,
For us to raise
A house of prayer!

2 Though once estranged afar,
  We now approach the throne,
For Jesus brings us near,
  And makes our cause his own:
Strangers no more,
To thee we come,
And find our home,
And rest secure.

AMHERST. H. M. BILLINGS.

3 May all the nations throng
To worship in thy house,
And thou attend their song,
And smile upon their vows;
Indulgent still, | To join the choir
Till earth conspire | On Zion's hill.

970. H. M. PRATT'S COL.

1 COME, let our voices join
In joyful songs of praise;
To God, the God of love,
Our thankful hearts we'll raise:
To God alone all praise belongs —
Our earliest and our latest songs.

2 Within these hallowed walls
Our wandering feet are brought,
Where prayer and praise ascend,
And heavenly truths are taught:
To God alone your offerings bring:
Let young and old his praises sing.

3 Lord, let this work of love
Be crowned with full success;
Let thousands, yet unborn,
Thy sacred name here bless:
To thee, O Lord, all praise to thee
We'll raise throughout eternity.

25*

1037. H. M. DWIGHT.

1 How pleasing is the voice
Of God, our heavenly King,
Who bids the frosts retire,
And wakes the lovely spring!
Bright suns arise, | And beauty glows
The mild wind blows, | Thro' earth and skies.

2 The morn, with glory crowned,
His hand arrays in smiles:
He bids the eve decline,
Rejoicing o'er the hills:
The evening breeze | His beauty blooms
His breath perfumes; | In flowers and trees.

3 With life he clothes the spring,
The earth with summer warms,
He spreads th' autumnal feast,
And rides on wintry storms:
His gifts divine | And round the year
Through all appear; | His glories shine.

6. DOXOLOGY. H. M.

To God the Father's throne
Your highest honors raise;
Glory to God the Son;
To God the Spirit praise:
With all our powers, | Thy name we sing,
Eternal King, | While faith adores.

ORGEL. C. H. M. — Joach. V. Burck. Died 1610.

Choral.

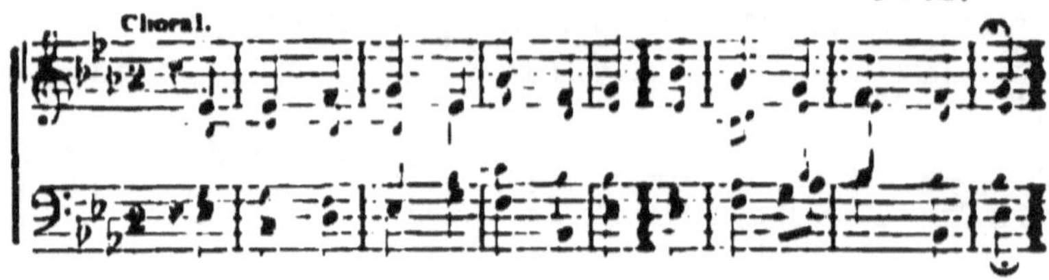

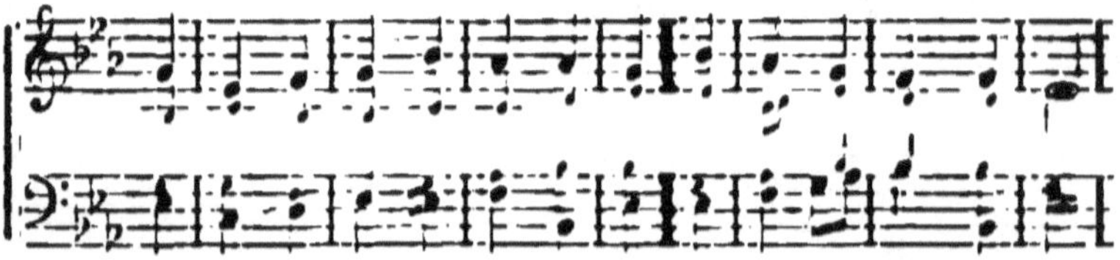

222. C. H. M. Hemans.

1 He knelt; the Saviour knelt and prayed,
When but his Father's eye
Looked, through the lonely garden's shade,
On that dread agony:
The Lord of all above, beneath,
Was bowed with sorrow unto death.

2 The sun went down in fearful hour;
The heavens might well grow dim,
When this mortality had power
To thus o'ershadow him,
That he who gave man's breath might know
The very depths of human woe.

3 He knew them all, — the doubt, the strife,
The faint, perplexing dread;
The mists that hang o'er parting life
All darkened round his head;
And the Deliverer knelt to pray;
Yet passed it not, that cup, away.

4 It passed not, though the stormy wave
Had sunk beneath his tread;
It passed not, though to him the grave
Had yielded up its dead;
But there was sent him, from on high,
A gift of strength, for man to die.

5 And was his mortal hour beset
With anguish and dismay:
How may we meet our conflict yet
In the dark, narrow way?
How, but through him that path who trod?
"Save, or we perish, Son of God."

583. C. H. M. Cowper.

1 When I can trust my all with God,
In trial's fearful hour,
Bow, all resigned, beneath his rod,
And bless his sparing power,
A joy springs up amid distress,
A fountain in the wilderness.

2 O, to be brought to Jesus' feet,
Though trials fix me there,
Is still a privilege most sweet,
For he will hear my prayer;
Though sighs and tears its language be,
The Lord is nigh to answer me.

3 O, blessed be the hand that gave,
Still blessed when it takes;
Blessed be he who smites to save,
Who heals the heart he breaks:
Perfect and true are all his ways,
Whom heaven adores and death obeys.

SOLACE. C. H. M. N. D. GOULD.

4 Come, let us pray: the mercy-seat
Invites the fervent prayer,
And Jesus ready stands to greet
The contrite spirit there:
O, loiter not, nor longer stay
From him who loves us; let us pray.

---

644. C. H. M. ANON.

1 COME, let us pray: 'tis sweet to feel
That God himself is near;
That, while we at his footstool kneel,
His mercy deigns to hear:
Though sorrows cloud life's dreary way,
This is our solace — let us pray.

2 Come, let us pray: the burning brow,
The heart oppressed with care,
And all the woes that throng us now,
Will be relieved by prayer:
Jesus will smile our griefs away;
O, glorious thought! — come, let us pray.

3 Come, let us pray: the sin-sick soul
Her weight of guilt must feel;
But, hark! the glorious tidings roll,
Whilst here we humbly kneel;
Jesus will wash that guilt away,
And pardon grant; then let us pray.

1064. C. H. M. JANE TAYLOR.

1 O, WHAT is life? — 'tis like a flower
That blossoms, and is gone;
It flourishes its little hour,
With all its beauty on:
Death comes, and, like a wintry day,
It cuts the lovely flower away.

2 O, what is life? — 'tis like the bow
That glistens in the sky;
We love to see its colors glow;
But while we look, they die:
Life fails as soon: to-day 'tis here;
To-morrow it may disappear.

3 Lord, what is life? — if spent with thee,
In humble praise and prayer,
How long or short our life may be,
We feel no anxious care:
Though life depart, our joys shall last
When life and all its joys are past.

CREATION. S. H. M.

HAYDN.‡

‡ From the Oratorio, The Creation.

512. S. H. M. ANON.

1 FAITH is the Christian's prop,
Whereon his sorrows lean ;
It is the substance of his hope,
His proof of things unseen ;
It is the anchor of his soul
When tempests rage and billows roll.

2 Faith is the polar star
That guides the Christian's way,
Directs his wanderings from afar
To realms of endless day ;
It points the course where'er he roam,
And safely leads the pilgrim home.

3 Faith is the rainbow's form
Hung on the brow of heaven,
The glory of the passing storm,
The pledge of mercy given ;
It is the bright, triumphal arch,
Through which the saints to glory march.

4 The faith that works by love,
And purifies the heart,
A foretaste of the joys above
To mortals can impart ;
It bears us through this earthly strife,
And triumphs in immortal life.

HALLELUJAH.‡

Hal - le - lu - jah! Hal - le - lu - jah! Hal - le - lu - jah! A - men.

‡ May be sung after the 4th, or the 3d and 4th stanzas.

TEMPLYN. S. H. M. J. HERMAN SCHEIN, 1627. Har. by Dr. Fillitz, 1846.

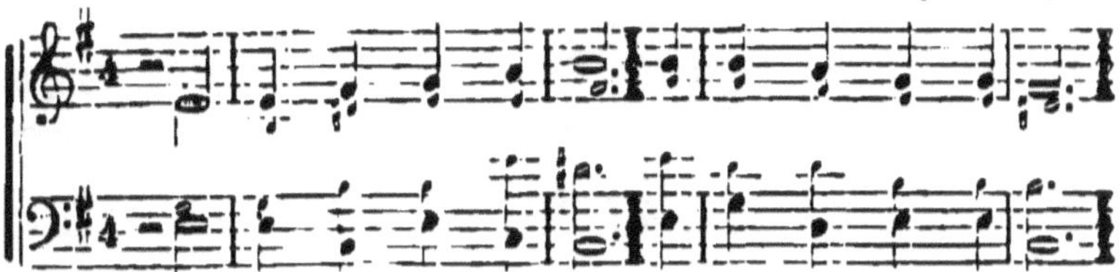

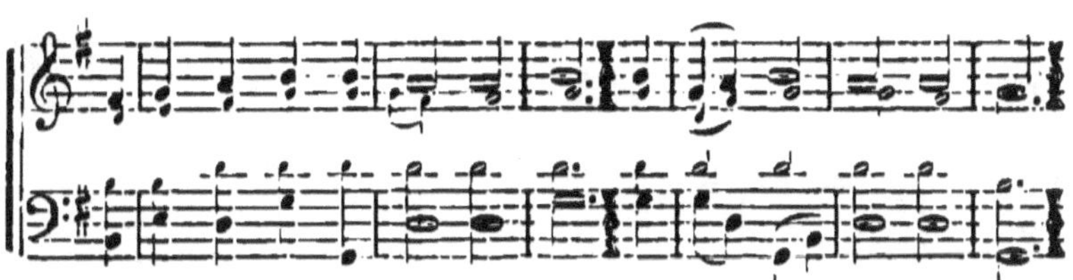

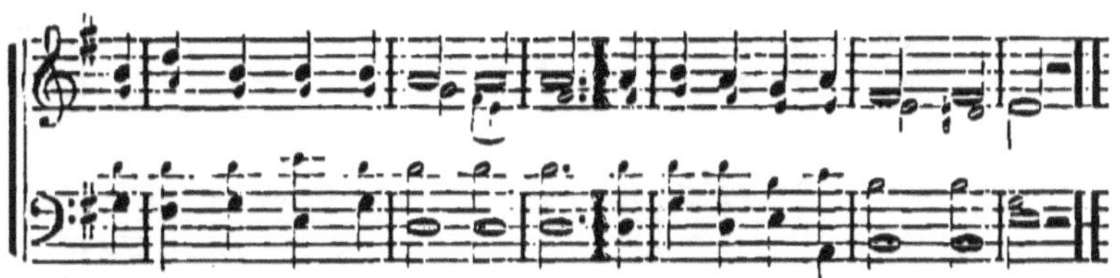

1090. S. H. M. MONTGOMERY.

1 FRIEND after friend departs:
   Who hath not lost a friend?
 There is no union here of hearts
   That finds not here an end:
Were this frail world our final rest,
Living or dying, none were blest.

2 Beyond the flight of time,
   Beyond the reign of death,
 There surely is some blessèd clime
   Where life is not a breath,
Nor life's affections transient fire,
Whose sparks fly upward and expire.

3 There is a world above,
   Where parting is unknown;
 A long eternity of love,
   Formed for the good alone;
And faith beholds the dying here
Translated to that glorious sphere.

4 Thus star by star declines,
   Till all are passed away;
 As morning high and higher shines
   To pure and perfect day;
Nor sink those stars in empty night,
But hide themselves in heaven's own light.

1099. S. H. M. MONTGOMERY.

1 THIS place is holy ground;
   World, with its cares, away;
 A holy, solemn stillness round
   This lifeless, mouldering clay;
Nor pain, nor grief, nor anxious fear
Can reach the peaceful sleeper here.

2 Behold the bed of death—
   The pale and mortal clay;
 Heard ye the sob of parting breath?
   Marked ye the eye's last ray?
No; life so sweetly ceased to be,
It lapsed in immortality.

3 Why mourn the pious dead?
   Why sorrows swell our eyes?
 Can sighs recall the spirit fled?
   Shall vain regrets arise?
Though death has caused this altered mien,
In heaven the ransomed soul is seen.

4 Bury the dead, and weep
   In stillness o'er the loss:
 Bury the dead; in Christ they sleep
   Who bore on earth his cross;
And from the grave their dust shall rise,
In his own image, to the skies.

TOLLAND. P. M.

SPOFFORTH.

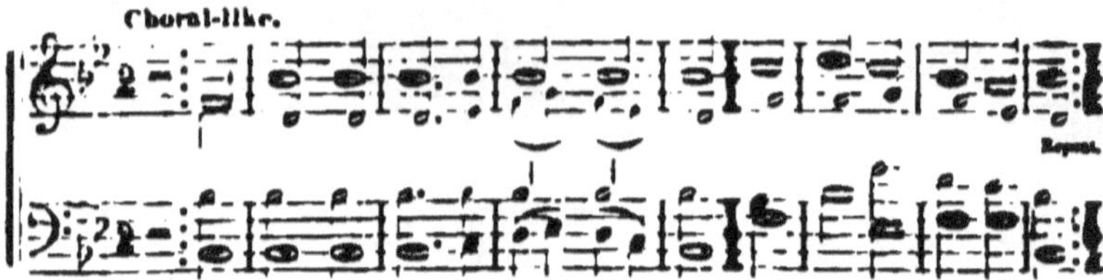

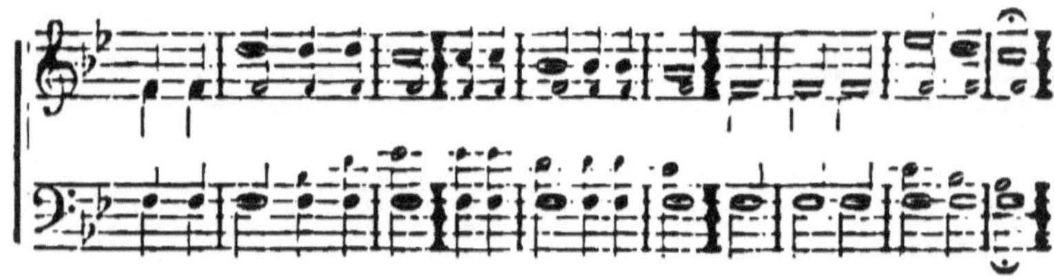

1005.

P. M. H. S. WASHBURN.

1 LET every heart rejoice and sing;
  Let choral anthems rise;
Ye reverend men and children, bring
  To God your sacrifice;
For he is good; the Lord is good,
  And kind are all his ways;
With songs and honors sounding loud,
  The Lord Jehovah praise,
    While the rocks and the rills,
    While the vales and the hills,
  A glorious anthem raise:
Let each prolong the grateful song,
  And the God of our fathers praise.

2 He bids the sun to rise and set;
  In heaven his power is known;
And earth, subdued to him, shall yet
  Bow low before his throne;
For he is good; the Lord is good,
  And kind are all his ways:
With songs and honors sounding loud,
  The Lord Jehovah praise,
    While the rocks and the rills,
    While the vales and the hills,
  A glorious anthem raise:
Let each prolong the grateful song,
  And the God of our fathers praise.

DALSTON. S. P. M.

WILLIAMS.

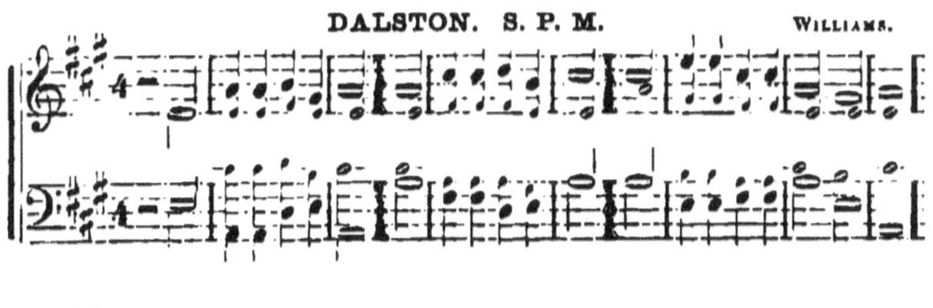

12. S. P. M. WATTS.

1 How pleased and blest was I,
To hear the people cry,
"Come, let us seek our God to-day!"
Yes, with a cheerful zeal,
We haste to Zion's hill,
And there our vows and honors pay.

2 Zion, thrice happy place,
Adorned with wondrous grace!
And walls of strength embrace thee round;
In thee our tribes appear,
To pray, and praise, and hear
The sacred gospel's joyful sound.

3 Here David's greater Son
Has fixed his royal throne;
He sits for grace and judgment here;
He bids the saint be glad;
He makes the sinner sad,
And humble souls rejoice with fear.

4 May peace attend thy gate,
And joy within thee wait,
To bless the soul of every guest;
The man who seeks thy peace,
And wishes thine increase,
A thousand blessings on him rest.

5 My tongue repeats her vows,
"Peace to this sacred house!"
For here my friends and kindred dwell;
And, since my glorious God
Makes thee his blest abode,
My soul shall ever love thee well.

145. S. P. M. WATTS.

1 The Lord Jehovah reigns,
And royal state maintains,
His head with awful glories crowned;
Arrayed in robes of light,
Begirt with sovereign might,
And rays of majesty around.

2 Upheld by thy commands,
The world securely stands,
And skies and stars obey thy word;
Thy throne was fixed on high
Ere stars adorned the sky;
Eternal is thy kingdom, Lord.

3 Let floods and nations rage,
And all their power engage;
Let swelling tides assault the sky;
The terrors of thy frown
Shall calm their fury down;
Thy throne forever stands on high.

4 Thy promises are true;
Thy grace is ever new;
There fixed, thy church shall ne'er remove;
Thy saints, with holy fear,
Shall in thy courts appear,
And sing thine everlasting love.

CODA. Hymn 145.

O, praise the Lord, Amen. Amen.

SHERBURNE. C. P. M. From Sacred Minstrel.

98. C. P. M. Ogilvie.

1 Begin, my soul, th' exalted lay;
Let each enraptured thought obey,
And praise th' almighty name;
Lo! heaven, and earth, and seas, and skies,
In one melodious concert rise,
To swell th' inspiring theme.

2 Thou heaven of heavens, his vast abode,
Ye clouds, proclaim your Maker God;
Ye thunders, speak his power;
Lo! on the lightning's fiery wing,
In triumph rides th' eternal King;
Th' astonished worlds adore.

3 Ye deeps, with roaring billows, rise
To join the thunders of the skies;
Praise him who bids you roll;
His praise in softer notes declare,
Each whispering breeze of yielding air,
And breathe it to the soul.

4 Wake, all ye soaring tribes, and sing;
Ye feathered warblers of the spring,
Harmonious anthems raise
To Him who shaped your finer mould,
Who decked your glittering wings with gold,
And tuned your voice to praise.

5 Let man — by nobler passions swayed —
Let man — in God's own image made —
His breath in praise employ,
Spread wide his Maker's name around,
Till heaven shall echo back the sound,
In songs of holy joy.

99. C. P. M. H. More.

1 My God, thy boundless love I praise;
How bright, on high, its glories blaze!
How sweetly bloom below!
It streams from thine eternal throne;
Through heaven its joys forever run,
And o'er the earth they flow.

2 'Tis love that paints the purple morn,
And bids the clouds, in air upborne,
Their genial drops distil:
In every vernal beam it glows,
And breathes in every gale that blows,
And glides in every rill.

3 But in the gospel it appears
In sweeter, fairer characters,
And charms the ravished breast:
There, love immortal leaves the sky,
To wipe the drooping mourner's eye,
And give the weary rest.

4 Then let the love that makes me blest,
With cheerful praise inspire my breast,
And ardent gratitude,
And all my thoughts and passions tend
To thee, my Father and my Friend,
My soul's eternal good.

BYZANTIUM. C. P. M. Dr. Hayes.

304. C. P. M. Medley.

1 O, could we speak the matchless worth,
O, could we sound the glories forth,
Which in our Saviour shine,
We'd soar, and touch the heavenly strings,
And vie with Gabriel, while he sings,
In notes almost divine.

2 We'd sing the precious blood he spilt—
Our ransom from the dreadful guilt
Of sin and wrath divine;
We'd sing his glorious righteousness,
In which all-perfect, heavenly dress
We shall forever shine.

3 We'd sing the characters he bears,
And all the forms of love he wears,
Exalted on his throne:
In loftiest songs of sweetest praise,
We would, to everlasting days,
Make all his glories known.

4 Well, the delightful day will come,
When our dear Lord will bring us home,
And we shall see his face:
Then, with our Saviour, Brother, Friend,
A blest eternity we'll spend,
Triumphant in his grace.

GANGES. C. P. M. Ancient Melody.

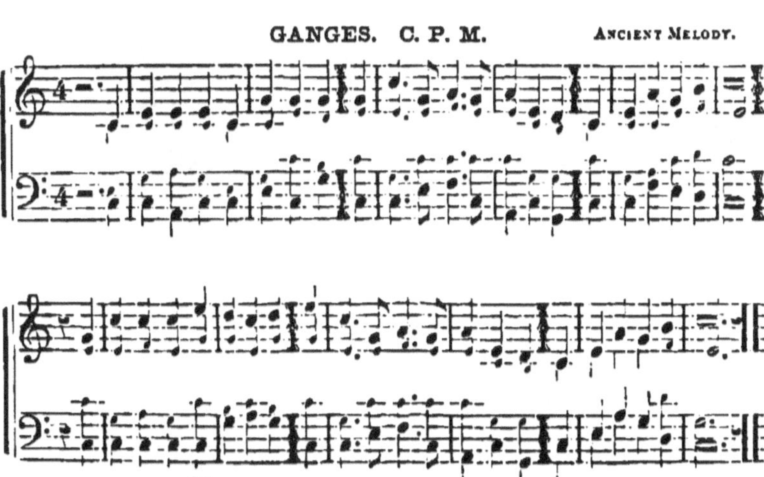

GERMAN.

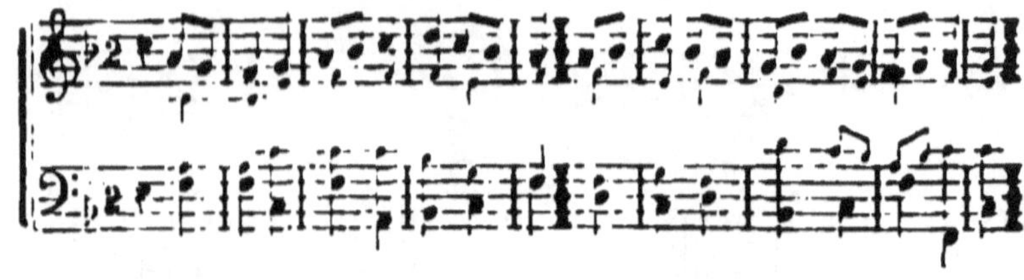

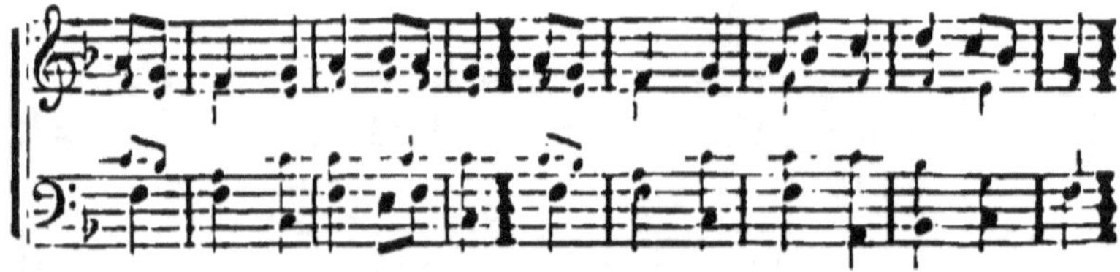

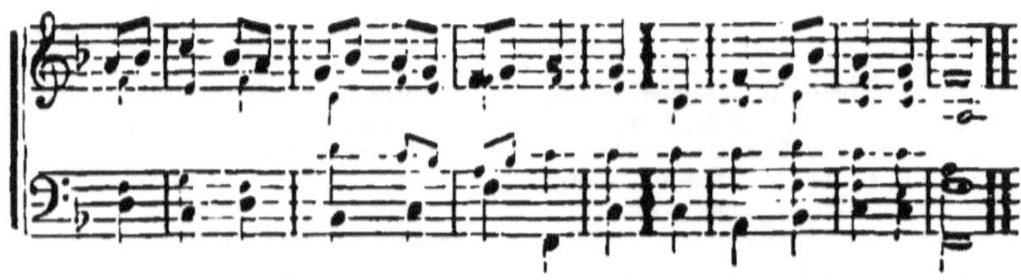

498. C. P. M. TOPLADY.

1 O THOU that hear'st the prayer of faith,
Wilt thou not save a soul from death
That casts itself on thee?
I have no refuge of my own,
But fly to what my Lord hath done
And suffered once for me.

2 Slain in the guilty sinner's stead,
His spotless righteousness I plead,
And his availing blood:
That righteousness my robe shall be;
That merit shall atone for me,
And bring me near to God.

3 Then save me from eternal death;
The Spirit of adoption breathe;
His consolations send;
By him some word of life impart,
And sweetly whisper to my heart,
"Thy Maker is thy Friend."

4 The king of terrors then would be
A welcome messenger to me,
To bid me come away:
Unclogged by earth, or earthly things,
I'd mount, I'd fly, with eager wings,
To everlasting day.

1133. C. P. M. C. WESLEY.

1 O GOD, my inmost soul convert,
And deeply on my thoughtful heart
Eternal things impress;
Cause me to feel their solemn weight,
And tremble on the brink of fate,
And wake to righteousness.

2 Before me place, in dread array,
The pomp of that tremendous day,
When thou with clouds shalt come
To judge the nations at thy bar;
And tell me, Lord, shall I be there
To meet a joyful doom?

3 Be this my one great business here,
With serious industry and fear,
Eternal bliss t' insure —
Thine utmost counsel to fulfil,
And suffer all thy righteous will,
And to the end endure.

4 Then, Father, then my soul receive,
Transported from this vale, to live
And reign with thee above,
Where faith is sweetly lost in sight,
And hope in full, supreme delight,
And everlasting love.

BURLINGTON. C. P. M.

CHARLES ZEUNER.:

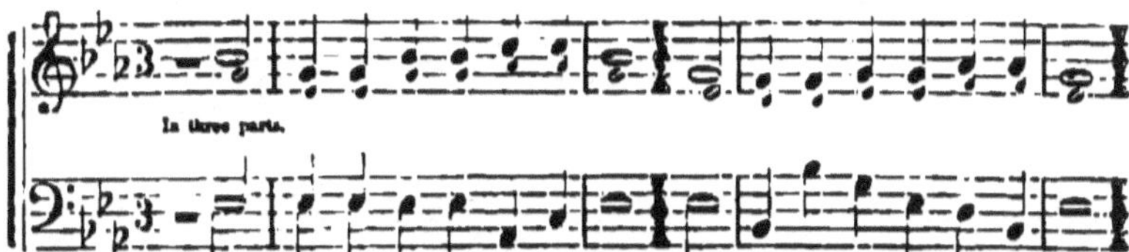

(: Rhythm changed.) From Zeuner's "Musical Manual," 1833.

1143. C. P. M. RIPPON'S COL.

1 WHEN thou, my righteous Judge, shalt come
To take thy ransomed people home,
Shall I among them stand?
Shall such a worthless worm as I,
Who sometimes am afraid to die,
Be found at thy right hand?

2 I love to meet thy people now,
Before thy feet with them to bow,
Though vilest of them all;
But—can I bear the piercing thought?—
What if my name should be left out,
When thou for them shalt call?

3 O Lord, prevent it by thy grace;
Be thou my only hiding-place,
In this th' accepted day;
Thy pardoning voice, O, let me hear,
To still my unbelieving fear,
Nor let me fall, I pray.

4 And when the final trump shall sound,
Among thy saints let me be found,
To bow before thy face:
Then in triumphant strains I'll sing,
While heaven's resounding mansions ring
With praise of sovereign grace.

DOXOLOGY.

12. C. P. M.

To Father, Son, and Holy Ghost,
Be praise amid the heavenly host,
And in the church below;
From whom all creatures draw their breath,
By whom redemption blest the earth,
From whom all comforts flow.

MERIBAH.

ARIEL.

CHARLES STREET. L. P. M.

Composed for Hymn 394. — Sumner Hill. Presented for this work.

394. L. P. M. WATTS.

1 I LOVE the volume of thy word;
What light and joy those leaves afford
To souls benighted and distressed!
Thy precepts guide my doubtful way;
Thy fear forbids my feet to stray;
Thy promise leads my heart to rest.

2 Thy threatenings wake my slumbering eyes,
And warn me where my danger lies;
But 'tis thy blessed gospel, Lord,
That makes my guilty conscience clean,
Converts my soul, subdues my sin,
And gives a free but large reward.

3 Who knows the errors of his thoughts?
My God, forgive my secret faults,
And from presumptuous sins restrain;
Accept my poor attempts of praise,
That I have read thy book of grace,
And book of nature, not in vain.

913. L. P. M. WATTS.

1 LET all the earth their voices raise,
To sing the choicest psalm of praise,
To sing and bless Jehovah's name:
His glory let the heathen know,
His wonders to the nations show,
And all his saving works proclaim.

2 He framed the globe; he built the sky;
He made the shining worlds on high,
And reigns complete in glory there;
His beams are majesty and light;
His beauties, how divinely bright!
His temple, how divinely fair!

3 Come, the great day, the glorious hour,
When earth shall feel his saving power,
And barbarous nations fear his name:
Then shall the race of men confess
The beauty of his holiness,
And in his courts his grace proclaim.

1004. L. P. M. KIPPIS.

1 WITH grateful hearts, with joyful tongues,
To God we raise united songs;
His power and mercy we proclaim:
Through every age, O, may we own
Jehovah here has fixed his throne,
And triumph in his mighty name.

2 Long as the moon her course shall run,
Or men behold the circling sun,
Lord, in our land support thy reign;
Crown her just counsels with success,
With truth and peace her borders bless,
And all thy sacred rights maintain.

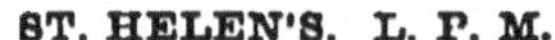

JENNINGS.

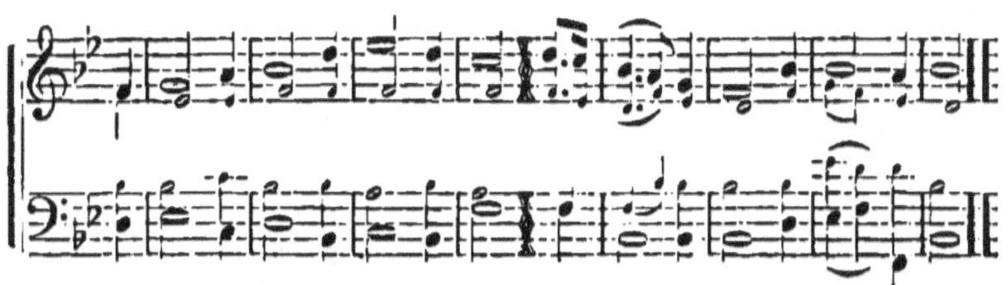

91. L. P. M. WATTS.

1 I'LL praise my Maker with my breath;
And, when my voice is lost in death,
Praise shall employ my nobler powers;
My days of praise shall ne'er be past,
While life, and thought, and being last,
Or immortality endures.

2 How blest the man whose hopes rely
On Israel's God! He made the sky,
And earth, and seas, with all their train;
His truth forever stands secure;
He saves th' oppressed, he feeds the poor,
And none shall find his promise vain.

3 I'll praise him while he lends me breath;
And, when my voice is lost in death,
Praise shall employ my nobler powers;
My days of praise shall ne'er be past,
While life, and thought, and being last,
Or immortality endures.

996. L. P. M. ROSCOE.

1 GREAT God, beneath whose piercing eye
The world's extended kingdoms lie,
We bow before thy heavenly throne;
Thy favoring smile upholds them all;
Thine anger smites them, and they fall;
Thy power we see, thy greatness own.

2 To thee, with grateful hearts, we raise
The tribute of exulting praise,
Our country's Guardian, Guide, and Friend;
Preserved by thee for ages past,
For ages let thy kindness last,
And e'er thy sheltering care extend.

DOXOLOGY.

11. L. P. M.

Now to the great and Sacred Three,
The Father, Son, and Spirit, be
Eternal praise and glory given,
Through all the worlds where God is known,
By all the angels near the throne,
And all the saints in earth and heaven.

NUREMBERG. 7s. J. R. Ahle. 1678.

25. 7s. Hammond.

1 Lord, we come before thee now;
At thy feet we humbly bow;
O, do not our suit disdain;
Shall we seek thee, Lord, in vain?

2 Lord, on thee our souls depend;
In compassion now descend;
Fill our hearts with thy rich grace;
Tune our lips to sing thy praise.

3 In thine own appointed way,
Now we seek thee; here we stay;
Lord, from hence we would not go
Till a blessing thou bestow.

4 Comfort those who weep and mourn;
Let the time of joy return;
Those that are cast down lift up;
Make them strong in faith and hope.

5 Grant that all may seek and find
Thee a God supremely kind;
Heal the sick; the captive free;
Let us all rejoice in thee.

28. 7s. Montgomery.

1 To thy temple we repair;
Lord, we love to worship there;
There, within the veil, we meet
Christ upon the mercy-seat.

2 While thy glorious name is sung,
Tune our lips, inspire our tongue;
Then our joyful souls shall bless
Christ, the Lord our Righteousness.

3 While to thee our prayers ascend,
Let thine ear in love attend;
Hear us when thy Spirit pleads;
Hear, for Jesus intercedes.

4 While thy word is heard with awe,
While we tremble at thy law,
Let thy gospel's wondrous love
Every doubt and fear remove.

5 From thy house when we return,
Let our hearts within us burn;
Then, at evening, we may say,
"We have walked with God to-day."

60. 7s. Kelly.

1 Saviour, bless thy word to all;
Quick and powerful let it prove:
O, may sinners hear thy call;
Let thy people grow in love.

2 Thine own gracious message bless;
Follow it with power divine;
Give the gospel great success;
Thine the work, the glory thine.

3 Saviour, bid the world rejoice;
Send, O, send thy truth abroad;
Let the nations hear thy voice,—
Hear it, and return to God.

61. 7s. Salisbury Col.

1 Glorious in thy saints appear;
Plant thy heavenly kingdom here;
Light and life to all impart;
Shine on each believing heart;—

2 And, in every grace complete,
Make us, Lord, for glory meet,
Till we stand before thy sight,
Partners with the saints in light.

WILMOT.

56. 7s. S. F. SMITH.

1 SOFTLY fades the twilight ray
Of the holy Sabbath day;
Gently as life's setting sun,
When the Christian's course is run.

2 Night her solemn mantle spreads
O'er the earth, as daylight fades;
All things tell of calm repose
At the holy Sabbath's close.

3 Peace is on the world abroad;
'Tis the holy peace of God —
Symbol of the peace within
When the spirit rests from sin.

4 Still the Spirit lingers near,
Where the evening worshipper
Seeks communion with the skies,
Pressing onward to the prize.

5 Saviour, may our Sabbaths be
Days of peace and joy in thee,
Till in heaven our souls repose,
Where the Sabbath ne'er shall close.

69. 7s. MONTGOMERY.

1 ALL ye nations, praise the Lord;
All ye lands, your voices raise;
Heaven and earth, with loud accord,
Praise the Lord, forever praise:

2 For his truth and mercy stand,
Past, and present, and to be,
Like the years of his right hand,
Like his own eternity.

3 Praise him, ye who know his love;
Praise him from the depths beneath;
Praise him in the heights above;
Praise your Maker, all that breathe.

73. 7s. WRANGHAM.

1 PRAISE the Lord; his glory bless;
Praise him in his holiness;
Praise him as the theme inspires;
Praise him as his fame requires.

2 Let the trumpet's lofty sound
Spread its loudest notes around;
Let the harp unite, in praise,
With the sacred minstrel's lays.

3 Let the organ join to bless
God, the Lord our Righteousness;
Tune your voice to spread the fame
Of the great Jehovah's name.

4 All who dwell beneath his light,
In his praise your hearts unite:
While the stream of song is poured,
Praise and magnify the Lord.

115. 7s. SALISBURY COL.

1 HEAVENLY Father, sovereign Lord,
Be thy glorious name adored;
Lord, thy mercies never fail:
Hail, celestial goodness, hail!

2 Though unworthy of thine ear,
Deign our humble songs to hear;
Purer praise we hope to bring,
When around thy throne we sing.

3 While on earth ordained to stay,
Guide our footsteps in thy way,
Till we come to dwell with thee,
Till we all thy glory see.

4 Then, with angel harps again,
We will wake a nobler strain;
There, in joyful songs of praise,
Our triumphant voices raise.

LISLEY.

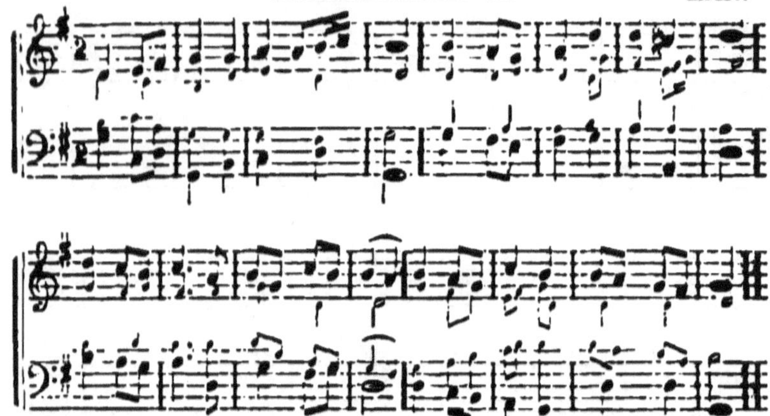

207. 7s. RIPPON'S COL.

1 HARK! the herald angels sing,
"Glory to the new born King;
Peace on earth, and mercy mild;
God and sinners reconciled."

2 Joyful, all ye nations, rise;
Join the triumph of the skies;
With th' angelic host proclaim,
"Christ is born in Bethlehem."

3 See, he lays his glory by,
Born, that man no more may die;
Born to raise the sons of earth;
Born to give them second birth.

4 Hail, the holy Prince of Peace!
Hail, the Sun of Righteousness!
Light and life to all he brings,
Risen with healing in his wings.

5 Let us, then, with angels sing,
"Glory to the new-born King;
Peace on earth, and mercy mild;
God and sinners reconciled."

233. 7s. COLLYER.

1 MORNING breaks upon the tomb;
Jesus scatters all its gloom;
Day of triumph! through the skies
See the glorious Saviour rise.

2 Ye who are of death afraid,
Triumph in the scattered shade;
Drive your anxious cares away;
See the place where Jesus lay.

3 Christian, dry your flowing tears;
Chase your unbelieving fears;
Look on his deserted grave;
Doubt no more his power to save.

234. 7s. GIBBONS.

1 ANGELS, roll the rock away;
Death, yield up thy mighty prey;
See! he rises from the tomb —
Rises with immortal bloom.

2 'Tis the Saviour; seraphs, raise
Your triumphant shouts of praise;
Let the earth's remotest bound
Hear the joy inspiring sound.

3 Lift, ye saints, lift up your eyes;
Now to glory see him rise;
Hosts of angels on the road
Hail and sing th' incarnate God.

4 Praise him, all ye heavenly choirs,
Praise him with your golden lyres;
Praise him in your noblest songs;
Praise him from ten thousand tongues.

235. 7s. CUDWORTH.

1 CHRIST, the Lord, is risen to-day,
Sons of men and angels say;
Raise your songs of triumph high;
Sing, ye heavens, and, earth, reply.

2 Love's redeeming work is done,
Fought the fight, the battle won;
Lo! our Sun's eclipse is o'er;
Lo! he sets in blood no more.

3 Vain the stone, the watch, the seal;
Christ hath burst the gates of hell;
Death in vain forbids his rise;
Christ hath opened Paradise.

4 Lives again our glorious King;
Where, O Death, is now thy sting?
Once he died our souls to save;
Where thy victory, boasting Grave?

5 Soar we now where Christ hath led,
Following our exalted Head;
Made like him, like him we rise;
Ours the cross, the grave, the skies.

245. 7s. SPIR. OF THE PSALMS.

1 "WIDE, ye heavenly gates, unfold,
Closed no more by death and sin;
Lo! the conquering Lord behold;
Let the King of glory in."

2 Hark! th' angelic host inquire,
"Who is he, th' almighty King?"
Hark again! the answering choir
Thus in strains of triumph sing:—

3 "He whose powerful arm, alone,
On his foes destruction hurled;
He who hath the victory won;
He who saved a ruined world;—

4 "He who God's pure law fulfilled;
Jesus, the incarnate Word;
He whose truth with blood was sealed;
He is heaven's all-glorious Lord."

5 "Who shall up to that abode
Follow in the Saviour's train?"
"They who in his cleansing blood
Wash away each guilty stain;—

6 "They whose daily actions prove
Steadfast faith and holy fear,
Fervent zeal and grateful love;
They shall dwell forever here."

275. 7s. LANGFORD.

1 NOW begin the heavenly theme;
Sing aloud in Jesus' name;
Ye who his salvation prove,
Triumph in redeeming love.

2 Ye who see the Father's grace
Beaming in the Saviour's face,
As to Canaan on ye move,
Praise and bless redeeming love.

3 Mourning souls, dry up your tears;
Banish all your guilty fears;
See your guilt and curse remove,
Cancelled by redeeming love.

4 Welcome, all by sin oppressed,
Welcome to his sacred rest;
Nothing brought him from above,
Nothing but redeeming love.

5 Hither, then, your music bring;
Strike aloud each cheerful string;
Mortals, join the host above—
Join to praise redeeming love.

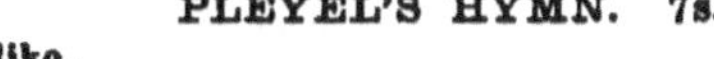

PLEYEL.

264. 7s. C. WESLEY.

1 JESUS, to thy wounds I fly;
Purge my sins of deepest dye;
Lamb of God, for sinners slain,
Wash away my crimson stain.

2 Plunge me in that sacred flood,
In that fountain of thy blood;
Then thy Father's eye shall see
Not a spot of guilt in me.

265. 7s. SELECT PSALMS.

1 SOVEREIGN Ruler, Lord of all,
Prostrate at thy feet I fall;
Hear, O, hear my earnest cry;
Frown not, lest I faint and die.

2 Vilest of the sons of men,
Chief of sinners I have been;
Oft have sinned before thy face,
Trampled on thy richest grace.

3 Justly might thy fatal dart
Pierce this bleeding, broken heart;
Justly might thy angry breath
Blast me in eternal death.

4 Jesus, save my dying soul;
Make my broken spirit whole;
Humbled in the dust I lie;
Saviour, leave me not to die.

JEPHTHAH. 7s, or 8s & 7s. HANDEL.

366. 7s. BATHURST.

1 HOLY Spirit, from on high,
Bend o'er us a pitying eye;
Now refresh the drooping heart;
Bid the power of sin depart.

2 Light up every dark recess
Of our heart's ungodliness;
Show us every devious way
Where our steps have gone astray.

3 Teach us, with repentant grief
Humbly to implore relief;
Then the Saviour's blood reveal,
And our broken spirits heal.

4 May we daily grow in grace,
And pursue the heavenly race,
Trained in wisdom, led by love,
Till we reach our rest above.

370. 8s & 7s. NOEL'S COL.

1 HOLY Source of consolation,
Light and life thy grace imparts;
Visit us in thy compassion;
Guide our minds, and fill our hearts.

2 Heavenly blessings, without measure,
Thou canst bring us from above;
Lord, we ask that heavenly treasure,
Wisdom, holiness, and love.

3 Dwell within us, blessèd Spirit;
Where thou art no ill can come;
Bless us now, through Jesus' merit;
Reign in every heart and home.

4 Saviour, lead us to adore thee,
While thou dost prolong our days;
Then, with angel hosts before thee,
May we worship, love, and praise.

371. 7s. STOCKER.

1 GRACIOUS Spirit — Love divine!
Let thy light within me shine;
All my guilty fears remove;
Fill me with thy heavenly love.

2 Speak thy pardoning grace to me;
Set the burdened sinner free;
Lead me to the Lamb of God;
Wash me in his precious blood.

3 Life and peace to me impart;
Seal salvation on my heart;
Dwell thyself within my breast,
Earnest of immortal rest.

4 Let me never from thee stray;
Keep me in the narrow way;
Fill my soul with joy divine;
Keep me, Lord, forever thine.

372. 7s. REED.

1 HOLY Ghost, with light divine,
Shine upon this heart of mine;
Chase the shades of night away;
Turn the darkness into day.

2 Holy Ghost, with power divine,
Cleanse this guilty heart of mine;
Long has sin, without control,
Held dominion o'er my soul.

3 Holy Ghost, with joy divine,
Cheer this saddened heart of mine;
Bid my many woes depart;
Heal my wounded, bleeding heart.

4 Holy Spirit, all divine,
Dwell within this heart of mine;
Cast down every idol throne;
Reign supreme, and reign alone.

PLEYEL'S HYMN. 7s, or 8s & 7s. PLEYEL.

365. 8s & 7s. JAY.

1 HOLY Ghost, dispel our sadness ;
Pierce the clouds of nature's night ;
Come, thou Source of joy and gladness,
Breathe thy life, and spread thy light.

2 Author of our new creation,
Bid us all thine influence prove ;
Make our souls thy habitation ;
Shed abroad the Saviour's love.

413. 7s. BARBAULD.

1 COME, saith Jesus' sacred voice,
Come, and make my paths your choice ;
I will guide you to your home ;
Weary pilgrims, hither come.

2 Hither come ; for here is found
Balm for every bleeding wound,
Peace which ever shall endure,
Rest, eternal, sacred, sure.

429. 7s CONVERT'S COMP.

1 WEEPING sinners, dry your tears ;
Jesus on the throne appears ;
Mercy comes with balmy wing,
Bids you his salvation sing.

2 Peace he brings you by his death,
Peace he speaks with every breath :
Can you slight such heavenly charms ?
Flee, O flee to Jesus' arms

NORWICH.

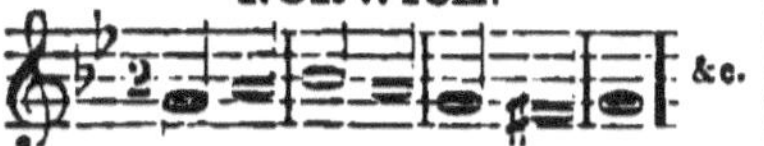

448. 7s. J. WESLEY.

1 SINNERS, turn ; why will ye die ?
God, your Maker, asks you why ;
God, who did your being give,
Made you with himself to live.

2 Sinners, turn ; why will ye die ?
God, your Saviour, asks you why :
Will ye not in him believe ?
He has died that ye might live.

3 Will ye let him die in vain ?
Crucify your Lord again ?
Why, unpardoned sinners, why
Will ye slight his grace, and die ?

4 Sinners, turn ; why will ye die ?
God, the Spirit, asks you why —
Often with you has he strove,
Wooed you to embrace his love.

5 Will ye not his grace receive ?
Will ye still refuse to live ?
O, ye dying sinners, why,
Why will ye forever die ?

455. 7s. S. F. SMITH.

1 WHEN thy mortal life is fled,
When the death-shades o'er thee spread,
When is finished thy career,
Sinner, where wilt thou appear ?

2 When the world has passed away,
When draws near the judgment day,
When the awful trump shall sound,
Say, O, where wilt thou be found ?

3 When the Judge descends in light,
Clothed in majesty and might,
When the wicked quail with fear,
Where, O, where wilt thou appear ?

4 What shall soothe thy bursting heart,
When the saints and thou must part ?
When the good with joy are crowned,
Sinner, where wilt thou be found ?

5 While the Holy Ghost is nigh,
Quickly to the Saviour fly ;
Then shall peace thy spirit cheer ;
Then in heaven shalt thou appear.

EDDYFIELD. 7s. Latrobe.

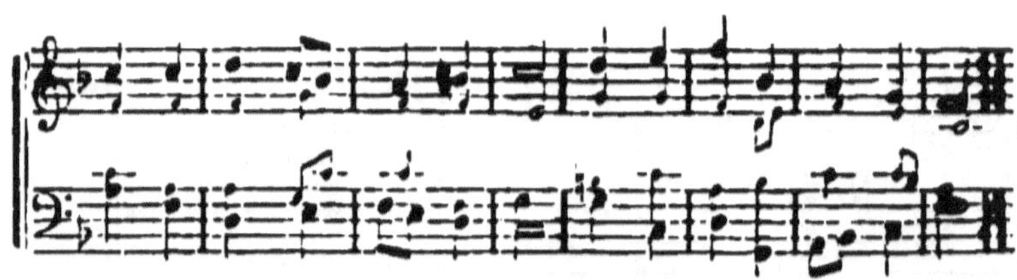

441. 7s. T. Scott.

1 Haste, O sinner; now be wise;
  Stay not for the morrow's sun;
Wisdom if you still despise,
  Harder is it to be won.

2 Haste, and mercy now implore;
  Stay not for the morrow's sun,
Lest thy season should be o'er
  Ere this evening's stage be run.

3 Haste, O sinner; now return;
  Stay not for the morrow's sun,
Lest thy lamp should cease to burn
  Ere salvation's work is done.

4 Haste, O sinner; now be blest;
  Stay not for the morrow's sun,
Lest perdition thee arrest
  Ere the morrow is begun.

444. 7s. Urwick's Col.

1 Sinner, what has earth to show
Like the joys believers know?
Is thy path, of fading flowers,
Half so bright, so sweet, as ours?

2 Doth a skilful, healing friend
On thy daily path attend,
And, where thorns and stings abound,
Shed a balm on every wound?

3 When the tempest rolls on high,
Hast thou still a refuge nigh?
Can, O, can thy dying breath
Summon one more strong than death?

4 Canst thou, in that awful day,
Fearless tread the gloomy way,
Plead a glorious ransom given,
Burst from earth, and soar to heaven.

457. 7s. Epis. Col.

1 Sinner, rouse thee from thy sleep;
Wake, and o'er thy folly weep;
Raise thy spirit, dark and dead;
Jesus waits his light to shed.

2 Wake from sleep; arise from death;
See the bright and living path;
Watchful, tread that path; be wise;
Leave thy folly; seek the skies.

3 Leave thy folly; cease from crime;
From this hour redeem thy time;
Life secure without delay;
Evil is thy mortal day.

4 O, then, rouse thee from thy sleep;
Wake, and o'er thy folly weep;
Jesus calls from death and night;
Jesus waits to shed his light.

462. 7s. J. Taylor.

1 God of mercy, God of grace,
  Hear our sad, repentant songs;
O, restore thy suppliant race,
  Thou, to whom our praise belongs.

2 Deep regret for follies past,
  Talents wasted, time misspent;
Hearts debased by worldly cares,
  Thankless for the blessings lent;—

3 Foolish fears and fond desires,
  Vain regrets for things as vain,
Lips too seldom taught to praise,
  Oft to murmur and complain;—

4 These, and every secret fault,
  Filled with grief and shame, we own;
Humbled at thy feet we lie,
  Seeking pardon from thy throne.

5 God of mercy, God of grace,
Hear our sad, repentant songs;
O, restore thy suppliant race,
Thou, to whom our praise belongs.

476. 7s. Luth. Col.

1 Depth of mercy! — can there be
Mercy still reserved for me?
Can my God his wrath forbear,
And the chief of sinners spare?

2 I have long withstood his grace;
Long provoked him to his face;
Would not hear his gracious calls;
Grieved him by a thousand falls.

3 Jesus, answer from above;
Is not all thy nature love?
Wilt thou not the wrong forget? —
Lo, I fall before thy feet.

4 Now incline me to repent;
Let me now my fall lament,
Deeply my revolt deplore,
Weep, believe, and sin no more.

---

528. 7s Anon.

1 Weeping saint, no longer mourn;
Surely Christ thy griefs hath borne;
Jesus, best of friends, for thee,
Numbered with transgressors, see!

2 He the wine-press trod alone;
Hear the Man of sorrows groan;
Mocked, and bruised, and crowned with thorns,
He his Father's absence mourns.

3 All thy sins, when Jesus bled,
Met on his devoted head;
All thy hope on Jesus place;
Plead his promise, trust his grace.

4 At his feet thy burden lay;
Christ shall smile thy fears away;
He thy guilt and sorrow bore;
Weeping saint, lament no more.

573. 7s. Anon.

1 Lord, my times are in thy hand;
All my fondest hopes have planned
To thy wisdom I resign,
And would make thy purpose mine.

2 Thou my daily task shalt give;
Day by day to thee I live:
So shall added years fulfil, —
Not my own, — my Father's will.

3 Fond ambition, whisper not;
Happy is my humble lot:
Anxious, busy cares, away;
I'm provided for to-day.

4 O, to live exempt from care,
By the energy of prayer,
Strong in faith, with mind subdued,
Yet elate with gratitude!

622. 7s. Spirit of the Psalms.

1 They who on the Lord rely,
Safely dwell, though danger's nigh;
Wide his sheltering wings are spread
O'er each faithful servant's head.

2 Vain temptation's wily snare;
Christians are Jehovah's care;
Harmless flies the shaft by day,
Or in darkness wings its way.

3 When they wake, or when they sleep,
Angel guards their vigils keep;
Death and danger may be near;
Faith and love have nought to fear.

PILGRIM. 7s. From Nat. Ch. Har.

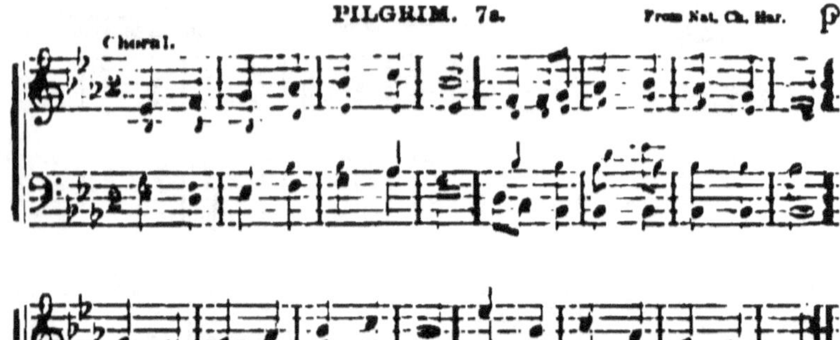

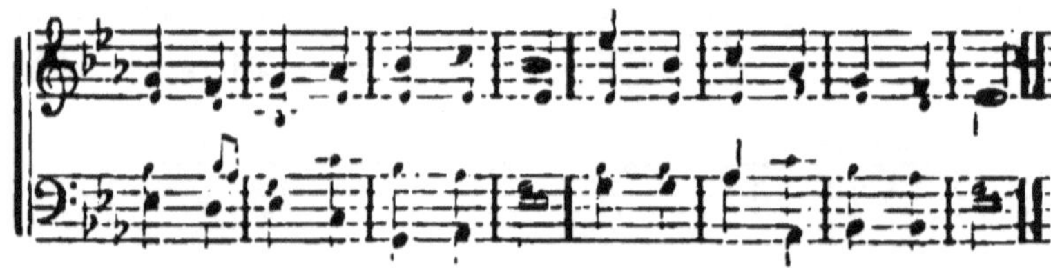

577. 7s. NEWTON.

1 'Tis a point I long to know, —
Oft it causes anxious thought, —
Do I love the Lord, or no?
Am I his, or am I not?

2 If I love, why am I thus?
Why this dull and lifeless frame?
Hardly, sure, can they be worse,
Who have never heard his name.

3 When I turn my eyes within,
All is dark, and vain, and wild;
Filled with unbelief and sin,
Can I deem myself a child?

4 If I pray, or hear, or read,
Sin is mixed with all I do;
You that love the Lord indeed,
Tell me, is it thus with you?

5 Yet I mourn my stubborn will,
Find my sin a grief and thrall;
Should I grieve for what I feel,
If I did not love at all?

6 Lord, decide the doubtful case;
Thou, who art thy people's sun,
Shine upon thy work of grace,
If it be indeed begun.

7 Let me love thee more and more,
If I love at all, I pray;
If I have not loved before,
Help me to begin to-day.

RHINE.

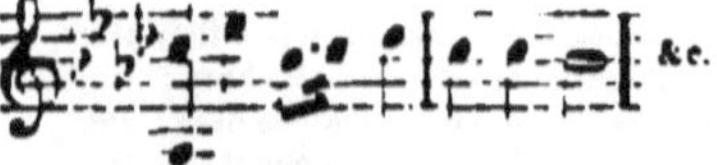

695. 7s. MONTGOMERY.

1 PEOPLE of the living God,
I have sought the world around,
Paths of sin and sorrow trod,
Peace and comfort nowhere found.

2 Now to you my spirit turns, —
Turns, a fugitive unblest;
Brethren, where your altar burns,
O, receive me into rest.

3 Lonely I no longer roam,
Like the cloud, the wind, the wave;
Where you dwell shall be my home,
Where you die shall be my grave.

4 Mine the God whom you adore;
Your Redeemer shall be mine;
Earth can fill my soul no more;
Every idol I resign.

847. 7s. CONDER.

1 BREAD of heaven, on thee we feed,
For thy flesh is meat indeed;
Ever let our souls be fed
With this true and living bread.

2 Vine of heaven, thy blood supplies
This blest cup of sacrifice;
Lord, thy wounds our healing give;
To thy cross we look, and live.

3 Day by day with strength supplied,
Through the life of him who died,
Lord of life, O, let us be
Rooted, grafted, built on thee.

BOTHNIA. 7s. GEORGE J. WEBB. Mass. Collection.

* If there be a choir, or competent soprano solo voice.

873. 7s. CONDER.

1 HASTEN, Lord, thy promised hour;
Come in glory and in power:
Still thy foes are unsubdued;
Nature sighs to be renewed.

2 Time has nearly reached its sum;
All things, with thy bride, say, "Come,
Jesus, whom all worlds adore,
Come, and reign forevermore."

893. 7s. BOWRING.

1 WATCHMAN! tell us of the night,
What its signs of promise are.
Traveller! o'er yon mountain's height
See that glory-beaming star.

2 Watchman! does its beauteous ray
Aught of hope or joy foretell?
Traveller! yes; it brings the day,
Promised day of Israel.

3 Watchman! tell us of the night;
Higher yet that star ascends.
Traveller! blessedness and light,
Peace and truth, its course portends.

4 Watchman! will its beams alone
Gild the spot that gave them birth?
Traveller! ages are its own;
See, it bursts o'er all the earth.

5 Watchman! tell us of the night,
For the morning seems to dawn.
Traveller! darkness takes its flight;
Doubt and terror are withdrawn.

6 Watchman! let thy wanderings cease;
Hie thee to thy quiet home.
Traveller! lo! the Prince of Peace,
Lo! the Son of God, is come.

915. 7s. BACON.

1 WAKE the song of jubilee;
Let it echo o'er the sea:
Now is come the promised hour;
Jesus reigns with sovereign power.

2 All ye nations, join and sing,
"Christ, of lords and kings is King:"
Let it sound from shore to shore;
Jesus reigns forevermore.

3 Now the desert lands rejoice,
And the islands join their voice;
Yea, the whole creation sings,
"Jesus is the King of kings."

916. 7s. MONTGOMERY.

1 HARK! the song of jubilee,
Loud as mighty thunders roar,
Or the fulness of the sea,
When it breaks upon the shore!

2 See, Jehovah's banner furled;
Sheathed his sword: he speaks—'tis done!
Now the kingdoms of this world
Are the kingdom of his Son.

3 He shall reign from pole to pole
With supreme, unbounded sway;
He shall reign, when, like a scroll,
Yonder heavens have passed away.

4 Hallelujah! for the Lord
God omnipotent shall reign:
Hallelujah!—let the word
Echo round the earth and main.

5 Hallelujah! hark! the sound,
From the centre to the skies,
Wakes, above, beneath, around,
All creation's harmonies.

‡ The small notes in this measure for Hymn 1033 only.

880. 7s. MARSDEN.

1 Go, ye messengers of God;
Like the beams of morning, fly;
Take the wonder-working rod;
Wave the banner-cross on high.

2 Go to many a tropic isle,
In the bosom of the deep,
Where the skies forever smile,
And th' oppressed forever weep.

3 O'er the pagan's night of care
Pour the living light of heaven;
Chase away his wild despair;
Bid him hope to be forgiven.

4 Where the golden gates of day
Open on the palmy east,
High the bleeding cross display,
Spread the gospel's richest feast.

956. 7s. HAMMOND.

1 Would you win a soul to God,
Tell him of a Saviour's blood,
Once for dying sinners spilt,
To atone for all their guilt.

2 Tell him how the streams did glide
From his hands, his feet, his side;
How his head with thorns was crowned,
And his heart in sorrow drowned;—

3 How he yielded up his breath;
How he agonized in death;
How he lives to intercede—
Christ our Advocate and Head.

4 Tell him it was sovereign grace
Led thee first to seek his face,
Made thee choose the better part
Wrought salvation in thy heart.

5 Tell him of that liberty
Wherewith Jesus makes us free;
Sweetly speak of sins forgiven,—
Earnest of the joys of heaven.

932. 7s. MONTGOMERY.

1 Lord of hosts, to thee we raise
Here a house of prayer and praise;
Thou thy people's hearts prepare
Here to meet for praise and prayer.

2 Let the living here be fed
With thy word, the heavenly bread;
Here, in hope of glory blest,
May the dead be laid to rest.

3 Here to thee a temple stand,
While the sea shall gird the land;
Here reveal thy mercy sure,
While the sun and moon endure.

4 Hallelujah!—earth and sky
To the joyful sound reply;
Hallelujah!—hence ascend
Prayer and praise till time shall end.

1033. 8s. HOGG.

1 Blessed be thy name forever,
Thou of life the glorious Giver;
Thou canst guard thy creatures, sleeping;
Heal the heart long broke with weeping.

2 Thou who slumberest not, nor sleepest:
Blest are they thou kindly keepest:
Thou of every good the Giver,
Blessèd be thy name forever

WARREN. 7s. GERMAN.

966. 7s. GRAY.

1 SUPPLIANT, lo! thy children bend,
Father, for thy blessing now;
Thou canst teach us, guide, defend;
We are weak; almighty thou.

2 With the peace thy word imparts
Be the taught and teachers blest;
In our lives, and in our hearts,
Father, be thy laws impressed.

3 Shed abroad in every mind
Light and pardon from above,
Charity for all our kind,
Trusting faith, and holy love.

976. 7s. CAMPBELL'S COL.

1 GOD of mercy, hear our prayer
For the children thou hast given;
Let them all thy blessings share —
Grace on earth, and bliss in heaven.

2 In the morning of their days
May their hearts be drawn to thee;
Let them learn to lisp thy praise
In their earliest infancy.

3 When we see their passions rise,
Sinful habits unsubdued,
Then to thee we lift our eyes,
That their hearts may be renewed.

4 Cleanse their souls from every stain,
Through the Saviour's precious blood;
Let them all be born again,
And be reconciled to God.

5 For this mercy, Lord, we cry;
Bend thine ever-gracious ear;
While on thee our souls rely,
Hear our prayer — in mercy hear.

999. 7s. SAC. LYRICS.

1 SWELL the anthem, raise the song;
Praises to our God belong;
Saints and angels, join to sing
Praises to the heavenly King.

2 Blessings from his liberal hand
Flow around this happy land:
Kept by him, no foes annoy;
Peace and freedom we enjoy.

3 Here, beneath a virtuous sway,
May we cheerfully obey, —
Never feel oppression's rod, —
Ever own and worship God.

4 Hark! the voice of nature sings
Praises to the King of kings;
Let us join the choral song,
And the grateful notes prolong.

1065. 7s. NEWTON.

1 FOR a season called to part,
Let us now ourselves commend
To the gracious eye and heart
Of our ever-present Friend.

2 Jesus, hear our humble prayer:
Tender Shepherd of thy sheep,
Let thy mercy and thy care
All our souls in safety keep.

3 In thy strength may we be strong;
Sweeten every cross and pain;
And our wasting lives prolong,
Till we meet on earth again.

ASCENSION. 7s. N. D. GOULD.

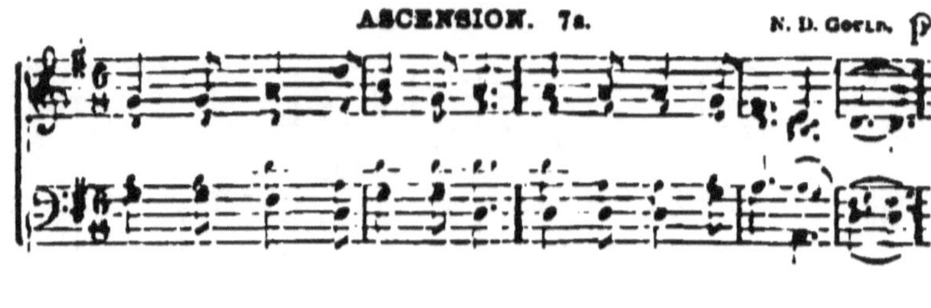

1013. 7s. EPIS. COL.

1 Now the shades of night are gone;
Now is passed the early dawn:
Lord, we would be thine to-day;
Drive the shades of sin away.

2 Make our souls as noonday clear;
Banish every doubt and fear:
In thy vineyard, Lord, to-day,
We would labor, we would pray.

3 When our work of life is past,
O, receive us all at last:
Labor then will all be o'er;
Sin's dark night will be no more.

1014. 7s. CH. PSALMODY.

1 Thou that dost my life prolong,
Kindly aid my morning song;
Thankful, from my couch I rise,
To the God that rules the skies.

2 Thou didst hear my evening cry;
Thy preserving hand was nigh:
Peaceful slumbers thou hast shed,
Grateful to my weary head.

3 Thou hast kept me through the night;
'Twas thy hand restored the light:
Lord, thy mercies still are new,
Plenteous as the morning dew.

4 Still my feet are prone to stray;
O, preserve me through the day:
Dangers every where abound;
Sins and snares beset me round.

5 Gently, with the dawning ray,
On my soul thy beams display;
Sweeter than the smiling morn,
Let thy cheering light return.

1026. 7s. EPIS. COL.

1 Softly, now the light of day
Fades upon our sight away;
Free from care, from labor free,
Lord, we would commune with thee.

2 Soon for us the light of day
Shall forever pass away;
Then from sin and sorrow free,
Take us, Lord, to dwell with thee.

1098. 7s. J. H. BANCROFT.

1 ~~Brother~~ Sister, though from yonder sky
Cometh neither voice nor cry,
Yet we know for thee to-day
Every pain hath passed away.

2 Not for thee shall tears be given,
Child of God, and heir of heaven;
For he gave thee sweet release;
Thine the Christian's death of peace.

3 Well we know thy living faith
Had the power to conquer death;
As a living rose may bloom
By the border of the tomb.

4 ~~Brother~~ Sister, in that solemn trust
We commend thee, dust to dust;
In that faith we wait, till, risen,
Thou shalt meet us all in heaven.

5 While we weep as Jesus wept,
Thou shalt sleep as Jesus slept:
With thy Saviour thou shalt rest,
Crowned, and glorified, and blest.

1089.

7s. TOPLADY.

1 DEATHLESS spirit, now arise;
Soar, thou native of the skies—
Pearl of price, by Jesus bought,
To his glorious likeness wrought.

2 Go to shine before the throne:
Deck the Mediator's crown;
Go, his triumphs to adorn;
Made for God, to God return.

3 Lo! he beckons from on high;
Fearless to his presence fly;
Thine the merit of his blood,
Thine the righteousness of God.

4 Angels, joyful to attend,
Hovering round thy pillow, bend,
Wait to catch the signal given,
And convey thee quick to heaven.

5 Burst thy shackles; drop thy clay;
Sweetly breathe thyself away;
Singing to thy crown remove,
Swift of wing, and fired with love.

6 Shudder not to pass the stream:
Venture all thy care on Him—
Him, whose dying love and power
Stilled its tossing, hushed its roar.

7 Safe is the expanded wave,
Gentle as a summer's eve;
Not one object of his care
Ever suffered shipwreck there.

8 See the haven full in view;
Love divine shall bear thee through;
Trust to that propitious gale;
Weigh thy anchor, spread thy sail.

9 Saints in glory, perfect made,
Wait thy passage through the shade;
Swiftly to their wish be given;
Kindle higher joy in heaven.

[For the odd verse omit the repeat, and sing the last two lines of stanza twice.]

ST. NICOLAI. 7s.‡ 2 STANZAS. J. ROSENMULLER. 1650.

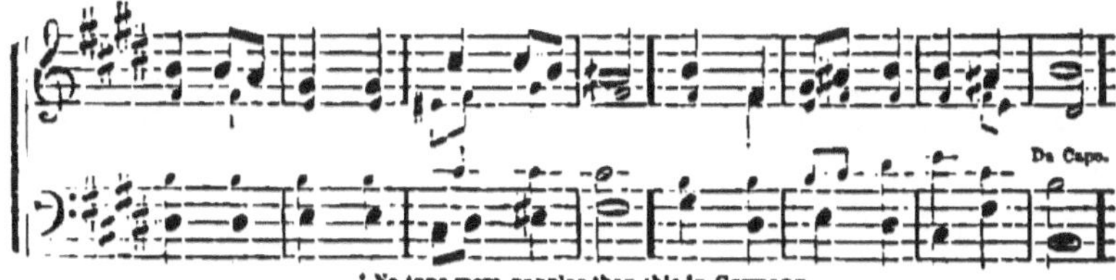

‡ No tune more popular than this in Germany.

[For the hymn below, and for general use, the signature of three flats may be better.]

1138.

7s. KELLY.

1 HARK! that shout of rapturous joy,
Bursting forth from yonder cloud;
Jesus comes, and through the sky,
Angels tell their joy aloud.

2 Hark! the trumpet's awful voice
Sounds abroad o'er sea and land;
Let his people now rejoice;
Their redemption is at hand.

3 See, the Lord appears in view;
Heaven and earth before him fly;
Rise, ye saints; he comes for you;
Rise to meet him in the sky.

4 Go and dwell with him above,
Where no foe can e'er molest;
Happy in the Saviour's love,
Ever blessing, ever blest.

FAIRFAX. 7s. Standard Ps. Tune Book.

1131. 7s. T. VON CELANO.

1 ON that great, that awful day,
This vain world shall pass away,
And, before the Maker, stand
All the creatures of his hand.

2 Then shall all the nations meet
At th' eternal judgment-seat,
And, unveiled before his eye,
All the works of man shall lie.

3 O, in that destroying hour,
Source of goodness, Source of power,
Show thou, of thine own free grace,
Help unto a helpless race.

4 Hear, and pity; hear, and aid;
Spare the creatures thou hast made;
Fold us with the sheep that stand
Pure and safe at thy right hand.

1026. 7s. EPIS. COL.

1 SOFTLY now the light of day
Fades upon our sight away;
Free from care, from labor free,
Lord, we would commune with thee.

2 Soon for us the light of day
Shall forever pass away;
Then, from sin and sorrow free,
Take us, Lord, to dwell with thee.

VOGLER. 7s. Arr. by B. F. EDMANDS, From Abbé Vogler. ‡

‡ The melody, composed about 1770, is the theme of the tune "Bowdoin Square," in C. M.

ELLENTHORPE. 7s. LINLEY.

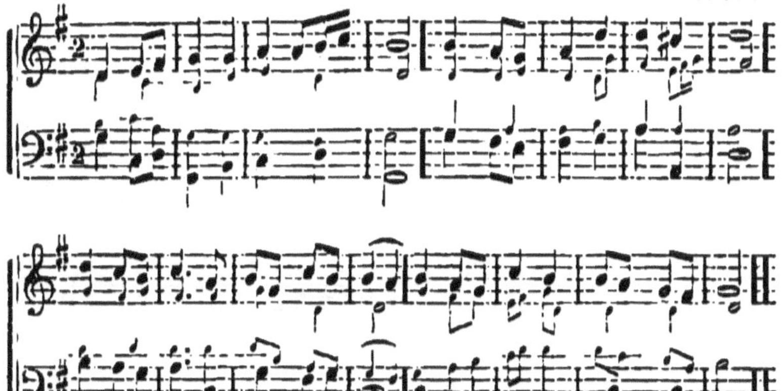

1151. 7s. SPIR. OF THE PSALMS.

1 WHO, O Lord, when life is o'er,
Shall to heaven's blest mansions soar?
Who, an ever-welcome guest,
In thy holy place shall rest?

2 He whose heart thy love has warmed;
He whose will, to thine conformed,
Bids his life unsullied run;
He whose words and thoughts are one;—

3 He who shuns the sinner's road,
Loving those who love their God;
Who, with hope and faith unfeigned,
Treads the path by thee ordained;—

4 He who trusts in Christ alone;
Not in aught himself has done;—
He, great God, shall be thy care,
And thy choicest blessing share.

1164. 7s. MONTGOMERY.

1 PALMS of glory, raiment bright,
Crowns which never fade away,
Gird and deck the saints in light;
Priests, and kings, and conquerors, they.

2 Yet the conquerors bring their palms
To the Lamb amidst the throne,
And proclaim, in joyful psalms,
Victory through his cross alone.

3 Kings for harps their crowns resign,
Crying, as they strike the chords,
"Take the kingdom; it is thine,
King of kings and Lord of lords."

4 Round the altar priests confess,
With their robes made white as snow,
'Twas their Saviour's righteousness,
And his blood, which made them so.

5 Who were these? on earth they dwelt,
Sinners once of Adam's race;
Guilt, and fear, and suffering felt,
But were saved by sovereign grace.

6 They were mortal, too, like us;
And when we, like them, shall die,
May our souls, translated thus,
Triumph, reign, and shine on high.

1177. 7s. RAFFLES.

1 HIGH, in yonder realms of light,
Dwell the raptured saints above,
Far beyond our feeble sight,
Happy in Immanuel's love.

2 Pilgrims in this vale of tears,
Once they knew, like us below,
Gloomy doubts, distressing fears,
Torturing pain, and heavy woe.

3 Happy spirits, ye are fled
Where no grief can entrance find,
Lulled to rest the aching head,
Soothed the anguish of the mind.

4 'Mid the chorus of the skies,
'Mid th' angelic lyres above,
Hark! their songs melodious rise—
Songs of praise to Jesus' love.

7. DOXOLOGY.

7s.

SING we to our God above,
Praise eternal as his love:
Praise him, all ye heavenly host—
Father, Son, and Holy Ghost.

278. 7s. 6 L. C. WESLEY.

1 CHRIST, whose glory fills the skies,
  Christ, the true, the only light,
Sun of Righteousness, arise,
  Triumph o'er the shades of night;
Dayspring from on high, be near;
Daystar, in my heart appear.

2 Dark and cheerless is the morn,
  If thy light is hid from me;
Joyless is the day's return,
  Till thy mercy's beams I see;
Till they inward light impart,
Warmth and gladness to my heart.

3 Visit, then, this soul of mine;
  Pierce the gloom of sin and grief;
Fill me, radiant Sun divine;
  Scatter all my unbelief;
More and more thyself display,
Shining to the perfect day.

339. 7s. 6 L. KELLY.

1 GLORY, glory to our King!
  Crowns unfading wreath his head;
Jesus is the name we sing —
  Jesus, risen from the dead;
Jesus, Conqueror o'er the grave;
Jesus, mighty now to save.

2 Now behold him high enthroned,
  Glory beaming from his face,
By adoring angels owned
  God of holiness and grace:
O for hearts and tongues to sing,
Glory, glory to our King!

3 Jesus, on thy people shine;
  Warm our hearts and tune our tongues,
That with angels we may join, —
  Share their bliss, and swell their songs:
Glory, honor, praise, and power,
Lord, be thine forevermore.

---

415. 7s. WINCHELL'S SEL.

1 YE who in his courts are found
Listening to the joyful sound,
Lost and helpless as ye are,
Sons of sorrow, sin, and care,
Glorify the King of kings;
Take the peace the gospel brings.

2 Turn to Christ your longing eyes;
View this bleeding sacrifice;
See in him your sins forgiven,
Pardon, holiness, and heaven;
Glorify the King of kings;
Take the peace the gospel brings.

SUMNER. 7s. 6 L.

282. 7s. TOPLADY.

1 ROCK of ages, cleft for me,
Let me hide myself in thee;
Let the water and the blood,
From thy side, a healing flood,
Be of sin the double cure,—
Save from wrath, and make me pure.

2 Should my tears forever flow,
Should my zeal no languor know,
All for sin could not atone;
Thou must save, and thou alone;
In my hand no price I bring;
Simply to thy cross I cling.

3 While I draw this fleeting breath,
When mine eyelids close in death,
When I rise to worlds unknown,
See thee on thy judgment throne,—
Rock of ages, cleft for me,
Let me hide myself in thee.

426. 7s. 6 L. HAWEIS.

1 FROM the cross uplifted high,
Where the Saviour deigns to die,
What melodious sounds we hear,
Bursting on the ravished ear!—
"Love's redeeming work is done;
Come and welcome, sinner, come.

2 "Sprinkled now with blood the throne,
Why beneath thy burdens groan?
On my piercéd body laid,
Justice owns the ransom paid;
Bow the knee, embrace the Son;
Come and welcome, sinner, come.

3 "Spread for thee, the festal board
See with richest dainties stored;
To thy Father's bosom pressed,
Yet again a child confessed,
Never from his house to roam,
Come and welcome, sinner, come.

4 "Soon the days of life shall end;
Lo, I come, your Saviour, Friend,
Safe your spirits to convey
To the realms of endless day,
Up to my eternal home;
Come and welcome, sinner, come."

427. 7s. 6 L. ANON.

1 WEARY sinner, keep thine eyes
On th' atoning Sacrifice;
View him bleeding on the tree,
Pouring out his life for thee:
There the dreadful curse he bore;
Weeping soul, lament no more.

2 Cast thy guilty soul on him;
Find him mighty to redeem;
At his feet thy burden lay;
Look thy doubts and care away;
Now by faith the Son embrace,
Plead his promise, trust his grace.

477. 7s. 6 L. HAR. SAC.

1 HEARTS of stone, relent, relent;
Break, by Jesus' cross subdued;
See his body mangled, rent,
Covered with a gore of blood;
Sinful soul, what hast thou done?
Crucified th' eternal Son.

2 Yes, thy sins have done the deed,
Driven the nails that fixed him there,
Crowned with thorns his sacred head,
Plunged into his side the spear,
Made his soul a sacrifice,
While for sinful man he dies.

3 Wilt thou let him bleed in vain?
Still to death thy Lord pursue?
Open all his wounds again!
And the shameful cross renew?
No; with all my sins I'll part;
Break, O, break, my bleeding heart.

SPANISH HYMN. 7s. 8 L.

19. 7s. J. TAYLOR.

FATHER of our feeble race,
 Wise, beneficent, and kind,
Spread o'er nature's ample face,
 Flows thy goodness unconfined:
Musing in the silent grove,
 Or the busy walks of men,
Still we trace thy wondrous love,
 Claiming large returns again.

2 Lord, what offerings shall we bring,
 At thine altars when we bow —
Hearts, the pure, unsullied spring,
 Whence the kind affections flow;
Soft compassion's feeling soul,
 By the melting eye expressed;
Sympathy, at whose control
 Sorrow leaves the wounded breast; —

3 Willing hands to lead the blind,
 Heal the wounded, feed the poor;
Love, embracing all our kind;
 Charity, with liberal store?
Teach us, O thou heavenly King,
 Thus to show our grateful mind,
Thus th' accepted offering bring, —
 Love to thee and all mankind.

285. 7s. C. WESLEY.

1 JESUS, refuge of my soul,
 Let me to thy bosom fly,
While the raging billows roll,
 While the tempest still is high:
Hide me, O my Saviour, hide,
 Till the storm of life is past;
Safe into the haven guide;
 O, receive my soul at last.

2 Other refuge have I none;
 Hangs my helpless soul on thee;
Leave, ah, leave me not alone;
 Still support and comfort me:
All my trust on thee is stayed,
 All my help from thee I bring;
Cover my defenceless head
 With the shadow of thy wing.

3 Thou, O Christ, art all I want;
 All in all in thee I find;
Raise the fallen, cheer the faint,
 Heal the sick, and lead the blind:
Just and holy is thy name;
 I am all unrighteousness;
Vile and full of sin I am;
 Thou art full of truth and grace.

BENEVENTO. 7s. Double. S. WEBBE.

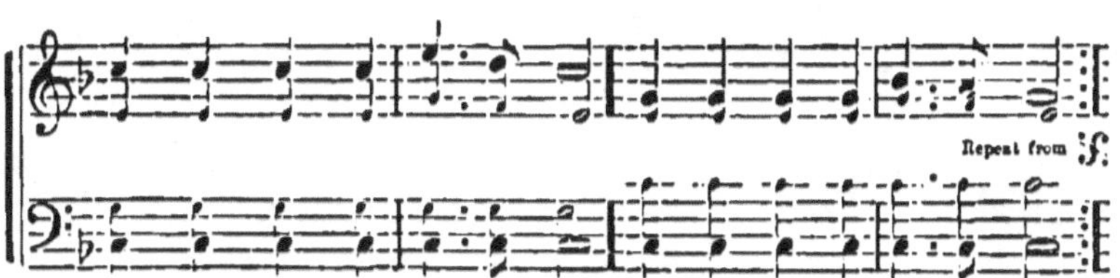

652. 7s. GRANT.

1 SAVIOUR, when, in dust, to thee
Low we bow th' adoring knee, —
When, repentant, to the skies
Scarce we lift our streaming eyes, —
O, by all thy pain and woe
Suffered once for man below,
Bending from thy throne on high,
Hear us when to thee we cry.

2 By thine hour of dark despair;
By thine agony of prayer;
By the cross, the nail, the thorn,
Piercing spear, and torturing scorn;
By the gloom that veiled the skies
O'er the dreadful sacrifice, —
Jesus, look with pitying eye;
Listen to our humble cry.

3 By the deep, expiring groan;
By the sealed, sepulchral stone;
By the vault whose dark abode
Held in vain the rising God, —
O, from earth to heaven restored,
Mighty, re-ascended Lord,
Saviour, Prince, exalted high,
Hear us when to thee we cry.

1049. 7s. NEWTON.

1 WHILE, with ceaseless course, the sun
Hasted through the former year,
Many souls their race have run,
Never more to meet us here:
Fixed in an eternal state,
They have done with all below:
We a little longer wait,
But how little none can know.

2 As the wingéd arrow flies,
Speedily the mark to find;
As the lightning from the skies
Darts, and leaves no trace behind;
Swiftly thus our fleeting days
Bear us down life's rapid stream:
Upward, Lord, our spirits raise;
All below is but a dream.

3 Thanks for mercies past receive;
Pardon of our sins renew;
Teach us, henceforth, how to live,
With eternity in view;
Bless thy word to old and young;
Fill us with a Saviour's love:
When our life's short race is run,
May we dwell with thee above.

STRELITZ. 7s. Double. From Dr. Filitz's‡ Choral Buch, 1846.

‡ The original was in $\frac{3}{2}$ time; may be so performed, as a choral, if preferred.

1083. 7s. Montgomery.

1 "Spirit, leave thy house of clay;
Lingering dust, resign thy breath;
Spirit, cast thy chains away;
Dust, be thou dissolved in death:"
Thus the mighty Saviour speaks,
While the faithful Christian dies;
Thus the bonds of life he breaks,
And the ransomed captive flies.

2 "Prisoner, long detained below,
Prisoner, now with freedom blest,
Welcome from a world of woe;
Welcome to a land of rest:"
Thus the choir of angels sing,
As they bear the soul on high,
While with hallelujahs ring
All the regions of the sky.

3 Grave, the guardian of our dust,
Grave, the treasury of the skies,
Every atom of thy trust
Rests in hope again to rise:
Hark! the judgment trumpet calls—
"Soul, rebuild thy house of clay;
Immortality thy walls,
And eternity thy day."

1176. 7s. Montgomery.

1 Who are these in bright array,
This exulting, happy throng,
Round the altar night and day,
Hymning one triumphant song?—
"Worthy is the Lamb, once slain,
Blessing, honor, glory, power,
Wisdom, riches, to obtain,
New dominion every hour."

2 These through fiery trials trod;
These from great affliction came;
Now, before the throne of God,
Sealed with his almighty name:
Clad in raiment pure and white,
Victor-palms in every hand,
Through their great Redeemer's might,
More than conquerors they stand.

3 Hunger, thirst, disease, unknown,
On immortal fruits they feed;
Them, the Lamb, amidst the throne,
Shall to living fountains lead:
Joy and gladness banish sighs;
Perfect love dispels all fears;
And forever from their eyes
God shall wipe away their tears.

47. 7s. 6 L. NEWTON.

1 SAFELY through another week
 God has brought us on our way;
Let us now a blessing seek,
 Waiting in his courts to-day —
Day of all the week the best,
Emblem of eternal rest.

2 While we seek supplies of grace,
 Through the dear Redeemer's name,
Show thy reconciling face,
 Take away our sin and shame
From our worldly cares set free,
May we rest, this day, in thee.

3 Here we come thy name to praise;
 Let us feel thy presence near;
May thy glory meet our eyes,
 While we in thy house appear
Here afford us, Lord, a taste
Of our everlasting feast.

4 May the gospel's joyful sound
 Conquer sinners, comfort saints,
Make the fruits of grace abound,
 Bring relief from all complaints:
Thus let all our Sabbaths prove,
Till we join the church above.

707. 7s. 6 L. MONTGOMERY.

1 Go to dark Gethsemane,
 Ye that feel temptation's power;
Your Redeemer's conflict see;
 Watch with him one bitter hour:
Turn not from his griefs away;
Learn of Jesus Christ to pray.

2 Follow to the judgment-hall;
 View the Lord of life arraigned:
O, the wormwood and the gall!
 O, the pangs his soul sustained!
Shun not suffering, shame, or loss;
Learn of him to bear the cross.

3 Calvary's mournful mountain climb;
 There, admiring at his feet,
Mark that miracle of time,
 God's own sacrifice complete:
"It is finished," hear him cry;
Learn of Jesus Christ to die.

4 Early hasten to the tomb
 Where they laid his breathless clay;
All is solitude and gloom:
 Who has taken him away?
Christ is risen; he meets our eyes:
Saviour, teach us so to rise.

WORTHING. 8s & 7s. SCHULTZ.

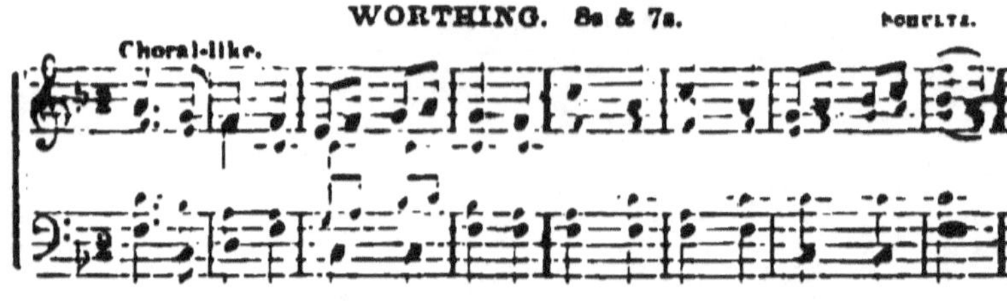

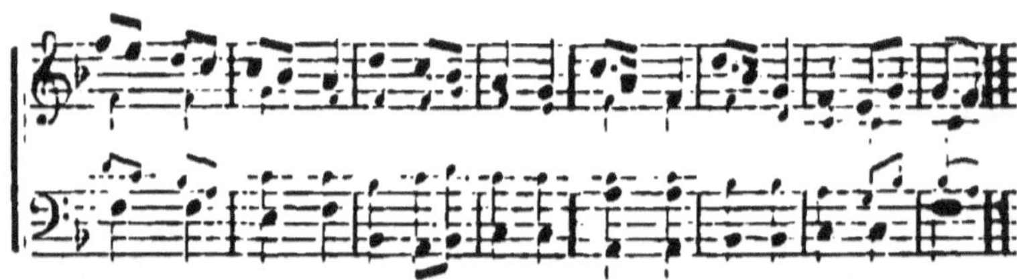

77. 8s & 7s. DUBLIN COL.

1 PRAISE the Lord; ye heavens, adore him;
Praise him, angels, in the height;
Sun and moon, rejoice before him;
Praise him, all ye stars of light.

2 Praise the Lord, for he hath spoken;
Worlds his mighty voice obeyed;
Laws which never can be broken,
For their guidance he hath made.

3 Praise the Lord, for he is glorious;
Never shall his promise fail;
God hath made his saints victorious;
Sin and death shall not prevail.

4 Praise the God of our salvation;
Hosts on high his power proclaim;
Heaven and earth, and all creation,
Praise and magnify his name.

109. 8s & 7s. FAWCETT.

1 PRAISE to thee, thou great Creator;
Praise be thine from every tongue;
Join, my soul, with every creature,
Join the universal song.

2 Father, source of all compassion,
Free, unbounded grace is thine:
Hail, the God of our salvation;
Praise him for his love divine.

3 For ten thousand blessings given,
For the hope of future joy,
Sound his praise through earth and heaven,
Sound Jehovah's praise on high.

4 Joyfully on earth adore him,
Till in heaven our song we raise;
There, enraptured, fall before him,
Lost in wonder, love, and praise.

155. 8s & 7s. BOWRING.

1 GOD is love; his mercy brightens
All the path in which we rove;
Bliss he wakes, and woe he lightens;
God is wisdom, God is love.

2 Chance and change are busy ever;
Man decays, and ages move;
But his mercy waneth never;
God is wisdom, God is love.

3 E'en the hour that darkest seemeth
Will his changeless goodness prove;
From the gloom his brightness streameth;
God is wisdom, God is love.

4 He with earthly cares entwineth
Hope and comfort from above:
Every where his glory shineth;
God is wisdom, God is love.

201. 8s & 7s. CAWOOD.

1 HARK! what mean those holy voices,
Sweetly sounding through the skies?
Lo! th' angelic host rejoices;
Heavenly hallelujahs rise.

2 Hear them tell the wondrous story;
Hear them chant, in hymns of joy
"Glory in the highest — glory!
Glory be to God most high!

3 "Peace on earth, good will from heaven,
Reaching far as man is found,
Souls redeemed, and sins forgiven,"
Loud our golden harps shall sound.

4 "Christ is born, the great Anointed;
Heaven and earth his praises sing;
O, receive whom God appointed,
For your Prophet, Priest, and King."

5 Haste, ye mortals, to adore him ;
Learn his name, and taste his joy ;
Till in heaven ye sing before him,
"Glory be to God most high !"

209. 8s & 7s. EPIS. COL.

1 HAIL, thou long-expected Jesus,
Born to set thy people free !
From our sins and fears release us ;
Let us find our rest in thee.

2 Israel's strength and consolation,
Hope of all the saints, thou art ;
Long desired of every nation,
Joy of every waiting heart.

3 Born thy people to deliver,
Born a child,—yet God our King,—
Born to reign in us forever,
Now thy gracious kingdom bring.

4 By thine own eternal Spirit,
Rule in all our hearts alone ;
By thine all-sufficient merit,
Raise us to thy glorious throne.

271. 8s & 7s. BOWRING.

1 IN the cross of Christ I glory ;
Towering o'er the wrecks of time,
All the light of sacred story
Gathers round its head sublime.

2 When the woes of life o'ertake me,
Hopes deceive and fears annoy,
Never shall the cross forsake me ;
Lo ! it glows with peace and joy.

3 When the sun of bliss is beaming
Light and love upon my way,
From the cross the radiance streaming
Adds new lustre to the day.

4 Bane and blessing, pain and pleasure,
By the cross are sanctified ;
Peace is there that knows no measure,
Joys that through all time abide.

5 In the cross of Christ I glory ;
Towering o'er the wrecks of time,
All the light of sacred story
Gathers round its head sublime.

62. 8s & 7s. NEWTON.

1 MAY the grace of Christ, our Saviour,
And the Father's boundless love,
With the Holy Spirit's favor,
Rest upon us from above.

2 Thus may we abide in union
With each other and the Lord,
And possess, in sweet communion,
Joys which earth cannot afford.

ONCKEN. 8s & 7s. From Oncken's Melodies.

327. 8s & 7s. Kelly.

1 Hark! the notes of angels, singing,
"Glory, glory to the Lamb!"
All in heaven their tribute bringing,
Raising high the Saviour's name.

2 Ye for whom his life is given,
Sacred themes to you belong:
Come, assist the choir of heaven;
Join the everlasting song.

3 Filled with holy emulation,
Let us vie with those above:
Sweet the theme — a free salvation!
Fruit of everlasting love.

4 Endless life in him possessing,
Let us praise his precious name;
Glory, honor, power, and blessing,
Be forever to the Lamb.

GLORIA. Coda for Hymn 327.

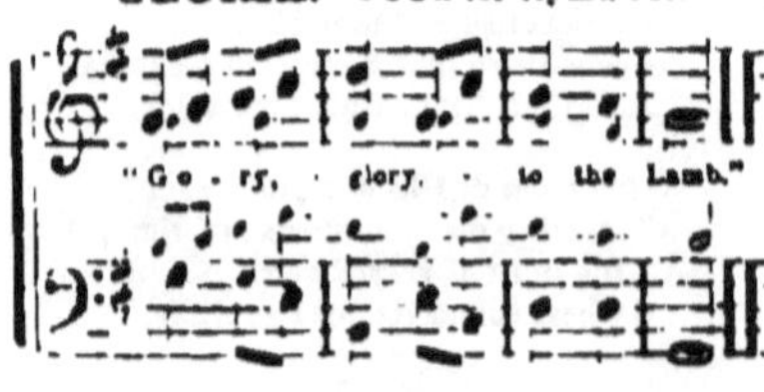

334. 8s & 7s. Pratt's Col.

1 Crown his head with endless blessing,
Who, in God the Father's name,
With compassion never ceasing,
Comes, salvation to proclaim.

2 Lo, Jehovah, we adore thee, —
Thee, our Saviour, — thee, our God;
From thy throne let beams of glory
Shine through all the world abroad.

3 Jesus, thee our Saviour hailing,
Thee our God, in praise we own;
Highest honors, never failing,
Rise eternal round thy throne.

4 Now, ye saints, his power confessing,
In your grateful strains adore;
For his mercy, never ceasing
Flows, and flows forevermore.

345 8s & 7s. Lock Hosp. Col.

1 Jesus, hail! enthroned in glory,
There forever to abide;
All the heavenly host adore thee
Seated at thy Father's side.

2 There for sinners thou art pleading,
There thou dost our place prepare;
Ever for us interceding,
Till in glory we appear.

3 Worship, honor, power, and blessing,
Thou art worthy to receive;
Loudest praises, without ceasing,
Meet it is for us to give.

4 Help, ye bright, angelic spirits;
Bring your sweetest, noblest lays;
Help to sing our Saviour's merits,
Help to chant Immanuel's praise.

CODA. For Hymn 345.

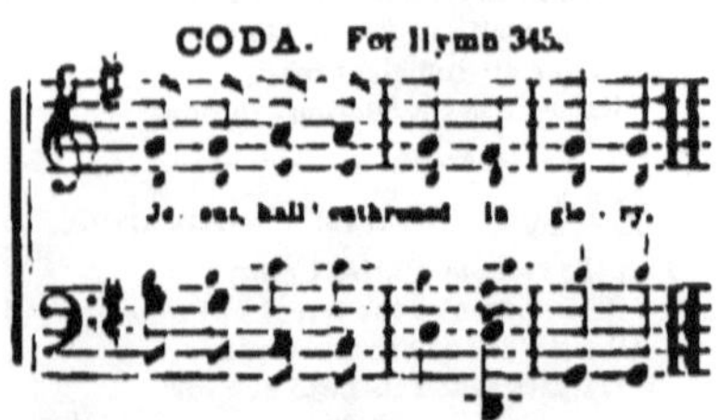

FAIRFAX. 8s & 7s. Standard Psalm Tune Book.

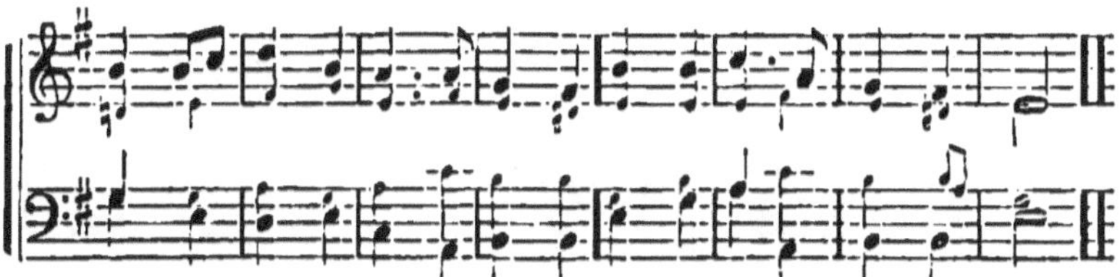

227. 8s & 7s. BICKERSTETH'S COL.

1 "STRICKEN, smitten, and afflicted,"
Lo! he dies upon the tree.
'Tis the Christ by man rejected;
Yes, believers — yes, 'tis he.

2 'Tis the long-expected Saviour,
David's Son and David's Lord,
Sacrificed to bring us favor;
'Tis a true and faithful word.

3 Tell us, ye who heard him groaning,
Was there ever grief like his?
Friends through fear his cause disowning,
Foes insulting his distress.

4 Many hands conspired to wound him;
None would interpose to save;
But the heaviest stroke that found him
Was the stroke that justice gave.

5 Mark the sacrifice appointed;
See! — who bears the awful load?
'Tis the Word, the Lord's Anointed,
Son of man and Son of God.

6 Lamb of God, for sinners wounded,
Sacrifice which cancels guilt,
None shall ever be confounded
Who on thee their hopes have built.

SICILY. 8s & 7s. MOZART. From a Latin Hymn.

ONCKEN. 8s & 7s. From Oncken's Melodies.

610. 8s & 7s. Robinson.

1 Come, thou Fount of every blessing,
Tune my heart to sing thy grace;
Streams of mercy, never ceasing,
Call for songs of loudest praise.

2 Teach me some melodious measure,
Sung by raptured saints above;
Fill my soul with sacred pleasure,
While I sing redeeming love.

3 By thy hand sustained, defended,
Safe through life, thus far, I've come;
Safely, Lord, when life is ended,
Bring me to my heavenly home.

4 Jesus sought me when a stranger,
Wandering from the fold of God;
He, to save my soul from danger,
Interposed his precious blood.

5 O, to grace how great a debtor
Daily I'm constrained to be!
Let thy grace, Lord, like a fetter,
Bind my wandering heart to thee.

6 Prone to wander, Lord, I feel it;
Prone to leave the God I love;
Here's my heart; O, take and seal it;
Seal it from thy courts above.

651. 8s & 7s. Toplady.

1 Light of those whose dreary dwelling
Borders on the shades of death,
Come, and, by thyself revealing,
Dissipate the clouds beneath.

2 Thou, new heaven and earth's Creator
In our deepest darkness rise,
Scattering all the night of nature,
Pouring day upon oureyes.

3 Still we wait for thy appearing;
Life and joy thy beams impart,
Chasing all our fears, and cheering
Every poor, benighted heart.

4 Come, extend thy wonted favor
To our ruined, guilty race;
Come, thou blest, exalted Saviour,
Come, apply thy saving grace.

5 By thine all-atoning merit
Every burdened soul release;
By the teachings of thy Spirit
Guide us into perfect peace.

674. 8s & 7s. Pratt's Col.

1 Let thy grace, Lord, make me lowly,
Humble all my swelling pride:
Fallen, guilty, and unholy,
Greatness from my eyes I'll hide.

2 I'll forbid my vain aspiring,
Nor at earthly honors aim,
No ambitious heights desiring,
Far above my humble claim.

3 Weaned from earth's delusive pleasures,
In thy love I'll seek for mine;
Placed in heaven my nobler treasures,
Earth I quietly resign.

4 Thus the transient world despising,
On the Lord my hopes rely;
Thus my joys, from him arising,
Like himself, shall never die.

MT. VERNON.

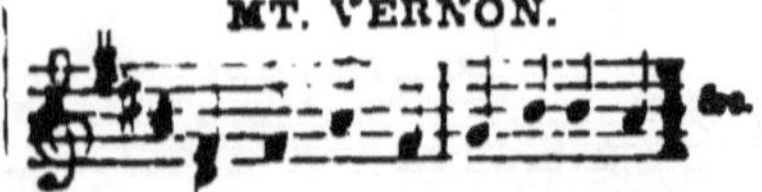

SICILY. 8s & 7s. MOZART. From a Latin Hymn.

711. 8s & 7s. J. TAYLOR.

1 FAR from mortal cares retreating,
Sordid hopes and vain desires,
Here, our willing footsteps meeting,
Every heart to heaven aspires.

2 From the fount of glory beaming,
Light celestial cheers our eyes,
Mercy from above proclaiming
Peace and pardon from the skies.

3 Who may share this great salvation?
Every pure and humble mind,
Every kindred, tongue, and nation,
From the stains of guilt refined.

4 Blessings all around bestowing,
God withholds his care from none,
Grace and mercy ever flowing
From the fountain of his throne.

871. 8s & 7s. URWICK'S COL.

1 O THOU Sun of glorious splendor,
Shine with healing in thy wing;
Chase away these shades of darkness;
Holy light and comfort bring.

2 Let the heralds of salvation
Round the world with joy proclaim,
"Death and hell are spoiled and vanquished
Through the great Immanuel's name."

3 Take thy power, almighty Saviour;
Claim the nations for thine own;
Reign, thou Lord of life and glory,
Till each heart becomes thy throne.

4 Then the earth, o'erspread with glory,
Decked with heavenly splendor bright,
Shall be made Jehovah's dwelling—
As at first, the Lord's delight.

MELODIEN. 8s & 7s. GERMAN.

WORTHING. 8s & 7s. SCHULTZ.

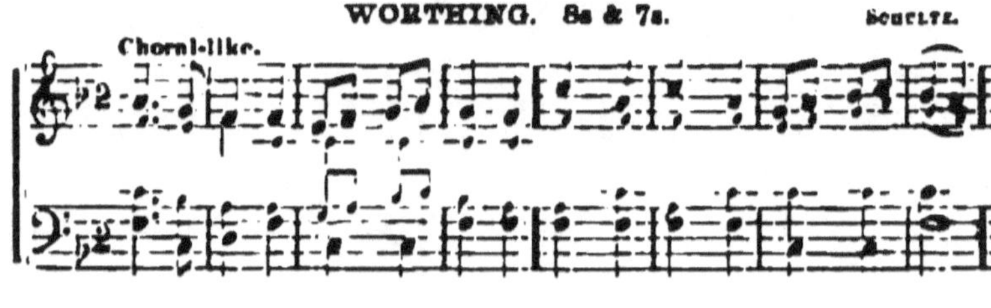

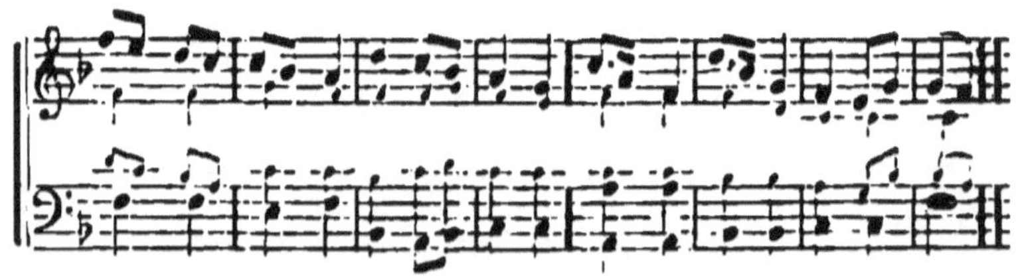

806. 8s & 7s. J. FAWCETT.

1 HUMBLE souls, who seek salvation
Through the Lamb's redeeming blood,
Hear the voice of revelation;
Tread the path that Jesus trod.

2 Hear the blest Redeemer call you;
Listen to his heavenly voice;
Dread no ills that can befall you,
While you make his ways your choice.

3 Plainly here his footsteps tracing,
Follow him without delay,
Gladly his command embracing;
Lo! your Captain leads the way.

819. 8s & 7s. FELLOWS.

1 JESUS, mighty King in Zion,
Thou alone our Guide shalt be;
Thy commission we rely on;
We would follow none but thee.

2 As an emblem of thy passion,
And thy victory o'er the grave,
We, who know thy great salvation,
Are baptized beneath the wave.

3 Fearless of the world's despising,
We the ancient path pursue,
Buried with our Lord, and rising
To a life divinely new.

930. 8s & 7s. NEWTON.

1 GLORIOUS things of thee are spoken,
Zion, city of our God;
He whose word can ne'er be broken
Chose thee for his own abode.

2 Lord, thy church is still thy dwelling,
Still is precious in thy sight,
Judah's temple far excelling,
Beaming with the gospel's light.

3 On the Rock of Ages founded,
What can shake her sure repose?
With salvation's wall surrounded,
She can smile at all her foes.

4 See, the streams of living waters,
Springing from eternal love,
Well supply her sons and daughters,
And all fear of want remove.

5 Round her habitation hovering,
See the cloud and fire appear,
For a glory and a covering,
Showing that the Lord is near.

6 Glorious things of thee are spoken,
Zion, city of our God;
He whose word can ne'er be broken
Chose thee for his own abode.

991. 8s & 7s. CROSBY.

1 LORD of heaven, and earth, and ocean,
Hear us from thy bright abode,
While our hearts, with true devotion,
Own their great and gracious God.

2 Health and every needful blessing
Are thy bounteous gifts alone;
Comforts undeserved possessing,
Here we bend before thy throne.

3 Thee, with humble adoration,
Lord, we praise for mercies past;
Still to this most favored nation
May those mercies ever last.

VESPER HYMN. 8s & 7s.

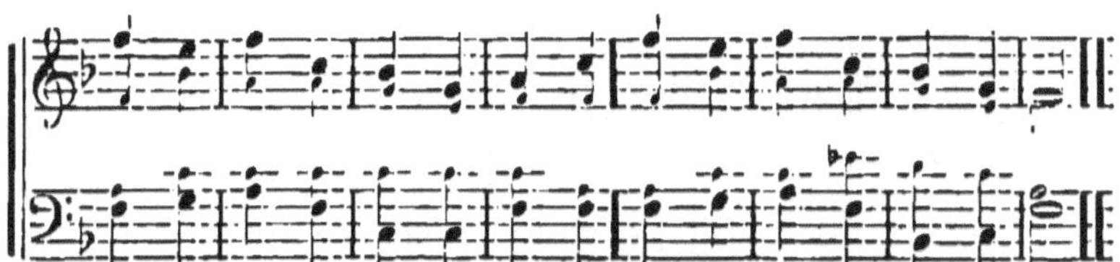

1032. 8s & 7s. EDMESTON.

1 SAVIOUR, breathe an evening blessing
Ere repose our spirits seal;
Sin and want we come confessing;
Thou canst save and thou canst heal.

2 Though destruction walk around us,
Though the arrows past us fly,
Angel guards from thee surround us;
We are safe, if thou art nigh.

3 Though the night be dark and dreary
Darkness cannot hide from thee;
Thou art he who, never weary,
Watcheth where thy people be.

4 Should swift death this night o'ertake us,
And command us to the tomb,
May the morn in heaven awake us,
Clad in bright, eternal bloom.

1041. 8s & 7s. HORNE.

1 SEE the leaves around us falling,
Dry and withered, to the ground,
Thus to thoughtless mortals calling,
In a sad and solemn sound, —

2 "Youth, on length of days presuming,
Who the paths of pleasure tread,
View us, late in beauty blooming,
Numbered now among the dead.

3 "What though yet no losses grieve you —
Gay with health and many a grace;
Let not cloudless skies deceive you;
Summer gives to autumn place."

4 On the tree of life eternal
Let our highest hopes be stayed:
This alone, forever vernal,
Bears a leaf that shall not fade.

FAIRFAX. 7s. Standard Ps. Tune Book.

SAXONIA. 8s & 7s. NAUMANN.

* These slurs for 2nd line only.

1096. 8s & 7s. S. F. SMITH.

1 SISTER, thou wast mild and lovely,
Gentle as the summer breeze,
Pleasant as the air of evening,
When it floats among the trees.

2 Peaceful be thy silent slumber —
Peaceful in the grave so low:
Thou no more wilt join our number;
Thou no more our songs shalt know.

3 Dearest sister, thou hast left us;
Here thy loss we deeply feel;
But 'tis God that hath bereft us:
He can all our sorrows heal.

4 Yet again we hope to meet thee,
When the day of life is fled,
Then in heaven with joy to greet thee,
Where no farewell tear is shed.

1107. 8s & 7s. BAP. MEMORIAL.

1 BROTHER, rest from sin and sorrow;
Death is o'er, and life is won;
On thy slumber dawns no morrow:
Rest; thine earthly race is run.

2 Brother, wake; the night is waning;
Endless day is round thee poured;
Enter thou the rest remaining
For the people of the Lord.

3 Brother, wake; for He who loved thee, —
He who died that thou mightst live, —
He who graciously approved thee, —
Waits thy crown of joy to give.

4 Fare thee well; though woe is blending
With the tones of earthly love,
Triumph high, and joy unending
Wait thee in the realms above.

1112. 8s & 7s. COLLYER.

1 CEASE, ye mourners, cease to languish
O'er the grave of those you love;
Pain, and death, and night, and anguish,
Enter not the world above.

2 While our silent steps are straying,
Lonely, through night's deepening shade,
Glory's brightest beams are playing
Round the happy Christian's head.

3 Light and peace at once deriving
From the hand of God most high,
In his glorious presence living,
They shall never, never die.

4 Endless pleasure, pain excluding,
Sickness, there, no more can come;
There, no fear of woe intruding,
Sheds o'er heaven a moment's gloom.

1117. 8s & 7s. L. H. SIGOURNEY.

1 PASTOR, thou art from us taken
In the glory of thy years,
As the oak, by tempest shaken,
Falls ere time its verdure sears.

2 Here where oft thy lip hath taught us
Of the Lamb who died to save, —
Where thy guiding hand hath brought us
To the deep, baptismal wave, —

3 Pale and cold, we see thee lying
In God's temple, once so dear,
And the mourners' bitter sighing
Falls unheeded on thine ear.

4 All thy love and zeal, to lead us
Where immortal fountains flow,
And on living bread to feed us,
In our fond remembrance glow.

5 May the conquering faith that cheered thee
When thy foot on Jordan pressed,
Guide our spirits while we leave thee
In the tomb that Jesus blessed.

MT. VERNON.

GREENVILLE. 8s & 7s. Double. ROUSSEAU. Previous to 1778.

341. 8s & 7s. ROBINSON.

1 MIGHTY God, while angels bless thee,
May a mortal lisp thy name?
Lord of men as well as angels,
Thou art every creature's theme:
Lord of every land and nation,
Ancient of eternal days,
Sounded through the wide creation
Be thy just and lawful praise.

2 For the grandeur of thy nature, —
Grand beyond a seraph's thought, —
For the wonders of creation, —
Works with skill and kindness wrought, —
For thy providence, that governs
Through thine empire's wide domain,
Wings an angel, guides a sparrow, —
Blessèd be thy gentle reign.

3 For thy rich, thy free redemption, —
Bright, though veiled in darkness long, —
Thought is poor, and poor expression;
Who can sing that wondrous song?
Brightness of the Father's glory,
Shall thy praise unuttered lie?
Break, my tongue, such guilty silence;
Sing the Lord who came to die; —

4 From the highest throne of glory,
To the cross of deepest woe,
Came to ransom guilty captives; —
Flow, my praise, forever flow:
Re-ascend, immortal Saviour,
Leave thy footstool, take thy throne;
Thence return and reign forever;
Be the kingdom all thy own.

530. 8s & 7s. MONTGOMERY.

1 JESUS, I my cross have taken,
All to leave, and follow thee;
Naked, poor, despised, forsaken,
Thou, from hence, my all shalt be:
And whilst thou shalt smile upon me,
God of wisdom, love, and might,
Foes may hate and friends disown me;
Show thy face, and all is bright.

2 Man may trouble and distress me;
'Twill but drive me to thy breast:
Life with trials hard may press me;
Heaven will bring me sweeter rest:
O, 'tis not in grief to harm me,
While thy love is left to me;
O, 'twere not in joy to charm me,
Were that joy unmixed with thee.

568. 8s & 7s. GRANT.

1 KNOW, my soul, thy full salvation;
Rise o'er sin, and fear, and care;
Joy to find, in every station,
Something still to do or bear:
Think what Spirit dwells within thee;
Think what Father's smiles are thine;
Think what Jesus did to win thee:
Child of heaven, canst thou repine?

2 Haste thee on from grace to glory,
Armed by faith and winged by prayer;
Heaven's eternal day's before thee;
God's own hand shall guide thee there:
Soon shall close thy earthly mission;
Soon shall pass thy pilgrim days;
Hope shall change to glad fruition,
Faith to sight, and prayer to praise.

653. 8s & 7s. C. WESLEY.

1 LOVE divine, all love excelling,
Joy of heaven, to earth come down;
Fix us in thy humble dwelling;
All thy faithful mercies crown:
Jesus, thou art all compassion;
Pure, unbounded love thou art;
Visit us with thy salvation;
Enter every trembling heart.

2 Breathe, O, breathe thy Holy Spirit
Into every troubled breast;
Let us all thy grace inherit;
Let us find thy promised rest:
Take away the love of sinning;
Take our load of guilt away;
End the work of thy beginning;
Bring us to eternal day.

3 Carry on thy new creation;
Pure and holy may we be;
Let us see our whole salvation
Perfectly secured by thee;
Change from glory into glory,
Till in heaven we take our place,
Till we cast our crowns before thee,
Lost in wonder, love, and praise.

883. 8s & 7s. L. H. SIGOURNEY.

1 ONWARD, onward, men of heaven;
Bear the gospel banner high;
Rest not till its light is given —
Star of every pagan sky:
Send it where the pilgrim stranger
Faints beneath the torrid ray;
Bid the hardy forest ranger
Hail it, ere he fades away.

2 Where the Arctic Ocean thunders,
Where the tropics fiercely glow,
Broadly spread its page of wonders,
Brightly bid its radiance flow:
India marks its lustre stealing;
Shivering Greenland loves its rays;
Afric, 'mid her deserts kneeling,
Lifts the untaught strain of praise.

3 Rude in speech, or wild in feature
Dark in spirit, though they be,
Show that light to every creature —
Prince or vassal, bond or free:
Lo! they haste to every nation;
Host on host the ranks supply;
Onward! Christ is your salvation,
And your death is victory.

965. 8s & 7s. ANON.

1 We have met in peace together
In this house of God again;
Constant friends have led us hither,
Here to chant the solemn strain;
Here to breathe our adoration,
Here the Saviour's praise to sing;
May the Spirit of salvation
Come with healing in his wing.

2 We have met, and Time is flying;
We shall part, and still his wing,
Sweeping o'er the dead and dying,
Will the changeful seasons bring:
Let us, while our hearts are lightest,
In our fresh and early years,
Turn to Him whose smile is brightest,
And whose grace will calm our fears.

3 He will aid us, should existence
With its sorrows sting the breast;
Gleaming in the onward distance,
Faith will mark the land of rest:
There, 'midst day beams round him playing,
We our Father's face shall see,
And shall hear him gently saying,
"Little children, come to me."

9. DOXOLOGY. 8s & 7s.

Praise the God of all creation;
Praise the Father's boundless love;
Praise the Lamb, our expiation —
Priest and King, enthroned above;
Praise the Fountain of salvation —
Him by whom our spirits live;
Undivided adoration
To the one Jehovah give.

SPANISH HYMN. 7s & 4.

228. 7s & 4. G. F. HEAD.

1 Hark! from yonder mount arise
Notes of sadness — Jesus dies!
On the cross the Lord of lords
Love for guilty man records;
Sinner, sinner,
Hear your dying Saviour's words.

2 "Mortal, for your guilt I die —
Guilt that dared your God defy;
Blood for you I freely give;
Death I taste that you may live;
Will you, sinner,
Free salvation now receive?"

1084. 7s & 4. MRS. GILBERT.

1 When the vale of death appears,
Faint and cold this mortal clay,
Blest Redeemer, soothe my fears,
Light me through the gloomy way;
Break the shadows,
Usher in eternal day; —

2 Upward from this dying state
Bid my waiting soul aspire;
Open thou the crystal gate;
To thy praise attune my lyre:
Then, triumphant,
I will join th' immortal choir.

GREENVILLE. 8s, 7s & 4.

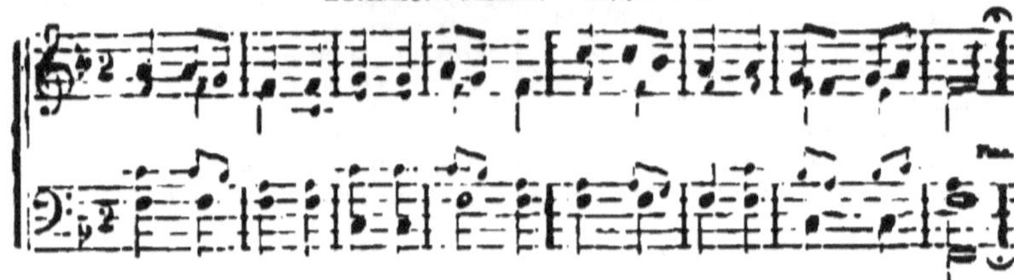

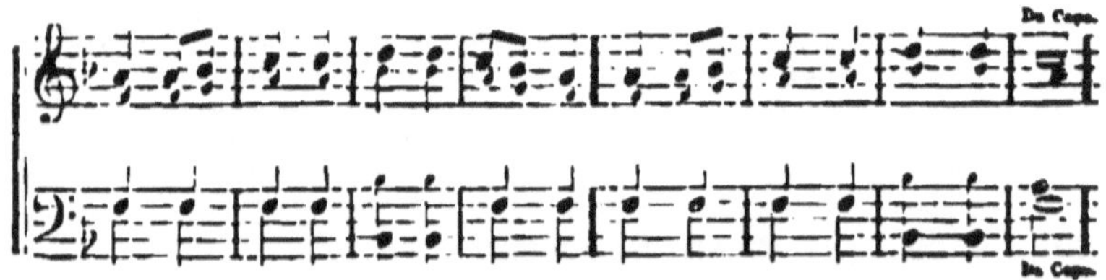

23. 8s, 7s & 4. KELLY.

1 IN thy name, O Lord, assembling,
We, thy people, now draw near;
Teach us to rejoice with trembling;
Speak, and let thy servants hear,—
Hear with meekness,—
Hear thy word with godly fear.

2 While our days on earth are lengthened,
May we give them, Lord, to thee;
Cheered by hope, and daily strengthened,
We would run, nor weary be,
Till thy glory,
Without clouds, in heaven, we see.

3 There, in worship purer, sweeter,
All thy people shall adore,
Tasting of enjoyment greater
Than they could conceive before,—
Full enjoyment,—
Holy bliss, forevermore.

3 Then, whene'er the signal's given
Us from earth to call away,
Borne on angels' wings, to heaven,—
Glad the summons to obey,—
May we ever
Reign with Christ in endless day.

63. 8s, 7s & 4. JAY.

1 COME, thou soul-transforming Spirit,
Bless the sower and the seed;
Let each heart thy grace inherit;
Raise the weak, the hungry feed;
From the gospel
Now supply thy people's need.

2 O, may all enjoy the blessing
Which thy word's designed to give,
Let us all, thy love possessing,
Joyfully the truth receive,
And forever
To thy praise and glory live.

---

65. 8s, 7s & 4. BURDER.

1 LORD, dismiss us with thy blessing;
Fill our hearts with joy and peace;
Let us each, thy love possessing,
Triumph in redeeming grace:
O, refresh us,
Travelling through this wilderness.

2 Thanks we give, and adoration,
For thy gospel's joyful sound;
May the fruits of thy salvation
In our hearts and lives abound;
May thy presence
With us evermore be found.

204. 8s, 7s & 4. MONTGOMERY.

1 ANGELS! from the realms of glory
Wing your flight o'er all the earth;
Ye, who sang creation's story,
Now proclaim Messiah's birth:
Come and worship—
Worship Christ, the new-born King.

2 Shepherds, in the field abiding,
Watching o'er your flocks by night,
God with man is now residing;
Yonder shines the heavenly light:
Come and worship—
Worship Christ, the new-born King.

SOMERSET STREET. 8s, 7s & 4. From Oncken's Melodies.

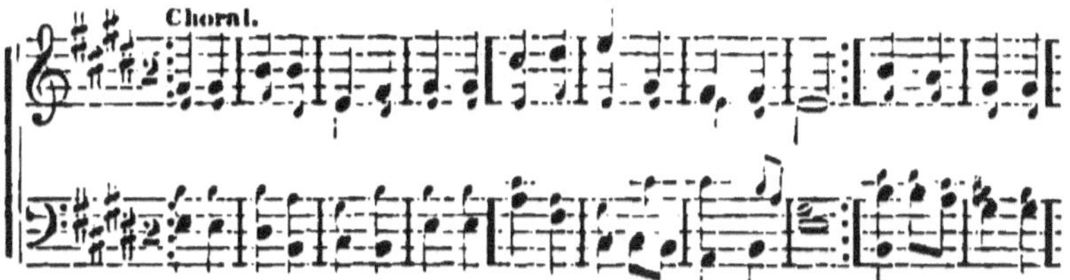

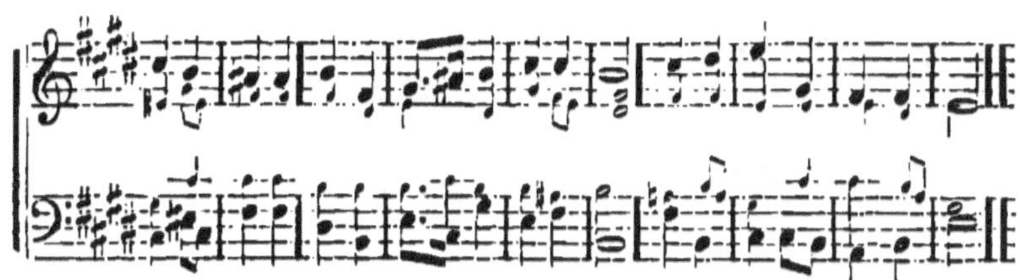

3 Saints, before the altar bending,
Watching long in hope and fear,
Suddenly the Lord, descending,
In his temple shall appear:
Come and worship —
Worship Christ, the new-born King.

4 Sinners, bowed in true repentance,
Doomed for guilt to endless pains,
Justice now revokes the sentence;
Mercy calls you; break your chains:
Come and worship —
Worship Christ, the new-born King.

225. 8s, 7s & 4. Francis.

1 Hark! the voice of love and mercy
Sounds aloud from Calvary:
See! it rends the rocks asunder,
Shakes the earth, and veils the sky:
"It is finished!"
Hear the dying Saviour cry.

2 "It is finished!" — O, what pleasure
Do these charming words afford!
Heavenly blessings, without measure,
Flow to us through Christ the Lord:
"It is finished!"
Saints, the dying words record.

3 Tune your harps anew, ye seraphs;
Join to sing the pleasing theme:
All in earth and heaven uniting,
Join to praise Immanuel's name:
Hallelujah!
Glory to the bleeding Lamb!

286. 8s, 7s & 4. Kelly.

1 See from Zion's sacred mountain,
Streams of living water flow;
God has opened there a fountain
That supplies the plains below:
They are blessèd
Who its sovereign virtues know.

2 Through ten thousand channels flowing,
Streams of mercy find their way;
Life, and health, and joy bestowing,
Making all around look gay:
O ye nations,
Hail the long-expected day.

3 Gladdened by the flowing treasure,
All-enriching as it goes,
Lo! the desert smiles with pleasure,
Buds and blossoms as the rose:
Every object
Sings for joy, where'er it flows.

4 Trees of life, the banks adorning,
Yield their fruit to all around;
Those who eat are saved from mourning;
Pleasure comes, and hopes abound:
Fair their portion —
Endless life with glory crowned.

HAMDEN.

TAMWORTH. 8s, 7s & 4. LOCKHART.

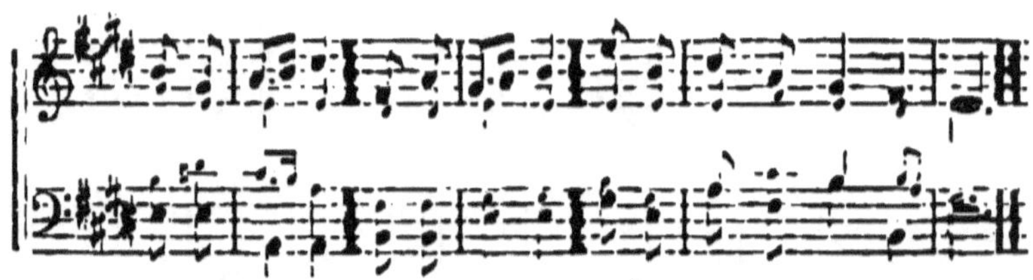

336. 8s, 7s & 4. KELLY.

1 LOOK, ye saints; — the sight is glorious; —
See the Man of sorrows now,
From the fight returned victorious;
Every knee to him shall bow:
Crown him, crown him;
Crowns become the Victor's brow.

2 Crown the Saviour, angels, crown him;
Rich the trophies Jesus brings;
In the seat of power enthrone him,
While the heavenly concave rings:
Crown him, crown him;
Crown the Saviour King of kings.

3 Sinners in derision crowned him,
Mocking thus the Saviour's claim;
Saints and angels crowd around him,
Own his title, praise his name:
Crown him, crown him;
Spread abroad the Victor's fame.

4 Hark! those bursts of acclamation!
Hark! those loud, triumphant chords!
Jesus takes the highest station;
O, what joy the sight affords!
Crown him, crown him,
King of kings, and Lord of lords.

340. 8s, 7s & 4. KELLY.

1 GLORY, glory everlasting,
Be to Him who bore the cross,
Who redeemed our souls by tasting
Death, — the death deserved by us:
Sound his glory,
While the soul with transport glows.

2 Jesus' love is love unbounded,
Without measure, without end;
Human thought is here confounded;
'Tis too vast to comprehend;
Praise the Saviour;
Magnify the sinner's Friend.

3 While we hear the wondrous story
Of the Saviour's cross and shame,
Sing we, "Everlasting glory
Be to God and to the Lamb!"
Saints and angels,
Give ye glory to his name.

---

606. 8s, 7s & 4. OLIVER.

1 GUIDE me, O thou great Jehovah,
Pilgrim through this barren land:
I am weak, but thou art mighty;
Hold me with thy powerful hand:
Bread of heaven,
Feed me till I want no more.

2 Open now the crystal fountain
Whence the healing streams do flow;
Let the fiery, cloudy pillar
Lead me all my journey through:
Strong Deliverer,
Be thou still my strength and shield.

3 When I tread the verge of Jordan,
Bid my anxious fears subside;
Bear me through the swelling current;
Land me safe on Canaan's side:
Songs of praises
I will ever give to thee.

OLIVER STREET. 8s, 7s & 4. GERMAN.

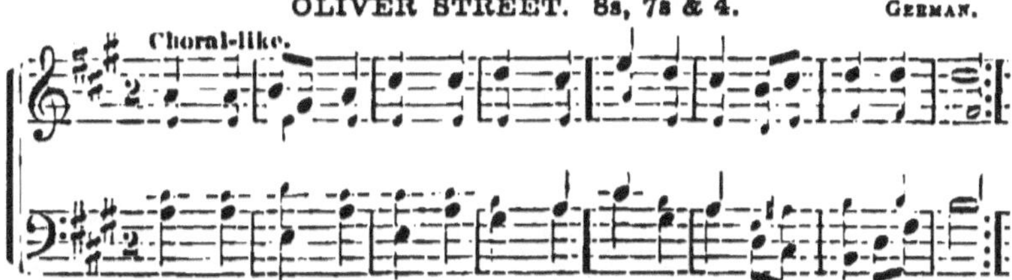

753. 8s, 7s & 4. FAWCETT.

1 O MY soul, what means this sadness?
Wherefore art thou thus cast down?
Let thy griefs be turned to gladness;
Bid thy restless fears be gone;
Look to Jesus,
And rejoice in his dear name.

2 What though Satan's strong temptations
Vex and grieve thee day by day,
And thy sinful inclinations
Often fill thee with dismay;
Thou shalt conquer,
Through the Lamb's redeeming blood.

3 Though ten thousand ills beset thee,
From without and from within,
Jesus saith he'll ne'er forget thee,
But will save from hell and sin;
He is faithful
To perform his gracious word.

4 Though distresses now attend thee,
And thou tread the thorny road,
His right hand shall still defend thee;
Soon he'll bring thee home to God;
Therefore praise him,
Praise the great Redeemer's name.

777. 8s, 7s & 4. UNION MINSTREL.

1 CHILDREN, hear the melting story
Of the Lamb that once was slain;
'Tis the Lord of life and glory:
Shall he plead with you in vain?
O, receive him,
And salvation now obtain.

2 Yield no more to sin and folly,
So displeasing in his sight:
Jesus loves the pure and holy;
They alone are his delight;
Seek his favor,
And your hearts to him unite.

3 All your sins to him confessing
Who is ready to forgive,
Seek the Saviour's richest blessing;
On his precious name believe:
He is waiting;
Will you not his grace receive?

---

439. 8s, 7s & 4. REED.

1 HEAR, O sinner! Mercy hails you;
Now with sweetest voice she calls;
Bids you haste to seek the Saviour,
Ere the hand of justice falls:
Trust in Jesus;
'Tis the voice of Mercy calls.

2 Haste, O sinner, to the Saviour;
Seek his mercy while you may;
Soon the day of grace is over;
Soon your life will pass away:
Haste to Jesus;
You must perish if you stay.

FENWICK.

UNION CHURCH. 8s, 7s & 4. Edw. Hamilton. From the Sanctus.

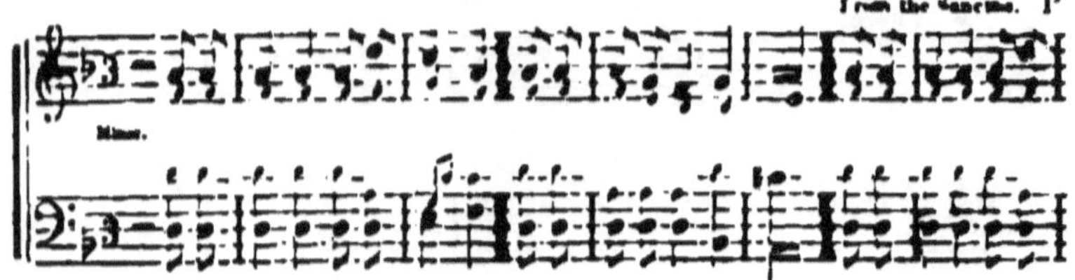

Comp. for Hymn 449.

449. 8s, 7s & 4. Allen.

1 Sinners, will you scorn the message
Sent in mercy from above?
Every sentence, O, how tender!
Every line is full of love:
Listen to it;
Every line is full of love.

2 Hear the heralds of the gospel
News from Zion's King proclaim
"Pardon to each rebel sinner;
Free forgiveness in his name:"
How important!
"Free forgiveness in his name."

3 Tempted souls, they bring you succor;
Fearful hearts, they quell your fears;
And, with news of consolation,
Chase away the falling tears;
Tender heralds,
Chase away the falling tears.

4 Who hath our report believéd?
Who received the joyful word?
Who embraced the news of pardon
Offered to you by the Lord?
Can you slight it,
Offered to you by the Lord?

5 O ye angels, hovering round us,
Waiting spirits, speed your way;
Haste ye to the court of heaven;
Tidings bear without delay:
Rebel sinners
Glad the message will obey.

416. 8s, 7s & 4. Hart.

1 Come, ye sinners, poor and wretched,
Come in mercy's gracious hour;
Jesus ready stands to save you,
Full of pity, love, and power:
He is able —
He is willing — doubt no more.

2 Let no sense of guilt prevent you,
Nor of fitness fondly dream;
All the fitness he requireth
Is to feel your need of him:
This he gives you;
'Tis the Spirit's rising beam.

3 Agonizing in the garden,
Lo! your Saviour prostrate lies;
On the bloody tree behold him;
There he groans, and bleeds, and dies:
"It is finished;"
Heaven's atoning sacrifice.

4 Lo! th' incarnate God, ascended,
Pleads the merit of his blood;
Venture on him — venture wholly;
Let no other trust intrude:
None but Jesus
Can do helpless sinners good.

HAMDEN.

WILMOT. 8s, 7s & 4. WEBER.

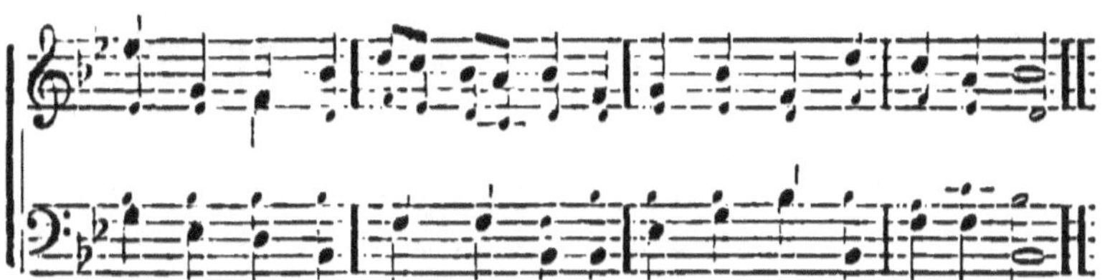

795. 8s, 7s & 4. KELLY.

1 ZION stands with hills surrounded—
Zion, kept by power divine:
All her foes shall be confounded,
Though the world in arms combine:
Happy Zion,
What a favored lot is thine!

2 Every human tie may perish;
Friend to friend unfaithful prove;
Mothers cease their own to cherish;
Heaven and earth at last remove;
But no changes
Can attend Jehovah's love.

3 In the furnace God may prove thee,
Thence to bring thee forth more bright,
But can never cease to love thee;
Thou art precious in his sight:
God is with thee—
God, thine everlasting light.

817. 8s, 7s & 4. J. E. GILES.

1 THOU hast said, exalted Jesus,
"Take thy cross and follow me;"
Shall the word with terror seize us?
Shall we from the burden flee?
Lord, I'll take it,
And, rejoicing, follow thee.

2 While this liquid tomb surveying,
Emblem of my Saviour's grave,
Shall I shun its brink, betraying
Feelings worthy of a slave?
No! I'll enter:
Jesus entered Jordan's wave.

3 Blest the sign which thus reminds me,
Saviour, of thy love for me;
But more blest the love that binds me
In its deathless bonds to thee:
O, what pleasure,
Buried with my Lord to be!

4 Should it rend some fond connection,
Should I suffer shame or loss,
Yet the fragrant, blest reflection,
I have been where Jesus was,
Will revive me
When I faint beneath the cross.

5 Fellowship with him possessing,
Let me die to earth and sin;
Let me rise t' enjoy the blessing
Which the faithful soul shall win:
May I ever
Follow where my Lord has been.

815. 8s, 7s & 4. S. S. CUTTING.

1 GRACIOUS Saviour, we adore thee;
Purchased by thy precious blood,
We present ourselves before thee,
Now to walk the narrow road:
Saviour, guide us—
Guide us to our heavenly home.

2 Thou didst mark our path of duty;
Thou wast laid beneath the wave;
Thou didst rise in glorious beauty
From the semblance of the grave;
May we follow
In the same delightful way.

JOHN CAMPBELL.

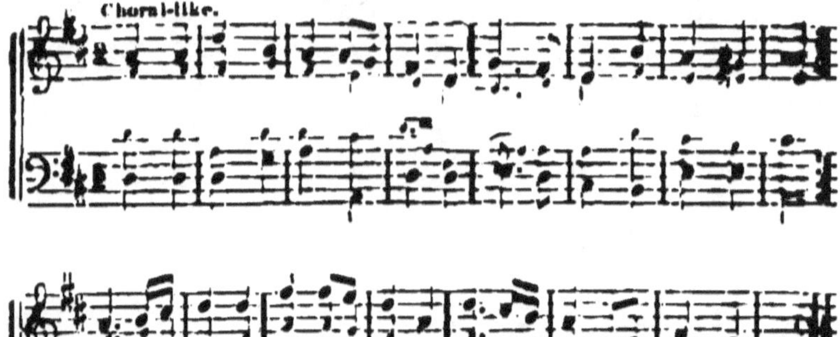

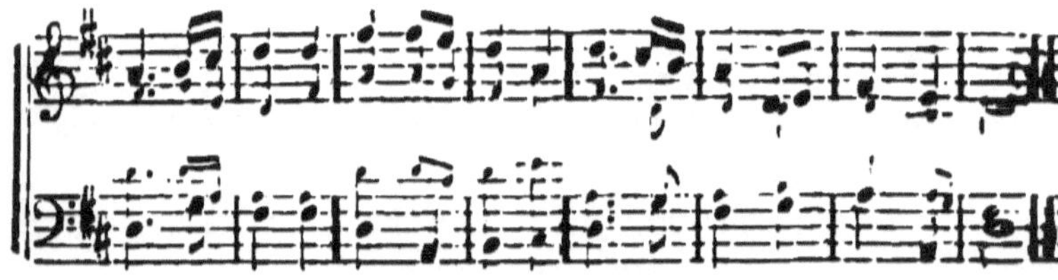

868. 8s, 7s & 4. J. RYLAND.

1 GIRD thy sword on, mighty Saviour;
Make the word of truth thy car;
Prosper in thy course, triumphant;
All success attend thy war:
Gracious Victor,
Bring thy trophies from afar.

2 Majesty combines with meekness,
Righteousness and peace unite,
To insure thy blessèd conquests;
Take possession of thy right:
Ride triumphant,
Dressed in robes of purest light.

3 Blest are they that touch thy sceptre;
Blest are all that own thy reign;
Freed from sin, that worst of tyrants,
Rescued from its galling chain:
Saints and angels,
All who know thee, bless thy reign.

877. 8s, 7s & 4. T. COTTERILL.

1 O'ER the realms of pagan darkness
Let the eye of pity gaze;
See the kindreds of the people
Lost in sin's bewildering maze;
Darkness brooding
O'er the face of all the earth.

2 Light of them that sit in darkness,
Rise and shine; thy blessings bring:
Light to lighten all the Gentiles,
Rise with healing in thy wing:
To thy brightness
Let all kings and nations come.

3 May the heathen, now adoring
Idol gods of wood and stone,
Come, and, worshipping before him,
Serve the living God alone:
Let thy glory
Fill the earth, as floods the sea.

4 Thou, to whom all power is given,
Speak the word; at thy command,
Let the company of heralds
Spread thy name from land to land;
Lord, be with them,
Alway, to the end of time.

881. 8s, 7s & 4. KELLY

1 MEN of God, go take your stations;
Darkness reigns throughout the earth.
Go proclaim among the nations
Joyful news of heavenly birth;
Bear the tidings
Of the Saviour's matchless worth.

2 Of his gospel not ashamèd,
As "the power of God to save,"
Go where Christ was never namèd,
Publish freedom to the slave —
Blessèd freedom!
Such as Zion's children have.

3 When exposed to fearful dangers,
Jesus will his own defend;
Borne afar 'midst foes and strangers,
Jesus will appear your Friend;
And his presence
Shall be with you to the end.

ZION. 8s, 7s & 4. DR. THOS. HASTINGS.

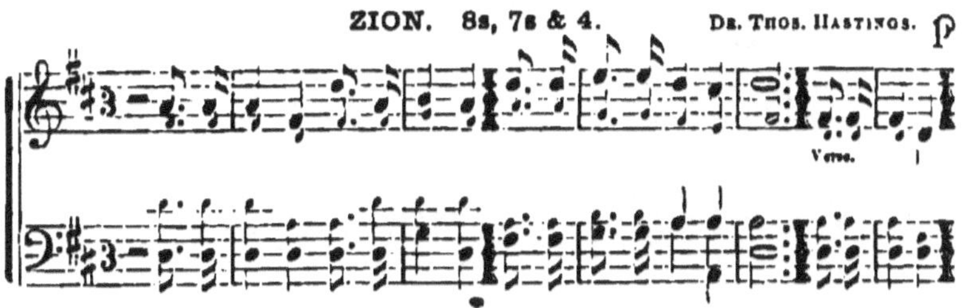

889. 8s, 7s & 4. S. F. SMITH.

1 YES, my native land, I love thee;
All thy scenes, I love them well:
Friends, connections, happy country,
Can I bid you all farewell?
Can I leave you,
Far in heathen lands to dwell?

2 Home, thy joys are passing lovely —
Joys no stranger-heart can tell:
Happy home, indeed I love thee:
Can I, can I say, "Farewell"?
Can I leave thee,
Far in heathen lands to dwell?

3 Scenes of sacred peace and pleasure,
Holy days and Sabbath bell,
Richest, brightest, sweetest treasure,
Can I say a last farewell?
Can I leave you,
Far in heathen lands to dwell?

4 Yes, I hasten from you gladly —
From the scenes I loved so well:
Far away, ye billows, bear me:
Lovely, native land, farewell:
Pleased I leave thee,
Far in heathen lands to dwell.

5 In the deserts let me labor;
On the mountains let me tell
How he died — the blessèd Saviour
To redeem a world from hell:
Let me hasten,
Far in heathen lands to dwell.

6 Bear me on, thou restless ocean:
Let the winds my canvas swell:
Heaves my heart with warm emotion,
While I go far hence to dwell:
Glad I bid thee,
Native land, farewell, farewell.

902. 8s, 7s & 4. KELLY.

1 ON the mountain's top appearing,
Lo! the sacred herald stands,
Welcome news to Zion bearing —
Zion, long in hostile lands:
Mourning captive,
God himself will loose thy bands.

2 Has thy night been long and mournful?
Have thy friends unfaithful proved?
Have thy foes been proud and scornful,
By thy sighs and tears unmoved?
Cease thy mourning;
Zion still is well beloved.

3 God, thy God, will now restore thee;
He himself appears thy Friend;
All thy foes shall flee before thee;
Here their boasts and triumphs end:
Great deliverance
Zion's King will surely send.

4 Peace and joy shall now attend thee;
All thy warfare now be past;
God thy Saviour will defend thee;
Victory is thine at last:
All thy conflicts
End in everlasting rest.

SOMERSET STREET. 8s, 7s & 4. From Oncken's Melodien

Choral.

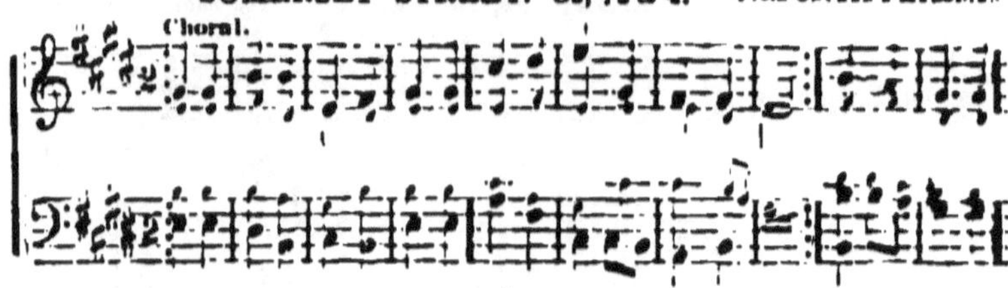

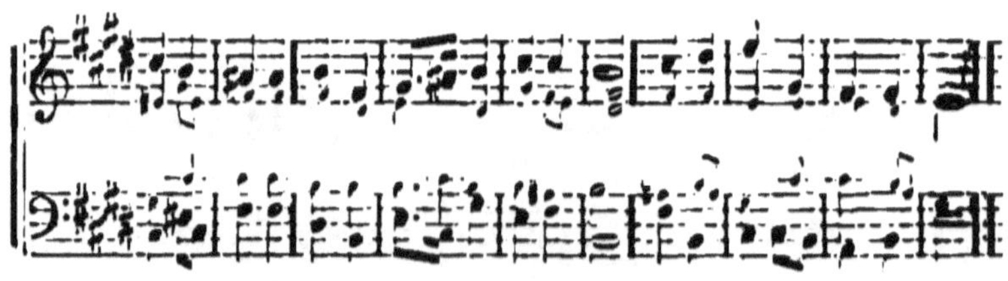

874. 8s, 7s & 4. Winchell's Sel.

1 Who but thou, almighty Spirit,
Can the heathen world reclaim?
Men may preach, but, till thou favor,
Heathens still will be the same:
Mighty Spirit,
Witness to the Saviour's name.

2 Thou hast promised, by the prophets,
Glorious light in latter days:
Come, and bless bewildered nations;
Change our prayers and tears to praise:
Promised Spirit,
Round the world diffuse thy rays.

3 All our hopes, and prayers, and labors
Must be vain without thy aid;
But thou wilt not disappoint us;
All is true that thou hast said:
Gracious Spirit,
O'er the world thy influence shed.

891. 8s, 7s & 4. P. Williams.

1 O'er the gloomy hills of darkness,
Look, my soul, be still and gaze;
See the promises advancing
To a glorious day of grace:
Blessed jubilee,
Let thy glorious morning dawn.

2 Let the dark, benighted pagan,
Let the rude barbarian, see
That divine and glorious conquest
Once obtained on Calvary:
Let the gospel
Loud resound, from pole to pole.

3 Kingdoms wide, that sit in darkness,
Grant them, Lord, the glorious light;
Now, from eastern coast to western,
May the morning chase the night:
Let redemption,
Freely purchased, win the day.

4 Fly abroad, thou mighty gospel;
Win and conquer — never cease;
May thy lasting, wide dominions
Multiply, and still increase:
Sway thy sceptre,
Saviour, all the world around.

904. 8s, 7s & 4. Kelly.

1 Yes, we trust the day is breaking;
Joyful times are near at hand;
God, the mighty God, is speaking,
By his word, in every land:
When he chooses,
Darkness flies at his command.

2 While the foe becomes more daring,
While he enters like a flood,
God, the Saviour, is preparing
Means to spread his truth abroad:
Every language
Soon shall tell the love of God.

3 O, 'tis pleasant, 'tis reviving
To our hearts, to hear, each day,
Joyful news, from far arriving,
How the gospel wins its way,
Those enlightening
Who in death and darkness lay.

TAMWORTH. 8s, 7s & 4. LOCKHART.

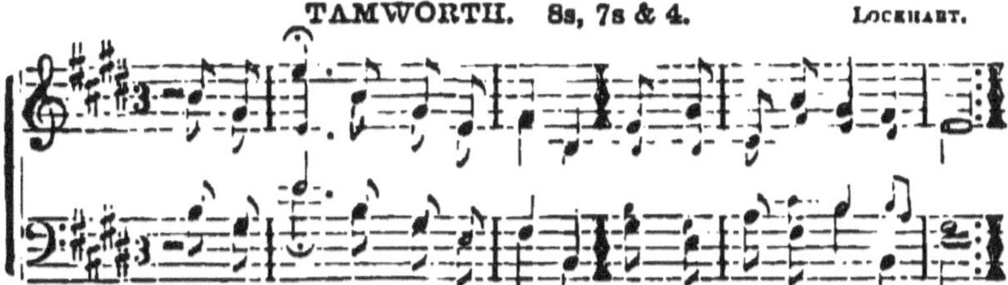

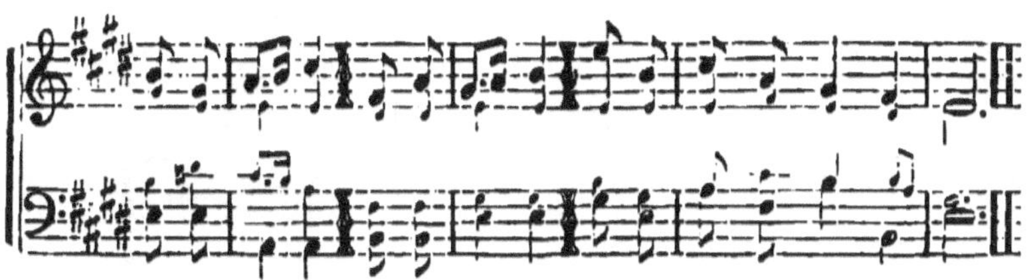

4 God of Jacob, high and glorious,
Let thy people see thy hand;
Let the gospel be victorious,
Through the world, in every land;
Then shall idols
Perish, Lord, at thy command.

1136. 8s, 7s & 4. OLIVER.

1 Lo! he comes, with clouds descending,
Once for favored sinners slain;
Thousand thousand saints, attending,
Swell the triumph of his train:
Hallelujah!
Jesus shall forever reign.

2 Every eye shall now behold him,
Robed in dreadful majesty:
Those who set at nought and sold him,
Pierced, and nailed him to the tree,
Deeply wailing,
Shall the true Messiah see.

3 When the solemn trump has sounded,
Heaven and earth shall flee away;
All who hate him must, confounded,
Hear the summons of that day —
"Come to judgment! —
Come to judgment! — come away!"

4 Now the Saviour, long expected,
See, in solemn pomp, appear;
All his saints, by man rejected,
Now shall meet him in the air:
Hallelujah!
See the day of God appear.

30

1140. 8s, 7s & 4. RIPPON'S COL.

1 Lo! he cometh: countless trumpets
Wake to life the slumbering dead;
'Mid ten thousand saints and angels
See their great, exalted Head:
Hallelujah!
Welcome, welcome, Son of God.

2 Full of joyful expectation,
Saints behold the Judge appear;
Truth and justice go before him;
Now the joyful sentence hear:
Hallelujah!
Welcome, welcome, Judge divine.

3 "Come, ye blessèd of my Father;
Enter into life and joy;
Banish all your fears and sorrows;
Endless praise be your employ:"
Hallelujah!
Welcome, welcome to the skies.

HAMDEN.

DOXOLOGY.

10. 8s, 7s & 4.

GREAT Jehovah, we adore thee,
God the Father, God the Son,
God the Spirit joined in glory
On the same eternal throne:
Endless praises
To Jehovah, three in one.

JUDGMENT. 8s, 7s & 4. Joacuim V. Burck.

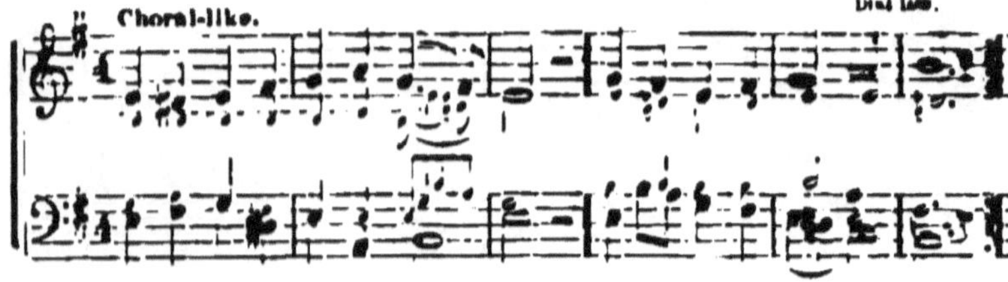

1144.

8s, 7s & 4. Newton.

1 Day of judgment, day of wonders !
Hark ! the trumpet's awful sound,
Louder than a thousand thunders,
Shakes the vast creation round :
How the summons
Will the sinner's heart confound !

2 See the Judge, our nature wearing,
Clothed in majesty divine :
You, who long for his appearing,
Then shall say, " This God is mine : "
Gracious Saviour,
Own me in that day for thine.

3 At his call the dead awaken,
Rise to life from earth and sea ;
All the powers of nature, shaken
By his looks, prepare to flee :
Careless sinner,
What will then become of thee ?

4 But to those who have confessèd,
Loved and served the Lord below,
He will say, " Come near, ye blessèd ;
See the kingdom I bestow :
You forever
Shall my love and glory know."

GREENVILLE. 8s, 7s. 7. 7.

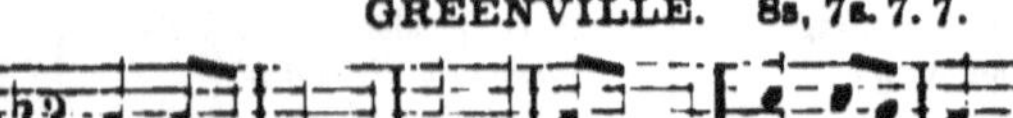

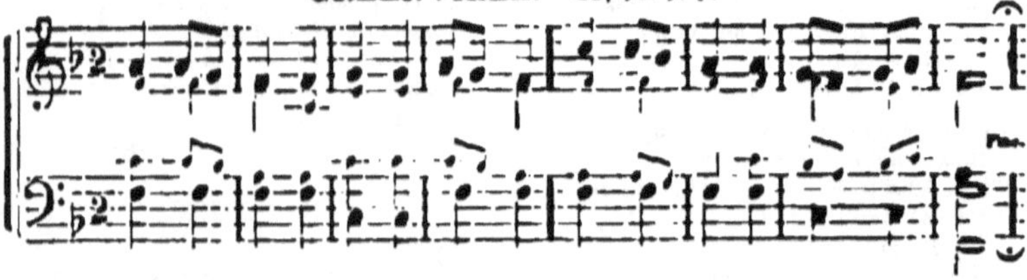

745.

8s & 7s. 7. 7. Anon.

1 When thy harvest yields thee pleasure,
Thou the golden sheaf shalt bind ;
To the poor belongs the treasure
Of the scattered ears behind :
This thy God ordains to bless
Th' widow and the fatherless.

2 When thine olive plants, increasing,
Pour their plenty o'er the plain,
Grateful thou shalt take the blessing,
But not search the boughs again :
This thy God ordains to bless
Th' widow and the fatherless.

HARVARD STREET. 8s & 7s. 7. 7. Adapted from the German.

3 When thy favored vintage, flowing,
Gladdens thine autumnal scene,
Own the bounteous hand bestowing,
But the vines the poor shall glean:
So thy God ordains to bless
Th' widow and the fatherless.

323. 8s & 7s. 7. 7. Kelly.

1 Hark! ten thousand harps and voices
Sound the note of praise above;
Jesus reigns, and heaven rejoices;
Jesus reigns, the God of love;
See, he sits on yonder throne;
Jesus rules the world alone.

2 Jesus, hail! whose glory brightens
All above, and gives it worth;
Lord of life, thy smile enlightens,
Cheers, and charms thy saints on earth;
When we think of love like thine,
Lord, we own it love divine.

3 King of glory, reign forever;
Thine an everlasting crown:
Nothing from thy love shall sever
Those whom thou hast made thine own;
Happy objects of thy grace,
Destined to behold thy face.

4 Saviour, hasten thine appearing;
Bring, O, bring the glorious day,
When, the awful summons hearing,
Heaven and earth shall pass away:
Then, with golden harps, we'll sing,
"Glory, glory to our King."

1161. 8s & 7s. 7. 7. Kelly.

1 When we pass through yonder river,
When we reach the farther shore,
There's an end of war forever;
We shall see our foes no more:
All our conflicts then shall cease,
Followed by eternal peace.

2 After warfare, rest is pleasant:
O, how sweet the prospect is!
Though we toil and strive at present,
Let us not repine at this:
Toil, and pain, and conflict, past,
All endear repose at last.

3 When we gain the heavenly regions,
When we touch the heavenly shore,—
Blessèd thought!—no hostile legions
Can alarm or trouble more:
Far beyond the reach of foes,
We shall dwell in sweet repose.

4 O, that hope! how bright, how glorious!
'Tis his people's blest reward;
In the Saviour's strength victorious,
They at length behold their Lord:
In his kingdom they shall rest,
In his love be fully blest.

DOXOLOGY.

8. 8s & 7s. 7. 7.

Glory be to God the Father,
Glory be to God the Son,
Glory be to God the Spirit,
Everlasting three in one:
Thee, let heaven and earth adore,
Now, henceforth, and evermore.

TREMONT. 8s & 7s. Peculiar. J. Heinrich Hesse.

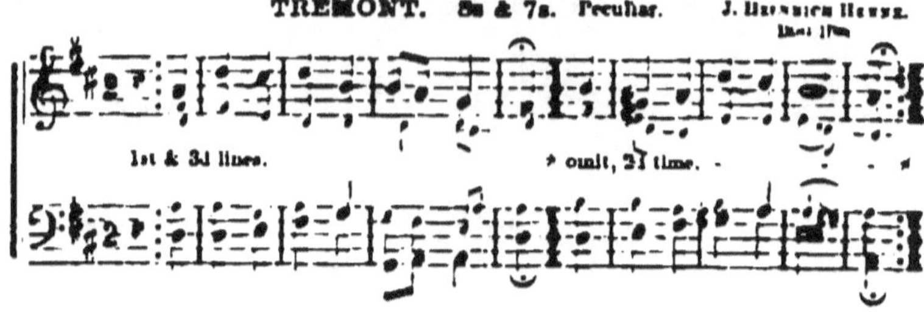

580. 8s & 7s. Peculiar. Anon.

1 O, LAY not up upon this earth
Your hope, your joy, your treasure;
Here sorrow clouds the pilgrim's path,
And blights each opening pleasure.

2 Earth's joys, like dewdrops, fade away;
Like clouds its visions vanish;
Above, no night can chase the day;
Those joys no change can banish.

3 All, all below must fade and die;
The dearest hopes we cherish,
Scenes touched with brightest radiancy,
Are all decreed to perish.

4 Then, man, be wise; thy constant care
To purer joys be given,
Nor let delusive objects share
The place of bliss and heaven.

5 Let things unseen, with potent force,
Alone possessing merit,
Lead upward to its holy source
Thy pure, immortal spirit.

1066. 8s & 7s. Peculiar. Parting Gift.

1 When forced to part from those we love,
Though sure to meet to-morrow,
We still a painful anguish prove—
We feel a pang of sorrow.

2 But who can e'er describe the tears
We shed when thus we sever,
If doomed to part for months, for years—
To part, perhaps, forever?

3 Yet, if our aims are fixed aright,
A sacred hope is given,
Though here our prospects end in night,
We'll meet again in heaven.

4 Then let us form those bonds above
Which time can ne'er dissever,
Since, parting in a Saviour's love,
We part to meet forever.

HARMONY. 8s & 7s. Peculiar. N. D. Gould.

892.

7s & 5s. S. F. SMITH.

1 ONWARD speed thy conquering flight;
Angel, onward speed;
Cast abroad thy radiant light,
Bid the shades recede;
Tread the idols in the dust,
Heathen fanes destroy,
Spread the gospel's holy trust,
Spread the gospel's joy.

2 Onward speed thy conquering flight;
Angel, onward haste;
Quickly on each mountain's height
Be thy standard placed;
Let thy blissful tidings float
Far o'er vale and hill,
Till the sweetly-echoing note
Every bosom thrill.

3 Onward speed thy conquering flight;
Angel, onward fly;
Long has been the reign of night;
Bring the morning nigh:
'Tis to thee the heathen lift
Their imploring wail;
Bear them Heaven's holy gift
Ere their courage fail.

4 Onward speed thy conquering flight;
Angel, onward speed:
Morning bursts upon our sight—
'Tis the time decreed:
Jesus now his kingdom takes,
Thrones and empires fall,
And the joyous song awakes,
"God is all in all."

PURITY. 7s & 6s, Iambic. N. D. GOULD.

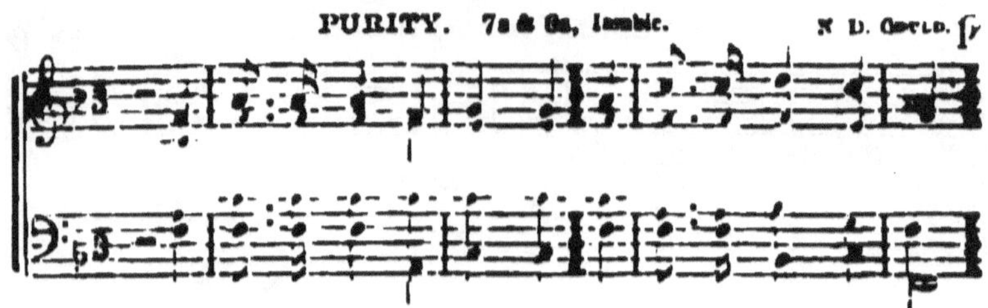

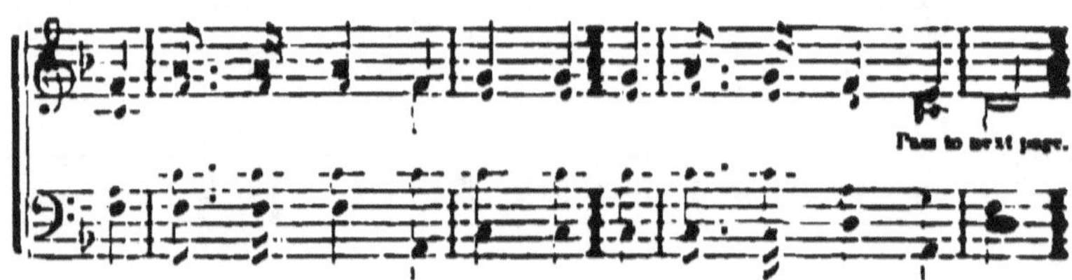

Turn to next page.

194. 7s & 6s. MONTGOMERY.

1 GOD is my strong salvation;
What foe have I to fear?
In darkness and temptation,
My light, my help, is near:
Though hosts encamp around me,
Firm in the fight I stand;
What terror can confound me,
With God at my right hand?

2 Place on the Lord reliance;
My soul, with courage wait;
His truth be thine affiance,
When faint and desolate;
His might thy heart shall strengthen,
His love thy joy increase;
Mercy thy days shall lengthen;
The Lord will give thee peace.

3 Or, if 'tis e'er denied thee
In solitude to pray,
Should holy thoughts come o'er thee
When friends are round thy way,
E'en then the silent breathing,
Thy spirit raised above,
Will reach his throne of glory,
Where dwells eternal love.

4 O, not a joy or blessing
With this can we compare—
The grace our Father gave us
To pour our souls in prayer;
Whene'er thou pin'st in sadness,
Before his footstool fall;
Remember, in thy gladness,
His love who gave thee all.

638. 7s & 6s. EDIN. LIT. REV.

1 GO when the morning shineth,
Go when the noon is bright,
Go when the eve declineth,
Go in the hush of night;
Go with pure mind and feeling,
Fling earthly thought away,
And, in thy closet kneeling,
Do thou in secret pray.

2 Remember all who love thee,
All who are loved by thee;
Pray, too, for those who hate thee,
If any such there be;
Then for thyself, in meekness,
A blessing humbly claim,
And blend with each petition
Thy great Redeemer's name.

778. 7s & 6s. S. F. SMITH.

1 "REMEMBER thy Creator"
While youth's fair spring is bright,
Before thy cares are greater,
Before comes age's night;
While yet the sun shines o'er thee,
While stars the darkness cheer,
While life is all before thee,
Thy great Creator fear.

2 "Remember thy Creator"
Ere life resigns its trust,
Ere sinks dissolving nature,
And dust returns to dust;
Before with God, who gave it,
The spirit shall appear:
He cries, who died to save it,
"Thy great Creator fear."

PURITY, Concluded. Com. for Hymn 638.

1040. 7s & 6s. BRIT. MAG.

1 THE leaves, around me falling,
Are preaching of decay;
The hollow winds are calling,
"Come, pilgrim, come away:"
The day, in night declining,
Says—I must, too, decline;—
The year its bloom resigning,
Its lot foreshadows mine.

2 The light my path surrounding,
The loves to which I cling,
The hopes within me bounding,
The joys that round me wing,
All, all, like stars at even,
Just gleam and shoot away,
Pass on before to heaven,
And chide at my delay.

3 The friends gone there before me,
Are calling from on high,
And happy angels o'er me
Tempt sweetly to the sky:
"Why wait," they say, "and wither,
'Mid scenes of death and sin?
O, rise to glory, hither,
And find true life begin."

4 I hear the invitation,
And fain would rise and come,
A sinner, to salvation,
An exile, to his home;
But while I here must linger,
Thus, thus, let all I see
Point on, with faithful finger,
o heaven, O Lord, and thee.

1059. 7s & 6s. S. F. SMITH.

1 As flows the rapid river,
With channel broad and free,
Its waters rippling ever,
And hasting to the sea,
So, life is onward flowing,
And days of offered peace;
And man is swiftly going
Where calls of mercy cease.

2 As moons are ever waning,
As hastes the sun away,
As stormy winds, complaining,
Bring on the wintry day,
So, fast the night comes o'er us—
The darkness of the grave;
And death is just before us:
God takes the life he gave.

3 Say, hath thy heart its treasure
Laid up in worlds above!
And is it all thy pleasure
Thy God to praise and love?
Beware, lest death's dark river
Its billows o'er thee roll,
And thou lament forever
The ruin of thy soul.

GOODWIN.

912.

7s & 6s. S. F. Smith.

1 The morning light is breaking;
  The darkness disappears;
The sons of earth are waking
  To penitential tears:
Each breeze that sweeps the ocean
  Brings tidings from afar
Of nations in commotion,
  Prepared for Zion's war.

2 Rich dews of grace come o'er us,
  In many a gentle shower,
And brighter scenes before us
  Are opening every hour:
Each cry, to heaven going,
  Abundant answers brings,
And heavenly gales are blowing,
  With peace upon their wings.

3 See heathen nations bending
  Before the God we love,
And thousand hearts ascending
  In gratitude above;
While sinners, now confessing,
  The gospel call obey,
And seek the Saviour's blessing —
  A nation in a day.

4 Blest river of salvation,
  Pursue thy onward way;
Flow thou to every nation,
  Nor in thy richness stay:
Stay not till all the lowly
  Triumphant reach their home;
Stay not till all the holy
  Proclaim, "The Lord is come."

SHARAIM. 7s & 6s. Iambic. DR. L. MASON. From Gould's Sac. Minstrel.

890. 7s & 6s. NOEL'S COL.

1 ROLL on, thou mighty ocean;
And, as thy billows flow,
Bear messengers of mercy
To every land below:

2 Arise, ye gales, and waft them
Safe to the destined shore,
That man may sit in darkness
And death's deep shade no more.

3 O thou eternal Ruler,
Who holdest in thine arm
The tempests of the ocean,
Protect them from all harm:

4 O, be thy presence with them,
Wherever they may be;
Though far from us who love them,
O, be they still with thee.

910. 7s & 6s. MONTGOMERY.

1 HAIL to the Lord's Anointed,
Great David's greater Son!
Hail, in the time appointed,
His reign on earth begun!
He comes to break oppression,
To set the captive free,
To take away transgression,
And rule in equity.

2 He comes, with succor speedy,
To those who suffer wrong;
To help the poor and needy,
And bid the weak be strong;
To give them songs for sighing,
Their darkness turn to light,
Whose souls, condemned and dying,
Were precious in his sight.

3 He shall descend like showers
Upon the fruitful earth,
And love and joy, like flowers,
Spring, in his path, to birth;
Before him, on the mountains,
Shall peace, the herald, go;
And righteousness, in fountains,
From hill to valley flow.

4 For him shall prayer unceasing,
And daily vows ascend,
His kingdom still increasing—
A kingdom without end:
The tide of time shall never
His covenant remove:
His name shall stand forever;
That name to us is love.

MISSION SONG. 7s & 6s. Iambic. (Rhodes.) GEORGE J. WEBB. From Mass. Coll.

Composed for Hymn 917.

907. 7s & 6s. ANON.

1 WHEN shall the voice of singing
  Flow joyfully along?
When hill and valley, ringing
  With one triumphant song,
Proclaim the contest ended,
  And Him, who once was slain,
Again to earth descended,
  In righteousness to reign?

2 Then from the craggy mountains
  The sacred shout shall fly,
And shady vales and fountains
  Shall echo the reply:
High tower and lowly dwelling
  Shall send the chorus round,
The hallelujah swelling
  In one eternal sound.

917. 7s & 6s. HEBER.

1 FROM Greenland's icy mountains,
  From India's coral strand,—
Where Afric's sunny fountains
  Roll down their golden sand,—
From many an ancient river,
  From many a palmy plain,—
They call us to deliver
  Their land from error's chain.

2 What though the spicy breezes
  Blow soft o'er Ceylon's isle,
Though every prospect pleases,
  And only man is vile;
In vain, with lavish kindness,
  The gifts of God are strown;
The heathen, in his blindness,
  Bows down to wood and stone.

3 Shall we, whose souls are lighted
  By wisdom from on high,
Shall we to man benighted
  The light of life deny?
Salvation! O, salvation!
  The joyful sound proclaim,
Till earth's remotest nation
  Has learned Messiah's name.

4 Waft, waft, ye winds, his story,
  And you, ye waters, roll,
Till, like a sea of glory,
  It spreads from pole to pole;
Till o'er our ransomed nature
  The Lamb, for sinners slain,
Redeemer, King, Creator,
  In bliss returns to reign.

BURGHAM. 7s & 6s. Iambic.

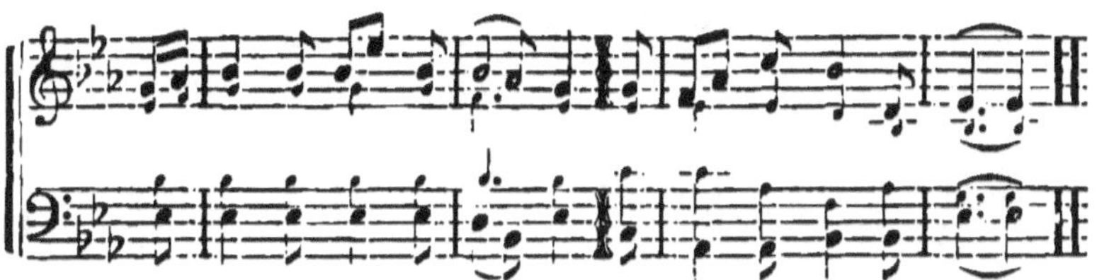

919. 7s & 6s. LYTE.

1 O THAT the Lord's salvation
Were out of Zion come,
To heal his ancient nation,
To lead his outcasts home!

2 How long the holy city
Shall heathen feet profane?
Return, O Lord, in pity;
Rebuild her walls again.

3 Let fall thy rod of terror;
Thy saving grace impart;
Roll back the veil of error;
Release the fettered heart.

4 Let Israel, home returning,
Her lost Messiah see;
Give oil of joy for mourning,
And bind thy church to thee.

971. 7s & 6s. ANON.

1 To thee, O blessèd Saviour,
Our grateful songs we raise;
O, tune our hearts and voices
Thy holy name to praise;
'Tis by thy sovereign mercy
We're here allowed to meet,
To join with friends and teachers
Thy blessing to entreat.

2 O, may thy precious gospel
Be published all abroad,
Till the benighted heathen
Shall know and serve the Lord;
Till o'er the wide creation
The rays of truth shall shine,
And nations now in darkness
Arise to light divine.

1027. 7s & 6s. SAC. SONGS.

1 THE mellow eve is gliding
Serenely down the west;
So, every care subsiding,
My soul would sink to rest.

2 The woodland hum is ringing
The daylight's gentle close;
May angels, round me singing,
Thus hymn my last repose.

3 The evening star has lighted
Her crystal lamp on high;
So, when in death benighted,
May hope illume the sky.

4 In golden splendor dawning
The morrow's light shall break;
O, on the last bright morning
May I in glory wake.

DOXOLOGY.

14. 7s & 6s.

To thee be praise forever,
Thou glorious King of kings:
Thy wondrous love and favor
Each ransomed spirit sings:
We celebrate thy glory,
With all the saints above,
And shout the joyful story
Of thy redeeming love.

MISSIONARY HYMN.

AMSTERDAM. 7s & 6s. Trochaic. Dr. Nares.

Choral-like.

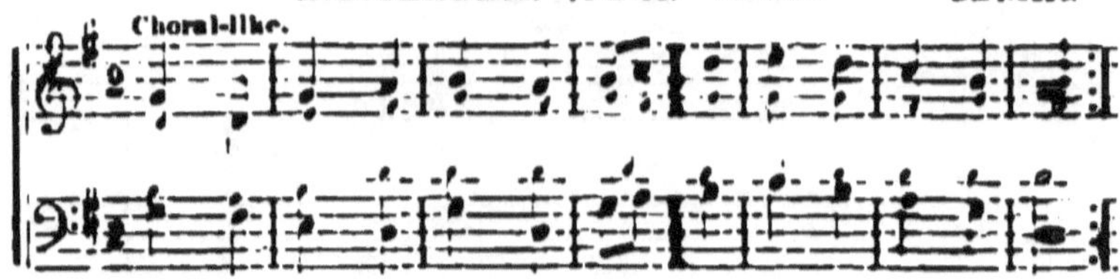

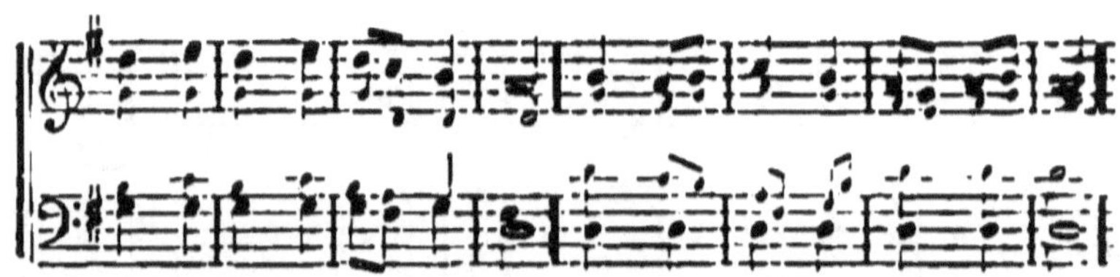

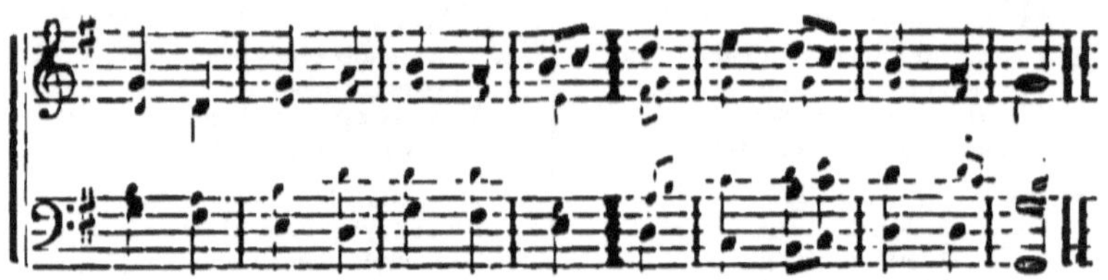

374. 7s & 6s. Peculiar. Toplady.

1 Saviour, I thy word believe;
  My unbelief remove;
Now thy quickening Spirit give,
  The unction from above;
Show me, Lord, how good thou art;
  Now thy gracious word fulfil;
Send the witness to my heart;
  The Holy Ghost reveal.

2 Blessèd Comforter, come down,
  And live and move in me;
Make my every deed thine own,
  In all things led by thee;
Bid my sin and fear depart,
  And within, O, deign to dwell;
Faithful witness, in my heart
  Thy perfect light reveal.

3 Whom the world cannot receive,
  O Lord, reveal in me;
Son of God, I cease to live,
  Unless I live to thee:
Make me choose the better part;
  O, do thou my pardon seal;
Send the witness to my heart;
  The Holy Ghost reveal.

719. 7s & 6s. Peculiar. Cennick.

1 Rise, my soul, and stretch thy wings;
  Thy better portion trace;
Rise from all terrestrial things,
  Towards heaven, thy native place:
Sun, and moon, and stars, decay;
  Time shall soon this earth remove;
Rise, my soul, and haste away
  To seats prepared above.

2 Rivers to the ocean run,
  Nor stay in all their course;
Fire, ascending, seeks the sun;
  Both speed them to their source:
So a soul that's born of God
  Pants to view his glorious face,
Upward tends to his abode,
  To rest in his embrace.

3 Cease, ye pilgrims, cease to mourn;
  Press onward to the prize;
Soon our Saviour will return,
  Triumphant in the skies:
Yet a season, and you know
  Happy entrance will be given,
All our sorrows left below,
  And earth exchanged for heaven.

1060.

7s & 6s. Peculiar. J. Burton.

1 Time is winging us away
To our eternal home;
Life is but a winter's day —
A journey to the tomb:
Youth and vigor soon will flee,
Blooming beauty lose its charms;
All that's mortal soon shall be
Enclosed in death's cold arms.

2 Time is winging us away
To our eternal home;
Life is but a winter's day —
A journey to the tomb;
But the Christian shall enjoy
Health and beauty soon above,
Where no worldly griefs annoy,
Secure in Jesus' love.

MARSHALL. 7s & 8s. Leonard Marshall. From the Hosanna.

1101.

7s & 8s. Doane.

1 Lift not thou the wailing voice;
Weep not; 'tis a Christian dieth:
Up, where blessed saints rejoice,
Ransomed now, the spirit flieth:
High in heaven's own light she dwelleth;
Full the song of triumph swelleth;
Freed from earth, and earthly failing:
Lift for her no voice of wailing.

2 They who die in Christ are blest:
Ours be, then, no thought of grieving:
Sweetly with their God they rest,
All their toils and troubles leaving:
So be ours the faith that saveth,
Hope that every trial braveth,
Love that to the end endureth,
And, through Christ, the crown secureth.

‡ NEW YEAR. 5s, 11, 6s & 12s. Anapestic. L. MARSHALL

‡ Slightly altered.

1050. 5s, 11, 6s & 12s. C. WESLEY.

1 COME, let us anew
Our journey pursue—
Roll round with the year,
And never stand still till the Master appear;
His adorable will
Let us gladly fulfil,
And our talents improve
By the patience of hope and the labor of love.

2 Our life is a dream;
Our time, as a stream,
Glides swiftly away;
The fugitive moment refuses to stay;
Lo, the arrow is flown,
And the moment is gone;
The millennial year
Rushes on to our view, and eternity's near.

3 May each, in the day
Of His coming, say,
"I've fought my way through;
I've finished the work thou didst give me to do:"
O that each from his Lord
May receive the glad word,
"Well and faithfully done;
Enter into my joy, and sit down on my throne."

RESURRECTION. 6s. Iambic.

1120.

6s. LUTHER.

1 FLUNG to the heedless winds,
Or on the waters cast,
Their ashes shall be watched,
And gathered at the last:
And from that scattered dust,
Around us and abroad,
Shall spring a plenteous seed
Of witnesses for God.

2 Jesus hath now received
Their latest living breath;
Yet vain is Satan's boast
Of victory in their death:
Still, still, though dead, they speak,
And, triumph-tongued, proclaim
To many a wakening land
The one availing Name.

ITALIAN HYMN. 6s & 4s. F. GIARDINI.

74. 6s & 4s. GOODE.

1 PRAISE ye Jehovah's name;
Praise through his courts proclaim;
Rise and adore;
High o'er the heavens above
Sound his great acts of love,
While his rich grace we prove,
Vast as his power.

2 Now let the trumpet raise
Triumphant sounds of praise,
Wide as his fame;
There let the harp be found;
Organs, with solemn sound,
Roll your deep notes around,
Filled with his name.

3 While his high praise ye sing,
Shake every sounding string:
Sweet the accord!
He vital breath bestows:
Let every breath that flows
His noblest fame disclose:
Praise ye the Lord.

120. 6s & 4s. DOBELL'S COL.

1 COME, thou Almighty King,
Help us thy name to sing,
Help us to praise;
Father all glorious,
O'er all victorious,
Come, and reign over us,
Ancient of Days.

2 Jesus, our Lord, descend;
From all our foes defend,
Nor let us fall;
Let thine almighty aid
Our sure defence be made,
Our souls on thee be stayed;
Lord, hear our call.

3 Come, thou incarnate Word,
Gird on thy mighty sword;
Our prayer attend;
Come, and thy people bless;
Come, give thy word success;
Spirit of holiness,
On us descend.

Come, holy Comforter,
Thy sacred witness bear,
In this glad hour;
Thou, who almighty art,
Now rule in every heart,
And ne'er from us depart,
Spirit of power.

5 To thee, great One in Three,
The highest praises be,
Hence evermore;
Thy sovereign majesty
May we in glory see,
And to eternity
Love and adore.

314. 6s & 4s. PRATT'S COL.

1 COME, all ye saints of God;
Wide through the earth abroad
Spread Jesus' fame:
Tell what his love has done;
Trust in his name alone;
Shout to his lofty throne,
"Worthy the Lamb."

2 Hence, gloomy doubts and fears!
Dry up your mournful tears;
Swell the glad theme;
Praise ye our gracious King;
Strike each melodious string;
Join heart and voice to sing,
"Worthy the Lamb."

From J. Tolmie.
Abridged.

3 Hark! how the choirs above,
Filled with the Saviour's love,
Dwell on his name!
There, too, may we be found,
With light and glory crowned,
While all the heavens resound,
"Worthy the Lamb."

320. 6s & 4s. Kingsbury.

1 Let us awake our joys;
Strike up with cheerful voice;
Each creature, sing;
Angels, begin the song;
Mortals, the strain prolong,
In accents sweet and strong,
"Jesus is King."

2 Proclaim abroad his name;
Tell of his matchless fame;
What wonders done;
Above, beneath, around,
Let all the earth resound,
Till heaven's high arch rebound,
"Victory is won."

3 He vanquished sin and hell,
And our last foe will quell;
Mourners, rejoice;
His dying love adore;
Praise him, now raised in power;
Praise him forevermore,
With joyful voice.

4 All hail the glorious day,
When, through the heavenly way,
Lo, he shall come,
While they who pierced him wail;
His promise shall not fail;
Saints, see your King prevail:
Great Saviour, come.

328. 6s & 4s. Sac. Lyrics.

1 Glory to God on high!
Let heaven and earth reply;
Praise ye his name;
His love and grace adore,
Who all our sorrows bore;
And sing forevermore,
"Worthy the Lamb."

2 Ye who surround the throne,
Join cheerfully in one,
Praising his name:
Ye who have felt his blood
Sealing your peace with God,
Sound his dear name abroad,
"Worthy the Lamb."

3 Join, all ye ransomed race,
Our Lord and God to bless;
Praise ye his name;
In him we will rejoice,
And make a joyful noise,
Shouting with heart and voice,
"Worthy the Lamb."

4 Soon must we change our place;
Yet will we never cease
Praising his name:
To him our songs we'll bring,
Hail him our gracious King,
And through all ages sing,
"Worthy the Lamb."

AMERICA.

&c.

ITALIAN HYMN. 6s & 4s. F. GIARDINI.

876. 6s & 4s. PRATT'S COL.

1 THOU, — whose almighty word
Chaos and darkness heard,
And took their flight, —
Hear us, we humbly pray;
And where the gospel day
Sheds not its glorious ray,
"Let there be light."

2 Thou, who didst come to bring,
On thy redeeming wing,
Healing and sight,
Health to the sick in mind,
Sight to the inly blind,
O, now to all mankind
"Let there be light."

3 Spirit of truth and love,
Life-giving, Holy Dove,
Speed forth thy flight;
Move on the waters' face,
Bearing the lamp of grace;
And in earth's darkest place
"Let there be light."

884. 6s & 4s. URWICK'S COL.

1 SOUND, sound the truth abroad;
Bear ye the word of God
Through the wide world;
Tell what our Lord has done;
Tell how the day is won,
And from his lofty throne
Satan is hurled.

2 Swiftly, on wings of love,
Jesus, who reigns above,
Bids us to fly;
They who his message bear
Should neither doubt nor fear;
He will their Friend appear;
He will be nigh.

3 When on the mighty deep,
He will their spirits keep,
Stayed on his word;
When in a foreign land,
No other friend at hand,
Jesus will by them stand —
Jesus, their Lord.

4 Ye who, forsaking all,
At your loved Master's call,
Comforts resign,
Soon will your work be done;
Soon will the prize be won;
Brighter than yonder sun
Ye soon shall shine.

---

993. 6s & 4s. MONTGOMERY.

1 THE God of harvest praise;
In loud thanksgiving raise
Hand, heart, and voice;
The valleys smile and sing,
Forests and mountains ring,
The plains their tribute bring,
The streams rejoice.

2 Yea, bless his holy name,
And purest thanks proclaim
Through all the earth;
To glory in your lot
Is duty: but be not
God's benefits forgot
Amidst your mirth.

3 The God of harvest praise;
Hands, hearts, and voices raise,
With sweet accord;
From field to garner throng,
Bearing your sheaves along,
And in your harvest song
Bless ye the Lord.

EBELING. 6s & 4s. Arranged from EBELING. Melody of 1666.

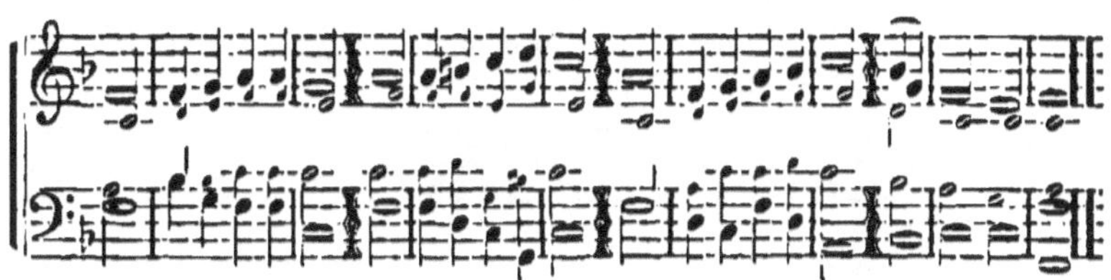

1000. 6s & 4s. S. F. SMITH.

1 MY country, 'tis of thee,
Sweet land of liberty,
Of thee I sing;
Land where my fathers died,
Land of the pilgrim's pride,
From every mountain side
Let freedom ring.

2 My native country, thee —
Land of the noble, free —
Thy name — I love;
I love thy rocks and rills,
Thy woods and templed hills;
My heart with rapture thrills
Like that above.

3 Let music swell the breeze,
And ring from all the trees
Sweet freedom's song:
Let mortal tongues awake;
Let all that breathe partake;
Let rocks their silence break —
The sound prolong.

4 Our fathers' God, to thee,
Author of liberty,
To thee we sing:
Long may our land be bright
With freedom's holy light;
Protect us by thy might,
Great God, our King.

AMERICA.

1007. 6s & 4s. S. F. SMITH.

1 AUSPICIOUS morning, hail!
Voices from hill and vale
Thy welcome sing:
Joy on thy dawning breaks;
Each heart that joy partakes,
While cheerful music wakes,
Its praise to bring.

2 When on the tyrant's rod
Our patriot fathers trod,
And dared be free,
'Twas not in burning zeal,
Firm nerves, and hearts of steel,
Our country's joy to seal,
But, Lord, in thee.

3 Thou, as a shield of power,
In battle's awful hour,
Didst round us stand;
Our hopes were in thy throne;
Strong in thy might alone,
By thee our banners shone,
God of our land.

4 Long o'er our native hills,
Long by our shaded rills,
May freedom rest;
Long may our shores have peace,
Our flag grace every breeze,
Our ships the distant seas,
From east to west.

5 Peace on this day abide,
From morn till even-tide;
Wake tuneful song;
Melodious accents raise;
Let every heart, with praise,
Bring high and grateful lays,
Rich, full, and strong.

680. 6s & 4s. Peculiar. HEMANS.

1 LOWLY and solemn be
Thy children's cry to thee,
Father divine, —
A hymn of suppliant breath,
Owning that life and death
Alike are thine.

2 O Father, in that hour,
When earth all helping power
Shall disavow, —
When spear, and shield, and crown,
In faintness are cast down, —
Sustain us, thou!

3 By Him who bowed to take
The death-cup for our sake,
The thorn, the rod, —
From whom the last dismay
Was not to pass away, —
Aid us, O God.

4 While trembling o'er the grave,
We call on thee to save,
Father divine:
Hear, hear our suppliant breath;
Keep us, in life and death,
Thine, only thine.

783. 6s & 4s. R. PALMER.

1 MY faith looks up to thee,
Thou Lamb of Calvary:
Saviour divine,
Now hear me while I pray;
Take all my guilt away;
O, let me, from this day,
Be wholly thine.

2 May thy rich grace impart
Strength to my fainting heart;
My zeal inspire;
As thou hast died for me,
O, may my love to thee
Pure, warm, and changeless be —
A living fire.

3 While life's dark maze I tread,
And griefs around me spread,
Be thou my Guide;
Bid darkness turn to day,
Wipe sorrow's tears away,
Nor let me ever stray
From thee aside.

4 When ends life's transient dream,
When death's cold, sullen stream
Shall o'er me roll,
Blest Saviour, then, in love,
Fear and distress remove;
O, bear me safe above —
A ransomed soul.

---

952. 6s & 4s. J. YOUNG.

1 O HOLY Lord, our God,
By heavenly hosts adored,
Hear us, we pray:
To thee the cherubim,
Angels and seraphim,
Unceasing praises bring;
Their homage pay.

2 Here give thy word success;
And this thy servant bless;
His labors own;
And, while the sinner's Friend
His life and words commend,
Thy Holy Spirit send,
And make him known.

3 May every passing year
More happy still appear
Than this glad day:
With numbers fill the place,
Adorn thy saints with grace;
Thy truth may all embrace,
O Lord, we pray.

4 O Lord, our God, arise;
And now, before our eyes,
Thy arm make bare;
Unite our hearts in love,
Till, raised to heaven above
We all its fulness prove,
And praise thee there.

13. DOXOLOGY.
6s & 4s.

To God — the Father, Son,
And Spirit — three in one —
All praise be given:
Crown him, in every song;
To him your hearts belong;
Let all his praise prolong,
On earth — in heaven.

SPANISH HYMN. 6s & 5s.

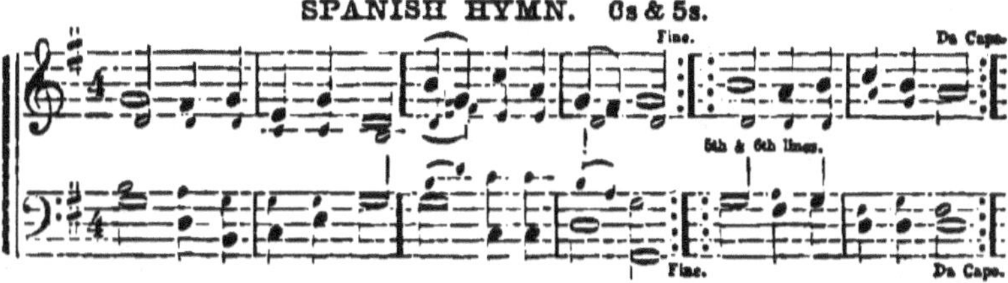

1020. 6s & 5s. ANON.

1 THROUGH thy protecting care,
Kept till the dawning,
Taught to draw near in prayer,
Heed we the warning:
O thou great One in Three,
Gladly our souls would be
Evermore praising thee,
God of the morning.

2 God of our sleeping hours,
Watch o'er us waking,
All our imperfect powers
In thine hands taking:
In us thy work fulfil,
Be with thy children still,
Those who obey thy will
Never forsaking.

1030. 6s & 5s. ANON.

1 O THOU who hearest prayer,
Through his submission
Who did our sorrows bear,
Hear our petition:
Lead us in thine own way;
Grant us, we humbly pray,
For all our sins this day,
Holy contrition.

2 They shall lie down in peace,
Lord, whom thou keepest;
Thy mercies never cease;
Thou never sleepest:
Guard us till morning's ray
Bids us again essay
Who shall pour forth the lay
Loudest and deepest.

1070. 6s & 5s. SEL. HYMNS.

1 WHEN shall we meet again? —
Meet ne'er to sever?
When will Peace wreathe her chain
Round us forever?
Our hearts will ne'er repose
Safe from each blast that blows
In this dark vale of woes —
Never — no, never!

2 When shall love freely flow
Pure as life's river?
When shall sweet friendship glow
Changeless forever?
Where joys celestial thrill,
Where bliss each heart shall fill,
And fears of parting chill
Never — no, never!

3 Up to that world of light
Take us, dear Saviour;
May we all there unite,!
Happy forever:
Where kindred spirits dwell,
There may our music swell,
And time our joys dispel
Never — no, never!

4 Soon shall we meet again —
Meet ne'er to sever;
Soon will Peace wreathe her chain
Round us forever:
Our hearts will then repose
Secure from worldly woes;
Our songs of praise shall close
Never — no, never!

317. 6s, 8s & 4s. Urwick's Col.

1 Proclaim the lofty praise
  Of Him who once was slain,
But now is risen, through endless days,
  To live and reign:
He lives and reigns on high,
  Who bought us with his blood,
Enthroned above the farthest sky,
  Our Saviour God.

2 The Son of God adore:
  Ye ransomed, spread his fame;
With joy and gladness, evermore
  Laud his great name:
Let every tongue confess
  That Jesus Christ is Lord,
And every creature join to bless
  Th' incarnate Word.

3 All honor, power, and praise,
  To Jesus' name belong;
With hosts seraphic, glad, we raise
  The sacred song:
"Worthy the Lamb," they cry,
  "That on the cross was slain;
But now, ascended up on high,
  He lives to reign."

4 He lives to bless and save
  The souls redeemed by grace,
And rescue from the dreary grave
  His chosen race:
And soon we hope, above,
  A louder strain to sing;
With all our powers to praise and love
  Our Saviour King.

574. 6s, 8s & 4s. Olivers.

1 Yes, God himself hath sworn,—
  I on his oath depend,—
I shall, on eagle's wings upborne,
  To heaven ascend:
I shall behold his face,
  I shall his power adore,
And sing the wonders of his grace
  Forevermore.

2 Though nature's strength decay,
  And death and hell withstand,
To Canaan's bounds I urge my way,
  At his command:
The watery deep I pass,
  With Jesus in my view,
And through the howling wilderness
  My way pursue

WARNING. 6s, 8s & 4s. Arr. from W. Arnold.

3 The goodly land I see,
With peace and plenty blest,
The land of sacred liberty
And endless rest:
There milk and honey flow,
And oil and wine abound,
And trees of life forever grow,
With mercy crowned.

4 There dwells the Lord our King,
The Lord our Righteousness;
Triumphant o'er the world and sin:
The Prince of Peace,
On Zion's sacred height,
His kingdom still maintains,
And, glorious with his saints in light,
Forever reigns.

5 He keeps his own secure;
He guards them by his side;
Arrays in garments white and pure
His spotless bride:
With streams of sacred bliss,
With groves of living joys,
With all the fruits of Paradise,
He still supplies.

6 Before the great Three-One
They all exulting stand,
And tell the wonders he hath done
Through all their land:
The listening spheres attend,
And swell the growing fame.
And sing, in songs which never end,
The wondrous Name.

687. 6s, 8s & 4s. Urwick's Col.

1 The awful message came;
The Lord of spirits said,
"I know thou hast a living name,
But thou art dead.
Thy dying gifts revive,
And strengthen what remain;
Repent, remember, watch, and strive
To live again.

2 "But if thou wilt not hear
This warning of my grace,
Nor bow, with penitential fear,
Before my face,
Lo! as a thief I come,—
The hour thou canst not tell,—
To drive thee from thy peaceful home
In flames to dwell.

3 "The undefiled shall see
My promise fixed and sure,
And he who conquers walk with me
In garments pure:
Recorded by my love,
His name I will declare
Before my Father's throne above,
And angels there."

SALVATION. 6, 7s & 8. From N. D. Gould. Slightly altered.

901. 6, 7s & 8. H. Y.

1 Hark! hark! a shout of joy!
The world, the world is calling;
In east and west, in north and south,
See Satan's kingdom falling.

2 Wake! wake! the church of God,
And dissipate thy slumbers;
Shake off thy deadly apathy,
And marshal all thy numbers.

3 Trust, trust the faithful God;
His promise is unfailing;
The prayer of faith can pierce the skies;
Its breath is all-prevailing.

4 Look! look! the fields are white;
And stay thy hand no longer;
Though Satan's mighty legions fight,
The arm of God is stronger.

5 See! see! the cross is raised;
The crescent droops before it;
The pagan nations feel its power,
And prostrate ranks adore it.

6 Joy! joy! the Saviour reigns;
See prophecy fulfilling;
The hearts of stubborn Jews relent,
In God's own time made willing.

7 Pray! pray! then, Christian, pray;
Though faint, be yet pursuing,
And cease not, day by day, the prayer
Of lively faith renewing.

8 Soon, soon your waiting eyes
Shall see the heavens rending,
And rich and richer blessings still
From God's bright throne descending.

Tune for Hymn 453 at foot of next page.

453. 6s & 4s. Sac. Songs.

1 To-day the Saviour calls:
Ye wanderers, come;
O ye benighted souls,
Why longer roam?

2 To-day the Saviour calls:
O, hear him now,
Within these sacred walls
To Jesus bow.

3 To-day the Saviour calls:
For refuge fly;
The storm of justice falls,
And death is nigh.

4 The Spirit calls to-day:
Yield to his power;
O, grieve him not away;
'Tis mercy's hour.

WON. 6s & 10s. From Sabbath Bell.

553.

6s & 10s. Martineau's Col.

1 Thou, who didst stoop below,
To drain the cup of woe,
And wear the form of frail mortality, —
Thy blessèd labors done,
Thy crown of victory won, —
Hast passed from earth — passed to thy home on high.

2 It was no path of flowers,
Through this dark world of ours,
Belovèd of the Father, thou didst tread;
And shall we, in dismay,
Shrink from the narrow way,
When clouds and darkness are around it spread?

3 O Thou, who art our life,
Be with us through the strife;
Thy own meek head by rudest storms was bowed;
Raise thou our eyes above,
To see a Father's love
Beam, like a bow of promise, through the cloud.

4 E'en through the awful gloom,
Which hovers o'er the tomb,
That light of love our guiding star shall be;
Our spirits shall not dread
The shadowy way to tread,
Friend, Guardian, Saviour, which doth lead to thee.

TO-DAY. 6s & 10s. For Hymn 453, opposite. B. F. Edmands.

MELTA. 8s & 6s, or 8s & 4s. Adapted from G. F. Root.

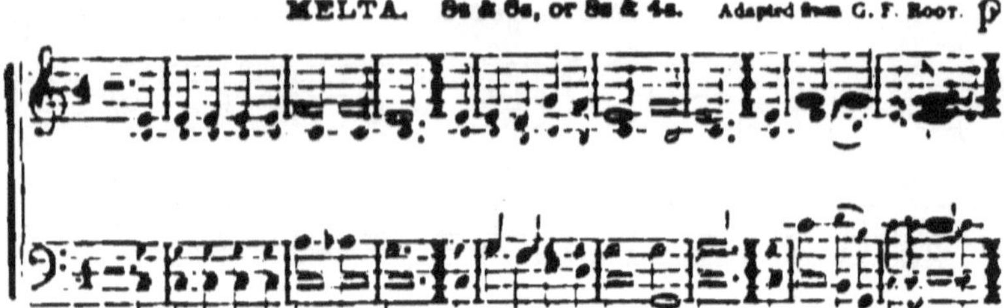

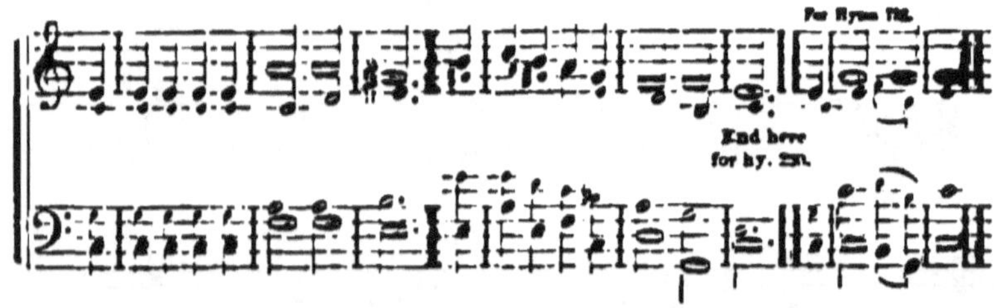

In singing Hymn 220, use the small notes in last measure of upper brace, and end at the first close.

In singing Hymn 752, sing the pointed half notes in the last measure of upper brace.

220. 8s & 6. S. F. Smith.

1 Beyond where Cedron's waters flow,
Behold the suffering Saviour go
To sad Gethsemane;
His countenance is all divine,
Yet grief appears in every line.

2 He bows beneath the sins of men;
He cries to God, and cries again,
In sad Gethsemane;
He lifts his mournful eyes above —
"My Father, can this cup remove?"

3 With gentle resignation still,
He yielded to his Father's will,
In sad Gethsemane;
"Behold me here, thine only Son;
And, Father, let thy will be done."

4 The Father heard; and angels, there,
Sustained the Son of God in prayer,
In sad Gethsemane;
He drank the dreadful cup of pain —
Then rose to life and joy again.

5 When storms of sorrow round us sweep,
And scenes of anguish make us weep,
To sad Gethsemane
We'll look, and see the Saviour there,
And humbly bow, like him, in prayer.

752. 8s & 4s. Anon.

1 Alas! how poor and little worth
Are all those glittering toys of earth
That lure us here! —
Dreams of a sleep that death must break:
Alas! before it bids us wake,
They disappear.

2 Where is the strength that spurned decay,
The step that rolled so light and gay,
The heart's blithe tone?
The strength is gone, the step is slow,
And joy grows weariness and woe
When age comes on.

3 Our birth is but a starting-place;
Life is the running of the race,
And death the goal:
There all those glittering toys are brought;
That path alone, of all unsought,
Is found of all.

4 O, let the soul its slumbers break,
Arouse its senses, and awake
To see how soon
Life, like its glories, glides away,
And the stern footsteps of decay
Come stealing on.

VERNON. 8s, 6 & 4. 2 STANZAS. GEORGE J. WEBB.

Composed for Hymn 352. Presented for this work.

678. 8s, 6 & 4. HEMANS.

1 FATHER, who in the olive shade,
When the dark hour came on,
Didst, with a breath of heavenly aid,
Strengthen thy Son, —

2 O, by the anguish of that night,
Send us down blest relief;
Or, to the chastened, let thy might
Hallow this grief.

3 And thou, that when the starry sky
Saw the dread strife begun,
Didst teach adoring faith to cry,
" Thy will be done," —

4 By thy meek spirit, thou, of all
That e'er have mourned the chief,
Blest Saviour, if the stroke must fall,
Hallow this grief.

Hymn 678 may be sung to some common metre tunes, by the use of slurs in the last line, as below.

PHUVAH. Page 122.

352. 8s, 6 & 4. SPIR. OF THE PSALMS.

1 OUR blest Redeemer, ere he breathed
His tender, last farewell,
A Guide, a Comforter, bequeathed
With us to dwell.

2 He came in tongues of living flame,
To teach, convince, subdue;
All powerful as the wind he came,
As viewless too.

3 He came sweet influence to impart,
A gracious, willing guest,
While he can find one humble heart
Wherein to rest.

4 He breathes that gentle voice we hear,
Soft as the breeze of even,
That checks each fault, that calms each fear,
And speaks of heaven.

5 And every virtue we possess,
And every victory won,
And every thought of holiness,
Are his alone.

6 Spirit of purity and grace,
Our weakness, pitying, see;
O, make our hearts thy dwelling-place,
And worthier thee.

REDEMPTION. 8s, or 8s & 9s. Anapestic. N. D. Gould.

Chant Style.

567. 8s. Toplady.

1 A DEBTOR to mercy alone,
Of covenant mercy I sing;
Nor fear, with thy righteousness on,
My person and offering to bring;
The terrors of law, and of God,
With me can have nothing to do;
My Saviour's obedience and blood
Hide all my transgression from view.

2 The work which his goodness began,
The arm of his strength will complete;
His promise is yea, and amen,
And never was forfeited yet;
Things future, nor things that are now,
Not all things, below nor above,
Can make him his purpose forego,
Or sever my soul from his love.

3 My name from the palms of his hands
Eternity will not erase:
Impressed on his heart it remains,
In marks of indelible grace:
Yes, I to the end shall endure,
As sure as the earnest is given;
More happy, but not more secure,
The glorified spirits in heaven.

598. 8s. Searle.

1 How sweet on thy bosom to rest,
When nature's affliction is near!
The soul that can trust thee is blest;
Thy smiles bring my freedom from fear.

2 The Lord has in kindness declared
That those who will trust in his name
Shall in the sharp conflict be spared,
His mercy and love to proclaim.

3 This promise shall be to my soul
A messenger sent from the skies,
An anchor when billows shall roll,
A refuge when tempests arise.

4 O Saviour, the promise fulfil;
Its comfort impart to my mind;
Then calmly I'll bow to thy will,
To the cup of affliction resigned.

599. 8s. Bath Col.

1 O THOU whose compassionate care
Forbids my fond heart to complain,
Now graciously teach me to bear
The weight of affliction and pain.

2 Though cheerless my days seem to flow,
Though weary and wakeful my nights,
What comfort it gives me to know
'Tis the hand of a Father that smites.

3 A tender physician thou art,
Who woundest in order to heal,
And comfort divine dost impart
To soften the anguish we feel.

4 O, let this correction be blest,
And answer thy gracious design;
Then grant that my soul may find rest
In comforts so healing as thine.

1086. 8s. COWPER.

1 To Jesus, the crown of my hope,
My soul is in haste to be gone;
O, bear me, ye cherubim, up,
And waft me away to his throne.

2 My Saviour, whom, absent, I love;
Whom, not having seen, I adore;
Whose name is exalted above
All glory, dominion, and power,—

3 Dissolve thou these bonds that detain
My soul from her portion in thee;
O, strike off this adamant chain,
And make me eternally free.

4 When that happy era begins,
When arrayed in thy glories I shine,
Nor grieve any more, by my sins,
The bosom on which I recline,—

5 O, then shall the veil be removed,
And round me thy brightness be poured;
I shall see Him whom, absent, I loved,
Whom, not having seen, I adored.

1119. 8s & 9s. BACON.

1 WEEP not for the saint that ascends
To partake of the joys of the sky;
Weep not for the seraph that bends
With the worshipping chorus on high;
Weep not for the spirit now crowned
With the garland to martyrdom given;
O, weep not for him: he has found
His reward and his refuge in heaven.

2 But weep for their sorrows who stand
And lament o'er the dead by his grave;
Who sigh when they muse on the land
Of their home far away o'er the wave;
And weep for the nations that dwell
Where the light of the truth never shone,
Where anthems of peace never swell,
And the love of the Lord is unknown.

1163. 8s. DE FLEURY.

1 YE angels, who stand round the throne,
And view my Immanuel's face,
In rapturous songs make him known;
O, tune your soft harps to his praise.

2 Ye saints, who stand nearer than they,
And cast your bright crowns at his feet,
His grace and his glory display,
And all his rich mercy repeat.

3 He snatched you from hell and the grave;
He ransomed from death and despair;
For you he is mighty to save,
And faithful to bring you safe there.

4 O, when will the moment appear
When I shall unite in your song?
I'm weary of lingering here;
For I to your Saviour belong.

5 I'm fettered and chained here in clay;
I struggle and pant to be free;
I long to be soaring away,
My God and my Saviour to see.

178. 8s. HART.

1 THIS God is the God we adore,
Our faithful, unchangeable Friend,
Whose love is as large as his power,
And neither knows measure nor end.

2 'Tis Jesus, the first and the last,
Whose Spirit shall guide us safe home;
We'll praise him for all that is past,
And trust him for all that's to come.

37. 10s. W. Mason.

1 Again returns the day of holy rest,
Which, when he made the world, Jehovah blest;
When, like his own, he bade our labor cease,
And all be piety, and all be peace.

2 Let us devote this consecrated day
To learn his will, and all we learn obey;
So shall he hear, when fervently we raise
Our supplications and our songs of praise.

3 Father of heaven, in whom our hopes confide,
Whose power defends us, and whose precepts guide,
In life our Guardian, and in death our Friend,
Glory supreme be thine, till time shall end.

42. 10s. Browne.

1 Hail, happy day! thou day of holy rest!
What heavenly peace and transport fill my breast!
When Christ, the God of grace, in love descends,
And kindly holds communion with his friends!

2 Let earth and all its vanities be gone,
Move from my sight, and leave my soul alone,
Its flattering, fading glories I despise,
And to immortal beauties turn my eyes.

3 Fain would I mount and penetrate the skies,
And on my Saviour's glories fix my eyes:
O, meet my rising soul, thou God of love,
And waft it to the blissful realms above.

SAVANNAH. 10s. Iambic. Pleyel.

900. 10s. Pope.

1 Rise, crowned with light, imperial Salem, rise,
Exalt thy towering head, and lift thine eyes;
See heaven its sparkling portals wide display,
And break upon thee in a flood of day.

2 See a long race thy spacious courts adorn;
See future sons and daughters, yet unborn,
In crowding ranks on every side arise,
Demanding life, impatient for the skies.

3 See barbarous nations at thy gates attend,
Walk in thy light, and in thy temple bend;
See thy bright altars thronged with prostrate kings,
While every land its joyous tribute brings.

4 The seas shall waste, the skies to smoke decay,
Rocks fall to dust, and mountains melt away;
But, fixed his word, his saving power remains;
Thy realm shall last, thy own Messiah reigns.

1116. 10s. Montgomery.

1 Go to the grave in all thy glorious prime,
In full activity of zeal and power;
A Christian cannot die before his time;
The Lord's appointment is the servant's hour.

2 Go to the grave; at noon from labor cease;
Rest on thy sheaves; thy harvest task is done,
Come from the heat of battle, and in peace,
Soldier, go home; with thee the fight is won.

3 Go to the grave; for there thy Saviour lay
In death's embrace, ere he arose on high;
And all the ransomed by that narrow way,
Pass to eternal life beyond the sky.

4 Go to the grave:—no; take thy seat above,
Be thy pure spirit present with the Lord,
Where thou for faith and hope hast perfect love,
And open vision for the written word.

LYONS. 10s & 11s; or 12, 11, 12, 8. Anapestic. HAYDN.

* For Hymn 906, omit, and pass to 2d Ending. - - * Fine.
2d Ending.
For 4th line of Hymn 906.
And na - - tions are own - ing his sway.

72. 10s & 11s. GRANT.

1 O, WORSHIP the King, all glorious above,
And gratefully sing his wonderful love,
Our Shield and Defender,
[the Ancient of days,
Pavilioned in splendor,
[and girded with praise.

2 O, tell of his might, and sing of his grace,
Whose robe is the light, whose canopy space;
His chariots of wrath
[the deep thunder clouds form,
And dark is his path
[on the wings of the storm.

3 Thy bountiful care what tongue can recite?
It breathes in the air, it shines in the light,
It streams from the hills,
[it descends to the plain,
And sweetly distils
[in the dew and the rain.

4 Frail children of dust, and feeble as frail,
In thee do we trust, nor find thee to fail;
Thy mercies how tender!
[how firm to the end!
Our Maker, — Defender, —
[Redeemer, and Friend.

5 Father Almighty, how faithful thy love!
While angels delight to hymn thee above,
The humbler creation,
[though feeble their lays,
With true adoration
[shall lisp to thy praise.

326. 10s & 11s. WINCHELL'S SEL.

1 YE servants of God, your Master proclaim,
And publish abroad his wonderful name;
The name all-victorious of Jesus extol;
His kingdom is glorious; he rules over all.

2 God ruleth on high, almighty to save;
And still he is nigh; his presence we have:
The great congregation his triumph shall sing,
Ascribing salvation to Jesus our King.

3 "Salvation to God, who sits on the throne,"
Let all cry aloud, and honor the Son;
The praises of Jesus the angels proclaim,
Fall down on their faces, and worship the
[Lamb.

4 Then let us adore, and give him his right, —
All glory and power, and wisdom and might,
All honor and blessing, with angels above,
And thanks never ceasing, for infinite love.

906. 12s, 11 & 8. S. F. SMITH.

1 THE Prince of salvation in triumph is
[riding,
And glory attends him along his bright
[way;
The tidings of grace on the breezes are
[gliding,
And nations are owning his sway.

2 Ride on in thy greatness, thou conquering
[Saviour;
Let thousands of thousands submit to thy
[reign,
Acknowledge thy goodness, entreat for thy
And follow thy glorious train. [favor,

3 Then loud shall ascend, from each sanctified
[nation,
The voice of thanksgiving, the chorus of
[praise;
And heaven shall reëcho the song of salva-
In rich and melodious lays. [tion

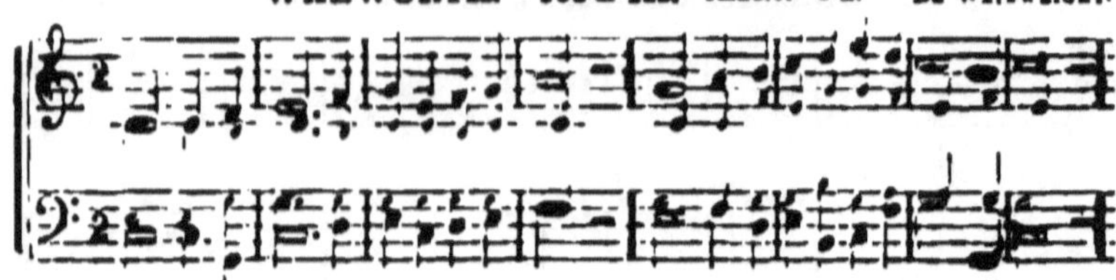

144. 10s & 11s. WATTS.

1 The Lord of glory reigns; he reigns on high,
His robes of state are strength and majesty;
This wide creation rose at his command,
Built by his word, and 'stablished by his hand:
Long stood his throne ere he began creation,
And his own Godhead is the firm foundation.

2 God is th' eternal King; thy foes in vain
Raise their rebellion to confound thy reign;
In vain the storms, in vain the floods, arise,
And roar, and toss their waves against the skies;
Foaming at heaven, they rage with wild commotion,
But heaven's high arches scorn the swelling ocean.

3 Ye tempests, rage no more; ye floods, be still;
And all the world submissive to his will;
Built on his truth, his church must ever stand;
Firm are his promises, and strong his hand:
See his own sons, when they appear before him,
Bow at his footstool, and with fear adore him.

1139. 10s & 11s. WATTS.

1 The God of glory sends his summons forth,
Calls the south nations, and awakes the north;
From east to west the sovereign orders spread,
Through distant worlds and regions of the dead:
The trumpet sounds; hell trembles; heaven rejoices;
Lift up your heads, ye saints, with cheerful voices.

2 No more shall atheists mock his long delay;
His vengeance sleeps no more: behold the day;
Behold, the Judge descends: his guards are nigh:
Tempest and fire attend him down the sky;
When God appears, all nature shall adore him:
While sinners tremble, saints rejoice before him.

3 Sinners, awake betimes; O, now be wise;
Awake before this dreadful morning rise:
Change your vain thoughts, your crooked works amend;
Fly to the Saviour make the Judge your Friend:
Then join the saints; wake every cheerful passion;
When Christ returns, he comes for your salvation.

WEBSTER. 11s & 8s. Iambic. GERMAN.

71.

11s & 8s. CH. PSALMODY.

1 THE Lord is great; ye hosts of heaven, adore him,
And ye who tread this earthly ball;
In holy songs rejoice aloud before him,
And shout his praise who made you all.

2 The Lord is great; his majesty how glorious!
Resound his praise from shore to shore;
O'er sin, and death, and hell, now made victorious,
He rules and reigns forevermore.

3 The Lord is great; his mercy how abounding!
Ye angels, strike your golden chords;
O, praise our God, with voice and harp resounding,
The King of kings and Lord of lords.

PRAISE. 11s & 8s. Anapestic.

990.

11s & 8s. MONTGOMERY.

1 BE joyful in God, all ye lands of the earth;
O, serve him with gladness and fear;
Exult in his presence with music and mirth;
With love and devotion draw near.

2 Jehovah is God, and Jehovah alone,
Creator and Ruler o'er all;
And we are his people; his sceptre we own;
His sheep, and we follow his call.

3 O, enter his gates with thanksgiving and song;
Your vows in his temple proclaim;
His praise in melodious accordance prolong,
And bless his adorable name.

4 For good is the Lord, inexpressibly good,
And we are the work of his hand;
His mercy and truth from eternity stood,
And shall to eternity stand.

Hymn 635. COME, YE DISCONSOLATE. 11s & 10s. Dactylic. S. Webbe.

635. 11s & 10s. Spir. Songs.

1 Come, ye disconsolate, where'er ye languish:
Come to the mercy-seat, fervently kneel;
Here bring your wounded hearts, here tell
[your anguish;
Earth has no sorrow that heaven cannot heal.

2 Joy of the desolate, light of the straying,
Hope of the penitent, fadeless and pure,
Here speaks the Comforter, tenderly saying,
Earth has no sorrow that heaven cannot cure.

3 Here see the bread of life; see waters flow-
[ing
Forth from the throne of God, pure from
[above;
Come to the feast of love; come, ever know
[ing
Earth has no sorrow but heaven can re-
[move.

202. 11s & 10s. Heber.

1 Brightest and best of the sons of the
[morning,
Dawn on our darkness, and lend us thine aid;
Star of the east, the horizon adorning,
Guide where the infant Redeemer is laid.

2 Cold, on his cradle, the dew-drops are shin-
[ing;
Low lies his bed with the beasts of the stall;
Angels adore him, in slumber reclining,
Maker, and Monarch, and Saviour of all.

3 Say, shall we yield him, in costly devotion,
Odors of Eden and offerings divine?
Gems of the mountain, and pearls of the
[ocean,
Myrrh from the forest, and gold from the
[mine?

Tune and 4th stanza of Hymn 202 on opposite page.

4 Vainly we offer each ample oblation;
Vainly with gifts would his favor secure:
Richer by far is the heart's adoration;
Dearer to God are the prayers of the poor.

---

792. 11s. Peculiar. Anon.

1 Daughter of Zion, awake from thy sadness;
Awake, for thy foes shall oppress thee no more;
Bright o'er thy hills dawns the daystar of gladness;
Arise, for the night of thy sorrow is o'er.

2 Strong were thy foes; but the arm that subdued them,
And scattered their legions, was mightier far;
They, like the chaff, fled the scourge that pursued them;
Vain were their steeds and their chariots of war.

3 Daughter of Zion, the power that hath saved thee
Extolled with the harp and the timbrel should be;
Shout, for the foe is destroyed that enslaved thee;
Th' oppressor is vanquished, and Zion is free.

HANOVER. 11s. Anapestic. From Handel, By Dr. [illegible]

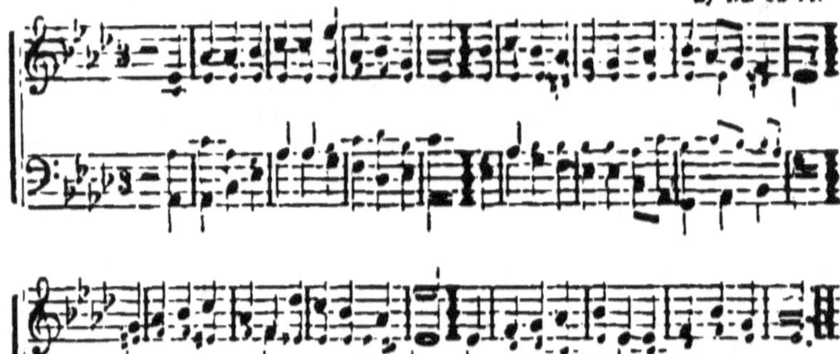

An additional note for the first syllable of the 1st and 3d lines will adapt [illegible] (on previous page, — 3d.)

347. 11s. De Fleury.

1 Come, saints, let us join in the praise of the Lamb,
The theme most sublime of the angels above;
They dwell with delight on the sound of his name,
And gaze on his glories with wonder and love.

2 Come, saints, and adore him; come, bow at his feet;
Let grateful hosannas unceasing arise;
O, give him the glory and praise that are meet,
And join the full chorus that gladdens the skies.

3 Behold to what honors the Saviour is raised;
He sits on the throne, and he rules over all;
By man once rejected, by seraphs now praised,
While powers and dominions, him worshipping, fall.

4 They worship the Lamb who for sinners was slain;
Their loftiest songs never equal his love:
The claims of his mercy will ever remain,
Transcending the anthems in glory above.

5 Yet even our service he will not despise,
When we join in worship and tell of his name;
Then let us unite in the song of the skies,
And, trusting his mercy, sing, "Worthy the Lamb."

---

843. 11s. E. Y. Reese.

1 "Do this," and remember the blood that was shed,
Ere Calvary's Victim to slaughter was led,
When, sad and forsaken, the garden alone
Gave ear to his sorrow, and echoed his moan.

2 Remember the conflict with insult and scorn,
The robe of derision, the chaplet of thorn,
The sin-cleansing fountain that streamed from his side,
When, "Father, forgive them," he uttered, and died.

3 Remember that, Victor o'er death and the grave,
He liveth forever, his people to save:
O, take with thanksgiving this pledge of his love —
The foretaste of rapture eternal above.

1148. 11s. Muhlenberg.

1 I would not live alway; I ask not to stay
Where storm after storm rises dark o'er the way;
The few lucid mornings that dawn on us here
Are followed by gloom or beclouded with fear.

2 I would not live alway thus fettered by sin —
Temptation without and corruption within:
E'en th' rapture of pardon is mingled with fears,
And th' cup of thanksgiving with penitent tears.

3 I would not live alway; no — welcome the tomb;
Since Jesus hath lain there, I dread not its gloom:
There sweet be my rest till he bid me arise
To hail him in triumph descending the skies.

4 Who, who would live alway away from his God —
Away from yon heaven, that blissful abode,

DELAY NOT.‡ 11s, or 12s & 11s Anapestic. DR. T. HASTINGS.

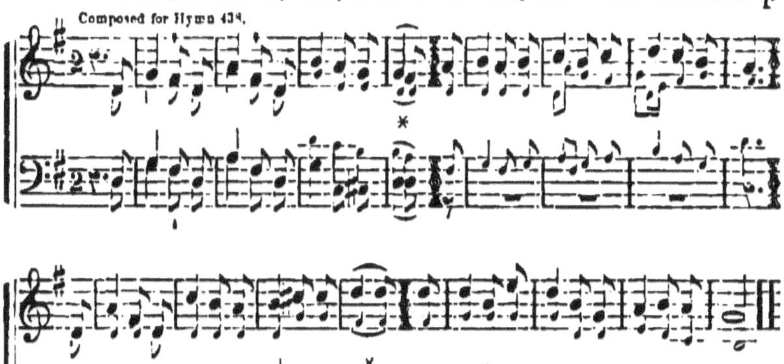

‡ Called also Ziklag. * Omit the slurs in 12s.

Where rivers of pleasure flow bright o'er the plains,
And th' noontide of glory eternally reigns?

5 There saints of all ages in harmony meet,
Their Saviour and brethren transported to greet;
While anthems of rapture unceasingly roll,
And th' smile of the Lord is the feast of the soul.

438. 11s. T. HASTINGS.

1 DELAY not, delay not; O sinner, draw near;
The waters of life are now flowing for thee;
No price is demanded; the Saviour is here;
Redemption is purchased, salvation is free.

2 Delay not, delay not; why longer abuse
The love and compassion of Jesus thy God?
A fountain is opened; how canst thou refuse
To wash and be cleansed in his pardoning blood!

3 Delay not, delay not, O sinner, to come,
For Mercy still lingers, and calls thee to-day;
Her voice is not heard in the shades of the tomb;
Her message, unheeded, will soon pass away.

4 Delay not, delay not; the Spirit of grace,
Long grieved and resisted, may take his sad flight,
And leave thee in darkness to finish thy race,
To sink in the gloom of eternity's night.

5 Delay not, delay not; the hour is at hand;
The earth shall dissolve, and the heavens shall fade;
The dead, small and great, in the judgment shall stand:
What helper, then, sinner, shall lend thee his aid?

454. 12s & 11s. J. B. HAGUE.

1 HARK, sinner, while God from on high doth entreat thee,
And warnings with accents of mercy doth blend;
Give ear to his voice, lest in judgment he meet thee;
"The harvest is passing, the summer will end."

2 How oft of thy danger and guilt he hath told thee!
How oft still the message of mercy doth send!
Haste, haste, while he waits in his arms to enfold thee;
"The harvest is passing, the summer will end."

3 Despiséd, rejected, at length he may leave thee:
What anguish and horror thy bosom will rend!
Then haste thee, O sinner, while he will receive thee;
"The harvest is passing, the summer will end."

4 Ere long, and Jehovah will come in his power,
Our God will arise, with his foes to contend:
Haste, haste thee, O sinner; prepare for that hour;
"The harvest is passing, the summer will end."

5 The Saviour will call thee in judgment before him:
O, bow to his sceptre, and make him thy Friend;
Now yield him thy heart, and make haste to adore him;
"Thy harvest is passing, thy summer will end."

COMPOSURE. 11s, or 12s & 11s, or 12s. Anapæstic. N. D. Gould.

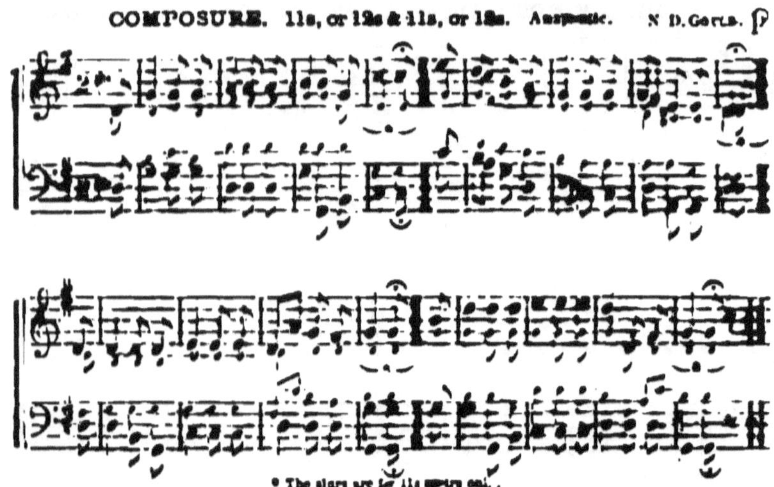

* The stars are for 11s metre only.

200. 11s. Montgomery.

1 The Lord is my Shepherd; no want shall I know;
I feed in green pastures, safe folded to rest;
He leadeth my soul where the still waters flow,
Restores me when wandering, redeems when oppressed.

2 Through th' valley and shadow of death though I stray,
Since thou art my Guardian, no evil I fear;
Thy rod shall defend me, thy staff be my stay;
No harm can befall with my Comforter near.

3 In th' midst of affliction, my table is spread;
With blessings unmeasured my cup runneth o'er,
With oil and perfume thou anointest my head;
O, what shall I ask of thy providence more?

4 Let goodness and mercy, my bountiful God,
Still follow my steps, till I meet thee above:
I seek, by the path which my forefathers trod,
Thro' th' land of their sojourn, thy kingdom of love.

960. 12s. Heber.

1 When thro' the torn sail the wild tempest is streaming,
When o'er the dark wave the red lightning is gleaming,
Nor hope lends a ray, the poor seaman to cherish,
We fly to our Maker — "Save, Lord, or we perish."

2 O Jesus, once rocked on the breast of the billow,
Aroused by the shriek of despair from thy pillow —
Now seated in glory, the mariner cherish,
Who cries in his anguish, "Save, Lord, or we perish."

3 And O, when the whirlwind of passion is raging,
When sin in our hearts its sad warfare is waging,
Then send down thy grace, thy redeemed to cherish;
Rebuke the destroyer — "Save, Lord, or we perish."

1021. 12s & 11s. C[illegible]man.

1 See, daylight is fading o'er earth and o'er ocean,
The sun has gone down on the far-distant seas;
O, now, in the hush of life's fitful commotion,
We lift our tired spirits, blest Saviour, to thee.

2 Full oft wast thou found afar off on the mountain,
As eventide spread her dark wing o'er the wave:
Thou Son of the Highest, and life's endless fountain,
Be with us, we pray thee, to bless and to save.

3 And oft as the tumult of life's heaving billow
Shall toss our frail bark, driving wild o'er night's deep,
Let thy healing wing be stretched over our pillow,
And guard us from evil, though death watch our sleep.

4 To God, our great Father, whose throne is in heaven,
Who dwells with the lowly and contrite in heart,
To th' Son, and the Spirit, all glory be given:
One God, ever blessed and praised thou art.

Comp. for Hymn 1106. **KANAH.** 13s & 11s. Anapestic. W. B. Bradbury.

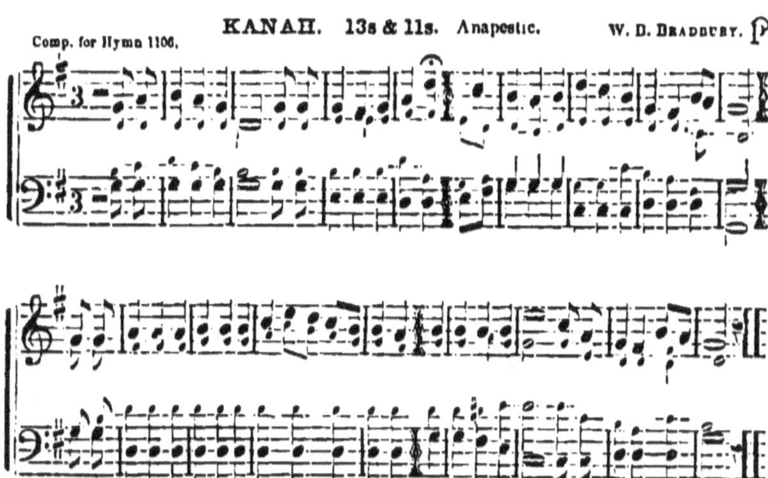

1106.

13s & 11s. Heber.

1 Thou art gone to the grave; but we will not deplore thee,
Though sorrows and darkness encompass the tomb;
The dear Saviour has passed thro' its portals before thee,
The lamp of his love is thy guide through the gloom.

2 Thou art gone to the grave; we no longer behold thee,
Nor tread the rough paths of the world by thy side;
But the wide arms of mercy are spread to enfold thee,
And sinners may hope, since the Saviour hath died.

3 Thou art gone to the grave; and its mansion forsaking,
Perchance thy weak spirit in doubt lingered long;
But the sunshine of heaven beamed bright on thy waking,
The sound thou didst hear was the seraphim's song.

4 Thou art gone to the grave; but we will not deplore thee;
Since God was thy Ransom, thy Guardian, thy Guide;
Since he gave thee, he took thee, and he will restore thee;
And death has no sting, since the Saviour hath died.

Adapted to Hymn 1106. **KANAAN.** 13s & 11s. Anapestic. Favorite Melody. Newly arranged by B. F. E.

VITAL SPARK, 1st & 2d Stanzas.

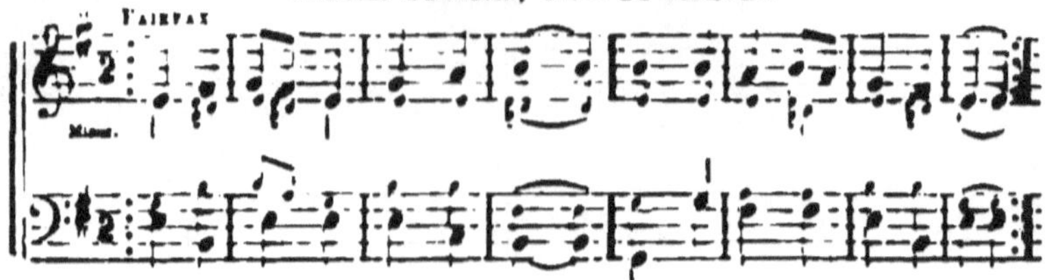

1080.

7s & 8s;—7s;—C. P. M. Pope.

1 VITAL spark of heavenly flame,
Quit, O, quit this mortal frame:
Trembling, hoping, lingering, flying,
O, the pain, the bliss, of dying!
Cease, fond nature, cease thy strife,
And let me languish into life.

2 Hark! — they whisper; angels say,
"Sister spirit, come away:"
What is this absorbs me quite? —
Steals my senses, shuts my sight,
Drowns my spirits, draws my breath? —
Tell me, my soul, can this be death?

3 The world recedes; it disappears;
Heaven opens on my eyes; my ears
With sounds seraphic ring:
Lend, lend your wings! I mount! I fly!
"O Grave, where is thy victory?
O Death, where is thy sting?"

VITAL SPARK, 3d Stanza.

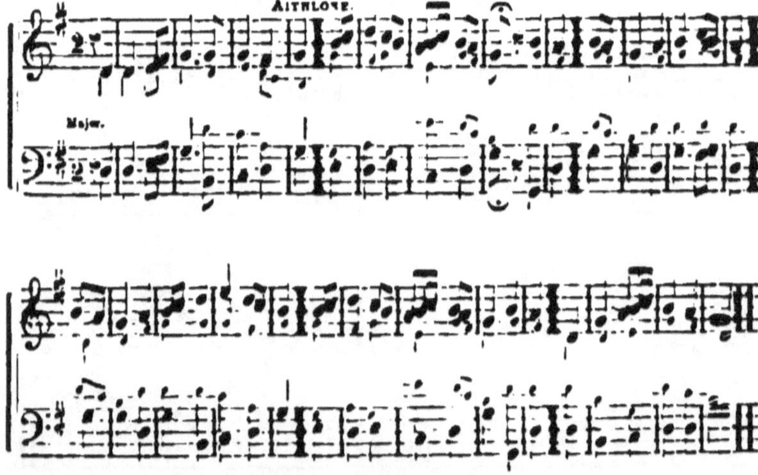

SUPPLEMENT.

PREFACE

TO THE SUPPLEMENT IN THE ORIGINAL EDITION.

THE Psalmist contains a copious supply of excellent hymns for the pulpit. We are acquainted with no collection of hymns combining, in an equal degree, poetic merit, evangelical sentiment, and a rich variety of subjects, with a happy adaptation to pulpit services. There is, however, a serious obstacle to its general use, especially in the South. Many hymns have acquired a high local popularity. Having been long in use, they are prized, not merely for their intrinsic worth, but for their tender and delightful associations. Old songs, like old friends, are more valued than new ones. A number of the hymns best known, most valued, and most frequently sung in the South are not found in the Psalmist. Without them, no hymn book, whatever may be its excellences, is likely to become generally or permanently popular in that region. To supply this deficiency in the Psalmist, as far as may be, is the design of the following Supplement.

These hymns have been mostly selected, not on account of their poetic beauty, but their established popularity. They will, we think, be found not seriously defective as metrical compositions, but their chief excellence consists in their adaptation to interest and affect the heart. They are, with few exceptions, inserted as they are known and sung among us without abridgment, or any attempt at improvement. If we are not deceived, they will form an acceptable appendix to the Psalmist. Adapted chiefly to *social worship*, they will, we trust, contribute greatly to the interest and profit of our prayer and protracted meetings.

Though this selection has been made with special reference to the taste and wants of the South, we know no reason why it should not be acceptable to other portions of the country. Many of the hymns in the Supplement are of high reputation in all parts of our country, as appears from the fact that they are found in almost every collection enjoying a local popularity.

Supplying the place of the Chants in the Psalmist, which in many portions of our country are seldom used, the Supplement will add very little to the bulk, and nothing to the price, of the book.

We now dedicate this small offering to the churches, earnestly imploring the "Father of Lights" that it may tend to increase the fervor of their devotions, and the spirituality of their minds.

RICHARD FULLER,
J. B. JETER.

SUPPLEMENT.

INDEX,

FROM HYMNS IN THE SUPPLEMENT TO PAGES.

1.

50.

100.

SUPPLEMENT

TO

THE PSALMIST.

PROVIDENCE.

GREGORY. L. M.

3. L. M. BEDDOME.

1 WAIT, O my soul, thy Maker's will;
Tumultuous passions, all be still;
Nor let a murmuring thought arise;
His ways are just, his counsels wise.

2 He in the thickest darkness dwells,
Performs his work, the cause conceals;
But, though his methods are unknown,
Judgment and truth support his throne.

3 In heaven, and earth, and air, and seas,
He executes his firm decrees;
And by his saints it stands confessed,
That what he does is ever best.

4 Wait, then, my soul, submissive wait,
Prostrate before his awful seat;
And, 'midst the terror of his rod,
Trust in a wise and gracious God.

CLARE. L. M.

EDWARD HAMILTON.
From The Sanctus.

6. L. M. METH. HYMNS.

1 GOD of my life, whose gracious power
Through various depths my soul hath led,
Or turned aside the fatal hour,
Or lifted up my sinking head, —

2 In all my ways thy hand I own,
Thy ruling providence I see;
Assist me still my course to run,
And still direct my paths to thee.

3 Whither, O whither, should I fly,
But to my loving Saviour's breast?
Secure within thine arms to lie,
And safe beneath thy wings to rest.

4 I have no skill the snare to shun,
But thou, O Christ, my wisdom art;
I ever into ruin run,
But thou art greater than my heart.

5 Foolish, and impotent, and blind,
Lead me a way I have not known;
Bring me where I my heaven may find —
The heaven of serving thee alone.

4. L. M. Rippon's Sel.

1 Through all the various, passing scene
Of life's mistaken ill or good,
Thy hand, O God, conducts, unseen,
The beautiful vicissitude.

2 Thou givest, with paternal care,
Howe'er unjustly we complain,
To each their necessary share
Of joy and sorrow, health and pain.

3 Trust we to youth, or friends, or power?
Fix we on this terrestrial ball?
When most secure, the coming hour,
If thou see fit, may blast them all.

4 When lowest sunk with grief and shame,
Filled with affliction's bitter cup,
Lost to relations, friends, and fame,
Thy powerful hand can raise us up;—

5 Thy powerful consolations cheer;
Thy smiles suppress the deep-fetched sigh;
Thy hand can dry the trickling tear
That secret wets the widow's eye.

6 All things on earth, and all in heaven,
On thy eternal will depend;
And all for greater good were given,
And all shall in thy glory end.

7 This be my care; to all beside
Indifferent let my wishes be:
"Passion be calm, and dumb be pride,
And fixed, O God, my soul on thee."

11. L. M. Cennick.

1 Jesus, my all, to heaven is gone—
He whom I fix my hopes upon;
His track I see, and I'll pursue
The narrow way, till him I view,—

2 The way the holy prophets went;
The road that leads from banishment;
The king's highway of holiness—
I'll go, for all his paths are peace.

3 This is the way I long have sought,
And mourned because I found it not;
My grief and burden long has been
Because I could not cease from sin.

4 The more I strove against its power,
I sinned and stumbled but the more;
Till late I heard my Saviour say,
"Come hither, soul; I am the way."

5 Lo! glad I come; and thou, blest Lamb,
Shalt take me to thee as I am,
My sinful self to thee I give;
Nothing but love shall I receive.

6 Then will I tell to sinners round
What a dear Saviour I have found,
I'll point to thy redeeming blood,
And say, "Behold the way to God!"

18. L. M. Hyde.

1 Say, sinner, hath a voice within,
Oft whispered to thy secret soul,
Urged thee to leave the ways of sin,
And yield thy heart to God's control?

2 Hath something met thee in the path
Of worldliness and vanity,
And pointed to the coming wrath,
And warned thee from that wrath to flee?

3 Sinner, it was a heavenly voice;
It was the Spirit's gracious call;
It bade thee make the better choice,
And haste to seek in Christ thine all.

HEBRO. L. M. Arranged by the Editor for this work.

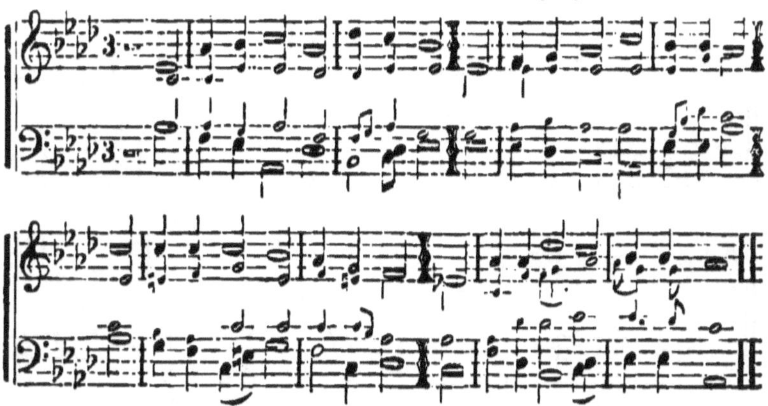

4 Spurn not the call to life and light;
Regard in time the warning, kind;
That call thou mayst not always slight,
And yet the gate of mercy find.

5 God's Spirit shall not always strive
With hardened, self-destroying man;
Ye who persist his love to grieve
May never hear his voice again.

33. L. M. Wesley.

1 O THAT my load of sin were gone!
O that I could at last submit
At Jesus' feet to lay it down,
To lay my soul at Jesus' feet!

2 Rest for my soul I long to find;
Saviour, if mine indeed thou art,
Give me thy meek and lowly mind,
And stamp thine image on my heart.

3 Fain would I learn of thee, my God,
Thy light and easy burden prove;
The cross, all stained with hallowed blood,
The labor of thy dying love.

4 I would; but thou must give the power;
My heart from every sin release;
Bring near, bring near the joyful hour,
And fill my soul with heavenly peace.

5 Come, Lord, the drooping sinner cheer,
Nor let thy chariot wheels delay;
Appear, in my poor heart appear;
My God, my Saviour, come away.

37. L. M. Kelly.

1 I HEAR a voice that comes from far;
From Calvary it sounds abroad;
It soothes my spirit, calms my fear;
It speaks of pardon bought with blood.

2 And is it true that many fly
The sound that bids my soul rejoice,
And rather choose in sin to die,
Than turn an ear to Mercy's voice?

3 Alas for those! — the day is near
When Mercy will be heard no more;
Then may they ask in vain to hear
The voice they would not hear before.

4 With such, I own, I once appeared;
But now I know how great their loss;
For sweeter sounds were never heard
Than Mercy utters from the cross.

5 But let me not forget to own
That, if I differ aught from those,
'Tis due to sovereign grace alone,
That conquers oft its proudest foes.

GREGORY. L. M.

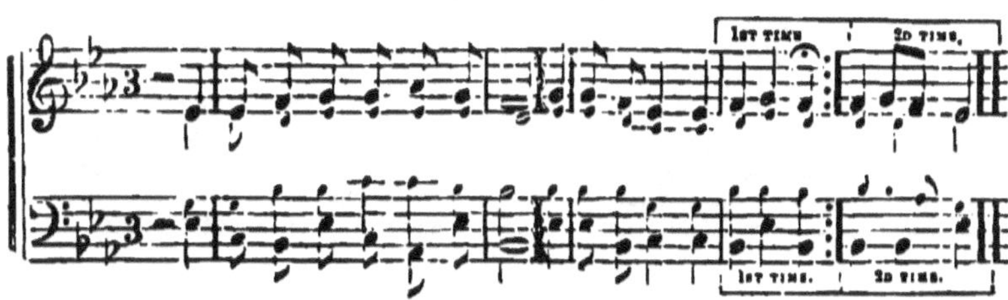

NAZARETH. L. M. (Malcombe.) {Arranged to [illegible]

Choral.

21. L. M. STEELE.

1 ETERNITY is just at hand!
And shall I waste my ebbing sand,
And careless view departing day,
And throw my inch of time away?

2 Eternity! — tremendous sound!
To guilty souls a dreadful wound;
But, O, if Christ and heaven be mine,
How sweet the accents, how divine!

3 Be this my chief, my only care,
My high pursuit, my ardent prayer —
An interest in the Saviour's blood,
My pardon sealed, my peace with God.

4 Search, Lord, O, search my inmost heart,
And light, and hope, and joy impart:
From guilt and error set me free,
And guide me safe to heaven and thee.

41. L. M. DODDRIDGE.

1 JESUS, our soul's delightful choice,
In thee believing, we rejoice;
Yet still our joy is mixed with grief,
While faith contends with unbelief.

2 Thy promises our hearts revive,
And keep our fainting hopes alive;
But guilt, and fears, and sorrows rise,
And hide the promise from our eyes.

3 O, let not sin and Satan boast,
While saints lie mourning in the dust,
Nor see that faith to ruin brought,
Which thy own gracious hand hath wrought.

4 Do thou the dying spark inflame;
Reveal the glories of thy name,
And put all anxious doubt to flight,
As shades dispersed by opening light.

38. L. M. DODDRIDGE.

1 LORD, shed a beam of heavenly day
To melt this stubborn stone away;
Now thaw, with rays of love divine,
This heart, this frozen heart, of mine.

2 The rocks can rend; the earth can quake;
The seas can roar; the mountains shake;
Of feeling all things show some sign,
But this unfeeling heart of mine.

3 To hear the sorrows thou hast felt;
What but an adamant would melt?
Goodness and wrath in vain combine
To move this stupid heart of mine.

4 But ONE can yet perform the deed;
That One in all his grace I need;
Thy Spirit can from dross refine
And melt this stubborn heart of mine.

5 O, Breath of Life, breathe on my soul!
On me let streams of mercy roll;
Now thaw, with rays of love divine,
This heart, this frozen heart, of mine.

104. L. M. KELLY.

1 HOW sweet to leave the world a while,
And seek the presence of our Lord!
Dear Saviour, on thy people smile,
According to thy faithful word.

2 From busy scenes we now retreat,
That we may here converse with thee;
O Lord, behold us at thy feet!
Let this the gate of heaven be.

3 "Chief of ten thousand," now appear,
That we by faith may view thy face;
O, speak, that we thy voice may hear,
And let thy presence fill the place.

WELLS. L. M. Composed before 1740. ‡

‡ Ascribed to Broderip, and to Holdrayd.

43. L. M. NEWTON.

1 I ASKED the Lord that I might grow
In faith, and love, and every grace,
Might more of his salvation know,
And seek, more earnestly, his face.

2 'Twas he who taught me thus to pray,
And he, I trust, has answered prayer;
But it has been in such a way
As almost drove me to despair.

3 I hoped that in some favored hour,
At once he'd answer my request,
And by his love's constraining power
Subdue my sins and give me rest.

4 Instead of this, he made me feel
The hidden evils of my heart,
And let the angry powers of hell
Assault my soul in every part.

5 Yea, more, with his own hand he seemed
Intent to aggravate my woe;
Crossed all the fair designs I schemed,
Blasted my gourds, and laid me low.

6 "Lord, why is this?" I trembling cried;
"Wilt thou pursue thy worm to death?"
"'Tis in this way," the Lord replied,
"I answer prayer for grace and faith.

7 "These inward trials I employ,
From self and pride to set thee free,
And break thy schemes of earthly joy,
That thou mayst seek thy all in me."

46. L. M. COWPER.

1 WHAT various hindrances we meet
In coming to the mercy-seat!
Yet who, that knows the worth of prayer,
But wishes to be often there?

2 Prayer makes the darkened cloud withdraw;
Prayer climbs the ladder Jacob saw,
Gives exercise to faith and love,
Brings every blessing from above.

3 Restraining prayer, we cease to fight;
Prayer makes the Christian's armor bright;
And Satan trembles, when he sees
The weakest saint upon his knees.

4 Have you no words? Ah, think again;
Words flow apace when you complain,
And fill your fellow-creature's ear
With the sad tale of all your care.

5 Were half the breath thus vainly spent
To Heaven in supplication sent,
Your cheerful songs would oftener be,
"Hear what the Lord has done for me!"

49. L. M. STENNETT.

1 To God, my Saviour and my King,
Fain would my soul her tribute bring;
Join me, ye saints, in songs of praise,
For ye have known and felt his grace.

2 Wretched and helpless once I lay,
Just breathing all my life away;
He saw me weltering in my blood,
And felt the pity of a God.

3 With speed he flew to my relief,
Bound up my wounds and soothed my grief,
Poured joy divine into my heart,
And bade each anxious fear depart.

4 These proofs of love, my dearest Lord,
Deep in my breast I will record:
The life which I from thee receive,
To thee, behold, I freely give.

5 My heart and tongue shall tune thy praise,
Through the remainder of my days;
And when I join the powers above,
My soul shall better sing thy love.

KINDNESS. L. M. Concluded on opposite page.

For Hymn 47.

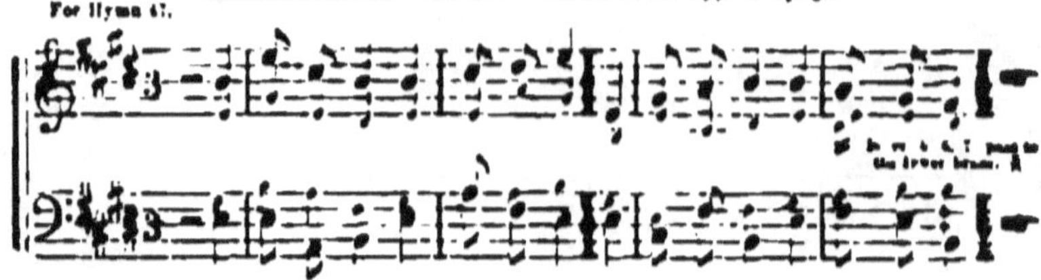

47. L. M. MEDLEY.

1 AWAKE, my soul, in joyful lays,
And sing thy great Redeemer's praise
He justly claims a song from me:
His loving kindness, O, how free!

2 He saw me ruined by the fall,
Yet loved me, notwithstanding all;
He saved me from my lost estate:
His loving kindness, O, how great!

3 Though numerous hosts of mighty foes,
Though earth and hell my way oppose,
He safely leads my soul along:
His loving kindness, O, how strong!

4 When trouble, like a gloomy cloud,
Has gathered thick and thundered loud,
He near my soul has always stood:
His loving kindness, O, how good!

In singing "Kindness" to this hymn, omit in the verses below the upper braces on next page, and sing the lower brace.

5 Often I feel my sinful heart
Prone from my Jesus to depart;
But though I have him oft forgot,
His loving kindness changes not.

6 Soon shall I pass the gloomy vale,
Soon all my mortal powers must fail;
O, may my last, expiring breath
His loving kindness sing in death.

7 Then let me mount and soar away
To the bright world of endless day,
And sing, with rapture and surprise,
His loving kindness in the skies.

LOVING KINDNESS. L. M.

Coda.—His lov - ing kindness, Loving kindness, His lov - ing, &c.

KINDNESS, Concluded. D. F. EDMANDS. ‡

This brace for verses 1, 2, 3 & 4 only.

This brace for verses 5, 6, & 7 only.

‡ Arranged partly from a Choral by J. Schop, 1660. Though specially adapted for hymn 47, it may be sung to hymn 57 by omitting the upper brace of this page.

57. L. M. STEELE.

1 DEAR Lord, and shall thy Spirit rest
In such a wretched heart as mine?
Unworthy dwelling, glorious Guest!
Favor astonishing, divine!

2 When sin prevails, and gloomy fear,
And hope almost expires in night,
Lord, can thy Spirit then be here,
Great Spring of comfort, life, and light?

3 Sure the blest Comforter is nigh;
'Tis he sustains my fainting heart;
Else would my hopes forever die,
And every cheering ray depart.

4 When some kind promise cheers my soul,
Do I not find his healing voice
The tempest of my fears control,
And bid my drooping powers rejoice?

5 Whene'er to call the Saviour mine
With ardent wish my heart aspires,
Can it be less than power divine,
Which animates these strong desires?

6 What less than thy almighty word
Can raise my heart from earth and dust,
And bid me cleave to thee, my Lord,
My Life, my Treasure, and my Trust?

7 And, when my cheerful hope can say,
"I love my God, and taste his grace,"
Lord, is it not thy blissful ray
Which brings this dawn of sacred peace?

8 Let thy kind Spirit in my heart
Forever dwell, O God of love,
And light and heavenly peace impart,
Sweet earnest of the joys above.

CLARE. L. M. EDWARD HAMILTON. From The Sanctus.

WINCHELSEA. L. M. PHILLIPS.

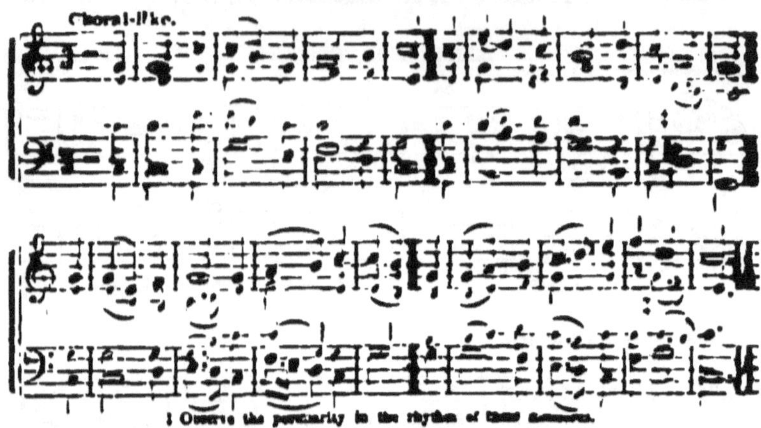

† Observe the peculiarity in the rhythm of these measures.

74. L. M. WATTS.

1 FROM age to age exalt his name;
God and his grace are still the same;
He fills the hungry soul with food,
And feeds the poor with every good.

2 But if their hearts rebel, and rise
Against the God that rules the skies,—
If they reject his heavenly word,
And slight the counsels of the Lord,—

3 He'll bring their spirits to the ground,
And no deliverer shall be found;
Laden with grief they waste their breath
In darkness and the shades of death.

4 Then to the Lord they raise their cries;
He makes the dawning light arise,
And scatters all that dismal shade,
That hung so heavy round their head.

5 He cuts the bars of brass in two,
And lets the smiling prisoners through;
Takes off the load of guilt and grief,
And gives the laboring soul relief.

6 O, may the sons of men record
The wondrous goodness of the Lord!
How great his works! how kind his ways!
Let every tongue pronounce his praise.

83. L. M. FAWCETT.

1 AFFLICTED saint, to Christ draw near;
Thy Saviour's gracious promise hear;
His faithful word declares to thee
That as thy days thy strength shall be.

2 Let not thy heart despond, and say
"How shall I stand the trying day?"
He has engaged, by firm decree,
That as thy days thy strength shall be.

3 Thy faith is weak; thy foes are strong;
And, if the conflict should be long,
Thy Lord will make the tempter flee;
For as thy days thy strength shall be.

4 Should persecution rage and flame,
Still trust in thy Redeemer's name;
In fiery trials thou shalt see,
That as thy days thy strength shall be.

5 When called to bear the weighty cross,
Or sore affliction, pain, or loss,
Or deep distress, or poverty,—
Still as thy days thy strength shall be.

6 When ghastly death appears in view,
Christ's presence shall thy fears subdue;
He comes to set thy spirit free;
And as thy days thy strength shall be.

88. L. M. D TURNER.

1 YES, I would love thee, blessed God!
Paternal goodness marks thy name;
Thy praises, through thy high abode,
The heavenly hosts with joy proclaim.

2 Freely thou gav'st thy dearest Son
For man to suffer, bleed, and die,
And bidd'st me, as a wretch undone,
For all I want on him rely.

3 In him, thy reconciled face,
With joy unspeakable I see,
And feel thy powerful, wondrous grace,
Draw and unite my soul to thee.

4 Whene'er my foolish, wandering heart,
Attracted by a creature's power,
Would from this blissful centre start,
Lord, fix it there to stray no more.

ROSEDALE. L. M. George F. Root.‡ 1853.

‡ By his permission.

61. L. M. Cowper.

1 When darkness long has veiled my mind,
And smiling day once more appears,
Then, my Redeemer, then I find
The folly of my doubts and fears.

2 I chide my unbelieving heart,
And blush that I should ever be
Thus prone to act so base a part,
Or harbor one hard thought of thee.

3 O, let me, then, at length, be taught —
What I am still so slow to learn —
That God is love, and changes not,
Nor knows the shadow of a turn.

4 Sweet truth, and easy to repeat;
But when my faith is sharply tried,
I find myself a learner yet,
Unskilful, weak, and apt to slide.

5 But, O my Lord, one look from thee
Subdues the disobedient will,
Drives doubt and discontent away,
And thy rebellious worm is still.

6 Thou art as ready to forgive
As I am ready to repine;
Thou, therefore, all the praise receive;
Be shame and self-abhorrence mine.

79. L. M. Gisborne.

1 Saviour, when night involves the skies,
My soul, adoring, turns to thee —
Thee — self-abased in mortal guise,
And wrapt in shades of death for me

2 On thee my waking raptures dwell,
When crimson gleams the east adorn;
Thee — Victor of the grave and hell —
Thee — Source of life's eternal morn.

3 When noon her throne in light arrays,
To thee my soul triumphant springs —
Thee — throned in glory's endless blaze —
Thee — Lord of lords, and King of kings.

4 O'er earth when shades of evening steal,
To death and thee my thoughts I give —
To death — whose power I soon must feel —
To thee — with whom I trust to live.

87. L. M. Fawcett.

1 Thus far my God hath led me on,
And made his truth and mercy known;
My hopes and fears alternate rise,
And comforts mingle with my sighs.

2 Through this wide wilderness I roam,
Far distant from my blissful home;
Lord, let thy presence be my stay,
And guard me in this dangerous way.

3 Temptations every where annoy,
And sins and snares my peace destroy;
My earthly joys are from me torn,
And oft an absent God I mourn.

4 My soul, with various tempests tossed,
Her hopes o'erturned, her projects crossed,
Sees, every day, new straits attend,
And wonders where the scene will end.

5 Is this, dear Lord, that thorny road
Which leads us to the mount of God?
Are these the toils thy people know,
While in the wilderness below?

6 'Tis even so thy faithful love
Doth all thy children's graces prove;
'Tis thus our pride and self must fall,
That Jesus may be all in all.

‡ Originally in equal notes; may be so sung, as a choral.

76. L. M. Epis. Col.

1 Be still, my heart; these anxious cares
To thee are burdens, thorns, and snares;
They cast dishonor on thy Lord,
And contradict his gracious word.

2 Brought safely by his hand thus far,
Why wilt thou now give place to fear?
How canst thou want if he provide,
Or lose thy way with such a Guide?

3 Did ever trouble yet befall,
And he refuse to hear thy call?
And has he not his promise passed
That thou shalt overcome at last?

4 Though rough and thorny be the road,
It leads thee home apace to God;
Then count thy present trials small,
For heaven will make amends for all.

80. L. M. Cowper.

1 Lord, unafflicted, undismayed,
In pleasure's path how long I strayed!
But thou hast made me feel thy rod,
And turn my soul to thee, my God.

2 What though it pierced my fainting heart?
I bless thy hand which caused the smart;
It taught my tears a while to flow,
But saved me from eternal woe.

3 O, hadst thou left me unchastised,
Thy precepts I had still despised;
And still the snare, in secret laid,
Had my unwary feet betrayed.

4 I love thy chastenings, O my God;
They fix my hopes on thy abode,
Where, in thy presence, fully blest,
Thy stricken saints forever rest.

68. L. M. Doddridge.

1 Arise, my tenderest thoughts, arise,
To torrents melt my streaming eyes;
And thou, my heart, with anguish feel
Those evils which thou canst not heal.

2 See human nature sunk in shame;
See scandals poured on Jesus' name;
The Father wounded through the Son;
The world abused; the soul undone.

3 See the short course of vain delight
Closing in everlasting night,
In flames that no abatement know,
Though briny tears forever flow.

4 My God, I feel the mournful scene;
My bowels yearn o'er dying men;
And fain my pity would reclaim,
And snatch the firebrands from the flame.

5 But feeble my compassion proves,
And can but weep where most it loves;
Thy own all saving arm employ,
And turn these drops of grief to joy.

102. L. M. Steele.

1 Ah, wretched souls, who strive in vain,
Slaves to the world, and slaves to sin;
A nobler toil may I sustain,
A nobler satisfaction win.

2 May I resolve, with all my heart,
With all my powers, to serve the Lord;
Nor from his precepts e'er depart,
Whose service is a rich reward.

3 O, be his service all my joy;
Around let my example shine,
Till others love the blest employ,
And join in labors so divine.

‡ The rhythm changed.

4 Be this the purpose of my soul,
My solemn, my determined choice,
To yield to his supreme control,
And in his kind commands rejoice.

5 O, may I never faint or tire,
Nor, wandering, leave his sacred ways;
Great God, accept my soul's desire,
And give me strength to live thy praise.

86. L. M. HEBER.

1 THOUGH sorrows rise, and dangers roll
In waves of darkness o'er my soul —
Though friends are false, and love decays,
And few and evil are my days —
Though conscience, fiercest of my foes,
Swells with remembered guilt my woes, —
Yet, even in nature's utmost ill,
I love thee, Lord; I love thee still.

2 Though Sinai's curse, in thunder dread,
Peals o'er my unprotected head,
And memory points, with busy pain,
To grace and mercy given in vain,
Till nature, shrinking in the strife,
Would fly to hell t' escape from life,
Though every thought has power to kill,
I love thee, Lord; I love thee still.

3 O, by the pangs thyself hast borne,
The ruffian's blow, the tyrant's scorn;
By Sinai's curse, whose dreadful doom
Was buried in thy guiltless tomb;
By these my pangs, whose healing smart
Thy grace hath planted in my heart,
I know, I feel, thy bounteous will;
Thou lov'st me, Lord; thou lov'st me still.

In Edwd. Ireland's "Tunes of the Psalms," [illegible] ‡

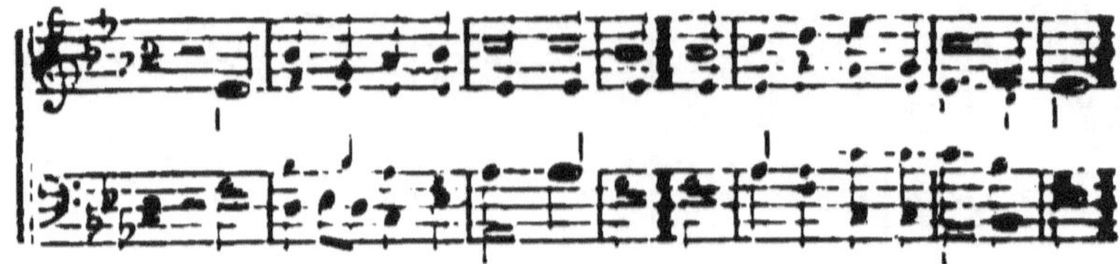

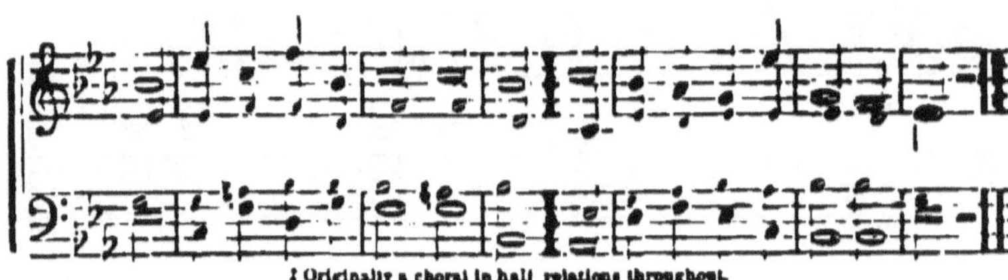

‡ Originally a choral in half relations throughout.

78. L. M. 6 L. Epis. Col.

1 As, panting in the sultry beam,
The hart desires the cooling stream,
So, to thy presence, Lord, I flee;
So longs my soul, O God, for thee;
Athirst to taste thy living grace,
And see thy glory face to face.

2 But rising griefs distress my soul,
And tears on tears successive roll;
For many an evil voice is near,
To chide my woe and mock my fear;
And silent memory weeps alone
O'er hours of peace and gladness flown

3 For I have walked the happy round
That circles Zion's holy ground,
And gladly swelled the choral lays
That hymned my great Redeemer's praise;
What time the hallowed arches rung,
Responsive to the solemn song.

4 Ah, why, by passing clouds oppressed,
Should vexing thoughts distract my breast?
Turn, turn to him in every pain,
Whom suppliants never sought in vain—
Thy strength in joy's ecstatic day,
Thy hope, when joy has passed away.

94. L. M. 6 L. Newton, alt'd.

1 This is the field, the world below,
Where wheat and tares together go;
Where oft we see, in mingled band,
Sinners and saints together stand;
But soon the reaping-time will come,
And angels shout the harvest home.

2 We seem as one, when thus we meet,
And bow before the mercy-seat;
But to the Lord's all-searching eyes,
Each heart appears without disguise;
And soon the reaping time, &c.

3 To love my sins, a saint t' appear,
To grow with wheat, and be a tare,
May serve me while on earth below,
Where tares and wheat together grow;
But soon the reaping time, &c.

4 Most awful truth! And is it so?
Must all mankind the harvest know?
Is every one a wheat or tare?—
Me for the harvest, Lord, prepare;
For soon the reaping time, &c.

5 Then all who truly righteous are,
Shall in their Father's kingdom share;

But tares in bundles shall be bound,
And cast in hell. O, doleful sound!
And soon the reaping-time will come,
And angels shout the harvest home.

12. L. M. 6 l. Grant.

1 When gathering storms around I view,
And days are dark, and friends are few,
On Him I lean, who not in vain
Experienced every human pain:
He sees my wants, allays my fears,
And counts and treasures up my tears.

2 If aught should tempt my soul to stray
From heavenly virtue's narrow way,
To fly the good I would pursue,
Or do the sin I would not do,
Still he who felt temptation's power
Shall guard me in that dangerous hour.

3 When vexing thoughts within me rise,
And, sore dismayed, my spirit dies,
Yet He, who once vouchsafed to bear
The sickening anguish of despair,
Shall sweetly soothe, shall gently dry,
The throbbing heart, the streaming eye.

4 When, sorrowing, o'er some stone I bend
Which covers all that was a friend,
And from his voice, his hand, his smile,
Divides me for a little while,
Thou, Saviour, seest the tears I shed,
For thou didst weep o'er Lazarus dead.

5 And O, when I have safely passed
Through every conflict but the last,
Still, still unchanging, watch beside
My painful bed, for thou hast died;
Then point to realms of cloudless day,
And wipe the latest tear away.

ZEPHYR. L. M. Wm. B. Bradbury. From Mendelssohn Col.

‡ Upper brace to be repeated for Hymn 12.

92. L. M. Village Hymns.

1 Lift up your eyes, ye sons of light;
Behold the fields already white;
The glorious harvest now is come;
See ransomed sinners flocking home.

2 Moved by the Spirit's softest wind,
Their hearts are all as one inclined;
Their former sins and follies mourn;
They bow, and to their God return.

3 Improve the harvest, fleeing fast,
Ere yet the shining season 's past,
When all the work of life shall end,
The last, the long, dark night descend.

MISS'Y CHANT.

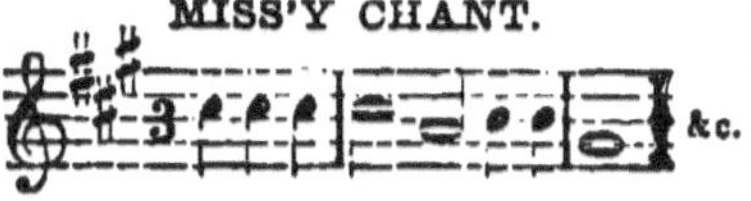

95. L. M. Newton.

1 As when the weary traveller gains
The height of some commanding hill,
His heart revives, if o'er the plains
He sees his home, though distant still,—

2 So, when the Christian pilgrim views,
By faith, his mansion in the skies,
The sight his fainting strength renews,
And wings his speed to reach the prize.

3 The hope of heaven his spirit cheers;
No more he grieves for sorrows past;
Nor any future conflict fears,
So he may safe arrive at last.

4 O Lord, on thee our hopes we stay,
To lead us on to thine abode,
Assured thy love will far o'erpay
The hardest labors of the road.

MADISON. 8s. Double. Arr. from S. B. Pond.

From the Selah.

42.

8s. TOPLADY.

1 ENCOMPASSED with clouds of distress,
Just ready all hope to resign,
I pant for the light of thy face,
And fear it will never be mine:
Disheartened with waiting so long,
I sink at thy feet with my load;
All plaintive I pour out my song,
And stretch forth my hands unto God.

2 Shine, Lord, and my terror shall cease;
The blood of atonement apply;
And lead me to Jesus for peace, —
The Rock that is higher than I:
Speak, Saviour! for sweet is thy voice;
Thy presence is fair to behold;
Attend to my sorrows and cries —
My groanings that cannot be told.

3 If sometimes I strive, as I mourn,
My hold of thy promise to keep,
The billows more fiercely return,
And plunge me again in the deep:
While harassed and cast from thy sight,
The tempter suggests, with a roar,
"The Lord has forsaken thee quite;
Thy God will be gracious no more."

4 Yet, Lord, if thy love hath designed
No covenant blessing for me,
Ah, tell me, how is it I find
Some pleasure in waiting for thee?
Almighty to rescue thou art;
Thy grace is my shield and my tower:
Come, succour and gladden my heart;
Let this be the day of thy power.

65.

8s. Double. NEWTON.

1 How tedious and tasteless the hours
When Jesus no longer I see!
Sweet prospects, sweet birds, and sweet flowers,
Have all lost their sweetness with me.
The midsummer sun shines but dim;
The fields strive in vain to look gay;
But when I am happy in him,
December 's as pleasant as May.

2 His name yields the richest perfume,
And sweeter than music his voice;
His presence disperses my gloom,
And makes all within me rejoice:
I should, were he always thus nigh,
Have nothing to wish for, or fear;
No mortal so happy as I;
My summer would last all the year.

3 Content with beholding his face,
My all to his pleasure resigned,
No changes of season or place
Would make any change in my mind:
While blest with a sense of his love,
A palace a toy would appear;
And prisons would palaces prove,
If Jesus would dwell with me there.

4 Dear Lord, if indeed I am thine,
If thou art my sun and my song,
Say, why do I languish and pine,
And why are my winters so long?
O, drive these dark clouds from my sky;
Thy soul-cheering presence restore;
Or take me unto thee on high,
Where winter and clouds are no more.

UNION HYMN. 8s, or 8s & 9s. Anapestic. BILLINGS.

67.

8s. BALDWIN.

1 From whence doth this union arise,
That hatred is conquered by love?
It fastens our souls in such ties
As distance and time can't remove.

2 It cannot in Eden be found,
Nor yet in a paradise lost;
It grows on Immanuel's ground,
And Jesus' dear blood it did cost.

3 My brethren are dear unto me,
Our hearts all united in love:
Where Jesus is gone we shall be,
In yonder blest mansions above.

4 Why, then, so unwilling to part,
Since there we shall all meet again?
Engraved on Immanuel's heart,
At a distance we cannot remain.

5 O, when shall we see that bright day,
And join with the angels above,
Set free from these prisons of clay,
United in Jesus's love?

6 With Jesus we ever shall reign,
And all his bright glories shall see,
Singing, Hallelujah! amen!
Amen! even so let it be.

NORTHFIELD 8s.

Treble part.

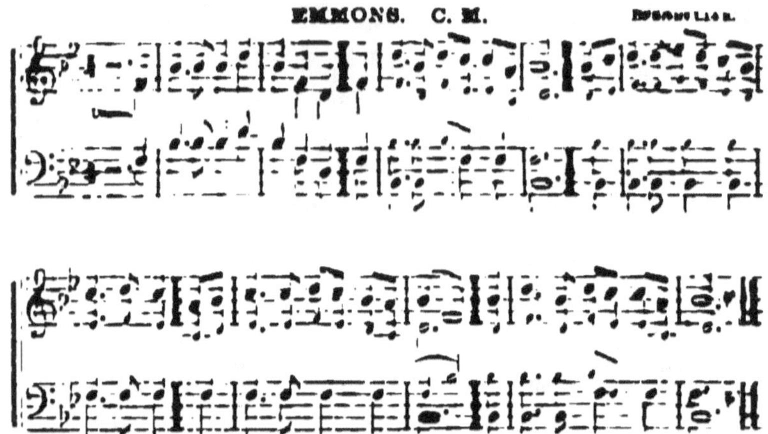

5. C. M. PRES. HYMNS.

1 O THOU, my light, my life, my joy,
My glory, and my all,
Unsent by thee, no good can come,
Nor evil can befall.

2 Such are thy schemes of providence,
And methods of thy grace,
That I may safely trust in thee
Through all the wilderness.

3 'Tis thine outstretched and powerful arm
Upholds me in my way;
And thy rich bounty well supplies
The wants of every day.

4 For such compassions, O my God,
Ten thousand thanks are due;
For such compassions, I esteem
Ten thousand thanks too few.

---

8. C. M. MEDLEY.

1 MORTALS, awake; with angels join,
And chant the solemn lay:
Joy, love, and gratitude combine
To hail th' auspicious day.

2 In heaven the rapturous song began,
And sweet, seraphic fire
Through all the shining legions ran,
And strung and tuned the lyre.

3 Swift through the vast expanse it flew,
And loud the echo rolled:
The theme, the song, the joy, was new;
'Twas more than heaven could hold.

4 Down through the portals of the sky
Th' impetuous torrent ran;
And angels flew, with eager joy,
To bear the news to man.

5 Hark! the cherubic armies shout,
And glory leads the song;
Good will and peace are heard throughout
Th' harmonious, heavenly throng.

6 O for a glance of heavenly love,
Our hearts and songs to raise,
Sweetly to bear our souls above,
And mingle with their lays.

7 With joy the chorus we'll repeat,
"Glory to God on high!
Good will and peace are now complete;
Jesus was born to die."

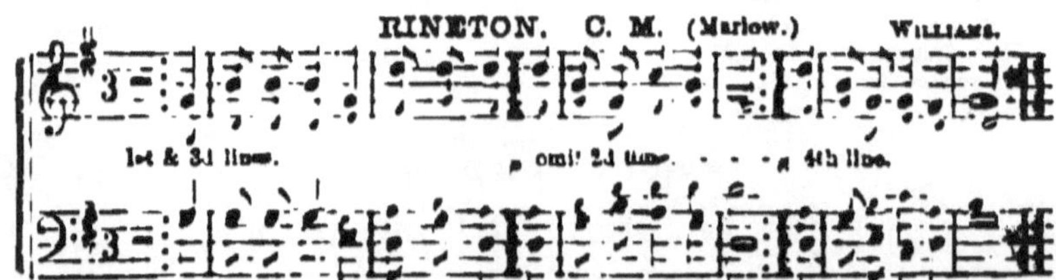

BROWN. C. M. W. B. BRADBURY. 1845.

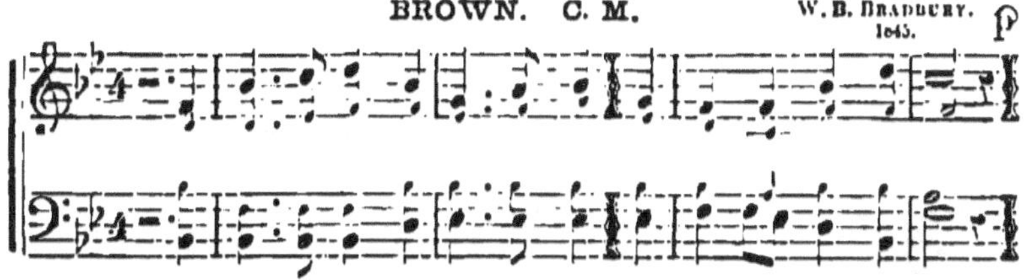

8 Hail, Prince of Life! forever hail,
Redeemer, Brother, Friend;
Though earth, and time, and life, should fail,
Thy praise shall never end.

13. C. M. NEWTON.

1 How sweet the name of Jesus sounds
In a believer's ear!
It soothes his sorrows, heals his wounds,
And drives away his fear.

2 It makes the wounded spirit whole,
And calms the troubled breast;
'Tis manna to the hungry soul,
And to the weary rest.

3 Dear name! the rock on which I build,
My shield and hiding-place,
My never-failing treasury, filled
With boundless stores of grace.

4 By thee my prayers acceptance gain,
Although with sin defiled;
Satan accuses me in vain,
And I am owned a child.

5 Jesus, my Shepherd, Husband, Friend,
My Prophet, Priest, and King,
My Lord, my Life, my Way, my End,
Accept the praise I bring.

6 Weak is the effort of my heart,
And cold my warmest thought;
But, when I see thee as thou art,
I'll praise thee as I ought.

7 Till then, I would thy love proclaim
With every fleeting breath;
And may the music of thy name
Refresh my soul in death.

14. C. M. DODDRIDGE.

1 Do not I love thee, O my Lord?
Behold my heart, and see;
And turn each cursèd idol out
That dares to rival thee.

2 Do not I love thee from my soul?
Then let me nothing love;
Dead be my heart to every joy,
When Jesus cannot move.

3 Is not thy name melodious still
To mine attentive ear?
Doth not each pulse with pleasure bound
My Saviour's voice to hear?

4 Hast thou a lamb in all thy flock
I would disdain to feed?
Hast thou a foe before whose face
I fear thy cause to plead?

5 Would not my ardent spirit vie
With angels round the throne,
To execute thy sacred will,
And make thy glory known?

6 Would not my heart pour forth its blood
In honor of thy name,
And challenge the cold hand of death
To damp th' immortal flame?

7 Thou know'st I love thee, dearest Lord;
But O, I long to soar
Far from the sphere of mortal joys,
And learn to love thee more.

MELODY.

COMFORT. C. M. With Coda. ‡ MRS. P. GIBSON.

CODA.
O Lord, O Lord, O Lord, Re mem ber me.

‡ The Coda is for Hymn 34. To other hymns the tune may be sung without the Coda.

34. C. M. ANON.

1 JESUS, thou art the sinner's Friend;
As such I look to thee;
Now, in the bowels of thy love,
O Lord, remember me.

2 Remember thy pure word of grace;
Remember Calvary;
Remember all thy dying groans;
And then remember me.

3 Thou wondrous Advocate with God,
I yield myself to thee;
While thou art sitting on thy throne,
O Lord, remember me.

4 I own I'm guilty, own I'm vile,
But thy salvation 's free;
Then in thy all abounding grace,
O Lord, remember me.

5 Howe'er forsaken or distressed,
Howe'er oppressed I be,
Howe'er afflicted here on earth,
Do thou remember me.

6 And when I close my eyes in death,
And creature-helps all flee,
Then, O my great Redeemer God,
I pray, remember me!

32. C. M. COWPER.

1 THE Lord will happiness divine
On contrite hearts bestow;
Then tell me, gracious God, is mine
A contrite heart, or no?

2 I hear, but seem to hear in vain,
Insensible as steel;
If aught is felt, 'tis only pain
To find I cannot feel.

3 I sometimes think myself inclined
To love thee if I could;
But often feel another mind,
Averse to all that's good.

4 My best desires are faint and few;
I fain would strive for more;
But when I cry, "My strength renew,"
Seem weaker than before.

5 Thy saints are comforted, I know,
And love thy house of prayer;
I sometimes go where others go,
But find no comfort there.

6 O, make this heart rejoice or ache;
Decide this doubt for me;
And, if it be not broken, break;
And heal it, if it be.

COMMUNION NEW. C. M.

SUMNER HILL.
From The Sanctus.

31. C. M. DR. S. STENNETT.

1 As on the cross the Saviour hung,
And wept, and bled, and died,
He poured salvation on a wretch
That languished at his side.

2 His crimes, with inward grief and shame,
The penitent confessed,
Then turned his dying eyes to Christ,
And thus his prayer addressed: —

3 "Jesus, thou Son and Heir of heaven!
Thou spotless Lamb of God!
I see thee bathed in sweat and tears,
And weltering in thy blood.

4 "Yet quickly, from these scenes of woe,
In triumph thou shalt rise,
Burst through the gloomy shades of death,
And shine above the skies.

5 "Amid the glories of that world,
Dear Saviour, think on me,
And in the victories of thy death,
Let me a sharer be."

36. C. M. NEWTON.

1 AFFLICTIONS, though they seem severe,
In mercy oft are sent;
They stopped the prodigal's career,
And forced him to repent.

2 Although he no relenting felt,
Till he had spent his store,
His stubborn heart began to melt,
When famine pinched him sore.

3 "What have I gained by sin," he said,
"But hunger, shame, and fear?
My father's house abounds with bread,
While I am starving here.

4 "I'll go and tell him all I've done,
And fall before his face;
Unworthy to be called his son,
I'll seek a servant's place."

5 His father saw him coming back;
He saw, and ran, and smiled,
And threw his arms around the neck
Of his rebellious child.

6 "Father, I've sinned; but, O, forgive!"
"Enough!" the Father said;
"Rejoice, my house; my son's alive,
For whom I mourned as dead.

7 "Now let the fatted calf be slain,
And spread the news around;
My son was dead, but lives again,
Was lost, but now is found."

8 'Tis thus the Lord his love reveals,
To call poor sinners home;
More than a father's love he feels,
And welcomes all that come.

39. C. M. WATTS.

1 'TWAS for my sins, my dearest Lord
Hung on the cursèd tree,
And groaned away a dying life,
For thee, my soul, for thee.

2 O, how I hate those lusts of mine
That crucified my God —
Those sins that pierced and nailed his flesh
Fast to the fatal wood!

3 Yes, my Redeemer, they shall die;
My heart has so decreed;
Nor will I spare the guilty things
That made my Saviour bleed.

4 Whilst with a bleeding, broken heart,
My murdered Lord I view,
I raise revenge against my sins,
And slay the murderers too.

HERMON.

PHUVAH. C. M.

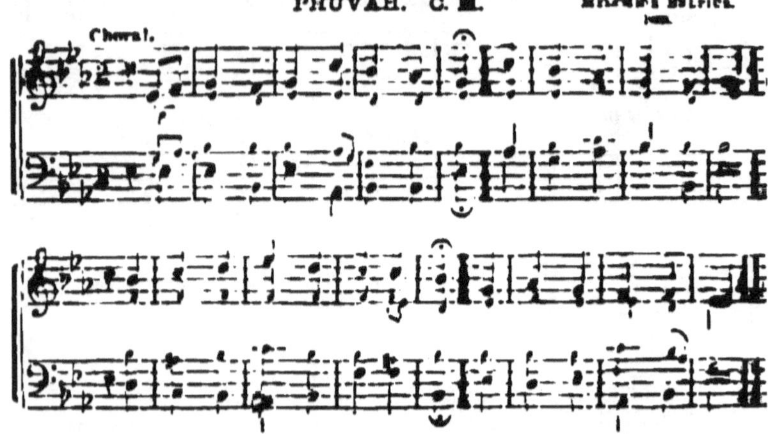

59. C. M. WATTS.

1 WHY is my heart so far from thee,
My God, my chief delight?
Why are my thoughts no more by day
With thee? no more by night?

2 Why should my foolish passions rove?
Where can such sweetness be,
As I have tasted in thy love,
As I have found in thee?

3 When my forgetful soul renews
The savor of thy grace,
My heart presumes I cannot lose
The relish all my days.

4 But ere one fleeting hour is past,
The flattering world employs
Some sensual bait to seize my taste,
And to pollute my joys.

5 Then I repent and vex my soul,
That I should leave thee so;
Where will those wild affections roll,
That let a Saviour go?

6 Wretch that I am to wander thus
In chase of false delight!
O, let me sit beneath thy cross,
And never lose the sight.

73. C. M. DR. S. STENNETT.

1 AND have I, Christ, no love for thee,
No passion for thy charms?
No wish my Saviour's face to see,
And dwell within his arms?

2 Is there no spark of gratitude,
In this cold heart of mine,
To Him whose generous bosom glowed
With friendship all divine?

3 Can I pronounce his charming name,
His acts of kindness tell,
And, while I dwell upon the theme,
No sweet emotion feel?

4 Such base ingratitude as this,
What heart but must detest
Sure Christ deserves the noblest place
In every human breast.

5 A very wretch, Lord, I should prove,
Had I no love for thee:
Rather than not my Saviour love,
O, may I cease to be.

77. C. M. STEELE.

1 HEAR, gracious God, my humble moan;
To thee I breathe my sighs,
When will the mournful night be gone?
When shall my joys arise?

2 Yet though my soul in darkness mourns,
Thy promise is my stay;
Here would I rest till light returns;
Thy presence makes my day.

3 Come, Lord, and with celestial peace
Relieve my aching heart;
O, smile, and bid my sorrows cease,
And all their gloom depart.

4 Then shall my drooping spirit rise,
And bless thy healing rays,
And change these deep, complaining sighs,
For songs of sacred praise.

EVAN.

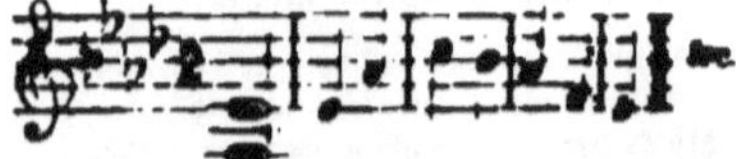

This and other of Dr. Hastings' tunes inserted by his special permission.

70. C. M. Anon.

1 From all that's mortal, all that's vain,
And from this earthly clod,
Arise, my soul, and strive to gain
Sweet fellowship with God.

2 Say, what is there beneath the skies,
Wherever thou hast trod,
Can suit thy wishes or thy joys,
Like fellowship with God?

3 Not life, nor all the toys of art,
Nor pleasure's flowery road,
Can to my soul such bliss impart,
As fellowship with God.

4 Not health, nor friendship here below,
Nor wealth, that golden load,
Can such delight or comfort show,
As fellowship with God.

5 When I am made in love to bear
Affliction's needful rod,
Light, sweet, and kind the strokes appear,
Through fellowship with God.

6 In fierce temptation's fiery blast,
When dangerous is the road,
I'm happy if I can but taste
Some fellowship with God.

7 And when the icy hand of death
Shall chill my flowing blood,
O, may I yield my latest breath
In fellowship with God.

8 When I at last to heaven ascend,
And gain my blest abode,
Then an eternity I'll spend
In fellowship with God.

82. C. M. Moore.

1 O Thou who dry'st the mourner's tear!
How dark this world would be,
If, pierced by sin and sorrows here,
We could not fly to thee.

2 The friends who in our sunshine live,
When winter comes, are flown;
And he who has but tears to give,
Must weep those tears alone.

3 But thou wilt heal that broken heart,
Which, like the plants that throw
Their fragrance from the wounded part,
Breathes sweetness out of woe.

4 When joy no longer soothes or cheers,
And e'en the hope that threw
A moment's sparkle o'er our tears,
Is dimmed and vanished too, —

5 O, who could bear life's stormy doom,
Did not thy wing of love
Come brightly wafting through the gloom
Our peace-branch from above?

6 Then sorrow, touched by thee, grows bright
With more than rapture's ray,
As darkness shows us worlds of light
We never saw by day.

HERMON.

&c.

ROCHESTER. C. M.

Composer unknown.

Generally ascribed to Williams. It is in Dinsmore's "Standard Tune Book" in notes of equal length.

60. C. M. Cowper.

1 O Lord, my best desires fulfil,
And help me to resign
Life, health, and comfort to thy will,
And make thy pleasure mine.

2 Why should I shrink at thy command,
Whose love forbids my fears?
Or tremble at the gracious hand
That wipes away my tears?

3 No! let me rather freely yield
What most I prize to thee,
Who never hast a good withheld,
Nor wilt withhold, from me.

4 Thy favor all my journey through
Thou art engaged to grant;
What else I want, or think I do,
'Tis better still to want.

5 Wisdom and mercy guide my way:
Shall I resist them both —
A poor, blind creature of a day,
And crushed before the moth?

6 But ah! my inmost spirit cries,
Still bind me to thy sway,
Else the next cloud that veils my skies
Drives all these thoughts away.

LITCHFIELD.

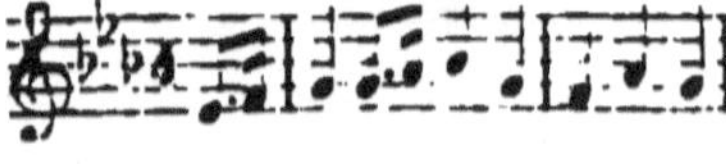

66. C. M. Newton.

1 Amazing grace — how sweet the sound! —
That saved a wretch like me;
I once was lost, but now am found;
Was blind, but now I see.

2 'Twas grace that taught my heart to fear,
And grace my fears relieved:
How precious did that grace appear,
The hour I first believed!

3 Through many dangers, toils, and snares,
I have already come;
'Tis grace has brought me safe thus far,
And grace will lead me home.

4 The Lord has promised good to me;
His word my hope secures;
He will my shield and portion be,
As long as life endures.

5 Yes, when this flesh and heart shall fail,
And mortal life shall cease,
I shall possess within the veil
A life of joy and peace.

6 The earth shall soon dissolve like snow,
The sun forbear to shine;
But God, who called me here below,
Will be forever mine.

CORINTH.

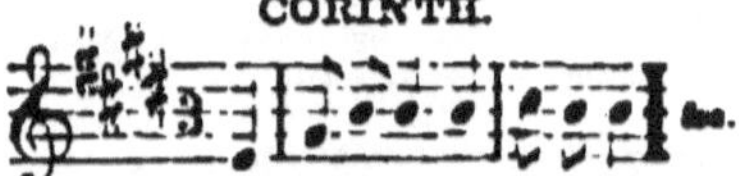

72. C. M. Dr. S. Stennett.

1 Why should a living man complain
Of deep distress within,
Since every sigh and every pain
Is but the fruit of sin?

2 No, Lord, I'll patiently submit,
Nor ever dare rebel;
Yet sure I may, here at thy feet,
My painful feelings tell.

MEMPHIS. C. M. Southern Tune.

3 Thou seest what floods of sorrow rise,
And beat upon my soul:
One trouble to another cries;
Billows on billows roll.

4 From fear to hope, from hope to fear,
My shipwrecked soul is tost,
Till I am tempted, in despair,
To give up all for lost.

5 Yet through the stormy clouds I'll look
Once more to thee, my God;
O, fix my feet upon the rock,
Beyond the raging flood.

6 One look of mercy from thy face
Will set my heart at ease;
One all-commanding word of grace
Will make the tempest cease

75. C. M. Watts.

1 My drowsy powers, why sleep ye so?
Awake, my sluggish soul!
Nothing has half thy work to do,
Yet nothing's half so dull.

2 The little ants, for one poor grain,
Labor, and tug, and strive;
Yet we, who have a heaven t' obtain,
How negligent we live! —

3 We, for whose sake all nature stands,
And stars their courses move;
We, for whose guard the angel bands
Come flying from above; —

4 We, for whom God the Son came down,
And labored for our good,
How careless to secure that crown
He purchased with his blood!

5 Lord, shall we lie so sluggish still,
And never act our parts?
Come, holy Dove, from th' heavenly hill,
And sit, and warm our hearts.

6 Then shall our active spirits move;
Upward our souls shall rise;
With hands of faith and wings of love,
We'll fly and take the prize.

97. C. M. Watts.

1 Earth has engrossed my love too long;
'Tis time I lift mine eyes
Upward, dear Father, to thy throne,
And to my native skies.

2 There the blest Man, my Saviour, sits;
The God! how bright he shines!
And scatters infinite delights
On all the happy minds.

3 Seraphs, with elevated strains,
Circle the throne around,
And move and charm the starry plains
With an immortal sound.

4 Jesus, the Lord, their harps employs;
Jesus, my love, they sing!
Jesus, the life of both our joys,
Sounds sweet from every string.

5 Now let me mount and join their song,
And be an angel, too;
My heart, my hand, my ear, my tongue,
Here's joyful work for you.

6 I would begin the music here,
And so my soul should rise;
O, for some heavenly notes to bear
My passions to the skies!

NEW HAVEN. C. M. Double. GIARDINI.

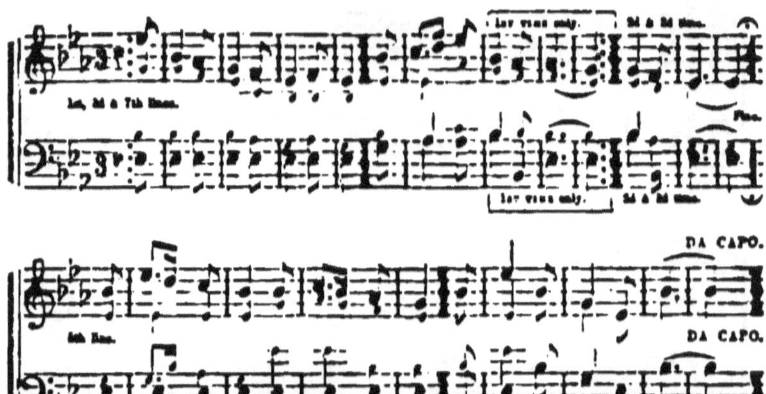

71. C. M. C. WESLEY.

1 How happy's every child of grace,
  Who feels his sins forgiven!
"This world," he cries, "is not my place;
  I seek a place in heaven, —
A country far from mortal sight;
  Yet, O, by faith, I see
The land of rest, the saints' delight,
  The heaven prepared for me.

2 "To that Jerusalem above,
  With singing I'll repair;
While in the world, by hope and love,
  My heart and soul are there:
There my exalted Saviour stands,
  My merciful High Priest,
And still extends his wounded hands,
  To take me to his breast.

3 "O, what a blessèd hope is ours,
  While here on earth we stay!
We more than taste the heavenly powers,
  And antedate that day:
We feel the resurrection near,
  Our life in Christ concealed,
And with his glorious presence here
  Our earthen vessels filled.

4 "O, would he more of heaven bestow,
  And let this vessel break;
And let my ransomed spirit go
  To grasp the God I seek;
In rapturous awe on Him to gaze,
  Who bled and died for me,
And shout and wonder at his grace,
  Through all eternity!"

96. C. M. WESLEY.

1 And let this feeble body fail,
  And let it faint and die;
My soul shall quit this mournful vale,
  And soar to worlds on high;
Shall join the disembodied saints,
  And find its long-sought rest —
That only bliss for which it pants —
  In the Redeemer's breast.

2 In hope of that immortal crown,
  I now the cross sustain,
And gladly wander up and down,
  And smile at toil and pain;
I suffer on, my threescore years,
  Till my Deliverer come
And wipe away his servant's tears,
  And take his exile home.

3 O, what hath Jesus done for me!
  Before my raptured eyes
Rivers of life divine I see,
  And trees of Paradise.
I see a world of spirits bright,
  Who taste the pleasures there;
They all are robed in spotless white,
  And conquering palms they bear.

4 O, what are all my sufferings here,
  If, Lord, thou count me meet
With that enraptured host t' appear,
  And worship at thy feet!
Give joy or grief, give ease or pain,
  Take life or friends away;
But let me find them all again
  In that eternal day.

‡ May be sung, without the repeat, to a double C. M. hymn.

105.

C. M. SUTTON.

1 HAIL, sweetest, dearest tie, that binds
Our glowing hearts in one;
Hail, sacred hope, that tunes our minds
To harmony divine.
It is the hope, the blissful hope,
Which Jesus' grace has given —
* The hope, when days and years are past,
We all shall meet in heaven;
We all shall meet in heaven at last,
We all shall meet in heaven;
The hope, when days and years are past,
We all shall meet in heaven.

2 What though the northern wintry blast
Shall howl around our cot;
What though beneath an eastern sun
Be cast our distant lot;
Yet still we share the blissful hope,
Which Jesus' grace has given, —
The hope, when days and years are past,
We all shall meet in heaven. *We all, &c.*

3 From Burmah's shores, from Afric's strand,
From India's burning plain,
From Europe, from Columbia's land,
We hope to meet again;
It is the hope, the blissful hope,
Which Jesus' grace has given, &c. v. 1,*

4 No lingering look, no parting sigh,
Our future meeting knows;
There friendship beams from every eye
And love immortal glows.
O sacred hope! O blissful hope!
Which Jesus' grace has given, &c. v. 1,*

7. S. M. J. WESLEY.

1 COMMIT thou all thy griefs
And ways into his hands,
To his sure truth and tender care,
Who earth and heaven commands,—

2 Who points the clouds their course,
Whom winds and seas obey;
He shall direct thy wandering feet;
He shall prepare thy way.

3 Put thou thy trust in God;
In duty's path go on;
Fix on his word thy steadfast eye;
So shall thy work be done.

4 No profit canst thou gain
By self consuming care;
To him commend thy cause; his ear
Attends thy softest prayer.

5 Give to the winds thy fears;
Hope, and be undismayed;
God hears thy sighs and counts thy tears;
God shall lift up thy head.

6 Through waves, and clouds, and storms,
He gently clears thy way;
Wait thou his time; thy darkest night
Shall end in brightest day.

---

10. S. M. WATTS.

1 WELL, the Redeemer's gone
T' appear before our God,
To sprinkle o'er the burning throne
With his atoning blood.

2 No fiery vengeance now,
Nor burning wrath comes down;
If Justice calls for sinners' blood,
The Saviour shows his own.

3 Before his Father's eye
Our humble suit he moves;
The Father lays his thunder by,
And looks, and smiles, and loves.

4 Now, may our joyful tongues
Our Maker's honor sing;
Jesus, the Priest, receives our songs,
And bears them to the King.

5 We bow before his face,
And sound his glories high:
"Hosanna to the God of grace,
Who lays his thunder by.

6 "On earth thy mercy reigns,
And triumphs all above;"
But, Lord, how weak are mortal strains
To speak immortal love!

---

23. S. M. DODDRIDGE.

1 OUR heavenly Father calls,
And Christ invites us near;
With both our friendship shall be sweet,
And our communion dear.

2 God pities all our griefs;
He pardons every day;
Almighty to protect our souls,
And wise to guide our way.

3 How large his bounties are!
What various stores of good,
Diffused from our Redeemer's hand,
And purchased with his blood!

4 Jesus, our living head,
We bless thy faithful care —
Our Advocate before the throne,
And our Forerunner there.

5 Here fix, my roving heart!
Here wait, my warmest love!
Till the communion be complete
In nobler scenes above.

6 My life, my portion, thou,
Thou all-sufficient art;
My hope, my heavenly treasure, now
Enter and keep my heart.

35.

S. M. WESLEY.

1 AND can I yet delay
My little all to give?
To tear my soul from earth away,
And Jesus to receive?

2 Nay, but I yield, I yield!
I can hold out no more;
I sink, by dying love compelled,
And own thee Conqueror.

3 Though late, I all forsake;
My friends, my all resign;
Gracious Redeemer, take, O take,
And seal me ever thine.

4 Come, and possess me whole,
Nor hence again remove;
Settle and fix my wavering soul
With all thy weight of love.

5 My one desire be this,
Thy only love to know;
Freely to yield all other bliss,
All other good, below.

63.

S. M. VA. SEL.

1 I LOVE the sons of grace,
The heirs of bliss divine,
Who walk in paths of righteousness,
And fly from every sin.

2 They will my faults reprove,
When heedlessly I err:
How do I prize their faithful love,
Their kind and tender care!

3 They Jesus' image bear;
How lovely is the sight!
They shall at length with him appear
In everlasting light.

4 They love the Father's name,
And gladly do his will;
They humbly follow Christ, the Lamb,
In purity and zeal.

5 Their footsteps I'll pursue
With vigor till I die,
Rejoicing in the pleasing view
Of meeting them on high.

6 It is a sweet employ
To join in worship here;
But how divine will be the joy
To see each other there!

Read.

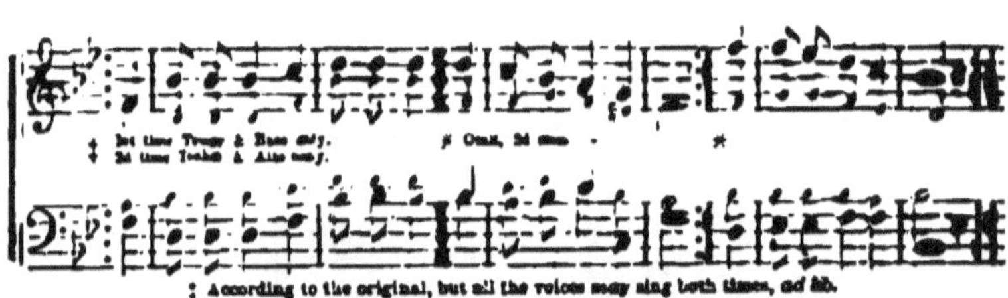

‡ According to the original, but all the voices may sing both times, ad lib.

90. S. M. Montgomery.

1 Ah! now my spirit faints
To reach the land I love,
The bright inheritance of saints,
Jerusalem above.

2 Yet clouds will intervene,
And all my prospect flies;
Like Noah's dove I flit, between
Rough seas and stormy skies.

3 Anon the clouds disperse,
The winds and waters cease,
And sweetly o'er my gladdened heart
Expands the bow of peace.

4 Beneath the flowery arch,
Along the hallowed ground,
I see cherubic armies march;
A camp of fire around.

5 Then, then I feel that He, —
Remembered or forgot, —
The Lord, is never far from me,
Though I perceive him not.

6 All that I am, have been,
All that I yet may be
He sees, as he hath ever seen
And shall forever see.

7 How can I meet his eyes!
Mine on the cross I cast,
And own my life a Saviour's prize;
Mercy from first to last.

8 Then shall I upward fly;
That resurrection word
Shall be my shout of victory,
"Forever with the Lord."

100. S. M. Montgomery.

1 "Forever with the Lord;"
Amen! so let it be;
Life from the dead is in that word;
'Tis immortality.

2 Here in the body pent,
Absent from him, I roam,
Yet nightly pitch my moving tent
A day's march nearer home.

3 My Father's house on high —
Home of my soul — how near,
At times, to faith's foreseeing eye,
The golden gates appear!

4 "Forever with the Lord!"
Father, if 'tis thy will,
The promise of that faithful word
E'en here to me fulfil.

5 So when my latest breath
Shall rend the veil in twain,
In death I shall escape from death,
And life eternal gain.

6 Knowing as I am known,
How shall I love that word,
And oft repeat before the throne,
"Forever with the Lord!"

7 The trump of final doom
Shall speak the self-same word,
And heaven's voice sound through the tomb,
"Forever with the Lord!"

8 That resurrection word!
That shout of victory!
Once more! "Forever with the Lord!"
Amen! so let it be.

BARON. S. M.

W. B. BRADBURY. 1843.

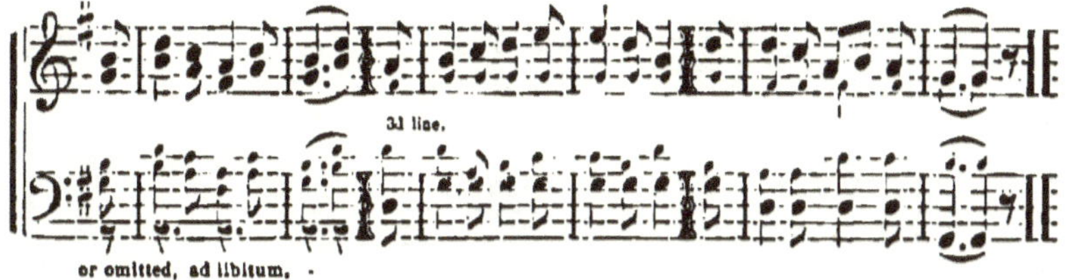

103.

S. M. STENNETT.

1 How charming is the place
Where my Redeemer, God,
Unveils the beauties of his face,
And sheds his love abroad!

2 Not the fair palaces,
To which the great resort,
Are once to be compared with this,
Where Jesus holds his court.

3 Here, on the mercy-seat,
With radiant glory crowned,
Our joyful eyes behold him sit,
And smile on all around.

4 To him their prayers and cries
Each humble soul presents;
He listens to their broken sighs,
And grants them all their wants.

5 To them his sovereign will
He graciously imparts,
And, in return, accepts with smiles,
The tribute of their hearts.

6 Give me, O Lord, a place
Within thy blest abode,
Among the children of thy grace,
The servants of my God.

HARTLAND. S. M. (Kentucky.) ‡

INGALS, 1805. Arr. by J. OSGOOD.

‡ Called also "Iowa," arranged in $\frac{2}{2}$ time.

LENOX. H. M. Edson.

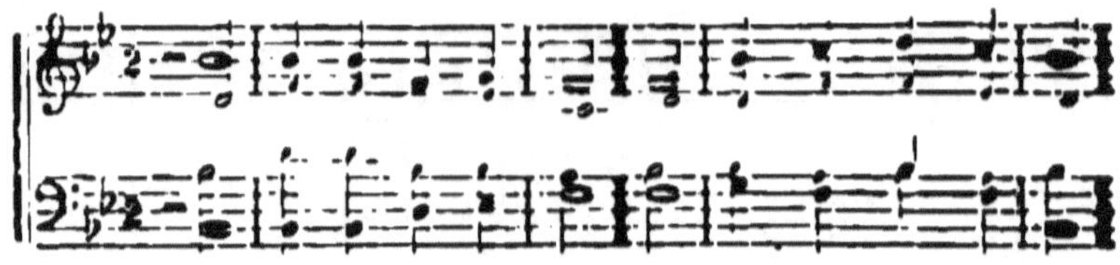

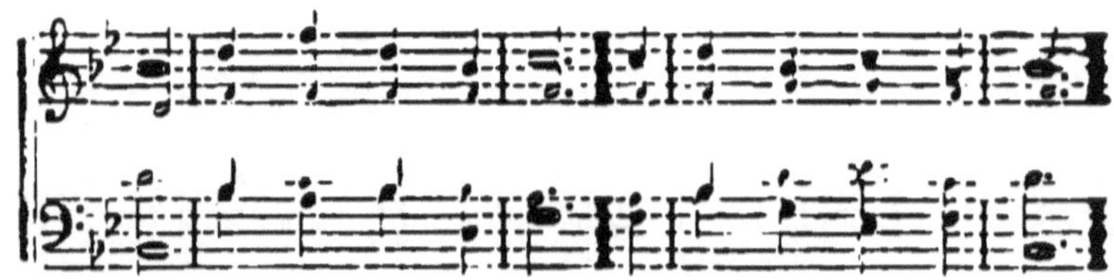

24.

H. M. Boden.

1 Ye dying sons of men, —
  Immerged in sin and woe,
The gospel's voice attend,
  While Jesus sends to you:
Ye perishing and guilty, come;
In Jesus arms there yet is room.

2 No longer now delay,
  Nor vain excuses frame:
He bids you come to day,
  Though poor, and blind, and lame:
All things are ready; sinners, come;
For every trembling soul there's room.

3 Believe the heavenly word
  His messengers proclaim;
He is a gracious Lord,
  And faithful is his name.
Backsliding souls, return and come;
Cast off despair; there yet is room.

4 Compelled by bleeding love,
  Ye wandering sheep, draw near;
Christ calls you from above;
  His charming accents hear:
Let whosoever will now come:
In mercy's breast there still is room.

FLANDERS.‡ H. M. or C. H. M. Old Flemish Air. Arr. by Dr. T. Hastings.

‡ For H. M. sing the half notes, and for C. H. M. the small notes, in this measure.

55.

C. H. M. — Spir. Songs.

1 Go watch and pray; thou canst not tell
How near thine hour may be;
Thou canst not know how soon the bell
May toll its notes for thee:
Death's countless snares beset thy way;
Frail child of dust, go watch and pray.

2 Fond youth, while free from blighting care,
Does thy firm pulse beat high?
Do hope's glad visions, bright and fair,
Dilate before thine eye?
Soon these must change, must pass away;
Frail child of dust, go watch and pray.

3 Thou agéd man, life's wintry storm
Hath seared thy vernal bloom;
With trembling limbs, and wasting form,
Thou'rt bending o'er thy tomb:
And can vain hope lead thee astray?
Go, weary pilgrim, watch and pray.

4 Ambition! stop thy panting breath!
Pride! sink thy lifted eye!
Behold the caverns, dark with death,
Before you open lie:
The heavenly warning now obey;
Ye sons of pride, go watch and pray.

HEAVEN.* C. H. M.

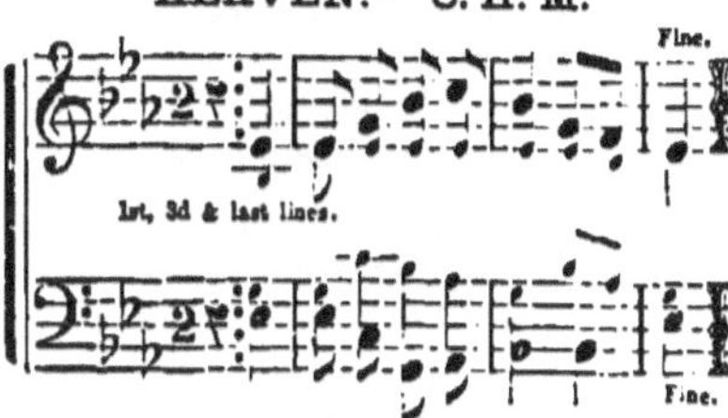

* Arr. from A. Lamond, by B. F. Edmands, for hymn below.

98.

C. H. M. — Sac. Lyrics.

1 Heaven is the land where troubles cease,
Where toils and tears are o'er;
The blissful clime of rest and peace,
Where cares distract no more;
And not the shadow of distress
Dims its unsullied blessedness.

2 Heaven is the dwelling-place of joy,
The home of light and love,
Where faith and hope in rapture die,
And ransomed souls above
Enjoy, before th' eternal throne,
Bliss everlasting and unknown.

WARNING VOICE. C. P. M. Dr. T. Hastings.
From [illegible]

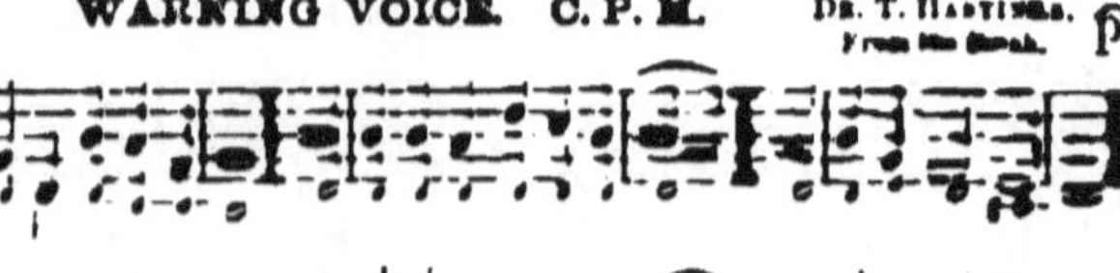

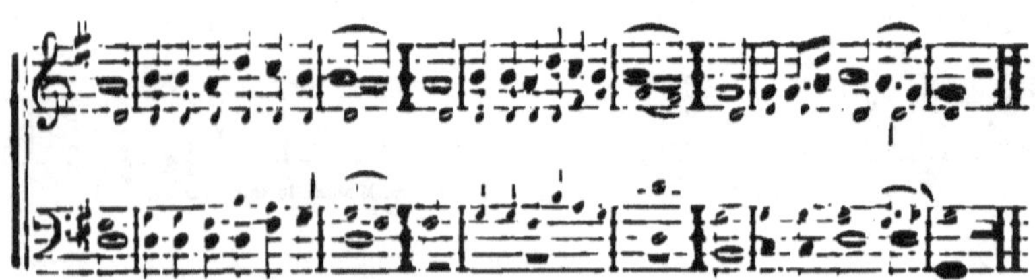

19. C. P. M. Wesley.

1 Thou God of glorious majesty,
To thee, against myself, to thee,
A sinful worm, I cry;
A half-awakened child of man,
An heir of endless bliss or pain,
A sinner born to die.

2 Lo! on a narrow neck of land,
'Twixt two unbounded seas, I stand;
Yet how insensible!
A point of time, a moment's space,
Removes me to that heavenly place,
Or shuts me up in hell.

3 O God, my inmost soul convert,
And deeply on my thoughtful heart
Eternal things impress;
Give me to feel their solemn weight,
And save me ere it be too late—
Wake me to righteousness.

20. C. P. M. Occum.

1 Awaked by Sinai's awful sound,
My soul in guilt and thrall I found,
And knew not where to go.
O'erwhelmed in sin, with anguish slain,
The sinner must be born again,
Or sunk in endless woe.

2 Amazed I stood, but could not tell
Which way to shun the gates of hell,
For death and hell drew near;
I strove, indeed, but strove in vain;
"The sinner must be born again"
Still sounded in my ear.

3 When to the law I trembling fled,
It poured its curses on my head;
I no relief could find.
This fearful truth increased my pain;
"The sinner must be born again"
O'erwhelmed my tortured mind.

4 Again did Sinai's thunder roll,
And guilt lay heavy on my soul,
A vast, unwieldy load.
Alas! I read, and saw it plain,
"The sinner must be born again,
Or drink the wrath of God."

5 The saints I heard with rapture tell
How Jesus conquered death and hell,
And broke the fowler's snare;
Yet when I found this truth remain,
"The sinner must be born again,"
I sunk in deep despair.

6 But while I thus in anguish lay,
Jesus of Naz'reth passed that way,
And felt his pity move.
The sinner, by his justice slain,
Now by his grace is born again,
And sings redeeming love.

7 To heaven the joyful tidings flew;
The angels tuned their harps anew,
And loftier notes did raise:
"All hail the Lamb that once was slain!
Unnumbered millions, born again,
Shall sing thine endless praise."

NUREMBERG. 7s.

J. R. AHLE. 1673.

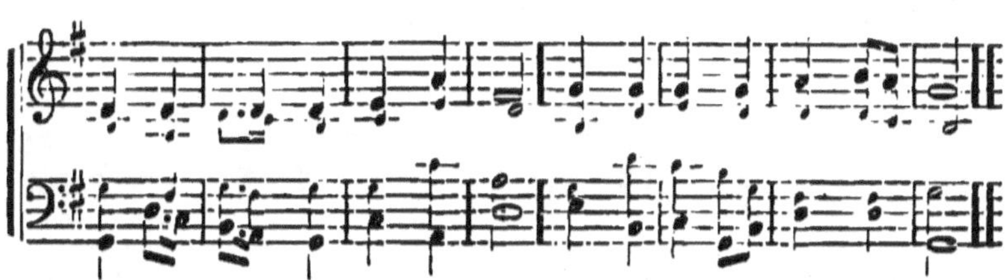

2. 7s. DR. RYLAND.

1 SOVEREIGN Ruler of the skies,
Ever gracious, ever wise,
All my times are in thy hand —
All events at thy command.

2 His decree, who formed the earth,
Fixed my first and second birth;
Parents, native place, and time,
All appointed were by him.

3 He that formed me in the womb,
He shall guide me to the tomb;
All my times shall ever be
Ordered by his wise decree.

4 Times of sickness, times of health,
Times of penury and wealth,
Times of trial and of grief,
Times of triumph and relief, —

5 Times the tempter's power to prove,
Times to taste a Saviour's love, —
All must come, and last, and end,
As shall please my heavenly Friend.

6 Plagues and deaths around me fly;
Till he bids, I cannot die;
Not a single shaft can hit,
Till the God of love sees fit.

7 O thou gracious, wise, and just,
In thy hands my life I trust,
Have I somewhat dearer still,
I resign it to thy will.

8 May I always own thy hand;
Still to thee surrendered stand;
Know that thou art God alone;
I and mine are all thy own.

9 Thee, at all times, will I bless;
Having thee, I all possess.
How can I bereavéd be,
Since I cannot part with thee?

---

17. 7s. SPIR. SONGS.

1 BLEEDING hearts, defiled by sin,
Jesus Christ can make you clean;
Contrite souls, with guilt oppressed,
Jesus Christ can give you rest.

2 You that mourn your follies past,
Precious hours and years laid waste,
Turn to God, O, turn and live;
Jesus Christ can still forgive.

3 You that oft have wandered far
From the light of Bethlehem's star,
Trembling, now your steps retrace;
Jesus Christ is full of grace.

4 Souls benighted and forlorn,
Grieved, afflicted, tempest-worn,
Now in Israel's Rock confide;
Jesus Christ for man has died.

5 Fainting souls, in peril's hour,
Yield not to the tempter's power;
On the risen Lord rely;
Jesus Christ now reigns on high.

RHINE.

ASCENSION. 7s. N. D. Gould.

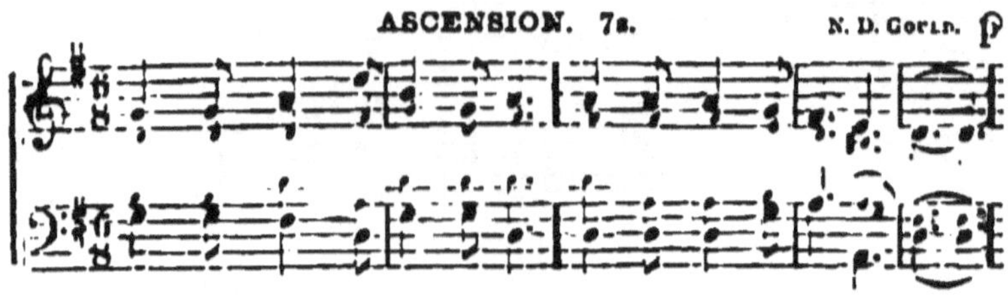

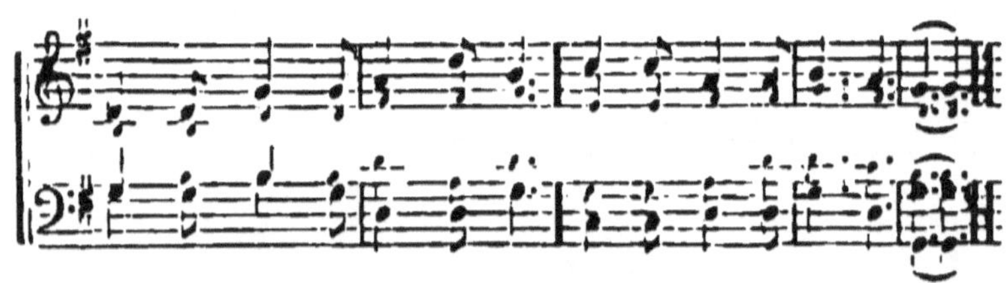

40. 7s. Spir. Songs.

1 Jesus, save my dying soul;
Make the broken spirit whole;
Humble in the dust I lie;
Saviour, leave me not to die.

2 Jesus, full of every grace,
Now reveal thy smiling face;
Grant the joys of sin forgiven,
Foretaste of the bliss of heaven.

3 All my guilt to thee is known;
Thou art righteous, thou alone.
All my help is from thy cross;
All beside I count but loss.

4 Lord, in thee I now believe;
Wilt thou, wilt thou not forgive?
Helpless at thy feet I lie;
Saviour, leave me not to die.

44. 7s. Rippon's Sel.

1 Gracious Lord, incline thine ear,
My requests vouchsafe to hear;
Hear my never-ceasing cry;
Give me Christ; or else I die.

2 Wealth and honor I disdain;
Earthly comforts, Lord, are vain;
These can never satisfy;
Give me Christ; or else I die.

3 Lord, deny me what thou wilt,
Only ease me of my guilt:
Suppliant at thy feet I lie;
Give me Christ; or else I die.

4 All unholy and unclean,
I am nothing else but sin:
On thy mercy I rely;
Give me Christ; or else I die.

5 Thou dost freely save the lost;
In thy grace alone I trust;
With my earnest suit comply;
Give me Christ; or else I die.

6 Thou dost promise to forgive
All who in thy Son believe:
Lord, I know thou canst not lie;
Give me Christ; or else I die.

7 Father, dost thou seem to frown?
Let me shelter in thy Son!
Jesus, to thine arms I fly;
Come and save me; or I die.

48. 7s. Cennick.

1 Children of the heavenly King,
As ye journey, sweetly sing;
Sing your Saviour's worthy praise,
Glorious in his works and ways.

2 Ye are travelling home to God,
In the way the fathers trod;
They are happy now, and ye
Soon their happiness shall see.

3 O ye banished seed, be glad!
Christ our Advocate is made,
Us to save our flesh assumes,
Brother to our souls becomes.

4 Shout, ye little flock and blest;
You on Jesus' throne shall rest;
There your seat is now prepared,
There your kingdom and reward.

5 Fear not, brethren; joyful stand
On the borders of your land;
Christ, your Father's darling Son,
Bids you undismayed go on.

LATROBE.

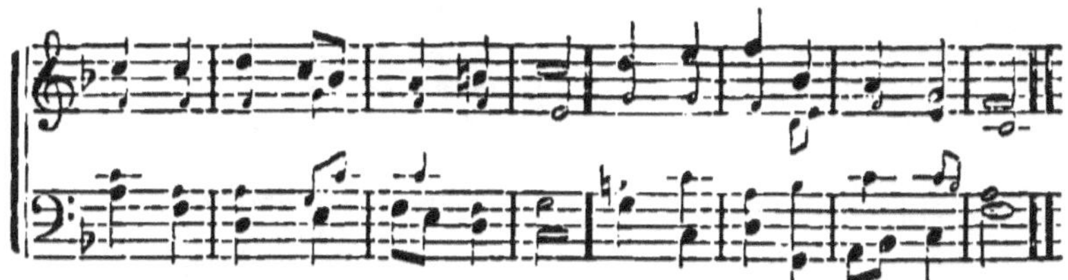

6 Lord, submissive make us go,
Gladly leaving all below;
Only thou our Leader be,
And we still will follow thee.

---

64. 7s. COWPER.

1 HARK, my soul; it is the Lord;
'Tis the Saviour; hear his word;
Jesus speaks, and speaks to thee,
"Say, poor sinner, lov'st thou me?

2 "I delivered thee when bound,
And when wounded, healed thy wound;
Sought thee wandering, set thee right,
Turned thy darkness into light.

3 "Can a woman's tender care
Cease towards the child she bare?
Yes, she may forgetful be;
Yet will I remember thee.

4 "Mine is an unchanging love,
Higher than the heights above,
Deeper than the depths beneath,
Free and faithful, strong as death.

5 "Thou shalt see my glory soon,
When the work of grace is done;
Partner of my throne shalt be;
Say, poor sinner, lov'st thou me?"

6 Lord, it is my chief complaint,
That my love's so weak and faint;
Yet I love thee, and adore;
O for grace to love thee more!

81. 7s. EPIS. PSALMS.

1 LORD, forever at thy side
Let my place and portion be;
Strip me of the robe of pride;
Clothe me with humility.

2 Meekly may my soul receive
All thy Spirit hath revealed;
Thou hast spoken; I believe,
Though the oracle be sealed.

3 Humble as a little child,
Weanéd from the mother's breast,
By no subtleties beguiled,
On thy faithful word I rest.

4 Israel, now and evermore
In the Lord Jehovah trust;
Him in all his ways adore,
Wise, and wonderful, and just.

89. 7s. H. K. WHITE.

1 MUCH in sorrow, oft in woe,
Onward, Christians, onward go;
Fight the fight; and, worn with strife,
Steep with tears the bread of life.

2 Onward, Christians, onward go;
Join the war, and face the foe;
Faint not; much doth yet remain;
Dreary is the long campaign.

3 Shrink not, Christians, — will ye yield?
Will ye quit the battle-field?
Fight till all the conflict's o'er,
Nor your foes shall rally more.

4 But when loud the trumpet blown,
Speaks their forces overthrown,
Christ, your Captain, shall bestow
Crowns to grace the conqueror's brow.

101. 7s. FAWCETT.

1 I MY Ebenezer raise
To my kind Redeemer's praise;
With a grateful heart I own,
Hitherto thy help I've known.

2 What may be my future lot,
Well I know, concerns me not;
This should set my heart at rest,—
What thy will ordains is best.

3 I my all to thee resign;
Father, let thy will be mine!
May but all thy dealings prove
Fruits of thy paternal love.

4 Guard me, Saviour, by thy power;
Guard me in the trying hour;
Let thy unremitted care
Save me from the lurking snare.

5 Let my few remaining days
Be directed to thy praise;
So the last, the closing scene,
Shall be tranquil and serene.

6 To thy will I leave the rest;
Grant me but this one request,
Both in life and death to prove
Tokens of thy special love.

---

85. 7s. STENNETT.

1 'Tis religion that can give
Sweetest pleasures while we live;
'Tis religion must supply
Solid comfort when we die.

2 After death, its joys will be
Lasting as eternity;
Be the living God my Friend,
Then my bliss shall never end.

PILGRIM. 7s. From Nat. Ch. Har.

27. 7s. PRES. SEL.

1 Am I called? and can it be!
Has my Saviour chosen me?
Guilty, wretched, as I am,
Has he named my worthless name?
Vilest of the vile am I;
Dare I raise my hopes so high?

2 Am I called? I dare not stay,
May not, must not, disobey;
Here I lay me at thy feet,
Clinging to the mercy seat;
Thine I am, and thine alone;
Lord, with me thy will be done.

3 Am I called? What shall I bring
As an offering to my King?
Poor, and blind, and naked, I
Trembling at thy footstool lie:
Nought but sin I call my own;
Nor for sin can sin atone.

4 Am I called? — an heir of God!
Washed, redeemed, by precious blood!
Father, lead me in thy hand,
Guide me to that better land,
Where my soul shall be at rest,
Pillowed on my Saviour's breast.

52. 7s. SPIR. SONGS.

1 SAVE me, Lord, in this distress;
Clothe me in thy righteousness;
Good and merciful thou art;
Heal this bleeding, broken heart;
Cast me not despairing hence;
Be my hope, my confidence.

2 Send thy light and truth to guide;
Leave me not to turn aside;
On thy holy hill I'll rest,
In thy courts forever blest:
There to God, my Love, my Joy,
Praise shall all my powers employ.

56. 7s. SEL. HYMNS.

1 IF 'tis sweet to mingle where
Christians meet for social prayer,—
If 'tis sweet with them to raise
Songs of holy joy and praise,—
O, how sweet that state must be,
Where they meet eternally!

2 Saviour, may these meetings prove
Preparations from above;
While we worship in this place,
May we go from grace to grace,
Till we each, in his degree,
Fit for endless glory be.

54. 7s. 6 L. NEWTON.

1 QUIET, Lord, my froward heart,
Make me teachable and mild,
Upright, simple, free from art,
Make me as a weanéd child;
From distrust and envy free,
Pleased with all that pleases thee.

2 What thou shalt to-day provide,
Let me as a child receive;
What to-morrow may betide,
Calmly to thy wisdom leave.
'Tis enough that thou wilt care;
Why should I the burden bear?

3 As a little child relies
On a care beyond his own,—
Knows he's neither strong nor wise,
Fears to stir a step alone,—
Let me thus with thee abide,
As my Father, Guard, and Guide.

4 Thus preserved from Satan's wiles,
Safe from dangers, free from fears,
May I live upon thy smiles,
Till the promised hour appears,
When the sons of God shall prove
All their Father's boundless love.

16. 7s. Toplady.

1 Object of my first desire,
  Jesus, crucified for me,
I to happiness aspire
  Only to be found in thee.
Thee to praise, and thee to know,
Constitute our bliss below;
Thee to see, and thee to love,
Constitute our bliss above.

2 Lord, it is not life to live,
  If thy presence thou deny;
Lord, if thou thy presence give,
  'Tis no longer death to die;
Source and Giver of repose,
Singly from thy smile it flows;
Peace and happiness are thine;
Mine they are, if thou art mine.

3 Whilst I see thy love to me,
  Every object teems with joy;
Here, O, may I walk with thee,
  Then into thy presence hie.
Let me but thyself possess,
Total sum of happiness,
Real bliss I then shall prove, —
Heaven below, and heaven above.

30. 7s. Divine Sal.

1 Saved by grace, I live to tell
  What the love of Christ has done;
He redeemed my soul from hell;
  Of a rebel made a son.
O, I tremble still to think
  How secure I lived in sin,
Sporting on destruction's brink,
  Yet preserved from falling in.

2 In a kind, propitious hour,
  To my heart the Saviour spoke;
Touched me by his Spirit's power,
  And my dangerous slumber broke:
Then I saw and owned my guilt;
  Soon my gracious Lord replied,
"Fear not; I my blood have spilt;
  'Twas for such as thee I died."

3 Shame and wonder, joy and love,
  All at once possessed my heart: —
Can I hope thy grace to prove,
  After acting such a part?
"Thou hast greatly sinned," he said,
  "But I freely all forgive:
I myself thy debt have paid;
  Now I bid thee rise and live."

4 Come, my fellow-sinners, try;
  Jesus' heart is full of love;
O, that you, as well as I,
  May his wondrous mercy prove!
He has sent me to declare
  All is ready, all is free.
Why should any soul despair,
  When he saved a wretch like me?

62. 7s. SWAIN.

1 BRETHREN, while we sojourn here,
Fight we must, but should not fear;
Foes we have, but we've a Friend,
One that loves us to the end:
Forward, then, with courage go;
Long we shall not dwell below;
Soon the joyful news will come,
"Child, your Father calls; come home!"

2 In the way a thousand snares
Lie, to take us unawares;
Satan, with malicious art,
Watches each unguarded part;
But from Satan's malice free,
Saints shall soon victorious be;
Soon the joyful news will come,
"Child, your Father calls; come home!"

3 But, of all the foes we meet,
None so oft mislead the feet,
None betray us into sin,
Like the foes that dwell within:
Yet let nothing spoil our peace;
Christ will also conquer these;
Then the joyful news will come,
"Child, your Father calls; come home!"

84. 7s. COWPER.

1 'TIS my happiness below,
Not to live without the cross,
But the Saviour's power to know,
Sanctifying every loss:
Trials must and will befall;
But with humble faith to see
Love inscribed upon them all,—
This is happiness to me.

2 God in Israel sows the seeds
Of affliction, pain, and toil;
These spring up and choke the weeds
Which would else o'erspread the soil.
Trials make the promise sweet;
Trials give new life to prayer;
Trials bring me to his feet,
Lay me low, and keep me there.

3 Did I meet no trials here,
No chastisement by the way,
Might I not with reason fear
I should prove a castaway?
Bastards may escape the rod,
Sink in earthly, vain delight;
But the true-born child of God,
Must not, would not, if he might.

PRECIOUS BIBLE. 8s & 7s. 7.7.‡ Adapt. fr G. F. [illegible]
[illegible] 1849.

‡ Or 8s & 7s by omitting the repeat, and singing the small diamond notes.

1.

8s & 7s. 7.7. NEWTON.

1 PRECIOUS Bible! what a treasure
Does the word of God afford!—
All I want for life or pleasure,
Food and medicine, shield and sword:
Let the world account me poor;
Having this, I need no more.

2 Food to which the world's a stranger,
Here my hungry soul enjoys;
Of excess there is no danger;
Though it fills, it never cloys:
On a dying Christ I feed:
He is meat and drink indeed.

3 When my faith is faint and sickly,
Or when Satan wounds my mind,
Cordials to revive me quickly,
Healing medicines, here I find:
To the promises I flee;
Each affords a remedy.

4 In the hour of dark temptation,
Satan cannot make me yield;
For the word of consolation
Is to me a mighty shield:
While the Scripture truths are sure,
From his malice I'm secure.

5 Vain his threats to overcome me,
When I take the Spirit's sword;
Then with ease I drive him from me;
Satan trembles at his word:
'Tis a sword for conquest made;
Keen the edge, and strong the blade.

6 Shall I envy, then, the miser,
Doting on his golden store?
Sure I am, or should be, wiser;
I am rich; 'tis he is poor;
Jesus gives me, in his word,
Food and medicine, shield and sword.

LOTHROP. 8s & 7s.

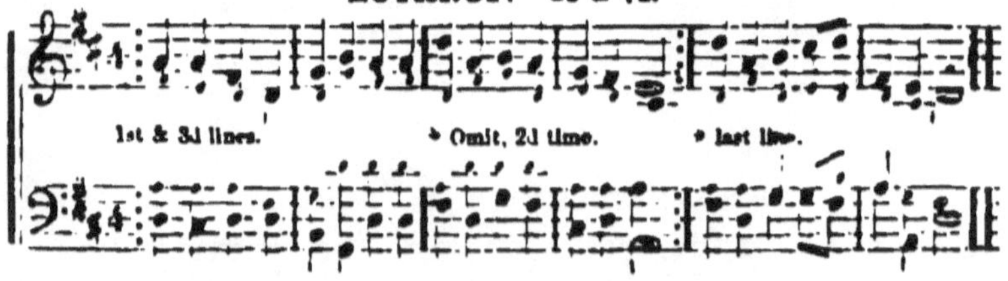

9.

8s & 7s. PRES. HYMNS.

1 ONE there is, above all others,
Well deserves the name of Friend;
His is love beyond a brother's,
Costly, free, and knows no end.

2 Which, of all our friends, to save us,
Could or would have shed his blood?
But this Saviour died, to have us
Reconciled in him to God

ZION. 8s, 7s & 4. DR. THOS. HASTINGS.

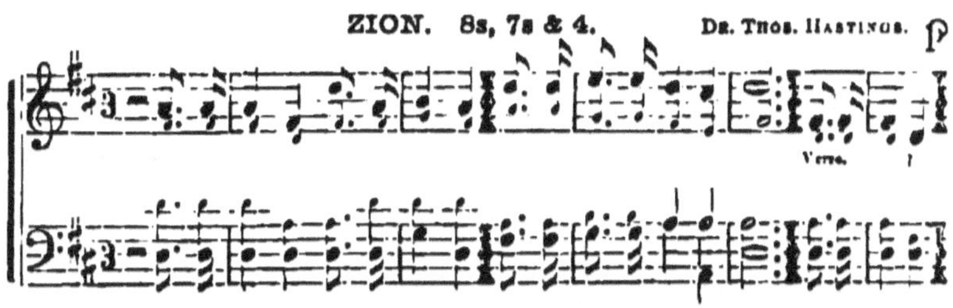

3 When he lived on earth, abaséd,
Friend of Sinners was his name;
Now, above all glory raiséd,
He rejoices in the same.

4 O for grace our hearts to soften!
Teach us, Lord, at length to love;
We, alas! forget too often
What a Friend we have above.

91. 8s, 7s & 4. NEWTON, altered.

1 SAVIOUR, visit thy plantation;
Grant us, Lord, a gracious rain;
All will come to desolation,
Unless thou return again.
Lord, revive us!
All our help must come from thee.

2 Surely once thy garden flourished;
Every part looked gay and green;
All its plants by thee were nourished;
Then how cheering was the scene!
Lord, revive us!
All our help must come from thee.

3 Keep no longer at a distance;
Shine upon us from on high,
Lest, for want of thine assistance,
Every plant should droop and die.
Lord, revive us!
All our help must come from thee.

4 Dearest Saviour, hasten hither;
Thou canst make them bloom again;
O, permit them not to wither;
Let not all our hopes be vain.
Lord, revive us!
All our help must come from thee.

5 Let our mutual love be fervent;
Make us prevalent in prayers;
Let each one, esteemed thy servant,
Shun the world's bewitching snares.
Lord, revive us!
All our help must come from thee.

6 Break the tempter's fatal power,
Turn the stony heart to flesh,
And begin, from this good hour,
To revive thy work afresh.
Lord, revive us!
All our help must come from thee.

25. 8s, 7s & 4s. VA. SEL.

1 COME, ye sinners, come to Jesus;
Think upon your gracious Lord;
He has pitied your condition;
He has sent his gospel word:
Mercy calls you;
Mercy flows in Jesus' blood.

2 Dearest Saviour, help thy servant
To proclaim thy wondrous love;
Pour thy grace upon this people,
That thy truth they may approve:
Bless, O bless them,
From thy shining courts above.

3 Now thy gracious word invites them,
To partake the gospel feast;
Let thy Spirit sweetly draw them;
Every soul be Jesus' guest:
O, receive us!
Let us find thy promised rest.

GREENVILLE. 8s & 7s. Double.

ROUSSEAU.
Previous to 1778.

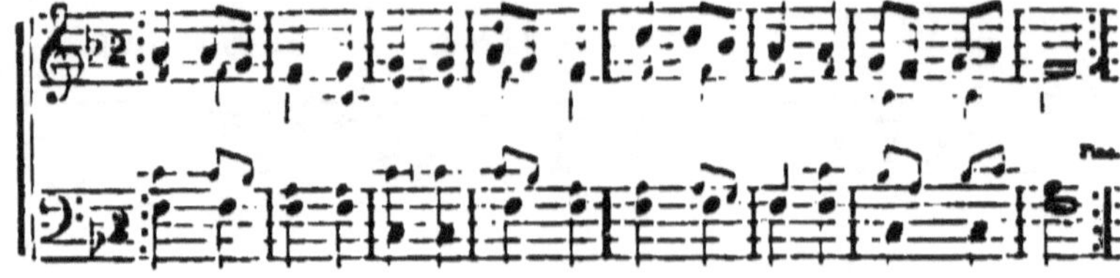

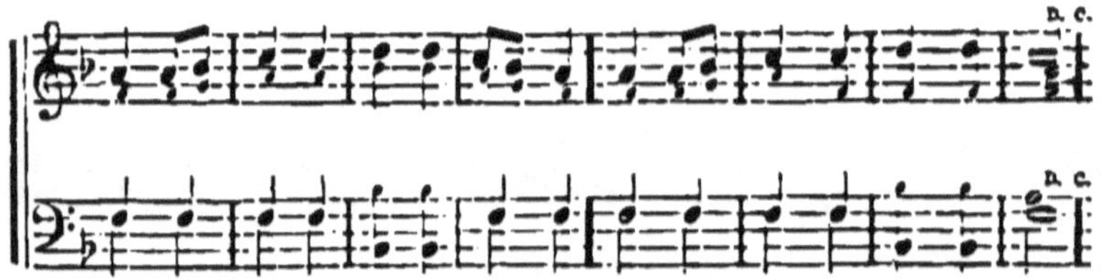

53.

8s & 7s. EPISCOPAL SEL.

1 LORD, with glowing heart I'd praise thee
For the bliss thy love bestows,
For the pardoning grace that saves me,
And the peace that from it flows:
Help, O God, my weak endeavor;
This dull soul to rapture raise;
Thou must light the flame, or never
Can my love be warmed to praise.

2 Praise, my soul, the God that sought thee,
Wretched wanderer, far astray,
Found thee lost, and kindly brought thee
From the paths of death away;
Praise, with love's devoutest feeling,
Him who saw thy guilt-born fear,
And, the light of hope revealing,
Bade the blood-stained cross appear.

3 Lord, this bosom's ardent feeling
Vainly would my lips express;
Low before thy footstool kneeling,
Deign thy suppliant's prayer to bless.
Let thy grace, my soul's chief treasure,
Love's pure flame within me raise,
And, since words can never measure,
Let my life show forth thy praise.

BAVARIA. 8s & 7s. Double

HARMONIA. 7s & 6s. Iambic, 8 lines. Arr. by B. F. Edmands.‡

‡ From the "Ode to Harmony," by Rousseau and Vogler.

15.

7s & 6s. NEWTON.

1 How lost was my condition,
Till Jesus made me whole!
There is but one physician
Can cure a sin-sick soul.
Next door to death he found me,
And snatched me from the grave,
To tell to all around me
His wondrous power to save.

2 The worst of all diseases
Is light, compared with sin;
On every part it seizes,
But rages most within;
'Tis palsy, plague, and fever,
And madness, all combined;
And none but a believer
The least relief can find.

3 From men great skill professing,
I thought a cure to gain;
But this proved more distressing,
And added to my pain;
Some said that nothing ailed me,
Some gave me up for lost;
Thus every refuge failed me,
And all my hopes were crossed.

4 At length this great Physician—
How matchless is his grace!—
Accepted my petition,
And undertook my case;
First gave me sight to view him,—
For sin my eyes had sealed,—
Then bade me look unto him:
I looked: and I was healed.

5 A dying, risen Jesus,
Seen by the eye of faith,
At once from danger frees us,
And saves the soul from death.
Come, then, to this Physician;
His help he'll freely give;
He makes no hard condition;
'Tis only, Look and live.

AMSTERDAM. 7s & 6s. Trochaic. Dr. Nares.

Choral-like.

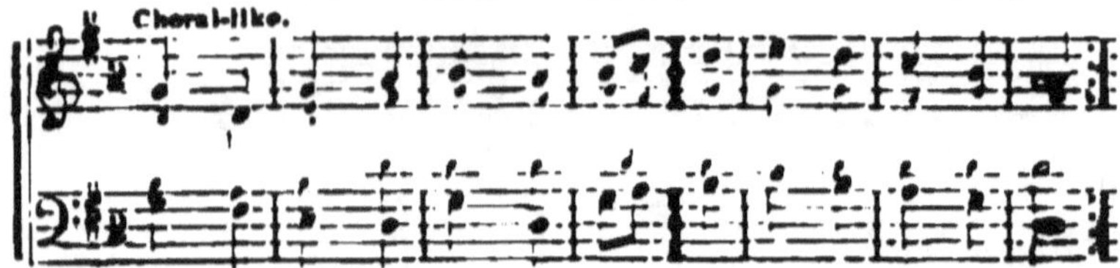

26.

7s & 6s. Newton.

1 Sinner, hear the Saviour's call;
He now is passing by;
He has seen thy grievous thrall,
And heard thy mournful cry;
He has pardons to impart,
Grace to save thee from thy fears;
See the love that fills his heart,
And wipes away thy tears.

2 Why art thou afraid to come,
And tell him all thy case?
He will not pronounce thy doom,
Nor frown thee from his face:
Wilt thou fear Immanuel?
Wilt thou dread the Lamb of God,
Who, to save thy soul from hell,
Has shed his precious blood?

3 Think how on the cross he hung,
Pierced with a thousand wounds!
Hark! from each, as with a tongue,
The voice of pardon sounds!
See from all his bursting veins
Blood of wondrous virtue flow!
Shed to wash away thy stains,
And ransom thee from woe.

4 Though his majesty be great,
His mercy is no less;
Though he thy transgressions hate,
He feels for thy distress:
By himself the Lord has sworn,
He delights not in thy death,
But invites thee to return,
That thou may'st live by faith.

5 Raise thy downcast eyes, and see
What throngs his throne surround!
These, though sinners once like thee,
Have full salvation found:
Yield not then to unbelief,
While he says, "There yet is room;"
Though of sinners thou art chief,
Since Jesus calls thee, come.

29. 11s & 10s. Peculiar. A. Broaddus.

1 Restless thy spirit, poor wandering sinner,
Restless and roving: O, come to thy home!
Turn to the arms, to the bosom of Mercy:
The Saviour of sinners invites thee to come.

2 Darkness surrounds thee, and tempests are rising,
Fearful and dangerous the path thou hast trod;
Mercy shines forth in the rainbow of promise,
To welcome the wanderer home to his God.

3 Peace to the storm in thy soul shall be spoken,
Guilt from thy bosom be banished away;
Heaven's sweet breezes, o'er death's rolling billows,
Shall waft thee at last to the regions of day.

4 But, if regardless of God's gracious warning,
Far from his favor your soul must remove,
May you ne'er hear, never feel the dread sentence,
But live to his glory, and die in his love.

106. 10s & 11s. Spir. Songs.

1 Hail to the brightness of Zion's glad morning!
Joy to the lands that in darkness have lain!
Hushed be the accents of sorrow and mourning:
Zion in triumph begins her mild reign.

2 Hail to the brightness of Zion's glad morning,
Long by the prophets of Israel foretold!
Hail to the millions from bondage returning!
Gentiles and Jews the blest vision behold.

3 Lo, in the desert rich flowers are springing;
Streams ever copious are gliding along;
Loud, from the mountain-tops, echoes are ringing;
Wastes rise in verdure, and mingle in song.

4 See from all lands, from the isles of the ocean,
Praise to Jehovah ascending on high;
Fallen are th' engines of war and commotion!
Shouts of salvation are rending the sky.

FOLSOM, or AURORA.

LYONS. 10s & 11s, or 11s. Anapestic. HAYDN.

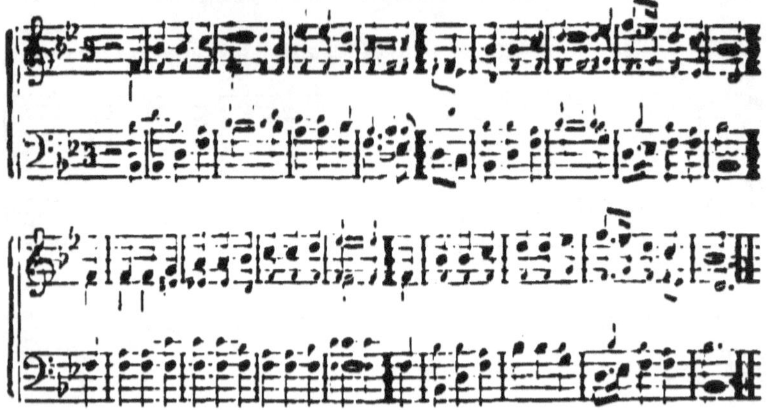

58. 10s & 11s. NEWTON.

1 BEGONE, unbelief! my Saviour is near,
And for my relief will surely appear;
By prayer let me wrestle, and he will perform;
With Christ in the vessel, I smile at the storm.

2 Tho' dark be my way, since he is my Guide,
'Tis mine to obey, 'tis his to provide;
Tho' cisterns be broken, and creatures all fail,
The word he has spoken will surely prevail.

3 His love, in times past, forbids me to think
He'll leave me at last in trouble to sink;
Each sweet Ebenezer I have in review,
Confirms his good pleasure to help me quite [through.

4 Determined to save, he watched o'er my path,
When, Satan's blind slave, I sported with [death;
And can he have taught me to trust in his [name,
And thus far have bro't me, to put me to shame?

5 Why should I complain of want or distress,
Temptation, or pain? He told me no less.
The heirs of salvation, I know from his word,
Through much tribulation must follow their [Lord.

6 How bitter that cup, no heart can conceive,
Which he drank quite up that sinners might [live.
His way was much rougher and darker than [mine;
Did Christ, my Lord, suffer, and shall I repine?

7 Since all that I meet shall work for my good,
The bitter is sweet, the medicine is food:
Tho' painful at present, 'twill cease before long,
And then, O how pleasant the conqueror's song!

69. 11s. KIRKHAM.

1 How firm a foundation, ye saints of the Lord,
Is laid for your faith in his excellent word!
What more can he say than to you he hath [said—
You, who unto Jesus for refuge have fled?

2 In every condition—in sickness, in health,
In poverty's vale, or abounding in wealth,
At home and abroad, on the land, on the [sea,—
As thy days may demand, shall thy strength [e'er be.

3 Fear not; I am with thee; O, be not dis- [mayed;
I, I am thy God, and will still give thee aid;
I'll strengthen thee, help thee, and cause thee [to stand,
Upheld by my righteous, omnipotent hand.

4 When thro' the deep waters I call thee to go,
The rivers of woe shall not thee overflow;
For I will be with thee, thy troubles to bless,
And sanctify to thee thy deepest distress.

5 When thro' fiery trials thy pathway shall lie,
My grace, all-sufficient, shall be thy supply;
The flame shall not hurt thee; I only design
Thy dross to consume, and thy gold to refine.

6 Even down to old age, all my people shall [prove
My sovereign, eternal, unchangeable love;
And when hoary hairs shall their temples [adorn,
Like lambs they shall still in my bosom be [borne.

7 The soul that on Jesus hath leaned for repose,
I will not, I will not, desert to his foes;
That soul, though all hell should endeavor [to shake,
I'll never, no, never, no, never, forsake.

BEETHOVEN. 11s. Anapestic. Arr. fr. BEETHOVEN.

* When accent requires these small notes, observe the slur near the end of the tune.

50.

11s. RIPPON'S SEL.

1 THY mercy, my God, is the theme of my [song.
The joy of my heart, and the boast of my [tongue;
Thy free grace alone, from the first to the [last,
Hath won my affections and bound my soul [fast.

2 Without thy sweet mercy I could not live [here;
Sin soon would reduce me to utter despair;
But through thy free goodness my spirits [revive,
And He that first made me still keeps me [alive.

3 Thy mercy is more than a match for my [heart,
Which wonders to feel its own hardness de- [part;
Dissolved by the sunshine, I fall to the [ground,
And weep to the praise of the mercy I found.

4 The door of thy mercy stands open all day
To the poor and the needy who knock by the [way;
No sinner shall ever be empty sent back,
Who comes seeking mercy for dear Jesus' [sake.

5 Thy mercy in Jesus exempts me from hell;
Its glories I'd sing, and its wonders I'd tell;
'Twas Jesus, my Friend, when he hung on [the tree,
Who opened the channel of mercy for me.

6 Great Father of mercies, thy goodness I own,
And the covenant love of thy crucified Son;
All praise to the Spirit, whose whisper di- [vine
Seals mercy, and pardon, and righteousness [mine.

HINTON. 11s. GERMAN.

THE CHARIOT. 11s & 12s. Anapestic. Leyser's Monmouth. Arr. for Hymn 93.

93. 11s & 12s. Christian Lyre.

1 The chariot! the chariot! its wheels roll in fire,
As the Lord cometh down in the pomp of his ire;
Lo! self-moving, it drives on its pathway of cloud,
And the heavens with the burden of Godhead are bowed.

2 The glory! the glory! around him are poured
Mighty hosts of the angels that wait on the Lord;
And the glorified saints and the martyrs are there,
And there all who the palm-wreaths of victory wear.

3 The trumpet! the trumpet! the dead have all heard;
Lo! the depths of the stone-covered charnel are stirred;
From the sea, from the earth, from the south, from the north
All the vast generations of man are come forth.

4 The judgment! the judgment! the thrones are all set,
Where the Lamb and the white-vested elders are met;
There all flesh is at once in the sight of the Lord,
And the doom of eternity hangs on his word.

5 O mercy! O mercy! look down from above,
Great Creator, on us, the sad children, with love,
When beneath, to their darkness, the wicked are driven,
May our justified souls find a welcome in heaven.

28. 12s. Thearby.

1 The voice of free grace, cries, Escape to the mountain;
For Adam's lost race Christ has opened a fountain:
For sin and uncleanness, for every transgression,
His blood flows most freely in streams of salvation.
Hallelujah to the Lamb! &c.

[See words with the tune on opposite page.

OLD HUNDRED.‡ Anapestic.

‡ May thus be sung in Unison to Hymn 93, the organ playing the harmony.

SCOTLAND. 12s, or 12s & 11s. Anapestic. Dr. Clarke.

Repeat for Hy. 90.
Repeat this
for Hymn 99.
the Eden of—
omit.
—love.
4th line again in Hymn 23.
Repeat for Hymn 23.
Hal-le-lu-jah to th' Lamb, He hath pur-chas'd our pardon We'll praise him a-
gain, when we pass ov-er Jordan. We'll praise him again, when we pass over Jordan.

2 Ye souls that are wounded, O, flee to the [Saviour!
He calls you in mercy; 'tis infinite favor;
Your sins are increasing; escape to the moun- [tain;
His blood can remove them, which flows from
Hallelujah, &c. [the fountain.

3 O Jesus, ride on triumphantly glorious;
O'er sin, death, and hell, thou art more than [victorious;
Thy name is the theme of the great congre- [gation,
While angels and men raise the shout of sal-
Hallelujah, &c. [vation—

99. 12s & 11s. Va. Sel.

1 How sweet to reflect on those joys that [await me
In yon blissful region, the haven of rest,
Where glorified spirits with welcome shall [greet me,
And lead me to mansions prepared for the [blest!
Encircled in light, and with glory enshrouded,
My happiness perfect, my mind's sky un- [clouded,
I'll bathe in the ocean of pleasure unbounded,
And range with delight thro' the Eden of love.

2 While angelic legions, with harps tuned, [celestial,
Harmoniously join in the concert of praise,
The saints, as they flock from the regions [terrestrial,
In loud hallelujahs their voices will raise;
Then songs to the Lamb shall reëcho through [heaven;
My soul will respond, "To Immanuel be [given
All glory, all honor, all might, and dominion,
Who brought us thro' grace to the Eden [of love."

3 Then hail, blesséd state; hail, ye songsters [of glory;
Ye harpers of bliss, soon I'll meet you above;
And join your full choir in rehearsing the [story,
"Salvation from sorrow, thro' Jesus' love;"
Tho' prisoned in earth, yet, by anticipation,
Already my soul feels a sweet prelibation
Of joys that await me when freed from proba- [tion;
My heart's now in heaven, the Eden of love.

22.

12s & 8s. S. F. Smith.

1 When the harvest is past and the summer is gone,
And sermons and prayers shall be o'er, —
When the beams cease to break of the blest Sabbath morn,
And Jesus invites thee no more; —
When the rich gales of mercy no longer shall blow,
The gospel no message declare, —
Sinner, how canst thou bear the deep wailings of woe?
How suffer the night of despair?

2 When the holy have gone to the regions of peace,
To dwell in the mansions above; —
When their harmony wakes, in the fulness of bliss,
Their song to the Saviour they love, —
Say, O sinner, that livest at rest and secure,
Who fearest no trouble to come,
Can thy spirit the swellings of sorrow endure,
Or bear the impenitent's doom?

NONANTUM.* 12s & 8s, (or 5. 6. 9. — 2 stanzas.) Anapestic.

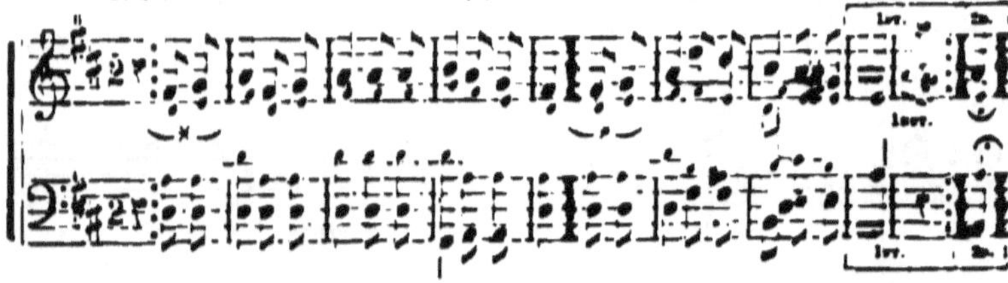

* The slurs to be observed only when the accent of the stanza requires them.

51.

5, 6, 9, or 6, 6, 9. Select Hymns.

1 How happy are they
Who the Saviour obey,
And whose treasures are laid up above
Tongue cannot express
The sweet comfort and peace
Of a soul in its earliest love.

2 That comfort was mine,
When the favor divine
I first found in the blood of the Lamb;
When my heart first believed,
O, what joy I received!
What a heaven in Jesus's name!

3 'Twas a heaven below
The Redeemer to know;
And the angels could do nothing more
Than to fall at his feet,
And the story repeat,
And the Lover of sinners adore.

Jesus, all the day long,
Was my joy and my song;
O, that all his salvation might see!
He hath loved me, I cried,
He hath suffered and died
To redeem such a rebel as me.

5 On the wings of his love,
I was carried above
All sin, and temptation, and pain;
I could not believe
That I ever should grieve,
That I ever should suffer again.

6 O! the rapturous height
Of that holy delight,
Which I felt in the life giving blood!
Of my Saviour possessed,
I was perfectly blessed,
As if filled with the fulness of God.

7 What a mercy is this!
What a heaven of bliss!
How unspeakably favored am I!
Gathered into the fold,
With believers enrolled,
With believers to live and to die.

8 Now my remnant of days
Would I spend to his praise,
Who hath died, my poor soul to redeem;
Whether many or few,
All my years are his due;
May they all be devoted to him.

JUDEA. 6. 6. 8. 4. Iambic. Arr. by B. F. Edmands. From Rev. De Core.

45.

6. 8. 4. Oliver.

1 The God of Abram praise,
Who reigns enthroned above;
Ancient of everlasting days,
And God of love!
Jehovah! great I AM,
By earth and heaven confessed,
I bow, and bless the sacred name,
Forever blessed.

2 The God of Abram praise,
At whose supreme command,
From earth I rise, and seek the joys
At his right hand:
I'd all on earth forsake,
Its wisdom, fame, and power,
And him my only portion make,
My shield and tower.

3 The God of Abram praise,
Whose all-sufficient grace
Shall guide me all my happy days,
In all his ways:
He calls a worm his friend;
He calls himself my God;
And he shall save me to the end,
Through Jesus' blood.

4 He by himself hath sworn;
I on his oath depend;
I shall, on eagle's wings upborne,
To heaven ascend:
I shall behold his face,
I shall his power adore,
And sing the wonders of his grace
Forevermore.

INDEX TO FIRST LINES OF HYMNS.

This Page embraces all the Hymns in the Supplement.

INDEX TO FIRST LINES OF HYMNS.

INDEX TO FIRST LINES OF HYMNS.

INDEX TO FIRST LINES OF HYMNS.

I.

J.

K.

L.

INDEX TO FIRST LINES OF HYMNS.

INDEX TO FIRST LINES OF HYMNS.

INDEX TO FIRST LINES OF HYMNS.

U.

V.

W.

Y.

Z.

INDEX OF TUNES,

METRICALLY ARRANGED.

THE tunes are recognized in the Index in four classes, viz.: 1st, The Chorals; 2d, The Choral-like tunes; 3d, The Chant-style tunes; and 4th, The Hymn tunes. Chorals have, in their melodies, but one note to a syllable, except perhaps an occasional passing note; they are of simple rhythm, and are considered best for congregational singing. Choral-like tunes of course stand next in order of availability; and tunes of the Chant-style may be considered as between them and the Hymn tunes; which last, being more varied in rhythm, are less easy of performance; and some of them can only be profitably used by congregations where there exists considerable musical culture, or which have the aid of a good choir.

The dates and annotations serve to show that standard music, which has stood the test of time and use in the Church, greatly predominates in this work. The dates marked with a star (*) refer to the composers, or the collections from which the tunes have been copied, or to the sources from which they are believed to have emanated, rather than to the *precise dates* of composition; and the mark (+) indicates the date of the death of the composer: of course such tunes may be of still earlier date. In this column is condensed much historical information relative to Psalmody.

The letter s, attached to the page figures, indicates that the tune is in the Supplement.

LONG METRE TUNES.

Tunes.	Pages.	Class.	Composers.	Collections, with Dates and Annotations.
All Saints,	74, 90,	*Choral-like,*	Dr. Croft,	1703. Tate & Brady's Supplement.
Alden,	56, 63,	*Chant style,*	E. F. Gould,	1833. National Church Harmony.
Alfreton,	30, 66,	*Choral-like,*	W. Beastall,	1703. Supple. to New Version.
Alton,	33, 35, 49,	*Chant style,*	N. D. Gould,	1833. National Church Harmony.
Angels' Hymn,	20,	*Choral,*	O. Gibbons,	1623.+ Withers' Church Songs.
Arnheim,	79,	*Choral-like,*	S. Holyoke,	1816.+ Harmonia Americana.
Audi, Israel,	18, 37,	*Choral,*	J. B. Bonometti,	1560. In German Psalter, 1562.
Bava,	18, 37,	*Choral,*	J. B. Bonometti,	1560. In German Psalter.
Bertram,	52,	*Choral,*	W. H. Havergall,	1853.* Cong. Tune Book, Lond.
Bridgewater,	69,	*Hymn tune,*	Edson,	Popular old American.
Brighton,	85,	*Hymn tune,*	. . . . . .	Called also Glasgow.
Boyce's Chant,	22, 35,	*Chant style,*	Dr. Boyce,	1779.+ English.
Burroughs,	65,	*Hymn tune,*	S. D. Hadley,	From the Well-Spring.
Castle Hill,	64,	*Choral-like,*	N. Minshall,	London Cong. Tune Book.
Chard,	90,	*Choral-like,*	England,	Lond. Cong. Tune Bk., 1853.
Clare,	391s, 43, 72, 81,	*Hymn tune,*	Edw. Hamilton,	1857. The Sanctus.
Crasselius,	21,	*Choral,*	Crasselius,	1650. Dusseldorf.
Croatia,	54,	*Choral,*	Spangenberger's	Cantiones Eccles., 1545.
Devotion,	23,	*Hymn tune,*	D. Read,	American; about 1793.
Duke Street,	25, 59,	*Hymn tune,*	J. Hatton,	Attributed also to Read.
Eventide,	45, 48,	*Hymn tune,*	Edw. Hamilton,	1857. The Sanctus.
Ecknuhl,	50,	*Choral,*	Mich. Weiss,	1530. Bohemian.
Erfurt,	90,	*Choral,*	Martin Luther,	1543. Klug's Gesangbuch.
Glasgow,	85,	*Hymn tune,*	. . . . . .	1833.* Sacred Minstrel.
Germania,	77, 82,	*Choral,*	J. H. Schein,	1620. In many collections.
Gregory,	391s, 75,	*Chant style,*	Arranged,	From Gregorian tone.
Gould's Chant,	36,	*Chant style,*	N. D. Gould,	1839. Sacred Minstrel.
Groton,	26,	*Choral,*	Zinck,	Old German style.

INDEX OF TUNES.

L. M. Continued.

Tunes.	Pages.	Class.	Composers.	Collections, with Dates and Abbreviations
Hamborough,	22, 35, 45, 64,	*Hymn tune,*	Arranged,	From Anc. Florentine Mel'y.
Hayti,	44,	*Choral,*	L. Marshall,	1836. The Hosanna.
Heber,	22,	*Chant style,*	N. D. Gould,	1839. The Sacred Minstrel.
Hebro,	393[a], 27, 45,	*Hymn tune,*	Arranged,	From old German Choral.
Iosco,	58, 78,	*Choral,*	John Huss,	1415.+ Burnt at the stake.
Jah,	28,	*Choral,*	. . . . .	1853.* Cong. Tune Book, London.
Leland,	62,	*Hymn tune,*	Josiah Osgood,	Presented for this work.
Lewis,	21, 80,	*Hymn tune,*	H. H. Hawley,	Modern American.
Lotha (Leipsic),	77, 82,	*Choral,*	J. H. Schein,	1620. Called also Germania.
Luton	38, 67,	*Choral-like,*	G. Burder,	An old standard tune.
Medway,	29, 60,	*Choral-like,*	Pergolesi,	1737.+ Arrangement from.
Melcombe,	32, 64, 88,	*Choral,*	S. Webbe,	1816.+ London.
Meroe,	392[a], 57,	*Hymn tune,*	W. B. Bradbury,	1847. Mendelssohn Collection.
Monmouth,	87,	*Choral,*	M. Luther,	1516, about. (Judgment Hymn.)
Nantwich,	76,	*Hymn tune,*	Dr. Madan,	Popular 30 years ago.
Nazareth,	394[a], 32, 64,	*Choral,*	S. Webbe,	1816.+ A universal favorite.
Old Hundred,	17, 24, 36, 46, 70, 91,	*Choral,*	Guilliam. Franc,	1543.* Beza & Marot's Psalms.
Old X. Command'ts,	18,	*Choral,*	J. B. Bonometti,	1560. In German Psalter, of 1562.
Olivet,	31, 89,	*Hymn tune,*	. . . . .	A new tune.
Prague,	58, 78,	*Choral,*	John Huss,	1415.+ (Called also Iosco.)
Peace, troubled s.,	63,	*Hymn tune,*	Mazzinghi,	Known as Palestine.
Prospect Hill,	39,	*Hymn tune,*	R. Gilchrist,	1854.* Glasgow Collection.
Rest,	86,	*Hymn tune,*	W. B. Bradbury,	1843. The Jubilee.
Resurgam,	83,	*Hymn tune,*	Handel,	From Dead March in Saul.
Rosedale,	399[a], 84,	*Hymn tune,*	G. F. Root,	1843. Sabbath Bell.
St. Austin,	60, 69,	*Choral,*	Unknown,	1595. The Psalter.
Sterling,	21, 36, 46,	*Chant style,*	Harrison,	Ancient tune.
Shoel,	46,	*Hymn tune,*	Shoel,	Popular old tune.
Stonefield,	68,	*Hymn tune,*	S. Stanley,	English style.
Ten Command'ts,	18, 37,	*Choral,*	J. B. Bonometti,	1632.* German Psalter.
The Saviour lives,	40,	*Hymn tune,*	Handel,	Arr. from "The Messiah."
Timsbury,	34,	*Choral,*	I. Smith,	1770, about.
Truro,	42,	*Hymn tune,*	Dr. C. Burney,	1814.+ English.
Ware,	19, 55,	*Chant style,*	N. D. Gould,	1833. National Church Harmony.
Wells,	395[a], 51,	*Hymn tune,*	. . . . .	1740, or before.
Windham,	400[a], 53,	*Hymn tune,*	M. Luther,	Arr. by D. Read, 1800.
Winchelsea,	396[a], 47,	*Choral-like,*	Prelleur,	1731. French tune.
Winchester,	41,	*Choral-like,*	Dr. Croft,	1725.+ The old favorite.
Zephyr,	403[a], 61,	*Hymn tune,*	W. B. Bradbury,	1847. Mendelssohn Collection.

COMMON METRE TUNES.

Tunes.	Pages.	Class.	Composers.	Collections, with Dates and Abbreviations
Adagio,	126, 131, 209,	*Choral,*	Arranged,	From a Gregorian tone.
Archdale,	117, 190,	*Hymn tune,*	Belcher,	1786.* A. Law's Collection.
Attalia,	108, 134, 162, 184, 211,	*Choral,*	T. Tallis,	1565.* Parker's Psalter.
Abridge,	113, 196,	*Hymn tune,*	I. Smith,	1770. Standard tune.
Arlington,	124, 175,	*Hymn tune,*	Dr. T. Arne,	1744, about. English.
Andover,	[illegible], 137,	*Hymn tune,*	. . . . .	1839. The Sacred Minstrel.
Avon,	161, 179,	*Hymn tune,*	H. Wilson,	Modern Scotch tune.

INDEX OF TUNES.

Tunes.	Pages.	Class.	Composers.	Collections, with Dates and Annotations.
Augustus,	97, 179,	*Hymn tune,*	W. W. Johnsen,	1839. The Sacred Minstrel.
Baldwin Place,	133, 143,	*Hymn tune,*	B. F. Edmands,	1859. Arr. from a German Choral.
Balerma,	186, 227,	*Hymn tune,*	R. Simpson,	1855. Davis's Appendix, London.
Bangor,	210, 218,	*Choral-like,*	W. Tansur,	1735. Tansur's Collection.
Barby,	149,	*Choral-like,*	W. Tansur,	1735. Tansur's Collection.
Blandford,	158, 216,	*Choral-like,*	J. Battishill,	1801.+ English style.
Bray,	115,	*Hymn tune,*	N. Herrman,	1550. Theme, same as Lutzen.
Bedford,	202,	*Choral,*	W. Wheall,	1729. Psalm Singer's Magazine.
Belcher,	121,	*Hymn tune,*	B. F. Edmands,	1859. Arranged for this work.
Billings' Jordan,	230,	*Hymn tune,*	W. Billings,	1800.+ American Composer.
Bowdoin Street,	169, 193, 205,	*Hymn tune,*	B. F. Edmands,	1859. Composed for this work.
Canterbury,	112, 209,	*Choral,*	Unknown,	1592.* Este's Psalter.
Charity,	173,	*Hymn tune,*	N. D. Gould,	1833. The Sacred Minstrel.
Clarendon,	94,	*Choral-like,*	J. Tucker,	An old favorite.
Christmas,	182,	*Choral-like,*	Handel,	1759.+ Arrangement.
Comfort,	408^s, 171,	*Hymn tune,*	Mrs. P. Gibson,	1854.* From a Glasgow Collect'n.
Communion, New,	139, 409^s, 151, 219,	*Hymn tune,*	Sumner Hill,	1857. The Sanctus.
Consecration,	174,	*Hymn tune,*	Rev. J. Aldrich,	1859. The Sacred Lyre.
Coronation,	128,	*Hymn tune,*	O. Holden,	1844.+ Old favorite tune.
Cupar,	119,	*Choral,*	Unknown,	1635.* Scotch Psalter.
Crucifix,	160, 226,	*Hymn tune,*	B. F. Edmands,	1859. Composed for this work.
Dedham,	123, 191,	*Hymn tune,*	W. Gardiner,	Author of Music of Nature.
Devizes,	129,	*Hymn tune,*	Tucker,	The old arrangement.
Dundee,	98, 154, 157, 191,	*Choral,*	Uncertain,	1615.* Scotch Psalter.
Dundee (Original),	142,	*Choral,*	Unknown,	1592. Now known as Windsor.
Dunfermline,	125, 180, 197, 222,	*Choral,*	Uncertain,	1621.* In Ravenscroft's Collect'n.
Durham,	137,	*Hymn tune,*	Uncertain,	1635.* Scotch Psalter.
Fountain,	121,	*Hymn tune,*	Dr. T. Hastings,	Spiritual Songs.
French,	98,	*Choral,*	Unknown,	1615. Now known as Dundee.
Funeral Thought,	220,	*Choral,*	J. Smith,	1791. Arnold's Psalms.
Gideoni,	189,	*Hymn tune,*	J. Osgood,	1853. Mel. Sacra. and other coll.
Haeffner,	176,	*Choral-like,*	Arranged,	1820.* From a German Collect'n.
Hammond,	147, 232, 233,	*Hymn tune,*	N. D. Gould,	1833. National Church Harmony.
Hillside,	229,	*Hymn tune,*	Sumner Hill,	1857. The Sanctus.
Holden's Glasgow,	135,	*Hymn tune,*	O. Holden,	1844.+ Old American melody.
Howards,	109, 126, 158,	*Hymn tune,*	Dr. Howard,	1782.+ In Weyman's Collection.
Inverness,	161, 179,	*Hymn tune,*	H. Wilson,	A Scotch melody.
Jordan,	230,	*Hymn tune,*	W. Billings,	1800.+ Popular American melo'y.
Lanesboro',	97,	*Hymn tune,*	Unknown,	An English melody.
Lauenburg,	130,	*Choral,*	Uncertain,	1820.* Svensk Choralbuch.
Lind,	109,	*Choral,*	Unknown,	1819.* Stockholm Choralbuch.
London,	92, 214,	*Choral,*	Unknown,	1635.* "Newton" of the Psalter.
Lutzen,	102, 200,	*Choral,*	N. Herrman,	1560. German.
Marlow,	406^s, 98, 116, 125, 141, 157,	*Hymn tune,*	Williams,	Called also Rineton.
Martyrs,	148,	*Choral,*	Unknown,	1621. Ravenscroft's Psalter.
Martyrdom,	161, 179,	*Hymn tune,*	H. Wilson,	Scotch tune.
Mear,	204,	*Choral,*	Unknown,	An ancient melody.
Melbourne,	97, 158,	*Hymn tune,*	Unknown,	An English tune.
Miles' Lane,	128,	*Hymn tune,*	Shrubsole,	Peculiar to hymn 338.
Milford,	168,	*Choral,*	Unknown,	1833. National Church Harmony.
New Haven,	414^s, 170,	*Hymn tune,*	Giardini,	1796.+ An Italian melody.
Norway,	195, 201,	*Hymn tune,*	A. A. Gould,	1833. National Church Harmony.

INDEX OF TUNES.

C. M. Continued.

Tunes.	Pages.	Class.	Composers.	Collections, with Dates and Annotations.
Northfield,	203,	*Hymn tune,*	Ingalls,	American fugue style.
Nottingham,	132, 164,	*Choral,*	J. Clark,	1700, or about that date.
Ortonvill,	411^{b}, 120, 221,	*Hymn tune,*	Dr. T. Hastings,	1849.* Mendelssohn Collection.
Peterboro',	93, 180, 213,	*Hymn tune,*	Harrison,	Webbe's Collection, old.
Phillips,	166,	*Hymn tune,*	F. Hunten,	—— Coblentz, modern.
Phuvah,	410^{b}, 122, 146, 152,	*Choral,*	M. Bulpius,	—— or Vulpius, 1609.
Refuge,	127, 179, 212,	*Hymn tune,*	N. Dougall,	1854.* Glasgow Collection.
Resignation,	221,	*Choral,*	T. Clark,	1833. National Church Harmony.
Rineton,	406^{a}, 98, 116, 125, 141, 157,	*Hymn tune,*	Williams,	1833.* National Ch'ch Harmony.
Rochester,	412^{a}, 95,	*Hymn tune,*	Unknown,	Originally a choral.
St. Ann's,	114, 110,	*Choral,*	Unknown,	1700, or about that date.
St. Magnus,	132, 161,	*Choral,*	J. Clark,	1707.+ Called also Nottingham.
St. Martin's,	110, 177, 180,	*Hymn tune,*	Tansur,	1735. Universally popular.
St. Sebastian,	97, 227,	*Hymn tune,*	Unknown,	English origin.
St. Stephen's,	138, 172,	*Choral-like,*	Rev. W. Jones,	1800.+ An English composer.
Stamford,	104, 136,	*Choral-like,*	Tansur,	1735, or about that date.
Stilt,	106, 141, 155, 188,	*Choral,*	John Milton.	Called also York.
Solomon,	178, 194,	*Choral-like,*	Handel,	Arranged from oratorio.
Stonington,	192,	*Chant style,*	N. D. Gould,	1833. The Sacred Minstrel.
Syme,	109,	*Choral,*	Edw. Hamilton,	1857. The Sanctus.
Tallis,	108, 118, 134, 162, 194,	*Choral,*	T. Tallis,	1565.* Parker's Psalter.
Tallis' Chant,	96, 156,	*Chant style,*	T. Tallis,	1585.+ Arranged from a chant.
Warwick,	215,	*Hymn tune,*	S. Stanley,	An English melody.
Watts,	234,	*Hymn tune,*	N. D. Gould,	1833. The Sacred Minstrel.
Windsor,	142, 145, 227,	*Choral,*	Unknown,	1592. The original "Dundee."
Woodland,	198, 206, 217, 228, 231,	*Hymn tune,*	N. D. Gould,	1833. The Sacred Minstrel.
Woodruff,	217, 228,	*Hymn tune,*	H. H. Hawley,	Modern tune.
Woodstock,	131, 208, 228,	*Hymn tune,*	Dutton,	American tune.
Worcester,	150,	*Hymn tune,*	Rev. J. Aldrich,	1859. Presented for this work.
York,	106, 144, 155, 188,	*Choral,*	John Milton,	1615. The father of the poet.

SHORT METRE TUNES.

Tunes.	Pages.	Class.	Composers.	Collections, with Dates and Annotations.
Aylesbury,	242, 248,	*Hymn tune,*	Dr. M. Greene,	1756.+ An English composer.
Admonition,	267,	*Hymn tune,*	Rev. J. Aldrich,	1859.* From the Sacred Lyre.
Battishill,	245,	*Chant style,*	J. Battishill,	1801.+ An English composer.
Bladen,	250,	*Choral,*	Unknown,	—— An old German tune.
Cambridge Old,	243,	*Choral-like,*	Rev. R. Harrison,	—— Called also "Hudson."
Caswell,	245,	*Hymn tune,*	B. F. Edmands,	1859. For this work.
Claytonville,	417^{a}, 270,	*Hymn tune,*	W. B. Bradbury,	1851. From the Psalmist.
Chester,	248,	*Hymn tune,*	S. Stanley,	1786.+ An English composer.
Command,	241,	*Hymn tune,*	Edw. Hamilton,	1857. From the Sanctus.
Concord,	258,	*Hymn tune,*	O. Holden,	1844.+ American style.
Croydon,	268,	*Hymn tune,*	Unknown,	1806. C. J. Latrobe's Selection.
Crucifix,	253, 273, 275,	*Choral like,*	B. F. Edmands,	1859. For this work (minor).
Doomsday,	274,	*Hymn tune,*	Wood,	—— American composer.
Dover,	266,	*Hymn tune,*	Uncertain,	—— Derived from an old choral.
Fairfield,	239,	*Choral like,*	Rev. R. Harrison,	—— An old favorite tune.

INDEX OF TUNES.

Tunes.	Pages.	Class.	Composers.	Collections, with Dates and Annotations.
Franconia,	274,	*Choral,*	Unknown,	1770. In Havergal's Psalmody.
Golden Hill,	249,	*Hymn tune,*	Unknown,	—— A Western melody.
Hartland,	419[s], 256, 262,	*Hymn tune,*	Ingalls,	1805. Called also "Kentucky."
Hudson,	243,	*Choral-like,*	Rev. R. Harrison,	—— Called also Cambridge Old.
Iowa, (Kentucky,)	256, 262,	*Hymn tune,*	Ingalls,	1805. Iowa in $\frac{3}{2}$ time.
Kinnicut,	239,	*Hymn tune,*	H. H. Hawley,	—— Modern American tune.
Lisbon,	418[s], 236,	*Hymn tune,*	D. Read,	—— Old American tune.
Loudon,	260,	*Choral,*	T. Olmsted,	—— Old American tune.
Mt. Ephraim,	244,	*Hymn tune,*	B. Milgrove,	1770, or about that date.
My Father's House,	275,	*Hymn tune,*	H. H. Hawley,	—— Presented for this work.
Nolen,	259,	*Hymn tune,*	Josiah Osgood,	1849.* Bay State Collection.
Olmutz,	416[s], 235, 249,	*Hymn tune,*	. . . . . .	—— Gregorian; "Magnificat."
Paddington,	257, 264,	*Choral,*	Unknown,	—— A fine composition.
Pentonville,	263,	*Choral,*	F. Linley,	1800.+ Blind from his birth.
Swabia,	240, 273,	*Choral,*	Unknown,	—— In Dibdin's Standard Coll.
Selah,	264, 266, 271,	*Hymn tune,*	Unknown,	
Silver Street,	237,	*Hymn tune,*	I. Smith,	1800.+ Called also Falcon Street.
St. Bride,	251,	*Choral,*	Dr. Howard,	1760. In Riley's Psalms, 1762.
St. Michael's,	261,	*Choral,*	Unknown,	1588. In Day's Psalter.
St. Thomas,	238, 247, 265,	*Hymn tune,*	G. F. Handel,	1759.+ First arr. by A. Williams.
Tenderness,	254,	*Hymn tune,*	Edw. Hamilton,	1857. From the Sanctus.
Watchman,	246,	*Hymn tune,*	Leach,	—— An old favorite melody.
Westminster,	269,	*Chant style,*	Dr. W. Boyce,	1779.+ An English composer.

HALLELUJAH METRES.

Tunes.	Pages.	Class.	Composers.	Collections, with Dates and Annotations.
Altar,	H. M. 288,	*Hymn tune,*	Dr. John Bull,	1622.+ Queen Elizabeth's Instr.
Amherst,	" 278, 293,	*Hymn tune,*	W. Billings,	1781, or about that date.
Bethesda,	" 276, 284,	*Choral-like,*	Dr. Green,	—— Dates prior to 1755.
Darwells,	" 286, 291,	*Hymn tune,*	Rev. W. Darwell,	—— In many old collections.
Flanders,	" 421[s], 287,	*Hymn tune,*	Dr. T. Hastings,	—— From an old Flemish air.
Haddam,	" 277, 292,	*Choral-like,*	. . . . . .	—— An old English tune.
Hampton,	" 283,	*Choral-like,*	Haydn,	1810.+ Arranged by J. Osgood.
Lenox,	" 420[s], 279,	*Hymn tune,*	Edson,	—— American fugue tune.
Lubec,	" 280,	*Hymn tune,*	Unknown,	—— Geneva Collect'n, ancient.
Rowe St.	" 282,	*Hymn tune,*	B. F. Edmands,	1859. For this work. Gregorian.
Warsaw,	" 281, 290,	*Hymn tune,*	T. Clark,	
Creation,	S. H. M. 296,	*Choral-like,*	Haydn,	1795. From the Oratorio.
Templyn,	" 297,	*Choral-like,*	J. H. Schein,	1627. Har. by Dr. Filitz, 1846.
Orgel,	C. H. M. 294,	*Choral,*	Joach. V. Burck,	1580.+ From a German collect'n.
Solace,	" 295,	*Hymn tune,*	N. D. Gould,	1844. Companion for Psalmist.

PARTICULAR METRES.

Tunes.	Pages.	Class.	Composers.	Collections, with Dates and Annotations.
Dalston,	S. P. M. 299,	*Choral-like,*	A. Williams,	—— In most old collections.
Aithlone,	C. P. M. 302,	*Choral-like,*	Unknown,	—— An old German, tune.
Burlington,	" 303,	*Choral-like,*	Charles Zeuner,	1833. New Village Harmony.
Byzantium,	" 301,	*Hymn tune,*	Dr. Hayes.	1779.+ An English composer.
Ganges,	" 301,	*Hymn tune,*	Unknown,	—— An ancient melody.
Sherburne,	" 300,	*Hymn tune,*	Unknown,	1833.* National Church Har.
Charles St.	L. P. M. 304,	*Hymn tune,*	Sumner Hill,	1859. Presented for this work.
St. Helens,	" 305,	*Choral-like,*	Jennings,	1819.* Old Village Harmony.

INDEX OF TUNES.

SEVENS (7s) METRE.

Tunes.	Pages.	Class.	Composers.	Collections, with Dates and Annotations.
Ascension,	424*, 318,	*Hymn tune,*	N. D. Gould,	1839.* From "Sacred Minstrel."
Benevento,	[illegible], 325,	*Choral like,*	S. Webbe,	1800, about. English.
Bothnia,	315,	*Hymn tune,*	Geo. J. Webb,	1840. Massachusetts Collection.
Cotbus,	313,	*Choral,*	J. Ublich,	1674. Har. by Dr. Filitz, 18[illegible].
Eddyfield,	425*, 312,	*Choral-like,*	C. J. Latrobe,	18[illegible]. Music of the Church.
Ellenthorpe,	308, 321,	*Hymn tune,*	Linley,	1800.+ An English composer.
Fairfax,	320,	*Choral like,*	Unknown,	—— Dibdin's Stand. Tune B'k.
Jephthah,	310,	*Choral-like,*	Handel,	—— From Oratorio "Jephthah."
Nuremberg,	423*, 306,	*Choral,*	J. R. Ahle,	1673.+ A universal favorite.
Pleyel's Hymn,	309, 311,	*Choral,*	Pleyel,	1795, or about that date.
Pilgrim,	314,	*Choral,*	Unknown,	1833.* Nat'al. Church Harmony.
Roselawn,	427*, 322,	*Choral-like,*	Unknown,	—— Arr. from a German choral.
Sabbath, 6 lines,	327,	*Hymn tune,*	Samuel Barr,	1861.* Glasgow Collection.
Spanish Hymn,	429*, 324,	*Hymn tune,*	Unknown,	—— An old favorite melody.
St. Nicolai, 2 stanz.,	319,	*Choral,*	C. F. Becker,	—— A melody of 17th Century.
Strelitz, 8 lines,	326,	*Hymn tune,*	Unknown,	1846.* Dr. Filitz's Collection.
Spring,	316,	*Choral-like,*	Unknown,	1839.* From "Sacred Minstrel."
Sumner, 6 lines,	323,	*Hymn tune,*	Anonymous,	1849. Composed for this work.
Vogler,	426*, 320,	*Choral-like,*	Abbé Vogler,	1770. Arr. by B. F. Edmands.
Warren,	317,	*Choral,*	Unknown,	—— Of German origin.
Worship,	307,	*Choral,*	Haeffner,	1819.* Svensk Choralbok.

EIGHTS & SEVENS (8s. & 7s.) METRE.

Tunes.	Pages.	Class.	Composers.	Collections, with Dates and Annotations.
Bavaria,	432*, 338,	*Hymn tune,*	Unknown,	—— In many collections.
Fairfax,	331, 335,	*Choral-like,*	Unknown,	—— Dibdin's Stand. Tune B'k.
Greenville,	337,	*Hymn tune,*	Rousseau,	1775, or about that date.
Melodien,	333,	*Hymn tune,*	Unknown,	1850.* Rev. J. G. Oncken's Coll.
Oncken,	330, 332,	*Choral-like,*	Unknown,	1850.* From "The Melodien."
Saxonia,	336,	*Choral-like,*	Naumann,	1785.+ German composer.
Tremont (Peculiar),	352,	*Choral-like,*	J. H. Henne,	179[illegible].+ Choralund Melodienbuch.
Sicily,	331, 333,	*Choral-like,*	Mozart,	—— From a Latin hymn.
Vesper Hymn,	335,	*Choral-like,*	Unknown,	—— A Russian melody.
Westborough,	329,	*Choral-like,*	Haydn,	1810.+ Arranged from Haydn.
Worthing,	328, 334,	*Choral-like,*	Schultze,	—— Saxon, born in 1759.

EIGHTS, SEVENS & FOUR (8s 7s & 4.) METRE.

Tunes.	Pages.	Class.	Composers.	Collections, with Dates and Annotations.
Greenville,	432*, 340,	*Hymn tune,*	Rousseau,	1775, or about that year.
Harvard Street,	351,	*Choral-like,*	Unknown,	—— Arr. from German choral.
Judgment,	350,	*Choral-like,*	J. V. Burck,	1[illegible]0.+ German composer.
Oliver Street,	343,	*Choral-like,*	Unknown,	1850.* Oncken's "Melodien."
Spanish Hymn,	339,	*Hymn tune,*	Unknown,	—— A popular old air.
Somerset St.,	341, 348,	*Choral,*	Unknown,	1850.* Oncken's "Melodien."
Tamworth,	342, 349,	*Hymn tune,*	Lockhart,	—— An old Scotch melody.
Trinity,	346,	*Choral like,*	J. Campbell,	1854.* His collection of tunes.
Union Church	344,	*Hymn tune,*	Edw. Hamilton,	—— From "The Sanctus."
Wilmot,	345,	*Hymn tune,*	C. V. Weber,	1826.+ Arranged from Weber.
Zion,	431*, 347,	*Hymn tune,*	Dr. T. Hastings,	—— From "Spiritual Songs."

MIXED AND PECULIAR METRES,

METRICALLY ARRANGED.

Tunes.	Pages.	Style.	Peculiarities of Metre.		Composers.	Collections, with Dates and Associations.	
[illegible]AR,	362,	*Hymn tune,*	5, 5, 5, 11; 6, 6, 6, 12,	Anapestic,	L. Marshall,	1840.*	From Marshall's Hosanna.
[illegible]NS,	363,	*Hymn tune,*	6, 6, 6, 6,	Iambic,	Unknown,	—	A German melody.
[illegible]	373,	*Chant style,*	6, 4, 6, 4,	Iambic,	B. F. Edmands,	1859.	For this work. Hymn 153.
[illegible]	369,	*Hymn tune,*	6, 5, 6, 5; 6, 6, 6, 5,	Iambic,	Unknown,	—	A favorite melody.
[illegible]	368,	*Hymn tune,*	6, 6, 4; 6, 6, 4,	Iambic,	E. Hamilton,	1857.+	From The Sanctus.
[illegible]	364, 366,	*Hymn tune,*	6, 6, 4; 6, 6, 6, 4,	Iambic,	Giardini,	1795.+	In many collections.
[illegible]	367,	*Choral like,*	6, 6, 4; 6, 6, 6, 4,	Iambic,	Ebeling,	1666.	Dibdin's Standard Collection.
[illegible]	365,	*Hymn tune,*	6, 6, 4; 6, 6, 6, 4.	Iambic,	J. Tolmie,	1854.[illegible]	Campbell's Collection.
[illegible]	372,	*Hymn tune,*	6, 7, 8, 7,	Iambic,	N. D. Gould,	1841.	Companion for the Psalmist.
[illegible]	371,	*Choral-like,*	6, 6, 8, 4; 6, 6, 8, 4,	Iambic,	W. Arnold,		
[illegible]	3[illegible]0,	*Hymn tune,*	6, 6, 8, 4; 6, 6, 8, 4,	Iambic,	Unknown,	—	A German melody.
[illegible]	[illegible]	*Hymn tune,*	6, 6, 10; 6, 6, 10,	Iambic,	Geo. F. Root,	1856.	From the "Sabbath Bell."
[illegible]	[illegible]	*Hymn tune,*	7, 5, 8 lines,	Trochaic,	N. D. Gould.	1841.	Companion for the Psalmist.
[illegible]	[illegible]	*Choral-like,*	7, 6, 8 lines,	Trochaic,	Dr. J. Nares,	17[illegible]3.	An English composer.
[illegible]	[illegible]	*Hymn tune,*	7, 6, 7, 6,	Iambic,	Unknown,	[illegible]	J. G. Oncken's Mel[illegible]
[illegible]	[illegible]	*Choral like,*	7, 6, 8 lines,	Iambic,	C. W. B[illegible]		Called also "Pom[illegible]"
[illegible]	[illegible]	*Hymn tune,*	7, 6, 8 lines,	Iambic,	George J. Webb,	1840.	Massachusetts Ps[illegible]
[illegible]	[illegible]	*Hymn tune,*	7, 6, 8 lines,	Iambic,	N. D. Gould,	1841.	Companion for the [illegible]
[illegible]	[illegible]	*Hymn tune,*	7, 6, 8 lines,	Iambic,	Dr. L. Mason,	1839.	From the Sacred Mel[illegible]
[illegible]	[illegible]	*Hymn tune,*	7, 7, 7, 7, 4, 7,	Trochaic,	Unknown,	—	A favorite melody.
[illegible]	[illegible]	*Choral-like,*	7, 8, 7, 8; 8, 8, 8, 8,	Trochaic,	L. Marshall,	1856.	From Marshall's Hosanna.
[illegible]	[illegible]	*Chant style,*	[illegible]s, 8 lines,	Anapestic,	N. D. Gould,	1841.	Companion for the [illegible]
[illegible]	[illegible]	*Hymn tune,*	8, 8, 8, 8,	Anapestic,	W. Billings,	[illegible]	An old American [illegible]
[illegible]	[illegible]	*Hymn tune,*	8, 6, 8, 4,	Iambic,	George J. Webb,	1859.	Presented for this work.
[illegible]	[illegible]	[illegible]	8, 8, 4; 8, 8, 4,	Iambic,	George F. Root,	[illegible]	From the "Sabbath Bell."
[illegible]	[illegible]	[illegible]	8, 8, 6; 8, 8, 6,	Iambic,	George F. R[illegible]	[illegible]	From the "S[illegible]"
[illegible]	[illegible]	[illegible]	8, 8, 8, 6,	Iambic,	Mrs. P. G[illegible]	1854.	[illegible]
[illegible]	[illegible]	[illegible]	8, 7, 8, 7,	Iambic,	N. D. Gould,	1841.	Companion for th[illegible]

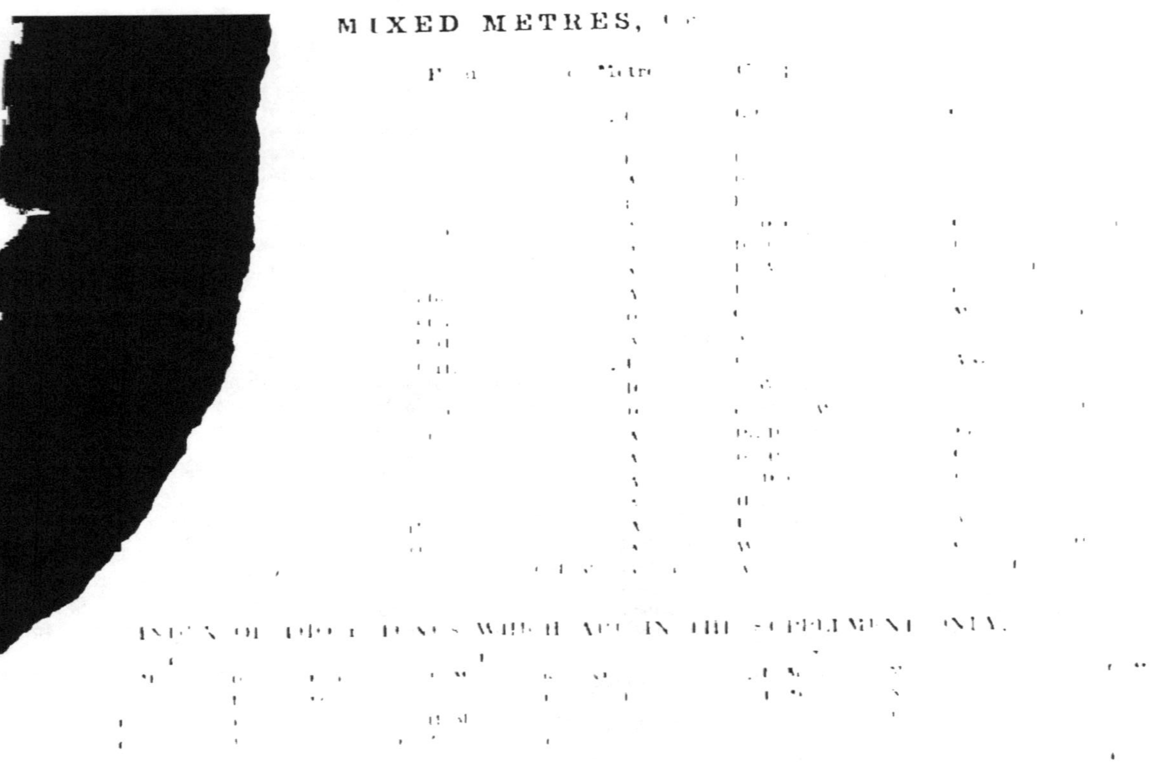

MIXED METRES, ...

INDEX OF ... TUNES WHICH ARE IN THE SUPPLEMENT ONLY.

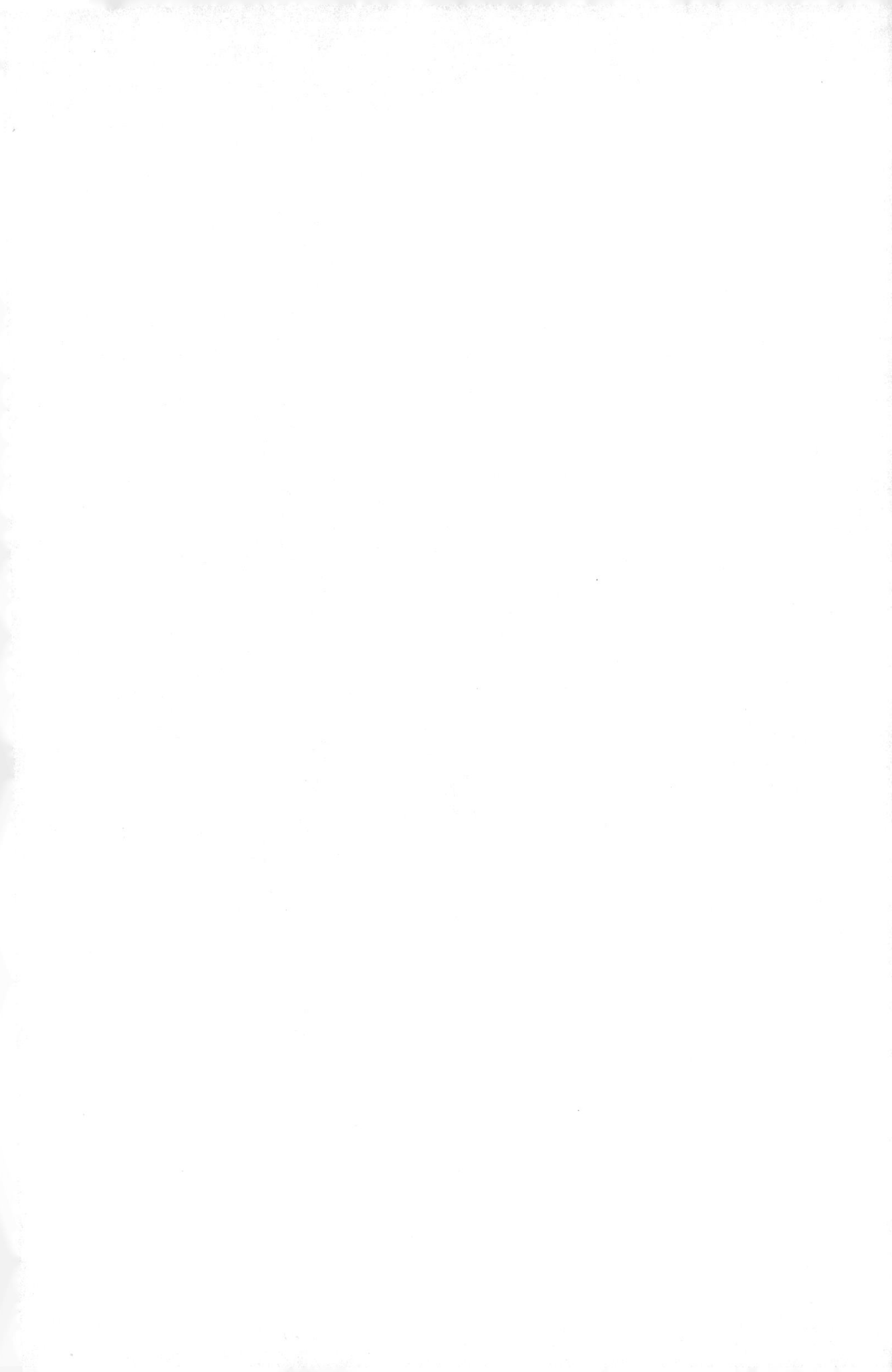

www.ingramcontent.com/pod-product-compliance
Lightning Source LLC
Chambersburg PA
CBHW032006300426
44117CB00008B/924

* 9 7 8 3 3 3 7 2 9 6 7 7 3 *